WO

T

The Law of Con

Tolley

The Law of Contract

Fourth edition

by Laurence Koffman, *Reader in Law, University of Sussex*
and
Elizabeth Macdonald, *Reader in Law, University of Wales, Aberystwyth*

Tolley

A member of the Reed Elsevier plc group

ISBN 0 7545 1276 2

First published 1992
Second edition 1995
Third edition 1998
Fourth edition 2001 (reprinted 2002)

Published by
Tolley
2 Addiscombe Road
Croydon
Surrey
CR9 5AF
020 8686 9141

Typeset in Great Britain by
Kerrypress Ltd, Luton, Bedfordshire

Printed in Great Britain by
The Cromwell Press, Trowbridge, Wiltshire

Preface to the first edition

The impetus for writing this book came from our experience, over many years, of teaching the Law of Contract to first year law students. We found that although the established textbooks on the subject are admirable in many respects, they are longer and more detailed than required by the average student. Our aim was to produce a book which has sufficient detail to meet the needs of students taking law degrees, but which does not contain more information than students ever require. Obviously we have been selective in deciding which topics merit more detailed exposition, but we hope that our selection reflects the emphasis of most Contract courses.

Although the book is written primarily with law students in mind, we hope that our approach to the subject will also appeal to those studying Contract as part of business studies courses. We think that a book on Contract should be readily intelligible to students new to law — as the subject is usually taught in the first year of a law degree. For this reason, the emphasis of the book is on explanation of the law in clear and non-technical terms. In particular, we have tried to give a full explanation of the important case law in order to assist students towards an understanding of how the common law works. We have preferred to provide a firm grounding in the case law, rather than to espouse or develop any individual "theory" of Contract law.

In writing the book we have been helped by more people than it is possible to name individually. But we are particularly grateful to those tutoring in Contract at Aberystwyth for reading and commenting helpfully on drafts of certain chapters. We also wish to thank Lillian Stevenson and the staff of the Hugh Owen library for their good-natured and patient assistance. We are indebted to our publishers for their initial interest in the idea of the book and for the encouragement which they gave us to write it. Special thanks are owed to Indira Carr for her advice on computers, and to Valerie Koffman for her help with proof reading. Our greatest debt of gratitude is owed to our families and friends who encouraged and supported us throughout the writing of the book. More particularly, Laurence Koffman wishes to thank his wife Valerie, and daughter Angela, for their patience and constant support. Elizabeth Macdonald would like to express her thanks to her parents, Pat and Stan Macdonald, for all their support and help.

We have attempted to state the law as at 15 September 1991.

Aberystwyth
February 1992

Laurence Koffman
Elizabeth Macdonald

Preface to the fourth edition

Our aims in writing the fourth edition remain much the same as in relation to the earlier editions of this book, as does our approach. We have been gratified by the popularity of the book with law students, and by the many favourable comments which the earlier editions have received.

This edition has been revised substantially to take account of the leading decisions and legislative changes of the last three years. In particular, there have been major changes to the chapter on the Unfair Terms in Consumer Contracts Regulations, to take account of the 1999 Regulations, and to the chapter on privity and third party rights, to include a reconsideration of this subject in the light of the Contracts (Rights of Third Parties) Act 1999. We have attempted to state the law as at 1 January 2001.

As in previous editions, Elizabeth has been primarily responsible for the areas now covered by Chapters 7, 8, 9, 10, 11, 13, 14, 17, 19, 21, 22 and 23. Laurence has been primarily responsible for the areas now covered by Chapters 1, 2, 3, 4, 5, 6, 12, 15, 16, 18 and 20.

In view of recent changes to civil procedure, what was formerly termed a "plaintiff" is now referred to as a "claimant". We have not altered references to plaintiffs in cases which were decided before this change was introduced, but in very recent cases the reader will come across references to claimants.

Elizabeth wishes to thank the staff of the Hugh Owen Library in Aberystwyth for their assistance, and also her parents, Stan and Pat Macdonald, for their encouragement and support. Laurence would like to thank his wife, Valerie, and daughter, Angela, for their constant support, patience and encouragement.

April 2001

Laurence Koffman
Elizabeth Macdonald

Contents

Table of cases

Chapter 1

Introduction to the study of contract law

1. What is a contract?

A contract is a legally enforceable agreement giving rise to obligations for the parties involved. The law of contract determines which agreements are enforceable and regulates those agreements, providing remedies if contractual obligations (undertakings or promises) are broken. Under a contract, the parties voluntarily assume their obligations or undertakings: for example, S promises to supply a new car to B by the end of the month, whilst B promises to pay, on delivery, the price of the vehicle. Their agreement to perform these undertakings is a contract. There is no legal duty to enter into such an agreement, but if the parties choose to do so, it will give rise to legal obligations. Therefore, the law of contract is distinct from branches of law where duties are imposed: for example, there is a general duty (in the law of tort) to take care that we do not injure other people by our careless actions. The doctor whose treatment of a patient falls below the professional standard expected of an ordinary practitioner of medicine will be liable for negligence. This liability is not based on a contract (indeed, there is no contractual relationship between a general practitioner and a National Health Service patient); it is a general duty of care imposed by law.

The word "contract" suggests to most people a formal or technical document drawn up and understood only by lawyers. Contracts can take this form, and certain types of contract (for instance, for the sale of land or any interest in land) must be in writing; but generally a contract can be made orally, without any legal jargon or formality. We all make numerous contracts as part of everyday life and we rarely give thought to legal technicalities. Making a contract is simply a way of facilitating, amongst other things, the exchange of goods and services. It is merely a method of commercial transaction. Of course, the transaction can vary enormously in complexity and in value — from the purchase of a chocolate bar to the multi-million pound take-over of a large company — but it is based on a contract nevertheless.

To illustrate the importance of contracts in our society, let us consider a day in the life of a fairly typical person (X), from the point of view of his contractual relationships. In the morning, the milkman delivers two pints to X's house and X buys a newspaper on his way to work. Both transactions are contracts for the sale of goods. X goes to work on the train, riding under a contract of carriage. X performs various tasks at work under a contract of employment and, on the way home from work, he stops to place a bet on a horse (an unenforceable wagering contract). X returns to his house which is probably subject to a very important contract, namely a lease or a mortgage. He is having the house redecorated, under a contract for the provision of services and materials. X takes his family for a ride in the car, which is protected by a contract of insurance. On his return, X watches his television which he hires under a contract. Finally, X walks his dog — no contract here!

2. The law of contract

There are particular types of contract, such as contracts of employment, which are subject to their own specialised rules of law and detailed legislation. A number of areas of law are concerned with the study of specific types of contract: eg commercial law involves the study of sale of goods and consumer credit agreements and labour law deals with contracts of employment. The law of contract is the study of the legal principles which underlie all contracts, it is not (generally) concerned with particular types of contracts and their specialised rules. The subject is an important foundation for the understanding of these other subjects. It also provides an essential introduction to the common law. For the law of contract is based primarily on the decisions of the courts (precedent), and these judicial rulings constitute the relevant law. Many principles of contract law owe their existence to decisions dating back hundreds of years, whilst some are of comparatively recent origin. There are some important statutes in the law of contract, for example the Law Reform (Frustrated Contracts) Act 1943 and the Misrepresentation Act 1967, but they build on a legal framework provided by the common law. It is in the area of consumer protection that Parliament has most frequently intervened in the development of contract law and, in addition to sale of goods legislation, there is now the Unfair Contract Terms Act 1977. Membership of the European Union has also affected our law; eg further powers have been given to our courts to regulate unfair terms in consumer contracts by the EC Directive on Unfair Terms in Consumer Contracts (1993)[1].

However, this concentration on the general principles of contract law, rather than on specific types of contract, can also be misleading. It presents the relevant law as almost exclusively based on case law and decided on narrow issues contested by the parties to a legal action. It fails to acknowledge the importance of public law and regulation to the law of contract. The diverse areas of specific contracts, eg employment, sale of goods, and the transfer of land may well raise different questions of public interest and government policy. The traditional approach to the study of contract law tells us very little about the importance of regulation; yet without this knowledge, no legal education would be complete. For instance, the study of consumer and commercial law will build on an understanding of the basic principles of contract and the relevant sale of goods statutes. But it goes further in considering public law approaches to the subject, such as fair trading, product safety, and the law relating to trade descriptions, especially where the civil law has proved ineffective in protecting consumers[2].

Another way in which the teaching of contract law can mislead is by an emphatically "legal" approach to what is essentially a pragmatic and practical subject. A study of appeal court decisions can give the impression that contracts lead inevitably to disputes and conflict. A contract law book or course presents what is comparatively rare (namely a legal action in the courts) as somehow typical. Traditional approaches tell us little about business practice and how it differs from the formal law. It is particularly important in the area of contractual remedies that we do not over-emphasise the importance of lawyers and the courts. As we have noted, a contract is simply a means of facilitating exchange (of goods, services etc) and if there is a dispute over its interpretation, or even if one party clearly breaks the agreement, this does not inevitably lead to litigation and the courts. The costs of a legal action can be prohibitive; only the very wealthy companies can contemplate protracted litigation without considerable unease.

Even where the parties can afford to go to court there are good reasons to try to avoid doing so. In commercial practice, some breaches of contract are seen less as a legal problem and more as a commercial one. Companies will want to avoid any damage to their reputation that might be caused by litigation. A legal action with its formal style, its conflict approach and its demands on time and money, can be damaging to continuing relationships in the business world. Even if successful, a party will normally fail to recover all the expenses that were incurred. For these and other reasons, business people try to resolve disputes without recourse to the courts. The same also applies to the consumer who, generally, can ill afford to take a claim to law. It is better to try negotiation and persuasion in the event of a contractual dispute. A seller of goods will often be more concerned about maintaining his reputation with the public than about an isolated dispute with a customer and he may be willing to settle a claim (for instance, by refunding the purchase price) even where he thinks that the customer is unlikely to sue or to succeed with a legal action[3]. In this way, informal pressure can be more effective than a legalistic or aggressive approach.

3. "Freedom of contract" — ① HISTORY OF CONTRACT.

Many important contractual principles, as expounded by the leading decisions of the courts, were established in the eighteenth and nineteenth centuries. It is interesting, at the outset, to assess their relevance to the law today. The "classical" view of contract was that the parties freely enter into an agreement or bargain as equals and therefore there should be as little state regulation or intervention as possible. It was not the task of the law to ensure that a fair bargain had been struck or to enquire whether the parties had in fact met as equals. This attitude was consistent with the *laissez-faire* philosophy which was so influential in the thinking of the time; it was consistent with the idea that contracts should be made by the parties (with freedom of choice) and not imposed on them by the state. It was thought to be consonant with a free market economy and the spirit of competition.

Even in its historical context, this approach raises obvious questions. It assumes a particular model of contractual activity; namely that between business people of fairly equal resources. It assumes the existence of genuine competition. Of course there never was true equality — a prerequisite for freedom of contract. How could such a doctrine apply as between employer and employee or between business people of disparate wealth and resources? In a more modern context, such a *laissez-faire* "world-view" seems absurd. It fails to take account of groups who are particularly susceptible to exploitation, such as consumers, tenants, and employees. Freedom of contract was always more illusory than real. In practice, the law of contract is often engaged in trying to balance the upholding of traditional market liberalism with the need to protect those who may be easily exploited.

There are now many circumstances in which there is neither freedom nor equality in matters of contracting. People are forced to make certain contracts in their lives, such as the compulsory insurance of motor vehicles for the protection of other road users, and contracts for public utilities such as gas or electricity (arguably privatisation has made little difference). There are many other instances where freedom of choice is minimal. But, more generally, there is less genuine choice than one would suppose in many areas. Many small companies are swallowed up by larger ones and in many industries there is relatively little, if any, genuine choice for the consumer. Despite the theory of competition there is an inexorable tendency towards monopoly. Different trades and industries form associations which standardise their dealings with the consumer and this is harmful to choice and competition. The customer finds, in selecting his or her new car for example, that despite the large number of different retailers and dealers, there is little difference in many of the standard terms that they employ. It is unrealistic to suppose that the consumer can renegotiate the terms of such a contract. The use of standard form contracts is a fact of commercial life and has been for a long time.

It has been argued that the 1980s witnessed a renaissance of classical principles[4]. The political emphasis upon freedom of choice, the value of a free market economy, and a less paternalistic role for the state are all associated with Conservative governments between 1979 and 1997. This political and economic climate fostered (or so it is argued) a resurgence in the idea of freedom of contract. There can be little doubt that such a political climate emphasised greater self-reliance on the part of the individual and less dependence on a benevolent state. It is also true that this had some repercussions for certain types of contracts. For example, the political aim of these governments was to remove some of the regulation pertaining to rents and employment, under the rallying cry of "freedom of contract". There was also some reduction in the amount of government regulation of the business community, especially in relation to small businesses[5]. However, it is debatable how far these political changes affected the common law. It is even questionable whether there was, in fact, a return to classical principles — at least to any significant extent. It is submitted that the supposed swing of the pendulum back towards freedom of contract was not far reaching. Also it is not simply government policy that influences statutory intervention in contractual matters. It is possible to point to other developments, emanating from the work of the Law Commission, which have made further inroads into freedom of contract. For example, s 2(1) Law of Property (Miscellaneous Provisions) Act 1989 provides that contracts for the sale or other disposition of an interest in land can only be made in writing, altering the law which previously required only that such contracts be evidenced in writing[6].

4.   Inequality of bargaining power

An important concept in the law of contract is that of inequality of bargaining strength. It is this concept that was ignored by the classical theory, with its emphasis on freedom (or even "sanctity") of contract. Without genuine economic equality, freedom of contract can be merely a recipe for exploitation and injustice. A major influence in the decline of the freedom of contract philosophy has been the emergence of the consumer as a contractual force. The traditional model of contracts as a means of exchange between business people must now accommodate the idea of exchange between a business person and a consumer. This means that the inevitable inequality of bargaining strength (in relation to wealth, resources and experience) must be acknowledged by the law. The twentieth century saw a move towards greater state regulation of many types of contract, including commercial and consumer contracts. A good example is the Unfair Contract Terms Act 1977 which went further in regulating and restricting the use of exclusion clauses than any previous control provided by the courts. There is also public law regulation of consumer affairs through the imposition, *inter alia*, of fair trading standards.

There is, then, acceptance of the idea that certain contracting parties need the protection of the law against economic exploitation and oppression. This interventionist approach — "welfare" or "paternalistic" are other descriptions — is now seen as a legitimate function of the law. Major legislation has gradually helped to prevent the exploitation of tenants and employees and to reduce the incidence of sex discrimination. The classical theory of contract has less relevance today: there is formal acknowledgment that the parties do not always meet as equals when it comes to striking a bargain.

For the above reasons, it might be questioned why many important principles of the law of contract, laid down by the courts under the influence of the classical theory, still appear to survive today. This is a paradox which is not always explained in the teaching of contract law. The key to understanding lies partly in the distinction between the theory and the practice of the law. We have seen earlier how the traditional teaching of contract tends to over-emphasise the importance of the common law and the courts and tends to understate the importance of regulation. Also, in the courts, judges are more flexible and innovative than it might appear from some textbook discussions of the subject. The judge possesses a variety of techniques that can be utilised to avoid an undesirable or an unjust result; for instance, by implying terms, by the use of equity, or by construction of ambiguities against the less deserving party.

Many apparent principles of contract law are not so firmly established or so unequivocal as they seem at first sight. The essentially flexible and pragmatic nature of the common law should be clearly understood from the outset. The law is a living and developing thing and cannot be reduced to a set of axioms or precepts as if it were an exact science. This is the challenge of the subject and from this it derives its enduring interest.

Footnotes

(1) See the Unfair Terms in Consumer Contracts Regulations 1999 (SI 1999 No 2083) which implemented the Directive.

(2) For example, see the Trade Descriptions Act 1968 which was enacted to deal with misleading descriptions applied to goods, misleading prices and statements in respect of services.

(3) Also see the Law Commission Report, No 160, *Sale and Supply of Goods*, Cm 137, 1987.

(4) See P Atiyah, *Introduction to the Law of Contract*, 5th ed, 1995, pp 27–34.

(5) See the White Paper, *Building Businesses... Not Barriers*, Cmnd 9794, 1986. This states (at p 1) that "the government recognize that all too often the energies of people can be diverted away from their main wealth-creating activities by rules and regulations which are complicated or obsolete".

(6) Section 2(8) Law of Property (Miscellaneous Provisions) Act 1989 repeals s 40 Law of Property Act 1925.

Chapter 2

Formation of the contract

1. The need for agreement

Whichever definition of the law of contract we use, the word "agreement" will be central to it; put simply, it is the law relating to and regulating agreements. A contract is a legally enforceable agreement giving rise to obligations for the parties to it. However, not all agreements are legally binding contracts and no legal system could enforce all agreements; it would be both impracticable and inconvenient. For example, in our law, social and domestic agreements are generally not legally enforceable, unless there is clear evidence of an intention to create legal relations between the parties (see *Balfour* v *Balfour* [1919] 2 KB 571). The law also requires that something of value must be given by both parties to an agreement; it will not enforce gratuitous promises. This is the requirement of consideration which is fundamental to simple contracts (see Chapter 4). In *Re Hudson* (1885) 54 LJ Ch 811:

> Hudson had promised to pay £4,000 a year for five years to a religious charity to help it pay off chapel debts. He died before the two final instalments could be paid and his executors claimed that his estate was not liable for the remaining £8,000 as there was no binding contract in law. The judge ruled that no consideration had been given by the charity in exchange for Hudson's promise. The promise was gratuitous, and there was no contract in any legal sense of the word. Thus Hudson's estate was not liable for the remaining instalments.

If a promise like Hudson's were made in writing by deed, it would be enforceable even in the absence of consideration, because then the formality of the contract would give it legal force. But, most contracts are not made in this way and, generally, we are concerned with "simple" contracts which require consideration. A contract, therefore, is an agreement with undertakings (promises or obligations) on both sides; and it is an agreement that is intended to have legal consequences.

The agreement is often said to require a meeting of the minds between the contracting parties; this is sometimes described as a *consensus ad idem*. However, this supposed requirement is rather misleading, as the law tends to take an objective approach to agreement. The law is not so much concerned with what is in the minds of the parties, but with what can be inferred from their conduct. In *Storer* v *Manchester City Council* [1974] 3 All ER 824 at p 828, Lord Denning stated:

"In contracts you do not look into the actual intent in a man's mind. You look at what he said and did. A contract is formed when there is, to all outward appearances, a contract."

The reason for a predominantly objective approach is that it is not possible to ascertain a person's private or subjective intention when bargaining for a contract. In the interests of fairness, certainty and commercial convenience, the parties are deemed to have reached agreement if, viewed objectively, they *appear* to have agreed. However, it should be noted that there are differing conceptions of what precisely is meant by an objective approach to agreement. For example, it could mean that it is to be assessed in relation to a reasonable person in the position of the offeree, as in *First Energy (UK) Ltd* v *Hungarian International Bank Ltd* [1993] BCLC 1409 (per Steyn LJ at p 1417). Alternatively, the objective approach could be interpreted as the understanding of the parties' actions from the perspective of a reasonable, but uninvolved bystander[1].

In most cases there will, of course, be both actual and objective agreement. But, if one party knows that the other has no intention of contracting with him, despite an objective appearance of agreement, there will be no contract between them. In this situation, the law would not pursue an objective approach.

The objective principle helps to prevent a party to a contract resiling from the agreement simply because he did not make a good bargain. For example, in 1984 some small investors in British Telecom sold their shares over the telephone to dealers and then tried to sell the same shares several times over as the market rose very rapidly. The contract for the sale of the shares was concluded over the telephone and therefore the sellers were bound by their original agreements. Whatever the innermost or subjective intention of the sellers may have been, they gave the outward appearance of having reached agreement[2]. In the interests of certainty and fairness a person is bound by his apparent agreement. A further illustration of the objective approach is provided by the case of *Moran* v *University College Salford (No 2)* [1993] The Times 23 November where M, an applicant for a place on a physiotherapy course, was sent an unconditional offer from the defendants as a result of a clerical error. M accepted the offer in the prescribed manner, but was later informed by the defendants of the error. The Court of Appeal stated that the unconditional offer of a place, despite the defendants' error, was capable of being accepted by M thus creating a binding agreement under which the university was committed to accept him for the course.

In *Trentham Ltd* v *Archital Luxfer* [1993] 1 Lloyd's Rep 25 (see below), Steyn LJ stated (at p 27):

"our law generally ignores the subjective expectations and unexpressed mental reservations of the parties. Instead the governing criterion is the reasonable expectations of honest men".

In *Cheddar Valley Engineering Ltd* v *Chaddlewood Homes Ltd* [1992] 4 All ER 942, a disagreement arose over whether negotiations between the parties' solicitors, about an existing dispute, were conducted on a "without prejudice" basis, or whether they were "open" — ie fully disclosable to the court. The negotiations commenced on a "without prejudice" basis, and the parties gave conflicting accounts of whether a later communication by telephone altered this understanding. The defendant's contention, that the negotiations had become "open", failed because a reasonable person (in the plaintiff's position) would not have understood this to be the case from the communications between the parties.

In *The "Bay Ridge"* [1999] 2 Lloyd's Rep 227, the parties entered into negotiations for the sale of an oil tanker, agreeing on certain main terms. As further terms and conditions were still to be agreed between the parties, the issue for the High Court was whether the initial negotiations resulted in a binding contract of sale. Cresswell J held that there was no concluded contract as the intentions of the parties, judged objectively, were that negotiations would continue as further terms were still to be agreed. He stated (at p 241) that the judge's task is:

> "[T]o review what the parties said and did and from that material to infer whether the parties' objective intentions as expressed to each other were to enter into a mutually binding contract ... to discern and give effect to the objective intentions of the parties."

2. Offer and acceptance — the traditional approach

In deciding whether the parties have reached agreement, the law looks for an offer by one party and an acceptance of the terms of that offer by the other. In the bargaining process leading up to an agreement (or meeting of the minds), one party will finally propose terms (price, date of delivery etc) and express a willingness to be bound by them if the other party signifies his acceptance of them. This is the traditional analysis of offer and acceptance which has been applied by the courts to the formation of contracts. It must be firmly stated that this approach, whilst convenient for analytical purposes (indeed a great many contracts are in fact made by such a process), does have its limitations. Judges differ in their attitudes to the need for a strict adherence to the offer and acceptance analysis (see *Gibson* v *Manchester City Council,* below). For example, in a recent Court of Appeal decision, *Trentham Ltd* v *Archital Luxfer* [1993] 1 Lloyd's Rep 25, Steyn LJ's approach (at pp 29–30) to the formation of a construction contract showed more concern for the parties' intentions and for commercial reality than it did for any technical requirement of "matching" offer and acceptance. Also, in certain everyday consumer transactions, such as buying goods in a supermarket, it is difficult to detect any genuine process of negotiation or bargaining between the parties.

Moreover, some agreements cannot be explained by the traditional approach — for example, see *Clarke* v *Dunraven* [1897] AC 59. There are also exceptional cases where, contrary to legal theory, the courts adopt a public policy approach and appear to impose an agreement on the parties in the interest of fairness. This type of "agreement" does not result from any bargaining process and clearly does not conform to the traditional offer and acceptance analysis. Examples of this judicial approach, and the limitations of the traditional analysis, are considered at the end of this chapter.

3. Offer

An offer is a proposal or promise by one party (the offeror) to enter into a contract, on a particular set of terms, with the intention of being bound as soon as the party to whom the promise is made (the offeree) signifies his acceptance. An offer may be made either to an individual person, or to a particular group of people, or it may be made to the general public (as in the case of a reward offered for the provision of information). An offer may be written, spoken or implied by conduct; it may be made with varying degrees of complexity. Although this sounds straightforward, in fact what amounts to an offer can give rise to differences of opinion. During the bargaining process, there may be a series of communications between the parties as they move towards a final agreement, and it may be difficult to state with confidence whether a particular statement was an offer, or whether it was part of continuing negotiations between the parties. A possible test which can be applied is to ask whether further bargaining was still expected or whether the statement shows a clear willingness to be bound if the other party assents. This test, although valid, is probably simpler to state than it is to apply, and the cases on this subject are not always easy to reconcile.

(a) Offer or invitation to treat?

A good illustration of the difficulty in distinguishing between an offer and an invitation to the other party to make an offer (an "invitation to treat") can be found in the important House of Lords' decision in *Gibson v Manchester City Council* [1979] 1 WLR 294. The facts were:

> The Conservative-controlled Manchester City Council advertised details of a scheme for tenants to buy their council houses from the corporation and P expressed interest and asked to be told the price of buying his house. The city treasurer wrote in reply: "The corporation may be prepared to sell the house to you at . . . £2,180", but the letter was not to be "regarded as a firm offer of a mortgage". P had to fill in a form to make a formal application, which he did, leaving blank the purchase price and listing certain defects in the property. He was told by the Council that the price had been fixed in accordance with the condition of the property, and P wrote that he wished to go ahead on the basis of his application. The Council took the house off the list of tenant-occupied houses which had to be maintained by them, and put it on their house purchase list. As a result of a local election, Labour gained control of the Council and reversed the policy of selling council houses. They would sell only those houses where a legally binding contract had already been concluded.

The trial judge and the Court of Appeal decided that there was a contract and ordered specific performance (that is, an order compelling the Manchester Council to sell the property to P). In the Court of Appeal, Lord Denning stated that the parties appeared to have reached agreement on all the material terms and this was evidenced by their correspondence and conduct. He thought that it did not matter that "all the formalities had not been gone through"[3]. He was overtly critical of the traditional approach which tries to analyse all contracts into the form of offer and acceptance.

The House of Lords allowed the Council's appeal and made it clear that the Council's statement of the price of the house was not an offer to Mr Gibson. It was merely one stage in the negotiating process. The language of the treasurer's letter indicated this with the phrases: "may be prepared to sell" and "this letter is not to be regarded as a firm offer of a mortgage". In reply to the argument that the parties' agreement could be shown by their conduct, it can be said that their conduct was equivocal. The house was taken off the list of properties maintained by the Council but this could merely indicate that the house was to be sold in the near future and not that agreement had been reached. The most damaging fact for the plaintiff to overcome was the uncertainty over whether he would be granted a mortgage: would he have gone ahead if he had been unable to obtain one? Would any court have ordered him to do so? The successive communications between the parties show that they were feeling their way towards agreement, but that the negotiations had not yet ripened into a contract.

The case can be contrasted with *Storer* v *Manchester City Council* [1974] 3 All ER 824, which also arose out of the change of policy in relation to council house sales. The main difference between the cases is that in *Storer* the plaintiff received a letter from the Council's representative which stated: "I understand you wish to purchase your council house and enclose the Agreement for Sale. If you sign the agreement and return it to me I will send you the agreement signed on behalf of the Corporation in exchange". He signed and returned the Council's standard form "Agreement for Sale" before control of the Council changed.

Despite the fact that the agreement had not been signed on behalf of the Council, the Court of Appeal decided that there was a binding contract and specific performance was ordered. The conclusion which can be drawn (albeit tentatively) is that, in *Storer*, the letter from the Council was more capable of being interpreted as an offer to sell the property than it was in *Gibson*. The Court of Appeal was keen to enforce the apparent agreement in *Storer* in spite of any technical objections that there had been no exchange of contracts between the parties. But it should be observed that the Council's letter in *Storer* also left certain important details to be decided later. The date for the termination of the tenancy and the start of the mortgage repayments was left blank; yet the property was to be at P's risk from this unspecified date.

As *Gibson* illustrates, the statement of a price by one party does not necessarily indicate that there is an offer to sell at that price, that is, without further negotiations. It is important to look at all the surrounding circumstances. Stating a price might be simply a response to a request for information. In *Harvey* v *Facey* [1893] AC 552, P sent a telegram to D: "Will you sell us Bumper Hall Pen? Telegraph lowest cash price". D's telegram replied: "Lowest price for Bumper Hall Pen, £900". P's final telegram purported to accept this "offer" and "agreed" to buy the property for £900. The Privy Council held that there was no contract as D was not making an offer merely by responding to P's request for information and stating a price. There was no clear intention to be bound simply by the other party's expression of assent. (For a similar result, see *Clifton* v *Palumbo* [1944] 2 All ER 497.)

The distinction between an offer and an invitation to treat is, therefore, often difficult to draw. One has to consider the communications between the parties and try to ascertain the intention with which a statement was made; does the statement evince a willingness to be bound if the other party expresses agreement? It may be necessary to look at a series of statements or letters which pass between the parties, during the negotiating process, to assess the overall impression conveyed by these communications. In *Bigg* v *Boyd Gibbins Ltd* [1971] 2 All ER 183, during the course of negotiations for the sale of his property to D, P stated that "for a quick sale [he] would accept £26,000". D replied by letter that he accepted this offer. P wrote back, expressing his pleasure at D's decision and stating that he was putting the matter in the hands of his solicitor to proceed with the sale. The Court of Appeal held that the impression given by these communications was that the parties "intended to and did achieve the formation of a . . . contract" (per Russell LJ at p 185).

The use of the word "offer" by one party is not decisive; the courts might still interpret a statement as an invitation to treat. In *Spencer v Harding* (1870) LR 5 CP 561, D sent out a circular: "We are instructed to offer [certain business stock] to the wholesale trade for sale by tender . . .". P's tender for the stock was the highest that D received, but D refused to accept it. P's contention was that the circular amounted to an offer and contained a promise to sell to the highest bidder. Generally, advertisements are not regarded as offers, but P tried to draw an analogy with advertisements of rewards for information (dealt with below) where there is a promise to pay the first person who supplies the information. But the court rejected this line of reasoning; there was no promise to sell to the highest bidder. In finding for the defendant, Willes J stated (at p 563):

> "[T]he question is, whether there is here any offer to enter into a contract at all, or whether the circular amounts to anything more than a mere proclamation that the defendants are ready to chaffer for the sale of goods, and to receive offers for the purchase of them . . . Here there is a total absence of any words to intimate that the highest bidder is to be the purchaser. It is a mere attempt to ascertain whether an offer can be obtained within such a margin as the sellers are willing to adopt".

Where a party invites bids (eg for property or shares), it is necessary to look at all the circumstances in deciding whether he intends to bind himself to the highest bidder. The question is whether the invitation goes beyond a mere invitation to treat and amounts to an offer capable of being accepted by the successful bidder. In *Harvela Investments Ltd v Royal Trust Co of Canada* [1984] 2 All ER 65:

> D(1) owned a parcel of shares which would give effective control of a company to either P or D(2), who were rivals bidding for the shares. D(1) invited both parties to submit, by sealed bid, a "single offer" for the whole parcel by a particular time and date. In making the invitation, they stated that: "we bind ourselves to accept [the highest] offer." P made a single bid, but D(2)'s bid was really two bids, being (a) for a fixed monetary amount (which was less than that bid by P); and (b) a referential bid which offered $101,000 in excess of any other offer that D(1) received. D(1) accepted D(2)'s referential bid and entered into a contract with them for the sale of the shares. P claimed that D(2)'s successful bid was not valid as it was not within the terms of the original invitation to bid (because it was not a "single offer"). P succeeded in this action. (NB Despite reversal in the Court of Appeal, the House of Lords restored the original decision in P's favour.)

In this case we can see a different intention on the part of the sellers, when inviting bids, from that in *Spencer v Harding*. In *Harvela*, the sellers bound themselves to accept the highest offer; this statement was itself an offer rather than a mere invitation to treat. A binding contract for the sale of the parcel of shares was made with the highest (valid) bidder at the time of the closing of bids. No further bargaining was either intended or necessary due to the way in which the invitation was expressed. (See the House of Lords' analysis of the transaction into two contracts: [1986] AC 207. *Quaere*: Is such an explanation necessary?)

Where X invites tenders from a small selected group of potentially interested parties, and tenders are received in accordance with the stipulated conditions of tender, is X under a contractual obligation to consider all the tenders when making his decision? This question arose in the case of *Blackpool & Fylde Aero Club Ltd* v *Blackpool Borough Council* [1990] 3 All ER 25. The facts were as follows:

> The defendant council owned an airport, from which it permitted an air operator to run pleasure trips. This concession had been granted to the plaintiff club on previous occasions and, on the expiry of the last concession, the council invited the club and six other parties to tender for the rights to operate pleasure flights from the airport. A very clear procedure for submitting bids was laid down by the council, and it was stated that tenders received after noon, 17 March 1983, would not be considered. Only the plaintiff club and two others responded to this invitation. The plaintiff's tender was put in the Town Hall letter box one hour before the deadline, but due to an oversight the letter box was not cleared by council staff at noon that day as it was supposed to be. (The council accepted that this was due to administrative error.) The plaintiff's tender was recorded as late and was therefore not considered. The club contended that the council was contractually bound to consider any tender that was validly made and received by the deadline. It sought damages from the council.

It was clear from the wording of the council's invitation to tender that it was not promising to accept the highest tender it received. But was it bound at least to consider all tenders submitted within the specified period? The Court of Appeal held that the council was liable in damages to the club for breach of contract. It held that, in certain circumstances, an invitation to tender could give rise to a contractual undertaking by the invitor to consider tenders which conformed with the stipulated conditions of tender. Bingham LJ stated (at p 30):

> "[W]here, as here, tenders are solicited from selected parties all of them known to the invitor, and where a local authority's invitation prescribes a clear, orderly and familiar procedure . . . the invitee is in my judgement protected at least to this extent: if he submits a conforming tender before the deadline he is entitled, not as a matter of mere expectation but of contractual right, to be sure that his tender will after the deadline be opened and considered in conjunction with all other conforming tenders or at least that his tender will be considered if others are."

The council was not obliged to accept any tender. Alternatively, it could have awarded the concession to any tenderer, so long as the decision was taken in good faith. But the council was contractually bound to consider the plaintiff's tender before making its decision. The outcome of the case is perhaps surprising. In effect the court implied a contract between the parties, who were merely in the process of negotiation[4].

(b) Offer or invitation to treat: practical examples

Because of the difficulty in distinguishing between an offer and an invitation to treat, the law has attempted to clarify the position in certain common types of transaction. For the sake of convenience, and for technical reasons, it is important to understand the process of offer and acceptance in shops, and auction sales, and in connection with tenders, advertisements, and automatic vending machines.

(i) Advertisements

As a general rule the advertisement of goods for sale is not to be regarded as an offer. In *Partridge* v *Crittenden* [1968] 2 All ER 421 the appellant was charged, under legislation for the protection of wild birds, with unlawfully offering for sale a wild bird. He had placed an advertisement in a magazine: "Bramblefinch cocks and hens, 25s each". The Divisional Court held that the appellant was not liable for the statutory offence as he had not offered the birds for sale; the advertisement was an invitation to treat.

The issuing of a catalogue or circular with a price-list, is not to be regarded as an offer to sell those goods. If a person sees a price-list and places an order, the seller is not normally bound to supply the goods. (See *Grainger & Son* v *Gough* [1896] AC 325.) A seller of goods has to be free to give information about his goods (ie advertise them) in the interests of a competitive market. It would inhibit this flow of information if he were to be contractually bound to supply to anyone who placed an order, as the seller might not have sufficient stock to meet the demand. Similarly, the advertisement of an auction of specific goods will not be construed as an offer to sell those goods. There is no promise to sell the goods and the auctioneer will not be liable for withdrawing them from the sale without notice. For example, in *Harris* v *Nickerson* (1873) LR 8 QB 286, P attended an auction in order to buy furniture which the auctioneer had advertised for sale. When the furniture was not put up for sale, P's subsequent claim for damages (for his loss of time) failed as the court held that the advertisement was not an offer of sale. Blackburn J stated that to hold otherwise "would be excessively inconvenient".

The reasoning behind the rule that advertisements are not to be treated as offers is that further bargaining between the parties is still possible or even necessary. This is thought to serve the interests of commercial convenience, albeit the seller's rather than the buyer's convenience. But there are situations where an advertisement is couched in terms which will be interpreted as an offer because no further bargaining between the parties is possible or intended. Advertisements of rewards (eg for information or the return of lost property) fall into this category. In the famous case of *Carlill* v *Carbolic Smoke Ball Co* [1893] 1 QB 256:

> The defendant company placed an advertisement in the newspaper offering a reward of £100 to anyone who bought one of its smoke balls, and used it in the prescribed manner, and yet caught influenza. To show its "sincerity in the matter", the company deposited £1,000 with its bank. Relying upon this advertisement, the plaintiff bought a smoke ball and used it as directed — and still caught influenza! The plaintiff sued successfully for the £100 reward and the defendant company appealed against the decision.

A variety of arguments were put forward by the defendants to defeat the plaintiff's claim for the reward. It was argued that the advertisement was too vague and that the defendants did not intend to be bound by it. These arguments were rejected by the Court of Appeal which held that both the meaning and the effect of the advertisement were clear. It was immaterial that the plaintiff did not notify the company of her acceptance before using the

smoke ball and catching influenza. Where an offer takes the form (
or reward in exchange for a particular act or acts — in what is kn
unilateral offer — there is no need for notification of acceptance. The on
accepted by performance of the act or condition. Hence the plaintiff was
entitled to the reward. The advertisement of the reward was an offer as no
further bargaining or negotiation was intended by the offeror.

This decision was relied upon recently in the Court of Appeal case of
Bowerman v *Association of British Travel Agents Ltd* [1996] CLC 456. This
case involved the cancellation of a school skiing holiday booked with
Adventure Express, an Association of British Travel Agents (ABTA) tour
operator. Adventure Express became insolvent and, although the holiday was
rearranged with another firm, the ABTA reimbursement did not include the
plaintiffs' holiday insurance premium paid on behalf of each pupil going on the
holiday. The plaintiffs' claim for a refund of this insurance payment was
rejected at the trial and the plaintiffs appealed relying on ABTA's notice, which
was displayed in all its members' offices, detailing the protection given to
customers in the event of financial failure of ABTA members. The plaintiffs'
appeal was based on the argument that the ABTA notice amounted to a
unilateral offer to all customers of failed ABTA tour operators, containing
promises which were legally enforceable by customers. This argument had
been rejected by the trial judge on the basis that the ABTA notice was merely
to inform the public of the ABTA protection scheme, and was not an offer by
ABTA to the customer, and also that it was too vague to be construed as an
offer.

The plaintiffs' appeal was allowed by a majority (Hirst LJ dissenting). It was
held that the ABTA notice was intended to be understood by members of the
public as containing an offer which the customer accepted by contracting with
an ABTA member. There was the necessary intention to create legal relations
on ABTA's part, and the promises contained in the notice were not too vague
to be legally enforceable. It was also held that customers provided consideration for ABTA's promise, as it was to ABTA's benefit that customers chose to
contract with its members. Waite LJ (at p 457) thought that the ABTA notice,
despite its complexities, would be understood by a potential customer as
importing an intention to create legal relations with customers of ABTA
members. In particular, he relied on the words in the notice which stated:
"Where holidays or other travel arrangements have not yet commenced at the
time of failure, ABTA arranges for you to be reimbursed the money you have
paid in respect of your holiday arrangements". Waite LJ thought that these
words would be understood by a reasonable person as a clear promise.
Hobhouse LJ stated (at p 463):

> "In my judgement this document is intended to be read and would reasonably
> be read by a member of the public as containing an offer of a promise which
> the customer is entitled to accept by choosing to do business with an ABTA
> member ... it satisfies the criteria for a unilateral contract and contains
> promises which are sufficiently clear to be capable of legal enforcement. The
> principles established in the *Carbolic Smoke Ball* case apply."

(ii) Items displayed in shops

It might be supposed that goods displayed in shop windows, or on shop
counters, with the prices clearly marked, are being offered for sale. In certain

types of shops or markets a limited degree of bargaining (or "haggling") may be possible. But in the vast majority of shops, stores and supermarkets, this is neither possible nor expected; goods are to be sold at the prices shown and no negotiation takes place between retailer and customer. Yet it is firmly established by the decided cases that the display of goods in a shop is not an offer to sell those goods. In *Pharmaceutical Society of Great Britain* v *Boots Cash Chemists* [1953] 1 QB 401:

> It had to be decided at what point a contract is concluded in a "self-service" shop where the goods are priced and displayed on shelves, selected by customers, and then taken to the cash-desk for payment. The case arose under s 18(1) Pharmacy and Poisons Act 1933 which stated that "... it shall not be lawful — (a) for a person to sell any [listed] poison, unless ... the sale is effected by, or under the supervision of a registered pharmacist". It was brought to establish whether the defendants were breaking the law by positioning their registered pharmacist (who was supposed to supervise sales) adjacent to the cash-desk. If the display of goods on the shelves were regarded as an offer to sell and could be accepted by the customer when they were picked up and put into the basket provided, then the defendants were breaking the law, as the sale would not be supervised by the pharmacist as required by the statute. But if the display of items were merely an invitation to treat and it was the customer who made the offer at the cash-desk, then Boots were complying with the law.

It was decided that the contract was concluded at the cash-desk; the customer made the offer and this could be accepted or rejected by the defendants. Therefore, sales were supervised by the registered pharmacist. The court argued (*per* Somervell LJ, below) that if the display of items on the shelf amounted to an offer, a customer who picked up items and put them into the basket provided would thereby accept the offer and be contractually bound to pay for the goods even if he later changed his mind and did not want the goods. Somervell LJ stated (at p 406):

> "I can see no reason for implying from this self-service arrangement any implication other than that ... it is a convenient method of enabling customers to see what there is and choose, and possibly put back and substitute, articles which they wish to have, and then go up to the cashier and offer to buy what they have so far chosen".

It could be argued with equal force that if the display of goods were regarded as an offer, the acceptance by the customer would take place only when the goods are presented at the cash-desk for payment and not when they are placed into the basket. However, this view does not represent the law as it stands, which is that the display of goods in a self-service shop, supermarket, or shop window does not amount to an offer to sell those goods. (See *Fisher* v *Bell* [1961] 1 QB 394, where it was held that the display of a "flick-knife" in a shop window was not an offer to sell this item.) It is interesting that the cases which have arisen have involved the sale of prohibited or restricted items to the public and not from any dispute between buyer and seller as to when the contract was formed. It is also important to consider whether there is any statutory regulation of the way goods are advertised, priced and displayed in shops[5]. Should shops be allowed to lure customers in with tempting "offers" if either they have no intention of selling at the advertised price, or they intend to impose some restriction on the type of person to whom they will sell their goods? (For an interesting American case which raises similar issues, see *Lefkowitz* v *Great Minneapolis Surplus Stores* (1957) 86 NW 2d 689).

(iii) Auctions

Where an auctioneer asks for bids, he is not making an offer to sell the goods to the highest bidder. It was established in *Payne* v *Cave* (1789) 3 Term Rep 148 that the auctioneer is merely inviting offers from bidders, which he can either accept or reject. This rule is now encapsulated in s 57(2) Sale of Goods Act 1979 which states:

> "A sale by auction is complete when the auctioneer announces its completion by the fall of the hammer, or in other customary manner; and until the announcement is made any bidder may retract his bid."

We have seen that the advertisement of an auction sale is not an offer to sell particular goods. But is there a binding promise to sell the goods to the highest bidder where an auction sale, which is advertised as "without reserve", actually takes place? The point is not resolved satisfactorily by the case of *Warlow* v *Harrison* (1859) 1 E & E 309, despite *obiter dicta* supporting the view that such an advertisement may include a separate and binding promise by the auctioneer to sell to the highest bona fide bidder. (However, *Warlow* v *Harrison* was applied recently in *Barry* v *Davies* [2000] 1 WLR 1962.)

(iv) Automatic machines

It seems that the display of goods in an automatic vending machine is an offer to sell those goods, rather than a mere invitation to treat. In this situation, no further bargaining between the parties is either possible or necessary. The customer accepts the offer by putting money into the machine and receives the goods or ticket. If the machine is empty it must be implied that the offer continues only whilst stocks last. (The same argument could be used to support the view that goods displayed in shops ought to be regarded as offered for sale; but, in theory, bargaining is still possible.)

It might be argued that analysing a sale by vending machine into offer and acceptance is of merely academic, rather than practical, significance. But there may be disputes as to precisely when a contract was formed and which terms were incorporated. If one party seeks to rely on terms printed on a ticket (such as an exclusion clause), it becomes important to know whether these terms were incorporated into the contract or whether they were ineffective for being introduced too late. For example, is the acceptance already complete when a ticket is taken by a motorist entering a multi-storey car park, having put money into a machine? If so, does this mean that terms printed on such a ticket have no contractual effect as the motorist is not given notice of them until after the contract is concluded? In *Thornton* v *Shoe Lane Parking* [1971] 2 QB 163, a similar issue was raised and Lord Denning explained the transaction as follows:

> "The customer pays his money and gets a ticket. He cannot refuse it . . . he was committed at the very moment when he put his money into the machine. It can be translated into offer and acceptance in this way: the offer is made when the proprietor of the machine holds it out as being ready to receive the money. The acceptance takes place when the customer puts his money into the slot."

4. Acceptance

According to traditional analysis, contracts are usually arrived at by one party proposing terms and the other party agreeing to them. The law looks for an offer by one party (the offeror) and an acceptance of the terms of that offer by the other (known as the offeree), as the best method of establishing agreement between them. Although this is an accurate way of representing the bargaining process in the majority of cases, there are transactions which do not fit easily into this traditional approach (see earlier discussion). Also, it should be remembered that the law takes an objective view of agreement. A further problem is that during the negotiating process the parties may add or withdraw terms, and it may be disputed whether the parties did in fact reach agreement.

What constitutes acceptance of an offer? It is the final expression of assent, by words or conduct, to the offer or proposal. It should be conveyed in the manner indicated by the offeror, where a particular means of communication is requested or implied. It is important that the acceptance is both final and unequivocal; put simply, it must be an acceptance of the offeror's proposal without varying the terms or adding new terms. A purported acceptance which attempts to introduce new terms, or vary those contained in the offer, will be regarded as a counter offer and not as an acceptance of the original offer.

In *Jones* v *Daniel* [1894] 2 Ch 332, D wrote and offered to buy P's property for £1,450 and received a reply from P's solicitor which purported to accept the offer and enclosed a contract for D's signature. However, the document contained important new terms that were not part of D's original offer, and D refused to sign it. It was held that there was no contract between the parties; the letter from P's solicitor (with its draft contract) was not an acceptance, but a counter offer which D was free to accept or reject. Similarly, if a person offers to pay a fixed price for services and materials, this will not be accepted by a promise to provide those services and materials at a variable price. (See *North West Leicestershire District Council* v *East Midlands Housing Association* [1981] 1 WLR 1396.)

A counter offer amounts to a rejection of the original offer. In *Hyde* v *Wrench* (1840) 3 Beav 334, D made a written offer to sell his farm to P for £1,000, to which P replied that he would give £950 for it. D refused to sell at the lower price and, a few days later, P wrote to D agreeing to pay £1,000 for the property. D had not withdrawn his original offer, but he now refused to sell to P. The court held that there was no contract; P's counter offer (of £950) was a rejection of D's original offer and brought it to an end. It could not be revived afterwards by P simply purporting to accept it. (See also *Norfolk County Council* v *Dencora Properties Ltd* (1995) EGCS 173, in which the Court of Appeal referred approvingly to the well-established rule in *Hyde* v *Wrench*.) However, there are situations where the offeree does not put forward a new proposal but merely seeks clarification of the offer or further information about it from the offeror. In such a case the offer is not to be regarded as rejected and it is still open to the offeree to accept it. This is illustrated by the case of *Stevenson* v *McLean* (1880) 5 QB 346:

> D wrote to P offering to sell a quantity of iron at "40s per ton net cash", and stating that the offer would remain open until the following Monday. It was clear from communications between the parties that P, in turn, was looking for buyers and that the market was unsettled. Early on Monday morning, P sent D a telegram: "Please

wire whether you would accept forty for delivery over two months, or if not, longest limit you would give". D did not answer P's question and sold the iron to a third party. On Monday afternoon, P (having had no reply) sent another telegram accepting D's offer to sell at 40s cash. P's final telegram was sent before D's withdrawal of the offer reached P. P sued for breach of contract, and D claimed that P's telegram of Monday morning amounted to a counter offer and therefore a rejection of D's offer.

Was the plaintiff's first telegram a fresh proposal, or did it merely seek to clarify an aspect of D's offer? The distinction can be a fine one, but the court ruled in P's favour. Lush J held that P did not make a counter offer: "Here there is no counter proposal ... there is nothing specific by way of offer or rejection, but a mere enquiry, which should have been answered and not treated as a rejection of the offer" (at p 350). But where one party offers to supply goods to another at a certain price and the offeree purports to accept, but adds a new stipulation requiring delivery within a fixed period of time, this will probably be regarded as a counter offer. (See *Northland Airliners Ltd* v *Dennis Ferranti Meters Ltd* (1970) 114 SJ 845.)

(a) Acceptance by conduct

In a unilateral contract the offeree signifies acceptance by conduct; that is, by performance of the act or condition stipulated in the offer. In *Carlill* v *Carbolic Smoke Ball Co* the court rejected the argument that the plaintiff failed to notify the defendant company of her acceptance of their offer before using the product. She accepted by buying the smoke ball and using it as instructed; by claiming the reward after catching influenza, she was entitled to succeed. In a bilateral contract, acceptance may be signified by words or documents, or by the conduct of the parties. (Whether an offer is unilateral or bilateral may be a matter for debate and it should not be supposed that the distinction is unproblematic. Also see *Dawson* v *Helicopter Exploration Co Ltd* [1955] 5 DLR 404.) In *Brogden* v *Metropolitan Railway Co* (1877) 2 App Cas 666:

> B had supplied the Metropolitan Railway Co with coal for some years without a formal agreement. The parties decided to formalise their transactions and the Metropolitan Railway Co sent B a draft agreement. B completed certain details in the draft which had been left blank, including the name of an arbitrator, and B then signed it and wrote "approved", and returned it to the Metropolitan Railway Co whose manager put it in his desk. Nothing further was done formally with the document, but for some time the parties acted in accordance with its arrangements by supplying and paying for the coal. Finally a disagreement arose and Brogden denied that there was a binding contract between the parties.

The addition of the arbitrator's name by B was a new term and therefore a counter offer. Did the Metropolitan Railway Co accept this offer? It might be thought that putting the document into the manager's desk was an equivocal act, incapable of amounting to a valid acceptance. But no objection was made to the terms suggested by B; instead the Metropolitan Railway Co placed an order for and accepted coal on the strength of the agreement. As Lord Cairns stated (at p 680): "[A]pprobation was clearly given when the company commenced a course of dealing which is referable ... only to the contract, and when that course of dealing was accepted and acted upon by [B] in the supply of coals".

Thus there was a clear acceptance by the company's conduct, of which B was aware. This principle was applied (and potentially extended) in *Trentham Ltd* v *Archital Luxfer* [1993] 1 Lloyd's Rep 25. Here, work began on a construction "contract" apparently before negotiations were complete; but the parties obviously intended to enter into an agreement and the work, when finished, was paid for. The Court of Appeal held that there was a binding contract which "came into existence during performance even if it cannot be precisely analysed in terms of offer and acceptance" (*per* Steyn LJ at p 30).

The *Brogden* case was considered recently in *Jayaar Impex Ltd* v *Toaken Group Ltd* [1996] 2 Lloyd's Rep 437, where it was emphasised by Rix J (at p 446) that the conduct of the parties in *Brogden* was "only referable to the contract document, since there was no other contract between the parties". In *Jayaar*, there was a dispute as to whether the contract between the parties for a quantity of Nigerian gum arabic was on the basis of an oral agreement, or a later written agreement which contained a specific set of terms on which the sellers wished to rely. The Commercial Court was not prepared to infer that the parties had agreed to amend their oral contract so as to incorporate the sellers' written terms. The court held, distinguishing *Brogden*, that the buyers were entitled to performance of their oral contract.

(b) "Battle of the forms"

We have noted that an acceptance, to be valid, should show unqualified assent to the terms of the offer; it should not introduce new proposals or stipulations. This is the position in theory, but in practice business people may try to exploit the process of offer and acceptance so as to contract on their own standard terms. (For example, see *Chichester Joinery* v *John Mowlem* (1987) 42 Build LR 100.) In business negotiations it is frequently difficult to decide at which precise moment the parties have reached agreement. Sometimes they cannot be said to be *ad idem* at all. The parties may wish to keep the situation uncertain in the hope that their own standard terms will prevail in the event of a dispute. For instance, X makes an offer to sell goods using his standard form with its own printed terms, and Y "accepts" the offer by using his own standard order form and its conflicting terms. If a dispute arises at this point, before there has been any performance of the undertakings (such as delivery of the goods), it seems that the parties have not reached agreement and there is no contract. However, the parties in this situation normally intend to proceed with the "contract" and they actually go beyond an exchange of promises; the dispute arises over whose terms prevail and not over the existence of a contract. (But see *Midland Veneers Ltd* v *Unilock HCP Ltd* (1998) LTL, 12 March 1998, where it was held that there was no contract, despite goods being delivered, as both parties had been attempting to impose their standard conditions and this indicated continuing negotiations rather than agreement.)

This illustrates how the "rules" of contract law are not always applicable, in a strict sense, to commercial practice. It seems that there are "non-contractual business dealings" which do not fit neatly into the traditional analysis of offer and acceptance[6]. In these situations where legal theory and commercial practice diverge, it is difficult to state precisely what the rules of law are[7]. It is possible to argue that the party who gets in his terms last, without the other party raising any objection, succeeds in contracting on his own standard terms.

He can be said to have "fired the last shot". This approach is illustrated by *British Road Services* v *Crutchley (Arthur V) & Co* [1968] 1 All ER 811. Under a well-established course of business between the parties, the plaintiffs delivered goods to the defendants' warehouse and presented a delivery note which stated: "All goods are carried on [the plaintiffs'] conditions of carriage . . .". However, as on previous occasions, when the plaintiffs' driver presented the delivery note to the defendants, it was "rubber-stamped" by the defendants with the words: "Received under [the defendants'] conditions". In this way the delivery note was transformed into a note of receipt and handed back to the plaintiffs' driver. In the course of an action for negligence against the defendants, it was disputed whose conditions prevailed. Although the defendants were liable to the plaintiffs in negligence for not adequately protecting the goods against theft, the Court of Appeal held that the defendants' liability was limited in accordance with their conditions which were incorporated into the contract between the parties. It seems that the defendants', rather than the plaintiffs', conditions prevailed as they got in the final word or "shot", without any further riposte from the plaintiffs. However, on the facts, it was regarded as important that there was a long-established course of dealing between the parties. If this had not been the case, it might have been questioned whether the plaintiffs' driver had the authority to receive an important contractual document from the defendants.

Although a useful starting point, the "final shot" approach cannot solve all the problems that arise in the "battle of the forms" cases. What if one party stipulates at the outset of the negotiations that he will contract only on his own printed terms? What if the exchange of printed terms by the two parties (or their agents) is virtually simultaneous? Should the court, if litigation arises, attempt to strike out any disputed terms? In truth, it is impossible to lay down a rule to cover the variety of situations and disputes that can occur in the commercial world. Different trades may have their own ways of conducting business dealings. The judge will need commercial sense as well as legal knowledge and he or she must look carefully at the particular facts of each case that arises.

For these reasons, the leading case of *Butler Machine Tool Co* v *Ex-cell-o Corp* [1979] 1 All ER 965 should be regarded as an illustration of the difficulties inherent in "battle of the forms" cases, rather than as a definitive statement of the legal position. The facts were:

> In response to D's enquiry, P made a quotation on 23 May, offering to sell a machine tool to D for £75,535. The offer was stated to be subject to certain conditions which were to "prevail over any terms in the buyer's order". These conditions included a price variation clause; ie that any increase in the cost of the goods, by the date of delivery (which was to be in ten months' time), would be added to the purchase price. On 27 May, D replied, ordering the machine, but on their own terms and conditions which did not include a price variation clause. At the foot of D's order form there was an acknowledgment section to be torn off, stating that "We accept your order on the terms and conditons stated thereon". On 5 June, P completed and signed the acknowledgment, returning it to D, together with a letter stating that D's order was being entered in accordance with P's quotation of 23 May. When the machine was delivered, P claimed the price had increased by £2,892, and D refused to pay the increase in price. P's action was based on the contention that they were entitled to increase the price under the price variation clause contained in their offer. D argued that the contract was on the buyer's terms and these did not include such a clause.

The Court of Appeal decided that the contract did not include the price variation clause and P could not claim the extra £2,892. It was held that D's order of 27 May was a counter offer which brought to an end the offer made by P on 23 May, and that P accepted D's counter offer by completing and returning the acknowledgment of the order on 5 June. The contract was therefore on D's terms and the price variation clause did not apply.

Although the decision was said to be in accordance with the doctrine of offer and acceptance, it could be argued that the parties had failed to reach agreement over a most important issue, namely the price of the goods. Had the dispute arisen before the goods were made and delivered, it might have been concluded that there was no legally enforceable agreement. However, both parties intended to proceed with the "agreement" and actually did so; the dispute was as to whose standard forms and terms prevailed. In deciding in favour of the defendant company, the Court of Appeal correctly concluded that there was doubt whether the parties had agreed to the price variation clause and that this condition should not be included in the "agreement". There is no simple solution to "battle of the forms" cases. Lord Denning in *Butler* (at p 969) thought that the documents must be considered as a whole: "If [the terms and conditions of both parties] can be reconciled so as to give a harmonious result, all well and good. If differences are irreconcilable, so that they are mutually contradictory, then the conflicting terms may have to be scrapped and replaced by a reasonable implication". (Also of interest, see *Sauter Automation* v *Goodman (HC) (Mechanical Services)* (1986) 34 Build LR 81.)

(c) Communication of acceptance

As a general principle, acceptance must be communicated to the offeror if it is to lead to a binding agreement. The offeree must do more than simply make an uncommunicated decision to accept an offer. In *Brogden* v *Metropolitan Railway Co* (see earlier) it was not the decision of the respondent company's manager to accept the amended draft contract that concluded the agreement with the appellant, but rather the ordering of coal and the subsequent course of dealing between the parties. An acceptance may be by words (spoken or written) or by conduct, but mere silence is insufficient. The law takes an objective view of agreement and some external evidence, beyond a mental resolution, is required for there to be a valid acceptance. If a particular form of acceptance is requested by the offeror, then generally the offeree must comply with this request.

Although there is a need to communicate acceptance to the offeror, what amounts to a communicated acceptance depends on the type of case we are considering. Furthermore, in unilateral contracts, the offeror does not request a counter promise from the offeree(s); he asks for the performance of some act or acts. As we saw in *Carlill*, there was no need for the plaintiff to notify the defendant company of her acceptance of their offer before using the product. She accepted by buying the smoke ball, using it as instructed and catching influenza.

The law requires the offeree to provide some objective manifestation of acceptance. After all, contracts are based (theoretically) on agreement and it would lead to considerable uncertainty and unfairness if the offeror were bound merely by an uncommunicated resolution by the offeree to accept. If O offers to sell his car to A for £1,000, he would not be bound simply by A's silent decision to accept. But what if O, having previously negotiated with A, writes to him, stating: "I will sell you my car for £1,000. If I do not hear from you within seven days, I shall assume that you accept". Can A's ensuing silence be regarded as a valid acceptance of the offer?

Generally, it is correct that the offeree should not be put to the trouble of either having to reject an offer, or risk being contractually bound if he fails to take active steps to do so. If it were otherwise, a salesman could make a nuisance of himself by sending goods to members of the public and stating in a letter that, if he hears no more from them within a certain period, he will consider the goods sold (although it should be noted that the problem of "inertia selling" is, to some extent, dealt with by the Unsolicited Goods and Services Act 1971, as amended in 1975).

But what is the position if O waives the requirement of a communicated acceptance and A, thinking that silence will amount to a valid acceptance, does nothing further? In the instructive case of *Felthouse* v *Bindley* (1862) 11 CB (NS) 869 the facts were:

> P entered into negotiations with his nephew, J, for the purchase of J's horse. He wrote to J, shortly after, offering to buy the horse and stating: "If I hear no more about him, I consider the horse is mine at £30 15s". J did not reply to his uncle's letter, but he did instruct the auctioneer (D) not to sell the horse along with his, J's, farming stock. D forgot this instruction and six weeks after P's letter, the horse was sold by D to another person. P sued D for conversion (in tort) basing his action on the contention that there was a concluded contract between P and J for the sale of the horse and therefore the horse belonged to P at the time of the auction. But was there a binding agreement between P and his nephew?

The court decided that the action for conversion failed. Although the nephew may have decided to sell the horse to his uncle, there was no communication of this decision to the uncle. Accordingly, there was no binding agreement between P and J and the horse never became the uncle's property. The decision is a useful illustration of the general rule that mere silence is not sufficient to constitute acceptance of an offer. Silence is equivocal, and if the law did not follow this approach, much uncertainty could arise in negotiations between parties.

But the decision in *Felthouse* v *Bindley* can be criticised. The parties had negotiated for the sale of the horse previously and the uncle waived the requirement of a communicated acceptance. There was no suggestion that he was taking advantage of his nephew's silence or making a nuisance of himself by putting the onus on his nephew to either reject the offer or be bound. Indeed, it is apparent that J intended his silence to constitute acceptance, and his conduct (in instructing D) was consistent with this. However, it could be argued that J did not accept P's offer by conduct, as there was no communication of J's conduct to P, and on this ground it is distinguishable from *Brogden*. (*Quaere*: If D had heeded the instructions and the uncle had then changed his mind and refused to purchase the horse from J, would the court have held that there was no contract between the parties?)[8]

(i) The need for communication: the general rule

Subject to certain exceptions, "communication" of acceptance requires that it is actually brought to the offeror's notice. (Where the offeree notifies the offeror's agent of his acceptance, this will be effective communication, so long as the agent has the authority to receive acceptance.) In situations which involve "instant" communication, such as face-to-face negotiations, telephone conversations, and telex messages, the acceptance must be actually received by the offeror (see *Entores* v *Miles Far East Corporation*, below). The contract is made at the place where the acceptance is received. But what if it is the offeror's own fault that he fails to receive the acceptance and the offeree thinks that his message has reached the offeror? In *Entores* v *Miles Far East Corporation* [1955] 2 QB 327, Lord Denning explained:

> "This may happen if the listener on the telephone does not catch the words of acceptance, but nevertheless does not trouble to ask for them to be repeated; or if the ink on the teleprinter fails at the receiving end, but the clerk does not ask for the message to be repeated; so that the man who sends an acceptance reasonably believes that his message has been received. The offeror in such circumstances is clearly bound, because he will be estopped from saying that he did not receive the message of acceptance. It is his own fault that he did not get it."

Where the offeror fails to receive the message of acceptance through no fault of his own, but the offeree reasonably (but wrongly) thinks that the message was received, there is no contract (*per* Lord Denning). Although the *Entores* decision is still good law today, it should be remembered that the use of instantaneous forms of communication has increased since the time of that decision. For example, telex and fax[9] are now popular means of business communication and there are a variety of ways in which they may be used. This was explained by Lord Wilberforce, in relation to the use of telex, in *Brinkibon Ltd* v *Stahag Stahl und Stahlwarenhandelsgesellschaft mbH* [1983] 2 AC 34:

> "The senders and the recipients may not be the principals to the contemplated contract. They may be servants or agents with limited authority. The message may not reach, or be intended to reach, the designated recipient immediately: messages may be sent out of office hours, or at night, with the intention, or on the assumption, that they will be read at a later time. There may be some error or fault at the recipient's end which prevents receipt at the time contemplated and believed in by the sender. The message may have been sent and/or received through machines operated by third persons. And many other variations may occur. No universal rule can cover all such cases; they must be resolved by reference to the intentions of the parties, by sound business practice and in some cases by a judgement where the risks should lie."

Despite these reservations, the House of Lords in *Brinkibon* supported the *Entores* decision as a *general* rule in relation to acceptance by telex. Perhaps clearer guidance might have been given by their Lordships on how to approach cases where the equipment proves to be faulty, or where messages are not read by the recipient until some time after transmission. (Lord Wilberforce's speech was considered by Gatehouse J in the recent case of *Mondial Shipping and Chartering BV* v *Astarte Shipping Ltd* [1995] CLC 1011, a case involving telex communications and contractual notice, rather than acceptance of an offer).

Recently, there has been speculation about when a contract is concluded by e-mail[10]. As e-mail communication is not "instantaneous", it could be argued that such transactions may be subsumed within the postal rule of acceptance. However, it is submitted that the courts will be unwilling to extend the postal rule in this way, and that acceptance by e-mail will come within the *Entores* rule.

(ii) Acceptance by post

As a general rule, then, an acceptance must be brought to the offeror's attention for it to be effective. However, communication through the post provides an important exception to this general rule. In *Adams* v *Lindsell* (1818) 1 B & Ald 681 the facts were:

> D wrote to P offering to sell wool and requested a reply "in the course of post". D misdirected the letter and this caused it to be delayed for a couple of days. On receiving the letter, P replied immediately, by posting a letter of acceptance. After P's acceptance was posted, but before it arrived, D sold the wool to a third party, in the belief that P was not interested.

The court decided that a contract was concluded between D and P when the letter of acceptance was posted by P. This approach might appear to contradict the idea of contracts being based on a "meeting of the minds"; in fact, it is a further illustration of the objective, rather than the subjective, nature of agreement in contract law. The "postal rule", as it is known, requires some explanation. If a posted acceptance were not effective until actually delivered to (or even read by) the offeror, then this could be unfair to the offeree in the event of his letter being delayed or lost in the post. Conversely, the offeror is at a disadvantage if he is bound by a posted acceptance that has not yet reached him. The law had to choose which party to favour, in postal communications, and for a number of reasons it chose to favour the offeree.

It is worth observing that the rule laid down in *Adams* v *Lindsell* originated at a time when there was no general rule that acceptance need be communicated [11]. The decision in *Adams* v *Lindsell* is defensible, moreover, on the basis that D was careless in addressing his offer and that it was fair for P's action to succeed. Whether this is a sufficient basis for the postal rule that has existed since that decision (surviving a few attempts at its overthrow), is more contentious. Much time has been spent by academics debating the merits and demerits of the rule. But, in truth, it is to some extent an arbitrary solution to the problem of which of two parties should be favoured where they communicate through the post. The argument that it is easier to prove posting than receipt is far from convincing. So too is the explanation that it is the offeror who chooses to use the post and therefore it is he who should be at a disadvantage; as it might have been the offeree who originally started the negotiations by letter.

Despite the lack of a convincing rationale, the postal rule is firmly established in the law of contract. (It also applies to acceptance by telegram or, to be more accurate, by telemessage.) The rule applies even in cases where the letter of acceptance is delayed or lost in the post (see *Household Fire Insurance* v *Grant* (1879) 4 Ex D 216), but the letter must have been correctly addressed and stamped. However, the rule does not apply if it was unreasonable to use the post as a means of communicating acceptance. The offeror can stipulate the mode of acceptance, expressly or by implication, and he can make it clear that a postal acceptance is not enough, by emphasising the need for a speedy reply.

Alternatively, the offeror may request a written reply, but may also stipulate that this reply must actually arrive before a contract is concluded. In *Holwell Securities* v *Hughes* [1974] 1 All ER 161:

> D offered to sell a house to P in the form of an option "exercisable by notice in writing to the intending vendor [D] at any time within six months". Within the six month period, P's solicitors wrote to D, notifying him of P's acceptance of the offer. The letter was correctly stamped, addressed and posted, but it never arrived. (A copy was received by D's solicitor, but P admitted that this was not sufficient notice.) No other written acceptance was given or sent to D before the time limit expired. P claimed specific performance, arguing that a contract was concluded on posting the letter of acceptance to D.

The Court of Appeal decided that the offer, by stipulating actual "notice to [D]", could not be accepted merely by P posting a letter of acceptance. The offer was so framed as to require that the acceptance be communicated to the offeror and therefore the postal rule did not apply in this instance. Thus the rule can be ousted by the express provision of the offeror. Similarly, the rule does not apply if it causes severe inconvenience or absurdity. (See *Holwell Securities*, above, at pp 166–167.)

(iii) Prescribed method of acceptance

As we saw in *Holwell Securities* (above), the offeror can stipulate that the acceptance must be made in a particular way. He may require it to be sent to a certain place, or to take a particular form, such as by letter or telex. In order to complete a binding agreement the offeree must normally comply with the prescribed method of acceptance. If the offeror stipulates a particular form of acceptance, and states that only the stipulated form will suffice, the offeree must comply with the offeror's requirement in order for there to be an effective acceptance. But the offeror may have requested a particular method of acceptance for a specific purpose, for example to obtain a speedy reply. If the offeree uses some other method which equally achieves the offeror's purpose, this will be a valid acceptance. (See *Tinn* v *Hoffman* (1873) 29 LT 271.)

In some instances, such as where the offeree supplies forms of tender to other business people to make offers to buy property, it is the offeree who stipulates the mode of acceptance. Can the offeree depart from the method of acceptance that he himself has prescribed? In *Manchester Diocesan Council of Education* v *Commercial & General Investments Ltd* [1970] 1 WLR 241:

> P invited offers to buy property and supplied forms of tender on which the offers were to be made. Clause 4 provided: "The person whose tender is accepted shall be the purchaser and shall be informed of the acceptance of his tender by letter sent to him by post addressed to the address given in the tender". A letter accepting D's tender was sent, not to the address given in the tender, but to D's surveyor. This did not affect D adversely, as it was P (the offeree) which had introduced this requirement in its standard form and now P waived it. D claimed that the acceptance failed to comply with the method of communication stipulated in the offer.

The court decided that P's acceptance was valid. P included the stipulation, about the method of communicating acceptance, in the form of tender for P's own purpose. P was entitled to waive the requirement if doing so did not adversely affect D. Buckley J stated (at p 246):

"Where . . . the offeror has prescribed a particular method of acceptance, but not in terms insisting that only acceptance in that mode shall be binding, I am of the opinion that acceptance communicated to the offeror by any other mode which is no less advantageous to him will conclude the contract . . . If an offeror intends that he shall be bound only if his offer is accepted in some particular manner, it must be for him to make this clear. Condition 4 in the present case had not, in my judgement, this effect."

(d) Is knowledge of the offer required?

Can an offer be accepted by a person who has no knowledge that the offer exists? This situation can occur where someone performs an act or service, for example by returning an item of lost property to the owner, and later learns that a reward was in fact offered for the performance of this act. In one sense, such a person has fulfilled the terms of the offer, and it could be argued that he is entitled to claim the reward. But, in this type of case, there is no agreement or meeting of the minds. The "acceptance" is accidental, as the act or service is not given in exchange for the offeror's promise. Yet, in *Gibbons* v *Proctor* (1891) 64 LT 594, the court appeared to decide that ignorance of an offer did not preclude a person from claiming a reward where he gave information and then later learned of the existence of the offer. (The case is open to criticism, but another report of it suggests that it was significant that P did know of the reward by the time the information was passed, via P's agents, to the appropriate person. See (1891) 55 JP 616.)

The Australian case of *R* v *Clarke* (1927) 40 CLR 227 is a more widely approved statement of the law. It concerned an offer of a reward for information leading to the arrest of certain murderers and a pardon to any accomplice giving the information. C gave the required information but admitted that he had forgotten about the reward at the time that he supplied it (ie when he was in custody, himself charged with the murders). C's claim for the £1,000 reward was rejected by the High Court of Australia, and the case was treated as if he had never known of the reward. Higgins J stated (at p 241):

"Clarke had seen the offer indeed; but it was not present to his mind — he had forgotten it, and gave no consideration to it, in his intense excitement as to his own danger. There cannot be assent without knowledge of the offer; and ignorance of the offer is the same thing whether it is due to never hearing of it or forgetting it after hearing . . . But for this candid confession of Clarke's it might fairly be presumed that Clarke, having once seen the offer, acted on the faith of it, in reliance on it; but he has himself rebutted that presumption."

Despite the less than satisfactory case law on the point, it seems that knowledge of an offer is required for there to be a valid acceptance. However, the motive for performing an act, which fulfils the terms of an offer, is irrelevant. So where a person knows of an offer of a reward for information, but gives the requested information for another reason (such as remorse), he is still entitled to claim the reward. (See *Williams* v *Cowardine* (1833) 5 C & P 566.)

A related issue is that of "cross offers". For example, A writes to B offering to sell him his computer for £100 and B, without knowing of the offer, writes to

A and offers to buy that computer for £100. It could be argued that there is a meeting of the minds, but clearly any "agreement" between the parties is merely by chance. It is thought that there is no contract in this situation unless one of the parties replies to the other and accepts the other's offer. It would lead to uncertainty if cross offers, with nothing further, amounted to a binding agreement. The problem is hardly one of great practical significance as indicated by the paucity of case law on the subject. (The one case which discusses the problem, *obiter*, is *Tinn v Hoffman* (1873) 29 LT 271. The majority of the judges thought there was no contract.)

(e) Acceptance in unilateral contracts

In a unilateral contract, the offeror promises payment or a reward in exchange for the offeree performing a particular act or acts. (See *Carlill v Carbolic Smoke Ball Co*, discussed earlier.) This is in contrast to a bilateral contract which, normally, is formed by the exchange of promises between the parties, resulting in reciprocal undertakings. In a unilateral contract, however, one party binds himself (eg to pay a reward) and the offeree accepts by performing the requested act (such as finding lost property). It is not necessary for the offeree to communicate to the offeror his intention to accept and the offeree is under no obligation to perform the requested act. The contract is "unilateral" because only one party (the offeror) is bound, and the contract is concluded by the offeree's act.

Although offers of rewards are frequently given as examples of unilateral contracts, it should not be supposed that this is the full extent of the practical application of this type of contract. For example, the issuing of cheque cards by banks to their customers is now commonplace. The reason for this is that retailers were wary of parting with goods in exchange for a cheque which might not be honoured. The cheque guarantee card ensures that, so long as the card is used correctly, the retailer will receive payment from the bank, regardless of whether the customer has sufficient funds in his account to meet the cheque. On what basis is the bank contractually bound to retailers who give customers value for their cheques? The transaction can be explained as a unilateral contract. The bank's issuing of the card is an offer to retailers who do not have to communicate their acceptance. A contract with the bank is concluded when a retailer parts with goods in exchange for a guaranteed cheque.

The essence of a unilateral contract, then, is that O does not bargain for a counter promise by A; instead he requires the performance by A of some act. As we shall see later, an offer may generally be revoked at any time before a valid acceptance is made. This is normally fair as neither party is bound until this time. But can O, in a unilateral contract, withdraw the offer once A has commenced the performance of the stipulated act? To take the classic example known to generations of law students: O offers a reward of £100 to anyone who walks from, say, Aberystwyth to Cardigan. It is evident that O is bargaining for the completed act of walking the whole distance of thirty-eight miles. (A mere promise by someone to do the walk does not conclude a contract.) Can O revoke his offer once A has started, but not yet completed, the walk to Cardigan? In theory, there is no effective acceptance where the act in question is only partly performed, but it could lead to manifest injustice if O were able to revoke the offer once A is in the process of accepting. Hence some departure from strict legal theory is necessary, as illustrated by *Errington* v *Errington and Woods* [1952] 1 KB 290. The facts were:

> A father wanted to provide his son and daughter-in-law with a home and he bought a house for £750, borrowing £500 on a mortgage from the building society. The conveyance remained in the father's name and he also paid the rates. He promised his son and daughter-in-law that if they continued to occupy the house and paid all the mortgage instalments, he would transfer the property to them. Until the father's death nine years later, the couple occupied the house and paid the mortgage. On the death of the father, all his property (including the house occupied by the couple) was left to his widow. The son left the daughter-in-law and moved out of the house. The widow brought an action for possession against the daughter-in-law.

The Court of Appeal decided that the widow was not entitled to possession. *Per* Denning LJ (at p 295):

> "The father's promise was a unilateral contract — a promise of the house in return for their act of paying the instalments. It could not be revoked by him once the couple entered on performance of the act, but it would cease to bind him if they left it incomplete and unperformed, which they have not done."

It seems that although a unilateral offer may be accepted only by performance of the requested act, the offer cannot normally be withdrawn once the offeree has started to perform. But in *Luxor (Eastbourne)* v *Cooper* [1941] AC 108, C was promised commission if he introduced a buyer for two cinemas and if this introduction resulted in the sale of these properties. Although C introduced a willing purchaser, the vendors changed their minds and decided against selling the properties. C claimed damages, arguing that the offer implied that the vendors would not refuse to sell to a buyer that he had introduced. The Court of Appeal refused to imply such a term and rejected C's claim. It is submitted that the *Errington* approach is to be preferred; it provides a fairer solution, but is there any theoretical basis for it? The usual explanation is that a unilateral offer contains two promises: the promise of the reward, and an implied (or collateral) promise that the offer will not be withdrawn once the offeree has embarked upon performance of the act. *Errington* v *Errington and Woods* can be explained in this way and the decision is supported, *obiter*, in *Daulia* v *Four Millbank Nominees Ltd* [1978] 2 All ER 557 (at pp 561, 566, and 570).

5.   Termination of offers

There are a number of ways in which an offer may be terminated before an acceptance has taken place. These are explained in the following sections.

(a) Revocation (or withdrawal)

Although an offer cannot be withdrawn once it has been accepted, it may be revoked at any time before acceptance has occurred (see *Payne* v *Cave* (1789) 3 Term Rep 148). The offeror may withdraw his offer even if it was expressly stated that it would remain open for a fixed period. This is because a promise to leave an offer open is not, generally, supported by any consideration given by the offeree. (This is explained more fully in Chapter 4.) In *Routledge* v *Grant* (1828) 130 ER 920 the defendant offered to take a lease of the plaintiff's premises, giving the plaintiff six weeks to make up his mind. Three weeks later, the defendant withdrew the offer and, afterwards, the plaintiff purported to accept within the six week period. The court held that there was no contract, as the defendant was free to withdraw the offer at any time before acceptance by the offeree. Despite the defendant's promise, the offer did not have to remain open for six weeks:

> "..[I]f six weeks are given on one side to accept an offer, the other side has six weeks to put an end to it. One party cannot be bound without the other" (*per* Best CJ at p 923).

A promise to keep an offer open for a fixed period will, of course, be binding if the offeree gives something in return for the offeror's promise. In this case there will be a separate or "collateral" contract between the parties; the offeror's promise will no longer be one-sided. In *Daulia v Four Millbank Nominees Ltd* [1978] 2 All ER 557, although the plaintiff's action in fact failed due to technicalities of land law, it is clear that there was a collateral contract to the effect that the offer would remain open for a fixed period, as promised by the offeror. The offeree gave consideration for the promise (to enter into a written contract) by complying with the offeror's stipulated conditions. (For a more recent illustration, see *Pitt v PHH Asset Management Ltd* [1993] 4 All ER 961.)

Although an offer may be withdrawn at any time before the offeree has accepted it, the withdrawal has to be communicated to the offeree. It is not sufficient for the offeror merely to change his mind without informing the offeree. It should be noted that even where the revocation is made by letter it must still be actually communicated to the offeree. This is in contrast to a letter of acceptance of an offer which is effective on posting. These rules are conveniently illustrated by *Byrne v Van Tienhoven* (1880) 5 CPD 344:

> The defendants wrote from Cardiff on 1 October offering to sell a quantity of tinplates to the plaintiffs in New York. On 8 October, the defendants posted a letter withdrawing the offer. On 11 October, the offer reached the plaintiffs, who accepted at once by telegram (and the plaintiffs also confirmed this in writing on 15 October). The defendants' letter of withdrawal reached the plaintiffs on 20 October.

It was decided that the mere posting of a letter of revocation does not amount to an effective communication to the offeree. The plaintiffs' acceptance (on 11 October) completed a contract with the defendants and this was not affected by the defendants' letter of revocation which did not arrive until later. The decision was intended to promote certainty for if the defendants' arguments had succeeded, "no person who had received an offer by post and accepted it would know his position until he had waited such a time as to be quite sure that a letter withdrawing the offer had not been posted before his acceptance of it" (*per* Lindley J at p 348). The case is also a vivid example of the objective view of agreement taken by the law of contract. At no time was there a meeting of the minds in fact, but it was held that there was a binding agreement.

Although the withdrawal of an offer must be communicated to the offeree, it appears that the offeree does not have to be notified of the withdrawal by the offeror in person. In *Dickinson v Dodds* (1876) 2 Ch D 463, P was given the option to buy certain land from D for £800, with D promising that the offer would remain open for two days (until 9 am on 12 June). But D sold the land to someone else on 11 June, and P learned of this later the same day, by chance, via a third party. P then proceeded to notify D of his acceptance of the offer before 9 am on 12 June. The Court of Appeal held that P's action for specific performance failed as there was no contract between P and D. We have seen already that a promise to keep an offer open for a specific period is not, by itself, binding on the offeror. But was the withdrawal of the offer effectively communicated to the offeree? James LJ (at p 472) had no doubts that it was:

> "..[I]n this case, beyond all question, the plaintiff knew that Dodds was no longer minded to sell the property to him as plainly and clearly as if Dodds had told him in so many words, 'I withdraw the offer'."

The case is generally regarded as deciding that communication of the withdrawal of an offer can be made to the offeree by any "reliable source". What matters is that the offeree has knowledge of the revocation, and not that notification comes directly from the offeror. Yet it might be contended that, in the interests of certainty, the withdrawal of an offer ought to be communicated by the offeror (or some person authorised by him) if it is to be effective. Otherwise, as the law stands, the offeree is in the unfortunate position of having to decide whether his source of information is reliable or not. There is no convincing reason why the offeree should shoulder this burden.

(b) Rejection

An offer is terminated if the offeree rejects the offer. It is not possible for him simply to change his mind and accept. It will be remembered that a counter offer amounts to a rejection of the original offer (see *Hyde* v *Wrench* (1840) 3 Beav 334). If D offers to sell goods to P for £1,000 and P replies that he will give D £950 for them, this is a rejection of D's offer which brings it to an end. P cannot revive D's offer later by simply purporting to accept it. It does not matter that D has not formally withdrawn the original offer. In contrast, where the offeree does not make a counter offer, but merely seeks further information from the offeror, an offer is not to be regarded as rejected. (See *Stevenson* v *McLean* (1880) 5 QB 346.)

(c) Lapse of time

An offer may come to an end due to the lapse of time. If A, on Monday, offers to sell his car to B and says: "I must have your answer by Friday at the latest", B cannot accept the offer on Saturday. In many cases, the offeror does not stipulate that the offer must be accepted within a specified period. However, it would be impracticable if an offer could be accepted after an unreasonable delay on the part of the offeree. So where the offeror does not specify a time limit for acceptance, the offer will lapse unless it is accepted within a reasonable time. What amounts to a reasonable time will depend on the circumstances of the case and must take account of the subject matter of the offer. For instance, in *Ramsgate Victoria Hotel* v *Montefiore* (1866) LR 1 Ex 109, it was held that an offer to buy shares which was made in June could not be accepted as late as the following November. The offer had not been accepted within a reasonable period, bearing in mind the fluctuating nature of the subject matter. (For another illustration of what amounts to a "reasonable time", see *Loring* v *City of Boston* (1844) 7 Metcalf 409.)

(d) Where the offer is conditional

An offer may be expressed as subject to the occurrence of some condition. For example, A may offer to sell goods to B subject to his being able to obtain supplies himself. If A subsequently cannot obtain supplies, the offer will come to an end. The offer was conditional on a particular state of affairs which did not occur. The courts can also imply a condition into an offer where it has not been expressly stated by the offeror. If A offers to buy goods, or to take them on hire purchase, it will be implied that the offer is subject to the condition that the goods will remain in (substantially) the same state that they were in at the time of the offer. (See *Financings Ltd* v *Stimson* [1962] 3 All ER 386, especially the words of Donovan LJ at p 390.)

(e) Death

What is the position where the offeror dies after making an offer but before the offeree has accepted? If it is an offer of a "personal" contract (involving a personal service such as employment or agency), it is sensible that the offer should come to an end with the death of the offeror. (In these circumstances a resulting contract would in any case be brought to an end by death even if the offer was not regarded as terminated.) Otherwise, it is possible for an offer to continue even after the death of the offeror, where the offeree accepts without knowing of the offeror's death (see *Bradbury* v *Morgan* (1862) 1 H & C 249). In this event the contract will be performed by the offeror's personal representatives. A good example is where the offer takes the form of a continuing guarantee of a bank overdraft. If, unknown to the bank, the guarantor dies, and the bank makes a further loan to the customer, then the personal representatives of the deceased may well be obliged to perform the contract. Of course there may be some other reason for refusing to allow the bank to charge the offeror's estate; for instance, it may be inequitable to do so.

Where the offeree dies after an offer has been made, it seems both likely and sensible that the offer comes to an end. It must be acknowledged, however, that the decided cases are not particularly helpful or conclusive on this rather esoteric point. (In *Reynolds* v *Atherton* (1921) 125 LT 690, Warrington LJ stated that an offer "made to a living person who ceases to be a living person before the offer is accepted ... is no longer an offer at all". But it must be emphasised that the case was actually decided on different grounds and the above statement was merely *obiter*.)

6. Offer and acceptance — a critical view of the traditional approach

The traditional approach of the law of contract is to analyse the formation of contracts in terms of an offer by one party and a "matching" acceptance by the other. The House of Lords in *Gibson* v *Manchester City Council* (discussed earlier) affirmed this method of analysis and it was stated that the types of contract which cannot be so analysed are "exceptional". In contrast, Lord Denning, in the Court of Appeal's decision in the same case, advocated a more flexible and less formal approach. He stated ([1978] 2 All ER 583 at p 586):

"To my mind it is a mistake to think that all contracts can be analysed into the form of offer and acceptance. I know in some textbooks it has been the custom to do so; but, as I understand the law, there is no need to look for a strict offer and acceptance. You should look at the correspondence as a whole and at the conduct of the parties and see therefrom whether the parties have come to an agreement on everything that was material."

Although this approach found no favour with the House of Lords, it is possible that Lord Denning's statement is a more accurate reflection of business practice than the traditional or "formalist" view. (It received some support recently in *Trentham Ltd* v *Archital Luxfer* [1993] 1 Lloyd's Rep 25, *per* Steyn LJ at pp 29–30.) The established legal principles which apply to the formation of contracts, for example in relation to offer and acceptance and consideration, were developed largely in the nineteenth century and some critics maintain that these principles are of marginal relevance to the conduct of business today. It is true that the various "rules" that we have considered relating to the formation of contracts give the appearance of a "technical and schematic" law of contract. (See the comments of Lord Wilberforce in *New Zealand Shipping Co* v *Satterthwaite (AM) & Co* [1975] AC 154.) But, the law, in practice, is capable of adopting a fairly flexible and pragmatic approach. In areas such as the "battle of the forms", disputes may be settled by reference to business practice as well as legal doctrine. Judges conventionally use the language of legal doctrine, even whilst adopting a more flexible approach, but this should not disguise the fact that there are limitations to the traditional or "formal" approach.

Even if we maintain that the process of offer and acceptance represents the way in which most contracts are made, there are certain agreements that cannot be explained convincingly by the traditional approach. A notable example is provided by *Clarke* v *Dunraven* [1897] AC 59:

> The case involved two yachts entered by their respective owners for a club race — the Mudhook Yacht Club Regatta. On entering for the race, each owner signed a letter to the club secretary undertaking to be bound by the yacht club sailing rules whilst participating in the race. These rules included an obligation to "pay all damages" caused by any contravention of the sailing rules which were to be observed during races. One of the yachts (*Satanita*), in breach of one of the sailing regulations, fouled another yacht (*Valkyrie*) and sank her. The owner of *Valkyrie* sued the owner of *Satanita* for damages. The defendant argued that his liability was limited by statute (s 54(1) Merchant Shipping Act 1862) to the payment of £8 per ton on the registered tonnage of the sunken vessel. The plaintiff claimed that the defendant was bound to "pay all damages" under a contract made between the competitors entering the race and undertaking to be bound by the rules of the club.

The Court of Appeal held that there was such a contract and that the defendant was liable for all damages. This was affirmed by the House of Lords. Lord Herschell stated (at p 63):

> "I cannot entertain any doubt that there was a contractual relation between the parties to this litigation. The effect of their entering for the race, and undertaking to be bound by these rules to the knowledge of each other, is sufficient, I think, where those rules indicate a liability on the part of the one to the other, to create a contractual obligation to discharge that liability."

There is no reason to criticise the actual outcome of this case: the various competitors entered into an agreement, on entering for the race, to be bound by certain rules. But was there a contract between the plaintiff and the defendant created by a process of offer and acceptance? There can be little doubt that the owners of the various yachts entered into a contract with the yacht club by their letter to the club secretary. Yet it is not easy to see how one owner can be said to have accepted the offer of any other owner to participate in the race (other than by a tortuous and artificial process).

Similarly, where A and B are negotiating for, say, the provision of certain services and they fail to reach agreement, a third party (C) may suggest a solution to their points of difference. If A and B both agree, at the same time, to C's proposal, it is impossible to argue that one of the contracting parties offered and the other accepted the offer. But they have reached a binding agreement nevertheless (assuming that all the other requirements of a contract are met).

Contracts imposed by the courts

We have seen (above) that not all agreements made by contracting parties can be analysed convincingly in terms of the conventional process of offer and acceptance. These instances can be viewed perhaps as comparatively rare departures from the norm. Moreover, the recognition of these exceptional cases does little violence to strict contractual theory as the contracts in question are still the result of agreement between the parties. However, there are cases which are harder to reconcile with traditional theory; contracts which do not result from any express agreement between the parties, but as a consequence of being imposed or implied by the courts. In theory this is not supposed to occur, as it is for the contracting parties to strike bargains and not for the courts to make contracts for them. This is another example of how legal theory and legal practice may diverge.

A contract might be implied by the courts on the grounds of public policy or expediency. This is a difficult matter to predict or analyse. Consider the unusual case of *Upton-on-Severn RDC v Powell* [1942] 1 All ER 220:

> Discovering that his farm was on fire, Powell rang the local police in the Upton police district and asked them to get "the fire brigade". The police rang the local (Upton) fire brigade and alerted them about the fire. Powell's farm was in the Pershore, not the Upton fire district, but the Upton fire brigade was called and it went to the fire at once. Powell was entitled to the services of the Pershore brigade without charge, but the Upton brigade was entitled to charge for its services, if it went outside its own district. At the time of the emergency, all the parties involved thought that the farm was in the Upton fire district. Later, on discovering that it was not, Upton Council claimed that a contract had been created by implication, under which it was entitled to be paid for its services.

The Court of Appeal decided that there was a contract and Powell's appeal was dismissed. He was bound by contract to pay for the Upton fire brigade's services. Lord Greene thought that public policy necessitated such a conclusion. He thought it would be quite "wrong in principle" (at p 221) if Powell could avoid paying because Upton thought it was rendering free services. But it is hard to understand why Powell should have to pay, when he was entitled to the free services of another brigade. Assuming that the Upton Council should have been allowed to recover for its services, the remedy should perhaps have been a quasi-contractual one (see Chapter 22).

It is difficult to agree with the conclusion reached by the Court of Appeal that there was a contract between the parties. There was clearly no process of offer and acceptance. It is fanciful to claim that Powell's telephone call was an offer. It is even more of a distortion to argue that the Upton fire brigade, by rendering a service which they thought was performed free of charge, was in fact accepting an offer of payment for that service. There was, in truth, no agreement between the parties in this unusual case. In the interest of fairness to the Council, the court decided that the defendant should have to pay. A contract was accordingly "invented" to achieve this result. Cases such as this might be dismissed as rare departures from established principles and, to a certain extent, there is some force in this assertion. But it is salutary to realise that not all cases can be fitted neatly into the established "slots" of legal doctrine and governed by a set of invariable rules. The law is not such an exact discipline, involving, as it does, judgements concerning fairness and the exigencies of public policy.

It might be contended that the cases which fail to fit within the established rules and lines of authority are not simply anomalies or "hard cases", but that rather they are illustrations of the flexibility of judge-made law; that is, that contracts can be imposed retrospectively by the courts as a "remedial" device to achieve a just solution to an essentially non-contractual dispute. This point is made cogently by Professor Atiyah[12]:

> "[I]t is important for students to understand that the law of contract has nearly always had room for cases of this character. Judges have rarely hesitated to use whatever instruments they can lay hands on in order to achieve a just result in a particular case; and the law of contract is one of those instruments."

The same writer gives the example, *inter alia*, of informal property transactions which are not based on any express agreement between the parties concerned. In *Tanner* v *Tanner* [1975] 1 WLR 1346:

> P and D were not married; D gave birth to twins and P was the father. (D also took P's name.) P bought a house with the help of a mortgage for them both to live in, together with the children. D relinquished her rent-controlled flat in order to move in with P. After a period of time, P moved out and tried to evict D. At first instance, D lost the case and was evicted. (She was rehoused by the local authority.)

On appeal, it was decided that D had, under an implied contract, a right to stay in the house with her children whilst they were of school age. As she had already lost her right to remain in the house (having been evicted), the order of the Court of Appeal was to award compensation of £2,000. Lord Denning was unabashed by the lack of any agreement between the parties to this effect. There was no pretence that the court's decision could be reconciled with established contractual principles. He stated (at p 1350):

> "... It is to be implied that she had a ... contractual licence — to have accommodation in the house for herself and the children so long as they were of school age ... There was no express contract to that effect, but the circumstances are such that the court should imply a contract by the plaintiff — or, if need be, impose the equivalent of a contract by him."

Few judges have declared their law-making potential quite so overtly and unreservedly as Lord Denning was prepared to do on this occasion. Indeed, some effort was subsequently made to decide these informal property disputes more strictly in accordance with recognizable contractual principles (see *Burns v Burns* [1984] Ch 317, for example). But this does not alter the fact that, in certain circumstances, contracts can be imposed retrospectively by the courts on the parties, so as to achieve a just solution. This process has little or nothing to do with the established "rules" of contract law that we have considered in this chapter. Here, the parties are not entering into an agreement to undertake certain obligations in the future; there is no offer and acceptance, nor any bargaining process.

Footnotes

(1) For further discussion, see Howarth, 100 LQR 265, and De Moor, 106 LQR 632.

(2) See *The Times* (9 December 1984). For a good example of the objective approach, see *Centrovincial Estates* v *Merchant Investors Assurance Co* [1983] Com LR 158.

(3) See [1978] 2 All ER 583 at p 586.

(4) For further discussion, see McKendrick, *Invitations to Tender and the Creation of Contracts*, [1991] Lloyd's Maritime and Commercial Law Quarterly, pp 31–36.

(5) For example, s 20(1) Consumer Protection Act 1987 states: ". . . a person shall be guilty of an offence if, in the course of any business of his, he gives . . . to any consumers an indication which is misleading as to the price at which any goods, services, accommodation or facilities are available (whether generally or from particular persons)."

(6) See J Adams, *Non-Contractual Business Dealings* (1983) New Law Journal, vol 133, pp 789–791.

(7) See Beale and Dugdale, *Contracts Between Businessmen* (1975) 2 Br Jo Law & Soc 45.

(8) See Miller, *Felthouse* v *Bindley Revisited* (1972) 35 MLR 489; also see *Fairline Shipping Corporation* v *Adamson* [1975] QB 180. Also, for a discussion of exceptions to the general rule, see P Owsia (1991) 40 ICLQ 784.

(9) Facsimile (or fax) machines are now widely used for sending text electronically. Presumably a contract made by fax will be concluded when the acceptance is received. For a discussion of the use of facsimile transmission in conveyancing contracts, see P Kenny, *Exchanging Contracts By Fax* (1988) Law Society's Gazette, vol 85, No 34, pp 11–12. Also see *Hastie and Jenkerson* v *McMahon* [1990] 1 WLR 1575.

(10) In relation to contracts made by e-mail, for a full discussion see D. Rowland and E. Macdonald, *Information Technology Law*, 2000, Cavendish. Also, see: Niemann, "Cyber Contracts — A Comparative View on the Actual Time of Formation" (2000) 5 Communications Law 48; and Downing and Harrington, "The Postal Rule in Electronic Commerce: A Reconsideration" (2000) 5 Communications Law 43.

(11) See Simpson, 91 LQR 247.

(12) Atiyah, *Introduction to the Law of Contract*, 5th ed, 1995, p 90.

Chapter 3

Certainty and completeness

1. Introduction

In Chapter 2 we saw that contracts are normally based on agreement. Although courts will try to give effect to apparent agreements, it may be difficult to do so in cases where the parties have expressed themselves in vague or incomplete terms. Much will depend on how far a court is willing to go in filling in any gaps left by the parties. Whilst not wishing to "incur the reproach of being the destroyer of bargains" (*per* Lord Tomlin in *Hillas & Co* v *Arcos* (1932) 147 LT 503 at p 512), a court may find it impossible to give effect to an uncertain "agreement". These situations must be viewed within the confines of legal principle; if no contractual bargain exists, it is not for a court to invent one.

However, in the business world it is not uncommon for negotiating parties to leave matters vague for as long as possible. This may be desirable in certain circumstances because the "agreement" in question might be conditional on one of the parties securing another contract with a third party. (For example, where company A uses a "letter of intent" to indicate to company B that a sub-contract is likely to be entered into with them if A's tender for a major contract with company C is successful.) They may even proceed as if a concluded contract has been made, despite the fact that in a technical (legal) sense there is no final agreement. (For a good example of this problem, see *British Steel Corporation* v *Cleveland Bridge and Engineering Co Ltd* [1984] 1 All ER 504; and for a more recent approach, see *Trentham Ltd* v *Archital Luxfer* [1993] 1 Lloyd's Rep 25.) We have considered further examples of this in relation to the "battle of the forms" (see Chapter 2) and it will be recalled that commercial practice may depart from the finer points of legal theory. It is difficult to lay down general rules about the extent of a court's power to fill in the gaps left by the parties and, for this reason, some of the cases that follow may appear to be inconsistent with one another. Much depends on the factual situation in each case rather than on any consistent or underlying precepts.

2. The need for certainty

Where contractual intention is expressed in such imprecise terms that no clear meaning can be given to it, there will be no binding agreement. For example, in *Gould* v *Gould* [1969] 3 All ER 728, a husband promised his wife £15 per week "so long as he could manage it", ie as long as his business was doing all right. On appeal, it was held that this agreement was too vague and uncertain to be enforceable. In other cases, the parties may clearly have intended to enter into a contract, but may have used some vague or ambiguous expression. In *Scammell (G) and Nephew* v *Ouston* [1941] AC 251, the facts were:

> Ouston (P) wrote to the defendant company (D) ordering a new Commer motor van, stating that the "order is given on the understanding that the balance of purchase price can be had on hire purchase terms over a period of two years". The order was accepted, but the defendants dropped out before any specific hire purchase agreement was entered into. P sued D for non-delivery and D claimed that there was no final agreement between the parties. The trial court and the Court of Appeal decided that there was a binding contract between the parties, and D appealed to the House of Lords.

It was held that there was no contract, as the phrase "on hire purchase terms" was too vague to constitute a binding agreement. This was because different types of hire purchase agreements existed (imposing different obligations on the parties) and therefore there was an ambiguity in the apparent agreement. If P could have shown, by reference to previous dealings with D or by reference to trade practice, that one particular meaning could be given to the phrase "hire purchase terms", he may well have succeeded. But this was not possible in this instance and the contractual intention of the parties may not have been identical.

In *Lind (Peter) and Co* v *Mersey Docks and Harbour Board* [1972] 2 Lloyd's Rep 234, P submitted two tenders to build a container freight terminal. The first offer was to build the terminal for a fixed price, whilst the second was to do the work for a price which was subject to variations in the cost of labour and materials. D purported to accept P's tender without making it clear which one. It was decided that there was no contract on the terms of either of P's tenders as there was an obvious ambiguity that could not be resolved by the court.

In contrast, there are instances where a court is able to make sense of vague statements and to give effect to the contractual intention of the parties. For example, in *Hillas & Co* v *Arcos* (1932) 147 LT 503, P had previously agreed to buy a quantity of timber, "of fair specification", from D. The contract gave P an option to buy a further 100,000 standards of timber the following year, but it failed to specify the size or type of timber. D argued that the vagueness of this "agreement" prevented it from being binding on the parties. But this argument was rejected by the House of Lords. In contrast to the case of *Scammell (G) and Nephew* v *Ouston*, the uncertainty in the agreement could be resolved by the court. It was possible to make reference to the previous dealings between the parties and the custom of the timber trade. In this way, the court could fill in the gaps left by the parties without making an entire contract for the parties. Clearly, the distinction between this type of case and that of *Scammell (G) and Nephew* v *Ouston* is a fine one[1].

The issue of lack of certainty was also raised in *Walford* v *Miles* [1992] 1 All ER 453. This case involved negotiations for the sale of a photographic business. The parties entered into a so-called "lock-out" agreement whereby the seller, in exchange for good consideration, agreed not to negotiate with any other party in respect of the sale of the business. Although such agreements can be enforceable, the House of Lords held that this one was not because it was of unspecified duration. It was stated that no term could be implied by the court to give effect to the agreement. However, if the seller had agreed not to negotiate with any other party for a specified period of time, the agreement could have been enforced (see Lord Ackner's judgment at pp 461–462).

It is important to distinguish between a clause in a contract which has still to be agreed (such as "hire purchase terms" in *Scammell (G) and Nephew* v *Ouston*) and a clause which is simply meaningless. The former may lead to a court deciding that no contract exists, whereas the latter can often be disregarded. Much will depend on the importance attached to the clause by the parties. For example, if it is of central importance in defining the contractual obligations of the parties, the vagueness of the clause may negate agreement (see *Bushwall Properties Ltd* v *Vortex Properties Ltd* [1976] 2 All ER 283). In *CPC Consolidated Pool Carriers GmbH* v *CTM CIA Trans-Mediterranea SA* [1994] 1 Lloyd's Rep 68, the negotiations between the parties, for the shipment of a jet foil, were said to be "subject to details/logical amendments". Potter J held that there was no concluded contract as it was intended by the parties that a formal contract was still to be drawn up later. The expression "subject to details" left matters too vague, as these terms and details needed to be finalised. But if the clause is "severable" from the main part of the agreement (ie of little significance, or even superfluous), then it can be ignored without affecting the validity of the contract. If this were not so, those in breach of contract might look for any vague phrase in the agreement as a means of escaping liability.

In *Nicolene* v *Simmonds* [1953] 1 QB 543, for example, P ordered 3,000 tons of steel bars from D. D's letter of acceptance of the order included the phrase that it was assumed that "the usual conditions of acceptance apply". D, who failed to supply the steel and was sued for breach of contract, claimed that due to the uncertainty caused by the words "usual conditions of acceptance", there was no binding agreement. This argument was rejected by the Court of Appeal. In the words of Lord Denning (at p 552):

> "... [T]here was nothing yet to be agreed. There was nothing left to further negotiation. All that happened was that the parties agreed that the 'usual conditions of acceptance apply'. That clause was so vague and uncertain as to be incapable of any precise meaning. It is clearly severable from the rest of the contract. It can be rejected without impairing the sense or reasonableness of the contract as a whole, and it should be so rejected. The contract should be held good and the clause ignored."

3. Is there a complete contract?

Provided that all the main terms of a contract have been agreed by the parties, the fact that further terms have still to be negotiated will not prevent there being a concluded contract (see *Pagnan SpA* v *Feed Products* [1987] 2 Lloyd's Rep 601). In other instances the parties may negotiate a contract and reach agreement in principle but leave certain details to be decided later. As a matter of strict theory it might appear that this does not constitute a binding agreement, especially if important terms are left undecided. This may well be the result in practice too, but much will depend on the circumstances (as discussed recently in *J Murphy and Sons Ltd* v *ABB Daimler-Benz Transportation (Signal) Ltd* (1999) CILL 1461). It is not the role of a court to make an agreement for the parties where none exists, but it may be able to give effect to contractual intention (eg by implying terms) where there is an agreement which has not been fully expressed. (For a discussion of this distinction, see *Scancarriers A/S* v *Aotearoa International Ltd* [1985] 2 Lloyd's Rep 419.)

In some commercial contexts it may be necessary to allow the price to be fixed, or adjusted, after the agreement has been concluded. For example, in a contract between an oil company and a petrol station owner for the supply of petrol over a number of years, it would not be too uncertain an agreement to allow the price to be adjusted periodically by the supplier. In *Shell (UK) Ltd* v *Lostock Garage Ltd* [1977] 1 All ER 481, the buyer agreed to pay for his supply of petrol "at a price which shall be the wholesale schedule price ruling at [the] date and place of delivery". Of course, such an agreement may be declared unenforceable by the court where it gives rise to an unreasonable restraint of trade, or even (perhaps) where it simply operates in an unfair and unconscionable way (*Shell* case at pp 489–493). But it is not void for lack of completeness.

As examples of contracting parties leaving important points unsettled, it is instructive to contrast the cases of *May and Butcher* v *The King* [1934] 2 KB 17 and *Foley* v *Classique Coaches Ltd* [1934] 2 KB 1. In the former, the facts were:

> P agreed to buy surplus tentage from the Controller of the Disposals Board. The agreement provided that: "The price . . . to be paid, and the date or dates on which payment is to be made by the purchasers to the Commission for such old tentage shall be agreed upon from time to time between the Commission and the purchasers . . ." The trial judge decided that this "agreement" did not amount to a contract, and this was affirmed by the Court of Appeal.

The House of Lords held that such a vague and incomplete agreement was not enforceable and that there was no binding contract between the parties. Lord Buckmaster stated (at p 20):

> "It is, of course, perfectly possible for two people to contract that they will sign a document which contains all the relevant terms, but it is not open to them to agree that they will in future agree upon a matter which is vital to the arrangement between them and has not yet been determined."

The failure of the parties to an agreement to fix a price for the goods need not prevent a binding contract from being concluded. Under the Sale of Goods Act 1979, s 8(1) provides that if the price of goods is not fixed by the contract of sale, it may alternatively "be left to be fixed in a manner agreed by the contract, or may be determined by the course of dealing between the parties". If the parties have not fixed a price for the goods then, under s 8(2), the buyer must pay a reasonable price. These provisions were not applicable in *May and Butcher* v *The King* because the parties had made it clear that the price was to be settled by future negotiation between them. This tends to indicate an incomplete agreement. (Also note *King's Motors (Oxford) Ltd* v *Lax* [1970] 1 WLR 426 where a lease contained an option for the tenant to accept a further lease "at such rental as may be agreed upon between the parties". It was held that, in the absence of an arbitration clause or some supplementary agreement fixing the rent to be paid, the option was void for uncertainty.)

Although the decision in *May and Butcher* v *The King* is defensible and probably correct, the law must be careful not to thwart the reasonable expectations of business people. Wherever possible, an attempt should be made to give effect to the clear contractual intention of the parties. For example, in *Foley* v *Classique Coaches* [1934] 2 KB 1, the following facts occurred:

> P agreed to sell a piece of land, adjoining P's garage, to the defendants. The sale of the land ("Contract One") was conditional on the defendants, who ran a motor coach business, entering into a second agreement with P for the supply of all their petrol requirements ("Contract Two"). Although the two agreements were contained in separate documents, the sale of the land was clearly conditional on the defendant's agreement to buy petrol from P "at a price to be agreed by the parties in writing and from time to time". (*Note:* There was also an arbitration clause included in the second contract to deal with any dispute between the parties arising out of the agreement.) After the conveyance of the land, the defendants bought their petrol from P for three years, but then they repudiated the second agreement. P sued for damages and sought a declaration that the agreement concerning the supply of petrol was binding on the defendants.

The Court of Appeal held that there was a binding contract despite the fact that the price was "to be agreed by the parties ... from time to time". It may seem that this decision is inconsistent with that of *May and Butcher* v *The King*; but on closer examination the decisions are clearly distinguishable. In *Foley*, the agreement had been acted upon by the parties for three years. (Also see *F & G Sykes (Wessex) Ltd* v *Fine Fare Ltd* [1967] 1 Lloyd's Rep 53.) This was not the case in *May and Butcher*. Furthermore, the arbitration clause in *Foley* enabled the parties to resolve any problems caused by an incomplete agreement. One of the grounds put forward by the defendants in *Foley* for repudiating the second agreement with the plaintiff was that it constituted an unreasonable restraint of trade. This argument was rejected by the court and it was stated that it would have been unfair to allow the defendants to escape from their contractual obligations, having obtained a good deal on the purchase of the land in the first place. Therefore the respective behaviour of the parties in *Foley* also appears to be of some significance[2].

An interesting point arose in *Sudbrook Trading Estate Ltd* v *Eggleton* [1982] 3 All ER 1. If the parties to an agreement provide some procedure for resolving the uncertainty of that agreement, and that procedure is subsequently unsuccessful, can the court still give effect to the clear contractual intention of the parties? The facts were as follows:

> The plaintiffs were tenants of four adjoining properties let to them by the defendants. Each lease gave the plaintiffs an option to purchase the freehold reversion of the leased properties at a price to be agreed by two valuers. Each party was to nominate a valuer, and if agreement was not reached by them, an umpire was to be appointed by both valuers. When the plaintiffs tried to exercise the options contained in the four leases, the defendants argued that the option clauses were void for uncertainty and refused to name a valuer. (They argued that the options were nothing more than agreements to agree in the future.) Although the options to purchase were declared valid by the trial court judge, the defendants' appeal was allowed by the Court of Appeal on the basis that there was no complete agreement which the court could enforce. The plaintiffs appealed to the House of Lords.

The plaintiffs' appeal was allowed and the options were ordered to be specifically performed. The purpose of the option clauses had been to provide for the sale of the properties at a fair and reasonable price and a procedure had been provided to ensure this. The machinery for ascertaining the value of the property was merely subsidiary and non-essential to this main purpose. It would have been unfair if the defendants, by their own breach of contract, had been able to defeat this clear contractual purpose by their refusal to appoint a valuer. Because the procedure laid down by the parties was not essential, there was no reason why the court could not substitute its own machinery to prevent the contract from being unenforceable. Accordingly, it ordered an enquiry into the fair value of the properties. (But see Lord Russell's dissenting judgment in this case.)[3]

A different problem arises where parties negotiate the terms of a contract, expressing their agreement "subject to contract", and one of the parties incurs costs in preparing for the intended contract which then fails to materialise. This occurred in *Regalian Properties plc* v *London Dockland Corporation* [1995] 1 All ER 1005 where P's offer to build a residential development was accepted by D subject to contract. There were long delays for various reasons and, two years later, after a sharp decrease in land prices, D abandoned the project. There was clearly no complete contract between the parties, but could P claim £3 million for costs already incurred in relation to the proposed contract? This claim was rejected by Rattee J who stressed that the dealings between P and D had been "subject to contract" only, and that D had not led P to believe that such costs would be paid for. The judge stated (at p 1024) that in this situation the parties should understand "that pending the conclusion of a binding contract any costs incurred by [P] in preparation for the intended contract will be incurred at his own risk in the sense that [P] will have no recompense for these costs if no contract results"[4].

4. Conclusion

The apparent willingness of both parties to make a contract does not necessarily amount to a legally binding agreement. Essential terms (such as price and date of completion) should not normally be left incomplete and the intentions of the parties should not be couched in vague or ambiguous terms. However, this basic principle is limited by the desire of the courts to give effect, particularly in business contexts, to the contractual intentions of the parties (for example, see *Perry* v *Suffields Ltd* [1916] 2 Ch 187). The law has to remain in touch with commercial reality and it is correct that problems of uncertainty and incompleteness are not decided purely on the basis of technical legal requirements. As we have seen, the courts are frequently able to fill in gaps left by the parties, and this judicial invention is assisted by the provisions of the Sale of Goods Act 1979 (s 8, for example). Furthermore, a court is more likely to give effect to an incomplete or uncertain agreement which has been acted on by one or both of the parties, than one where the obligations on each party are in the future.

Footnotes

(1) *Quaere:* In *Hillas & Co* v *Arcos* did the option to buy timber constitute an agreement, or was it merely an agreement to make an agreement?

(2) See the speech of Scrutton LJ [1934] 2 KB at p 7.

(3) His lordship (at p 12) made the following observations: "Why should it be thought that the potential vendor and purchaser intended the price to be 'fair'? The former would intend the price to be high, even though unfairly so. And the latter vice versa. Vendors and purchasers are normally greedy". *Quaere:* Is this an apposite criticism of the view of the majority in *Sudbrook Ltd* v *Eggleton?*

(4) If D had encouraged P to incur costs beyond those which fell within the category of normal business risks in this situation, the result may have been different, especially if D had encouraged P to think such costs would be remunerated. See *Lacey (Hounslow) Ltd* v *Davis* [1957] 2 All ER 712, which was distinguished by Rattee J in the *Regalian* case.

Chapter 4

Consideration

1. Introduction

The law of contract has to have some means of distinguishing between those agreements which are enforceable and those which are not. It would be clearly impracticable and inconvenient if all agreements were legally binding. Some agreements may lack certainty or completeness (see Chapter 3) and will be ineffective for this reason. In certain situations, such as social and domestic agreements, the law presumes a lack of intention to create legal relations, when in reality it is restricting the enforceability of such agreements for policy reasons (see Chapter 6). Another method of limiting the enforceability of agreements is to require that the contract be expressed in a particular form, such as in writing. This is a rather time-consuming and inflexible method which tends to be employed either for evidential reasons or in circumstances where the law wishes to protect certain groups from possible exploitation. (For example, a regulated consumer credit agreement must comply with the Consumer Credit (Agreements) Regulations 1983, made under ss 60 and 61 Consumer Credit Act 1974.)

A gratuitous promise made in writing by deed is legally binding because of the form in which it is expressed. It does not matter whether anything is given in return for such a promise. However, most contracts are not of this type. "Simple" contracts do not normally require any particular form in order to be effective. As we have seen, an enforceable agreement can be made orally, or in writing. The test of enforceability which is used under our law of contract is the requirement of consideration. This is the symbol of bargain and reciprocal obligations. The law does not enforce gratuitous promises; the promise of a gift, for example, to a charity will not be binding unless it is by deed (see *Re Hudson* (1885) 54 LJ Ch 811). Similarly, a promise is not enforceable simply because it is morally right that the promisor should keep his word (see *Eastwood* v *Kenyon* (1840) 11 A & E 438). The law requires that the promisor asks for and receives something in return for his promise. The courts are not generally concerned with whether the promisor made a good bargain. (For further discussion, see Chapter 16). All that is required is that there is some element of exchange, that is, some degree of mutuality.

The historical origins of the doctrine of consideration are still the subject of academic debate, but this need not concern us here. It is sufficient to note that the doctrine survived the challenge of an eminent judge, Lord Mansfield, in the mid-eighteenth century, when he attempted to argue that it was not a necessary contractual requirement, but merely one method of proving the intention of the parties to be bound. In other words, some other evidence of the parties' contractual intention, such as writing, would equally suffice. This view was rejected in *Rann* v *Hughes* (1778) 7 Term Rep 350n. Despite many criticisms of the doctrine, which we will consider in due course, consideration is a basic requirement of all simple contracts and it is therefore central to our understanding of the subject.

Although we refer to "the" doctrine of consideration, it must be stressed that this doctrine, in fact, consists of a number of different rules, developed over a long period, some of which are more defensible than others. To debate whether the doctrine is a good or bad thing is to miss the point of its importance. The various rules which we call "consideration" simply represent the method that our law has developed for distinguishing between enforceable and unenforceable promises. In doing so, it has emphasised the idea of bargain and exchange in contractual dealings. This was clearly in keeping with the spirit of classical contract law and the *laissez faire* philosophy which influenced it.

If the doctrine were to be abolished, some alternative test of enforceability would still be required. This is not to suggest that all the present rules are satisfactory. It is only the resourcefulness of the judiciary and the malleability of the common law which have enabled the doctrine to survive in its present form without being subjected to the attentions of the legislature (for instance, see the development of the doctrine of promissory estoppel, in Chapter 5). Some of the rules of consideration appear to be capable of producing unfair results, whilst others are perhaps out of touch with commercial practice. Some of these anomalies have been smoothed out by the judges, but certain fundamental issues still need to be resolved. For example, what is the nature of the interrelationship between the traditional exchange model of contracts and the more modern emphasis on estoppel and reliance? These are matters to which we shall return.

2.　Can consideration be defined?

As the doctrine is in fact a loose assortment of different rules, it tends to defy any standard or broadly accepted definition. Yet attempts at such a definition abound. The traditional definitions tended to concentrate on the ideas of benefit and detriment. For example, in *Currie* v *Misa* (1875) LR 10 Ex 153, Lush J stated (at p 162):

> "A valuable consideration, in the eyes of the law, may consist either in some right, interest, profit, or benefit accruing to the one party, or some forbearance, detriment, loss, or responsibility given, suffered or undertaken by the other".

This type of definition stressed the exchange nature of contracts in terms of some kind of economic advantage. (Also see *Thomas* v *Thomas* (1842) 2 QB 851 at p 859.) In other words, the promisor must receive something which the law recognizes as a "benefit", namely something of value. If a seller promises to deliver goods to a customer, the latter provides consideration by paying for them, or by his promise to pay for them. The customer suffers a detriment by so doing, in exchange for the benefit conferred upon him by the seller. In many commercial transactions there is such a benefit and detriment, although some might argue that there is no detriment where the contract is wholly executory (ie by the exchange of promises)[1].

The problem with the traditional definition is that in many instances the consideration in question does not, in fact, confer any economic benefit on the promisor. The idea of something of value, given in exchange for a promise, is interpreted very widely. In the absence of fraud or any other vitiating factor, the courts are not generally concerned with the nature of the bargain struck by the parties. It may well be that, in economic terms, the consideration is inadequate; the courts will not interfere. The doctrine represents the symbol of bargain, rather than the reality of bargain. It is a technical requirement of the law of contract and the parties can easily ensure that it is met by the provision of some nominal consideration.

For these reasons, more modern definitions of consideration tend not to be expressed in terms of benefit and detriment. Reference is made more loosely to one party paying the "price" of the other's promise. (For example, Sir Frederick Pollock stated: "An act or forbearance of one party, or the promise thereof, is the price for which the promise is bought and the promise thus given for value is enforceable"[2]; this statement was approved in *Dunlop Pneumatic Tyre Co Ltd v Selfridge & Co Ltd* [1915] AC 847 at p 855.) If a party promises something and asks for nothing in return, there is no consideration and, therefore, the promise is not legally enforceable. But where the promisor asks for something in exchange for his promise, the promisee provides consideration by giving the promisor what he has requested. The promisor might have requested a specific act, such as the provision of information in exchange for a reward. This is referred to as "executed" consideration (see below). Alternatively, the promisor might request a promise (for example, of payment for goods to be delivered in the future). This is known as "executory" consideration.

The various definitions of consideration have their respective supporters, but it scarcely matters which one we adopt. This is because the courts take an essentially pragmatic view of the requirement. The decisions under the different rules which are discussed below are not always consistent with one another. In some circumstances, where justice demands, the courts will invent consideration so as to make the promise in question binding. As we saw in the earlier chapters of this book, the common law is flexible and the law of contract cannot be reduced to a set of axioms. With this warning in mind, the main rules which comprise the doctrine of consideration will now be considered.

3. Consideration must not be past

Where the promisor (P) requests a specific act in return for his promise, then performance of the act by the promisee will be good consideration. If all the other ingredients of a binding contract are present, P's promise will be enforceable. It will be remembered that in *Carlill v Carbolic Smoke Ball Co* [1893] 1 QB 256, the defendant company offered a reward of £100 to anyone who bought one of their smoke balls, used it in the prescribed manner, and yet caught influenza. The plaintiff, who bought a smoke ball, and used it, provided consideration for the company's promise. (Obviously she could not have claimed the reward unless she in fact caught 'flu, but this can hardly be described as part of the consideration.) This exchange of a promise for a particular act or acts is referred to as executed consideration.

An exchange of promises by the parties, known as executory consideration, will also amount to an enforceable agreement. For example, X promises to deliver a new car to Y in three weeks' time, and Y promises to pay for the vehicle on delivery. Despite the fact that no performance of the undertakings has yet taken place — the obligations are still in the future — there is good consideration. Both parties are getting what they requested in return for their promises. For commercial reasons it is important that the law recognizes the validity of such agreements as this facilitates forward planning by the parties.

Executed and executory consideration are commonly referred to as "good consideration". However, a promise which is made after an act has been performed is generally not enforceable. This is rather confusingly referred to as "past consideration", and is not recognized as good consideration. The reason for this is that the act or performance in question was not part of any bargain or exchange; it was gratuitous. Therefore, any subsequent promise is not part of any contractual bargain and remains unenforceable (although there are some important exceptions which will be considered later). A vivid illustration of the basic rule is provided by *Eastwood* v *Kenyon* (1840) 11 A & E 438:

> The plaintiff had become the guardian of Sarah, a young heiress, on the death of Sarah's father. He spent money on improving her estate, and on her education, and he had to borrow £140 in order to do so. When she came of age, she promised to pay the plaintiff the amount of the loan. After her marriage to the defendant, he (her husband) repeated this promise of reimbursement to the plaintiff.

The plaintiff could not enforce the defendant's promise, due to lack of consideration. The guardian's acts were gratuitous; they were not given in return for the defendant's (or Sarah's) promise. The case clearly shows that a moral obligation to fulfil a promise is not sufficient to lead the court to enforce that promise. Even when confronted by an unjust result, as in this case, the court will require something given in exchange for a promise for it to be enforceable. A similar decision was reached in *Re McArdle* [1951] Ch 669, which also shows that the use of the term "consideration" by the parties themselves is not of any significance. The facts were:

> The five children of a family were to inherit a house (by their father's will) after the death of their mother. One of the sons, and his wife, lived in the house with his mother until she died. During this period the daughter-in-law made some improvements and alterations to the property, which she paid for herself. She had not been asked to do this. However, about a year later, all five children signed a document addressed to her, in which they promised to repay her £488 from the estate when it was eventually distributed. The document specifically stated that this payment was "in consideration of [her] carrying out certain alterations and improvements to the property". When the mother died, the daughter-in-law tried to enforce the promise made in this document.

The Court of Appeal held that her claim failed. The promise was not given in exchange for her act. She had already carried out the improvements without any such promise of reimbursement being made. This was a clear instance of past consideration and the promise was, accordingly, unenforceable, despite the apparently unequivocal way in which the document expressed the contractual intention of the five children. This appears to be a rather unfair result. It is possible, however, that in the case of a commercial transaction the courts might be more willing to imply that the work was done at the promisor's request (see *Re Casey's Patents*, below).

The rule about past consideration is probably not applied so strictly as to defeat obvious commercial (especially consumer) expectations. Otherwise the case of *Roscorla* v *Thomas* (1842) 3 QB 234 could have serious implications for those who buy guaranteed goods. In that case, P bought a horse from D for £30. After the sale, D promised that the horse was "sound and free from vice", a fact which turned out to be untrue. It was held that this promise was not enforceable, as it was given after the contract between the parties had been concluded; nothing was given by P in exchange for D's promise (or guarantee).

How far would this decision be applied today when the giving of guarantees by manufacturers is commonplace? The buyer provides consideration under the contract with the retailer by paying the price of the goods. But if those goods turn out to be guaranteed by the manufacturer, who is not a party to the contract between the retailer and the buyer, does the buyer provide any consideration for the manufacturer's promise? If the buyer knows that the goods in question are guaranteed, he may have chosen them for that reason and, in so doing, have provided the consideration for the guarantee. But surely the guarantee is equally enforceable against the manufacturer even where the buyer does not buy the goods because they are guaranteed and learns of this only after the purchase?

It could be argued that the buyer provides consideration by filling in a card (which is often, but not always required) and sending it off to the manufacturer. It could be analysed as follows: the main contract is between the retailer and the buyer for the sale of goods. The guarantee is a unilateral offer by the manufacturer, which can be accepted by buying the goods, filling in the appropriate card or form, and sending it off to the manufacturer within a specified period. A slightly different way of expressing this is that the guarantee is the subject of a collateral contract; ie one that exists alongside the main contract. This is something of a judicial device enabling the courts to enforce certain promises which would otherwise be unenforceable. Whichever analysis is preferred, it seems that manufacturers' guarantees will not be rendered ineffective by the rules relating to consideration. (For an interesting case which raises some analogous issues, see *Shanklin Pier* v *Detel Products Ltd* [1951] 2 KB 854.)

Instances where consideration is not past

There are certain well-established circumstances where what appears to be past consideration will be regarded as good consideration by the courts. They will look at the whole transaction between the parties and not rely simply on whether the promise was made after a particular act or service was performed by the promisee. These circumstances have been helpfully summarised by Lord Scarman in the Privy Council decision in *Pao On* v *Lau Yiu Long* [1979] 3 All ER 65 at p 74, where he stated:

"An act done before the giving of a promise to make a payment or to confer some other benefit can sometimes be consideration for the promise. The act must have been done at the promisor's request, the parties must have understood that the act was to be remunerated either by a payment or the conferment of some other benefit, and payment, or the conferment of a benefit, must have been legally enforceable had it been promised in advance".

To explain the matter more clearly, let us return to the facts of *Re McArdle* (see page 47). The daughter-in-law carried out the improvements on the house on her own initiative, and not as a result of any request by the five children. Thus her attempt to enforce their subsequent promise failed. If the children had asked her to carry out the work, but promised no particular amount of remuneration until afterwards, the result may well have been different. The outcome would then have depended on whether there was an understanding between the parties, express or implied, that the work would be remunerated in some way. As we have seen, it is more likely that such an understanding will be implied in commercial dealings than in domestic arrangements.

A useful illustration of the first requirement mentioned by Lord Scarman is provided by the early seventeenth century case of *Lampleigh* v *Brathwait* (1615) Hob 105. The facts were:

> Brathwait had killed a man and he requested that Lampleigh should try to get him a pardon from the King. Lampleigh did as requested, which involved making journeys at his own expense, and obtained a pardon for Brathwait. Afterwards, Brathwait promised to pay him £100 for his endeavours. He then failed to pay Lampleigh and was sued by him. Brathwait's defence was that the act had been performed before the promise of a reward was made.

The court found in favour of Lampleigh and rejected the argument that the consideration was past. It stressed that the plaintiff's service was performed at the request of the defendant and his later promise to pay for it was binding. This is because the later promise was clearly related to the earlier request for help; essentially, it was all part of the same transaction. It is also likely, given the facts of the case, that in Brathwait's request for help there was an implied promise that a reward would follow if Lampleigh was successful. This is certainly the interpretation given to the case in *Kennedy* v *Broun* (1863) 13 CB 677. Of course, it is unlikely that any such promise would be implied where the service was rendered out of friendship rather than out of any thought of reward.

The second test put forward by Lord Scarman is illustrated by *Re Casey's Patents; (Stewart* v *Casey)* [1892] 1 Ch 104. The facts were as follows:

> Stewart and Charlton, the joint owners of certain patent rights wrote to Casey stating that, in consideration for his services as practical manager in working their patents, they promised to give him a one-third share of the patents. They later transferred the letters patent to Casey. After the death of Stewart, it was argued by Charlton and by Stewart's executor that Casey was not entitled to possession of the letters patent. Casey contested this and argued that, as owner of a one-third share in the patents, he was entitled to possession.

The question for the Court of Appeal to decide was whether Casey provided consideration for the promise made to him by Stewart and Charlton in the letter. The plaintiffs contended that it was a case of past consideration, but this argument was rejected by the court which found in favour of the defendant. The court was willing to imply an understanding between the parties, at the time the services by Casey were performed, that they would be remunerated.

The later promise was, therefore, part of the same transaction; it merely fixed the amount of remuneration for which the service was originally rendered. Accordingly, consideration is not past in these circumstances, despite appearances to the contrary.

The general rule that past consideration is not good consideration can thus be evaded by judicial ingenuity, as in *Re Casey's Patents*. A more logical approach might be to do away with the rule altogether as it is difficult to see what useful purpose it serves. The Law Reform Committee, 6th Interim Report, 1937 (Cmnd 5449, para 32), did in fact recommend the abolition of the rule, but to no avail. It should be noted that the general rule about past consideration is also subject to certain statutory exceptions; for example, in relation to negotiable instruments. Under the Bills of Exchange Act 1882, s 27(1) provides that "valuable consideration for a bill may be constituted by: (a) Any consideration sufficient to support a simple contract; (b) An antecedent debt or liability. Such a debt or liability is deemed valuable consideration whether the bill is payable on demand or at a future time"[3].

4. Consideration must move from the promisee

As a general principle, a person can enforce a promise made to him only if he himself provided consideration for that promise (see *Price* v *Easton* (1833) 4 B & Ad 433). But, what if A is promised some benefit by B, but the consideration for the promise has been supplied by C? In such a situation, A has given nothing in exchange for B's promise; he has not paid the price of it, or suffered any detriment. The traditional view of the law has been that A will not normally be able to enforce B's promise as consideration has not been provided by him. For example, in *Tweddle* v *Atkinson* (1861) 1 B & S 393, the facts were:

> John Tweddle and William Guy agreed (at first orally, and later in writing) each to pay a sum of money to a couple on their marriage. The couple in question were their son and daughter, respectively. The plaintiff, John Tweddle's son, tried to enforce his father-in-law's promise, when William Guy failed to make the agreed payment. (In fact, the action was brought against the executor of the deceased William Guy).

The son's action failed as he did not provide any consideration for his father-in-law's promise. Crompton J stated (at p 398) that:

> "... [T]he consideration must move from the party entitled to sue upon the contract. It would be a monstrous proposition to say that a person was a party to a contract for the purpose of suing upon it for his own advantage, and not a party to it for the purpose of being sued."

An alternative way of expressing the justification for not allowing the son's action to succeed in *Tweddle* v *Atkinson* is that there was no privity of contract between him and his father-in-law. (The contract was between John Tweddle and William Guy). This principle of contract law is dealt with in Chapter 18, together with the important Contracts (Rights of Third Parties) Act 1999, which has introduced significant changes to this area of law. The extent to which the rule that "consideration must move from the promisee" has been affected by the new legislation, implicitly if not formally, will be considered in

Chapter 18, as this principle is closely related to the doctrine of privity. It was the view of the Law Commission that it is not possible "even at a formal level, [to] reform the privity doctrine while leaving untouched the rule that consideration must move from the promisee." (See Law Commission No 242, *Privity of Contract: Contracts for the Benefit of Third Parties*, 1996, para 6.5).

5. Must the consideration be adequate?

The doctrine of consideration represents the idea of bargain and mutual obligations. The law will enforce only those promises for which something is given in return; it will not enforce gratuitous promises. One of the difficulties with the traditional definition of consideration in terms of "benefit" and "detriment" is that the promisor might request some act or forbearance from the promisee which is of little or no economic value. But as long as this is what he requests, and is given, the court will not interfere with the "bargain" struck by the parties (see *Bainbridge* v *Firmstone* (1838) 1 P & D 2). Thus consideration represents the idea of bargain rather than the reality of it. Certain acts or promises, which we will consider, are regarded by the law as sufficient consideration for a promise, whilst others are not. It is often said (rather unhelpfully) that consideration must be sufficient. On the other hand, the courts will generally not judge the adequacy of consideration; ie whether adequate value has been given in exchange for a promise.

This apparent failure to question the adequacy of consideration is perhaps more defensible than it seems at first sight. If the parties have bargained for a particular consideration, then it can usually be assumed that they achieved what they wanted from the exchange. Where a party appears to have made a particularly bad bargain there may be some other factor present which may vitiate the agreement, such as fraud or duress. But in the absence of any vitiating factor, the courts will not (in theory) intervene in order to ensure a fair bargain has been struck. An important point here is that the law of contract is not the most suitable means of monitoring or controlling prices and ensuring fairness. Regulation through other measures can achieve this end more effectively. Moreover, although there is perhaps no general doctrine in our law which protects parties simply on the basis that they have entered into a bad bargain or an unconscionable agreement, the law of contract is capable of considerable flexibility in the pursuit of a fair result. In other words, the courts may rely on the various techniques at their disposal in order to promote the idea that a contract should not involve an unfair exchange or a very one-sided bargain[4].

Before we go on to consider the traditional cases which are illustrative of the general rule that the courts will not enquire into the adequacy of consideration, it is salutary to look at a few examples of the courts taking an obvious interest in this very question. It is conceded that these decisions may have been explained on different grounds, and that they do not disprove the general rule about adequacy of consideration, but they do show that the courts will attempt, where possible, to ensure that a contract involves a fair exchange. An interesting example is provided by a case on undue influence, *Lloyds Bank* v *Bundy* [1974] 3 All ER 757, where the facts were:

> Herbert Bundy, the defendant, was an elderly farmer. His only financial asset was the farmhouse which he owned. However, he guaranteed his son's company's

overdraft with Lloyds Bank, by charging his house to the bank to secure progressively larger amounts. His son owned a plant-hire business which was in trouble. Both Herbert Bundy and his son's company banked at the same branch of the plaintiff bank. Herbert Bundy had received a warning from his solicitor that he should not commit more than £10,000 to his son's business, as any greater sum would exceed the value of his house. But when a new assistant manager called to see Herbert Bundy, taking a guarantee and a charge form for the latter to sign, the defendant did not heed his solicitor's warning. Mr Bundy had no adviser present at the meeting between himself, his son, and the assistant bank manager. It was made clear that the bank would continue to support the company only if the defendant increased the guarantee and charge up to an amount of £11,000. The assistant manager did explain the company's financial position, but did not explain its accounts very fully. Herbert Bundy signed the documents. Six months later the bank stopped overdraft facilities for the company, which was still in trouble, and proceeded to enforce the charge and guarantee against Herbert Bundy. In effect, this meant the bank selling his house, and an action for possession was brought against the defendant.

The Court of Appeal set aside the guarantee and charge signed by Herbert Bundy and dismissed the action for possession against him. The bank should have advised the defendant to seek independent financial advice before committing himself in such a potentially far-reaching way. Failure to do so was a breach of the bank's fiduciary duty to the defendant, and it would not be allowed to retain the benefit of the transaction. This finding of undue influence would have been sufficient to dispose of the matter, but Lord Denning went further in his judgment. He made reference (at p 765) to the fact that "the consideration moving from the bank was grossly inadequate". By this he meant that both Mr Bundy and his son's company received very little benefit from the contract. His lordship also tried to identify a general principle of "inequality of bargaining power". He stated (at p 765):

"...the English law gives relief to one who, without independent advice, enters into a contract on terms which are very unfair or transfers property for a consideration which is grossly inadequate, when his bargaining power is grievously impaired by reason of his own needs or desires, or by his own ignorance or infirmity, coupled with undue influences or pressures brought to bear on him by or for the benefit of the other".

Lord Denning's statement was merely *obiter* and it is probably too broad a statement of principle to find favour with the majority of judges. (Indeed, it was criticised by Lord Scarman in *National Westminster Bank* v *Morgan* [1985] 1 All ER 821 at p 830.) However, it does illustrate the fact that inadequate consideration may be a relevant factor for the courts to consider in some instances. (For another example of a contract where the inadequacy of the consideration was an important factor, see *Schroeder (A) Music Publishing Co* v *Macaulay* [1974] 3 All ER 616, especially the judgment of Lord Diplock at pp 623–624.) The courts may prefer to explain their judgments in more technical terms, but they may well be reluctant to uphold an agreement that provides for a very unequal exchange between the parties. In *Staffordshire Area Health Authority* v *South Staffordshire Waterworks Co* [1978] 3 All ER 769, the court's decision, to allow a seemingly indefinite contract for the supply of water to be brought to an end by giving reasonable notice, was influenced by the fact that the defendants should not be permitted to go on receiving their water at one-fifteenth of the economic rate.

6. Adequacy of consideration: the general rule

Although it is commonly stated that consideration must be of economic value, it is generally not a matter for the courts to judge the adequacy of consideration. Subject to the observations made in the previous section, the courts will not enquire whether the parties in fact made a fair bargain or exchange. So the provision of nominal consideration will suffice to meet the technical requirement of the law. For example, in *Mountford v Scott* [1975] Ch 258 the payment of £1 by P was sufficient to secure an option to purchase D's house. The Court of Appeal held that this option agreement was enforceable against D and that it was irrelevant that the consideration provided by P could be described as a token payment. In reaching this conclusion, reference was made to the "mass of English authority to the effect that anything of value, however small the value, is sufficient consideration to support a contract at law" (*per* Cairns LJ at p 265). There is nothing objectionable in principle about this general rule. If the parties strike a particular bargain with the promisor requesting, and being given, something of minimal economical value in exchange for his promise, there is no reason for the court to interfere. There may, occasionally, be problems in differentiating between a contract supported by consideration and a conditional gift. These issues are well illustrated by the case of *Thomas v Thomas* (1842) 2 QB 851. The facts were:

> P's husband had made it clear that if his wife survived him, she should have the use of his house. After her husband's death, P agreed with the defendant, her husband's executor, that she should have the use of the house as long as she did not remarry. Her husband's executor made the agreement largely in deference to the deceased's clearly expressed wishes. But P was also asked to pay £1 per year to the executors under the agreement. Had P provided consideration for the promise, or was the payment of £1 per year no more than a condition attached to a gift?

It was held that the plaintiff provided consideration for the executor's promise. It would not have been a legally enforceable agreement if the executor had merely wished to honour the deceased's wishes and requested nothing further, for this would have been a gratuitous promise. But, in this case, something of value, no matter how inadequate, was asked for by the promisor. It was more than a conditional gift, it was a binding agreement; the court did not have to enquire into the adequacy of the consideration provided by the promisee under the contract.

In theory, consideration must be of some economic value, no matter how slight. For this reason, a promise which confers less tangible benefits may fail to satisfy this requirement. In *White v Bluett* (1853) 23 LJ Ex 36, the defendant borrowed money from his father and gave him a promissory note. This was followed by bitter complaints from the defendant that he had been treated less favourably by his father than the other children in the family. In order to gain some peace, and out of affection for his son, the father promised to discharge the defendant from his obligation to repay the loan. On the father's death, his executor brought a successful action to recover the loan. It was held that no consideration had been provided by the defendant for his father's promise, as refraining from making complaints was thought not to be of any economic value.

It is impossible to be dogmatic on the question of what is regarded as being of economic value, and *White v Bluett* is far from conclusive. It can be contrasted with the interesting case of *Ward v Byham* [1956] 2 All ER 318. The facts were:

> The plaintiff (P) lived with the defendant (D) for five years as an unmarried couple. P gave birth to their daughter during this period, but the couple eventually separated. Initially, D was responsible for looking after the child, as P had been forced to leave their home. But when P found a housekeeping job, where she could have the daughter with her, D agreed to let her have the child and an allowance of £1 per week, provided that P could prove that their daughter was "well looked after and happy". The daughter, who was allowed to decide with which parent she wanted to live, went to her mother's. D made the £1 weekly payments, but stopped these when P married her employer. P brought an action for the £1 per week promised by D.

The Court of Appeal decided in favour of P and held that she did provide consideration for D's promise. In fact, P was under a legal obligation (as the mother of an illegitimate child) to look after her daughter (s 42 National Assistance Act 1948). However, it was argued that she went beyond her statutory duty by undertaking that the child was well looked after and happy. The judges offered various reasons for enforcing the agreement, but it is difficult to escape the conclusion that the plaintiff failed to provide anything of economic value in exchange for the defendant's promise. There was undoubtedly a benefit of some kind to D, as indeed there was in *White* v *Bluett*, but it can hardly be claimed that it was of economic rather than emotional value. This contrast between the two cases illustrates the point that the court can exercise some discretion in deciding what will and what will not amount to consideration. The apparent "rules" are not so precisely formulated as to exclude some room for judicial manoeuvre.

In certain circumstances the parties themselves might not dispute the binding nature of their agreement, but the consideration requested by the promisor might have a bearing on the rights of another party. For example, in *Chappell & Co* v *Nestlé Co* [1960] AC 87, the facts were:

> The Nestlé Company (D) offered a record entitled "Rockin' Shoes" to the public for 1s 6d (7p) plus three Nestlé's chocolate bar wrappers. The requirement of sending in the wrappers, in addition to the money, was in order to promote the company's chocolate; the wrappers were worthless and were thrown away on receipt. The action arose because the plaintiff, who owned the copyright in "Rockin' Shoes", claimed that he received insufficient royalties on the sale of the record. D paid a percentage based on the price of the record, which was 1s 6d. The plaintiff argued that the wrappers were also part of the consideration.

The House of Lords decided the case in favour of the plaintiff. The wrappers were part of the consideration. They were requested by the Nestlé Company and were given by members of the public, together with money, in exchange for the record. It was held to be irrelevant that the wrappers were of no intrinsic value to the company (*per* Lord Somervell at p 114). Parties to a contract could ask for whatever consideration they wanted, and it was not for the court to assess its adequacy. It might also be observed that although the wrappers were worthless they represented something of value to the Nestlé Company, namely the successful promotion of the company's products. This was acknowledged by Lord Reid (at p 108) who stated that "the requirement that wrappers should be sent was of great importance to the Nestlé Co... it seems to me quite unrealistic to divorce the buying of the chocolate from the supplying of the records".

The courts can be fairly inventive in finding consideration for a promise where it is felt that justice requires such an approach. *Ward* v *Byham* (see above) is a good example of such flexibility. A further illustration is provided by *De La Bere* v *Pearson* [1908] 1 KB 280, where a newspaper owned by D advertised a financial advice section which answered readers' questions. P wrote in and asked for advice on investments but received faulty advice, as a result of which, he lost money. D was held to be liable for breach of contract. (It is, perhaps, more likely that if similar facts occurred today an action would be brought for negligent misstatement in tort.) The problem with the Court of Appeal's decision in P's favour is that he did not appear to provide any consideration for the newspaper's promise to supply him with financial advice. It is fanciful to suggest that the purchase of the newspaper was consideration for the promise, as the paper contained many other features for which a reader would presumably buy a copy. But it was of benefit to the paper to receive readers' letters and to publish replies and therefore P provided consideration by requesting advice from the newspaper's financial advice section. D presumably hoped to boost sales by running such a service and this benefit was (however slightly) assisted by the plaintiff.

7. Forbearance to sue and compromise as consideration

Where X is threatened by Y with legal action to enforce a claim, they might reach a compromise whereby Y's promise to refrain from suing is "bought" by X's counter promise to pay an agreed amount. This exchange of promises is binding, because something of value is given by both parties. (For example, see *Horton* v *Horton (No 2)* [1961] 1 QB 215: in this case there was only a possibility that an action might have been brought by the wife against her husband in relation to their separation agreement. But giving up this possible claim was still regarded by the court as consideration.) One party gives up a claim whilst the other agrees to pay compensation. It is in the interest of the legal system to encourage parties, wherever possible, to reach a compromise over disputes. Similarly, if X is faced with a claim by Y (eg for an outstanding debt), and requests further time to pay, Y's forbearance from pursuing the claim can amount to consideration for any new promise made by X. So where a debtor promises to give additional security for a debt, in exchange for more time to pay, this will again be regarded as a binding agreement.

If X is threatened with a legal action which Y knows to be without foundation, Y's forbearance from proceeding will not amount to consideration for any new promise given by X. To hold otherwise would encourage vexatious and frivolous claims and be contrary to public policy (see *Wade* v *Simeon* (1846) 2 CB 548). But as long as Y honestly believes that the action is reasonable, and might succeed, then forbearance from proceeding with a doubtful or even a bad claim is capable of amounting to consideration. (For a recent discussion of this issue, see *Freedman* v *Union Group plc and another* [1997] EGCS 28). Of course, Y must not conceal any information from X which might affect his ability to resist the claim (see *Miles* v *New Zealand Alford Estate Co* (1886) 32 Ch D 266).

Is it necessary for Y specifically to promise X some degree of forbearance from bringing an action, or need there only be some forbearance in fact which can be inferred from the dealings between the parties? This question was considered in *Alliance Bank* v *Broom* (1864) 2 Dr & Sm 289, where the facts were:

The defendants, a firm of Liverpool merchants, owed £22,000 to the plaintiff bank and were asked by the bank to provide additional security for the debt. The defendants promised to assign to them the documents of title to certain goods by way of additional security. It is important to note that, in return, the bank made no express counter promise not to sue the defendants. The defendants failed to provide the promised security and the bank tried to enforce the promise. Had the bank given anything in return for the defendants' promise?

It was held that the bank had given consideration by their actual forbearance and were entitled to claim specific performance. The reason given was that in the circumstances the defendants received the benefit of "a certain amount of forbearance which [they] would not have derived if [they] had not made the agreement" (at p 292). Apparently, it did not matter that no specific promise to forbear was given by the bank, nor was it necessary that the actual forbearance should last for a substantial period of time. The decision is, perhaps, unfortunate. The court seems to have enforced a very one-sided exchange in circumstances where the extent of any forbearance was, to say the least, unclear. (For a contrasting decision, see *Miles* v *New Zealand Alford Estate Co* (1886) 32 Ch D 266.)

8. Performance of a legal duty as consideration

The rules relating to sufficiency of consideration are not always entirely consistent, and they tend more accurately to reflect the exigencies of public policy than the dictates of logic. This is particularly the case in relation to the performance of an existing legal duty in exchange for another person's promise. This can arise in three distinct factual situations, which will be considered in turn: (a) the performance of a public duty; (b) the performance of a duty owed already to the promisor; and (c) the performance of a duty owed already to a third party. If a person performs (or promises to perform) an act which he is already legally obliged to perform for one of the three reasons listed above, can this be regarded as "buying" the other party's promise? As a matter of logic it might be doubted whether there is any consideration provided in such instances, although it is certainly possible that the other party might, in fact, receive some benefit.

(a) Public duty imposed by law

We have already seen an illustration of this type of case. In *Ward* v *Byham* (see page 53) the plaintiff was under a statutory duty to look after her illegitimate daughter, but it was held that she provided consideration for the defendant's promise to pay her £1 per week for doing precisely that. It was argued by Morris LJ that the consideration consisted of ensuring that the child was both well looked after and happy, as requested by the promisor. But, as we have seen, it is unlikely that keeping the child "happy" can itself amount to something of value for the purposes of the law (see *White* v *Bluett*, discussed on page 53). Lord Denning's assessment of the facts in *Ward* v *Byham* was, perhaps, more realistic. He acknowledged that, in looking after her daughter, the plaintiff was only fulfilling her legal obligation. However, he thought that such a performance of an existing duty (or the promise of such performance) was good consideration. He concentrated on the benefit that this performance conferred upon the promisor. In support of such a view it might well be asked why the promisor made the promise if it was to have no legal effect. (See the discussion of this issue in the Law Revision Committee's 6th Interim Report, 1937, Cmnd 5449, para 36.)

The traditional view is not in accord with Lord Denning's opinion, as expressed in *Ward* v *Byham*, but it is fair to say that the case law is far from conclusive on the matter. In *Collins* v *Godefroy* (1831) 1 B & Ad 950, P was subpoenaed to give evidence on D's behalf at a trial in which D was involved. P claimed that D promised him one guinea (£1.05) per day for attending court. But P was unsuccessful in his attempt to enforce D's promise as he failed to provide consideration for this promise. P was already under a legal duty to attend court because of the subpoena. Although this decision does not represent court practice today, it is thought to have established a general principle that a person does not provide consideration for another person's promise (of payment) by simply performing an existing legal duty.

Such a principle is, however, open to question. There can be no doubt that it is in the public interest to prevent certain professional groups from bargaining for services that they are under a public duty to render. It would be unthinkable for a policeman or a fireman to be able to enforce a promise of a reward made to them by a member of the public, in urgent need of their help, simply for carrying out their public duties. But the reason for not upholding such an agreement is not necessarily based on lack of consideration, but rather on the grounds of public policy and the prevention of extortion. It will be remembered that in *Gibbons* v *Proctor* (1891) 64 LT 594 a policeman was able to claim a reward for providing information leading to the arrest of an offender. (Also see *England* v *Davidson* (1840) 11 Ad & El 856.) So it appears that the true test of whether such promises are enforceable is not whether consideration is given, but whether upholding these agreements is contrary to public policy.

One method of circumventing this problem is for the court to find that the promisee did, in fact, go beyond the mere performance of an existing legal duty. (This was the explanation given by the majority of the court for the decision in *Ward* v *Byham*.) A good example of this reasoning is provided by *Glasbrook Brothers Ltd* v *Glamorgan County Council* [1925] AC 270, where mine-owners, during a miners' strike, were fearful of violence occurring. Their assessment of the amount of police protection that they needed differed from that of the police whose job it was to provide it. Eventually, the police did agree to mount a stationary guard, which they did not think necessary, but they did so on the basis that it would be paid for by the company. The company agreed to pay £2,200 for this more extensive police operation, but later refused to make the payment, claiming that there was no consideration given for their promise. The House of Lords held that the police were entitled to recover the payment as they had done more than perform their existing legal duty.

The decision in *Glasbrook Brothers* is not open to criticism as long as the police's original assessment of the company's security requirements was a reasonable one. If it was, the police clearly gave something of value, over and above their public duty, in exchange for the company's promise. Of course, if there is the slightest suggestion of extortion in this type of case, the agreement should not be enforceable on the grounds of public policy. It is submitted that cases of this type cannot be resolved purely on the basis of any technical requirement of consideration in the law of contract. In reality, they involve issues of public policy and should be explained on this basis.

(b) Performance of a duty owed to promisor

This type of case involves the following conundrum: X makes a promise to Y in exchange for Y doing (or promising to do) something which Y is already obliged to do under an existing contract with X. If Y does (or promises) nothing more than he is already bound to do, it is difficult to see how he can be said to have provided consideration for X's promise. Once again, questions of public policy may be involved, and it would be clearly undesirable if a person who had already contracted to perform a particular service could extort more money from the promisor for performing the same service. On the other hand, if it is worthwhile to X to make such a promise (eg to be absolutely sure that Y will do what he contracted to do), it could be argued that X gets what he asks for and should not be allowed to escape liability for the further promise. The law has to try to distinguish between genuine agreements of this type and situations where there is some element of economic duress. (Increasingly, duress has become the central issue in such cases rather than the technical requirements of the doctrine of consideration. This subject is dealt with in detail in Chapter 14.)

The traditional view was that the performance of an existing duty already owed to the promisor (as described above) could not amount to consideration. This is well illustrated by *Stilk* v *Myrick* (1809) 2 Camp 317 and 6 Esp 129. The facts arose out of a return voyage from London to the Baltic, during which two sailors had deserted and the captain was unable to find replacements for them. He therefore promised to divide the wages of the two deserters amongst the remaining crew members in exchange for them sailing the ship short-handed on the home voyage. Largely on the grounds of public policy, to deter extortion, the action brought by one of the crew, to enforce this promise, failed. An alternative reason for the decision was that the crew members provided no consideration for the captain's promise, as they were only fulfilling their existing contractual obligations by sailing the ship home.

There may well have been sound policy reasons for the courts refusing to enforce promises of this kind. It was presumably felt that this type of situation gave seamen an undesirable opportunity to bargain for higher wages to complete voyages which they were already bound to complete. But there appears to be no evidence of the seamen making any demand in *Stilk* v *Myrick* and thus there was no evidence of extortion in the case itself. The objection to this general rule was that it struck down quite legitimate bargains as well as potentially extortionate ones. It should be noted, however, that if the circumstances on a voyage were to change so radically as to make the trip a positively dangerous one, seamen were probably able to enforce any additional promise of remuneration made by the captain.

For example, in *Hartley* v *Ponsonby* (1857) 7 El & Bl 872, a crew of thirty-six was reduced by desertions to one of nineteen, of which only a handful were experienced sailors. This situation was distinguishable from that of *Stilk* v *Myrick* and the plaintiff was able to enforce the captain's promise of an additional £40. But it was clear from the judgments in the case that this was an exceptional set of circumstances, where continuing with the voyage was so dangerous that the remaining crew members were not simply fulfilling their existing obligations, and they were free to make a fresh bargain. Accordingly, consideration was provided for the captain's promise.

The basic rule laid down in *Stilk* v *Myrick* has increasingly been questioned. There is no reason why the promisor in such a situation cannot derive a benefit from the other party's promise; he achieves peace of mind in knowing that the other person will do the thing bargained for. If this benefit matters sufficiently to him to make a promise of further remuneration to the other party, then why should he be able to go back on the promise, having obtained the benefit? The main objection to changing the basic rule is that it would allow a party to a contract to put pressure on the other, for greater remuneration, having embarked upon performance. But this is a problem more suitably dealt with by the concept of economic duress rather than that of lack of consideration. Let us consider the case of *North Ocean Shipping Co Ltd* v *Hyundai Construction Co Ltd; (The Atlantic Baron)* [1979] QB 705. The facts were:

> Shipbuilders contracted to build a tanker for the owners for a fixed price of US$30,950,000. The contract price was to be paid in five instalments while the ship was being built. After payment of the first instalment, the dollar was devalued and the builders claimed an additional 10 per cent on the four remaining payments. The owners did not agree to this proposal, but they were given little choice. The builders threatened to terminate the agreement if they were not paid the extra 10 per cent. It was important to the owners to secure completion of the ship as they had agreed to a lucrative charter of the tanker to a major oil company. So, reluctantly, they agreed to pay for the ship at the increased rate "without prejudice to [their] rights". The tanker was eventually delivered to the owners who had paid the remaining instalments at the increased rate. After a period of eight months from delivery, the owners sought the return of the 10 per cent extra payment.

Mocatta J gave judgment for the shipbuilders. He thought that the facts of the case did establish that the "agreement" to increase the price of the tanker by 10 per cent was brought about by economic duress; it was clearly made under compulsion. But by making the final payment without protest, and then by waiting eight months before bringing an action to reclaim the additional payment, the owners affirmed the variation of the original contract contained in the agreement to pay an extra 10 per cent. It was far from clear in this case whether the shipbuilders provided any consideration for the owner's promise of extra payment, although (rather hesitantly) the judge thought that they had.

Although the action of the owners failed in this particular case, it does illustrate that the way of preventing extortion in this type of situation is better pursued through the idea of duress, rather than on the basis of lack of consideration. After all, the rule in *Stilk* v *Myrick* was more truly rooted in public policy than in technical questions about the presence or absence of consideration. If this is accepted, the way is now clear to reconsider the basic rule and to modify it. If X makes a promise to Y in exchange for Y performing (or promising to perform) some act which he is already obliged to do under an existing contract with X, the following questions must be considered: Was there any duress used by Y? Did X obtain a benefit in exchange for his new promise? In other words, the emphasis is on whether the amended agreement between the parties represents a reasonable commercial renegotiation.

For these reasons, the rule in *Stilk* v *Myrick* has been refined and limited by *Williams* v *Roffey & Nicholls (Contractors) Ltd* [1990] 1 All ER 512, where the facts were:

> The defendant building contractors were under contract to refurbish a block of twenty-seven flats. They sub-contracted the carpentry work to the plaintiff (P) for

£20,000. After completing some of the work, and receiving interim payments under the sub-contract, P found that he was in financial difficulties because the remuneration under his contract with the defendants was too low and he had failed to supervise his workmen properly. The defendants were liable under a penalty clause in the main contract if the work was not completed on time and they were aware that P was in difficulties because the carpentry work had been underpriced. They called a meeting with P at which they promised an extra £10,300 to ensure that P continued with the work and finished it on time. The extra payment thus agreed was to be at the rate of £575 per flat on completion. P continued working, but the defendants did not keep up the additional payments which they had agreed. P then stopped work on the remaining flats and sued the defendants for the additional sum promised. The defendants argued that no consideration had been provided by P for the promise of extra payment.

The Court of Appeal held that P was entitled to the additional payments for the flats completed under the agreement. There was no evidence of economic duress; the original contract underpriced the work and the defendants understood this and themselves commenced the process of renegotiation. The defendants also gained a benefit under this later agreement. It was important to them to be sure that the work was completed promptly; they were faced with a penalty clause under the main contract. Accordingly, P did provide consideration for the defendants' promise of additional payment. Without being under duress, the defendants asked for and received something of value from P. This constituted a binding agreement.

It might be objected that the plaintiff in *Williams* v *Roffey & Nicholls* agreed to do nothing more than he was already bound to do by the original sub-contract with the defendants. In finding in his favour, it appears that the court did (despite its protestations to the contrary) seek to depart from, rather than apply, the decision in *Stilk* v *Myrick*. Glidewell LJ rationalised the decision in the following way (at p 522):

> "If it be objected that the propositions above contravene the principle in *Stilk* v *Myrick*, I answer that in my view they do not: they refine and limit the application of that principle, but they leave the principle unscathed, eg where [the promisor] secures no benefit from his promise. It is not in my view surprising that a principle enunciated in relation to the rigours of seafaring life during the Napoleonic wars should be subjected during the succeeding 180 years to a process of refinement and limitation in its application in the present day".

The decision in *Williams* v *Roffey & Nicholls* provides a sensible solution to the conundrum posed at the start of this section. It comes close to acknowledging that the true reason for the decision in *Stilk* v *Myrick* was on the grounds of public policy rather than want of consideration. The important test to be applied to a promise of this type in the future will be whether it was obtained by some form of duress. If it was not, then it will be enforceable if the promisor received some benefit or obviated some disadvantage. Of course, this latter test will normally be satisfied; otherwise why would the promisor have made the promise in the first place?

One interesting consequence of the case is that it seems to permit commercially reasonable renegotiation under an existing contract. In *Williams* v *Roffey & Nicholls* the plaintiff undervalued his services in the original sub-contract and also failed to supervise his workmen adequately. Yet he was able to enforce a promise of further payment made during the course of the work contracted for. However, in *Davis Contractors Ltd* v *Fareham UDC* [1956] AC 696 (discussed in Chapter 20), the plaintiffs agreed to build seventy-eight houses for a local council in eight months at a price of £92,425. Due to shortages of labour and materials, the work took much longer than planned and it meant that the contractors had undervalued their services. The contractors tried to claim that the contract was frustrated so that they could claim greater remuneration for their work on a *quantum meruit* basis. The House of Lords held that their claim failed as mere hardship or inconvenience to one of the parties was not sufficient to frustrate a contract.

In other words, no reasonable renegotiation was possible where the contractors had fulfilled their obligations and then claimed additional payment for the benefit conferred by completing in adversity. It now seems that if, during the course of the building of the houses, the council had agreed (without duress) to pay more money to the contractors to ensure that the work was finished on time, the promise would have been enforceable. The benefits to the council would have been fairly obvious. No such promise was in fact made in *Davis* v *Fareham UDC*, but there now appears to be a curious difference in policy, in relation to renegotiated contractual obligations, between these two areas of contract law.

The decision in *Williams* v *Roffey & Nicholls* represents a change of emphasis by the courts, with a movement away from technical questions of consideration towards a growing interest in the *factual* benefit which the promisor obtained. The long-term implications of this development for the doctrine of considera-tion are still a matter for debate[5]. But if a promise to perform an existing obligation can be good consideration so long as there are practical benefits for the other party, why should this approach be restricted to one particular factual situation? (For an unsuccessful attempt to extend the *Williams* v *Roffey & Nicholls* approach to the issue of part payment of a debt, see *Re Selectmove Ltd* [1995] 2 All ER 531 — discussed below.)

(c) Performance of a duty owed to a third party

This type of problem can be summarised as follows: X makes a promise to Y in exchange for Y doing (or promising to do) something which Y is already obliged to do under an existing contract with Z. At first sight it seems, as a matter of logic, that Y provides no consideration for X's promise. He merely performs, or promises to perform, an act which he is already bound to do. However, it could be argued that performance of the existing duty owed to Z might be more onerous for Y than paying damages for breach of contract. He might also confer some benefit on X by performance of his contractual obligations to Z.

It might be thought that, traditionally, this situation would have been regarded in the same way as the performance of a duty owed to the promisor, considered above. If it was argued that there was no consideration given by the promisee in *Stilk* v *Myrick*, then how could there be any consideration provided by Y for X's promise here? But, as we have seen, the decision in *Stilk* v *Myrick* was more a reflection of public policy than legal doctrine. The policy reasons for refusing to uphold X's promise to Y, in consideration of Y performing his existing obligations to Z, were never so compelling. Once again, this illustrates that the legal rules relating to the doctrine of consideration have not always followed a consistent or coherent pattern. For example, in *Shadwell* v *Shadwell* (1860) 9 CB(NS) 159, the facts were:

> Lancey Shadwell (P), who was engaged to be married to Ellen, received a letter from his uncle, Charles Shadwell. The letter expressed Charles' pleasure at hearing of his nephew's engagement, and it continued: ". . . as I promised to assist you at starting, I am happy to tell you that I will pay to you £150 yearly during my life". It also stated that, if the nephew's annual income as a barrister reached 600 guineas, then the uncle's payments would cease. P married Ellen and his income as a barrister never amounted to 600 guineas a year. Charles Shadwell did not make all the payments that he promised, and after his death, P sued his uncle's personal representatives for the arrears. The defendants argued that P had provided no consideration for his uncle's promise, as he was already bound to marry Ellen before the promise was made.

It might be thought that the nephew's action was bound to fail. The promise contained in the letter appears to be gratuitous; nothing of value was given by Lancey in exchange for it. The only benefit to Charles, even assuming that the payment was being promised as a consequence of his nephew's intended marriage, was of a sentimental rather than an economic nature. It may also be doubted whether there was any contractual intent in the letter. But despite a persuasive dissenting judgment by Byles J, the majority found in favour of the plaintiff. It was held that Lancey had suffered a detriment because, in reliance upon the promise, he might have incurred financial liabilities. It was also held that a benefit was conferred on the uncle because his nephew's marriage was clearly a matter of some importance to him.

The decision in *Shadwell* v *Shadwell* is obviously open to criticism (see Salmon LJ's comments in *Jones* v *Padavatton* [1969] 1 WLR 328 at p 333). Nevertheless, it is supported by *Chichester* v *Cobb* (1866) 14 LT 433 and *Scotson* v *Pegg* (1861) 6 H & N 295, both decided shortly afterwards. Thus it appears that X's promise to Y, given in exchange for Y fulfilling his contractual obligations to Z, is enforceable. This is supported more recently by the case of *New Zealand Shipping Co Ltd* v *Satterthwaite (AM) & Co Ltd* (discussed below) where *Scotson* v *Pegg* was approved. It is further supported by the Privy Council decision in *Pao On* v *Lau Yiu Long* [1979] 3 All ER 65, where Lord Scarman stated (at p 76):

> "Their lordships do not doubt that a promise to perform, or the performance of, a pre-existing contractual obligation to a third party can be valid consideration".

In *New Zealand Shipping Co Ltd* v *Satterthwaite (AM) & Co Ltd; (The Eurymedon)* [1974] 1 All ER 1015, the plaintiff cargo owners promised the defendant stevedore company that they would not be liable for any damage to the goods arising out of their (D's) negligence. The cargo was damaged as a result of D's negligence during unloading. P's action raised issues of privity (see Chapter 18). But of relevance here, is the fact that D was already bound to unload the goods under an existing contract with a third party, the carrier. Could the unloading of the goods be regarded as consideration provided by D in exchange for P's promise not to sue in the event of damage to the goods? The Privy Council held (pp 1020–1021) that the work done in unloading the cargo was good consideration for P's promise, as the plaintiffs thereby obtained the benefit of a direct obligation which they could enforce.

9. Part payment of a debt

Under the rule in *Stilk* v *Myrick*, we saw that X's promise made to Y, in return for Y's performance (or promise to perform) some act which Y was already contractually bound to X to perform, was traditionally not regarded as good consideration. So it is not surprising that where Y owes a debt to X, and X promises to accept from Y payment of part of the debt in exchange for releasing Y from the rest of it, that this promise is unenforceable. It appears that nothing of value is given by Y in such circumstances. He is doing (or promising to do) nothing in addition to that which he is already obliged to do. It cannot be said that Y suffers any detriment by paying part of the debt in return for X's promise to forgo the balance. However, it could be argued that some benefit is, in fact, conferred on X by Y's part payment (or promise thereof). There is undoubtedly the peace of mind of collecting some of the debt and obviating a financial disadvantage. In practice, this is certainly the view taken by many creditors who will accept part payment of a debt in full settlement.

Once again, the justification for the rule may be found in the requirements of public policy. Without such a rule, a debtor might be encouraged to delay paying for an unreasonable amount of time, in the hope of securing the agreement of his creditor to accept part payment of the debt in full settlement. This could lead to a form of economic duress and unconscionable behaviour on the part of debtors. This might particularly affect small firms desperate to collect some part of a debt owed to them in order to survive (for example, see *D & C Builders* v *Rees* [1966] 2 QB 617). The main problem with the general rule about part payment (laid down in *Pinnel's Case*, and *Foakes* v *Beer*, which are discussed below), is that it fails to distinguish between genuine cases where the creditor is content to secure part payment of an existing debt and to forgo the balance, and those situations where he is given virtually no choice. It simply states that part payment cannot be regarded as consideration for the creditor's promise. In so stating, it is out of step with commercial practice. (In view of the decision in *Williams* v *Roffey & Nicholls* [1990] 1 All ER 512, it might be thought that the whole question of part payment also may need to be reconsidered[6]. But there is little in the judgment itself to suggest that this was intended, and the recent decisions in *Re Selectmove Ltd* [1995] 2 All ER 531 and *Re C (A Debtor)* [1994] *The Times* 11 May have treated the two situations as distinguishable.)

First we will consider the origins and development of the basic rule and then we will look at more recent developments in the law. The classic statement is to be found in *Pinnel's Case* (1602) 5 Co Rep 117a, where it was held that payment of part of an existing debt could not amount to consideration for the creditor's promise to accept this lesser sum as full settlement and to forgo the balance. But if, in addition or instead, something other than money was given by the debtor in exchange for the creditor's promise, this would provide good consideration. Similarly, payment of a lesser sum by the debtor at an earlier time than originally agreed, at the creditor's request, can also amount to consideration. In these situations, some benefit to the creditor can be discerned. But where there was simply part payment, and nothing more, there was no consideration given by the debtor.

This rule was approved by the House of Lords in *Foakes* v *Beer* (1884) 9 App Cas 605. The facts were as follows:

Julia Beer had obtained a judgment in the High Court against John Foakes for £2,090 19s. More than a year later, Dr Foakes requested time to pay. It was agreed by the parties, in writing, that if Dr Foakes paid £500 immediately and then paid biannual instalments of £150 until the debt was fully paid, Mrs Beer would "not take any proceedings whatever on the said judgment". Dr Foakes paid the debt, in the agreed way, and then Mrs Beer claimed interest. (Dr Foakes was liable to pay interest on a judgment debt, but their agreement had made no reference to this.) Dr Foakes argued that Mrs Beer had promised not to take any action on the debt if he paid in the prescribed manner. But even assuming that the agreement covered the question of interest, did Dr Foakes provide any consideration in return for Mrs Beer's promise?

The House of Lords found in favour of Mrs Beer and upheld her claim for the interest. Opinion was divided on whether the agreement was, in fact, intended to cover the question of interest. But, whatever the true construction of the agreement might have been, it was held that payment of part of the debt could not be good consideration for Mrs Beer's promise to forgo the balance (ie the interest). Although one of the judges (at p 622) acknowledged that the rule was not in accordance with business practice, the court held that the rule was too well established to be rejected.

Much has been said in criticism of the rule laid down in *Pinnel's Case* and in *Foakes* v *Beer*. For example, it is capable of producing an unjust result where a debtor has relied on the creditor's promise to accept part payment. It is artificial, in so far as the giving of something other than money in exchange for the promise is capable of amounting to consideration, regardless of the value of the thing so given. It is unrealistic in view of the standard business practice by which creditors are often pleased to accept the prompt payment of part of a debt, rather than relying on their strict rights to enforce the whole debt. But having briefly stated these objections to the rule, it must be conceded that it can also serve a useful function. For example, in *D & C Builders* v *Rees* [1966] 2 QB 617, the facts were as follows:

> The plaintiffs were a small firm of builders, who had done some work for the defendant, as a result of which the defendant still owed them £482. The plaintiffs were in financial difficulties and the defendant, having delayed payment of the debt, instructed his wife to offer the builders £300 and no more. The financial problems of the plaintiffs (which were allegedly known to the debtors) led them to accept the offer of £300 in full settlement. They later sued for the balance.

The Court of Appeal held that the builders were entitled to claim the rest of the debt from the defendant, who had given no consideration in exchange for the plaintiffs' promise to accept part payment of the debt. The rule in *Foakes* v *Beer* was thus used to defeat the unconscionable behaviour of the debtor in this case. But the important point about *D & C Builders* v *Rees* is the use of economic duress by the debtor; the plaintiffs had little choice but to accept, as they were desperate to get some money. The problem with the rule in *Foakes* v *Beer* is that it fails to distinguish between this type of situation and that where the creditor willingly accepts the payment of a lesser sum than he is due.

D & C Builders v *Rees* was applied recently in the case of *Ferguson* v *Davies* [1997] 1 All ER 315. In this case, P sold a number of specialist recordings (discs, tapes, etc) to D, a dealer in such items. The parties agreed that D would provide, in return, records worth £600 by a specified date. If D failed to do so, it was agreed that D would pay the cash value of the individual items to P, to a total of £1,700. In fact, D failed to meet the time limit, having provided P with records to the value of £143.50 only; P brought an action, limiting his claim to £468.50. Later, D sent a cheque to P for £150 as full payment, also admitting P's claim but only in respect of £150. P cashed the cheque but told D that he was proceeding with the action until he received full payment, which he now claimed was £1,745. At first instance, the judge found that P had compromised his claim by a binding accord with D. The Court of Appeal reversed this decision, allowing P's appeal. It was held (per Henry and Aldous LJJ) that P's acceptance of the lesser sum did not amount to an accord and satisfaction so as to compromise his claim against D. In order to have compromised such an action, P would need to have received some additional benefit amounting to consideration. As D paid only what, by his own admission, he owed already to P, he provided no consideration in law for the accord. By cashing the cheque, P was not agreeing to let D off with the balance.

In the recent case of *Re Selectmove Ltd* [1995] 2 All ER 531, the Court of Appeal was invited to consider whether the practical benefit to the creditor, derived from a debtor's part payment, could amount to good consideration. In other words, it was given the opportunity to reconsider *Foakes* v *Beer*. In *Re Selectmove Ltd* the Inland Revenue, having at first seemed to accept S's payment of its debts by instalments, subsequently demanded immediate payment in full. The Inland Revenue obtained a compulsory winding-up order against S in the Companies Court. In its appeal against this order, S claimed that a promise to perform an existing obligation could now amount to good consideration as long as practical benefits accrued to the other party (following *Williams* v *Roffey & Nicholls*). However, dismissing S's appeal, the court refused to accept this argument in relation to part payment of a debt (see Peter Gibson LJ at p 538). It was stated that the *Williams* v *Roffey & Nicholls* decision concerned an obligation to supply goods and services, and did not apply to an obligation to pay a debt[7]. The court considered that the law was clearly settled by *Foakes* v *Beer*, which is of course a House of Lords authority[8]. The best way forward perhaps is for the subject of consideration and the performance of existing obligations (including part payment of a debt) to be dealt with by Parliament.

(a) Limitations on the rule in Foakes v Beer

There are limitations on the general rule. We have seen, in *Pinnel's Case* (above), that whilst part payment of a debt is not good consideration, "the gift of a horse, a hawk, or a robe, etc, in satisfaction is good" (*per* Lord Coke). Furthermore, it was established in *Sibree* v *Tripp* (1846) 15 M & W 23 that if a debtor gives his creditor promissory notes for a lesser amount than the actual debt, this could be good consideration for the creditor's promise not to demand the balance. Thus if X owes Y £1,000, and Y promises to accept £900 in full settlement, he can go back on this and later claim the full amount. But if Y promises to accept from X promissory notes for £500 in full settlement, he is bound by his promise and cannot claim the residue.

The justification for this rather strange distinction is that something different is being given by the debtor (ie a negotiable security). However, in *D & C Builders* v *Rees* the court was not willing to allow this limitation on the rule in

Foakes v *Beer* to extend to the payment of a lesser sum by cheque. Mrs Rees paid the builders £300 (see above) by cheque, but the defendant was not able to claim that something different, amounting to consideration, had been given in exchange for the creditors' promise. The case of *Sibree* v *Tripp* was, in fact, distinguished in *D & C Builders* v *Rees* (see Denning LJ at p 623), but perhaps it should now be treated with circumspection.

A practical note should also be added. It is common practice for services to be rendered, by plumbers, builders etc, under a contract which fails to fix the price of the work to be done. The amount owed will not necessarily be the amount claimed by the workman. It may well be that the customer disputes the account when it is finally presented. If the workman agrees to accept in full settlement a lesser sum than he originally claimed, he is bound by such an agreement. It is only where the creditor's claim is "liquidated" (and undisputed) that his promise to accept part payment of the debt in full settlement will not be binding.

A further limitation on the rule in *Foakes* v *Beer* can be illustrated as follows: X owes Y £1,000. Y promises to accept £700 from Z in full settlement of X's debt. Y is not able to go back on his promise and sue X for the balance (see *Hirachand Punamchand* v *Temple* [1911] 2 KB 330). It might be argued that in such a situation X provides no consideration for Y's promise to forgo the remainder of the debt. However, it would be manifestly unjust, to Z in particular, if Y were able to go back on his promise. (It would be a breach of Y's contract with Z.) Another restriction on the rule is where X owes money to a number of creditors and is unable to meet the debts in full. He may come to a composition agreement with them, under which they all promise to accept a lesser amount than they are in fact owed. If the creditors accept such a payment by X, based on a division of his assets, in full satisfaction of their claims against him, they cannot go back on this and sue for the balance.

(b) The equitable approach

Despite these limitations, the general rule laid down by *Foakes* v *Beer* still represents the common law approach to part payment of a debt. However, the rule (as we have seen) is open to criticism, and a means of evading it has been developed under the equitable principle of promissory estoppel — see Chapter 5.

Footnotes

(1) For an interesting discussion, see P Atiyah, *The Rise and Fall of Freedom of Contract* (Oxford, 1979), pp 448–454.

(2) See his work on *Contract*, 13th ed, p 133.

(3) Of interest on this subject, see *Thoni GmbH & Co KG* v *RTP Equipment* [1979] 2 Lloyd's Rep 282.

(4) This topic is dealt with in more detail in Chapter 16.

(5) See R Halson, *Sailors, Sub-Contractors and Consideration* (1990) 106 LQR 183; and A Phang, *Consideration at the Crossroads* (1991) 107 LQR 21.

(6) See J Adams and R Brownsword, (1990) 53 MLR 536. Also N Hird and A Blair (1996) JBL 254; Carter, Phang and Poole (1995) 8 JCL 248; and J O'Sullivan (1996) 55 CLJ 219.

(7) See also *Re C (A Debtor)* [1994] *The Times* 11 May, and the comments of Bingham MR.

(8) For an interesting discussion of the possible solutions to this problem, see E Peel, *Part Payment of a Debt is No Consideration* (1994) 110 LQR 353.

Chapter 5

Promissory estoppel

1. Introduction

It is a firmly established principle of the common law, as stated in the House of Lords in *Foakes* v *Beer* (1884) 9 App Cas 605, that a debtor's payment of part of an existing debt (or promise to do so) cannot amount to consideration for a creditor's promise to accept a lesser sum in full settlement. This rule has been reiterated many times since then, for example in *Re Selectmove Ltd* [1995] 2 All ER 531, where it was held that a company's agreement to pay off its existing debts (to the Inland Revenue) by instalments was unenforceable as no consideration was thereby provided; the company promised nothing more than it was already legally bound to do. The Inland Revenue was allowed to go back on its apparent agreement with the company (although there was some dispute as to whether such an agreement had, in fact, been reached), and demand immediate payment in full from the company. This decision was reached despite the fact that there was no evidence of duress used by the company, and that the alleged agreement conferred some practical benefit on the creditor.

In the light of *Williams* v *Roffey & Nicholls* [1990] 1 All ER 512 (see Chapter 4), the whole question of consideration and the performance of existing obligations may need to be re-examined in the near future. There seems to be little justification for the law to hold that A's promise to perform a service already owed to B is capable of amounting to consideration if it confers some practical benefit on B, whilst simultaneously maintaining that a promise to pay part of an existing debt can never provide good consideration for a creditor's promise regardless of the practical advantages to the creditor. (The only possible justification might be if an obligation under a debt were thought to be fundamentally different from a contractual obligation under an agreement for the provision of services — but this does not seem a particularly convincing argument.) But despite the apparent inconsistency of the law relating to the performance of existing obligations, it is clear that the decision in *Foakes* v *Beer* is still binding[1]. Unless the rule is to be reconsidered by the House of Lords or abolished by legislation (neither of which seems immediately likely), then other means have to be used to evade its harsher consequences.

There can be little doubt that the decision in *Foakes* v *Beer* is capable of producing unfair results and of defeating reasonable commercial expectations.

In *Re Selectmove Ltd* it appears that the company did not, in fact, manage to comply with the terms of the alleged agreement with the Inland Revenue and therefore the actual outcome of the case was not unjust. But if the company had complied with the terms of this agreement, should the Inland Revenue have been allowed to go back on its promise (if one *had* been made by an authorised employee)? In *Foakes* v *Beer* itself, Lord Blackburn expressed some misgivings about the validity of the rule (see (1884) 9 App Cas at p 622). He observed that businessmen frequently accept part payment in full satisfaction of an outstanding debt and, as a matter of commercial reality, that they are content to do so. There was further criticism in the report of the Law Revision Committee (1937, Cmnd 5449) on the doctrine of consideration. A major objection to the rule is that where a creditor (Y) promises to accept a lesser sum in full settlement and the debtor (X) relies on this promise, altering his position in some detrimental way, it is unjust to permit Y to go back on his promise. X may, for instance, incur other financial liabilities (eg to Z) in the belief that the debt owed to Y has been fully settled.

Although the rule is capable of producing unfair results, its abolition might leave creditors exposed to unconscionable behaviour by debtors. So the rule remains and, for the present at least, it is the doctrine of promissory estoppel which is used to provide some relief against the potential harshness of the decision in *Foakes* v *Beer*.

2. Development of the doctrine

The opportunity to put forward a different solution to the problem of part payment of a debt arose in *Central London Property Trust Ltd* v *High Trees House Ltd* [1947] KB 130. In this famous case, widely referred to as *High Trees*, the facts were as follows:

> The plaintiffs let a block of flats to the defendants, in September 1937, for a term of 99 years at a rent of £2,500 per year. A few years later, due to wartime conditions and fear of bombing raids, many of the flats were not let. The plaintiffs agreed, in 1940, to reduce the defendants' rent to £1,250. When the war ended in 1945, the flats were no longer empty, and the plaintiffs wanted to claim the full rent (ie £2,500) from the defendants. In order to test whether they could claim the full rate, retrospectively, for the period when many of the flats were empty, the plaintiffs claimed the full rent for the last two quarters of 1945.

After less than a year as a High Court judge, Denning J delivered a famous judgment. He held in favour of the plaintiffs' claim because the agreement to accept the lower rent was intended only to cover the period when many of the flats were empty. As this was no longer the case by the second half of 1945, the plaintiffs were entitled to go back to charging the defendants the full rent that had been agreed originally between the parties in 1937. The innovative aspect of his judgment, however, was his opinion that any attempt by the plaintiffs to recover the full rent for the period 1940–1945 would not be successful. In other words, contrary to the established rule in *Foakes* v *Beer*, the plaintiffs would not be permitted to go back on the promise made to the defendants (in 1940) to accept a lesser rent. This agreement was to last whilst war conditions prevailed and many flats remained empty. Thereafter, the plaintiffs could charge the full rent.

On the basis of the principles discussed in Chapter 4, it seems that Denning J's opinion was without legal foundation. The defendants did not provide any consideration for the plaintiffs' promise in 1940. Thus the 1940 agreement did not satisfy all the requirements that we would normally look for in a legally binding contract. But Denning J was undeterred in his search for a means of preventing the promisor from going back on his promise and insisting on his full legal rights. He chose the idea of estoppel as the basis for his assault on the rule in *Foakes* v *Beer*. Put simply, this doctrine encapsulates the idea that if X makes an unequivocal statement of fact to Y which he intends Y to rely upon, and which Y does in fact rely upon to his detriment, X is prevented from later acting inconsistently with that representation (ie by denying the truth of his statement). The difficulty with estoppel, as a means of evading the common law rule, was that it was held in *Jordan* v *Money* (1845) 5 HL Cas 185 that the doctrine applied only to a representation of existing fact (also see *Argy Trading Development Co Ltd* v *Lapid Developments Ltd* [1977] 3 All ER 785); whereas in *High Trees* the representation made by the plaintiffs, in relation to reducing the rent, was one of intention, rather than of existing fact.

Denning J did not allow this established meaning of the doctrine of estoppel to present an insurmountable problem. He distinguished *Jordan* v *Money* on rather tenuous grounds and proceeded to promulgate an analogous doctrine of promissory estoppel, which was equitable in nature. He argued that the law had moved on since *Jordan* v *Money* to cover a broader principle than that traditionally represented by the doctrine of estoppel by representation. This principle extended to cases in which a promise was made by X to Y with the intention that it would be acted upon by Y and was in fact acted upon by Y. Denning J thought that it was now established that X's promise must be honoured in so far as he would be prevented from acting inconsistently with it, despite a lack of consideration by Y. (It should be noted that X could not be sued for breach of such a promise.) Of course, this wider principle of promissory estoppel covered the *High Trees* situation. But was there any authority for Denning J's view? He argued in *High Trees* (at p 134) that the principle that he was putting forward was the "natural result of a fusion of law and equity". He continued:

> "In my opinion, the time has now come for the validity of such a promise to be recognized. The logical consequence, no doubt, is that a promise to accept a smaller sum in discharge of a larger sum, if acted upon, is binding notwithstanding the absence of consideration: and if the fusion of law and equity leads to this result , so much the better."

It might be objected, with some force, that Denning J's interpretation of the law appeared to ignore the binding precedent of the House of Lords in *Foakes* v *Beer*. He argued that the equitable principle had not been considered in *Foakes* v *Beer*, and instead he chose to rely on another House of Lords decision: *Hughes* v *Metropolitan Railway Co* (1877) 2 App Cas 439. The facts were:

> A landlord gave his tenant six months' notice to repair the premises. The tenant faced forfeiture of the lease if he did not comply with the notice. The tenant agreed to do the repairs but also suggested that the landlord might wish to purchase the lease. The tenant indicated that he would not start the repairs whilst negotiations for the sale of the lease were in progress. One month after giving him the notice to repair, the landlord began negotiations with the tenant for the purchase of the lease, but these

proved fruitless and were discontinued the following month. The tenant had, meanwhile, failed to repair the premises. When six months had passed from the date of giving the tenant notice to repair, the landlord tried to treat the lease as forfeited.

The House of Lords rejected the landlord's claim. The tenant was entitled to relief in equity against forfeiture. By starting negotiations for the purchase of the lease the landlord had led the tenant to believe that he would not enforce his strict legal rights while the negotiations continued. It would have been unfair to allow the landlord to go back on this implied promise. Once the negotiations did break down, he should have given the tenant reasonable time to do the repairs. Accordingly, the six months' notice was to run from when the negotiations were broken off. It was stated by Lord Cairns (at p 448):

"It is the first principle upon which all courts of equity proceed, that if parties who have entered into definite and distinct terms involving certain legal results — certain penalties or legal forfeiture — afterwards by their own act or with their own consent enter upon a course of negotiation which has the effect of leading one of the parties to suppose that the strict rights arising under the contract will not be enforced, or will be kept in suspense, or held in abeyance, the person who otherwise might have enforced those rights will not be allowed to enforce them where it would be inequitable having regard to the dealings which have thus taken place between the parties".

This statement offered possibilities of a broader doctrine, which can be summarised in the following way. Where X, who has contractual rights against Y, by his conduct induces Y to believe that these rights will be suspended or will not be strictly enforced for a certain period, he will be prevented (by a court of equity) from enforcing those rights until that period has elapsed. (See *Birmingham and District Land Co* v *London and NW Railway Co* (1888) 40 Ch D 268.) This was Denning J's solution to the problem posed by *Foakes* v *Beer*. The ingenuity of his approach cannot be questioned, but there are a number of objections to it on other grounds.

In a system based on precedent, a judge has an obligation to follow previous decisions of the higher courts and not to depart from established legal rules[2]. This is not to deny the flexibility of the common law and the creative element in judicial decision-making, but this is not the same thing as judges (especially those of the High Court) making the law or ignoring established rules because they do not like them. The answer to this might well take the form that the "Denning" approach was concerned with justice rather than a slavish adherence to precedent. Such a defence is not without foundation, but it can be overstated. Many people want to know what their legal position is without resort to expensive litigation. They can receive reliable advice only if decisions of the courts can be relied upon as establishing rules. However, if these decisions reflect little more than the personal view of a particular judge (no matter how influential), there can be little confidence in their authoritative value.

There are more specific objections to Denning J's approach in *High Trees*. It should not be forgotten that *Foakes* v *Beer* was decided seven years *after Hughes* v *Metropolitan Railway Co* and it is significant that the *Hughes* case was not seen as relevant in *Foakes*. It could hardly have been forgotten! It is more plausible that the House of Lords did not think that the two situations were truly analogous. In this respect their lordships were possibly correct. In

Hughes, the landlord was claiming that the lease should be forfeited because of the tenant's breach of contract (ie his failure to comply with the notice to repair). It can be argued that the plaintiffs' claim in situations like those of *Foakes* v *Beer* and *High Trees* is of a different nature. In *High Trees*, for example, there was no argument to the effect that the defendants were in breach of contract. It was not an action seeking termination of the lease or damages, but an action claiming the full rent under the original agreement.

There was, however, a link between cases like *Hughes* and *Foakes* v *Beer* in so far as they both dealt with the question of whether a person should be allowed to go back on a promise (express or implied) and retrospectively claim his full legal rights under the original agreement. In *Hughes* it would have been unfair to allow the landlord to do this and it was not possible for the tenant to comply with the notice at this stage. In *Foakes* v *Beer* it was possibly (but not necessarily) unfair to allow the promisor to go back on her promise. However, it was not impossible for Dr Foakes to pay the interest on the debt. Similarly, it would have been harsh, but not impossible, for the defendants in *High Trees* to have had to pay the full rent for the period 1940–1945.

A further objection to Denning J's judgment in *High Trees* is that it extended the scope of estoppel in contravention of well established principles (see above). His suggested doctrine of equitable estoppel was not restricted to representations of fact, but also covered promises and representations of intention. The doctrine of estoppel by representation requires detrimental reliance. But, in *High Trees* it seems that there was no such requirement. In assessing Denning J's novel formulation of an equitable doctrine of promissory estoppel, it is fair to conclude that it was born with a far from unimpeachable pedigree. But if his proposal of such a doctrine, which was only *obiter* in *High Trees*, was totally without foundation, it would presumably have been authoritatively rejected by now. Although its scope and status are still far from clear (see Lord Hailsham's comments in *Woodhouse AC Israel Cocoa SA* v *Nigerian Produce Marketing Co Ltd* [1972] AC 741 at p 758), the fact that the doctrine has received such extensive discussion, both in later cases and in academic literature, tends to suggest that it is not devoid of merit.

3. Scope of the doctrine

In suggesting the doctrine of promissory estoppel, Denning J was concerned, primarily, with finding a solution to the problem of part payment of a debt. But there was clearly potential for such a doctrine to be developed further and its more general impact on the law of contract needs to be assessed. It is, therefore, necessary to examine the scope and limitations of the doctrine. This is no easy matter as, despite much discussion of the doctrine, there have been relatively few cases decided exclusively on this ground.

(a) The doctrine does not create a cause of action

Promissory estoppel, by itself, does not create a cause of action; if it did, it would be difficult to reconcile with the doctrine of consideration. In *Combe* v *Combe* [1951] 2 KB 215, a husband agreed to pay his wife £100 a year (free of tax) at the time of their divorce. He failed to make any payment and she sued him, after six years, for £600 arrears. She gave no consideration for her husband's promise. She chose not to apply to the Divorce Court for maintenance; she did not refrain from doing so at her husband's request. (In fact, she had a greater annual income than her husband.) However, the trial judge, by applying the doctrine of promissory estoppel, held that the husband's promise was enforceable. The husband had made a clear promise, which he intended to be binding and to be acted upon, and which was acted upon by his wife.

This proposed extension of the doctrine was potentially far-reaching. Promissory estoppel was not being relied upon here as a defence, it was being used to create a cause of action. Such a radical interpretation had not been intended by the *High Trees* case. If the trial judge (Byrne J) in *Combe* v *Combe* had been correct, this would have been a fundamental challenge to the traditional requirement of consideration in contracts. The Court of Appeal allowed the husband's appeal, and Denning LJ (as he had now become) was quick to dispel fears that promissory estoppel posed such a threat to the doctrine of consideration. He explained that the *High Trees* principle did not create new causes of action where none previously existed. It operated only to prevent a person from insisting on his strict legal rights, when it would be unjust for him to do so in view of the dealings which had taken place between the parties. So where a party, by his words or conduct, made a promise to the other which was intended to affect the legal relations between them, and to be acted upon, and the other party did act upon it, the promisor should not be allowed to go back on his promise and revert to their earlier legal position. To this extent only was promissory estoppel intended to modify the legal requirement of consideration. Denning LJ continued (at p 220):

> "Seeing that the principle never stands alone as giving a cause of action in itself, it can never do away with the necessity of consideration when that is an essential part of the cause of action. The doctrine is too firmly fixed to be overthrown by a side-wind... it still remains a cardinal necessity of the formation of a contract, though not of its modification or discharge."

This limitation on the principle of promissory estoppel is not accurately encapsulated by the phrase that it is "a shield and not a sword". For such a phrase tends to suggest, misleadingly, that the principle cannot be relied upon by a plaintiff to an action. In fact the limitation means only that promissory estoppel cannot stand alone as giving a cause of action. If there is an independent cause of action, there is no reason why a plaintiff could not rely upon the principle.

(b) Does it merely suspend rights?

It will be remembered that in *Hughes* v *Metropolitan Railway Co* the landlord's right to treat the lease as forfeited was not lost altogether. The case simply decided that due to his implied promise to the tenant that he would not insist on his strict legal rights while negotiations for the purchase of the lease were in progress, he could rely on those rights only after six months' notice from the breakdown of their negotiations. It would represent a considerable extension if such a principle were to be reinterpreted as totally extinguishing the rights of the promisor. Yet this appears to be what Denning J proposed in *High Trees*. In the passage from his judgment quoted on page 69, he stated that a promise to accept a smaller sum in discharge of a larger sum is binding, if it is acted upon, even though there is no consideration. In *D & C Builders* v *Rees* [1966] 2 QB 617, he was even more forthright in stating that the equitable principle was capable not simply of suspending the promisor's strict legal rights, but could operate "so as to preclude the enforcement of them". Such a view poses a direct challenge to the House of Lords decision in *Foakes* v *Beer*.

The effect of the principle on the promisor's rights was considered by the House of Lords in *Tool Metal Manufacturing Co Ltd* v *Tungsten Electric Co Ltd* [1955] 1 WLR 761. The facts were:

> Tool Metal ("TM") owned the patents of certain hard metal alloys and, under a contract in 1938, they granted Tungsten Electric ("TE") a licence to manufacture and sell these metals. The agreement provided that the standard royalty to be paid by TE was 10 per cent, but that a higher rate of 30 per cent (described as "compensation") was payable if TE used more than a specified amount of the alloys in any month. After the outbreak of war, TE stopped paying compensation to TM at the higher royalty rate, and TM agreed (in the national interest) not to enforce their right to 30 per cent, and to allow payment at the basic rate of 10 per cent. In 1944, TM proposed a new agreement which included compensation payments once again, but this was rejected by TE. In 1945, TM sought compensation (ie the waived 20 per cent) in respect of the material used by TE since June 1945. The Court of Appeal held that, under the principle of *Hughes* v *Metropolitan Railway Co*, TM's agreement to suspend compensation payments was binding in equity until proper notice was given of their intention to resume insistence upon their strict legal rights. (The draft agreement of 1944 did not amount to reasonable notice.) In 1950, TM claimed compensation from TE dating from January 1947. Had TM given reasonable notice to TE of their intention to insist once more on their strict legal rights?

The House of Lords held in favour of TM's claim to compensation. They had effectively revoked their promise, made during the war, to suspend their strict legal rights. The first action, brought in 1945, constituted reasonable notice of their intention. The case suggests, therefore, that the promisor's strict legal rights are merely suspended and can be resumed by giving adequate notice of his intention to the other party. Presumably, if they had wished, the plaintiffs in *High Trees* could have given reasonable notice during the war of their intention to resume insistence upon their strict legal rights and, having done so, claimed full rent thereafter.

So it seems that the effect of the principle of promissory estoppel is merely suspensory. This was certainly the view taken in the Privy Council case of *Ajayi* v *Briscoe (RT) (Nigeria) Ltd* [1964] 1 WLR 1326 at p 1330, where a number of limitations on the equitable principle were listed. Amongst these was the qualification that the promisor is able to go back on his promise, on giving reasonable notice (which need not be formal notice), giving the promisee a reasonable opportunity of resuming his position. If it is not possible for the promisee to resume his original position, it seems that only then would the promise be regarded as irrevocable. In other words, the promisor's "rights" might be extinguished where the promisee acts to his detriment, undertaking new and more onerous commitments, in reliance on the promise, and where the promisee cannot be restored to his earlier position. (See *Brikom Investments Ltd* v *Carr* [1979] QB 467.)

There is still some confusion, however, over the precise effect of the equitable principle on the "rights" of the promisor. The cases that we have considered (eg *High Trees* and *Tool Metal*) were concerned not with a single obligation, but with continuing payments of rent or royalties. Here it is possible to argue that promissory estoppel has the effect of extinguishing existing obligations, but merely suspending future obligations until reasonable notice is given by the promisor of his intention to resume his strict rights. This interpretation is not without its critics and must be put forward with some caution. It is possible to argue that where the promisor gives reasonable notice that suspension of his strict legal rights is at an end, the debtor must resume full payment (of rent, royalties, etc) in the future *and* make up the outstanding sums still owed to the promisor. This is rather a harsh view, however, and if accepted it would seriously limit the utility of promissory estoppel. Whether the doctrine merely suspends or can actually extinguish rights remains uncertain.

(c) Other limitations on the doctrine of promissory estoppel

For the principle to operate, there must be a promise (by words or conduct), and its effect must not be vague or equivocal (see *Woodhouse AC Israel Cocoa SA* v *Nigerian Produce Marketing Co Ltd* [1972] AC 741). In *Re Selectmove Ltd* [1995] 2 All ER 531 (discussed earlier), one of the reasons why the company could not rely on the doctrine was that the official of the Inland Revenue who made the alleged promise, to accept payment by instalments, had no authority to make such an agreement. Thus the promise on which the estoppel was said to be based was not clear and unequivocal.

The principle is equitable in nature and therefore it should not be used to help a promisee or debtor who has behaved in an unconscionable or inequitable way. In *D & C Builders* v *Rees* [1966] 2 QB 617, for example, the defendant took advantage of the financial hardship of his creditor, who had little choice but to accept the defendant's offer of a lesser sum in full settlement of the debt (see page 64). The decision of the Court of Appeal was consistent with the common law rule in *Foakes* v *Beer*; the creditor was entitled to go back on his promise and sue successfully for the balance of the debt. However, the case was decided after the principle of promissory estoppel had been established, and Lord Denning's reason for finding in favour of the creditor was that the defendant had behaved inequitably and, therefore, should not be allowed to rely on the equitable defence.

It makes good sense that a principle which was introduced to remedy a potentially unfair common law rule should not be used to protect the unconscionable behaviour of debtors where they have used some form of economic duress. But where is the line to be drawn? Where a lesser degree of pressure is used by a debtor, falling short of intimidation, is he to be denied the equitable defence of promissory estoppel? The matter has not been settled by the courts.

(d) Reliance

The equitable principle draws upon an analogy with the doctrine of estoppel. As we have seen, estoppel by representation requires, *inter alia*, reliance by the representee to his detriment. The equitable principle of promissory estoppel, on the other hand, requires reliance, but must it be detrimental reliance? In *High Trees* itself there appears to have been no detriment suffered by the defendants; they simply paid less rent than was agreed under the original lease. They relied on the plaintiffs' promise and it would have been unjust to allow the plaintiffs to go back on that promise. Thus the idea of estoppel is possibly broadened under the equitable principle of promissory estoppel. Lord Denning has argued that detriment is not required for the *High Trees* principle to operate (see *WJ Alan & Co* v *El Nasr Export & Import Co* [1972] 2 QB 189 at p 212). Moreover, in his book, *The Discipline of Law* (1979), Lord Denning plays down the importance of "estoppel" in describing the equitable principle. He states (at p 223) that although lawyers use this "archaic word", he prefers to explain it, as follows, in ordinary language:

"It is a principle of justice and of equity. It comes to this: When a man, by his words or conduct, has led another to believe that he may safely act on the faith of them — and the other does act on them — he will not be allowed to go back on what he has said or done when it would be unjust or inequitable for him to do so."

This aspect of the doctrine is, however, by no means settled. In *Ajayi* v *Briscoe (RT) (Nigeria)* [1964] 1 WLR 1326, for example, the facts were:

D hired lorries from P under certain hire-purchase agreements. Owing to difficulties with the servicing of the lorries, P agreed, by letter, that D could withhold instalments due on the lorries as long as they were withdrawn from active service. As a result of the letter, D removed the lorries from service. (In fact, most of them were laid up with P.) P later sued to recover the instalments due and then D raised the equitable defence of promissory estoppel.

It was held by the Privy Council that P was able to recover the instalments due and that D failed to establish the equitable defence. The court rejected D's claim that no notice had been given to him that the lorries were available for active service. But it may well be that the promise made by P to D was not clear and unequivocal. The letter which agreed to D "withholding instalments due on [the lorries]" probably meant only that D could defer the payment of some instalments. It was not a promise that he could refrain altogether from making those payments. So the decision in the case is consistent with the parties' intention at the time of the promise. But Lord Hodson (at p 1330) went on to consider the limitations on the principle of promissory estoppel. One of these is that the equitable defence will be available only if the promisee has altered his position. This can presumably be taken to mean that the promisee must have altered his position in some detrimental way.

Perhaps the debate over whether the equitable principle requires detrimental reliance is not particularly apposite. The following reconciliation of views can be put forward. It is unlikely that "detriment" is a strict requirement. Even in the absence of detrimental reliance it may still be inequitable to allow the promisor to go back on his promise and enforce his legal rights, at least without giving reasonable notice. As a matter of common sense, however, it is more likely to be inequitable to allow a promisor to resile from his promise where the other party has acted on the promise, not only in reliance, but also to his disadvantage or "detriment". (For a useful discussion, see *Société Italo-Belge Pour le Commerce et l'Industrie SA (Antwerp)* v *Palm and Vegetable Oils (Malaysia) Sdn Bhd* [1982] 1 All ER 19, *per* Robert Goff J at pp 26–27.)

It is also worth noting the Privy Council's decision in *Maharaj (Sheila)* v *Chand (Jai)* [1986] 3 All ER 107. The facts were that P promised D that he would provide a permanent home for both of them and their children. Although the parties were not married, D was P's *de facto* wife. In reliance upon P's promise, D gave up her own flat, moved into P's house and looked after P and their children. Although P had paid for the building of the house, D contributed to household expenses from her earnings. When the relationship broke up, P left the house and told D that she could remain there. But P later tried to evict her, seeking vacant possession of the property. The court held that it would be inequitable to allow P to evict her and it allowed D's appeal. P had represented to D that he was providing her with a permanent home. She had acted in reasonable reliance on that representation: she had given up her flat, she had contributed to household expenses, and had looked after P and the children. On the facts, D had clearly altered her position in some detrimental way and it was not possible to restore her to her former position. The case appears to show that the doctrine of promissory estoppel can extinguish the future rights of the promisor, even after he has given notice of his intention to insist on his strict legal rights.

4. Conclusion

Since the decision in *High Trees* in 1947, there have not been very many cases decided on the basis of promissory estoppel alone. The scope and merits of the doctrine have been much discussed in cases that were eventually decided on other (more certain) grounds. We have considered the decision and its implications for the doctrine of precedent. It can be concluded that the common law rule in *Foakes* v *Beer* still stands despite recent challenges discussed in Chapter 4; and that the *High Trees* principle is an equitable way of mitigating the potential harshness of the common law rule. Where the common law rule does not lead to injustice (as in *D & C Builders* v *Rees*), the equitable principle will not apply. Similarly, a person cannot rely on promissory estoppel as a defence where he has behaved inequitably or unconscionably. In view of the origins of the doctrine of promissory estoppel, and its potential challenge to the requirement of consideration in contracts, it is hardly surprising that the judiciary have treated the subject with some circumspection. Its existence is acknowledged by leading judges, but they often appear to be reluctant to commit themselves to any precise interpretation. For example, in *Woodhouse AC Israel Cocoa SA* v *Nigerian Produce Marketing Co Ltd* [1972] AC 741, Lord Hailsham stated (at p 758):

> "The time may soon come when the whole sequence of cases based on promissory estoppel since the war, beginning with [the *High Trees* case], may need to be reviewed and reduced to a coherent body of doctrine by the courts. I do not mean to say that any are to be regarded with suspicion. But as is common with an expanding doctrine, they do raise problems of coherent exposition which have never been systematically explored."

A further challenge for the courts in the future is to clarify the relationship between the equitable doctrines of promissory estoppel and proprietary estoppel. (Rather confusingly, there are a number of distinct doctrines of estoppel.) Proprietary estoppel may apply in cases where a person acts in reliance on the belief that he has been, or will be, granted an interest in or over another person's land[3]. There is also the task of deciding upon the scope of "unconscionability" as a ground for equitable intervention, and, for example, the extent to which unconscionability may be used as a basis for enforcing non-contractual promises[4].

The decision of the High Court of Australia in *Walton Stores (Interstate) Ltd* v *Maher* (1988) 62 ALJR 110 represents an interesting and potentially far-reaching challenge to the traditional view of the relationship between estoppel and consideration. It is generally thought that for promissory estoppel to be invoked there must be an existing legal relationship between the parties. But this restriction on the scope of equitable intervention has been questioned by the *Walton Stores* decision. In this case, M (a builder) negotiated with W (a large retail company) for a construction and lease contract under which M would demolish an existing building on his own land, and build a new one to W's specifications, which would then be leased by W. The parties were very close to concluding the deal, but as no formal exchange of contracts had taken place, there was no binding agreement. Believing that W's completion of the relevant documents was no more than a formality, M started work on the project so as to enable him to meet the deadline for completion. He demolished the old building and laid the foundations for the new one. W was, in fact, having second thoughts about the deal, but did not communicate these to M despite being aware that M had already started work on his land. W told him of its decision to pull out only after he had carried out a substantial amount of work. Although no formal contract had been completed between the parties, M brought an action claiming specific performance or, as an alternative, damages against W. M argued that W had made an implied promise that it would enter into a binding agreement with him and that W was now estopped from resiling from this. The problem with this contention was that, as there was no existing contract between the parties, M was seeking to use the idea of estoppel to establish a cause of action.

The High Court of Australia found in favour of M, holding that in certain cases the ambit of promissory estoppel could be extended so as to permit the creation of a cause of action. It was argued (by the majority of the court) that as the decision was based on an estoppel and not on a contract, the absence of consideration was not a problem. The court held that the purpose of the equitable doctrine was to avoid the detriment which M suffered as a result of W's unconscionable behaviour in going back on its promise. (In other words, the object was not to compensate M for expectation loss for a breach of contract by W.) By this reasoning, the court found that promissory estoppel was not limited to cases where there is an existing legal relationship between the parties. It was argued that the doctrine has a wider function of providing equitable relief against unconscionable conduct, even in the context of non-contractual promises.

Although the actual outcome of the *Walton Stores* case may be applauded, the court achieved this result at the expense of introducing the potential for a great deal of uncertainty. If the use of promissory estoppel is not dependent on an existing legal relationship between the parties, the law of contract and that of equity may well be very difficult to reconcile in the future, and the exact meaning of unconscionable behaviour may prove difficult to define with precision. Whether the English courts will be tempted to adopt the Australian approach remains a matter for doubt.

Footnotes

(1)   See the judgment of Peter Gibson LJ in *Re Selectmove* [1995] 2 All ER 531 at p 538.

(2) In *Re Selectmove*, ibid, Peter Gibson LJ hinted at his dissatisfaction with *Foakes* v *Beer* but went on to state that it was "impossible, consistently with the doctrine of precedent, for this court to extend the principle in [*Williams* v *Roffey & Nicholls*] to any circumstances governed by the principle of *Foakes* v *Beer*".

(3) For example, see *Crabb* v *Arun District Council* [1976] Ch 179. (But also see *Re Bosham* [1987] 1 WLR 1498.)

(4) See Duthie, *Equitable Estoppel, Unconscionability, and the Enforcement of Promises* (1988) 104 LQR 362.

Chapter 6

Intention to create legal relations

1. Introduction

Not all agreements are legally enforceable. We have seen that the main test of enforceability which is applied in our law of contract is the requirement of consideration. Even if the parties intend to enter into a contract, the law requires an element of exchange between the parties; this represents, in theory at least, the idea of reciprocal obligations. It might be thought that if this requirement is satisfied, and if the contract does not need to be expressed in a particular form, then an agreement will be enforceable. There is, however, a further requirement that certain types of agreement must satisfy if they are to be enforceable. It is usually stated that there must also be an intention to create legal relations.

In fact, this term can be misleading as the law is not primarily concerned with whether the parties actually intended to enter into a legally binding agreement. In commercial transactions it will be presumed (usually correctly) that they did intend to create legal relations, unless there is an express statement to the contrary. In the case of social and domestic agreements it will usually be presumed that the parties did not intend such consequences. In the vast majority of such agreements this will undoubtedly be a valid assumption. But although the word "intention" is used, the test is really one of judicial policy. It is a method of restricting the enforceability of social and domestic arrangements. It could be argued that if both parties to an agreement provide consideration, there should be no need for any further requirement of an intention to create legal relations. But our law has not followed this line of reasoning. It has attempted to limit the enforceability of certain types of agreement. This may be a sound policy for pragmatic reasons, but it is difficult to see why it should be described today in terms of contractual intention.

2. Social and domestic agreements

Every day, people make family, or social, agreements. For instance, two friends might agree to operate a rota for taking their young children to school, so that only one car is required for each journey. Agreement and reciprocal obligations are both present here, but it is unlikely that the two friends intend any legal consequences to arise from their agreement. (Of interest on a related issue, see

Buckpitt v *Oates* [1968] 1 All ER 1145; and *Coward* v *Motor Insurers' Bureau* [1963] 1 QB 259.)[1] A parent may agree to give "pocket" money to his or her child in return for the performance of simple household chores; a person may agree to make a meal for a friend, who in turn promises to bring a bottle of wine.

In all of the above examples of social and domestic agreements it is fair to say that the parties do not intend legal consequences to flow from their arrangements. If such agreements are broken, it is not an appropriate use of the legal process to allow one party to pursue another[2]. To prevent frivolous claims and a waste of court time, it is better that disputes over such arrangements are left to the parties to settle for themselves, informally. It is not inaccurate, in the examples given, to defend this policy by saying that the parties did not intend to create legal relations.

But in certain other instances of family and domestic agreements, the presumed lack of intention to contract is more questionable. In *Balfour* v *Balfour* [1919] 2 KB 571, for example, the facts were:

> D, who worked as a civil servant stationed abroad, left his wife (P) in England; P had been advised by her doctor that her health was not sufficiently good to accompany her husband. Before departing, D promised to pay P an allowance of £30 a month whilst they were apart. P sued D for breach of his promise. The trial judge found that there was consideration given for D's promise and he ruled in P's favour.

The Court of Appeal reversed the trial judge's decision and held that D's promise was not enforceable. Even if P had given consideration for the promise (which is arguable), there was no intention to create legal relations. It was seen as a purely domestic agreement. Lord Atkin stated (at p 578):

> "[T]here are agreements between parties which do not result in contracts within the meaning of that term in our law . . . and one of the most usual forms of agreement which does not constitute a contract appears to me to be the arrangements which are made between husband and wife . . . and they do not result in contracts even though there may be what as between other parties would constitute consideration for the agreement."

Although the justification for the decision in *Balfour* v *Balfour* was expressed in terms of the parties' lack of contractual intention, it is clear from other parts of Lord Atkin's judgment that he was concerned by the prospect of the "small courts of this country" being inundated with domestic disputes (over "housekeeping" arrangements and the like). Although he perhaps overstated the likelihood of such a flood of litigation — one cannot really imagine many people wishing to go to court over this type of dispute — there is a sound policy reason for encouraging trivial domestic disputes to be settled by the parties without recourse to law. But did the agreement in *Balfour* v *Balfour* fall into this category? It was clearly a borderline case, and the court's bald assertion that the parties lacked contractual intention is not particularly helpful.

It might be argued that a husband and wife (unless separated) are unlikely to intend legal consequences to flow from any domestic agreement. But there may also be many other non-domestic agreements where the parties do not address their minds to the question of creating legal relations. It should be pointed out that the law takes an objective approach: would a reasonable person assume that the parties intended to contract? In the case of domestic agreements, particularly those between husband and wife, a reasonable person would not assume that the parties intended to create legal relations. But there are also cases where the answer is not so clear. The law appears to have adopted a rule of expediency, probably correctly, but seeks to justify it in terms of a requirement of contractual intention.

It is likely that many agreements between members of a family are not enforceable for other reasons. It could be argued that in many instances there is no consideration. This solution avoids reference to a separate, and often fictitious, requirement of an intention to create legal relations. Another ground for refusing to enforce certain family agreements is that of lack of certainty or clarity. In *Gould* v *Gould* [1969] 3 WLR 490, for example, a husband promised his wife, when leaving her, £15 per week as long as his business was all right. (The actual words used were disputed.) The majority of the court thought that the vagueness of the arrangement showed a lack of contractual intention. Many domestic arrangements, about housekeeping, spending money, clothing allowance etc, are vague and imprecise and subject to constant alteration. This might be a better way of explaining their lack of legal consequences.

It should also be noted that in *Balfour* v *Balfour* it was important that the parties were not separated at the time of making their agreement as to maintenance. In *Merritt* v *Merritt* [1970] 1 WLR 1211:

> A husband (H) left his wife (W), moving out of the house that was in their joint names, and went to live with another woman. H and W later met to discuss their financial arrangements for the future. They agreed that H would pay £40 per month to W, and W was to make the outstanding mortgage payments on the house out of this sum. W insisted upon a written acknowledgment by H of their agreement; this stated: "In consideration of the fact that you will pay all charges in connection with the house . . . until such time as the mortgage repayment has been completed . . . I will agree to transfer the property into your sole ownership". W paid off the mortgage, but H refused to transfer the house to her.

The Court of Appeal held that W was now the sole owner of the matrimonial home based on the enforceable agreement made between H and W. The court stated that the *Balfour* principle does not apply in the case of couples who are not on friendly terms, but are about to separate or, indeed, have separated. In such circumstances, it is important to the parties to sort out their financial arrangements in more precise terms and, therefore, it is easier to ascribe to them an intention to create legal relations. (*Quaere:* Are the facts in *Balfour* so different? It was clearly important for the parties in that case to sort out their financial arrangements before H went abroad to resume his work. Again, it can be suggested that the main ground for the decision in *Balfour* is questionable.) A further limitation of the *Balfour* principle relates to the situation where parties carry out promises, under what would otherwise be an unenforceable domestic agreement, by making improvements or additions to the matrimonial home. (See *Pettitt* v *Pettitt* [1970] AC 777 and especially Lord Diplock's comments at p 822.)

Family agreements may be made by parties other than husband and wife, but they give rise to similar problems. Once again, it can be questioned whether such cases truly turn on the issue of contractual intention, even though such an intention is to be judged objectively. In *Jones* v *Padavatton* [1969] 1 WLR 328, the facts were:

A mother (M) promised her daughter (D) that she would give her an allowance of $200 a month if she gave up her job in Washington DC and went to England to study for the bar. (M lived in Trinidad, where she hoped D would practise when qualified.) Despite not wishing to leave Washington, D accepted M's proposal and went to England and commenced her studies to become a barrister. Two years later, M and D varied the agreement. M bought a house in London for D to live in, and by renting out some of the rooms, D was able to maintain herself instead of receiving the $200 a month. Three years later, M and D quarrelled, and M claimed possession of the house. D had not yet passed her bar exams.

The Court of Appeal found in M's favour. It was held (by the majority) that the arrangement between the parties was not intended to have legal consequences and therefore M was entitled to possession. This followed the reasoning in *Balfour*. The opening comments of Danckwerts LJ (at p 329) reveal the majority's concern that disagreements of this type should not be aired in a court of law. He stated:

"This action . . . is really deplorable. The points of difference between the two parties appear to be comparatively small, and it is distressing that they could not settle their differences amicably and avoid the bitterness and expense which is involved in this dispute carried as far as this court".

The case is instructive. It shows not only the general presumption that family agreements are not enforceable, but also it illustrates that this is more for policy reasons than for any lack of contractual intention. In fact, although Salmon LJ arrived at the same decision as the other two judges, he reached it by way of a different route. He thought that there was an intention to create legal relations at the time of the original agreement, but that this agreement was to last only for a reasonable time and it had therefore ended by the time that five years had elapsed. M could never have intended to pay indefinitely whilst her daughter made repeated and unsuccessful efforts to pass the exams.

It is submitted that Salmon LJ's judgment represented a much sounder basis for deciding the case than those of his two colleagues. If the test is really one of an intention to create legal relations, then surely the agreement (at least initially) satisfied this requirement. D reluctantly gave up a good job and commenced studies in England at M's request. If M had ceased to pay D her allowance within a few months of D arriving in England, it was surely not intended by the parties that D would have no legal redress? The second agreement, concerning occupation of the house and the use of funds derived from letting out rooms, might be regarded as unenforceable because of its evident vagueness. There were several details left unsettled and this was perhaps a better basis for allowing M's claim for possession[3].

Household or domestic agreements can be made by people other than husband and wife or parent and child. A group of single people may share a house, for instance, and make housekeeping arrangements. It is unlikely that such agreements would be regarded as giving rise to legally enforceable obligations. But there may be agreements between people which precede the setting up of a household or joint habitation, whereby one party induces the other to come and live with him or her and perhaps to give up secure accommodation. In *Tanner* v *Tanner* [1975] 1 WLR 1346, D gave birth to twins of which P was the father. They were unmarried, but D took P's name. P bought a house for them both to live in with the children and D gave up her rent-controlled flat.

Later, P moved out and wanted to evict D (and he succeeded at first instance). On appeal, the court held that P was contractually bound by his promise to D, who was awarded compensation (having already been evicted).

The important fact about cases of this type is that one of the parties to the agreement has acted in reliance upon the other's promise and, in doing so, has given up something of value. It can be argued with some force that this evinces an intention to create legal relations, but such reasoning does not appear to have been accepted by the majority in *Jones v Padavatton*. It seems that in cases of this type (such as *Tanner v Tanner*, or *Parker v Clark*, below) the general policy of denying legal consequences to domestic agreements would produce such an unjust result that the courts depart from that policy. In *Parker v Clark* [1960] 1 WLR 286, the Clarks invited a younger couple, the Parkers, to share their house. (Mrs C was the aunt of Mrs P.) In order to go ahead with the arrangement the Parkers sold their own house. It was held that the agreement was legally binding.

The fact that people who are not related share accommodation does not automatically mean that any agreements they make are not enforceable. If they are of a commercial nature, or relate to matters other than the running of the household (and are not simply "social" agreements), there is no reason why they should not be regarded as legally binding. In *Simpkins v Pays* [1955] 1 WLR 975, a lodger (P), her landlady, and her landlady's grand-daughter entered a competition ran by a newspaper. Their weekly entries were a joint effort with an agreement that, if successful, the prize would be shared. The entries were sent in the landlady's name and she refused to share the prize which they won. It was held that there was a binding agreement, and that P was entitled to claim one-third of the prize.

3. Commercial agreements

In commercial transactions, it is generally presumed that there is an intention to create legal relations. The courts are anxious to uphold the validity of commercial dealings. But in certain situations, the general presumption may be rebutted. For example, manufacturers of products may make boastful, but vague claims about the effectiveness of their products. These statements (known as "mere puffs"), contained in advertisements and other promotional literature, will not generally be regarded as having any legal effect[4].

However, in exceptional cases, advertisements may be expressed in such a way that the courts will infer a definite intention to create legal relations. In *Carlill v Carbolic Smoke Ball Co* [1893] 1 QB 256, the company's advertisement of a reward was held to be an offer to members of the public who bought the smoke ball and used it in the prescribed manner, and still caught influenza. The company's attempt to argue that there was no contractual intention was rejected; the plaintiff was entitled to claim the reward. The fact that the company had deposited £1,000 with its bank as evidence of its "sincerity in the matter", indicated that the advertisement was more than just a mere puff.

In other commercial situations the parties might, as part of their agreement, expressly deny that they intend to create legal relations[5]. For example, in *Jones v Vernons Pools* [1938] 2 All ER 626, P claimed to have filled in his pools coupon and to have sent it off, but the Vernon Pools company alleged that they had not received it. (P's entry, if received, would have been successful.) It was a condition of entry, known to P, that the sending in of the coupon should not be attended by or give rise to any legal relationship, or be legally enforceable, or the subject of litigation. It was stated in the conditions of entry, therefore, that the arrangements of the pools were binding in honour only. Atkinson J held that the agreed conditions prevented P from succeeding against the defendants in any action to enforce payment of prize money. As there was no intention to create legal relations, there was no need for the court to decide whether P did, in fact, post the coupon. Atkinson J stated (at p 629):

> "It seems to me that the purpose of these rules [for entry] is this. The defendants wish it to be made quite clear that they are conducting these pools on certain clear lines, and they intend to say by these conditions: 'Everybody who comes into these pools must understand that there are no legal obligations either way in connection with these pools ... money must be sent in [with entries] on the clearest understanding that this is a gentlemen's agreement, an agreement which carries with it no legal obligations on either side, and confers no legal rights'".

Similarly, in *Rose and Frank Co* v *Crompton (JR) & Bros Ltd* [1925] AC 445, an arrangement was made between an American company and an English company whereby the American company was established as sole agents for the sale, in the United States, of tissues (for carbonising paper) supplied by the English company. Their original agreement was extended and a document was drawn up to regulate their dealings. This stated:

> "This arrangement is not entered into, nor is the memorandum written, as a formal or legal agreement, and shall not be subject to legal jurisdiction in the Law Courts either of the U.S. or England, but it is only a definite expression and record of the purpose and intention of the ... parties concerned, to which each honourably pledge themselves ...".

A dispute eventually arose between the parties and the English company determined the agreement without notice. Before this, the American firm had placed an order, which had been accepted by the English firm. The American company brought an action for breach of contract. The House of Lords held that the agreement did not constitute a legally binding contract[6]. Accordingly, there was no obligation on the American company to order goods or upon the English firm to accept an order. But any actual transaction between the parties gave rise to the usual legal rights, "for the fact that it was not of obligation to do the transaction did not divest the transaction when done of its ordinary legal significance" (*per* Lord Phillimore at p 455).

If a commercial transaction is not intended by the parties to give rise to legal relations, the courts will require clear evidence to that effect. It should be remembered that the presumption will be that the parties did intend to be legally bound. This is illustrated by *Edwards* v *Skyways Ltd* [1964] 1 All ER 494, where the facts were:

> P was employed as a pilot by the defendant company ("the company"), and he was a member of the company's contributory pension fund. The company informed P that he was to be made redundant. It also promised P an *ex gratia* payment "equivalent to" (the actual words were disputed) the defendants' contribution to the pension fund. Later, the defendant company failed to make the *ex gratia* payment

to P. The company defended P's action for breach of contract by arguing that the agreement, about the *ex gratia* payment, was not intended to create legal relations and that it was too vague to be enforceable.

It was held that where, (as in this case), the subject of the agreement between the parties related to business matters, the onus of negativing contractual intention was on the defendant company. It was a heavy onus and one which the company had failed to discharge. The court found in favour of P. The fact that the payment was described as *ex gratia* did not show that the company's promise lacked contractual intention. Accordingly, the company's promise to make this payment was duly accepted by P, who provided consideration for it.

There may be commercial transactions where the value of the goods involved is so small that the parties are most unlikely, in practice, to take the matter to court in the event of any breach of the agreement. For example, a "free gift" may be offered, as part of a sales promotion, to purchasers of certain goods. If the gift is of little intrinsic value, can it be said that there is any intention to create legal relations? This issue arose in *Esso Petroleum Co Ltd* v *Commissioners of Customs and Excise* [1976] 1 All ER 117, where the facts were:

> Esso distributed millions of "World Cup" coins to petrol stations which supplied their (Esso's) petrol, as part of a sales promotion scheme. One coin (depicting a member of the English soccer team) was to be given away with every four gallons of petrol bought by motorists. The coins were of little value, but the scheme was potentially lucrative because motorists were encouraged to buy Esso petrol in order to collect the set of thirty coins. Large posters and extensive advertisements were used to publicise the scheme. The Customs and Excise Commissioners claimed that the coins were chargeable to purchase tax (under the relevant legislation) on the basis that they had been "produced in quantity for general sale".

On the point of tax law in question the House of Lords held that the coins had not been "produced ... for ... sale" (within the relevant legislation) and were not therefore chargeable to purchase tax. The majority held (with Lord Fraser dissenting) that this was because the coins were not supplied under a contract of "sale". The consideration for the transfer of the coins was not a money payment, but the undertaking by the customer to enter into a collateral contract to buy the requisite amount of petrol. However, the majority were then divided on whether there was any intention to create a legally binding contract (of any sort) to supply the coins to customers who bought the petrol. The majority, including Lord Fraser, appear to have favoured the view that there was contractual intention. But it is possible that the dissenting judges (Lords Dilhorne and Russell) were correct in their interpretation of the transaction between the contracting parties; they doubted whether there was any intention to create legal relations because of the way in which the advertisements referred to "free gifts", and also because of the lack of intrinsic value of the coins.

4. "Letters of comfort"

The issue of contractual intention has recently been considered by the courts in relation to the use, in business practice, of "letters of comfort"[7]. This is a practice which occurs where a party is considering lending money to X, and receives some encouragement or "comfort" from Y (not amounting to a guarantee) to go ahead and do so. This can be illustrated by the facts of *Kleinwort Benson Ltd* v *Malaysia Mining Corp Sdn Bhd* [1989] 1 All ER 785, which were as follows:

> The plaintiff merchant bank (KB) agreed with the defendants (D) to make a loan of up to £10m available to D's wholly-owned subsidiary (M) which traded in tin on the London Metal Exchange. As part of this credit arrangement, D provided KB with two "letters of comfort" which both stated, in para 3, that "it is our policy to ensure that the business of [M] is at all times in a position to meet its liabilities to you under the [loan facility] arrangements". A year later, the tin market collapsed when the International Tin Council announced that it was unable to meet its liabilities, at a time when M owed KB the whole amount of the facility. M went into liquidation and KB sought from D payment of the amount owing. At first instance, the court held that KB could recover the money from D, who appealed on the ground that the letters of comfort did not have contractual effect.

It was held, allowing D's appeal, that the letters of comfort in question did not constitute a contractual promise. Ralph Gibson LJ stated (at p 792):

> "In my judgement the defendants made a statement as to what their policy was, and did not in para 3 of the comfort letter expressly promise that such policy would be continued in future. It is impossible to make up for the lack of express promise by implying such a promise, and indeed, no such promise was pleaded. My conclusion rests on what is the proper effect and meaning which . . . is to be given to para 3 of the comfort letters."

It might be argued that as the letters occurred in a commercial context, the usual presumption of contractual intention should have applied and that there should have been more than just a moral responsibility on D's part to meet M's debt. Of course the parties can, if they wish, expressly disclaim any contractual intention, but is it clear that this was done in the *Kleinwort Benson* case? It is possibly a borderline decision, and it is evident that the courts may experience difficulty in deciding what the wording of such letters actually means. In support of the Court of Appeal's decision it might be pointed out that the bank was happy to accept a letter of comfort rather than a guarantee, but on the basis that it "would probably have to charge a higher rate [of interest]". See *Kleinwort Benson* v *Malaysia Mining Corp Sdn Bhd* [1989] 1 All ER 785 at p 795.

5.   Collective agreements

Agreements relating to working conditions and pay may be made in industry between employers and trade unions. These are known as collective bargaining agreements and they are of a commercial nature. Where the terms of this type of agreement are incorporated into individual contracts of employment they are legally enforceable as between employer and employee. But what is the legal position in relation to the collective agreement as betweeen trade unions and employers? Such agreements might expressly state that they are not intended to be legally binding, but in the absence of such a declaration will it be presumed that there is an intention to be legally bound? A particular difficulty is that, although of a commercial nature, such agreements are often expressed in a rather general or vague manner. The matter was considered in *Ford Motor Co*

Ltd v *Amalgamated Union of Engineering and Foundry Workers* [1969] 1 WLR 339. The facts were:

> Ford Motors made an agreement with a number of trade unions which dealt, *inter alia*, with the procedure to be followed in the event of disputes arising. Some years later, certain unions declared a strike in contravention of the collective agreement. Ford sought an injunction against these unions on the basis that the agreement was legally enforceable. Was there a legally binding contract between the company and the trade unions arising out of the agreement?

It was held that the agreement was not legally enforceable. In this type of case the usual presumption relating to commercial dealings was apparently reversed. In the absence of a clear statement that the parties intended it to be legally binding, the courts will not enforce such an agreement; it will be binding in honour only (see Lane J at p 356). The decision in this case was probably correct, but it is far from clear that it was decided solely on the basis of lack of contractual intention.

The first problem in relation to such collective agreements is that they attempt to lay down a code of relations between employer and trade unions and they operate at a rather generalised level that makes legal enforceability difficult. Furthermore, there is the policy question of whether such disputes should be dealt with by the courts. The court process may be inimical to good industrial relations, and it is perhaps preferable that collective agreements are presumed to be unenforceable in law. This is now recognized by statute, under s 179 Trade Union and Labour Relations (Consolidation) Act 1992, which states that a collective agreement is "conclusively presumed" not to have been intended to be legally binding by the parties, unless it is in writing and expressly states otherwise.

6.   Other instances where contractual intention is relevant

There are other cases which are relevant to a discussion of contractual intent but which do not fall within any definite category. The case of *Upton-on-Severn RDC* v *Powell* [1942] 1 All ER 220, for example, suggests that the courts will not always regard an intention to create legal relations as an indispensable prerequisite of a contract. In that case, Powell rang the local police, on discovering that his farm was on fire, and asked them to call the fire brigade. The police rang the local (Upton) fire brigade which extinguished the fire. It turned out that Powell's farm was not in the Upton fire district, a fact which was not known to any of the parties at the time of the fire. Upton RDC's policy was to charge for its fire brigade's services if they were given outside its own district. The council claimed that Powell was liable under a contract to pay for the fire brigade's services and the court, upholding the council's claim, held that there was such a contract.

It has already been argued that there was no agreement between the parties in this case, but it can also be questioned whether the parties can be said to have intended to create legal relations. It is evident from the facts that such a thought did not enter the minds of the parties and it is unlikely that it would have entered the mind of any reasonable person in such circumstances. Perhaps it was thought that the transaction was of an essentially commercial nature and therefore contractual intention should be presumed in the absence of any express statement to the contrary. But such a rationalisation of the decision is far from convincing.

In some circumstances it is difficult to know whether an agreement is to be regarded as commercial or not. An interesting illustration is provided by *Methodist Conference (President of the)* v *Parfitt* [1983] 3 All ER 747, where the facts were:

> Parfitt (P), who had been a Methodist minister, was dismissed by the Church's governing body as a result of a disciplinary hearing. P claimed to have been unfairly dismissed and sought relief from an industrial tribunal under the Employment Protection (Consolidation) Act 1978. The Church argued that he was not entitled to such protection as he was not employed under a contract, and especially not a contract of service. P claimed that a contract of service had been created, either when he had been received into the Church as a minister, or when he accepted the invitation to become a minister of a circuit. P succeeded with his claim at the industrial tribunal and the Employment Appeal Tribunal dismissed the Church's appeal.

The Court of Appeal allowed the Church's appeal. It decided that the parties had not intended to create legal relations either at the time that P was ordained, or when he accepted the invitation to join the circuit of the Methodist Church. P did not have a contract of service with the Church and, therefore, he was not entitled to bring a complaint of unfair dismissal before an industrial tribunal. Dillon LJ stated (at p 752):

> "In the spiritual sense, the minister sets out to serve God as his master; I do not think it right to say that in a legal sense [P] is at the point of ordination undertaking by contract to serve the Church ... as his master throughout the years of his ministry ... Equally I do not think it is right to say that any contract, let alone a contract of service, comes into being between the Church and the minister when the minister accepts an invitation from a circuit steward to become a minister on a particular circuit."[8].

7. Conclusion

It might be argued that with the doctrine of consideration acting as a test of enforceability for agreements, there is no need for an additional requirement of an intention to create legal relations. However, this does not appear to be the position in our law. For there to be a valid contract, it is stated that the parties must have intended to create legal relations. In fact, such an intention is usually presumed in the context of commercial transactions, and it is for the parties expressly to negative such an intention if they wish to rebut the presumption. On the other hand, it is presumed that parties to agreements of a social or domestic nature do not intend to create legal relations unless they indicate very clearly to the contrary.

The requirement of an intention to create legal relations operates, to some extent, as an instrument of judicial policy for declining to enforce certain types of agreement. Most notably, it is clear that the courts do not wish to hear disputes between friends or family members over domestic and social agreements. We have seen other examples of agreements, such as collective bargaining agreements, which for policy reasons, the courts do not wish to enforce. The judicial policy behind the various decisions limiting the enforceability of such agreements is basically sound, but it is a little misleading to claim that there is a general requirement in the law of contract that the parties must intend to create legal relations. It is possible that many agreements that are not enforceable due to a presumed lack of contractual intent could also be regarded as invalid for other, more defensible reasons, such as lack of certainty.

Footnotes

(1) Cases on this issue have tended to arise as a result of accidents caused by the driver's negligence. But now see s 149 Road Traffic Act 1988.

(2) But, surprisingly, a prosecution for theft may succeed in the circumstances where a man gives his *de facto* wife a sum of money for her to pay certain debts and to meet household expenses and, instead of doing so, she spends the money on herself. In *Cullen* (1972) (unreported), the Court of Appeal seems to have assumed that the defendant was under an obligation to deal with the money in the manner prescribed and in no other way. Her conviction for theft overlooked the fact that it arose out of a domestic arrangement which was not intended to create legal relations. Her behaviour could not have amounted to a breach of contract — so why should it have been regarded as theft?

(3) *Quaere:* Why did the court in *Shadwell* v *Shadwell* (1860) 9 CB (NS) 159 not decide that the uncle's promise to his nephew was merely a family agreement and therefore unenforceable?

(4) See *Lambert* v *Lewis* [1982] AC 225.

(5) In agreements for the sale of houses, for instance, it is a common practice to state that they are "subject to contract". The agreement will not have legal force until a formal contract has been entered into. Also, in *Regalian Properties plc* v *London Dockland Corporation* [1995] 1 All ER 1005, an agreement for a building development was "subject to contract". The project was later abandoned and P's claim for wasted expenditure was unsuccessful as such costs were incurred at their own risk (see Chapter 3).

(6) Contrast *Home Insurance Co* v *Administration Asiguraliror* [1983] 2 Lloyd's Rep 674.

(7) Also see I Brown, *The Letter of Comfort: Placebo or Promise?* [1990] JBL, 281.

(8) It was also stated, at p 752, that secretaries and caretakers are employed by the Church on contracts of service, but that ministers are not. *Quaere:* Why should ministers' employment be regarded in a different light simply because of their spiritual position? More recently, an Anglican curate lost his appeal against an Employment Appeal Tribunal ruling; he was thus prevented from pursuing his case on the grounds of unfair dismissal. Staughton LJ stated: "A minister of religion serves God and his congregation but does not serve an employer. There is not a contract that he will serve a terrestrial employer in the performance of his duties" (as reported in *The Guardian*, 12 July 1997). Similar issues were also raised in *Mr A Kahn* v *Oxford City Mosque Society*, LTL, 13 October 1998, (unreported elsewhere).

Chapter 7

Express and implied terms

1. Introduction

Here we are concerned with the contents of the contract, its terms and the obligations undertaken by the parties. They may be either express or implied, and both possibilities are considered below. First we should consider the question of formalities, ie whether a contract must take any particular form to be effective, for example whether it has to be in writing.

2. Formalities

It is commonly assumed that a contract is something which is in writing and signed. Usually, however, contracts require no formalities — most can be made orally — although a deed may substitute for consideration. Formality requirements are restricted to a few specific types of contract and the requirements vary. Some examples will illustrate this. The Consumer Credit Act 1974 requires regulated consumer credit agreements to be in writing and in a specific form. For example, where the agreement is cancellable, it must contain a statement of the debtor's right to cancel. A contract for the sale or other disposition of an interest in land is unenforceable unless in writing (s 2 Law of Property (Miscellaneous Provisions) Act 1989). Certain contracts of guarantee are unenforceable unless evidenced in writing (Statute of Frauds 1677).

Formalities may be required for a number of reasons (Fuller (1941) 41 Col LR 799, Law Com Rep No 164 (1987)). They may be there to promote certainty by requiring clear evidence of the terms. They may be used to encourage the parties to give full consideration to the legal obligations being undertaken. They may even be required to provide protection to the person in the weaker bargaining position (eg the requirements of the Consumer Credit Act 1974).

Requirements of "writing" or "signature" may cause difficulties in the e-commerce context. It may be argued that they can be fulfilled by communications by e-mail or over the web, but mere uncertainty as to the position can be detrimental to the efficient growth of e-commerce and action has been taken at both the EC and UK levels. Article 9 of the EC Directive (2000/31/EC) on Electronic Commerce requires Member States to "ensure that their legal system allows contracts to be concluded by electronic means" and, in particular, to "ensure that the legal requirements applicable to the contractual process do not create obstacles for the use of electronic contracts or result in such contracts being deprived of legal effectiveness and validity on account of their having been made by electronic means". Member states are allowed to exempt from this:

> "(a) contracts that create or transfer rights in real estate, except for rental rights;
> (b) contracts requiring by law the involvement of the courts, public authorities or professions exercising public authority;
> (c) contracts of suretyship granted and collateral securities furnished by persons acting for purposes outside their trade, business, or profession;
> (d) contracts governed by family law or the law of succession."

This takes the approach of requiring the removal of any formality barriers to electronic contracting in all but a small number of exceptional cases. As has been indicated, the number of occasions in which formalities are required in contract formation is small in English law, but this may, for example, require changes to be made in relation to the current formality requirements applying to leases and sureties. Contracts creating or transferring rights in real estate are exempted under Article 9(2)(a) above, but "rental rights" are specifically taken outside that exemption. In addition, the exemption in relation to sureties, only extends to those "furnished by persons acting outside their trade, business or profession". The current formality requirements in that area, under s 4 of the Statute of Frauds, apply irrespective of whether the surety is acting for business or other purposes. There has been legislation in the UK in the form of the Electronic Communications Act 2000. The Act is more wide ranging than the EC Directive as its coverage goes beyond the contracting process to requirements for "signature", "writing", "documents", or "notices", for example, which are legally significant in other ways. However, it does not in itself make any changes to the legislation under which such requirements are set out but s 8 allows the "appropriate minister" to amend any such legislation by statutory instrument, "for the purpose of authorising or facilitating the use of electronic communications or electronic storage ... for any purpose mentioned in subsection (2)". The purposes mentioned in subsection (2) are wide ranging, but here it is relevant to note that they include:

> "(a) the doing of anything which under any such provision is required to be or may be done or evidenced in writing, or otherwise using a document notice or instrument;
>
> . . .
>
> (c) the doing of anything which under any such provision is required to be or may be authorised by a person's signature or seal, or is required to be delivered as a deed or witnessed;"

This legislation is more wide-ranging than the Directive — it is not confined to the contracting process. It may allow law in the UK to be brought into line with the requirements of the EC Directive, by appropriate ministerial decisions in relation to the amendment of legislation dealing with formality requirements relating to the "contracting process". (On "electronic signatures" see below p 142. Generally, see further Rowland & Macdonald *Information Technology Law* (2nd ed) Cavendish (2000) pp 308–327).

A. Express terms

1. Introduction

As we have seen, most contracts can be made orally or in writing, or there may be a combination of oral and written terms. The question of whether a written clause is a contract term is dealt with in relation to exemption clauses, a context in which that question often arises (see Chapter 9). Here we are concerned with the spoken word and the problem of determining whether what was said was part of the contract or was a mere representation.

It is possible that a statement may be found to be a term not of the main contract, but of a collateral contract. Collateral contracts often serve to avoid some difficulty involved in finding that the statement is a term of the main contract (for example the statement may be found to be a term of a collateral contract where the person injured is not a party to the main contract, thus evading the rule relating to privity of contract (see Chapter 18)). Collateral contracts are considered below.

2. Representations and terms

A statement made before the contract may become a term of the contract or it may be a mere representation. It may relate to some present fact or to some future act, event or circumstance. If the statement is a term, a remedy will lie for breach of contract if it is untrue or does not occur. If it is a mere representation, and it is untrue or does not occur, there will be no remedy for breach, although a remedy may be available for misrepresentation (see Chapter 13). The basic test for distinguishing terms and representations is that of the parties' intention. It is the type of test which leaves considerable scope for the court to be influenced by the result which will ensue from a decision. Such influence particularly needs to be borne in mind when considering some of the older decisions where terms were found. Before the mid-1960s, damages for misrepresentation were much more limited in their availability than they are now, with the result that the courts had a greater impetus to find that the statement in question was a term and not merely a representation.

A preliminary point should be made on the terminology adopted by the courts. The question whether or not X's statement was a term of his contract with Y may be put in terms of whether he warranted what he was saying. "Warrant" is being used simply to mean promise or guarantee, ie it is being used to ask whether X intended to take upon himself the risk that his statement was untrue, or would not be fulfilled, by making it a term. Similarly, "warranty" may be used simply to mean a term of the contract, but some care must be taken. The courts also use it more technically, to contrast with condition and innominate term, to mean a term with a particular legal consequence flowing from its breach (ie only a claim in damages with no right to terminate the contract for its breach as there would be for breach of a condition, and might be for breach of an innominate term). To avoid confusion, "term" will be used here to denote the simple fact that a statement was a term, but not to indicate that it was of any particular type. The use of "warranty" in that sense will be avoided wherever possible.

(a) The basic test

The basic test of whether a statement is a term is one of intention. This was recognized by the House of Lords in *Heilbut, Symons & Co v Buckleton* [1913] AC 30. The facts were:

Heilbut, Symons & Co were rubber merchants who were underwriting an issue of shares in a company called the Filisola Rubber and Produce Estates Ltd. Heilbut, Symons & Co contacted Johnston, their manager in Liverpool, and told him to obtain applications for shares in the Filisola company. Johnston had seen a prospectus for that company but he did not have one in the Liverpool office. Buckleton telephoned Johnston and said "I understand you are bringing out a rubber company". The reply was "we are". On being informed that Johnston did not have any prospectuses, Buckleton enquired "if it was all right". The response was, "we are bringing it out". Buckleton replied, "that is good enough for me". After Buckleton had bought shares in the company, it was discovered that there were considerably fewer rubber trees on the estate than the prospectus had stated. The shares fell in value. Buckleton tried to claim damages from Heilbut, Symons & Co on the basis (a) of a fraudulent misrepresentation, or (b) that Heilbut, Symons & Co had contracted with him that the company was a rubber company.

The claim of fraud was dismissed at first instance, but the assertion that there had been a breach of a contract term — that the company was a rubber company — was successful until the case reached the House of Lords. There it was held that, although the company could not properly be termed a rubber company, there was no contractual promise by Heilbut, Symons & Co that the company was a rubber company. When Buckleton had spoken to Johnston on the telephone, what had clearly been important was that the company was being "brought out" by Heilbut, Symons & Co. They had not been considering whether it should, or should not, technically be referred to as a "rubber company".

It should be emphasised that the intention test is not subjective but objective[1]. Denning LJ in *Oscar Chess Ltd v Williams* [1957] 1 WLR 370 said at p 375:

"It is sometimes supposed that the tribunal must look into the minds of the parties to see what they themselves intended. That is a mistake... The question of whether a warranty was intended depends on the conduct of the parties, on their words and behaviour, rather than on their thoughts. If an intelligent bystander would reasonably infer that a warranty was intended, that will suffice."

The objective nature of the test is well illustrated by *Thake v Maurice* [1986] 1 All ER 497. In that case, the facts were:

Mr and Mrs Thake did not wish to have any more children, and so Mr Thake decided to have an operation which would sterilise him. The defendant, the surgeon who undertook the operation, had explained beforehand that it was irreversible. He had not told them that there was a slight possibility that it might reverse itself naturally even after the usual checks on Mr Thake's sperm count had shown that the operation had been successful. The couple believed that Mr Thake must be sterile after the operation, and they did not realise that Mrs Thake was pregnant until it was too late for her to have an abortion. Mr Thake's operation had been carried out with due care, and his sperm count had been correctly checked, but a natural reversal of the operation had subsequently occurred.

Mr and Mrs Thake argued that it had been a term of their contract with the surgeon that the operation would render Mr Thake sterile and that term had been breached. The Court of Appeal did not accept that argument. It was held that the surgeon had merely guaranteed to carry out the operation with care and skill. However, Mr and Mrs Thake were awarded damages on the basis that the surgeon had been negligent in failing to warn them of the possibility of natural reversal.

On the question of whether the surgeon had guaranteed that the operation would render Mr Thake sterile, the court recognized the objective nature of the search for intention as the determinant of the terms of the contract. Mr and Mrs Thake both left the surgeon's consulting room thinking that he had guaranteed that the operation would render Mr Thake sterile but, equally, the surgeon had not intended to give any such guarantee. Both parties held opposing views of what the terms were. Objectively, no term guaranteeing the success of the operation was found. The court thought that a reasonable person, in the position of Mr and Mrs Thake, would have known that medical science was not certain and would not have thought that the surgeon was guaranteeing the success of the operation. Nourse LJ said (at p 511):

> "The function of the court in ascertaining, objectively, the meaning of words used by contracting parties is one of everyday occurrence. But it is often exceedingly difficult to discharge it where the subjective understandings of the parties are clear and opposed. Here the plaintiffs understood that Mr Thake would be permanently sterile. The defendant himself recognized they would have been left with that impression. On the other hand, he did not intend, and on the state of his knowledge he could not have intended, to guarantee that that would be the case. Both the understanding and the intention appear to them, as individuals, to have been entirely reasonable, but an objective interpretation must choose between them. In the end the question seems to be reduced to one of determining the extent of the knowledge which is to be attributed to the reasonable person standing in the position of the plaintiffs."

This illustrates the objective approach and the need for it.

(b) Indicators of intention

The test of the parties' intention can be difficult to apply but certain factors are regarded by the courts as indicators of whether a statement was intended as a term. Some of the factors have been given more importance than others but, as Lord Moulton emphasised in *Heilbut, Symons & Co v Buckleton* [1913] AC 30 (at p 50), none of them is decisive. They are all only aids to establish the parties' intention. With that in mind we may now consider some of the factors the courts have recognized as indicators of whether a statement was intended as a term.

Importance of the statement

It may be clear to both sides that a certain factor was very important to one of the parties in the decision to contract. A statement on that factor, by the other party, may then well be found to have been intended as a guarantee, as a term. In *Bannerman v White* (1861) 10 CBNS 844:

Brewers were refusing to use hops contaminated with sulphur. Bannerman offered hops to White, and White asked if sulphur had been used to grow them. Bannerman said "no" and White said that he would not even discuss the price if it had. A contract was made for the sale of the hops; later it was established that Bannerman had forgotten that sulphur had been used in growing a small proportion of them.

It was held that it was a term of the contract that sulphur had not been used in growing the hops. It had been clear to both parties that the question of the use of sulphur was very important to White and that he would not have contracted without the assurance that no sulphur had been used on Bannerman's hops.

Reliance

An indication that a statement by one party can be relied upon, and need not be verified, may show that it should be regarded as a term. For example, a prospective seller may indicate to a potential buyer that he can rely upon the seller's statement as to the condition of the goods and need not check the goods for himself. This may then lead to the conclusion that the seller's statement is a term of the contract of sale. In *Schawel* v *Reade* [1913] 2 IR 64:

> The plaintiff wished to purchase a horse for stud purposes. He visited the defendant's stables and while he was inspecting a horse, "Mallow Man", the defendant said "You need not look for anything; the horse is perfectly sound. If there was anything the matter with the horse I would tell you". The plaintiff ceased his inspection and three weeks later he bought "Mallow Man". The horse was unfit for stud purposes because of a hereditary eye disease.

The House of Lords held that the soundness of the horse was a term of the contract. It was clearly indicated that the buyer could rely upon the seller, ie that the seller was taking the risk of the horse being unsound. Lord Moulton said at p 86:

> "The essence of such warranty is that it becomes plain by the words, and the action, of the parties that it is intended that in the purchase the responsibility of the soundness shall rest upon the vendor; and how. . . could a vendor more clearly indicate that he is prepared and intends to take upon himself the responsibility of the soundness than by saying: 'You need not look at that horse because it is perfectly sound', and sees that the purchaser thereupon desists from his immediate independent examination."

This can be contrasted with *Ecay* v *Godfrey* (1947) 80 Lloyd's L Rep 286 where a boat was being sold. Although the seller, Mr Godfrey, said that it was sound he also suggested a survey to the buyer, Senor Ecay. It was held that it was not a term of the contract of sale that the boat was sound. Equally, a similar conclusion may be reached where, although the statement of soundness is not followed by any express warning to carry out a check, there is a trade practice that such statements are not terms[2].

Relative knowledge of the parties

It is relevant to consider the question of which of the two parties was in the best position to know or ascertain the truth of a statement made. It is connected with the above indicator. It could be put in terms of whether it was reasonable to rely upon the statement made or whether one party can be taken to have assumed the risk of the statement being untrue. The court will be more inclined to find that the statement is a term if it was made by the person in the best position to have ascertained its truth. Two cases can be contrasted here: *Oscar Chess* v *Williams* [1957] 1 WLR 370 and *Dick Bentley Productions Ltd* v *Harold Smith (Motors) Ltd* [1965] 1 WLR 623.

In *Oscar Chess* v *Williams*:

> The defendant sold a Morris car to the plaintiff, a car dealer who was familiar with the car as he had been given lifts in it. The log book had shown it to be a 1948 model and the defendant had innocently described it as such and produced the log book. Before the defendant acquired the car the log book had been tampered with and the car was, in fact, a 1939 model. There was no difference in appearance between a 1948 and a 1939 model. The plaintiff would have paid £115 less for a 1939 model than for a 1948 model. Eight months after the sale, the plaintiff discovered the alteration of the log book and claimed £115 from the defendant for breach of a term that the car was a 1948 model.

The Court of Appeal held that there was no term that the car was a 1948 model. The defendant was in no better position than the plaintiff to assess the age of the car. The defendant had simply relied upon the date stated in the log book. There was no reason to suppose that he had intended to take upon himself the risk that the car was not a 1948 model by making the age of the car a term of the contract.

Oscar Chess contrasts with *Dick Bentley Productions Ltd* v *Harold Smith (Motors) Ltd* where the person making the statement was in the better position to establish its truth, and the statement was found to be a term. In *Dick Bentley*:

> Dick Bentley asked a car dealer, Smith, to find him a well vetted Bentley car. Smith found a car and showed it to Dick Bentley, telling him that since a new engine had been fitted the car had done only 20,000 miles, the mileage shown on the odometer. Dick Bentley purchased the car, which proved to be unsatisfactory, and it was discovered that it had done far more than the mileage shown on the odometer since the new engine had been fitted.

The Court of Appeal held that the mileage had been a term of the contract. The case was distinguished from *Oscar Chess* on the basis of the position of the person making the statement. A car dealer was in a far better position than his customer to establish the accuracy of the mileage recorded on the odometer.

3. The parol evidence rule

Where there is a written document containing contract terms, the question arises whether evidence can be given to show that the parties agreed to additional terms which are not contained within the written document. It has been said that "it is firmly established as a rule of law that parol evidence cannot be admitted to add to, vary or contradict a deed or other written document" (*Jacobs* v *Batavia and General Plantations Trust* [1924] 1 Ch 287 *per* Lawrence J at p 295). However, although this is commonly referred to as the parol evidence *rule* its status as a rule is very doubtful. On closer examination it does nothing more than express a presumption. In *Gillespie*

Brothers & Co v *Cheney, Eggar & Co* [1896] 2 QB 59, Lord Russell CJ said (at p 62):

> "although when the parties arrive at a definite written contract the implication or presumption is very strong that such contract is intended to contain all the terms of their bargain, it is a presumption only, and it is open to either of the parties to allege that there was, in addition to what appears in the written agreement, an antecedent express stipulation not intended by the parties to be excluded, but intended to continue in force with the express written agreement".

In other words, a written agreement, which looks like a complete contract, leads to the presumption that it is the complete contract, but that presumption can be rebutted. If it is shown that other terms were intended, in addition to those contained in the written document, then there is no rule preventing the admission of evidence of those other terms. If the written document was intended to embody the entire contract between the parties, there is clearly no room to admit evidence of any other statements of the parties as terms; they cannot be terms. On this basis the Law Commission concluded that the parol evidence rule is "a proposition of law which is no more than a circular statement" (Law Com 154 (1986); Marston [1986] CLJ 192).

The Law Commission also concluded that even if the parol evidence rule was viewed as of some substance, it was unlikely to work injustice because of the numerous exceptions to it. For example, evidence can be used to show that it had been orally agreed that the contract embodied in the written document was not intended to be immediately effective but was to become so only when certain conditions had been fulfilled (*Pym* v *Campbell* (1856) 6 El & Bl 379 — see page 112), or evidence of custom can be used to add to written contracts on matters on which the writing is silent (*Hutton* v *Warren* (1836) 1 M & W 466 — see page 110). The device of the collateral contract has also been used to avoid the parol evidence rule, so that if the parol evidence rule meant that the court felt unable to find that a statement was a term of the main contract, it could still find that it was a term of a collateral contract. Collateral contracts are considered below. For further "exceptions" to the parol evidence "rule", see Treitel, *The Law of Contract* (10th ed), pp 174–183.

4.   Collateral contracts[3]

The courts may occasionally find that, although a statement is not part of the main contract, it is part of a collateral contract. The statement can then found an action for breach of contract just as it would have done had it been part of the main contract. The collateral contract is often of the form, "if you will enter into the main contract then I guarantee that. . .". In *Heilbut, Symons & Co* v *Buckleton* [1913] AC 30, Lord Moulton stated at p 47:

> "It is evident, both on principle and on authority, that there may be a contract the consideration for which is the making of some other contract. 'If you will make such and such a contract I will give you one hundred pounds,' is in every sense of the word a complete legal contract. It is collateral to the main contract, but each has an independent existence, and they do not differ in respect of their possessing to the full the character and status of a contract."

The collateral contract has proved to be a useful device when there is a reason why the court cannot find that the statement in question is a term of the main contract. It has, for example, provided the courts with a means of avoiding the rule as to privity of contract (see Chapter 18), formality requirements (see page 90), and the parol evidence rule (above) where it "eases the consciences of those who believe that the parol evidence rule is a strict and meaningful prohibition" (Wedderburn [1959] CLJ 58 at p 69).

It was originally thought that the parol evidence rule could be avoided by finding the statement in question was part of a separate collateral contract only if the statement merely added to the written document and did not vary or contradict it (*Mann* v *Nunn* (1874) 30 LT 526). However, in *City and Westminster Properties Ltd* v *Mudd* [1959] Ch 129 (see Wedderburn, *op cit*, at pp 83–84) a collateral contract was found to make legally effective a statement which contradicted the written contract in so far as it rendered unenforceable a right of one of the parties under the main contract. In that case:

> Mr Mudd leased a shop from the plaintiff, and he also lived on the premises. When the time came for the renewal of the lease the plaintiff wished to include a new term stating that the premises were only to be used for business purposes. Mr Mudd made it clear that he wished to go on residing on the premises and that he would not accept the new term. Mr Mudd accepted the new lease, with the new term, only after the plaintiff stated that, if he signed the lease, no objection would be made to his continuing to live on the premises. Had Mr Mudd not thought that he would be able to continue to live on the premises he would not have signed the new lease but moved to other premises which were available at the time.

Subsequently, the plaintiff sought forfeiture of Mr Mudd's lease on the basis that he was in breach of its terms by residing on the premises. Harman J dismissed the action for forfeiture: "There was a clear contract acted upon by the defendant to his detriment and from which the plaintiff [could not] be allowed to resile" (at pp 145–6), ie there was a collateral contract that if Mr Mudd entered into the new lease the plaintiff would not object to his continued residence on the premises.

The use of the collateral contract as a means of avoiding the problems posed by the privity rule is illustrated by *Shanklin Pier Ltd* v *Detel Products Ltd* [1951] 2 KB 854:

> The pier owners wished to have their pier painted. Detel Products assured the pier owners that a paint of theirs, known as DMU, was suitable for the job and would last for seven to ten years. On the basis of that assurance, the pier owners specified that the painters, with whom the pier owners contracted for the painting of the pier, should use Detel Products' DMU paint. The painters used the DMU paint but it proved unsatisfactory and lasted only about three months.

The pier owners wished to sue Detel Products but there was a problem. Detel Products had given their assurance of the suitability of the paint to the pier owners, but it was the painters who had made a contract with Detel Products as purchasers of the paint. McNair J nevertheless held that the pier owners could succeed in an action for breach of contract against Detel Products. The statement as to the suitability of the paint formed a collateral contract of the form "if Detel Products' paint is specified for purchase by the painters then we (Detel Products) undertake its suitability for the job". (Some of the difficulties posed by the privity rule have now been mitigated by the Contracts (Rights of Third Parties) Act 1999 — see Chapter 18.)

Record v *Bell* [1991] 1 WLR 853 provides a recent example of the collateral contract being used as a device to avoid a formality requirement. In that case a warranty as to the vendor's title to the land for sale was found to be part of a collateral contract. As such it did not prevent the main sale contract from being effective because of the requirement that contracts for the sale of land should be in writing (s 2 Law of Property (Miscellaneous Provisions) Act 1989).

The usual requirements for a valid contract apply to a collateral contract, just as to any other. The consideration for the promise in the collateral contract is usually the act of entering into the main contract, as in *City and Westminster* v *Mudd* above, ie "if you will enter into the main contract then I guarantee that...". As was pointed out in the *Shanklin Pier* case, however, there is "no reason why there may not be an enforceable warranty between A and B supported by the consideration that B should cause C to enter into a contract with A" ([1951] 2 KB 854 at p 856).

There is a terminological difficulty in this area. Warranties are sometimes referred to as "collateral terms" or "collateral warranties", ie terms subsidiary to the main terms, the conditions, but properly speaking still part of the main contract. Nevertheless, it is sometimes difficult to discern whether the judges think they are discussing a warranty in the main contract or in a collateral contract (eg *Heilbut, Symons & Co* v *Buckleton* [1913] AC 30) and sometimes, although recognizing the two different possibilities, they treat them as interchangeable (eg *Evans* v *Merzario* [1976] 2 All ER 930 — see page 170).

B. Implied terms[4]

1. Introduction

Often the parties will not expressly deal with every query which could arise under the contract. They may have intended to contract against a background of established trade custom, or they may have thought that some things were too obvious to express, or they may simply not have considered every possible eventuality. When a problem arises which has not been dealt with by the express terms of the contract, then it may be argued that a term can be implied. There are basically three types of implied term which we need to consider — terms implied in fact, terms implied in law, and terms implied by custom.

2. Terms implied in fact

In implying terms in fact, the courts will state that they are endeavouring merely to find the intention of the parties. In particular the courts will often emphasise that they are not rewriting the parties' bargain (eg *Trollope & Colls* v *North West Metropolitan Regional Hospital Board* [1973] 2 All ER 260 at p 268). To justify this view of the process being carried out, the courts have indicated that the circumstances in which such terms will be implied are very limited. It is said that the implication of the term must be "necessary to give the transaction such business efficacy as the parties must have intended" (*per*

Bowen LJ in *The Moorcock* (1889) 14 PD 64); ie the term must be required to make the contract workable. In addition, the "officious bystander" test is often cited:

> "*Prima facie* that which in any contract is left to be implied and need not be expressed is something so obvious that it goes without saying; so that, if while the parties were making their bargain an officious bystander were to suggest some express provision for it in the agreement, they would testily suppress him with a common 'Oh, of course'" (*Shirlaw* v *Southern Foundries Ltd* [1939] 2 KB 206 *per* Mackinnon LJ at p 227).

In *The Moorcock* (1889) 14 PD 64:

> The defendants owned a wharf on the Thames and made a contract with the plaintiff shipowner for him to unload his vessel at their wharf. Both parties knew that the vessel was such that, whilst at the wharf, it must ground at low tide. The vessel grounded and was damaged.

It was held to be an implied term of the contract that the defendants had taken due care to ascertain that the bed of the river adjoining the wharf was not such as to damage the vessel when it grounded. The defendants were in breach of the implied term.

In *Shirlaw* v *Southern Foundries Ltd* [1939] 2 KB 206:

> On 1 December 1933 Mr Shirlaw was appointed managing director of Southern Foundries for ten years. Subsequently, Federated Foundries became the beneficial owners of Southern Foundries and in 1936 they changed the articles of association of Southern Foundries to enable them to remove Mr Shirlaw as a director. They removed him from his directorship, and he could not continue as managing director once he ceased to be a director.

The original articles of association of Southern Foundries did not allow Mr Shirlaw's removal in that way. The court found a breach of an implied term that such removal would not occur before the ten year period expired.

However, the authorities by no means put it beyond doubt whether the "officious bystander" and "business efficacy" tests should be regarded as distinct, or cumulative, or with one, or the other, as dominant. In the Privy Council case of *BP Refinery (Westernport) Pty Ltd* v *Shire of Hastings Ltd* (1978) ALJR 20 they seem to have been regarded as cumulative. Lord Simon laid out the requirements for terms implied in fact generally, saying (at p 26):

> "for a term to be implied, the following conditions (which may overlap) must be satisfied: (1) it must be reasonable and equitable; (2) it must be necessary to give business efficacy to the contract, so that no term will be implied if the contract is effective without it; (3) it must be so obvious that 'it goes without saying'; (4) it must be capable of close expression; (5) it must not contradict any express term of the contract."

It has not, generally, been uncommon to find the tests treated cumulatively or equated, or joined as one test. In *Trollope & Colls Ltd* v *North West Metropolitan Regional Hospital Board* [1973] 2 All ER 260, for example, Lord Pearson said (at p 268):

> "it must have been a term that went without saying, a term *necessary* to give business efficacy to the contract, a term which, although tacit, formed part of the contract which the parties made for themselves".

However, they have also been referred to as separate tests. It has been said, for example, that they are "distinct tests with the result that a term may sometimes be implied on the basis of one but not the other" (*Ashmore* v *Corp of Lloyds (No 2)* [1992] 2 Lloyd's Rep 620, Gatehouse J at p 627). As a distinct test, the "officious bystander" test has been viewed as "broader in scope than the *Moorcock* test", but, nevertheless, as "a stringent test" (*Associated Japanese Bank (International) Ltd* v *Credit Du Nord* [1989] 1 WLR 255, Steyn J at p 263. See also *MJB Enterprsies Ltd* v *Defence Construction (1951) Ltd* (1999) 170 DLR (4th) 577 at p 587, Sup Ct Can). Even if viewed as two tests, it has been recognised that "they [would] often overlap" (*Ashmore* v *Corp of Lloyds (No 2)* above). Whilst these views of the tests may be logical if they are viewed in the abstract, there may be further legal restrictions to consider and there is considerable emphasis upon "necessity" as the test for the implication of all terms in fact. It has been said that "it is hornbook law that a term may only be implied [in fact] if it satisfies the legal test of strict necessity" (*The Society of Lloyds* v *Clementson* [1995] CLC 117, Steyn LJ at p 132; *White* v *Reflecting Roadstuds Ltd* [1991] ICR 735; *Ashmore* v *Corp of Lloyds (No 2)* [1992] 2 Lloyd's Rep 620, Gatehouse J at 627; *Baker* v *Black Sea & Baltic General Ins Co Ltd* [1998] CLC 820, Lord Lloyd at p 824), and if that is the case, then, if the two tests do not simply coincide, the business efficacy test must be the broader.

Whatever the relationship of the tests, both are "but a route to the presumed intention of the parties" (*Richco International Ltd* v *Alfred Toepfer International GmbH (The Bonde)* [1991] 1 Ll Rep 136). Even though the tests ensure that intention is sought within very restricted bounds, certain arguments naturally follow from the fact that it is that intention which is sought. Those arguments should now be considered.

(a) Knowledge

The stated search for the parties' intention makes one party's lack of knowledge of the subject matter of a proposed implied term relevant to the court's decision on whether a term should be implied. In *Spring* v *National Amalgamated Stevedores and Dockers Society* [1956] 1 WLR 585 such a factor was put in the context of the "officious bystander" test:

> In 1939, at Bridlington, the Trades Union Congress drew up an agreement for the transfer of members between one union and another — the Bridlington Agreement. In breach of that agreement the NASDS allowed Mr Spring to become a member. He had been a member of the Transport and General Workers Union. In deciding the ensuing dispute between the two unions, the TUC told the NASDS to exclude all the members, like Mr Spring, that it had enrolled in contravention of the Bridlington Agreement.

When the NASDS attempted to expel Mr Spring, he asked the court for a declaration that the union was acting *ultra vires*, illegally, and unconstitutionally, and that his expulsion was void. The union tried to argue that an implied term in Mr Spring's contract of membership justified his expulsion to bring the union back within the terms of the Bridlington Agreement.

The court granted Mr Spring's request for a declaration. On the question of the implied term, and applying the "officious bystander" test, Sir Leonard Sachs V-C said (at p 599):

"If... the bystander had asked the plaintiff... 'won't you put into it some reference to the Bridlington Agreement?', I think (indeed I have no doubt) the plaintiff would have answered 'What's that?'."

Mr Spring could not have been expected to say "Oh, of course" to the suggestion of the "officious bystander" when it concerned something he had not heard of, and could not reasonably have been expected to have heard of.

(b) Would both parties have agreed to the term?

National Bank of Greece SA v *Pinios Shipping Co* [1989] 1 All ER 213[5] illustrates another factor relevant to the implication of terms based on intention. The court asks whether, at the time of contracting, both parties would have agreed to the term which one of them is contending should be implied.

> A ship was built for Pinios in Japan. Pinios paid 30 per cent of the price on delivery but the rest of the purchase price was borrowed on the basis of a mortgage of the ship. Pinios failed to pay the first instalment of the money owed. The bank could have declared Pinios in default and the ship would have been sold, but the sale of the ship at that point would not have recovered all the money owed, and another course was taken. The bank made a three party agreement with Pinios and Glafki for Glafki to manage the ship in the best interest of Pinios and the bank. It was a term of the mortgage that Pinios should insure the ship for 130 per cent of the amount secured, and Pinios had done so when the ship was initially delivered. The management contract specifically made it an obligation of Glafki to insure the vessel in accordance with the requirements of the mortgage. Glafki allowed the value of the insurance to fall. When the ship sank the insurance did not cover the sums owed by Pinios. Pinios successfully sued Glafki for negligent management of the ship, but could not obtain payment. Pinios sued the bank for Glafki's neglect.

The question before the court was whether the bank was also responsible to Pinios for Glafki's failure to insure the vessel fully. Pinios argued that a term should be implied that the bank would oversee Glafki's insurance of the vessel and that they were liable for not doing so. Pinios contended that the term should be implied because otherwise their interests were not protected, as Glafki was only subject to control by the bank and not Pinios. The Court of Appeal rejected this argument as, although Pinios would have agreed to such a term, it was not thought that the bank would have done so. The "officious bystander" test could not be satisfied; both parties would not have said "Oh, of course". The management agreement had put Glafki under the control of the bank, and not Pinios, but the agreement was very much in Pinios's interests. But for the bank deciding on the management agreement, rather than simply selling the vessel, Pinios would not have remained the ship's owner. As long as Pinios owned the ship their financial situation would improve if the market improved. In addition, it was thought that the parties would have envisaged Pinios recovering from Glafki in the sort of situation which occurred. They would not have envisaged Glafki refusing to honour the judgment. Dealing with the "officious bystander" test, Lloyd LJ said (at p 218):

> "the judge was... understating the position when he said that it was by no means obvious that the bank would have agreed to act as 'guarantor' for Glafki, more especially as Glafki was Pinios's own nominee to act as manager. To my mind it is obvious that it would not."[6]

Once it is accepted that one party would not have agreed to the proposed implied term, it cannot be implied on the basis that the parties intended it.

(c) Several possible formulations of implied term; detailed express terms

Trollope & Colls v *North West Metropolitan Regional Hospital Board* [1973] 2 All ER 260 provides an example of two factors against the implication of a term based on the parties' intention. In that case:

> T&C had contracted to build a hospital for the Board. The hospital was to be constructed in phases. Phases I and II were concurrent but Phase III was to commence only six months after the issue of the Certificate of Practical Completion of Phase I. The date for the completion of Phase I was specified, and there was provision for extension of that time if the delay was due to certain specified factors. There was no provision for the alteration of the date for completing Phase III because of delay in completing Phase I, although there was provision for extension of the Phase III completion date in certain other specified circumstances. The completion of Phase I was delayed to such an extent that there were only sixteen months in which to construct Phase III by the specified date. There would have been thirty months available for construction of Phase III had Phase I been completed by the date specified.

The House of Lords had to decide whether to imply a term allowing the delay on completion of Phase I to extend the completion date for Phase III. Lord Pearson (with whom Lords Guest, Diplock and Cross agreed) stated that the court would not improve the parties' bargain for them, however desirable such an improvement might be, and then emphasised the strictness of the test for the implication of terms based on the parties' intention. He said (at p 268):

> "An unexpressed term can be implied if and only if the court finds that the parties must have intended that term to form part of their contract; it is not enough for the court to find that such a term would have been adopted by the parties as reasonable men if it had been suggested to them: it must have been a term that went without saying, a term necessary to give business efficacy to the contract, a term which, though tacit, formed part of the contract which the parties made for themselves."

In this case two factors indicated that no term should be implied. First, there were detailed express terms in the contract. Those terms even dealt with some reasons for extending the completion date of Phase III. Under those circumstances it was not clear that the omission of any reference to an extension because of the late completion of Phase I was not deliberate. Secondly, it was not clear how any implied term should be formulated. There were various reasons for the delay in the completion of Phase I. Some of that delay was allowed under the contract for one reason, and some for other reasons, and some of it was not allowed at all. It was not clear how much of the delay any implied term should encompass. There were four or five possibilities. Doubts over the substance of the term meant that the court was not prepared to find that the parties would have included any particular version of it[7]. Detailed express terms may indicate that no term should be implied, and the court will be unwilling to find that a term is to be implied if there are several possible versions of it.

3. Terms implied in law

Statutes imply terms into certain types of contract. For example, the Sale of Goods Act 1979 implies terms into contracts for the sale of goods that the goods should be of satisfactory quality and reasonably fit for the buyer's purpose (see s 14). In any particular case, whether a statute implies a term will depend upon whether the statutory requirements for its implication are present. In relation to s 14 of the Sale of Goods Act, for example, the above terms are only implied if the goods are sold "in the course of a business". Similarly, whether the parties can exclude the implication will depend upon the statute. Terms implied by statute are the most obvious type of term implied in law, but they will not be considered further here — as has been indicated the implication is dependent upon the particular statute. What requires further consideration here is the implication of terms in law at common law. Like statute, such implication is not based upon the particular contract, but on the type of contract, and there are many types of regularly occurring contracts where certain implied terms have become standard for the type of contract in question — contracts for the lease of a furnished house (eg *Smith* v *Marrable* (1843) 11 M & W 5), contracts of employment (eg *Lister* v *Romford Ice and Cold Storage Co* [1957] AC 555, *Malik* v *BCCI* [1997] 3 All ER 1), contracts between banker and customer (eg *London Joint Stock Bank Ltd* v *Macmillan* [1918] AC 777). The standard implied terms are implied in the particular case unless they would contradict the express terms[8]. However, although there are established terms which are implied in law, consideration must now be given to how a type of contract will be addressed and a term implied in law generated.

(a) Terms implied in law are not based on the intention of the parties

In *Liverpool City Council* v *Irwin* [1976] 2 All ER 39 Lord Cross distinguished between terms implied in fact on the basis of the intention of the parties, and terms implied in law because of the type of contract. He said (at p 47):

> "When it implies a term the court is sometimes laying down a general rule that in all contracts of a certain type — sale of goods, master and servant, landlord and tenant, and so on — some provision is to be implied unless the parties have expressly excluded it... Sometimes however there is no question of laying down any *prima facie* rule applicable to all cases of a defined type... Here... the court... must be able to say that the insertion of the term is necessary to give... 'business efficacy' to the contract and that if its absence had been pointed out at the time both parties — assuming them to be reasonable men — would have agreed to the insertion."

In other words, "terms implied in fact are individualised gap fillers, depending on the terms and circumstances of a particular contract. Terms implied in law are in reality incidents attached to standardised contractual relationships" (*The Society of Lloyds* v *Clementson* [1995] CLC 117, *per* Steyn LJ at p 131). "Such implied terms operate as default rules" (*Malik* v *BCCI* [1997] 3 All ER 1, Lord Steyn at p 15).

The *Liverpool* case itself provides an example of the difference between implying a term in fact and implying a term in law:

Liverpool City Council owned a tower block which was in a very bad state of repair. Many of the problems were due to vandalism. The lifts frequently did not work and stairwells were often unlit. Rubbish chutes were frequently blocked. When Liverpool City Council sued the tenants for non-payment of rent, the tenants claimed that Liverpool City Council was in breach of an implied term as to the maintenance of the premises.

The House of Lords implied a term that Liverpool City Council should take reasonable care to maintain the common parts of the block in a reasonable state of repair. Unfortunately for the tenants, the Court also found that a lack of reasonable care by Liverpool City Council had not been established and that the implied term had not been breached.

How did the House of Lords imply a term when the "officious bystander" test was not satisfied, as it was thought that Liverpool City Council would not have agreed to the term? The majority of the Court of Appeal had refused to imply a term on the only argument before them, that a term should be implied in fact on the basis of the parties' intention. The House of Lords was able to imply a term as it did not look to the parties' intention but to the type of contract in question. In this case the contract was a landlord and tenant contract, but in a building of multi-occupancy where the only access to the flats was via the common areas, the stairs and the lifts. The only express terms set out the obligations of the tenants and they did not deal with the maintenance of the common parts of the building, like the stairs and the lifts. There were no express obligations on Liverpool City Council. The situation demanded that someone had to be responsible for those common parts and, in the absence of any express allocation of responsibility among the tenants, the obligation was held to fall on Liverpool City Council which had kept control of those areas.

(b) When will a term be implied in law?

There are two basic requirements for the implication of a term in law:

> "the first requirement is that the contract in question should be a contract of a defined type... The second requirement is that the implication of the term should be necessary" (*El Awadi* v *Bank of Credit and Commerce International SA* [1989] 1 All ER 242 at p 253).

Each of these requirements is considered below.

(i) A contract of a defined type

We saw above that Lord Cross provided examples of the type of contract into which a term be implied in law — "sale of goods, master and servant, landlord and tenant". As he indicated, they are all commonly occurring types of contract. We can identify two basic factors relevant to determining whether the contract in question is a contract into which a term may be implied in law, a contract of a defined type. They are, first, that the contract is of a recognizable commonly occurring type and, secondly, that the express terms of the particular contract do not differ too greatly from the "ordinary" terms of those contracts normally regarded as falling within that type.

Sale of goods contracts, master and servant contracts, landlord and tenant contracts are all contracts of a recognizable commonly occurring type and there will often be no difficulty in deciding if the contract is of such a type. Hutchinson J had no doubts that he was dealing with a contract of that type in *El Awadi* v *Bank of Credit and Commerce International SA* where the contract was for the sale of traveller's cheques by a bank to its customer. Hutchinson J thought that the sale of traveller's cheques was "self evidently" a contract in which the implication of a term in law was a possibility. It was a contract of common occurrence. (But see *Shell UK Ltd* v *Lostock Garage Ltd* [1977] 1 All ER 481 *per* Lord Denning MR at p 488.)

However, the type of contract in which a term may be implied may be more specifically delimited. There is an interaction between the identification of the type of contract in which the term in question is to be implied and the "necessity" test, below. This is exemplified by *Scally* v *Southern Health and Social Services Board* [1991] 4 All ER 563. *Scally* was concerned with doctors' contracts of employment. They included a contributory pension scheme which required forty years' contribution for maximum benefit. However, the terms were varied to give the employees an opportunity, for a limited period, to purchase extra years of contribution to make their pensions equivalent to one based on forty years' service, if the employees would not achieve that period of actual service. The problem arose because the plaintiffs were not informed of that opportunity and did not exercise their right. The question was whether there was an implied term in the contract requiring the employer to give notice of that opportunity. It was held that a term, requiring notice, could be implied in law. The implication was necessary because the contract was one arrived at by collective bargaining, not individual negotiation, and the doctors could not reasonably be expected to know of the opportunity unless given notice. The contracts in which such an implication would be made were of a carefully stated "defined type", reflecting this rationale for the implication. Lord Bridge said (at p 571):

"I would define it as the relationship of employer and employee where the following circumstances obtain: (1) the terms of the contract of employment have not been negotiated with the individual employee but result from negotiation with a representative body or are otherwise incorporated by reference; (2) a particular term of the contract makes available to the employee a valuable right contingent upon action being taken by him to avail himself of its benefit; (3) the employee cannot, in all the circumstances, reasonably be expected to be aware of the term unless it is drawn to his attention."

The second point to be made here is that it is not simply a matter of commonly occurring contractual relationships (eg landlord and tenant) or contracts commonly occurring to deal with a specific subject matter (eg sale of goods, sale of traveller's cheques by bank to customer); the contents of the contract must also be such that in its express terms it is an "ordinary" contract of that type. *National Bank of Greece SA* v *Pinios Shipping Co* [1989] 1 All ER 213 has already been discussed in the context of whether or not a term could be implied in fact (see page 102). Here we need to consider the alternative argument, that a term should be implied in law. Lloyd LJ dismissed the possibility (at p 219):

"Can the present case be brought within a defined type? If we were concerned with the ordinary relationship of banker and customer the law would imply certain obligations ... But we are not here concerned with the ordinary relationship of banker and customer. We are concerned with a carefully drawn one-off contract between three parties, made for a particular purpose in special circumstances, and apparently making full provision for that purpose. I cannot imagine a contract which it would be more difficult to fit into a 'defined type'."

Although contracts between banker and customer could be of a "defined type" (see, for example, *Tai Hing Cotton* below), this contract was not. The court was not faced with the "ordinary" relationship of banker and customer but with a "one-off" contract. All contracts are "one-off" in the sense that they will have terms unique to them. The question therefore relates to the degree of departure from the "ordinary" contract of the type in question. For example, how far does the contract in question depart from the "ordinary" banker and customer contract? It will be relevant to consider which terms are specific to the particular contract. Are they those terms which are specific to the "ordinary" contract between banker and customer?

(ii) The necessity test

In *Liverpool City Council* v *Irwin* [1976] 2 All ER 39, Lord Cross thought that in implying a term in law (at p 47):

"the court will naturally ask itself whether in the general run of such cases the term in question would be one which it would be reasonable to insert."

In addition, Lord Denning MR is noted for his attempts to insist upon reasonableness as the basis of the implication of terms (eg *Liverpool City Council* v *Irwin* [1975] 3 All ER 658 CA, *Shell UK* v *Lostock Garage* [1977] 1 All ER 481). However, although it may be that the court will not imply a term which is not reasonable, Lord Wilberforce asserted that (at p 44):

"such obligations should be read into the contract as the nature of the contract itself requires, no more, no less; a test in other words of necessity".

It is "necessity", as the test for terms implied in law, which has since been followed. The Privy Council adopted it in refusing to imply the term contended for in *Tai Hing Cotton Mill Ltd* v *Liu Chong Hing Bank Ltd* [1985] 2 All ER 947[9]. The facts were:

For a number of years an employee of Tai Hing had not been properly supervised. He had been able to forge the signature of the managing director of Tai Hing on cheques and obtain payment of the cheque to his own benefit. The bank had debited Tai Hing's account on paying out on the cheques.

When the forgery was discovered, Tai Hing claimed from the bank the sums debited from its account because of the forged cheques. It stated that the bank had debited its account without proper authority to do so. The bank resisted this, claiming to be able to rely upon Tai Hing's breach of an implied term that Tai Hing would take reasonable precautions in the management of its business to prevent forged cheques being presented for payment. The Privy Council refused to imply such a term. It was not considered to be necessary.

The court said that the terms which it was necessary to imply in the banker-customer relationship had already been decided by the courts as (i) a duty to refrain from drawing a cheque in such a manner as to facilitate fraud or forgery (*London Joint Stock Bank Ltd* v *MacMillan* [1918] AC 777), and (ii) a duty to inform the bank of any forgery as soon as the customer discovered it (*Greenwood* v *Martins Bank Ltd* [1933] AC 51). The bank had argued that circumstances had changed. The development of banking business had made its obligations so burdensome that they should be met by some reciprocal expansion of responsibility imposed on the customer. The court, nevertheless, held that the banker-customer relationship did not make it necessary to imply the term contended for. The possibility of paying out on a forged cheque was part of the risk of the service which it was the business of the bank to offer.

Some further consideration must be given to the "necessity" test. It should be viewed in the context of what the courts are doing when they imply a term because the contract is of a certain type. When considering implication of a term in law the court is not looking for the intention of the parties. Their intention is only relevant in so far as it is shown by express contrary terms[10]. The court is openly interfering with the parties' bargain; the whole idea of such an implication is contrary to that of freedom of contract. It is not surprising that the test should be expressed so as to minimise what the court is doing by making the test appear as narrow as possible, ie a test which is stated to depend on "necessity". Of course, the point should also be made that, in any event, "necessity" is not viewed in absolute terms. In *Liverpool City Council* v *Irwin,* there were stairs in the flats. To that extent, lifts were not "necessary" but, in high rise flats, lifts would be said to be "necessary" in an everyday sense of the word. Similarly, in an absolute sense it was not necessary that the employers in *Scally* give the employees notice of their enhanced pension opportunities if the employees were to be able to avail themselves of them. The employees could have made enquiries and kept themselves informed but they could not "reasonably be expected to be aware of them" unless given notice by the employer. As was indicated above, the courts have stated that they will not imply a term simply because it is reasonable, but it could be said that they address the question of "necessity", not in absolute terms, but through the eyes of a reasonable person applying the label in everyday terms.

The "necessity" test may involve consideration of the relative bargaining powers, generally, of parties to such contracts. In the *Tai Hing* case, when faced with the argument that the term had to be implied because of the increased burden placed on banks by the modern world, Lord Scarman commented (at p 956):

> "One can fully understand the comment ... that the banks must today look for protection. So be it. They can increase the severity of their terms of business, and they can use their influence, as they have in the past, to seek to persuade the legislature that they should be granted further protection by statute. But it does not follow that because they may need protection as their business expands the necessary incidents of their relationship with their customer must also change."

The banks could look after their own interests and no implied term was necessary. This is to be contrasted with the situation in the *Liverpool City Council* case, above, where a term was implied to put the obligation to repair the common parts on Liverpool City Council, the landlords. Liverpool City Council could have included in their contracts a term allocating responsibility for the maintenance of the common parts but they did not do so and did not wish to do so. Clearly, the tenants needed the situation to be clarified and were not in a position to bargain for an express term.

It must be recognised, more generally, that whether a term is regarded as "necessary" in this context involves wider issues and differs from the "necessity" test applied in relation to terms implied in fact. This was acknowledged in *Scally* v *Southern Health and Social Services Board* [1991] 4 All ER 563, where Lord Bridge said (at p 571):

"A clear distinction is drawn ... between the search for an implied term necessary to give business efficacy to a particular contract and the search, based on wider considerations, for a term which the law will imply as a necessary incident of a definable category of contractual relationship." (See also *Spring* v *Guardian Assurance* [1994] 3 All ER 129, Lord Woolf at p 178.)

More broadly, the "necessity" test encompasses considerations of "justice and social policy" (*The Star Texas* [1993] 2 Lloyd's Rep 445 at 526, *Lister* v *Romford Ice* [1957] AC 555) and it was recognised in *Malik* v *BCCI* [1997] 3 All ER 1 that what that leads to will change over time, with changing social attitudes. In that case, the House of Lords accepted that there should be implied into contracts of employment a term that both parties would not engage in conduct likely to undermine the trust and confidence required if the employment relationship was to continue. They saw such implication as part of the "history of the development of employment law in this century" (at p 15). They recognised the:

"Changes which have taken place in the employer/employee relationship, with far greater duties imposed on the employer than in the past whether by statute or by judicial decision, to care for the physical, financial and even psychological welfare of the employee." (At p 15, quoting *Spring* v *Guardian Assurance* [1994] 3 All ER Lord Slynn at p 161.)

The term was regarded as making little difference to the obligations of employees, who had long been seen as under obligations to serve their employers loyally and not to act contrary to their business. Its importance was perceived to be in its impact upon the employer's obligations. The term was regarded as "apt to cover the great diversity of situations in which a balance has to be struck between an employer's interest in managing his business as he sees fit and the employee's interest in not being unfairly and improperly exploited" (Lord Steyn at pp 15–16).

At times, broad considerations of justice and social policy may lead to the conclusion that a term should be implied but the courts will, nevertheless, refuse to imply a term on the basis that the issue is not one which can appropriately be dealt with in that way. Public policy was looked at in *Reid* v *Rush & Tompkins Group plc* [1990] 1 WLR 212 and the implication of a term was viewed as desirable but the issue was regarded as too complex for the courts to deal with by such means. It was said (at p 220):

"As to treating such a term as implied by law, the arguments in favour of a social policy, which would require employers to provide some level of personal accident insurance for the benefit of men and women working overseas, and for their dependants, are obvious but there appears to be no way in which the court could 'embody this policy in the law without the assistance of the legislature'".

4. Terms implied by custom

There may be contractual terms which are implied on the basis that they are customary in a particular trade, profession or locality[11]. In *Hutton* v *Warren* (1836) 1 M & W 466:

> The tenant of a farm was given notice to quit by the landlord. He had worked and planted the land and the landlord would obtain the benefit of that when he left. It was held that the tenant was entitled to an allowance for the seeds and labour on leaving. There was no express term to that effect, but he was so entitled on the basis of a local custom.

Baron Parke indicated the rationale of implying terms on the basis of custom. He said (at p 475):

> "It has long been settled that, in commercial transactions, extrinsic evidence of custom and usage is admissible to annex incidents to written contracts, in matters with respect to which they are silent. The same rule has also been applied to contracts in other transactions of life, in which known usages have been established and prevailed; and this has been done upon the principle of presumption that, in such transactions, the parties did not mean to express in writing the whole of the contract by which they intended to be bound, but to contract with reference to those known usages."

However, despite the reference to intention by Baron Parke, the situation is more akin to terms implied in law than to terms implied on the basis of the parties' intention (ie terms implied in fact). Terms implied by custom are implied on the basis that the contract is of a certain type and there is a custom which implies certain terms into contracts of that type. Also, as with terms implied in law, the intention of the parties is only of limited relevance. Here, the term will be excluded if the contract evidences a contrary intention:

> "An alleged custom can be imported into a contract only if there is nothing in the express or necessarily implied terms of the contract to prevent such inclusion and further that a custom will only be imported into a contract where it can be so imported consistently with the tenor of the documents as a whole" (*London Export Corp Ltd* v *Jubilee Coffee Roasting Co* [1958] 1 WLR 661 *per* Lord Jenkins at p 675).

In *Walford's case* (*Les Affreteurs Réunis Société Anonyme* v *Walford* [1919] AC 801), for example, a custom that a broker's commission was payable only when hire was earned under a charter, could not be implied into a contract with an express term stating that the owners were to pay commission on the signing of a charter.

It is not easy to establish the existence of a particular custom or usage. It has been said that is must be:

> "certain, in the sense that the practice is clearly established; it must be notorious, in the sense that it is so well known in the market in which it is alleged to exist, that those who conduct business in the market contract with the usage as an implied term; and it must be reasonable" (*Cunliffe-Owen* v *Teather & Greenwood* [1967] 1 WLR 1421, *per* Ungoed Thomas J at p 1438).

More recently, the House of Lords has viewed the situation as requiring "evidence of a universal and acknowledged practice of the market" (*Baker* v *Black Sea Insurance* [1998] 2 All ER 833 at 842). If a custom is unreasonable, "the courts have said that they will not recognise it as binding on people who do not know of it and who have not consented to act upon it" (*Perry* v *Barnett* (1885) 15 QBD 388, *per* Brett MR at p 393).

5. Express contradictory terms and the Unfair Contract Terms Act 1977

A term will not be implied if there is an express contradictory term. The impact upon this of the Unfair Contract Terms Act 1977 is considered in Chapter 10. In *Johnstone* v *Bloomsbury Health Authority* [1991] 2 All ER 293 it was said that, had the relevant express term contradicted the term which it was contended should be implied in law, the express term would have been treated as one excluding liability and subject to s 2 of the Unfair Contract Terms Act 1977 (see page 216).

Footnotes

(1) On objectivity in contract, see generally Howarth (1984) 100 LQR 265; De Moor (1990) 106 LQR 632.
(2) Trade practice seems to be the explanation of *Hopkins* v *Tanqueray* (1864) 15 CB 130.
(3) Wedderburn [1959] CLJ 58.
(4) Phang [1990] JBL 394, [1993] JBL 242, [1994] JBL 255.
(5) The case went to the House of Lords on another point — [1990] 1 All ER 78.
(6) See also *Bank of Nova Scotia* v *Hellenic Mutual War Risk Association (Bermuda); (The Good Luck)* [1989] 3 All ER 628 at p 667; *El Awadi* v *Bank of Credit and Commerce International SA* [1989] 1 All ER 242 at p 252.
(7) See also *Shell UK* v *Lostock Garage* [1977] 1 All ER 481 at p 488; *Liverpool City Council* v *Irwin* [1975] 3 All ER 658 (CA).
(8) The Court of Appeal seems to be making an inroad on the parties' intention here in envisaging the application of the Unfair Contract Terms Act 1977 to an express term precluding the implied term — *Johnstone* v *Bloomsbury Health Authority* [1991] 2 All ER 293 (see page 216).
(9) At p 955; see also *Bank of Nova Scotia* v *Hellenic Mutual War Risk Association (Bermuda); (The Good Luck)* [1989] 3 All ER 628 at p 666; *El Awadi* v *Bank of Credit and Commerce International SA* [1989] 1 All ER 242 at p 253; *National Bank of Greece SA* v *Pinios Shipping Co* [1989] 1 All ER 213 at p 220.
(10) See note 8 above.
(11) For example, see *National Bank of Greece SA* v *Pinios Shipping Co* [1990] 1 All ER 78.

Chapter 8

Contingencies, classification of terms and entire contracts

A. Contingent conditions

Whether a contract is operative, or even exists, may depend upon a contingency. For example, the operation of a contract may be subject to a condition precedent. Until the condition precedent occurs the contract is inoperative and, as the fulfilment of the condition is not an obligation of the contract, there is no question of a claim for breach of contract if it is not fulfilled. However, there may also be promissory contingent conditions, and they will indicate the order of performance.

1. Conditions precedent — non-promissory

(a) Existence/enforceability of contracts

There are two basic possibilities in relation to a non-promissory condition precedent. A condition precedent may suspend entirely the formation of the contract, or it may not delay formation itself but merely the operation of some, or all, of the obligations under the contract. In *Pym* v *Campbell* (1856) 6 El & Bl 379 the situation was perceived as one where prior to the fulfilment of the contingency there was no contract in existence. In that case, the facts were:

> The plaintiff wished to sell to the defendant a share in an invention of the plaintiff. A written document appeared to contain an agreement for the purchase. The plaintiff sought to rely upon it but the defendant established that the parties had further agreed that the written document was to be the agreement only if the plaintiff's invention was approved of by a third party, Abernethie. Abernethie had not given his approval of the invention.

The court concluded that there was no contract at all. Abernethie's approval was a condition precedent to the existence of the contract.

Marks v *Board* (1930) 46 TLR 424 provides another example of a case where no contract was found to exist because of a condition. In that case there was a document, labelled as a "memorandum of agreement", which had been drawn up in relation to the sale of a house. It was stated to be "subject to survey". The court found that there was no contract in existence. It was intended that the prospective purchaser should be entirely free to say whether the surveyor's report was satisfactory or not. There was no contract as neither party was intended to be bound. (See also *Astra Trust* v *Adams and Williams* [1969] 1 Lloyd's Rep 81, but contrast *Ee* v *Kakar* (1979) 40 P & CR 223.)

Marten v *Whale* [1917] 2 KB 480 provides an example of a situation in which the contingency merely suspended the operation of the contract's main obligations, rather than its entire existence. In that case:

> Marten and Thacker entered into two linked sales. Marten agreed to buy a piece of land from Thacker "subject to purchaser's solicitor's approval of title and restrictions". In consideration of that sale Marten agreed to sell Thacker a car. The sale of the car was to be completed simultaneously with the sale of the land. However, Marten let Thacker take the car away and Thacker sold it to Whale, who acted in good faith. When Marten's solicitor did not approve the title to the land, and both sales could not be completed, the question was whether Marten could recover the car from Whale.

Under certain circumstances, what is now s 25(1) Sale of Goods Act 1979 allows good title to goods to pass to a third party in a sale by a non-owner. In order that the statute might operate, it was necessary that, when he sold the car to Whale, Thacker should have been a person who had "agreed to buy" the car. The Court of Appeal thought that there was a contract for the sale of the car in existence between the parties. It was the operation of the contract, rather than its existence, which was dependent upon the solicitor's approval of the sale of the land. As there was a contract in existence at the time of the sale to Whale, albeit a conditional one, Thacker sold as someone who had "agreed to buy" the car. Whale acquired good title to the car under s 25(1).

(b) Obligations relating to the occurrence of the contingency

In *Marten* v *Whale* the opinion was voiced that there was "an implied provision that [Marten] shall appoint a solicitor and shall consult him in good faith, and that the solicitor shall give an honest opinion" (*per* Scrutton LJ at p 487). In other words, the court thought that, as the contingency on which the operation of the main contract terms depended was the approval of Marten's solicitor, Marten had to ensure that it was possible for that approval to be given. It might not be given, as indeed it was not, but the court thought that he was obliged to make it possible for the opinion to be given, one way or the other. This illustrates the point that, although the main obligations are inoperative until a condition is fulfilled, there may still be subsidiary, operative obligations relating to the fulfilment of the condition.

The content of any subsidiary obligations will depend upon the nature of the condition. The subsidiary obligation may simply be not to prevent the condition from being fulfilled. In *Mackay* v *Dick* (1881) 6 App Cas 251 the agreement was for the sale of an excavating machine but subject to the requirement that the machine could work at a specified rate on the buyer's property. It was held that the buyer should have facilitated the trial of the machine. Where the condition relates to the approval of a third party, there may be subsidiary obligations to appoint the third party (see *Marten* v *Whale* above). Where the condition relates to the obtaining of planning permission, or an export licence, one party may be under an obligation to use reasonable efforts to obtain the necessary licence or permission (eg *Hargreaves Transport Ltd* v *Lynch* [1969] 1 WLR 215), although of course the parties may have made the obtaining of the permission/licence a contingent promissory condition, rather than a mere contingent condition, so that one party is obliged to obtain it and is in breach if he does not (eg *Peter Cassidy Seed Co Ltd* v *Osuustukkukauppa IL* [1957] 1 WLR 273).

(c) Waiver of conditions precedent

The condition precedent, preventing the immediate existence or enforceability of the contract, may be for the benefit of one party rather than both. If it is simply for the benefit of one party, that party can waive it and the contract will come into existence, or become enforceable, without the occurrence of the condition. In *Ee* v *Kakar* (1979) 40 P & CR 223:

> There was an agreement for the sale of a house "subject to survey of the property". The vendor then sought to repudiate the agreement but the purchaser asked for specific performance. The purchaser claimed that, as the condition as to survey was wholly in his favour, he could waive it.

Walton J concluded that the purchaser could waive fulfilment of the condition. The vendor had argued that it was also in his, the vendor's, interest that the state of the property be known but the judge found that the benefit of the condition was wholly one sided. There was no provision for disclosure of the report to the vendor. He might never have obtained any knowledge of its contents. The purchaser could waive the condition (see also *Graham* v *Pitkin* [1992] 2 All ER 235).

The condition could not be waived by one party in *Heron Garage Properties* v *Moss* [1974] 1 All ER 421. In that case:

> There was an agreement for the sale of land subject to the purchaser obtaining planning permission for the use of the land as a filling station. The vendor also owned adjoining land and he intended to build a car showroom on it. When planning permission for the filling station was refused, the purchaser claimed to be able to waive the condition on the basis that it was wholly for his benefit.

Brightman J held that the condition was for the benefit of both parties. It could not be waived by the purchaser. A filling station would be a complementary business to that intended by the vendor.

(d) Uncertainty and incompleteness

The condition may be such that the agreement will be considered invalid because of uncertainty (see Chapter 3). In *Lee-Parker* v *Izzet (No 2)* [1972] 2 All ER 800, land was sold "subject to the purchaser obtaining a satisfactory mortgage" but the phrase was considered to be too uncertain for there to be a binding agreement. Goulding J considered that "everything is at large, not only interest and ancillary obligations, on which evidence might establish what would be usual or reasonable, but also these two most essential points — the amount of the loan and the terms of the repayment". (But contrast *Lee-Parker* v *Izzet* [1971] 3 All ER 1099, and see Furmston (1983) 3 Ox Jo Legal Studies 438. See also *Graham* v *Pitkin* [1992] 2 All ER 235 at p 237.)

The phrase "subject to contract" usually has a different impact from that of the conditions considered above. It generally signifies that the parties have not yet reached complete agreement but are still bargaining. In chartering transactions the phrase "subject to details" is of similar effect (*The Junior K* [1988] 2 Lloyd's Rep 583; *The CPC Gallia* [1994] 1 Lloyd's Rep 68).

2.   Conditions precedent — promissory

These conditions relate to the order of performance and are discussed below, in that context.

3.   Concurrent conditions

See below in the context of promissory conditions and the order of performance.

4.   Conditions subsequent

A condition subsequent is a condition upon the fulfilment of which an existing contract is extinguished. *Head* v *Tattersall* (1871) LR 7 Ex 7 is the case usually quoted in this context (but see Stoljar 69 LQR 485, pp 506–511):

> A horse was sold on the basis that it had been hunted with the Bicester hounds. It was expressly stated by the seller that if it had not been so hunted the buyer could return it by 5 pm on the following Wednesday. Before that time arrived the horse was injured and the buyer discovered that it had not been hunted with the Bicester hounds. The buyer had not been at fault with regard to the injury to the horse.

It was held that the buyer could return the horse, despite its injury, because it had not been hunted with the Bicester hounds.

It should be noted that there is an overlapping use of terminology here. The term "conditions precedent" includes not only conditions which prevent a contract coming into existence, but also those which suspend obligations. Therefore, the use of the terminology "conditions precedent" and "conditions subsequent" overlap. In *Total Gas Marketing Ltd* v *Arco British Ltd* [1998] CLC 1275, Lord Steyn noted (at pp 1289–1290):

> "a fact is a condition precedent to a contract for the creation of which it is necessary, and ... a fact is a condition subsequent to a contract that it extinguishes. On the other hand, 'condition precedent' is sometimes used in the sense of a condition subsequent. That is not so surprising. The question is condition precedent to what? And in this case the question can only receive the answer: the operation of the contract."

5. Contingent promissory conditions and the order of performance

Contingent promissory conditions will indicate the order of performance. For example, the fulfilment by A of an obligation under the contract he has made with B may be a condition precedent to B's performance. If the performance of an obligation of one party, A, is a condition precedent to the other party's, B's, liability to perform then the contract is safer for B than for A; B will not be left in the situation where he has performed and A refuses to do so. The same, of course, does not apply to A. Whether the contract makes A's performance a condition precedent to B's liability may depend upon B's superior bargaining power, or the practicalities of the situation, or simply what is usual in a particular type of contract. In *Trans Trust SPRL* v *Danubian Trading Co Ltd* [1952] 1 All ER 970 there was a contract for the sale of one thousand tons of rolled steel. There was an obligation on the buyer to open a confirmed letter of credit to pay for the steel. It was necessary that the buyer should open the letter of credit before the seller became liable to deliver. It was known to both parties that the seller could not obtain the goods until the letter of credit was opened. The obligation to open the letter of credit was construed as a condition precedent to the seller's obligation to deliver. The seller did not have to perform until the buyer had done so.

Concurrent conditions also indicate the order of performance. For example in sale of goods contracts, in the absence of contrary intention, s 28 Sale of Goods Act 1979 makes the seller's obligation to deliver, and the buyer's obligation to pay, concurrent conditions. Each party must be willing to perform his obligation in order to claim that the other should do so. The concurrent condition provides some security for each party's performance.

Many contractual obligations are independent of each other. Their performance is not linked to that of the other party. For example, the landlord's obligation to repair and the tenant's to pay rent were held to be independent of each other and the landlord's failure to repair did not justify the tenant in refusing to pay the rent (*Taylor* v *Webb* [1937] 2 KB 283).

6. Promissory conditions — terminology

"Condition" is used in many senses in contract law and this can cause confusion. Here we need to consider further the term "promissory condition". It has been used above to indicate contingency and the order of performance. However, as we will see in the next section, "promissory condition" may also be used to indicate that a term is a "condition" rather than a warranty or an innominate term. When contrasted with warranties and innominate terms, the label of "promissory condition" is being used to indicate the legal consequences of the breach, in the sense of whether the injured party has a right to terminate the contract because of the breach. (When any breach of a term which is a condition occurs, the injured party has a right to terminate the contract as well as to claim damages (but see s 15A Sale of Goods Act 1979 — see page 119). In contrast, breach of a warranty gives rise only to the right to claim damages. Breach of an innominate term means that damages can always be claimed but the right to terminate depends upon the seriousness of the breach (see below).)

The label "promissory condition", in the sense of contingency, relates to the order of performance. Promissory conditions, when contrasted with warranties and innominate terms, relate to the conformity of the performance rendered with that promised (Treitel (1990) 106 LQR 183).

B. Distinguishing conditions, warranties and innominate terms

1. Introduction

We must now distinguish conditions from warranties and innominate terms. Basically the three types of term can be distinguished by the legal consequences that flow from the breach of each of them. As we noted above, when a condition is breached the injured party has the right to sue for damages and also to terminate the contract (but see s 15A Sale of Goods Act 1979 — see page 119). A breach of warranty gives rise only to the right to sue for damages. When an innominate term is breached, the legal consequences of the breach depend upon its factual consequences, ie there is a right to terminate the contract, in addition to suing for damages, only if the breach of an innominate term is such as to deprive the injured party of substantially all the benefit which he was intended to derive from the contract.

For a long time it was thought that terms were either conditions or warranties. That was probably due to the fact that the definitions of condition and warranty given above were only satisfactorily settled with the enactment of the Sale of Goods Act 1893 and that Act referred only to conditions and warranties. It was the judgment of Diplock LJ in *Hong Kong Fir Shipping Co* v *Kawasaki Kisen Kaisha* [1962] 2 QB 26 which made it clear that the division into conditions and warranties was not complete but had to be supplemented by the innominate term.

The Sale of Goods Act 1893 settled the technical meaning to be given to conditions and warranties in one context (ie when the effect of a breach is under consideration), but the words are still used in other senses. For example, both condition and warranty may be used non-technically simply to mean a term of the contract, without it carrying any implication as to the legal consequences of a breach. Warranty is often used non-technically in that way, to mean a term, when the question being asked is whether a statement is a term or a mere representation. The words condition and warranty must be approached with some caution to ascertain the sense in which they are being used. That caution must be all the greater when dealing with some of the older cases decided before the enactment of the Sale of Goods Act 1893.

2. The test

The question of how it is to be decided whether a term is a condition, a warranty, or an innominate term can be easily answered in theory. The application of the test is more problematic as it is based upon the parties' intention. The parties may have expressly classified the term[1]; otherwise the test to be applied derives from *Bentsen* v *Taylor, Sons & Co* [1893] 2 QB 274. In that case, it was held that the term in the charterparty describing the ship as "now sailed or about to sail from . . . to the United Kingdom" was a condition. Such a statement provided the charterer's only basis for his calculations as to when he would be able to load the ship in the United Kingdom. It was the importance of the term to the whole charter that led to its construction as a condition. In coming to that conclusion, Bowen LJ delivered what is now the classic test for distinguishing the different types of term. He said (at p 281):

> "There is no way of deciding that question except by looking at the contract in the light of the surrounding circumstances, and making up one's mind whether the intention of the parties, as gathered from the instrument itself, will best be carried out by treating the promise as a warranty sounding only in damages, or as a condition precedent by the failure to perform which the other party is relieved of his liability."

This provides the test for determining whether the term is a condition or a warranty, despite the reference to a "condition precedent" — there are difficulties with terminological usage in this area! To that formulation of the test should now be added the third possibility, that the intention of the parties will best be carried out by classifying the term as innominate. In *Bunge Corp* v *Tradax Export SA* [1981] 1 WLR 711 (see below) the House of Lords made it clear that this is the correct approach to the classification of terms, even innominate terms. The application of this test, for deciding if a term is a condition, warranty, or innominate term, is considered further below.

One aspect of the classification test should be emphasised here, if the importance of the innominate term is to be understood. That aspect is the point in time against which the intention of the parties is to be assessed in determining the classification of a term. In *Bentsen* v *Taylor, Sons & Co* [1893] 2 QB 274, after the above *dictum*. Bowen LJ continued (at p 281):

> "One of the first things you would look to is to what extent the accuracy of the statement — the truth of what is promised — would be likely to affect the substance and foundation of the adventure which the contract is intended to carry out . . . it may well be that such a test can only be applied after getting the jury to say what the effect of a breach of such a condition would be on the substance and foundation of the adventure; not the effect of the breach which has in fact taken place, but the effect likely to be produced on the foundation of the adventure by any such breach of that portion of the contract."

As will be seen, a term is more likely to be classified as a condition if it can be regarded as an important term of the contract; and the effect of any breach of it is relevant to an assessment of its importance. However, the point to be noted here, and which Bowen LJ emphasised, is that the importance of the term is to be assessed against the effect of possible breaches rather than the actual breach. The classification of terms is based upon the intention at the time of contracting and not the time of the breach[2]. Basically, the actual breach is considered only if the term is innominate. It is then that the actual breach becomes relevant to deciding if the injured party can terminate the contract.

However, there is a statutory exception to the above situation. The Sale of Goods Act 1979 was amended by the Sale and Supply of Goods Act 1994. A new section, s 15A, was inserted into the 1979 Act and that section deems a breach of the conditions implied by ss 13–15 of that Act to be merely a breach of warranty under certain circumstances. This deemed change of the status of the implied terms occurs if the buyer does not deal as a consumer and breach is so slight that it would be unreasonable to reject the goods. It is the second requirement which is relevant here and which creates the exception to the point made above. The implied terms are generally conditions but, because they can be deemed to be merely warranties in the light of the actual breach, the actual breach is relevant to the terms' "deemed" classification at least. Section 15A of the 1979 Act is considered further below (similar provision is made for other supply of goods contracts — see Sale and Supply of Goods Act 1994).

The point should additionally be made here that if the term is part of a standard form contract and it has a "usual" classification as a condition, warranty or innominate term, then the parties will generally be taken to have intended to classify it accordingly (*Maredelanto Compania Naviera SA v Bergbau-Handel GmbH; (The Mihalis Angelos)* [1971] 1 QB 164).

3. Recognition of the innominate term

In *Hong Kong Fir Shipping Co Ltd v Kawasaki Kisen Kaisha Ltd* [1962] 2 QB 26 it was shown that the traditional division of terms into conditions and warranties is not complete, and that there are also innominate terms. In that case:

> The shipowner hired a ship, *The Hong Kong Fir*, to the charterer for twenty-four months. On a voyage to deliver coal to Osaka, the ship spent five weeks being repaired. The engines were old and needed to be well maintained by efficient staff. The engine-room staff were insufficient in number and inefficient. When the ship arrived in Osaka the engine-room staff were replaced, and a further period of fifteen weeks was required to make it ready for sea again. The charterer claimed to be able to terminate the contract for failure to deliver a seaworthy ship because of the state of the engines and the inadequacy of the staff.

The shipowner sued the charterer for wrongful termination of the contract, ie the shipowner claimed that the breach of the term that the vessel was seaworthy did not entitle the charterer to terminate the contract. Although the owner had been in breach, in failing to provide a seaworthy ship, the Court of Appeal held that the breach had not entitled the charterer to terminate. The charterer was in breach in wrongfully terminating the contract. The owner was entitled to substantial damages as the market had dropped considerably since the charter had been made.

The importance of *Hong Kong Fir* lies in the treatment by Diplock LJ of the charterer's claim that seaworthiness was a condition and that, as such, any breach of it entitled the charterer to terminate the contract (see also Upjohn LJ). He made it clear that whether termination was possible, for the breach of the term as to seaworthiness, did not depend upon the classification of the term as a condition or warranty but upon the factual consequences of the breach. The factual consequences of the breach determined the legal consequences. If the factual consequences were sufficiently serious, termination was possible — but not otherwise. Diplock LJ said (at p 70):

"There are however many contractual undertakings of a more complex character which cannot be categorised as being 'conditions' or 'warranties' . . . Of such undertakings all that can be predicated is that some breaches will and others will not give rise to an event which will deprive the party not in default of substantially the whole benefit which it was intended that he should obtain from the contract; and the legal consequences of a breach of such an undertaking . . . depend upon the nature of the event to which the breach gives rise and do not follow automatically from a prior classification of the undertaking as a 'condition' or a 'warranty'".

The term as to seaworthiness is such that it is particularly appropriate that the legal consequences of a breach should depend upon the particular breach. It is a term which can be breached in many ways. Some of the possible defects which it encompasses are very serious whilst others may be fairly trivial. A ship will not be seaworthy "if a nail is missing from one of the timbers of a wooden vessel or if proper medical supplies or two anchors are not on board at the time of sailing" (Upjohn LJ at p 62). It is particularly inappropriate to label such a term as a condition or warranty from the inception of the contract. In *Hong Kong Fir* it was decided that the need for twenty weeks of repairs, and replacement of the engine-room staff, were not sufficiently serious to give the charterer the right to terminate when the charter, the hire of the ship, was for twenty-four months. The breach was not one which deprived the charterer of "substantially the whole benefit which it was the intention of the parties . . . that he should obtain" (see *dictum* of Diplock LJ above).

If the term is an innominate or intermediate term, what is the test which is applied to determine if the breach gives the injured party a right to terminate as well as to claim damages? What makes the breach of an innominate term equivalent, in the legal result it produces, to a breach of a condition? As has been indicated, the test has been put in terms of whether the breach substantially deprives the innocent party of the whole of the benefit he was intended to derive from the contract (see also *Bunge Corp v Tradax Export SA* [1981] 1 WLR 711). This was the formulation adopted by Diplock LJ in *Hong Kong Fir*, who equated it (at p 66) with the test of whether a contract has been frustrated (see Chapter 20) — an equation which was also made by Upjohn LJ (at p 65). The test has also been put in terms of whether the breach went to the root of the contract (eg *Cehave NV v Bremer Handelsgesellschaft mbH; (The Hansa Nord)* [1975] 3 All ER 739 *per* Lord Denning MR at p 747, Roskill LJ at p 757).

4.   Flexibility — the benefit of the innominate term classification[3]

If a term is a condition, then, outside the special statutory exceptions noted above (see page 119), even a trivial breach of it will justify the innocent party in terminating. There is no necessary connection between the seriousness of the factual consequences of the breach and its legal consequences. For example, in *Arcos v Ronaasen (EA) & Son* [1933] AC 470:

There was a contract for the sale of barrel staves half an inch thick. There was held to be a breach of the condition that the goods should correspond with their description when the staves varied from that thickness by up to one-sixteenth of an inch. The variation caused no problems with their use but this did not prevent the finding of a breach of condition.

(See also *Re Moore & Co Ltd and Landauer & Co Ltd* [1921] 2 KB 519 below.) The party in breach may lose the entire contract because of a breach of condition which has little practical effect. This is obviously not the case where the term is innominate and the factual consequences of the breach are directly related to the availability of the right to terminate. The innominate term classification allows the law to be flexible in its approach to the legal consequences of a breach.

One aspect of termination being related to the seriousness of the breach is that a minor breach cannot be used by the innocent party to escape from a contract which has ceased to be a "good deal" from his point of view. In *Hong Kong Fir* [1962] 2 QB 26 the owners of the vessel received substantial damages in the wake of the charterer's wrongful termination of the contract. This was because the charter market had dropped. Any substitute charter had to be at a much lower rate than that provided for by the relevant contract. The drop in the market probably explains why the charterer was eager to claim to be entitled to terminate the contract. By the time he did so he could get another ship more cheaply. Had the term been a condition, the charterer could have escaped from the contract and hired another ship more cheaply. This would have defeated part of the object of the contract, the allocation of the risk of market changes for the period of the charter. The flexibility of the innominate term classification prevents a minor breach from being used in this way.

The Hansa Nord (Cehave NV v Bremer Handelsgesellschaft mbH) [1975] 3 All ER 739 provides a good example of the benefits of the flexibility of the innominate term. The facts were as follows:

A German company had contracted to sell citrus pulp pellets to a Dutch company for about £100,000. The pellets had to come from Florida and it was a term of the contract that they should be shipped "in good condition". On arrival it was discovered that some of the pellets had been damaged by overheating, and by that time the market price for sound goods had dropped to about £86,000. The purchasers refused to take delivery and claimed to be entitled to terminate the contract on the basis that the goods had not been shipped "in good condition" and that it was a condition of the contract that they should be. Whilst the dispute was in progress the pellets were sold to a third party for about £30,000. That third party then sold them for that same reduced price, approximately £30,000, to the original purchasers. The original purchasers were able to use them as originally intended in the manufacture of cattle food, although in slightly reduced proportions.

The Court of Appeal had to decide whether the purchasers had been correct in their claim to be able to terminate for breach of the term that the goods would be shipped "in good condition". It was held that the purchasers were not correct. The breach entitled them to damages but not to terminate, and they were themselves liable for wrongful termination. The Court of Appeal refused to regard the term as a condition. It was a term, the legal consequences of the breach of which depended upon its factual consequences, ie an innominate term. The particular breach was not sufficiently serious to give rise to the right to terminate. It did not go to the root of the contract. This was evident from the fact that the pellets had been used to make cattle food in almost exactly the same way as they would have been, had they not been damaged.

The advantages of the innominate term classification are obvious in *Hansa Nord*. Had the term been a condition, the breach would have allowed the purchaser to terminate. This would have been his right despite the fact that the grounds for his decision to terminate were obviously purely pecuniary, rather than based on the actual breach. The damage to the goods barely affected the purchaser's use of them. The flexibility provided by the innominate term classification allowed the court to look at the seriousness of the breach to determine the availability of a right to terminate. (But see Weir [1976] CLJ 33.)

The *Hansa Nord* is also important on a more technical level. The sellers had argued that no terms of the contract could be classified as innominate because the contract was one dealing with the sale of goods, and what is now the Sale of Goods Act 1979 (formerly 1893) refers only to conditions and warranties (but see below). However, the Court of Appeal held that sale of goods contracts should be treated in the same way as other contracts, and that the innominate term classification should be recognized in such contracts. Section 62(2) preserves the common law in so far as the Act does not conflict with it, and this allows for a type of term additional to those specifically dealt with by the Act.

The attempt to avoid trivial breaches giving rise to the right to terminate can also be seen in other situations. As has already been indicated, the legal effect of breaches of the conditions implied by ss 13–15 Sale of Goods Act 1979 has been modified by a new s 15A, inserted by the Sale and Supply of Goods Act 1994. If the buyer does not deal as consumer, where the breach is so slight that it would be unreasonable for the buyer to reject, then the term is deemed not to be a condition but a warranty and the buyer cannot reject the goods but has only a right to claim damages. Before the amendment made by the 1994 Act, the implied terms always remained conditions in the full sense and the buyer had a right to reject the goods for any breach, even the most trivial. Under those circumstances, before the insertion of s 15A, the courts sought to use other means to diminish the impact of the statutory classification of the terms as conditions. In *Hansa Nord* if the buyer was to have no right to terminate, the court had to decide that, despite the damage, the citrus pulp pellets were merchantable, ie that there was no breach of the condition implied by s 14(2) Sale of Goods Act 1893. The court so found and the buyer had no right to reject. In effect, the flexible approach indicated in *Hong Kong Fir* was reflected in the courts' narrowing of the contents of the implied conditions for any breach of which the statute provided that the buyer had to have a right to reject the goods. Section 13 of the Sale of Goods Act 1979 implies a condition into a contract of sale that the goods should correspond with their description. In *Ashington Piggeries v Christopher Hill* [1972] AC 441 the House of Lords made it clear that not all terms describing the goods were part of the description for the purposes of s 13, but only those which "identified" the goods. The need for such restriction can be seen in the older decisions, to which a critical approach came to be taken. In the past a broader application of s 13 resulted in some quite minor breaches being treated as breaches of condition. In *Re Moore & Co Ltd and Landauer & Co Ltd* [1921] 2 KB 519:

> The contract concerned the sale of tinned fruit. The tins were stated to be packed in cases containing thirty tins each. The correct number of tins was delivered but they were packed in cases containing twenty-four tins each.

The court held that the difference in the number of tins per case meant that there was a breach of the condition that the goods should correspond with their description. This recognition of a minor technical breach as a breach of condition was criticised. It was seen as being out of line with the general approach taken in contract law since *Hong Kong Fir*, and as being "due for fresh examination" (see *Reardon Smith Line Ltd* v *Hansen-Tangen* [1976] 1 WLR 989 *per* Lord Wilberforce at p 998).

It was in keeping with the post-*Hong Kong Fir* approach that the Law Commission should recommend that, in contracts between business people, a breach of the implied conditions in the Sale of Goods Act 1979 should cease to give rise to an automatic right to terminate however trivial the breach (Law Com No 160, Cmnd 137, 1987). In relation to contracts between business people, the Law Commission recommended that a breach of such a term should be treated as a breach of warranty where the breach is so slight that it would be unreasonable for the buyer to terminate. It was this recommendation which led to the enactment of the Sale and Supply of Goods Act 1994 and the addition of s 15A to the Sale of Goods Act 1979, modifying the legal effect of breach of the conditions implied by ss 13–15 of that Act. This does not equate such terms with innominate terms, as the right to terminate is absent only if the breach is fairly minor. If a term is innominate, the right to terminate is present only if the breach is serious. The emphasis is different, but the changes in the law do move the sale of goods legislation more into line with the flexible *Hong Kong Fir* approach which links the availability of the right to terminate to the seriousness of the factual consequences of the breach.

The Law Commission's recommendation was based upon the potential injustice of the automatic right to terminate. It was also based upon the distorting effect which that known automatic right to terminate could have upon a court faced with an argument that one of the implied conditions had been breached in a trivial way. It could lead the court to construe the implied condition inventively so that it was not breached. This could have been unfortunate in relation to future attempts to apply the implied condition and, in the instant case, the injured party could have been left without any remedy. In *Hansa Nord*, had there not been an express term that the goods would be shipped "in good condition", the effect of construing the implied condition of merchantability so that it was not breached would have left the buyers without any remedy for the damage to the goods.

The Law Commission's approach to contracts between business people is to be contrasted with its recommendations in relation to the situation where one party "deals as consumer". In those cases it was recommended that the implied terms should continue to have full effect as conditions even in relation to the most trivial breach. The benefits of certainty were seen to outweigh those of flexibility. Most disputes over defective goods do not come before the court and, when trying to settle a dispute, the consumer was perceived to need the leverage which could be derived from an automatic right to tell the supplier that he was rejecting the goods for a breach of condition. The automatic right to terminate, with no scope for the business person to say, legitimately, that the goods were not sufficiently defective for that right to be present, was seen as some counterweight to the superior bargaining power of the business person. The Law Commission proposals have also been followed on this point. The new s 15A only affects the right to reject goods if the buyer does not "deal as consumer". (The definition of "deals as consumer" is the same as under the Unfair Contract Terms Act 1977 — s 61(5A) Sale of Goods Act 1979, as amended — see page 194.)

5. Conditions and the benefit of certainty

The development of the innominate term approach in *Hong Kong Fir* led to the argument that, in the absence of a label being placed on a term expressly by the parties, or by statute, the classification of the term depended entirely upon the factual effects of the breach. In other words the argument was that, in the absence of an express classification, all terms were innominate and a breach gave rise to the right to terminate only if it deprived the innocent party of substantially all the benefit that it was intended he should derive from the contract. This argument was dismissed by the House of Lords in *Bunge Corp v Tradax Export SA* [1981] 1 WLR 711 (see also *The Mihalis Angelos* [1971] 1 QB 164) where it was affirmed that the question whether the breach is such as substantially to deprive the innocent party of all the benefit it was intended that he should derive from the contract is relevant only after it has been decided that the term is innominate. The first question which must be asked is what sort of a term it is, ie a condition, a warranty, or an innominate term. If the term has not been labelled by statute or expressly by the parties, the test is that stated by Bowen LJ in *Bentsen* v *Taylor, Sons & Co* [1893] 2 QB 274 at p 281 (see above), ie which classification will fulfil the intention of the parties.

In *Bunge* [1981] 1 WLR 711 the term in question was found to be a condition despite the lack of any statutory or express classification. In that case:

> The contract concerned the sale of soya bean meal. The meal was to be shipped by the end of June 1975. By clause 7 the buyers had to give the sellers at least fifteen days' notice of the probable readiness of the vessel to load the meal. The fifteen days were to allow the sellers time to nominate a loading port and make sure the meal could be shipped from there at the appropriate time. The buyers gave notice on 17 June. The last shipment day within the contract was 30 June, and the notice provided less than the required fifteen-day interval. The sellers claimed to terminate the contract. The buyers disputed that termination.

The House of Lords held that clause 7 was a condition of the contract and breach of it gave the sellers the automatic right to terminate whatever the factual consequences of that breach. Lord Roskill said (at p 727):

> "While recognizing the modern approach and not being over-ready to construe terms as conditions unless the contract clearly requires the court so to do, none the less the basic principles of construction for determining whether or not a particular term is a condition remain as before, always bearing in mind on the one hand the need for certainty and on the other the desirability of not, when legitimate, allowing rescission where the breach complained of is highly technical and where damages would clearly be an adequate remedy."

In *Bunge* the court was dealing with a time clause in a mercantile contract, and this indicated the need for the certainty obtained by classifying the term as a condition — ie if the term is a condition, the innocent party knows that he has the right to terminate upon any breach of that term and he can do so immediately and can quickly try to find a substitute contract. He does not have to weigh up the seriousness of the consequences of the breach to see if he can terminate. If the term was innominate, he might decide that he had to wait to see further what the actual consequences of the breach were before he could risk claiming to be able to terminate.

Beyond the simple fact that the clause was a time clause in a mercantile contract, there were other factors pointing to the clause being a condition in *Bunge*. First, the contract was one of a chain of sales of the soya bean meal. Timely performance is obviously all the more important where a whole chain of sales is involved. Secondly, the sellers had to act upon the buyers' notification; they had to nominate a suitable port and ensure that the soya meal could be shipped from there on time. The dependence of the sellers' performance upon the buyers' timely notification indicated that the sellers should be able to terminate for any breach of the time clause.

6. Classification of terms not expressly labelled by the parties

The general impetus is towards the labelling of terms as innominate rather than as conditions because of the flexibility provided by that classification, but in "suitable cases" conditions will be found:

> "It remains true, as Lord Roskill said in *Cehave NV* v *Bremer Handelsge-sellschaft mbH (The Hansa Nord)*, that the courts should not be too ready to interpret contractual clauses as conditions. And I have myself commended, and continue to commend, the greater flexibility in the law of contracts to which *Hong Kong Fir* points the way ... But I do not doubt that in suitable cases, the courts should not be reluctant, if the intention of the parties as shown by the contract so indicates, to hold that an obligation has the force of a condition and that indeed they should usually do so in the case of time clauses in mercantile contracts" (Lord Wilberforce in *Bunge Corp* v *Tradax Export SA* [1981] 1 WLR 711 at pp 715–6).

Before addressing ourselves to what constitutes a "suitable case", it is worth noting that the question is basically "is the term a condition or an innominate term". The warranty label is unlikely to be used in the absence of a clear express or statutory classification (eg s 12(2) Sale of Goods Act 1979). The innominate term classification will be used instead. It does not matter if most breaches of the term in question would have minor factual consequences; they will give rise only to the right to damages and not to the right to terminate, but the innominate term classification also allows for termination in the odd case where the breach has very serious consequences (*Re Olympia & York Canary Wharf Ltd (No 2)* [1993] BCC 159 at pp 166–167).

In *Bunge Corp* v *Tradax Export SA* [1981] 1 WLR 711 Lord Wilberforce distinguished the time clause in that case and the seaworthiness clause in *Hong Kong Fir*. He pointed out (at p 715) that a term as to seaworthiness can be breached in many different ways:

> "the breaches which might occur of the [seaworthiness clause are] various. They might be extremely trivial, the omission of a nail; they might be extremely grave, a serious defect in the hull or in the machinery".

He considered that this made the term one in which it was appropriate for the legal consequences of the breach to depend upon the factual consequences. A time clause was "totally different in character":

"As to such a clause there is only one kind of breach possible, namely to be late".

However, although a clause like that in *Hong Kong Fir* can be breached in many different ways, and will usually be appropriately classified as an innominate term, the jump cannot be made from that conclusion to stating that a term which can be breached in only one way will normally be classified as a condition or a warranty. Even though a term may be breached in only one way, eg by being late, it may be capable of being breached to different degrees and there may be variations in the seriousness of the consequences which flow from any breach. The exception to this would seem to be in relation to an agreement to sell goods where the purported seller does not have title to the goods. In *Barber* v *NWS Bank plc* [1996] 1 All ER 906 the court had to consider the classification of an express term of a conditional sale agreement that, at the time the contract was made, the supplier was the owner of the goods. That was not the case as the goods were still subject to an earlier hire purchase agreement and the court found that the term was a condition, enabling the purchaser to terminate the contract. The view was taken that the term was distinguishable from those which admit "of different breaches, some of which are trivial" (at p 911). All breaches of the term were viewed as sufficiently serious to justify termination and thus the term had to be classified as a condition. This is based on the view that the transfer of ownership is fundamental to an agreement to sell, or a sale, and is consistent with the idea that any failure to transfer good title under a contract of sale leads to a total failure of consideration, allowing the purchaser to recover all the money paid, even though he, or she, has had considerable period of use of the goods (see page 528. See also the term implied by s 12(1) Sale of Goods Act 1979).

It should be emphasised that the question of classification is a matter of the parties' intention. However, as we have seen, the starting point should favour the innominate term and the basic question should be whether there is a reason to classify the term as a condition rather than as an innominate term. The basic pointers to a term being a condition are that the term is important to the contract as a whole and that certainty is required. The need for certainty, as an indicator of the intention that the term should be a condition, was referred to in *Bunge* (above) and reference to the importance of the term is well established (eg *Bentsen* v *Taylor, Sons & Co* [1893] 2 QB 274 *per* Bowen LJ at p 281 (see above)). The more important a term is perceived to be to the substance of the contract, the more likely it is to be found that it was intended to be a condition (see also *Glaholm* v *Hays* (1841) 2 Man & G 257 at p 266). More recently, consideration of the importance of the term, in deciding upon its classification, has been put in terms of its "commercial significance" (see below *State Trading Corporation of India* v *Golodetz Ltd* [1989] 2 Lloyd's Rep 277) — but the same point is being made. Although the main indicators of whether a term is to be construed as a condition are the importance of the term and the need for certainty, each case must be assessed as a whole to determine the parties' intention.

In *Bunge Corp* v *Tradax Export SA* [1981] 1 WLR 711 the House of Lords indicated that time clauses in mercantile contracts will normally be conditions because of the need for certainty. Consideration of time clauses will illustrate how the need for certainty and the importance of the term, or otherwise, aid its classification.

A time clause had to be considered in *Compagnie Commerciale Sucres et Denrées* v *C Czarnikow Ltd; (The Naxos)* [1990] 3 All ER 641:

> There was a contract for the sale of sugar. Delivery was to be to a vessel which was to be ready to load during May or June. The buyer was to give the seller not less than fourteen days' notice of expected readiness to load. By rule 14 of the standard term contract the buyer was entitled to call for delivery at any time within the contract period, provided he had given the requisite notice. The buyers gave the requisite notice for loading on 29 May. The sellers did not have the sugar ready to load on 29 May; on 3 June, having warned the sellers, the buyers terminated the contract and purchased a replacement cargo.

The House of Lords had to decide whether rule 14 was a condition giving the buyers the right to terminate when the sellers failed to deliver on the date specified for loading. The House of Lords held (Lord Brandon dissenting) that rule 14 was a condition and the buyers had been entitled to terminate. The clause was a time clause in a mercantile contract, but there were also more specific indications that the term was to be construed as a condition. The court found that compliance with the time clause was "crucially important" to the buyers. Had there been no delay it would in turn have enabled the buyers punctually to perform their own obligations to their customers. The situation was, as in *Bunge*, that of a chain of sales.

Time clauses in mercantile contracts will not always be construed as conditions. The situation as a whole must be considered. In *State Trading Corporation of India* v *Golodetz Ltd* [1989] 2 Lloyd's Rep 277, Kerr LJ said (at p 283):

> "At the end of the day, if there is no other more specific guide to the correct solution to a particular dispute, the court may have no alternative but to follow the general statement of Bowen LJ in *Bentsen* v *Taylor* . . . by making what is in effect a value judgement about the commercial significance of the term in question."

In that case the term in question contained a time limit and the contract was mercantile but its "commercial significance", or importance to the contract as a whole, meant that it was not construed as a condition. In that case:

> The contract was for the sale of a cargo of sugar. The sugar was to be paid for by a letter of credit which the buyers undertook to open within seven days. The sellers undertook to open two guarantees within seven days — one in respect of the sugar sale and the other in respect of another undertaking which they had made, to purchase from the buyers, within six months, goods to the value of 60 per cent of the sugar contract.

The Court of Appeal was asked to decide whether the provision of the second guarantee, the countertrade guarantee, within seven days was a condition of the contract. It was held that it was not. The "commercial significance of the term" indicated that it should not be treated as a condition. It did not affect the buyer's performance of the sugar contract. It was a time clause, but it did not relate to the main and immediate transaction but only to one which was to occur within six months. It was also relatively unimportant in financial terms. The more important guarantee was that relating to performance of the sugar contract, and the timely giving of that guarantee was expressly prevented from being a condition. It was felt that the provision of the countertrade guarantee within seven days could not be a condition when the undertaking to provide a guarantee of the sugar contract was much more important to the contract and was not a condition.

A time clause may be such that it does not require the certainty of the "condition" label. A time clause was not construed as a condition in *Bremer Handelsgesellschaft mbH* v *Vanden-Avenne Izegem PVBA* [1978] 2 Lloyd's Rep 109 because the clause did not set a definite time limit. The clause in question stated that the sellers were to advise the buyers "without delay" if shipment had become impossible for any one of a number of stated reasons. The question was whether it was a condition that such notification be made "without delay". Without a quantification of delay in terms of a stated time period, the House of Lords did not think that the term was to be construed as a condition. It was an innominate term. Similarly, "as soon as reasonably practicable" was too indefinite to be construed as a condition in *British and Commonwealth Holdings plc* v *Quadrex Holdings Inc* [1989] 3 All ER 492. In that case the contract was for the sale of shares in an unquoted private company trading in a very volatile sector. The possibility of changes in the value of the shares would have made the time of completion of the sale a condition had it been more specific. However, it must be remembered that the parties may have intended a term which looks indefinite to be a condition. For example, a term requiring notice "as soon as possible" might be construed as a condition if it was seen as very important to the contract. Such a conclusion would be assisted if trade practice made it possible to read "as soon as possible" as the more specific "within twenty-four hours" (see *Société Italo-Belge Pour le Commerce et l'Industrie SA* v *Palm and Vegetable Oils (Malaysia) Sdn Bhd* [1981] 2 Lloyd's Rep 695).

7. Express conditions and stated consequences

The parties can expressly make a term a condition, in the technical sense of that word, so that any breach of it, no matter how trivial, gives rise to the right to terminate. However, in considering whether the parties have expressly made a term a condition, in that sense, the courts are faced with the same opposing pulls of certainty and flexibility that we saw above. If it seems from the contract that the parties intended to make the term expressly a condition in the technical sense, then, if it is so construed, it will promote certainty and be in keeping with the ideal of freedom of contract. On the other hand, if the term can be breached in minor ways, a more inventive construction, which denies the term the status of a condition, will promote flexibility and will match the availability of the right to terminate to the seriousness of the breach. These opposing forces can be seen in the case law.

The word "condition" was used by the parties in *Schuler AG* v *Wickman Machine Tool Sales Ltd* [1973] 2 All ER 39 but it was not construed in its technical sense. In that case:

> Schuler, a German manufacturing company, made an agreement with Wickman for Wickman to have the sole right to sell Schuler's goods in the UK for about four and a half years. The agreement contained provisions relating to the promotion of Schuler's goods by Wickman. Clause 7 stated that it was a "condition" that one of

two named representatives of Wickman should visit six named UK automobile manufacturers each week. Clause 11 laid out the procedure for termination of the contract upon a "material breach" of the contract occurring, ie notice was to be given to remedy it within sixty days and if it was not remedied the contract could be terminated. In breach of clause 7, Wickman failed to carry out all of the specified visits to the six named automobile manufacturers.

Schuler argued that clause 7 was expressly made a condition of the contract and, as such, there was a right to terminate the contract for any breach of it no matter how trivial. Schuler argued that even one failure to visit, out of the 1,400 visits required during the course of the contract, gave them the right to terminate. The House of Lords (Lord Wilberforce dissenting) refused to accept that argument. It pointed out that the word "condition" had many meanings other than its technical one. In addition, their lordships thought that a construction was to be avoided if it produced an unreasonable result and there was an alternative construction available which did not. The court thought it would be unreasonable if any single breach of clause 7 gave the right to terminate, no matter how little at fault Wickman had been. The alternative which the court found, to help it avoid that unreasonable result, was to link clause 7 with clause 11. The use of the word "condition" in clause 7 was construed as relating to whether the breach was "material" within clause 11.

Lord Reid thought that the use of the word "condition" was a "strong indication" that the parties intended termination to be available on any breach of clause 7, but (at p 45):

"The fact that a particular construction leads to a very unreasonable result must be a relevant consideration. The more unreasonable the result the more unlikely it is that the parties can have intended it, and if they do intend it the more necessary it is that they should make that intention abundantly clear."

Any intention to use "condition" in its technical sense had not been made clear enough, under the circumstances, for Lord Reid and the other members of the majority in the House of Lords.

However, Lord Wilberforce thought that "condition" should have been construed technically. He gave little weight to the argument that such a construction was to be avoided on the grounds that it produced an unreasonable result. He said (at p 55):

"to call the clause arbitrary, capricious, or fantastic, or to introduce as a test of its validity the ubiquitous reasonable man ... is to assume, contrary to the evidence, that both parties to this contract adopted a standard of easygoing tolerance rather than one of aggressive, insistent punctuality and efficiency. This is not an assumption which I am prepared to make, nor do I think myself entitled to impose the former standard on the parties if their words indicate, as they plainly do, the latter."

The initial reaction to the construction put upon the word "condition" in *Schuler* v *Wickman* is that if the parties want to make it clear that they intend a term to be a condition in the technical sense, they should specify that breach of it is to give rise to the right to terminate. However, even if it is specified that one party has a right to terminate the contract upon the other party's failure to perform one of the contract terms, that term will not always be construed as a condition. In *Financings Ltd* v *Baldock* [1963] 2 QB 104:

Mr Baldock acquired a van from Financings Ltd under a hire purchase agreement. He paid £100 and was to pay monthly instalments of £28 for two years. Clause 8 provided that Financings had a right to terminate the contract if any instalment was more than ten days overdue. Clause 11 gave Financings the right to recover two-thirds of the total amount to be paid on any termination by them under Clause 8. Mr Baldock failed to make the first two payments on time and Financings terminated the contract and took back the van under Clause 8. Financings sold the van for £140.

Clause 11 was invalid as a penalty clause (see page 491), and Financings tried to claim a sum in excess of the two instalments due on the basis that Mr Baldock's breach had brought the contract to an end and they were entitled to receive damages to cover the loss of the contract. In effect, Financings tried to use their damages claim to achieve a result similar to that provided for in Clause 11, the clause which was ineffective because it was a penalty clause. The Court of Appeal denied them success by refusing to construe Clause 8 as a condition. The Court of Appeal held that although Clause 8 gave Financings the right to terminate, it was not a right to terminate on the basis of a breach of condition — nor was the breach sufficiently serious to give rise to the right to terminate (it was not a sufficiently serious breach of an innominate term). Financings had merely made use of a right to terminate which was expressly given by the contract, but that was their choice. Mr Baldock had not committed a breach which automatically entitled them to terminate. The court considered that any loss due to the termination of the contract was not due to his breach but merely to Financings' choice. On that basis their damages were limited to the two instalments owed. Even specifying a right to terminate may not be sufficiently specific for the term in question to be construed as a condition.

However, *Schuler* v *Wickman* and *Financings Ltd* v *Baldock* are to be contrasted with the more recent Court of Appeal decision in *Lombard North Central plc* v *Butterworth* [1987] 1 All ER 267. In that case:

Mr Butterworth obtained a computer from the finance company. The transaction was, in effect, one of hire purchase. Mr Butterworth was to pay £584 initially, followed by nineteen quarterly instalments of the same amount. Clause 2(a) made punctual payment "of the essence" of the contract. Clause 5 stated that failure to make due and punctual payment entitled the finance company to terminate the contract. Clause 6 provided that, on termination, the finance house was entitled to all arrears and to all future instalments which would have fallen due had the contract not been terminated. In the second year Mr Butterworth's payments were late but there was only one outstanding when the finance company terminated the contract under Clause 2(a). The computer was resold for only £172.88.

The Court of Appeal had to decide whether the finance company was restricted to the arrears owing at the time of termination of the contract or whether it could recover for the loss of the rest of the contract. The finance company could not claim under Clause 6 as such as it was a penalty clause (see page 492). After *Financings* v *Baldock* the question was whether it could claim for the loss of the rest of the contract on the basis that it had terminated for breach of a condition. It was decided that Clause 2(a), making "time of the essence", made payment on time a condition of the contract and any breach gave a right to terminate. The phrase "time of the essence" was well established as having that effect and the court thought that Clauses 5 and 6 strengthened that conclusion. Clause 6 was looked at in that way despite the fact that, as a penalty clause, it could not itself provide a basis for a similar claim. In short, putting in a clause stating that time was "of the essence" was seen as preventing the court from adopting the same line as that taken in *Financings* v *Baldock*. Clause 2(a), and its construction as a condition, prevented the court from saying that the finance company had a right to terminate but no right to claim for the loss of the rest of the contract. The effect was that the draftsman had largely managed to circumvent the risk of Clause 6 being struck down as a penalty. Nicholls LJ viewed the result "with considerable dissatisfaction". He contrasted the agreement in *Financings* v *Baldock* with that before the court (at p 280):

"The difference between these two agreements is one of drafting form, and wholly without substance. Yet under an agreement drafted in the first form, the owner's damages claim arising on his exercise of the power of termination is confined to damages for breaches up to the date of termination, whereas under an agreement drafted in the second form the owner's damages claim, arising on his acceptance of an identical breach as a repudiation of the agreement, will extend to damages for loss of the whole transaction."

But he also said (at p 278):

"it was a matter of importance to the plaintiffs that the agreed instalments should be paid, and should be paid promptly. I can see no reason to doubt that the interest charges were calculated by reference to the agreed hire instalment dates, on the footing that the instalments would be paid regularly and with reasonable promptness. To the plaintiffs a hirer who is repeatedly and significantly late with his payments and who has to be chased with reminders and warnings, time after time, is an unattractive hirer whose transaction may eventually become an unprofitable one".

There may well have been a good commercial reason for a clause which, at first sight, seems unreasonable.

The construction which the court arrived at in *Lombard North Central* v *Butterworth* is in keeping with the idea of freedom of contract and the promotion of certainty in commercial dealings. It does not match the availability of the right to terminate to the seriousness of the actual breach as would have occurred had the court construed the clause more inventively, as in *Schuler* v *Wickman*[4]. In *A/S Awilco of Oslo* v *Fulvia SpA di Navigazione of Cagliari; (The Chikuma)* [1981] 1 All ER 652, in the context of a charterparty Lord Bridge commented on the opposing principles which the court may face (at pp 658–9):

"It has often been pointed out that shipowners and charterers bargain at arm's length. Neither class has such a preponderance of bargaining power as to be in a position to oppress the other. They should be in a position to look after themselves by contracting only on terms which are acceptable to them. Where as here, they embody in their contracts common form clauses, it is, to my mind, of overriding importance that their meaning and legal effect should be certain and well understood. The ideal at which the courts should aim in construing such clauses, is to produce a result such that in any given situation both parties seeking legal advice as to their rights and obligations can expect the same clear and confident answer from their advisers and neither will be tempted to embark on long and expensive litigation in the belief that victory depends on winning the sympathy of the court. This ideal may never be fully attainable, but we shall certainly never even approximate to it unless we strive to follow clear and consistent principles and steadfastly refuse to be blown off course by the supposed merits of individual cases."

In other words where the parties are commercial people, of roughly equal bargaining power, the impetus towards certainty is greater than that towards achieving a situation where the availability of the right to terminate relates to the seriousness of the breach. In that case the contract for the charter of the ship (the charterparty) contained a clause which stated that payment of hire was "to be made . . . in cash in United States currency, monthly in advance . . . otherwise failing the punctual and regular payment of the hire . . . the owners shall be at liberty to withdraw the vessel from the service of the charterers". The eighty-first monthly hire payment was due on 22 January 1976. A transfer of money to the owners' bank was arranged for that date but on such terms that the owners would not start to receive interest on it until 26 January and would have to pay the bank "lost interest" to withdraw it before then. It had long been accepted that a commercially recognized transfer of funds which gave the payee immediate access to them sufficed instead of actual cash. The House of Lords held that, as the owners would have had to have paid about £70 to obtain the money on 22 January, the hire had not been paid on time and the owners had been right in claiming to be able to terminate.

C.   Entire contracts

We have already seen that contingent promissory conditions may set the order of performance. The performance of an obligation of one party may be a condition precedent to the other party becoming obliged to perform. This can lead to cases where the situation is that of an "entire contract" and one party is obliged to perform his side of the contract before the other party becomes obliged to pay him. The harsh result which can be achieved in such cases is illustrated by *Cutter* v *Powell* (1795) 6 Term Rep 320, 101 ER 573:

> Mr Cutter had signed on as second mate on the "Governor Parry" for a voyage from Jamaica to Liverpool. It was stated that he would receive 30 guineas "provided he proceeds, continues and does his duty" from Jamaica to Liverpool. The ship sailed on 2 August and arrived at Liverpool on 9 October. Unfortunately, Mr Cutter died on 20 September, before the ship reached Liverpool. His widow was suing for payment for the work he had done before his death. The usual rate of pay was £4 per month. The voyage was one which should have taken about two months.

The court held that the contract was entire. There was no obligation to pay for any work done unless the voyage was completed and, as Mr Cutter did not complete the voyage, his widow could not claim any payment. Mr Cutter's completion of the voyage was a condition precedent to the obligation to pay for the work he had done. This seems harsh, but the court was obviously influenced in its conclusion by the fact that 30 guineas was much greater than the sum which he would have expected to earn under a contract based on payment by the month rather than for the whole voyage. Lord Kenyon CJ said:

> "He stipulated to receive the larger sum if the whole duty were performed, and nothing unless the whole of that duty were performed; it was a kind of insurance."

In other words there was good reason, in the amount contracted for, to regard Mr Cutter's completion of the voyage as a condition precedent to any obligation to pay him. The conclusion reached in *Cutter* v *Powell* would have been otherwise if the contract had not been entire but severable, ie if the obligation to act as second mate from Jamaica to Liverpool had been divided up so that the corresponding obligation was to pay so much for each month of the voyage. Finding that a contract is severable, rather than entire, is one way of avoiding the sort of result that was reached in *Cutter v Powell*[5].

Sumpter v Hedges [1898] 1 QB 673 provides another example of the operation of the rule on entire contracts. In that case:

> Mr Hedges contracted with Mr Sumpter for Mr Sumpter to build two houses on his land for the sum of £565. Mr Sumpter did part of the work, to the value of £333, but his financial circumstances were such that he could not complete the work. Mr Hedges finished the houses himself. In doing so he made use of unused materials which belonged to Mr Sumpter and which he had left on Mr Hedges' land.

The question was whether Mr Sumpter could recover payment in relation to the work which he had carried out in erecting the houses. The court said that he could not. The contract was for a lump sum to be paid upon completion of the houses and he could not succeed in his claim when he had not done that.

Some mitigation of the entire contracts rule occurs when the work done by one party is adopted by the other party, whom it has benefited. The benefiting party will then have to pay for the work done. (The action is then one for *quantum meruit* — a restitutionary action, see Chapter 22.) On the same basis, Mr Hedges paid Mr Sumpter the value of Mr Sumpter's materials which he, Mr Hedges, had used on the houses after Mr Sumpter stopped work. He did not have to pay for the work Mr Sumpter had done on the houses because it could not be said that his adoption of the work was a matter on which he could act "voluntarily". He did not have sufficient choice in the matter. He either had to finish the houses himself or have the nuisance of incomplete buildings on his land. In contrast, he had a fully effective range of choices open to him when he decided to use Mr Sumpter's materials in the completion of the houses.

However, the greater mitigation of the entire contracts rule came with the idea of "substantial performance". In *Hoenig v Isaacs* [1952] 2 All ER 176:

> Mr Isaacs contracted with Mr Hoenig for the decoration and furnishing of his flat for £750. Mr Hoenig fulfilled the contract except in relation to some defects in a bookcase and a wardrobe, costing about £55 to rectify.

Mr Hoenig was able to recover the sum due under the contract less the sum Mr Isaacs could claim in damages for the defects (the cost of putting them right). Mr Hoenig had "substantially performed".

"Substantial performance" may simply be a matter of correctly identifying what is required for fulfilment of the condition precedent. Somervell LJ distinguished the case before him from that of *Cutter v Powell*. He said (at p 178):

> "[*Cutter v Powell*] clearly decided that his continuing as mate during the whole of the voyage was a condition precedent to payment. It did not decide that if he had completed the main purpose of the contract, namely serving as mate for the whole voyage, the defendant could have repudiated his liability by establishing that in the course of the voyage, the sailor had, possibly through inadvertence, failed on some occasion in his duty as mate whereby some damage had been caused".

He continued (at p 179):

> "The question here is whether in a contract for work and labour for a lump sum payable on completion the defendant can repudiate liability under the contract on the ground that the work though 'finished' or 'done' is in some respects not in accordance with the contract."

This indicates that the idea of "substantial performance" depends upon asking whether the work has been "done", albeit with defects. In *Bolton* v *Mahadeva* [1972] 2 All ER 1322, the idea of "substantial performance" did not entitle the contractor to recover. In that case:

> Mr Mahadeva had contracted with Mr Bolton for the installation of a central heating system for £560. The system was defective and it would have cost about £175 to make it function correctly. There were fumes in the living room and, on average, the house was 10 per cent less warm than it should have been, although in some rooms it was as much as 30 per cent colder.

Mr Bolton had not "substantially performed" and could not recover the contract price with damages for the defects set off against it. Here the judgments indicate a general assessment of the extent to which the performance carried out differs from that required by the contract. Cairns LJ said (at p 1324):

> "The main question in the case is whether the defects in workmanship ... were of such character and amount that the plaintiff could not be said to have substantially performed his contract. That is, in my view, clearly the legal principle which has to be applied in cases of this kind."

The explanation of substantial performance being sufficient to enable a claim to payment to be made may be that:

> "it is frequently correct to say that absolutely exact and complete performance by the plaintiff is not a condition precedent to the duty of the defendant. If substantial performance by the plaintiff was sufficient to charge the defendant, then such substantial performance was the only condition and the requirement has been exactly fulfilled." (Corbin, *Conditions in the Law of Contract* (1919) 28 Yale LJ 739 at p 759.)

The Law Commission has criticised cases like *Bolton* v *Mahadeva* and recommended that the party whose performance is not in keeping with the contract, and whom the entire contracts rule deprives of payment, should receive some payment for the benefit he has conferred on the other party (Law Com no 121, *Pecuniary Restitution for Breach of Contract* (1983)). But there has been no move to implement that recommendation and Brian Davenport QC added a strong note of dissent to the report. He concluded that, in almost all contracts of any substance, provision is now made for staged payment (ie payment as and when a stage of the work is completed) thus avoiding the problem posed by the entire contracts rule. However, he thought that the rule served a useful purpose which the majority's recommendation would undermine. He stated:

> "The so-called mischief which the report is intended to correct is therefore likely only to exist in relation to small, informal contracts of which the normal example will be a contract between a householder and a jobbing builder to carry out a particular item of work. Experience has shown that it is all too

common for such builders not to complete one job of work before moving on to the next. The effect of the report is to remove from the householder almost the only effective sanction he has against the builder not completing the job. In short he is prevented from saying with any legal effect, 'Unless you come back and finish the job I shan't pay you a penny'."

Footnotes

(1) Express classification itself may not be without difficulties. See p 128.

(2) Of course the actual breach will be known to the court — see *Poussard* v *Spiers* (1876) 1 QBD 410.

(3) Brownsword (1992) Journal of Contract Law 83.

(4) Bojczuk [1987] JBL 353; Beale (1988) 104 LQR 355; Opeskin (1990) 106 LQR 293; Wilkin (1990) LMCLQ 16.

(5) In relation to salaries or wages the common law is assisted by s 2 Apportionment Act 1870 which states that "all rents, annuities, dividends, and other periodical payments in the nature of income . . . shall . . . be considered as accruing from day to day".

Chapter 9

Exemption clauses

1. Introduction

Exemption clauses have proved to be one of the most interesting areas of contract law in recent years. It is an area which has provoked litigation and legislation and often involves a balancing of the competing interests of consumer protection and freedom of contract. The main general legislation in this area is the Unfair Contract Terms Act 1977, which is considered in detail in Chapter 10. In addition, although its application is not restricted to exemption clauses, this area is now also considerably affected by the EC Directive on Unfair Terms in Consumer Contracts ([1993] OJ L 95/29). The Regulations implementing the Directive are considered in Chapter 11.

2. Definitions

At a basic level an exemption clause is one which excludes or limits, or appears to exclude or limit, liability for breach of contract, or other liability arising by way of tort, bailment, or statute.

It should be noted that the exemption clause may seek to exclude totally a liability or merely to limit it. The terms exemption clause and exclusion clause are often loosely used to encompass both situations but, in an effort to avoid confusion, the practice adopted here is to use exemption clause as a general term, encompassing both exclusion and limitation clauses. The term exclusion clauses will be restricted to those clauses which remove, or purport to remove, liability. The label limitation clause will be used solely for those clauses which do not remove, or purport to remove, liability entirely but, for example, restrict or purport to restrict damages payable on a breach of contract to a specified sum. (See Yates, *Exclusion Clauses in Contracts* (2nd ed, 1982) pp 33–41, Beale, Bishop, Furmston, *Contract Cases and Materials* (2nd ed, 1990) pp 679–680 for a more extensive breakdown of types of exemption clause.)

Coote identified a problem with the above type of basic definition (Coote, *Exception Clauses* (1964) Chapters 1 and 10). An example will help to explain the difficulty. Consider the situation where X has agreed to sell goods to Y and to deliver them by a certain date. The contract contains a clause designed to prevent X having to pay damages for breach if late delivery is caused by industrial action. X may have put in a term stating that liability for late delivery is excluded where it is caused by industrial action. Alternatively, X may have specified that he is obliged to deliver by that stated date only if there is no industrial action. The same end result can be achieved by two different forms of clause. The first possible way of achieving the desired result is by using a straightforward exclusion clause. The second possibility is to use a clause which defines the initial obligation in such a way that there is no obligation to deliver by the stated time if industrial action occurs. The fact that the same result can be achieved by the two approaches leads to the argument that an exclusion clause cannot be regarded as a distinct type of clause but merely one of the clauses defining the obligations under the contract, whatever form it takes (for contrasting judicial approaches on this, see *Photo Production Ltd* v *Securicor Transport Ltd* [1980] AC 827 *per* Lord Wilberforce at pp 842–843 and *per* Lord Diplock at p 851). For the most part, the courts assume that an exclusion clause is a distinct type of clause, removing liability for breach of an existing obligation. They may even be content to regard a clause as an exclusion clause without any consideration of the fact that it is, in form, a definition of the obligation (eg *J Evans & Son (Portsmouth)* v *Andrea Merzario Ltd* [1976] 1 WLR 1078). However, it must be borne in mind that an exclusion clause can simply be seen as part of the definition of the obligation. In particular, difficult borderline cases arise under the Unfair Contract Terms Act 1977. It is sometimes necessary to determine whether a clause should be regarded as an exclusion clause, and subject to the Act, or merely a definition of the parties' obligations, and not subject to the Act (see Macdonald (1992) 12 LS 277; Adams & Brownsword (1988) 104 LQR 94).

It should be noted that this problem with definition cannot arise in relation to a limitation clause. Such a clause concedes the existence of the initial obligation and merely purports to place a limitation upon what happens when that obligation is not fulfilled. It is distinct from the definition of the initial obligation.

It should also be noted that basically the operation of the Unfair Contract Terms Act 1977 is confined to exemption clauses, whereas the Unfair Terms in Consumer Contracts Regulations 1999 apply more generally and may avoid the difficulties occassioned by the need to classify clauses.

3. Standard form contracts

Exemption clauses are often found in standard form contracts. This can lead to the allegation that they have been imposed as part of a "take it or leave it" package by the party with the superior bargaining position; hence the alternative label of contracts of adhesion. The effect of standard form contracts is often such that the party against whom the exemption clause is being used had no knowledge that it was a term of the contract (see below). In such circumstances it would hardly be surprising if the fairness of exemption clauses was questioned, particularly where a business person is seeking to rely upon an exemption clause against a consumer.

This sort of problem led to the enactment of the Unfair Contract Terms Act 1977. This Act prevents the use of some exemption clauses entirely and renders others ineffective unless they satisfy the requirement of reasonableness. Before the Act the common law tried to respond to the problem of objectionable exemption clauses. It was possible for the courts to take a restrictive approach to the construction of an exemption clause and limit its effectiveness by finding that it did not cover the particular breach which had occurred. Similarly, the courts found some flexibility in the rules relating to incorporation of contract terms. They could find that the exemption clause was not part of the contract at all. Some of the older case law relating to exemption clauses must now be viewed with caution. The existence of the Unfair Contract Terms Act 1977 means that the devices developed by the common law to deal with exemption clauses may now be used more sparingly by the courts. The Unfair Contract Terms Act 1977 has the advantage that it often allows the court openly to weigh the factors indicating whether the clause is "reasonable". Such calculations of reasonableness must have influenced the courts' approach to their use of the common law devices, but it can now often be considered openly, with arguments from both sides specifically directed to it. However, it should be borne in mind that not all types of contract are subject to the Unfair Contract Terms Act 1977 and the courts may be more willing to use the common law devices when faced with a contract excluded from the Act. It should also be noted that the EC Directive applies a "fairness" test to terms which have *not been individually negotiated* in contracts between consumers and sellers or suppliers, ie basically the Directive/Regulations focus on the problems of standard form contracts in the consumer context.

However, it should not be assumed that standard form contracts, with their exemption clauses, are always devices for the abuse of a superior bargaining position. There are advantages to be gained from the use of standard form contracts. A standard form contract may be used to speed up the contracting process and reduce the costs involved in arriving at a concluded contract. This is unobjectionable if the standard form contract is a fair allocation of risk. The standard form may be one used throughout a particular trade, arrived at by negotiation, on equal terms, between representatives of those using it on both sides (eg both buyers and sellers of a particular commodity, or hirers and those to whom they hire a type of equipment). Under such circumstances the exemption clause may merely represent an allocation of risk to the person best able to insure against it. A limitation of risk may be accompanied by a low charge to the other party.

4.   Three basic questions

When considering exemption clauses, there are three basic questions to be considered:

- (a) Incorporation — is the clause part of the contract?
- (b) Construction — is the clause appropriately worded to cover what has occurred?
- (c) Legislation — basically, is the clause affected by the Unfair Contract Terms Act 1977 or the Regulations implementing the EC Directive on Unfair Terms in Consumer Contracts?

Questions (a) and (b) are discussed on pages 139–159 and 159–174 respectively. Question (c) is dealt with in Chapters 10 and 11.

Exemption clauses and third parties

Before embarking upon a discussion of incorporation and construction, brief mention should be made of the additional problem of exemption clauses and third parties. The problem is one of privity of contract, and Chapter 18 should be consulted. A brief outline of the situation in relation to exemption clauses is, however, given at the end of this chapter (see p 174).

A. Incorporation

1. Introduction

The first question to be considered is whether the exemption clause has become a term of the contract. This is the issue of incorporation. It should be noted that the same basic rules apply to incorporation of all terms, whether they are exemption clauses or not. The discussion of incorporation largely takes place here, in the context of exemption clauses, because it is in relation to such clauses that the issue is often raised. Under consideration here are clauses in written documents; it is unlikely that an exemption clause will have simply been stated orally by one party to another, but on the question generally of whether an oral statement is a term of the contract see page 92.

At first sight the question of incorporation of a clause might be thought of as an uncomplicated matter, simply requiring the determination of what the parties agreed to. Certainly, incorporation poses no problems where both parties have actual knowledge of all the terms contained in the offer which was accepted. Problems arise because there is often no actual knowledge of all the terms, and incorporation cannot be said to be based upon any simple notion of what the parties agreed to. Even when one party has been alerted that a document contains important clauses, designed to be part of the contract, he will not always read it. He may even sign it without reading it. Such signature will ensure that the clauses become terms of the contract even though that party has no actual knowledge of their content (see p 140). Incorporation of clauses from unsigned documents can also occur, even though there is no actual knowledge of their content (see p 145). In short, incorporation is not a matter of subjective agreement to the terms. The "agreement" is looked for objectively. It has become a question of whether or not the parties are to be taken to have "agreed to" a particular set of terms according to the rules worked out by the court for determining the question of incorporation.

To allow incorporation without actual knowledge, and even without signature, obviously opens the way for one party to take advantage of another. This is particularly so where one party has a set of standard terms which he wishes to incorporate into each contract he makes. This is often the case with contracts between business people and consumers, and the lack of any real opportunity to become acquainted with terms may be relevant to their fairness under the Unfair Terms in Consumer Contracts Regulations 1999. It could be said that if one party is not sufficiently careful of his own interests to inform himself of all the terms on which he is contracting, then he can only blame himself for any unacceptable terms which he did not know about. However, with long standard form documents it is understandable if all clauses are not read before the document is signed and, where there has been incorporation without signature, there may not even have been knowledge of the existence of the clauses. Particularly in the business/consumer situation, there may also be a feeling that there is no point in reading the standard clauses as they will not be open to negotiation. Against this background, when the issue of incorporation has arisen, the courts have attempted to maintain some balance between the parties (see p 148). In other words, the cases show some reaction against the perceived unfairness produced by our current general rules on incorporation. It is interesting to note that Atiyah has identified these present rules as stemming from the courts' reaction to juries favouring consumers in litigation against railway companies and the perceived need then to protect those companies (Atiyah, *Rise and Fall of Freedom of Contract*, (1979) p 731). However, it should again be emphasised that the Unfair Contract Terms Act 1977 will now often provide a direct means of attacking "objectionable" exemption clauses which have become terms of the contract, and the Regulations on Unfair Terms in Consumer Contracts 1999 apply a test of fairness to standard terms in the consumer context more generally.

2. Signature

Incorporation of a clause by signature is basically a very mechanical process. It leaves little room for any questioning of the incorporation of the clause into the contract and has the benefit of certainty. The relevant clause will be incorporated into the contract if it is contained in a contractual document which has been signed by the person seeking to deny that the clause is part of the contract. This is obviously subject to a claim of fraud, or misrepresentation, or *non est factum* but, in the absence of such a claim, signature will act to incorporate the clause whether the person signing had any knowledge of the clause or not. *L'Estrange* v *F Graucob Ltd* [1934] 2 KB 394 illustrates this point:

> Miss L'Estrange was the owner of a cafe in Llandudno. She purchased a cigarette vending machine from Graucob Ltd. The machine proved to be defective. She claimed that Graucob Ltd were in breach of an implied term that the machine was reasonably fit for its purpose. Graucob Ltd denied that any such term could be implied. They relied upon a clause in the order form, which the plaintiff had signed, which said "any express or implied condition, statement, or warranty, statutory or otherwise not stated herein is hereby excluded". This clause was in "regrettably small print" and Miss L'Estrange had not read it and did not know of its contents.

The court decided that Miss L'Estrange's signature on the order form containing the clause meant that her total lack of awareness of the exemption clause was irrelevant. The clause prevented the term from being implied, and Graucob were not in breach of contract despite the defects in the vending machine.

In the recent case of *Grogan* v *Robin Meredith Plant Hire Ltd* [1996] CLC 1127, it was emphasised that in order for signature to incorporate terms, the document signed must be a contractual one. Therefore signature of a time sheet, which had an obvious and purely administrative purpose in the working of an existing contract, did not incorporate clauses printed on it as it did not "purport to have contractual effect". More generally, the question seems to be how the reasonable person would have viewed the document, taking account of "the nature and purpose of the document" and the "circumstances of its use between the parties", ie in that context would the reasonable person have viewed it as a document intended to contain contract terms. This does not make any significant inroad on the approach taken in *L'Estrange* v *Graucob* and should be distinguished from incorporation of unsigned documents through "reasonably sufficient notice" (see below). In the context of a signed document there is no requirement of notice. It is merely that in the absence of knowledge, a signing party should not be contractually bound by clauses printed on what the world at large would take to be a non-contractual document.

However, even where the contract terms were embodied in a signed contractual document, misrepresentation as to the effect of the exemption clause came to the aid of the person seeking to deny the effectiveness of that clause in *Curtis* v *Chemical Cleaning and Dyeing Co* [1951] 1 KB 805:

> Mrs Curtis took a white satin wedding dress to the defendants' shop to be cleaned. The assistant asked her to sign a document headed "Receipt". Mrs Curtis asked about the "Receipt" and was told that it stated that the cleaners would not accept liability for damage to beads and sequins. The "Receipt" actually contained a clause stating "This article. . . is accepted on condition that the company is not liable for any damage however arising". Owing to the cleaners' negligence the fabric of Mrs Curtis' dress was stained, but the cleaners argued that they were not liable for this damage because of the exemption clause in the "Receipt".

The wording of the exemption clause was very wide and could have covered damage to the fabric of the dress, but, despite Mrs Curtis' signature, the Court of Appeal held that the cleaners could not rely upon the clause to remove their liability. The contents of the exemption clause had been innocently misrepresented as confined to limiting liability for negligent damage to the beads and sequins. It could not assist them when damage had occurred to the fabric of the dress. (See also *Harvey* v *Ventilatoren-Fabrik Oelde GmbH* (1989) 8 Tr LR 138.)

The restrictions on the basic approach taken in *L'Estrange* v *Graucob* are very limited, and it is a very artificial approach to determining the content of the parties' agreement. On occasion, this artificiality has been noted. In *McCutcheon* v *David MacBrayne Ltd* [1964] 1 WLR 125 Lord Devlin considered what difference it should make whether the document in question had been signed or not. He said (at p 133):

> "If it were possible for your Lordships to escape from the world of make-believe which the law has created into the real world in which transactions of this sort are actually done, the answer would be short and simple. It should make no difference whatever. This sort of document is not meant to be read, still less to be understood. Its signature is in truth about as significant as a handshake that marks the formal conclusion of a bargain." (See, also *Jones* v *Northampton BC* (1990) *The Times* 21 May, Lexis, Ralph Gibson LJ; *Levison* v *Patent Steam Cleaning Co* [1978] 1 QB 69, Lord Denning MR at p 78; *Bridge* v *Campbell Discount* [1962] 1 All ER 385, Lord Denning at p 399.)

Elsewhere there has been a move away from the basic approach in *L'Estrange*. In the Canadian case of *Tilden Rent-A-Car* v *Clendenning* (1978) 83 DLR (3d) 400 unusual and onerous printed clauses were not incorporated and the line was taken that signature can only be relied upon as showing assent to a document when it is reasonable for the person relying on the signed document to believe that the signatory assented to its contents. There have been suggestions that such a line might not be that far away from development by the English courts. *Grogan* v *Robin Meredith Plant Hire Ltd,* above, for example, has been seen as potentially a movement in that direction (McKendrick *Contract Law* 4th ed at p 185) — but it is suggested above that it is of relatively limited significance. In addition, there have been suggestions that the reasoning on the "red hand" rule in *Interfoto Picture Library* v *Stiletto Visual Programmes* [1988] 1 All ER 348 in the context of incorporation by notice (see below p 148), could provide a basis for a requirement that the signatory's attention be drawn to unusual or unreasonable clauses if they are to be incorporated by signature (Rutherford & Wilson (1998) 148 NLJ 380; Downes *Textbook on Contract Law* (5th ed) at pp 160–161). The "red hand" rule mitigates the impact of the general rule, that clauses can be incorporated from unsigned documents or signs by using "reasonably sufficient notice", by requiring a greater degree of notice to pass that test in relation to unusual or unreasonable clauses. Support for the extension of that approach to unreasonable or unusual clauses into the context of incorporation by signature might be suggested by the *obiter* comment made by Evans LJ in *Ocean Chemical Transport Inc* v *Exnor Craggs Ltd* [2000] 1 All ER 519 at p 530. In response to council's suggestion that "the *Interfoto* test . . . has to be applied, even in a case where the other party has signed an acknowledgement of the terms and conditions and their incorporation", Evans LJ said that it seemed to him that council "could be right in what might be regarded as an extreme case, where signature was obtained under pressure of time or other circumstances . . .". However, despite the artificialities involved in the *L'Estrange* approach, it is suggested that the line taken by the Canadian court, or anything similar, is unlikely to be adopted here. It was developed by the Canadian court at about the same time as the Unfair Contract Terms Act 1977 was introduced in the UK to deal with objectionable exemption clauses and in the UK there are also now the Unfair Terms in Consumer Contracts Regulations 1999. Those Regulations may only cover consumer contracts but their operation is not restricted to exemption clauses. The *L'Estrange* approach provides a great deal of certainty in relation to the issue of incorporation, and the above comment of Evans LJ is to be contrasted with that of Hobhouse LJ in *AEG* v *Logic Resource Ltd* [1996] CLC 265. In the context of incorporation by notice, Hobhouse LJ indicated that, in the interests of certainty, the red hand rule should itself now be restricted in the light of the scope provided to the courts to deal with objectionable exemption clauses by the Unfair Contract Terms Act 1977 (see p 151). Artificiality of incorporation can itself be a factor in determining the "reasonableness" of a clause under the Unfair Contract Terms Act 1977 and, under the 1999 Regulations on Unfair Terms in Consumer Contracts, whether there was a realistic possibility for the consumer to become acquainted with the term, may be very important to the fairness test (see p 210 and p 243 respectively). (On the issue of the interaction of the common law rules on incorporation and legislation see further Macdonald (1999) 58 CLJ 413.)

One further point to be considered in relation to incorporation by signature relates to the context of electronic contracting by e-mail or on the web. As has been seen, the approach in *L'Estrange* makes a signature a very certain way of ensuring the incorporation of standard terms. The question is whether an "electronic signature" will be treated in the same way, to facilitate e-commerce. It should be noted that the discussion here of "electronic signatures" is not of electronically produced facsimiles of signed names. It is of a functional equivalent of a signature which can be produced cryptographically, for example. Cryptography can provide a form of electronic signature, serving the purposes of identifying the sender of a message (authenticating it) and also of ensuring that it has not been altered (ensuring its integrity). One cryptographic method of dealing with the need for authentication and integrity is through the use of two "keys" — "public key" or "asymmetric" cryptography. That is described in *Building Confidence in Electronic Commerce — A Consultation Document* (DTI 1999 URN 99/642):

> "Public Key cryptography uses two keys, also known as a *key pair.* (These keys are both large numbers with special mathematical properties). When this technique is used for signatures, the *private key* (which as the term suggests is known only to its owner) is used to transform a data file, by scrambling the information contained in it. The transformed data is the electronic signature and can be checked against the original file using the *public key* of the person who signed it. Anyone with access to the public key (which might, for example, be available on a website) can check the signature, so verifying that it could only have been used by someone with access to the private key. If the only one with access to the *private key* is its owner then the owner must have signed the message . . . If a third party had altered the message, the fact they had done so would be easily detectable."

Cryptography can produce something which could be regarded as an "electronic signature". Its status can be enhanced by the use of third parties to provide certificates to, for example, authenticate the identity of the private key holder. Under the Electronic Communications Act 2000, a certificate can be furnished by "any person" but the first part of the Act provides for the "registration" of "approved providers of cryptography support services". It is s 7 of the Act, however, which provides scope for cryptographically generated signatures to be treated as falling within the approach taken in *L'Estrange* to a more traditional signature. Section 7 states:

> "(1) In any legal proceedings—
>
> > (a) an electronic signature incorporated into or logically associated with a particular electronic communication or particular electronic data, and
> > (b) the certification by any such person of such a signature,
>
> shall each be admissible in evidence in relation to any question as to the authenticity of the communication or data as to the integrity of the communication or data.
>
> (2) For the purposes of this section an electronic signature is so much of anything in electronic form as—
>
> > (a) is incorporated into or otherwise associated with any electronic communication or electronic data; and
> > (b) purports to be so incorporated or associated for the purpose of being used in establishing the authenticity of the communication or data, the integrity of the communication or data, or both.
>
> (3) For the purposes of this section an electronic signature incorporated into or logically associated with a particular electronic communication or particular

electronic data is certified by any person if that person (whether before or after the making of the communication) has made a statement confirming that—

(a) the signature,
(b) a means of producing, communicating or verifying the signature, or
(c) a procedure applied to the signature,

is (either alone or in combination with other factors) a valid means of establishing the authenticity of the communication or data, the integrity of the communication or data, or both."

This section not only contains a definition of an electronic signature (s 7(2)), but also provides that, along with an appropriate certificate, it is admissible as evidence of the "authenticity" or "integrity" of the relevant communication or data (s 7(1)). If such signatures (and certificates) are being used as evidence of "authenticity" then, under s 15(2)(a), they are being used as evidence of "one or more of the following—

(i) whether the communication or data comes from a particular person or other source;
(ii) whether it is accurately timed and dated;
(iii) whether it is intended to have legal effect".

With its reference to the origin of the communication and "whether it is intended to have legal effect" this would seem to allow for the possibility of electronic reproduction of the effect the common law gives to a more traditional signature, to show that the document contains the terms of a contract to which the electronic signatory is a party, ie in the absence of fraud, misrepresentation or *non est factum*, to make those terms binding upon the relevant party whether he, or she, has read them or not (following *L'Estrange*). (See also the EC Directive (1999/93/EC) on a Community Framework for Electronic Signatures[1].)

3.   Notice[2]

Unsigned documents or signs provide the main problems in relation to incorporation. As there is no signature, it must be asked what other means can be used to establish that the clauses on the document or sign are part of the contract. There is no difficulty where there is actual knowledge of the clause. It will then clearly be part of the contract. It is the situation when this knowledge is absent which needs to be considered.

(a) Timing

The first point to be made is that clauses cannot be incorporated from unsigned documents or signs if those documents or signs are not introduced into the transaction until after the contract has been concluded. Once offer and acceptance have occurred, one party cannot say to the other: "Oh, by the way, these clauses are part of our agreement". The contract is on the terms of the offer, which was accepted. It will be remembered that in Chapter 2 *Thornton* v *Shoe Lane Parking* [1971] 2 QB 163 was seen to raise the question as to exactly when acceptance occurred (see p 17). The timing of acceptance was important because once it had taken place no further terms could be introduced into the contract. Another case which illustrates the need to ensure that the unsigned document or sign is introduced into the transaction before offer and acceptance are complete, and the contract is made, is *Olley* v *Marlborough Court Hotel* [1949] 1 KB 532. In that case:

> Mrs Olley and her husband made a contract to stay in the hotel. The contract was made at the reception desk on their arrival. They were then shown to their room. There was a sign in the room which purported to exclude the hotel's liability for the theft of guests' property unless deposited with the manageress for safekeeping. Mrs Olley returned to her room one day to discover that her furs had been stolen through the hotel's negligence. The hotel sought to rely upon its exemption clause to exclude its liability for her loss.

The Court of Appeal held that the clauses on the sign in the bedroom could not form part of the contract between the hotel and Mrs Olley. The contract had been made at the reception desk before there had been any opportunity to see the sign.

(b) The test

The basic rule for incorporation of a clause contained in an unsigned document or sign is that such a clause is part of the contract if there has been reasonably sufficient notice of it. This test is derived from *Parker* v *South Eastern Railway Co Ltd* [1877] 2 CPD 416 where the court was concerned with the terms on which goods were deposited in a railway station cloakroom. In that case:

> On depositing a bag in the cloakroom, Mr Parker was handed a ticket which he did not read and which contained a clause purporting to limit the railway company's responsibility to packages not exceeding £10 in value. Mr Parker's bag was of greater value than £10 and, on its loss from the cloakroom, the question was whether the clause on the ticket limited the liability of the railway company.

The result of the case was that a retrial was ordered. The judge at first instance had misdirected the jury on the test for incorporation. The court decided that the basic test to determine whether incorporation had occurred in this type of situation is that of reasonably sufficient notice, ie had reasonably sufficient notice of the clause been given (see also page 151).

The need to order a retrial in *Parker* emphasises the factual nature of the test (*Hood* v *Anchor Line* [1918] AC 837 at p 844). So, for example, there is unlikely to be reasonably sufficient notice of a clause printed on the back of a ticket if the front of the ticket does not say "for conditions see back" (*Henderson* v *Stephenson* (1875) LR 2 HL, Sc 470), but it will depend upon all the facts of the particular case. Equally, a ticket which would in normal circumstances provide reasonably sufficient notice might not do so if it had been folded over (*Richardson, Spence & Co* v *Rowntree* [1894] AC 217) or the relevant clause had been obscured by a date stamp (*Sugar* v *London, Midland and Scottish Railway* [1941] 1 All ER 172).

(c) Type of document

The type of document in which a clause is found is relevant to its incorporation. It may simply be said that a non-contractual document will not incorporate terms (see *Grogan* v *Meredith* [1996] CLC 1127 — page 140 above — in the context of signed documents). However, in the context of a general requirement of reasonably sufficient notice, the type of document is also relevant to that requirement. If the document is not of a type which the reasonable person would expect to contain contract terms then that indicates that reasonably sufficient notice of the clause has not been given. In *Parker* v *South Eastern Railway Co Ltd* [1877] 2 CPD 416 Mellish LJ gave an example of this (at p 422):

> "If a person driving through a turnpike-gate received a ticket upon paying the toll, he might reasonably assume that the object of the ticket was that by producing it he might be free from paying toll at some other turnpike-gate, and might put it in his pocket unread."

Although this is quite an old example, the general point is clear. It was referred to by Slesser LJ in *Chapelton* v *Barry UDC* [1940] 1 KB 532 (at p 538), and that case provides us with a further example:

> Mr Chapelton was at the beach at Cold Knap in Barry. There was a sign indicating the hire charge for deck chairs and requesting those using the chairs to obtain a ticket from the attendant and retain it for inspection. Mr Chapelton took a chair and obtained a ticket. He put the ticket in his pocket without reading what was printed on it. When he sat down in the chair the canvas gave way and he fell and injured himself. Barry UDC, from whom he had hired the chair, claimed to be able to rely upon a clause on the ticket to exclude liability for his injuries.

The court decided that the clause on the ticket was not part of the contract. The ticket was not the sort of document on which a contract term would be expected. It appeared merely to be proof that Mr Chapelton had paid his 2d hire charge.

When the type of document is discussed, in relation to the issue of incorporation, the point is sometimes put in terms of whether the document is a "mere receipt". Mellish LJ clearly envisaged the ticket from the turn-pike gate as a mere receipt and that is also how the court in *Chapelton* perceived the deck chair ticket, ie those tickets were seen as evidence of payment and nothing more. However, there is no reason why a document headed "receipt" should not be used to incorporate clauses into a contract successfully if the circumstances indicate its true role to the reasonable person (*Watkins* v *Rymill* (1883) 10 QBD 178). It should be borne in mind that a clause cannot be incorporated into a contract by a document which is introduced after the contract is concluded; if a document is intended to be a receipt, in the sense of evidence of payment, it may have been introduced too late, after offer and acceptance have occurred. The timing of the introduction of the ticket was another reason for the decision in *Chapelton*.

A further point, related to that of the type of document, is that the transaction may be one in which it is commonly known that there will be standard terms. The question of incorporation from a particular document will then be viewed against this background and it will be easier to establish that reasonably sufficient notice has been provided. In *Alexander* v *Railway Executive* [1951] 2 KB 882 it was regarded as relevant to the question of reasonably sufficient notice that "most people nowadays know that railway companies have conditions subject to which they take articles into their cloakrooms" (at p 886). (See also incorporation by a course of dealing and *British Crane Hire Corporation* v *Ipswich Plant Hire* [1975] QB 303 (p 157)).

(d) Reference

It is not necessary for the document or sign itself to contain the terms. There may be incorporation by reference to where the terms may be found. In *Thompson* v *LM & S Railway* [1930] 1 KB 41 the railway ticket said on its front, in "quite big print and quite legible print", "for conditions see back". On the back the passenger was referred to the railway timetable to ascertain the conditions. Despite the fact that the clause was only to be found upon page 552 of the timetable, which itself cost 6d when Mrs Thompson's ticket cost only 2s 7d, the clauses were held to be incorporated and removed the railway's liability for the negligent injury to Mrs Thompson.

The reaction to *Thompson* may be that it is a fairly extreme case. A decision by a passenger to ascertain the content of the terms would have entailed a search of the timetable and some expense. Undoubtedly it was easier for the court to accept that the terms were incorporated in this case because it did not regard the exemption clause as unreasonable. Mrs Thompson had purchased an excursion ticket, at half the ordinary fare for the journey. Restricted liability was not regarded as unreasonable when a reduced fare was being paid.

As will be seen, at common law the courts have now proved themselves willing to link the question of incorporation by notice and the unreasonableness, or unusualness, of the content of a clause. That occurs through the "red hand rule" (see below), which applies to incorporation by notice generally and in the context of incorporation by reference. It should, however, also be noted that artificiality of incorporation will also be relevant to the reasonableness test under the Unfair Contract Terms Act 1977 and the fairness test in the Regulations on Unfair Terms in Consumer Contracts 1999. In particular, the latter contains a list of terms which may be regarded as unfair (see page 236) and that list includes:

"Terms which have the object or effect of . . .

(i) irrevocably binding the consumer to terms with which he had no real opportunity of becoming acquainted before the conclusion of the contract."

In contracts between consumers and sellers or suppliers, this requires consideration of the accessibility of any clauses that it is sought to incorporate by reference. If they are inaccessible, then the term referring to them may be found to be unfair. Under those circumstances, it would not bind the consumer and there would then be no effective term to incorporate the clauses it had referred to.

(e) Objective nature of the test

A variation on the facts of *Thompson* provides a useful way to emphasise the objective nature of the notice test. In that case the passenger was illiterate but the ticket was purchased by her agent who could read. The legal position of an agent is such that what the agent had notice of Mrs Thompson would also have notice of, and her illiteracy could not be relevant to the question of incorporation. However, even without the agent, Mrs Thompson's illiteracy should not be relevant to the question of reasonably sufficient notice and this is the tenor of the judgments in the case. The test is objective. The question is one of sufficiency of notice for the reasonable person, not the particular individual. In *Parker* [1877] 2 CPD 416 Mellish LJ said (at p 423):

"The railway company ... must be entitled to make some assumptions respecting the person who deposits luggage with them; I think they are entitled to assume that he can read, and that he understands the English language. . ."

The situation would be modified if the person who wished to include his exemption clauses knew, or should have known, that the person he was contracting with was illiterate. That factor would then enter into the assessment of whether there had been reasonably sufficient notice (*Geier* v *Kujawa, Weston and Warne Bros (Transport)* [1970] 1 Lloyd's Rep 364). More generally, the situation may be that the person wishing to incorporate his standard terms knows, or should know, that he will be contracting with individuals from a particular group who share some characteristic affecting their ability to acquire knowledge from a particular form of notice. In *Richardson, Spence & Co* v *Rowntree* [1894] AC 217 one of the elements mentioned by the court in relation to sufficiency of notice of the exemption clause was that the tickets were for steerage class passengers, "many of whom have little education and some of them none" (at p 221). That specific factor is obviously a product of its time, but it is possible to conceive of situations where the problem of communication with a particular group might be raised today. For example, a travel company setting out to provide holidays suitable for the blind would have to give serious consideration to the method used to incorporate an exemption clause into the contract with a blind person for such a holiday.

(f) The red hand rule[3]

Thompson contains some comments on whether it is possible to incorporate an unreasonable clause by notice ([1930] 1 KB 41 at pp 53 and 56). Such comments can be found in various cases (eg *Parker* v *South Eastern Railway* (1877) 2 CPD 416 at p 428; *Van Toll* v *South Eastern Railway* (1862) 12 CBNS 75 at pp 85 and 88) but there is no such accepted restriction upon this method of incorporation. However it is understandable that there should be a reaction against the idea that unreasonable clauses can be incorporated into a contract by notice and used against someone who has not read them, and who has not even been alerted to be on guard by the necessity of signing the document containing the clauses. The courts have developed a technique for restricting incorporation of unusual or unreasonable clauses by notice. In *Spurling* v *Bradshaw* [1956] 1 WLR 461 Denning LJ, as he then was, said (at p 466):

"the more unreasonable a clause is, the greater the notice which must be given of it. Some clauses which I have seen would need to be printed in *red ink on the face of the document with a red hand* pointing to [them] before the notice could be held to be sufficient" (emphasis added).

Spurling itself provides no further guidance on what will, for obvious reasons, be termed the red hand rule. The reference to the rule in *Spurling* was a lone *obiter dictum*.

The rule was given further consideration in *Thornton* v *Shoe Lane Parking* [1971] 2 QB 163. It will be remembered that *Thornton* involved an attempt by the owners of a car park to escape liability for the negligently caused personal injury of Mr Thornton, who was injured when he returned to the car park to collect his car. The car park owners were seeking to rely upon an exemption clause printed on the sign inside the car park and referred to on a ticket received at the entrance to the car park. It was argued that the ticket arrived too late to incorporate any clause into the contract, but the court also considered what the situation would be if that was not the case. The clause purported to exclude liability not only for damage to property but also for personal injury. Lord Denning MR considered it (at p 170) to be an example of the type of clause which he had in mind in *Spurling* when propounding the red hand rule (ie an unreasonable clause) and one which would require additional notice to incorporate it. Megaw LJ also thought (at p 172) that the clause would require extra notice in order to be incorporated, but he considered it to be unusual clauses which should be treated in this way. (See Clarke [1976] CLJ 51, pp 69–71.)

After *Thornton* it seemed that the red hand rule should be stated as being that the more unreasonable or unusual a clause is, the greater the degree of notice required to incorporate it, and this is confirmed by the judgments of the Court of Appeal in *Interfoto Picture Library* v *Stiletto Visual Programmes* [1988] 1 All ER 348. In *Interfoto*:

> An advertising agency, Stiletto, telephoned Interfoto, who ran a library of photographic transparencies, to obtain material for a presentation to a client. Stiletto had not dealt with Interfoto before. Interfoto dispatched to Stiletto a bag containing forty-seven transparencies and a delivery note containing nine "Conditions". "Condition 2" stated that a holding fee of £5 per transparency per day would be charged for any transparency kept beyond a fourteen day period. Stiletto failed to return the transparencies within fourteen days and, on the basis of "Condition 2", Interfoto claimed over £3,500 from Stiletto. The question was whether or not that clause was a term of the contract.

At first instance it was held that "Condition 2" was part of the contract, but this was reversed by the Court of Appeal. The clause in question was not an exclusion clause but the court said that the same rules for incorporation applied and, in particular, what has here been termed the red hand rule. The judgments in the Court of Appeal can be synthesised into the formulation of the red hand rule indicated above, ie the more unusual or unreasonable a clause the greater the notice required for there to be reasonably sufficient notice. The court considered "Condition 2" to be both unusual and unreasonable. There was evidence of the holding fees of ten other agencies. Most of them charged less than £3.50 per transparency per week, only one charged more (£4 per week). The court held that there was not sufficient notice to incorporate "Condition 2", and Interfoto were entitled to a *quantum meruit* (see Chapter 22) of £3.50 per transparency per *week*, instead of the £5 per transparency per *day* claimed.

The importance here of the red hand rule does not simply lie in its impact within the law of contract as a specific rule. The development of the red hand rule is worth considering also because it will make us think about the way in which the common law evolves and this is of great importance in relation to an area of law, like contract, which is largely based upon judicial decisions rather than statute.

The red hand rule says that notice varies with the contents of a clause. Its effect is that where clauses (a), (b), and (c) are printed on a ticket, in exactly the same size type, and (b) is a very unreasonable clause whilst the other two are not, there may be sufficient notice to incorporate clauses (a) and (c) but not clause (b). Is this logical? How can the degree of notice required to incorporate a clause depend upon its contents? Can the contents of a clause affect its legibility? Consideration of these questions makes obvious the problem of establishing the basis of the rule. It certainly cannot be regarded as merely a logical derivation from *Parker* v *South Eastern Railway* [1877] 2 CPD 416 (Brownsword (1972) 35 MLR 183). The contents of a clause cannot affect its legibility. However, the common law develops in response to the problems which the courts encounter. The general principle of incorporation by notice can be perceived as producing unfairness in some situations. One party may use it to introduce very unreasonable or unusual terms into his contract with the other party and that other party will have no actual knowledge of the terms and will not even have been alerted to be on his guard by the necessity of signing the document. The decision in *Interfoto* represents the view that it is appropriate for the courts to interfere with the parties' apparent bargain in such circumstances. The court has acted to limit what it has seen as an abuse of the general notice principle and to protect the injured party against that common human failing of not reading everything. The decision will be approved by those who favour an interventionist role for the courts.

Interfoto will be criticised by those who strongly favour the idea of freedom of contract. The court has interfered with the parties' apparent bargain. It could, however, be argued that the form of the red hand rule does not place an absolute bar upon the incorporation of unusual or unreasonable clauses and is not a real interference with freedom of contract, being merely an interference with the manner of the terms' incorporation and not with their content. It can be seen as aimed at ensuring that there is real freedom of contract through trying to address the problem of the artificiality of incorporation of contract terms, and the lack of real choice and consent that engenders. *Interfoto* is the type of case in which the court has to base its decision upon its view of a very fundamental idea, such as that of freedom of contract, and precedent can be of only limited help. In the end the result will depend upon whether the court leans towards intervention in such situations.

However, different means of dealing with a problem can come into being and it may be that the "red hand" rule is in the process of further evolution — to narrow its scope. In *AEG (UK) Ltd* v *Logic Resource Ltd* [1996] CLC 265 the court was concerned with a business to business contract and an exemption clause dealing with breaches of the terms as to quality of the goods implied by the Sale of Goods Act 1979. The Court of Appeal was unanimous in finding that the clause did not satisfy the requirement of reasonableness and was ineffective under the Unfair Contract Terms Act 1977. However, what is of interest here is that the court also had to consider the issue of incorporation and, in particular, the application of the "red hand" rule and there was a difference of opinion as to the operation of the rule. The majority thought that in considering whether a clause was unusual or unreasonable (and so within the scope of the rule), it was the particular clause which had to be addressed. Hobhouse LJ took a different view, claiming that the rule only considered the type of clause ie that the clause had to be unusual or unreasonable as a type of clause in order for the rule to apply. An exemption clause dealing with the statutorily implied terms was neither unusual or unreasonable as a type of clause. It was the extent of the clause which put it within the scope of the red hand rule, and prevented its incorporation in the eyes of the majority.

Hobhouse LJ took the view that the red hand rule did not apply and that the clause was incorporated. This difference in view as to the scope of the red hand rule has been noted subsequently (see *Ocean Chemical Transport Inc* v *Exnor Craggs Ltd* [2000] 1 All ER (Comm) 519), but the point should be made here that clearly *Interfoto* (above) was concerned with whether the specific clause was unusual or unreasonable and not merely whether it was unusual or unreasonable as a type of clause — the court compared the clause in *Interfoto* with that used by ten other agencies. That does not, however, necessarily dismiss the line indicated by Hobhouse LJ, in his minority judgment. His approach must be viewed against the background of his wider comments as to the desirability of the red hand rule. He said (at p 277):

"In the past there may have been a tendency to introduce more strict criteria [for incorporation] but this is no longer necessary in view of the Unfair Contract Terms Act. The reasonableness of clauses is the subject matter of the Unfair Contract Terms Act and it is under the provisions of the Act that problems of unreasonable clauses should be addressed and the solution found."

Hobhouse LJ saw the rule as no longer required in the light of the Unfair Contract Terms Act 1977 and wished to see it restricted to limit the uncertainty which he saw it as generating. His approach to the rule — applying it only on the basis of the type of clause, rather than in relation to the particular clause — would considerably curtail the scope of the rule, and it might therefore be taken if it was considered generally that the rule now merely generated uncertainty without really being required (but see *Lacey's Footwear* v *Bowler International* [1997] 2 Lloyd's Rep 369 at 385). Of course, the point can be made that the Unfair Contract Terms Act 1977 basically only deals with exemption clauses, and although there are also now the 1999 Regulations on Unfair Terms in Consumer Contracts, the hirer of the transparencies in *Interfoto* would not gain protection from either piece of legislation. The clause was one imposing an onerous obligation — not removing a liability — and it could not fall within the 1977 Act, and, in addition, both parties were businesses and the 1999 Regulations only apply to contracts between consumers and sellers or suppliers. It will be asked whether there will be sufficient cases where intervention will be viewed as desirable, and which will fall outside the legislation, to justify any additional uncertainty created by the red hand rule. (For consideration of further potential interaction between the legislation and the common law rules see Macdonald (1999) 58 CLJ 413.)

(g) The general test — a further clarification of Parker

As we have seen, the basic test for incorporation of an unsigned document is that of reasonably sufficient notice. However, it is not uncommon to encounter a *dictum* of Mellish LJ in *Parker* v *South Eastern Railway Co* [1877] 2 CPD 416 which appears to provide a fuller test and which is worth considering now that the basic test has been explored. Mellish LJ thought the appropriate test was (at p 423):

"that if the person receiving the ticket did not see or know that there was any writing on the ticket, he is not bound by the conditions; that if he knew there was writing, and knew or believed that the writing contained conditions, then he is bound by the conditions; that if he knew there was writing on the ticket, but did not know or believe that the writing contained conditions, nevertheless he would be bound, if the delivering of the ticket to him in such a manner that he could see there was writing upon it, was... reasonable notice that the writing contained conditions."

A number of points must be noted here in order to avoid confusion. First, Mellish LJ said that there will not be incorporation if the person to whom the ticket was given did not know that there was writing on it. This cannot be regarded as a general rule. As has been seen, the test of reasonably sufficient notice depends upon the facts in each case, and is not dependent upon providing sufficient notice for the particular individual (see the discussion of *Thompson* v *LM & S Railway Co* above). That the person to whom the ticket was delivered did not know that there was any writing on it cannot determine the issue. At most it is evidence that the reasonable person would not have realised that there was writing on the ticket and that there was not reasonably sufficient notice.

The second point to be made is on Mellish LJ's second statement, that if the person to whom the ticket is handed knows that it contains conditions then he will be bound by them even though he does not know of the content of the conditions. An analogy can be made with incorporation by reference (see page 147). The individual is in a position to ascertain the contents of the terms. One qualification needs to be made: this situation should also be subject to the red hand rule. If the person to whom the ticket is given does not know of the content of the terms, but merely of their existence, he should be given extra notice of any unusual or unreasonable terms.

Finally, Mellish LJ's third point must be considered. It is close to a formulation of the general test. Again the point which needs to be made is that the test is one which depends upon the facts in each case (*Hood* v *Anchor Line* [1918] AC 837 at p 844). It cannot be regarded as a general rule that, in order for there to be reasonably sufficient notice, the ticket must be delivered so that the person to whom it is delivered can see that there is writing on it. The *dictum* of Mellish LJ should be treated with some care.

4. Consistent course of dealing[(4)]

(a) The test

There may sometimes be incorporation based upon the previous dealings between the parties. *Spurling* v *Bradshaw* [1956] 1 WLR 461 provides an illustration of this:

> Bradshaw stored casks of orange juice in Spurling's warehouse. When Bradshaw went to collect his casks it was discovered that the juice was either gone or ruined, and he refused to pay the storage charge. When Spurling sued for the storage charge, Bradshaw counterclaimed for breach of contract by negligent storage. To defeat the counterclaim, Spurling sought to rely upon an exemption clause contained in a document which was sent to Bradshaw only some days after the contract of storage had been concluded.

The document containing the exemption clause had obviously arrived too late to incorporate terms into that particular contract. However, Bradshaw conceded that he had received such documents on previous occasions when he had dealt with Spurling and this led the Court of Appeal to conclude that "by the course of business and conduct of the parties [the clause was] part of the contract" (at p 471).

In *Spurling* the clause had been incorporated despite the late arrival of the document containing it. It is in this sort of situation, where the document has arrived too late in the instant case, that the argument for incorporation by a course of dealing usually arises. *Kendall & Sons* v *Lillico & Sons* [1969] 2 AC 31 provides another example:

> The seller sold Brazilian ground nut extract to the buyer to be used to compound cattle and poultry food. The contract between the parties had been made over the telephone but was followed, the next day, by the dispatch of a document, a sold note, which contained an exemption clause. The conclusion of an oral contract, followed by the dispatch of the sold note, was the practice which the parties had followed for three years. During that time there had been three or four transactions a month following that pattern. In the instant case the ground nut extract contained a substance poisonous to poultry.

The question arose as to the seller's liability for the poisonous state of the Brazilian ground nut extract. One argument was that the seller was protected by the exemption clause. This raised the issue of incorporation. The House of Lords was willing to accept that, although the document arrived too late to incorporate the clause into the particular transaction, the clause was part of the contract on the basis of the previous dealings between the parties. In the event this did not assist the sellers as the court also concluded that the clause was not appropriately worded to cover the breach which had occurred.

Kendall v *Lillico* helps us towards a general test for incorporation by past dealings. In the Court of Appeal [1966] 1 WLR 287 (*sub nom Hardwick Game Farm* v *SAPPA*) Diplock LJ stated the test (at p 339) as:

> "what each party by his words and conduct reasonably led the other party to believe were the acts he was undertaking a legal duty to perform."

In the House of Lords, Lord Wilberforce agreed with Diplock LJ ([1969] 2 AC 31 at p 130) and Lord Pearce formulated a general test in similar terms. He said (at p 113):

> "The court's task is to decide what each party to an alleged contract would reasonably conclude from the utterances, writings or conduct of the other."

More recently, a similar formulation has been applied. It has been asked "what each party by his words and conduct would have led the other party as a reasonable man to believe he was accepting."[5]

To settle on an exact formula for the test for incorporation by a course of dealing we need to consider the mechanism by which such incorporation occurs. In each case the court is concerned with what was included, unspoken, in the offer and acceptance on the basis of the previous dealings between the parties and what they have said and done in the instant case in relation to the offer and acceptance. In both *Spurling* and *Kendall* v *Lillico* a document containing the clauses in question had been sent, but it had been sent after offer and acceptance had occurred. The lateness of this document did not prevent the clauses from being incorporated because it is not the document dispatched in relation to the particular transaction which is the basis of incorporation of the clauses in the instant case. In *Kendall* v *Lillico*, for example, the incorporation of the exemption clause should be seen as based upon the "sold note" delivered in relation to each of the previous transactions over the preceding three years. Because of the past transactions each party, as a reasonable person, should have assumed that the offer and acceptance, in the instant case, included the seller's standard terms. In *Petrotrade Inc* v *Texaco Ltd* [2000] CLC 1341, on the basis of five previous transactions on the same terms, and for the same commodity, in thirteen months, Clarke LJ concluded (at p 1349):

> "Given the course of dealing ... both parties will have made the oral agreement on the basis that the contract would be subject to the same terms as before".

Obviously the situation would be different if one party had indicated by his words or actions that the particular transaction was not to be on the same basis as previous transactions (see below). Bearing all this in mind, it is possible to formulate the test for incorporation from a course of dealings. The test should be whether, at the time of contracting, each party, as a reasonable person, is entitled to infer from the past dealings and the actions and words of the other in the instant case, that the standard clauses are part of the instant contract.

(b) Acts/words in the instant case

In the context of incorporation by a course of dealing, further consideration needs to be given to the relevance of the acts or words of the parties in the instant case. On a factual level their relevance is obvious. For many years the parties may have contracted frequently and always used one party's standard terms. In the instant case it may be clear that past practice is to be departed from and that the standard terms are not to form part of the contract. Equally, it should be possible to find incorporation by a course of dealing when there are some differences between the instant case and past transactions, provided that the situation as a whole is such that the parties, as reasonable people, would still assume the standard terms to be part of the contract. For example, incorporation of one party's standard terms should be possible where those terms have been incorporated in each previous transaction by a document providing reasonably sufficient notice and, in the instant case, the contract is concluded over the telephone without any express reference to those standard terms (see below *British Crane Hire Corporation* v *Ipswich Plant Hire* [1975] QB 303). However, *McCutcheon* v *David MacBrayne* [1964] 1 WLR 125 indicated that the acts or words in the instant case must be given some special legal significance beyond that which they would naturally have on a factual level and this should be considered.

In *McCutcheon* v *David MacBrayne* [1964] 1 WLR 125:

> McSporran arranged for a car belonging to his brother-in-law, McCutcheon, to be shipped from the Hebrides to the mainland by MacBrayne. McCutcheon had shipped various items three or four times in the past and so had McSporran. On each previous occasion McCutcheon had signed a risk note but McSporran had done so only twice. The ship sank and McCutcheon sought to recover the cost of his car from MacBrayne. MacBrayne sought to rely upon an exemption clause, and one of the ways in which he argued that it had been incorporated was by a course of

dealing. The clause was contained in the risk note which, on this occasion, McSporran had not been asked to sign.

In this case the House of Lords found that the past dealings were not appropriate to incorporate the clause. On the facts there is no difficulty with this. The previous transactions were limited in number and not consistent in the introduction of the risk note.

The reasoning in *McCutcheon* v *MacBrayne* must be considered. The judgment of Lord Reid poses no problems. He took the line which is the basis of the general test indicated above. He thought that the court's task (at p 128):

"is to decide what each [party] was reasonably entitled to conclude from the attitude of the other".

It is the judgments of the other members of the House of Lords which present some difficulties. They favour the idea that for incorporation by a course of dealing there must be complete consistency, not only in the past transactions, but also between the previous transactions and the instant case. If this were so, incorporation by a course of dealing could occur only in the *Kendall* v *Lillico* type of case, the "complete consistency" case, where the document containing the relevant clauses arrived too late in the instant case and has always arrived too late in the past, ie the document has always arrived after offer and acceptance.

Incorporation by a course of dealing should not be regarded as restricted to the situation where the instant case follows entirely the pattern of past dealings (and the Court of Appeal seems to have assumed that it was not so restricted in *PLM Trading Ltd v Georgiou* [1986] BTLC 404). Two points must be made. First, the need for complete consistency between past transactions and the instant case would create an unacceptable uncertainty. This is illustrated if we look again at the facts of *Kendall* v *Lillico*. The contract in the instant case was concluded over the telephone. In the previous dealings the telephone conversation had been followed by the dispatch of the "sold note" containing the exemption clause. If a course of dealing could not incorporate a clause unless there was complete consistency between past transactions and the instant case it would not be clear whether the instant contract included the clause until the "sold note" had been dispatched or, possibly, received. There would be a time, after the making of the contract, during which it would not be clear what the terms of the contract were. Clearly that would be an unacceptable situation (Hogget (1970) 33 MLR 518, 520–521).

The second point to be made is that circumstances have changed since *McCutcheon* [1964] 1 WLR 125 was decided, and the reason why the majority of the House of Lords favoured a restrictive approach to incorporation by a course of dealing no longer applies. The line taken by the majority in *McCutcheon* is explained by their view that such incorporation is another way in which the business person has an unfair advantage over the consumer (Lord Pearce at p 139, Lord Hodson at p 130, Lord Guest at p 131, Lord Devlin at p 136). They saw it as simply giving the business person yet another opportunity to rely upon standard terms with exemption clauses. It should be remembered that since *McCutcheon* was decided, the Unfair Contract Terms Act 1977 has been enacted. That Act helps the consumer to deal with exemption clauses and there is now the more general EC Directive/Regulations on Unfair Terms in Consumer Contracts. The courts need no longer place undue restriction upon incorporation to provide protection from such clauses.

It seems unlikely that the approach of the majority in *McCutcheon* will be revived today. Comments upon *McCutcheon*, such as that in *Circle Freight International* v *Medeast Gulf Exports* [1988] 2 Lloyd's Rep 427 (see page 158), therefore need to be treated with care. In that case Taylor LJ said, of *McCutcheon*, (at p 431):

> "[Lord Pearce] was pointing out that whereas some of the previous dealings in that case had involved a contractual document, on the occasion of the sinking the contract was purely oral. It was the departure from the ordinary course of business which excluded the condition".

Such a comment should merely be seen as an acceptance of the natural factual relevance of differences between the past transactions and the instant case.

(c) Failure to incorporate in past transactions

Incorporation by a course of dealing in the *Kendall* v *Lillico* [1969] 2 AC 31 type of case is worth further consideration. Each time the parties contracted, the document containing the standard terms was introduced by one party, only after offer and acceptance had occurred. It is the cumulative effect of these documents which means that a point is reached when the other party, as a reasonable person, must be taken to know that the offer is made on the basis of those standard terms and, in the absence of some indication to the contrary, his acceptance will encompass them. This is simply to re-emphasise the mechanism by which incorporation by a course of dealing occurs. The point to be made here is that there is no possibility of incorporation by a course of dealing when the failure to incorporate standard terms by the document produced in each particular past contract, and the instant case, is due not to the timing of delivery of that document but rather to its not providing "reasonably sufficient" notice, ie where, in relation to each transaction, the terms have been present before offer and acceptance but they are insufficiently prominent to be incorporated by notice. Under these circumstances the party seeking to rely upon his standard terms never puts the other party in the situation where, as a reasonable person, he should assume that the offer encompasses those terms. The reasonable person would make no such assumption in relation to terms of the existence of which he has never been given sufficient notice. By definition there is no reason why he should know of the terms. Where incorporation occurs because of the cumulative effect of a series of late deliveries of standard terms, the situation must be such that those terms would have been incorporated in each individual transaction had they arrived on time.

(d) Consumer/business distinction

When considering whether incorporation by a course of dealing has occurred, the courts have shown themselves less willing to find such incorporation where one party is a consumer than where both are business people. In *Hollier* v *Rambler Motors* [1972] 2 QB 71:

> Rambler Motors had repaired Mr Hollier's car on three or four occasions over a five year period. On at least two occasions Mr Hollier had signed a form containing Rambler's standard terms including an exemption clause. In the instant case the

parties contracted over the telephone, without any mention of the standard terms. Whilst the car was in the garage it was damaged by fire due to Rambler's negligence.

The court decided that the exemption clause did not cover the breach which had occurred, but it also considered the issue of incorporation. On that question the court concluded that three or four transactions over a five year period were not sufficient to incorporate the standard terms into the oral contract. This was obviously not a strong case for such incorporation, but it should be noted that in considering this case the Court of Appeal in *British Crane Hire Corporation* v *Ipswich Plant Hire* [1975] QB 303 (see below) emphasised that Mr Hollier was a consumer. It should be easier to incorporate terms by a course of dealing into a contract between two business people than into a contract between a business person and a consumer.

Hollier should be contrasted with *British Crane Hire Corporation* v *Ipswich Plant Hire* [1975] QB 303. In that case:

> Ipswich Plant Hire, IP, were draining marsh land and carrying out other engineering works on it. IP were also in the business of hiring out equipment but on this occasion they, themselves, needed to hire a crane. As their need was urgent they telephoned British Crane Hire, BC, and arranged to hire a crane from them. Subsequently BC sent IP a printed form setting out conditions of hire. IP did not sign or return the form to BC. On two previous occasions BC had hired equipment to IP and those contracts had been made on the basis of BC's printed form. The crane sank into the marsh.

The question arose as to who was to pay for the removal of the crane from the mud. BC relied on their standard terms to argue that IP should pay. The question was whether those terms were part of the contract. Both parties were business people involved in the same trade. BC's standard terms were similar to those used throughout the trade and resembled those used by IP themselves when they were hiring out their machinery. Two prior transactions, by themselves, might not have been sufficient to incorporate the terms but the question of incorporation had to be viewed against the background of trade practice and that decided the issue in BC's favour. BC's terms were incorporated because the contract was between two business people in the same trade.

The court seemed inclined to view trade background as a distinct basis of incorporation from course of dealing. However, even if it could work independently, trade background can add to the effect of past dealings between the parties when incorporation by a course of dealing is considered. In *SIAT di del Ferro* v *Tradax Overseas SA* [1978] 2 Lloyd's Rep 470 Donaldson J considered *British Crane Hire Corporation* v *Ipswich Plant Hire* and the course of dealing cases. He said (at p 490):

> "I do not think that they are different. They are two different examples of a much wider concept, namely, that a contract is not made in a vacuum, but against a background of present and past facts. . . and that its terms. . . are to be gathered. . . from conduct viewed against that background."

Common trade background affects what each party, as a reasonable person, is entitled to infer that the other is agreeing to (*Fal Bunkering of Sharjah* v *Grecale of Panama* [1990] 1 Lloyd's Rep 369). Trade background can feed into the test for incorporation by a course of dealing. The two may combine and they should be viewed as so doing in *British Crane Hire Corporation* v *Ipswich Plant Hire*. When two business people contract, it may well be easier to say that reasonable people in their situation would infer the use of one party's standard terms after a very brief course of dealing. The knowledge of business practice which can be imputed to business people, particularly within the same trade, is obviously greater than that which can be imputed to a consumer.

(e) Course of dealing and reasonably sufficient notice

In *Circle Freight International* v *Medeast Gulf Exports* [1988] 2 Lloyd's Rep 427 some consideration was given to the relationship between incorporation by a course of dealing and the rule from *Parker* v *South Eastern Railway Co* [1877] 2 CPD 416. The facts of *Circle Freight* provide us with another useful illustration of incorporation by a course of dealing. In *Circle Freight*:

> Medeast exported goods to the Middle East. Circle Freight were freight forwarding agents. They had acted as such for Medeast on a number of occasions when Medeast were exporting dresses. Circle Freight were suing Medeast for money owed. Medeast were counterclaiming in relation to a consignment of dresses stolen whilst Circle Freight's driver left them unattended in Fleet Street. In relation to the counterclaim, Circle Freight sought to rely upon an exemption clause in the standard terms of the Institute of Freight Forwarders. Each contract between the parties was made orally, over the telephone, and was followed by an "invoice". The standard terms were referred to on the "invoice" which had been sent to Medeast on at least eleven occasions over the six months preceding the lost consignment. Medeast were a commercial company and knew that freight forwarders usually dealt on standard terms.

The court concluded that the standard terms were incorporated. Taylor LJ said (at p 433):

> "I consider that [Medeast's] conduct in continuing the course of business after at least eleven notices of the terms and omitting to request a sight of them would have led and did lead [Circle Freight] reasonably to believe [Medeast] accepted their terms."

As can be seen, this is an application of the test indicated above for incorporation by a course of dealing, ie whether, at the time of contracting, each party, as a reasonable person, is entitled to infer from the past dealings and the actions and words of the other in the instant case, that the standard clauses are part of the instant contract. However, the question of reasonably sufficient notice was also raised and was regarded as interchangeable with the more specific test for incorporation by a course of dealing. There seems to be every justification for this. Both tests are based upon an objective view of the contracting process. Both are concerned with what a reasonable person should be taken to have agreed to. However, although it is desirable to recognize the link, as such recognition may help with any further development of the law, there is something to be said for maintaining a separate test for the course of dealing cases. The separate test draws attention to the factors specific to incorporation in that manner.

Why is incorporation by a course of dealing required? Some empirical work undertaken in relation to contract law revealed that business people do not always have the rules of contract law at the forefront of their minds when contracting[6]. The primary interest is in "clinching the deal". When this attitude is combined with the use of standard terms, it can create problems. Perhaps the best known example of this is the "battle of the forms" (see page 20). The contention that terms have been incorporated by a course of dealing can also be seen as a product of this attitude. It is usually raised when one party has attempted to introduce standard terms into the contract after it has been made, ie when not much thought has been given to the correct procedure, within the law of contract, to ensure that his standard terms are part of the contract.

B. Construction

1. Introduction

When considering the construction of the contract, we are looking at its interpretation. In relation to exemption clauses the question being asked is whether the clause used is appropriately worded to cover what has occurred. However, before considering in detail the interpretation of exemption clauses, we should first briefly look at construction more generally and the trends in approaches to the construction of exemption clauses.

(a) Construction in general

The objective when construing or interpreting a contract is that of determining the parties' intention, objectively ascertained. Traditionally, there has been an overwhelming emphasis upon the written words used and a restrictive approach to what further evidence of the parties' intention could be considered. However, in *Investors Compensation Scheme Ltd* v *West Bromwich Building Society* [1998] 1 All ER 98 at p 114, the House of Lords took the view that a "fundamental change ... has overtaken this branch of the law" and that the result has largely been (at p 114):

> "to assimilate the way in which such documents are interpreted by judges to the common sense principles by which any serious utterance would be interpreted in ordinary life. Almost all the old intellectual baggage of 'legal' interpretation has been discarded."

Lord Hoffmann provided a summary of principles, which is now frequently referred to by the courts. He said (at p 114):

> "(1) Interpretation is the ascertainment of the meaning which the document would convey to a reasonable person having all the background knowledge which would reasonably have been available to the parties in the situation in which they were at the time of the contract.
>
> (2) The background was famously referred to by Lord Wilberforce as the 'matrix of fact', but this phrase is if anything an understated description of what the background may include. Subject to the requirement that it should have been reasonably available to the parties and to the exception mentioned next, it includes absolutely anything which would have affected the way in

which the language of the document would have been understood by a reasonable man.

(3) The law excludes from the admissable background the previous negotiations of the parties and their declarations of subjective intent. They are admissable only in an action for rectification. The law makes this distinction for reasons of practical policy and, in this respect only, legal interpretation differs from the way we would interpret utterances in ordinary life. . . .

(4) The meaning which a document (or any other utterance) would convey to a reasonable man is not the same thing as the meaning of its words. The meaning of words is a matter of dictionaries and grammars; the meaning of the document is what the parties using those words against the relevant background would reasonably have been understood to mean. The background may not merely enable the reasonable man to choose between the possible meanings of words which are ambiguous but even (as occasionally happens in ordinary life) to conclude that the parties must, for whatever reason, have used the wrong words or syntax (see *Mannai Investments Co Ltd v Eagle Star Life Ass Co Ltd* [1997] 3 All ER 352) . . .

(5) The 'rule' that words should be given their 'natural and ordinary meaning' reflects the commonsense proposition that we do not easily accept that people have made linguistic mistakes, particularly in formal documents. On the other hand, if one would nevertheless conclude from the background that something must have gone wrong with the language, the law does not require judges to attribute to the parties an intention which they plainly could not have had. . . ."

Lord Hoffmann's first point states the basic rule as to how construction is to be carried out. In most cases, the starting point would seem to remain the "natural and ordinary meaning of words". However, the words must not be divorced from the context of the document as a whole and "a statement that words have a particular natural meaning may mean no more than that in many contexts they will have that meaning. In other contexts, their meaning may be different but no less natural" (*Charter Reinsurance Co Ltd v Fagan* [1996] 2 WLR 726, Lord Hoffmann at p 762). In addition, it must be emphasised that, the words must be considered not only in the context of the rest of the contract, but against the background of the "matrix of fact" ie subject to certain exceptions (see point 3 above), and "subject to the requirement that it should have been reasonably available to both parties" at the time of contracting, that includes "absolutely anything which would have affected the way in which the language of the document would have been understood by a reasonable man". The matrix of fact, includes "evidence of the 'genesis' and objectively of the 'aim' of the transaction" (*Prenn v Simmonds* [1971] 1 WLR 1381, Lord Wilberforce). Finally, it should be emphasised that, in general, business contracts should be construed in a way which makes "good commercial sense". "If a detailed semantic and syntactical analysis of words in a commercial contract is going to lead to a conclusion that flouts business common sense, it must be made to yield to business common sense" (*Antaios Cia Naviera SA v Salen Rederierna AB* [1985] AC 191, Lord Diplock at p 121). In addition, at a more general level than the impetus to achieve "good commercial sense", is the pressure against a construction which achieves an unreasonable result and the "more unreasonable the result the more unlikely it is that the parties can have intended it, and if they do intend it the more necessary it is that they [should] make that intention abundantly clear" (*L Schuler A G* v *Wickman Machine Tools Sales Ltd* [1974] AC 235, Lord Reid at p 251). Of course, the courts must nevertheless avoid substituting "for the bargain actually made one which the court believes could better have been made" (*Charter Reinsurance Co Ltd* v *Fagan* [1996] 2 WLR 726, Lord Mustill at p 759). (For an informative criticism of Lord Hoffmann's approach see Clarke "Freedom of Information in Commercial Disputes" in *Freedom of Expression and Freedom of Information*, Beatson and Cripps eds.)

(b) Trends in the approach to exemption clauses

The process of construing the contract, with its search for the "intention of the parties", is one which allows the courts sufficient flexibility for the desirability of the end result to play a part in the conclusion reached. Prior to the enactment of the controls imposed upon exemption clauses by the Unfair Contract Terms Act 1977, the courts used the rules of construction inventively in order to mitigate the effects of such clauses. This was described by Lord Denning MR in the Court of Appeal in *George Mitchell (Chesterhall) Ltd* v *Finney Lock Seeds Ltd* [1983] 1 QB 284 (at p 297):

"Faced with this abuse of power — by the strong against the weak — by the use of small print conditions — the judges did what they could to put a curb upon it. They still had before them the idol, 'freedom of contract'. They still knelt down and worshipped it, but they concealed under their cloaks a secret weapon. They used it to stab the idol in the back. This weapon was called 'the construction of the contract'. They used it with great skill and ingenuity. They used it so as to depart from the natural meaning of the words of the exemption clause and to put upon them a strained and unnatural construction."

The courts' ability to use the rules of construction so as to arrive at the result they thought appropriate was used to its fullest extent before the Unfair Contract Terms Act 1977. Since then the use of "strained construction" has been deprecated. In *Photo Production Ltd* v *Securicor Transport Ltd* [1980] AC 827 Lord Diplock said (at p 851):

"the reports are full of cases in which what would appear to be very strained constructions have been placed upon exclusion clauses, mainly in what today would be called consumer contracts and contracts of adhesion ... any need for this kind of judicial distortion of the English language has been banished by Parliament's having made these kinds of contracts subject to the Unfair Contract Terms Act 1977." (See also eg *George Mitchell (Chesterhall) Ltd* v *Finney Lock Seeds Ltd* [1983] 2 AC 803 at p 810.)

Of course, in the consumer context, the controls of the 1977 Act have now been added to by the EC Directive/Regulations on Unfair Terms in Consumer Contracts (previously the 1994 version, now the 1999 version). In addition, it is not yet clear to what extent the interpretation of exemption clauses will be affected by the evolution of the approach to construction in general, which was identified in the *Investors Compensation Scheme* case — an approach which, as indicated above, assimilates "the way in which such documents are interpreted by judges to the common sense principles by which any serious utterance would be interpreted in ordinary life".

2.   Basic approach

The *contra proferentem* rule applies here so that any ambiguity in the clause is resolved against the person seeking to rely upon it. Exemption clauses are strictly construed. The words used must clearly cover what has occurred if the clause is to be effective. *Wallis, Son & Wells* v *Pratt & Haynes* [1911] AC 394 provides an example of the strict construction of exemption clauses:

> P & H sold seed to W as "common English sanfoin" seed. In fact the seed supplied was giant sanfoin, a different and inferior variety. There was a clause in the sale contract stating that the "sellers give no warranty expressed or implied as to the growth, description or any other matters".

The House of Lords decided that the exemption clause did not cover what had occurred. It was a condition of the contract that the seed supplied was common English sanfoin. A breach of that term could not be covered by a clause which merely referred to warranties.

Andrews Bros (Bournemouth) Ltd v *Singer & Co Ltd* [1934] 1 KB 17 provides a further example of this strict construction:

> Singer & Co contracted to sell Andrews Bros a "new Singer car". The car they delivered had recorded such a mileage that it could no longer be described as a "new" car. Singer & Co sought to rely upon Clause 5 of the contract which stated, ". . . all conditions, warranties and liabilities implied by statute, common law or otherwise are excluded".

The court held that Clause 5 did not protect Singer & Co from failing to provide a "new" car. The clause referred to implied terms and it was an express term that the car should be "new".

The impact of the *Investors Compensation Scheme* case here is yet to be worked out. It has been questioned what "strict construction" means as opposed to the normal process of ascertaining the parties' intention. It may be that it "operates merely by way of intensification, so that the intention must be clear, unambiguous, incapable of misleading . . ."(*Mannai Investment Co Ltd* v *Eagle Star Life Assurance Co Ltd* [1997] 3 All ER 352 at p 377). The *contra proferentem* rule is still being applied (eg *ABTA* v *British Airways* [2000] 2 All ER 204 at p 213, *Zeus Tradition Marine Ltd* v *Bell* [2000] 2 Ll LR 587 at p 597). However, certainly it can be emphasised that it is a "rule of last resort" (*Sinochem* v *Mobil* [2000] 1 All ER (Comm) 474 at p 483) and that "it would be wrong to use it to create an ambiguity where none realistically exists, and then to resolve the question by reference to it" (*Singer* v *Tees & Hartlepool Port Authority* [1988] 2 Ll LR 164 at p 169).

The final point to be made here is that there is what can be regarded as a version of the *contra proferentem* rule in reg 7(2) of the Unfair Terms in Consumer Contracts Regulations 1999. Its operation and whether it works in the same way as the common law rule is considered below (see p 244). It should be noted that, in general, the Regulations contain considerable impetus to draft in "plain intelligible language" and that the use of unclear language may be seen as indicative of unfairness (see p 243).

3. Liability for negligence[7]

The courts have dealt with the issue of whether an exemption clause covers liability based on negligence by developing a three stage test — the *Canada*

Steamship rules (below). However, before considering that test, it should be emphasised that s 2 of the Unfair Contract Terms Act 1977 is concerned with attempts to exclude or restrict liability based on negligence. Where the negligence has caused personal injury or death any such clause will be automatically ineffective (s 2(1)) and in other cases it is subject to the test of reasonableness (s 2(2)). In addition, now where the exemption clause concerned with negligence is in a consumer contract, the 1999 Regulations on unfair terms may subject it to the fairness test. In considering clauses referred to it under the Regulations, the Office of Fair Trading has encountered clauses which are automatically ineffective under s 2(1), as they deal with liability for personal injury or death. Under the Regulations, such a clause is merely subject to the fairness test but the OFT has indicated that "it would be difficult to conceive of circumstances in which [such a clause] would be fair" (OFT Unfair Terms Bulletin 3 at 1.2) and the fact that, under the Regulations, enforcement is not left to the individual consumer may make the application of the fairness test more significant to the consumer than the automatic ineffectiveness of such clauses under the 1977 Act (see further p 219). Obviously exemption clauses dealing with other types of negligently caused loss or damage also fall within the scope of the test of fairness under the Regulations and the Director General of Fair Trading clearly views them as generally unfair in the consumer context (see eg Bulletin 3 at pp 30, 54, Bulletin 4 at p 65).

Consideration should now be given to the test used by the courts when faced with the question of whether an exemption clause covers negligence. The three stage test is:

(i) If the contract contains an express exemption from liability for negligence then effect must be given to it;

(ii) If there is no express reference to negligence, it must be asked whether the words used are wide enough, in their ordinary meaning, to cover liability for negligence; any doubt must be resolved against the party in breach;

(iii) Even if the words used are wide enough to cover liability for negligence, it must be asked whether the party in breach could be liable on some ground other than that of negligence. If he, or she, could be, and if that other ground is not so fanciful or remote that the party in breach cannot be supposed to have desired protection against it, then it is likely that the words will be taken to refer to the non-negligent liability only.

As has been indicated, this is based upon the three stage test formulated by Lord Morton in giving the judgment of the Privy Council in *Canada Steamship Lines Ltd* v *R* [1952] AC 192 at p 208[8]. Two initial points must be made before the stages of the test are considered further. Firstly, the approach is based upon the idea that "it is inherently improbable that one party to the contract should intend to absolve the other party from the consequences of the latter's own negligence" (*Gillespie Brothers & Co Ltd* v *Roy Bowles Transport Ltd* [1973] 1 All ER 193 at p 203). Secondly, it has been suggested that there is no such "high degree of improbability" that a limitation of liability (rather than an exclusion of liability) would be agreed to, and that a less strict approach should be taken to the construction of limitation than exclusion clauses. The idea of making a general distinction of this type between limitation clauses and exclusion clauses is considered more generally, and criticised, below (p 168). The impact on the *Canada Steamship* test of the general approach to construction indicated in the *Investors Compensation Scheme* case (above p 167) will be considered after the stages of the test have been considered further.

It is obvious that there should be no difficulty in finding that a clause covers negligence if it expressly refers to negligence. Any other conclusion would run contrary to the idea of freedom of contract and the basic principle that in construing a clause it is the intention of the parties which is being sought. Although it has been suggested that nothing short of the use of the term negligence itself will suffice (*Lamport & Holt Lines Ltd* v *Coubro & Scrutton (M&I) Ltd (The "Raphael")* [1982] 2 Lloyd's Rep 42 at p 48), what is required here is that the clause should use the term negligence or some synonym for it (*Smith* v *South Wales Switchgear Co Ltd* [1978] 1 WLR 165 at p 168 and p 172) such as the phrase "neglect or default" (*Monarch Airlines* v *London Luton Airport* [1997] CLC 698 at p 706). Clauses explicitly referring to negligence are not unknown (eg *Spriggs* v *Sotheby Parke Bernet & Co* [1986] 1 Lloyd's Rep 487), but do not occur very often. Such a clause could dissuade the party against whom it might be used from contracting. In *EE Caledonia Ltd* v *Orbit Valve plc* [1994] 2 L1 LR 239, Steyn LJ said (at p 246):

> "Why was an express reference to negligence not inserted? ... I have no doubt that the draftsman on the Underground to whom such a question was addressed would say 'one does not want to frighten off one or other of the parties'. Omissions of express reference to negligence in contracts drafted by lawyers tend to be deliberate."

More difficulties arise when general words are used ie once stages (ii) and (iii) (above) become relevant.

The second part of the rule would seem to require consideration of what the clause "plainly means to any ordinary literate and sensible person" (*Lamport & Holt Lines Ltd* v *Coubro Scrutton (The Raphael)* [1982] 2 Lloyd's Rep 42 at p 52), although in appropriate circumstances, specialised commercial knowledge may be relevant. A clause may refer to loss or damage "howsoever caused", directing attention to the cause of the loss (*Joseph Travers & Sons Ltd* v *Cooper* [1915] 1 KB 73 at p 93 and p 101), but less explicit general clauses may be sufficient. The words "any act or omission" have been seen as "certainly wide enough to comprehend negligence" (*Lamport & Holt Lines Ltd* v *Coubro Scrutton (The Raphael)* [1982] 2 Lloyd's Rep 42, Donaldson LJ at p 45). The second and third stages of the test can combine to put the person seeking to rely on the clause "on the horns of a dilemma" ie in some cases arguing that the clause is wide enough to satisfy the second part of the test, will result in it covering "other" liability within the third (*Shell Chemicals Ltd* v *P&O Roadtankers Ltd* [1995] 1 Lloyd's Rep 297, Balcombe LJ at p 301).

The third stage of the test indicated above could be regarded as part of the second stage. In considering whether there could be liability without negligence, the question being asked is merely whether a general clause is ambiguous because of one particular factor; the number of ways in which liability may occur. In some cases liability may occur in more than one way. It may arise on the basis of negligence or it may occur strictly, without fault. Where there can be liability without negligence the courts have tended to find that a generally worded exemption clause is intended to cover only the strict liability and not that based on negligence. In *Alderslade* v *Hendon Laundry Ltd* [1945] 1 KB 189 (see below) Lord Greene MR gave this example (at p 192):

"[a common carrier's] liability in respect of articles entrusted to him is not necessarily based on negligence. Accordingly if a common carrier wishes to limit his liability for lost articles and does not make it quite clear that he is desiring to limit it in respect of his liability for negligence, then the clause will be construed as extending only to his liability on grounds other than negligence."

(See also *Rutter* v *Palmer* [1922] 2 KB 87 at p 94.) A further illustration is provided by *White* v *John Warwick & Co Ltd* [1953] 2 All ER 1021 (Gower, (1954) 17 MLR 155):

Mr White was in business as a newsagent and tobacconist. He contracted with the defendants for the hire of a tradesman's tricycle. The defendants supplied him with a tricycle with a defective saddle which caused him to fall off and injure himself. The contract of hire contained a clause which stated "nothing in this agreement shall render the owners liable for any personal injury to the riders of the machines hired".

Mr White sued the defendants for damages for his injuries. He had two grounds for his claim:

(i) breach of contract for failure to supply a tricycle which was reasonably fit for its purpose (strict liability); and

(ii) liability for negligently failing to see that the cycle was kept in good repair.

The defendants sought to rely upon the exemption clause in the contract of hire. The Court of Appeal concluded that the exemption clause should be construed as merely applying to the strict liability and not to the liability for negligence. (In such a case the exclusion of liability for negligently caused personal injury would now be prevented by s 2 Unfair Contract Terms Act 1977.) See also *EE Caledonia Ltd* v *Orbit Valve plc* [1994] 2 Lloyd's Rep 239.

One point which should be emphasised is that not every alternative basis of liability will be relevant to the third part of the test. To be relevant to the question of construction, an alternative basis of liability must not be too "fanciful or remote" so that it "would not have been within the contemplation of the parties when the terms of the [contract] were agreed" (*Canada Steamship Lines Ltd* v *R* [1952] AC 192 at p 210). The question of whether or not any alternative basis of liability is too "fanciful or remote" will depend upon the facts of the particular case, but it should be borne in mind that:

"When two commercial concerns contract with one another, they do not. . . concern themselves with. . . legal subtleties. . . We should look at the facts and realities of the situation as they did or must be deemed to have presented themselves to the contracting parties at the time the contract was made, and ask what potential liabilities the one to the other did the parties apply their minds, or must be deemed to have done so". (*Lamport & Holt Lines Ltd* v *Coubro & Scrutton (M & I) Ltd; (The Raphael)* [1982] 2 Lloyd's Rep 42 at p 50 *per* May LJ (see also Stephenson LJ at p 51).)

In *The Raphael* the contract concerned the restowing of a derrick on board the plaintiff's vessel. The defendants negligently allowed the derrick to fall on to the deck, damaging the vessel. There was a general exemption clause in the contract, referring to "any act or omission" of the defendants. This was held to be wide enough to cover negligence. The court felt that the only alternative bases of liability were not such that the parties could be taken to have contemplated them at the time of contracting. (See also *Cert plc* v *George Hammond plc* [1999] 2 All ER (Comm) 976 at p 988.)

We have discussed up to this point the situation where there is a generally worded exemption clause and negligence is not the only basis of liability. The converse of that situation is where there is a generally worded clause but there is no liability, and no breach of contract, in the absence of negligence. Where the sole basis of liability is negligence, the courts more readily find that a generally worded exemption clause covers negligence. In *Alderslade* v *Hendon Laundry Ltd* [1945] 1 KB 189 it was successfully argued that the exemption clause covered negligence. In that case:

> Mr Alderslade left ten Irish linen handkerchiefs with the laundry to be washed. The laundry lost the handkerchiefs. The contract contained a clause which stated "The maximum amount allowed for lost or damaged articles is 20 times the charge made for laundering".

When sued by Mr Alderslade, the laundry sought to rely upon the clause to limit its liability. The loss of the handkerchiefs constituted a breach of contract only if the laundry had been negligent; there was no strict liability for the loss. It was decided that the clause covered the breach, the negligent loss of the handkerchiefs.

In *Alderslade* Lord Greene MR considered the third stage of the test and used language which indicated that the presence, or absence, of an alternative basis of liability to negligence is determinative of the question of construction of a widely worded, general, exemption clause. In that case there was no liability in the absence of negligence and he was influenced by the fact that, if the court had concluded otherwise, the exemption clause would have served no purpose at all. He said (at p 192) that the clause *must* be construed as relating to negligence, in the absence of other possible liability for it to cover (see also Lord Morton in *Canada Steamship Lines* v *R* [1952] AC 192 at p 208). However this is to take too rigid a line. In *Alderslade* Mackinnon LJ took the approach that "if the only liability of the party pleading the exemption is a liability for negligence, the clause will *more readily* operate to exempt him" (at p 195, quoting Scrutton LJ in *Rutter* v *Palmer* [1922] 2 KB 87 at p 92). Similarly, in relation to the converse case, it has been emphasised that the presence of an alternative, non-negligent, ground of liability is merely an indicator of the parties' intentions:

> "If there is a head of liability upon which the clause could bite in addition to negligence then, because it is more unlikely than not that a party will be ready to excuse his other contracting party from the consequence of the other's negligence, the clause will generally be construed as not covering negligence. . . the court asks itself what in all the relevant circumstances the parties intended the alleged exemption clause to mean" (*Lamport & Holt Lines Ltd* v *Coubro & Scrutton (M & I) Ltd; (The Raphael)* [1982] 2 Lloyd's Rep 42 *per* May LJ at p 50).

In short it must be borne in mind that in looking at the three stage test above, we are not considering a rule of law, merely an aid to construction (*Smith* v *South Wales Switchgear Co Ltd* [1978] 1 WLR 165 at p 178 *per* Lord Keith).

Hollier v *Rambler Motors Ltd* [1972] 2 QB 71 illustrates the point that the three part test merely assists construction. Mr Hollier's car was on the Rambler Motors' premises for repair when it was damaged by a fire caused by their negligence. Rambler Motors had a standard form document containing the clause, "The company is not responsible for damage caused by fire to customers' cars on the premises". The Court of Appeal decided that Rambler Motors had not incorporated that clause into the particular contract with Mr Hollier (see page 156). However, the court also considered whether the clause would have covered what had occurred had it been incorporated. It was argued that, as there was no breach unless the fire had been caused by Rambler Motors' negligence, the clause had to cover a negligent breach or it would serve no purpose. The court did not take that line. It considered how an ordinary person, in the position of Mr Hollier, would have viewed the clause and concluded that he would have seen it as merely indicating that there was no strict liability for fire damage. The case before the court was contrasted with *Alderslade* which the court thought had dealt with a situation where "any ordinary man or woman would have known that all that was being excluded was the negligence of the laundry" (at p 80). The clause before the court in *Hollier* was construed as not covering negligence but rather as a warning to customers that Rambler Motors were not liable if a car was damaged by a fire occurring without negligence. (For a discussion of the case see Barendt (1972) 85 MLR 644.)[9]

As we have seen, in applying the three stage test above the courts look at the clause in context; they consider such matters as the understanding of the ordinary person and whether a possible liability is too "fanciful or remote" for the parties to have considered it when contracting. Clearly this leaves sufficient flexibility for the courts' view of the justice of the case to influence their legal reasoning. It must be remembered that *Hollier* did not concern a dispute between two business people but rather between a consumer and a business-man. However, the tools which the courts have available to assist them to achieve a desired result vary from time to time. When they acquire a new tool their use of an old one may change. It must be emphasised that since the Unfair Contract Terms Act 1977 the courts have acknowledged that they should no longer resort to "strained construction" to restrict the operation of exemption clauses (for example, *Photo Production Ltd* v *Securicor Transport Ltd* [1980] AC 827 Lord Diplock at p 851; *George Mitchell (Chesterhall) Ltd* v *Finney Lock Seeds Ltd* [1983] 2 AC 803 at p 810 and there are now also the Unfair Terms in Consumer Contracts Regulations 1999 to consider.)

In addition, some final consideration should be given to the *Canada Steamship* approach in the light of the principles set out in the *Investors Compensation Scheme* case. The *Canada Steamship* case might simply be viewed as part of the "old intellectual baggage of legal interpretation" which is being dispensed with (see above p 159). However, it has been seen as based on the assumption about the probability of one party intending to excuse the other's negligence and it has been seen "when properly understood" as "according with ... common sense" (*E Scott (Plant Hire) Ltd* v *British Waterways Board,* 1982, 20 December, Lexis). In any event, the point can also be made that the approach is so well established that, at least in commercial cases, it could be seen as part of the "background knowledge which would reasonably have been available to the parties at the time of the contract" (see above p 159), and so to be taken into account in the construction process on that basis. Certainly, the analogous point can be made that a previous decision on the interpretation of a clause has been seen as still relevant to the interpretation of a related clause when the previous decision "would be likely to have been in the back of the minds of those negotiating [the instant] contract" (*MDIS Ltd* v *Swinbank* [1999] 2 All ER (Comm) 722 at p 728). It may be, however, that there will be more emphasis placed upon the fact that the *Canada Steamship* approach is simply an aid to construction and that it does not need to be considered where the clause can be regarded as "unambiguously" covering negligence. It may also be that that conclusion is more likely, currently, to be arrived at where what is in question is a limitation rather than an exclusion clause (*BHP Petroleum Ltd* v *British Steel plc* [2000] 2 All ER (Comm) 133; *Cert plc* v *George Hammond plc* [1999] 2 All ER (Comm) 976 at p 987) but that artificial distinction is criticised below.

4. Limitation of liability

The House of Lords has distinguished the construction of clauses which totally exclude liability from the construction of those which merely limit it. In *Ailsa Craig Fishing Co Ltd* v *Malvern Fishing Co Ltd* [1983] 1 WLR 964 the House of Lords stated that limitation clauses are to be construed differently from total exclusion clauses. In that case:

> Securicor had undertaken to provide a security service for the boats belonging to a fishing association whilst those vessels were in Aberdeen harbour. Ailsa Craig were members of that association. One night their vessel, the Strathallan, fouled another boat and sank. Ailsa Craig claimed £55,000 damages from Securicor. Securicor conceded that they had been negligent, and breached their contract, but sought to rely upon a clause in the contract to restrict their liability to £1,000.

The House of Lords decided that the clause was effective to limit Securicor's liability to £1,000.

The general comments on the construction of limitation clauses in *Ailsa Craig* should be noted. Such clauses are still to be construed *contra proferentem* (pp 966 and 971), but Lord Wilberforce stated that limitation clauses are not to be treated with "the same hostility as clauses of exclusion" (p 966). Lord Fraser thought that the rules for the construction of exclusion clauses should not be applied in "their full rigour" to limitation clauses (p 971). The same line was taken by the House of Lords in *George Mitchell (Chesterhall) Ltd* v *Finney Lock Seeds Ltd* [1983] 2 AC 803 (see above). There Lord Bridge, with whom the rest of the court agreed, stated that the principles used for the construction of total exclusion clauses "cannot be applied in their full rigour to limitation clauses" (p 814).

The natural reaction to this stated distinction between limitation and exclusion clauses is that it is wholly unrealistic as "a limitation clause may be so severe in its operation as to be virtually indistinguishable from that of an exclusion clause".

Such indeed was the reaction of the High Court of Australia when refusing to take the same approach to the construction of a limitation clause as the House of Lords (*Darlington Futures Ltd* v *Delco Australia Property* (1986) 68 ALR 385 at p 391). The Australian High Court thought that the same basic approach should be taken to the interpretation of limitation and exclusion clauses. It felt that the way in which any exemption clause, whether it limited or excluded liability, was construed was sufficiently flexible to take account of any case in which it was relevant that the clause was one which limited rather than totally excluded liability. This approach seems preferable to that of the House of Lords. Some support for a move towards it here might be found in the judgment of Evans LJ in *BHP Petroleum* v *British Steel* [2000] 2 All ER (Comm) 133 (at para 43) where he favoured the single line that:

"the more extreme the consequences are, in terms of excluding or modifying the liability that would otherwise arise, then the more stringent the court's approach should be in requiring that clause should be clearly and unambiguously expressed."

However, the House of Lords has put forward some justification for its approach. In *Ailsa Craig* Lord Wilberforce said (at p 966):

"Clauses of limitation are not to be regarded with the same hostility as clauses of exclusion; this is because they must be related to other contractual terms, in particular to the risks to which the defending party may be exposed, the remuneration which he receives, and possibly also the opportunity of the other party to insure."

(See also Lord Fraser at p 970.) This is to take the line that a limitation clause will represent a carefully agreed allocation of risks between the parties and, on that basis, is not to be construed "hostilely". There are two points to be made here. First, such a correlation of factors may be present when there is an exclusion clause and may not be present when there is a limitation clause. In *Photo Production Ltd* v *Securicor Transport Ltd* [1980] AC 827 the court considered the exclusion of liability for fire damage to be reasonable where Securicor was providing a relatively cheap service, particularly as it was more efficient for Photo Production to insure against the risk than for Securicor to do so. Conversely, in *Mitchell* v *Finney Lock Seeds*, although there was a low price in comparison with the potential loss, the clause merely limiting liability was considered to be unreasonable and the fact that the seedsmen could have insured against such liability, without materially affecting their prices, was one indication of "unreasonableness". Secondly, the true relevance of the above factors is in relation to the "reasonableness" of the exemption clause, whether it is one excluding or limiting liability. The Unfair Contract Terms Act 1977 will often now allow the courts to examine the "reasonableness" of the clause and factors relating to the issue of reasonableness must largely be left to be considered within the context of the Act if "strained construction" is to be avoided.

There is one situation in which there is a basic difference in principle between a clause which merely limits and one which excludes liability (see (1983) 99 LQR 163). An exclusion clause could be so extensive that the court would be faced with the question of whether the person relying upon it was under any obligation at all, ie if X and Y have made an agreement X could have inserted an exclusion clause which is so extensive that X appears to have no legal liability, whatever he does or does not do, and so has no initial legal obligation under the agreement. In this situation the court would have to determine whether X and Y had intended to make a legally enforceable contract at all. If it concluded that they had, it would have to find a way of construing the exclusion clause to leave some binding obligation upon X. This singular situation can never arise in relation to a limitation clause. In seeking to limit liability the parties acknowledge the existence of the obligation on which that liability is founded. When dealing with a limitation clause, the question of whether the parties in fact intended a legally enforceable contract cannot arise in the way that it can in relation to a total exclusion clause. (See *Mitchell* v *Finney Lock Seeds* [1983] 1 QB 284 *per* Oliver LJ at p 304.) However, interesting as this distinction may be (see Coote, *Exception Clause* (1964) Chapter 1), it would not justify the wide, and unqualified, general distinction made by the House of Lords between exclusion and limitation clauses. Certainly there is nothing to indicate that their lordships considered the approach they were taking to be restricted to this narrow point and every indication that they viewed their approach as being of general application. This narrow point of principle does not appear to provide a basis for the distinction made by the House of Lords.

5. Inconsistent terms

The exemption clause may appear to be inconsistent with one of the other terms of the contract, and an issue of construction will then arise. Did the parties intend the exemption clause to deprive the apparent term of its contractual force or is the exemption clause subject to that other term? *J Evans & Son (Portsmouth)* v *Andrea Merzario Ltd* [1976] 1 WLR 1078 provides an example of this type of problem. In that case:

> Evans were importers of machinery. Merzario were the freight forwarding agents that they used. From 1959 to 1967 Merzario shipped machinery for Evans on the basis that it would always be shipped below deck to prevent rusting. In 1967 Merzario wished to change to using containers to ship goods. Merzario discussed this with Evans. Evans did not want their goods to be carried on deck even in containers. Evans agreed to the change to containers on being given an assurance that the containers with their goods in would continue to be shipped below deck. None of this was in writing. Subsequently, Merzario agreed to ship an injection moulding machine for Evans in a container. Merzario failed to ensure that the container was shipped below deck and, in a swell, the container fell overboard and was lost. Evans sought to sue Merzario on the basis that the loss was due to breach of a term that the machinery would be shipped below deck. Merzario sought to rely upon the standard conditions of the freight forwarding trade. Clause 4 stated "subject to express instructions in writing given by the customer, [Merzario] reserves to itself complete freedom in respect of means, route and procedure to be followed in the handling and transportation of goods".

Obviously, on its face, clause 4 was inconsistent with any contention that there was an enforceable obligation on Merzario to ship the goods below deck. Nevertheless, reversing the decision of Kerr J, the Court of Appeal held that the express oral assurance, that the machinery would be shipped below deck, was an enforceable contractual obligation which prevailed over clause 4 (either on the basis that it was a collateral contract or because it was part of the main contract, which was partly oral and partly written). Roskill LJ said (at p 1084):

> "It is a question of construction. Interpreting the contract. . . one has to treat the promise that no container would be shipped on deck as overriding any

question of [an] exempting condition. Otherwise... the promise would be illusory."

This seems to represent the reality of the situation. There was a clear oral statement which both parties knew was essential to the contract. There was also a standard set of terms which conflicted with that oral statement. It seems clear that the parties were in full subjective agreement about the term which required shipment below deck. It is unlikely that there was much actual knowledge of the content and impact of the standard terms by either party.

The same conclusion has been reached in other cases where there has been a clear oral promise, essential to the contract, and a contradiction of that promise in one party's standard terms. *Harling* v *Eddy* [1951] 2 KB 739 provides another example:

> Mr Eddy had put a heifer up for sale at an auction. When his heifer came into the ring nobody bid for her until Mr Eddy said that there was nothing wrong with her and he would absolutely guarantee her in every respect. Mr Harling then bid for and purchased the heifer. Within three months the heifer was dead from tuberculosis. Mr Eddy sought to defend himself from a claim for breach of contract by relying on condition 12 of the printed conditions of sale at the auction. Condition 12 said "No animal... is sold with a warranty unless specifically mentioned at the time of offering, and no warranty so given shall have any legal force or effect unless the terms thereof appear on the purchaser's account." The statement Mr Eddy had made as to the heifer's condition had not appeared on Mr Harling's account.

The Court of Appeal concluded that the statement was a condition and not covered by a clause relating to a warranty but, even if this was not the case, the oral statement overrode the printed term. Bearing in mind the lack of any bidding until the statement was made the defendant implied "that the animal should be sold on the faith of what he stated, to the exclusion of condition 12, or any other condition which might be found in the auction particulars which would of itself appear to exclude any oral statement" (Lord Evershed MR at p 744. See also *Couchman* v *Hill* [1947] KB 554 at p 558). Although it is unlikely that the parties' thought processes were quite so analytical, this recognizes the reality of the situation.

Even commercial parties may concentrate on reaching agreement on a few basic terms without giving any thought to the contents of the standard terms[10]. This approach, and the problems it can create, has already been seen in the "battle of the forms", where the parties may well ensure that they agree on such terms as price and quantity whilst exchanging conflicting standard terms on other matters (see page 20). These cases can similarly be explained as being caused by a lack of consideration of the standard terms. In the above cases this meant that the parties had not considered the standard terms in the light of the terms on which they wished to reach specific agreement in the particular contract. The court was, in effect, faced with a question of priority, ie which term was to be read subject to which. In all the circumstances the court found it fairly easy to conclude that the individually agreed oral terms should prevail over the conflicting terms which were to be found only in the midst of the standard form which had been accepted as a whole.

6. Fundamental breach

There were attempts to introduce a rule of law preventing "fundamental breaches", or breaches of "fundamental terms", being covered by exemption clauses, no matter how aptly worded the clause (eg *Karsales (Harrow) Ltd* v *Wallis* [1956] 1 WLR 936). However, in *Suisse Atlantique Société d'Armement Maritime SA* v *NV Rotterdamsche Kolen Centrale* [1967] 1 AC 361 the House of Lords disagreed with any such attempts, and in *Photo Production Ltd* v *Securicor Ltd* [1980] AC 827, it "gave the final quietus to the doctrine that a 'fundamental breach' of contract deprived the party in breach of the benefit of a clause in the contract excluding or limiting his liability" *(George Mitchell (Chesterhall) Ltd* v *Finney Lock Seeds Ltd* [1983] 2 All ER 737, Lord Bridge at p 741). The purpose of the Court of Appeal, in attempting to create fundamental breach as a rule of law, was to deal with objectionable exemption clauses in a way which the draftsman would not overcome. However, the usefulness of fundamental breach as a rule of law had been considered in *Suisse Atlantique.* There it had been pointed out that it was an undiscrimating approach to the problem of objectionable exemption clauses as it could strike down clauses arrived at as a fairly negotiated allocation of risk between businesses. It was indicated that to deal with objectionable exemption clauses a more discriminating tool than fundamental breach would have to be provided by legislation. (See Lord Reid at p 406.) By the time *Photo Production* was decided, Parliament had provided the courts with a means of attacking exemption clauses in a more discriminating way: the Unfair Contract Terms Act 1977.

Once fundamental breach had been disposed of as a rule of law, the point could be made that it "is always necessary when considering an exemption clause to decide whether as a matter of construction, it extends to exclude or restrict the liability in question, but, if it does, it is no longer permissable at common law to reject or circumvent the clause by treating it as inapplicable to a 'fundamental breach'" *(Edmund Murray* v *BSP International Foundations* (1993) 33 Con LR 1, Neill LI at p 16). In this context, it was never entirely clear what was meant by a "fundamental breach" or a "fundamental term" and it now seems unnecessary to be overly concerned with those questions or to use the terminology. It may be that the more extensive, or significant, the breach the more explicit wording the courts will require in order to be convinced that it was intended to be covered by an exemption clause, but any such tendency does not need to be regarded as a named rule.

7. "Peas and beans", main purpose of the contract, four corners rule

Here brief consideration can be given to some of the approaches and rules which were, in effect, the foundations upon which the attempt was made to construct "fundamental breach" as a rule of law. Some care has to be taken, though, not to resurrect that idea.

The argument may arise that an exemption clause does not cover what has occurred, because it was only intended to relate to the situation in which the contract was being performed (albeit in some way defectively) and what has occurred is not a performance of the contract, even a defective one. In other words, it is argued that the clause was not intended to apply in such circumstances because they are beyond the boundaries of the contract, by which the clause was intended to be limited. In *Chanter* v *Hopkins* (1838) 4 M & W 399 Lord Abinger said (at p 404):

"If a man offers to buy peas of another, and he sends him beans, he does not perform his contract. But that is not a warranty; there is no warranty that he should sell him peas; the contract is to sell peas, and if he sends him anything else in their stead, it is a non-performance of it."

If there is a contract between two parties, X and Y, and X has contracted to deliver peas to Y, but he delivers beans instead, it will be contended that he cannot rely upon any clause of the contract excluding his liability for defective performance because what occurred was not a performance at all, even a defective one. (Of course, care must be taken in ascertaining exactly what the contractual obligations were. The contract may have been one for the supply of peas or beans or, even, any green vegetable — see Devlin [1966] CLJ 192 at p 212). But, this type of argument has been seen as going beyond delivery of goods which are clearly of an entirely different kind to that contracted for, to the situation where the goods delivered are, at one level, the type of goods contracted for, but which are argued to be so defective that their delivery cannot be regarded as within the performance of the contract (eg *Karsales* v *Wallis* [1956] 1 WLR 936). However, such an approach must now be regarded as of very restricted application. In *George Mitchell Ltd* v *Finney Lock Seeds Ltd* [1983] 2 AC 803 where there was a contract for the sale of Dutch winter white cabbage seed and an inferior autumn variety was supplied which led to a valueless crop, the House of Lords refused to apply this type of approach. The view was taken that acceptance of that argument in the Court of Appeal and at first instance "came dangerously near to re-introducing by the back door the doctrine of fundamental breach" (at p 741). The relevant clause was seen as applying to "seeds" and "seeds" had been supplied.

However, there are other situations, in which arguments arise, that an exemption clause was not intended to apply to what has occurred because it has gone beyond the boundaries of the contract. That line may be taken in relation to the situation in which a ship unjustifiably deviates from its route, or a bailee stores goods other than in the place contracted for, or hands them over to a sub-contractor without authority. In each case, it is, of course, necessary to determine what the boundaries of the contract are, a clause may give a ship "liberty to deviate" for example, and effect will be given to such a clause. However, faced with wide clauses, serving to stretch the contractual boundaries, the courts may find that such clauses are intended to be restricted by the "main purpose", or the "four corners", of the contract. In *Glynn* v *Margetson & Co* [1893] AC 351 when a clause in a contract for the shipment of a perishable cargo stated that the ship "should have liberty to proceed to and stay at any port or ports in any station in the Mediterranean, Levant, Black Sea, or Adriatic, or on the coasts of Africa, Spain, Portugal, France, Great Britain or Ireland, for the purpose of delivering coals, cargo, or passengers, or for any other purpose whatsoever", that clause did not prevent the shipowners from being liable for the damage to the cargo, when it had gone 350 miles off of the direct route. The clause provided a liberty to deviate but the approach taken was that it had to be read in the light of the main purpose of the contract, ascertained from reading it as a whole and that main purpose of getting a perishable cargo from A to B would be defeated if the liberty to deviate was not read as confined to ports along the route from A to B. Similarly, in *Sze Hai Tong Bank* v *Rambler Cycle Co* [1959] AC 576 where there was a clause stating that that "the responsibility of the carrier ... shall be deemed ... to cease absolutely after the goods are discharged from the ship" but the contract also provided that delivery should only be made on production of the bill of lading, the court viewed delivery of the goods without production of the bill of lading as defeating the main object of the contract and as outside the protection of the other clause. The situation was equated with what would have occurred if the carriers had burnt the goods or thrown them into the sea. However, this type of reasoning must be used with care to avoid resurrecting fundamental breach. The reasoning in the recent case of *Motis Exports Ltd* v *Dampskibsselskabet* [2000] 1 All ER (Comm) 91, in extending the *Rambler Cycle* case, above, to hold liable carriers who had handed over goods in response to a forged bill of lading, has been seen as "coming perilously close to, if not actually to be, the doctrine of fundamental breach" (Davenport [2000] LMCLQ 455 at p 456).

C. Exemption clauses and third parties

1. Introduction

Traditionally, the rule of privity of contract has meant that basically only the parties to a contract can enforce a benefit in it or be burdened by it and there is a full discussion of privity of contract in Chapter 18. However, where contracts confer benefits on third parties, this could thwart the intentions of the contracting parties and deny the reasonable expectation of the third parties. The common law developed various means of avoiding the privity rule and that has now been furthered by the Contracts (Rights of Third Parties) Act 1999. Here, brief consideration will be given to the situation in which a third party, C, can have the protection of an exemption clause in a contract between A and B. That issue is of particular importance when C is an employee, or subcontractor, of B and A is making a claim, in tort, against C, based on C's carrying out of a task which is part of the work dealt with by the contract between A and B. It has been seen as undesirable to allow the privity rule to be used effectively to undermine the contractual allocation of the risk and the concomitant insurance coverage. In *The Mahkutai* [1996] AC 650 (at p 651), for example, the point was made that:

> "Recognition has been given to the undesirability, especially in the commercial context, of allowing plaintiffs to circumvent the contractual exemption clause by suing in particular the servant or agent of the contracting party who caused the relevant damage, thereby undermining the purpose of the exemption, and so redistributing the contractual allocation of risk, which is reflected in the freight rate and the parties' respective insurance arrangements".

As has been indicated, the courts have developed various devices to circumvent the privity rule and allow the third party to rely upon the exemption clause in such cases. Probably the most successful are those based on a kind of agency and the negativing of the duty of care in tort. Some brief consideration will be given to those devices before the impact of the Contracts (Rights of Third Parties) Act 1999 is considered.

2. Common law devices

The "agency" device can be understood by brief consideration of *Midland Silicones Ltd* v *Scruttons Ltd* [1962] AC 446. The case was concerned with commonly occurring facts:

> A were cargo owners, B carriers, and C stevedores. A had contracted with B for the carriage of their goods. The stevedores, C, negligently damaged the cargo owner's, A's, goods. The stevedores had contracted with B, the carrier, and were third parties to the contract between A and B. The stevedores, C, were sued in tort by A.

It was held that the stevedores were unable to rely on an exemption clause in the contract between A and B, to which they were third parties. However, what is significant is that Lord Reid indicated a situation in which the third party, C, might be able to rely on the exemption clause in the contract between A and B. He said (at p 474):

> "I can see a possibility of the success of the argument if (first) the bill of lading makes it clear that the stevedore is intended to be protected by the provisions in it which limit liability, (secondly) the bill of lading makes it clear that the carrier, in addition to contracting for those provisions on his own behalf is also contracting as agent for the stevedore that those provisions should apply to the stevedore, (thirdly) the carrier has authority from the stevedore to do that, or perhaps later ratification by the stevedore would suffice, and (fourthly) that any difficulties about consideration moving from the stevedore were overcome."

Such an approach was unhelpful to the stevedores in the particular case as the exemption clause only referred to the "carrier" — there was nothing which could be said "to make it clear that the stevedore [was] intended to be protected" by it. However, the Privy Council accepted the effectiveness of the type of approach identified by Lord Reid in *The Eurymedon (New Zealand Shipping Co Ltd* v *A M Satterthwaite & Co Ltd)* [1975] AC 154 allowing the stevedores, in that case, the protection of the exemption clause, and similarly in *The New York Star (Port Jackson Stevedoring Pty Ltd* v *Salmond & Spraggon (Australia) Pty Ltd)* [1981] 1 WLR 138. This device has met with some success but it does depend upon the fulfilment of the technical requirements identified by Lord Reid. Obviously the clause must appropriately refer to C and, for example, it must be possible for it to be found that B contracted on behalf of C (ie acted as C's agent) in agreeing the exemption clause and that C supplied consideration for A's promise contained in the exemption clause. The point has been made that:

> "so long as the principles continue to be understood to rest upon an enforceable contract as between the cargo owners and the stevedores entered into through the agency of the shipowner, it is inevitable that technical points of contract and agency law will continue to be invoked by cargo owners seeking to enforce tortious remedies against stevedores and others uninhibited by the exceptions and limitations in the relevant bills of lading" (*The Mahkutai* [1996] AC 650 at p 664).

It will not always be possible to avoid the effects of such technicalities but there has been discouragement of a "search for fine distinctions which would

175

diminish the general applicability [of the approach] in the light of established commercial practice" (*The New York Star* [1981] 1 WLR 138 at p 144).

The second device to consider is the negativing of the duty of care. The contract between A and B may indirectly help to protect C from liability, in tort, for negligence by negativing or limiting, the duty of care which C owes to A. The "contractual background", particularly the allocation of the need to insure, may serve to prevent a duty of care arising between a contracting party and a third party — in particular between the owner of a building and the sub-contractor carrying out work on it. The contract terms and the background in each case will need to be considered. (See eg *Southern Water Authority* v *Carey* [1985] 2 All ER 1077; *Norwich City Council* v *Harvey* [1989] 1 All ER 1180; *Marc Rich & Co* v *Bishop Rock Marine Co (The Nicholas H)* [1995] 3 All ER 307; *British Telecommunications plc* v *James Thomson and Sons (Engineers) Ltd* [1999] 2 All ER 241).

3. Contracts (Rights of Third Parties) Act 1999

The common law has provided devices to mitigate the effects of the privity rule in this area. However, brief consideration should now be given to the Contracts (Rights of Third Parties) Act 1999 (see further Chapter 18). Section 1 sets out the basic test of enforceability. It states:

"1(1) Subject to the provisions of this Act, a person who is not a party to a contract (a "third party") may in his own right enforce a term of the contract if—
(a) the contract expressly provides that he may, or
(b) subject to subsection (2), the term purports to confer a benefit on him.
(2) Subsection 1(b) does not apply if on a proper construction of the contract it appears that the parties did not intend the term to be enforceable by the third party."

In other words, either (a) the contract must expressly provide that the third party may enforce the term or (b) the term must purport to confer a benefit on C and, on a proper construction of the contract, it does not appear that the parties did not intend the term to be enforceable by the third party. In addition, to acquire rights, the third party must be "expressly identified in the contract" to a stated extent (ie "by name, as a member of a class or as answering a particular description") (s 1(3)). The third party will not acquire rights to enforce a term "otherwise than subject to and in accordance with any other relevant terms of the contract" (s 1(4)). Where the original contract would confer rights on a third party, there are limitations on the abilities of the contracting parties to affect those rights by agreement, variation or rescission of the contract (s 2(1)). However, the point which must be emphasised here is that although the Act generally refers to the rights of a third party to enforce a term, s 1(6) makes it clear that it encompasses the situation in which a third party, C, seeks to avail himself, or herself, of the "benefit" of exclusions or limitations of liability in a contract between A and B. Where the third party, C, does seek to rely on an exemption clause in the contract between A and B, the Unfair Contract Terms Act 1977 may fall to be considered. Under s 1(6) a third party seeking to enforce a term of the contract (including an exemption clause) "cannot do so if he could not have done so ... had he been a party to the contract".

4. Further developments

Brief consideration has now been given to the common law's approach to the problem of the privity rule in this area. It produced a number of devices which in some situations could be used to allow third parties the protection of an exemption clause. The point was made however that there is some uncertainty in the use of such devices — they might be defeated by a technicality in a particular case — and in any event they did not cover all situations.

> "While most commentators welcome, at least in principle, the various judicial exceptions to privity of contract, concerns about the predictability of its use have been raised. Moreover, it is said, in cases where the recognised exceptions do not appear to apply, the underlying concerns of commercial reality and justice still militate for the recognition of a third party beneficiary right." (*London Drugs Ltd* v *Kuehne & Nagel International Ltd* (1992) 97 DLR (4th) 261, Iacobucci J at p 348.)

The Contracts (Rights of Third Parties) Act 1999 may supply a more uniform and certain approach where it applies, but its application is also limited. The point can be made that, in order for third parties to be able to rely on the Act, there must be sufficient express reference to the third parties for the situation to fall within s 1(1)(a) or (b). An employee, C, will not be able to make use of the Act to rely on an exemption clause in a contract between A and his, or her, employer in the absence of sufficient reference to employees in the clause. This leaves obvious scope for avoidance of the contractual allocation of risk through an action against an employee rather than the employer. However, there is still scope for judicial development in this area. The Act specifically states that it "does not affect any right or remedy of a third party that exists or is available apart from this Act" (s 7(1)) and the Law Commission envisaged that judicial development would continue. It was said (Law Com No 242, para 5.10):

> "We should emphasise that we do not wish our proposed legislation — which we believe to be a relatively conservative and moderate measure — to hamper the judicial development of third party rights. Should the House of Lords decide that in a particular sphere our reform does not go far enough and that, for example ... employees (even though not mentioned in the contract) should be able to rely on exclusion clauses that protect their employers under a doctrine of vicarious immunity, we would not wish our proposed legislation to be construed as hampering that development".

The point can be made that elsewhere there has been a move towards a doctrine of "vicarious immunity" for employees and that similar developments could take place here. In *London Drugs Ltd* v *Kuehne & Nagel International Ltd* (1992) 97 DLR (4th) 261 the Supreme Court of Canada has provided some such protection for employees. Employees were viewed as entitled to the benefit of limitation clauses if (at p 366):

> "(1) the limitation of liability clause must either expressly or impliedly extend its benefit to the employees ... seeking to rely on it; and

(2)   the employees ... seeking the benefit of the limitation of liability must have been in the course of their employment and must have been performing the very services provided for in the contract between the employer and the plaintiff (customer) when the loss occurred".

In that case the clause was seen as impliedly extending its benefit to employees. The court took the view that when most contracts are made between customer and employer it will be contemplated that it will be employees who will actually carry out the services contracted for. In those circumstances, there was seen to be such an identity of interest between employer and employee in relation to a limitation of liability clause in the customer/employer contract that "there was simply no reason for denying the benefit of the clause to employees who perform the contractual obligations" (at p 361). With its reference to *implied* extension of benefit to employees, (and a readiness to recognise such an implication) the *London Drugs* approach might make the protection of an exemption clause more widely available to employees than is the case under the Contracts (Rights of Third Parties) Act 1999[1].

Footnotes

(1)   The EC Directive (1999/93/EC) on a community framework for electronic signatures refers to different "types" of electronic signature and whilst providing for some recognition of electronic signatures generally, it gives a specific role to "advanced electronic signatures", based on a "qualified certificate" and created by a "secure-signature-creation device". Article 5 provides:

1. Member States shall ensure that advanced electronic signatures which are based on a qualified certificate and which are created by a secure-signature-creation device:
(a) satisfy the legal requirements of a signature in relation to data in electronic form in the same manner as a handwritten signature satisfies those requirements in relation to paper-based data; and
(b) are admissible as evidence in legal proceedings.
2. Member States shall ensure that an electronic signature is not denied legal effectiveness and admissability as evidence in legal proceedings solely on the grounds that it is:
– in electric form, or
– not based on a qulalified certificate, or
– not based upon a qualified certificate issued by an accredited certification-service-provider, or
– not created by a secure signature-creation device.

There is no direct reflection of the EC approach, with its "advanced electronic signature" in the Electronic Communications Act 2000. However, the Act does allow requirements to be made in relation to registered certification service providers and their certificates. It may be that English law will not be out of step with the EC measure, but compliance is by no means obvious. See Rowland & Macdonald *Information Technology Law* (2nd ed) pp 319–326.

(2)   Clarke [1976] CLJ 51.

(3)   Macdonald [1988] JBL 375; McClean [1988] CLJ 172; Macdonald, *Exemption Clauses and Unfair Terms* (1999) Butterworths pp 19–24.

(4)   Macdonald (1988) 8 LS 48; Macdonald, *Exemption Clauses and Unfair Terms* (1999) Butterworths pp 26–33.

(5)   *SIAT di del Ferro* v *Tradax Overseas SA* [1978] 2 Lloyd's Rep 470 at p 490; *Johnson Matthey Bankers* v *State Trading Corporation of India* [1984] 1 Lloyd's Rep 427 at p 433; *Circle Freight International* v *Medeast Gulf Exports* [1988] 2 Lloyd's Rep 427 at p 433.

(6)   Macauley, *Non-Contractual Relations in Business* [1963] Am Soc Rev 45; Beale and Dugdale, *Contracts Between Businessmen: Planning and the Use of Contractual Remedies* (1975) 2 Brit J Law and Soc 18.

(7) Palmer [1983] LMCLQ 557; Macdonald, *Exemption Clauses and Unfair Terms* (1999) Butterworths pp 50–61; *Carter* [1995] 9 JCL 69.

(8) See also *George Mitchell (Chesterhall) Ltd* v *Finney Lock Seeds Ltd* [1983] 1 QB 284 at p 312; *Alderslade* v *Hendon Laundry Ltd* [1945] 1 KB 189 at p 192.

(9) Where there is no other head of liability, the clause may be seen as not covering negligence but merely avoiding doubt about the existence of other liability — *Dorset County Council* v *Southern Felt Roofing* [1990] Tr L 96.

(10) See Macauley, *Non-Contractual Relations in Business* [1963] Am Soc Rev 45; Beale and Dugdale, *Contracts between Businessmen: Planning and Use of Contractual Remedies* (1975) 2 Brit J Law and Soc 18.

(11) More recently, the *London Drugs'* approach has been extended beyond employees by the Canadian courts in *Fraser River Pile & Dredge Ltd* v *Can Drive Services Ltd* [2000] 1 Ll Rep 199 but, of course, the Canadian courts do not have the benefit of the general exception to the privity rule which is contained in the Contracts (Rights of Third Parties) Act 1999.

Chapter 10

Exemption clauses and the Unfair Contract Terms Act 1977

1. Introduction

Logically, before any consideration is given to the effect of the Unfair Contract Terms Act 1977 on an exemption clause it should be asked whether the clause is part of the contract and whether it covers the breach which has occurred. Those two points were dealt with in Chapter 9.

The Act is the first piece of legislation to deal with exemption clauses on a fairly general basis rather than merely dealing with specific types of contracts[1] (although certain types of contract are excluded from its operation — see page 181). The name of the Unfair Contract Terms Act 1977 should not be regarded as a clear guide to what it does. It does not deal with "unfair terms" as such. It deals with exemption clauses. This contrasts with the EC Directive/Regulations on Unfair Terms in Consumer Contracts which strike down unfair non-individually negotiated terms in contracts between consumers and sellers or suppliers. There are, however, some exclusions from the terms which it covers (see Chapter 11).

In some circumstances the 1977 Act will strike down an exemption clause because it does not "satisfy the requirement of reasonableness" but in others the clause is struck down without any reference to its reasonableness. To see exactly what effect it will have on any given exemption clause requires careful consideration of its specific provisions.

In Chapter 9 the problem with definition of exclusion clauses was raised. The argument that there is no such distinct type of clause was referred to. It will be considered again in this chapter, as the Act is based upon the assumption that the exclusion clause is a distinct type of clause, and indeed it contains provisions for dealing with exclusion clauses which have been "disguised" in the form of part of the definition of the obligation (see ss 3 and 13 below).

The Act clearly interferes with freedom of contract. It affects the agreement which the parties made for themselves. However, as Lord Reid pointed out in *Suisse Atlantique* [1967] 1 AC 361, the situation in which an "objectionable" exemption clause is found may be one in which one party's freedom of contract is very limited. He said:

> "Probably the most objectionable are found in the complex standard conditions which are now so common. In the ordinary way the customer has

no time to read them, and if he did read them he probably would not understand them. And if he did understand and object to any of them, he would generally be told he could take it or leave it. And if he then went to another supplier the result would be the same. Freedom to contract must surely imply some choice or room for bargaining."

The aim of the Act is to strike down "objectionable" exemption clauses. However the variety of situations and clauses with which it has to deal means that it is not without difficulties.

A. Basic structure of the Act

1. Introduction

A mistake often made by students is to see an exemption clause and jump from there to the statement that the clause must be subject to the "requirement of reasonableness" under the Unfair Contract Terms Act 1977. This is not possible. The Act does not apply to all exemption clauses and it does not subject all of those clauses to which it does apply to the requirement of reasonableness. It renders some clauses automatically ineffective without their "reasonableness" coming into question. If the contract comes within the operation of the Act, a section must first be found which deals with the exemption clause in question and then it must be asked what that section does to the clause. If the section states that the clause is effective only if it satisfies the requirement of reasonableness, the question of the reasonableness of the clause then, and only then, becomes relevant.

The presence of two important types of section within the Act should be emphasised. The first type consists of those sections which state that a clause is totally ineffective or effective only if it satisfies the requirement of reasonableness. These can be termed the "active sections" (eg ss 2, 3, 6 and 7). The second type are the "definition" sections which merely help to explain the meaning of the terms used within the "active sections" (eg s 12 ("deals as consumer") and s 11 ("the requirement of reasonableness")). The key to using the Act is to remember to find an active section applicable to the exemption clause in question. The definition sections assist that active section by clarifying its meaning. It is not possible simply to use s 11, which indicates the meaning of the requirement of reasonableness. That section does not state that the requirement of reasonableness is to be applied to any exemption clause. An active section is required first to indicate that something is to happen to the particular exemption clause.

2. Exemption clauses within the operation of the Act

It should be emphasised that, basically, the Act only applies to business liability. Sections 2–7, subject to the exception in s 6(4) (which is limited in its practical effect, see page 191), apply only to business liability, ie liability for breach of obligations or duties arising (a) from things done or to be done by a person in the course of a business, or (b) from the occupation of premises used for the business purposes of the occupier (s 1(3)). Business is not defined but it includes "a profession and the activities of any government department or local or public authority" (s 14).

Schedule 1 lists certain types of contract which are excluded wholly, or in part, from the operation of the Act. They include contracts of insurance, or any contract in so far as it relates to the creation or transfer of an interest in land (see *Electricity Supply Nominees Ltd* v *IAF Group plc* [1993] 3 All ER 372) or intellectual property (patents, trade marks etc), the formation or dissolution of a company or its constitution, and the creation or transfer of securities (para 1), charterparties and carriage of goods by ship or hovercraft etc (paras 2 and 3), and contracts of employment (para 4) (see s 1(2)).

Sections 26, 27 and 29 set boundaries for the Act in relation to contracts with an international element.

B. The active sections

In considering the active sections, frequent reference will be made to the requirement of reasonableness (s 11), deals as consumer (s 12) etc. These concepts are considered in detail below, where the definition sections are dealt with.

1. Negligence (s 2)

Section 2 is an important and widely applicable section. It deals with liability arising from negligence which, for the purposes of the Act, is defined in s 1. Section 1 states that negligence means the breach:

"(a) of any obligation, arising from the express or implied terms of a contract, to take reasonable care or exercise reasonable skill in the performance of the contract;

(b) of any common law duty to take reasonable care or exercise reasonable skill (but not any stricter duty);

(c) of the common duty of care imposed by the Occupiers' Liability Act 1957".

The duty may arise in contract or tort or under the Occupiers' Liability Act 1957, and s 2 not only relates to contract terms purporting to exclude or restrict liability for negligence, but also covers non-contractual notices attempting to affect such liability in tort. Note that in this section it is irrelevant whether the person against whom an attempt is being made to use the exemption clause or notice deals as a consumer.

Section 2(1) prevents entirely the exclusion or restriction of liability for negligently caused death or personal injury. For example, this section would have provided another means of disposing of the argument in *Thornton Shoe Lane Parking Ltd* [1971] 2 QB 163 (see page 144) that the personal injury which Shoe Lane Parking negligently caused to Mr Thornton was covered by an exemption clause. The ban on such exclusion or restriction is absolute. There is no need to consider whether the clause is reasonable.

Section 2(2) deals with negligently caused loss or damage not covered by s 2(1). It states that a person *cannot* use a contract term or a notice to exclude or restrict his liability for such loss or damage *unless* the term or notice satisfies the requirement of reasonableness. The term or notice will only be effective to exclude or restrict liability for such negligently caused loss or damage if the term or notice satisfies the requirement of reasonableness.

Section 2(3) enigmatically states:

> "Where a contract term or notice purports to exclude or restrict liability for negligence a person's agreement to or awareness of it is not of itself to be taken as indicating his voluntary acceptance of any risk."

This seems to be intended to limit claims to rely upon the tort defence of *volenti non fit injuria*.

Section 2 covers the situation where a contract term would, in the absence of that section, exclude or restrict liability for negligence. This means that there is less need for a very restrictive approach to be taken to the construction of exemption clauses which are claimed to deal with liability for negligence. It is worth considering whether the Court of Appeal would have viewed the construction of the exemption clause in *Hollier* v *Rambler Motors Ltd* [1972] 2 QB 71 in the same way had the Unfair Contract Terms Act 1977 been available to it (see page 166).

It must also be remembered that there is now the additional protection of the Unfair Terms in Consumer Contracts Regulations 1999 (formerly 1994). Now, where an exemption clause concerned with negligence is in a consumer contract, the 1999 Regulations on unfair terms may subject it to the fairness test. In considering clauses referred to it under the Regulations, the Office of Fair Trading has encountered clauses which are automatically ineffective under s 2(1), as they deal with liability for personal injury or death. Under the Regulations, such a clause is merely subject to the fairness test but the OFT has indicated that "it would be difficult to conceive of circumstances in which [such a clause] would be fair" (OFT Unfair Terms Bulletin 3 at 1.2) and the fact that, under the Regulations, enforcement is not left to the individual consumer may make the application of the fairness test more significant to the consumer than the automatic ineffectiveness of such clauses under the 1977 Act (see further p 219). Obviously exemption clauses dealing with other types of negligently caused loss or damage also fall within the scope of the test of fairness under the Regulations and the Director General of Fair Trading clearly views them as generally unfair in the consumer context (see eg Bulletin 3 at pp 30, 54; Bulletin 4 at p 65).

2. Contracts where one party "deals as consumer" or on the other's "written standard terms of business" (s 3)

"Written standard terms"

Section 3 deals with two types of contracts: those where one party "deals as consumer" and those where he, or she, deals on the other party's "written standard terms of business". The two types will frequently overlap. "Deals as consumer" is defined in s 12 and is considered below (see page 194). There is no definition of "written standard terms of business", and this phrase raises a number of questions. In most cases, it will be clear that the terms are written (but see p 187), and what will fall to be determined is (i) whether the relevant party has standard terms, and (ii) whether the parties dealt on them in the instant case.

(i) The existence of the relevant party's standard terms

In the context of s 17 of the 1977 Act, which is the equivalent of s 3 in the Scottish part of the Act, the phrase used is "standard form contract", rather than "written standard terms of business". In the context of s 17, in *McCrone* v *Boots Farm Sales Ltd* [1981] SLT 103, Lord Dunpark referred (at p 105) to a standard form contract as one where there are:

> "a number of fixed terms or conditions invariably incorporated in contracts of the kind in question".

However, whilst a set of terms "invariably" incorporated into contracts of the appropriate type would clearly be standard terms, a set of terms may be "standard terms" even though not used "invariably". "If this were not so the statute would be emasculated" — s 3 could be avoided simply by not using the relevant terms on one or two isolated, and unimportant, occasions (*Chester Grosvenor Hotel* v *Alfred McAlpine Management Ltd* 56 Build LR 115). Certainly, it was indicated in *British Fermentation Products* v *Compair Reavell* [1999] 2 All ER (Comm) 389 that it would suffice if the terms were "usually used" by the relevant party. What can constitute standard terms should depend upon the pattern of dealing on the terms in question, when the contract is of the type to which they are appropriate. It can be suggested that even requiring their "usual" use could be seen as too strict, if that requires their use in more than half of the contracts of the appropriate type made by the relevant party. The relevant party may use them, for example, whenever he, or she, can, but in the course of negotiations, he, or she, can only ensure their use in a substantial minority of the contracts he, or she, makes. It should be a question of whether the whole pattern of the relevant party's use of the terms is sufficient for them to be regarded as that party's standard terms, and it may be that the relevant party's intention as to their use should be relevant. In *Chester Grosvenor Hotel* v *Alfred McAlpine Management Ltd* 56 Build LR 115 the Official Referee, Judge Stannard, indicated a "fact and degree" approach. He said (at p 133):

> "In my judgment the question is one of fact and degree. What are alleged to be standard terms may be used so infrequently in comparison with other terms that they cannot realistically be regarded as standard, or on any particular occasion may be so added to or mutilated that they must be regarded as having lost their essential identity. What is required for terms to be standard is that they should be regarded as standard by the party which advances them as its standard terms and that it should habitually contract on those terms. If it contracts also on other terms, it must be determined in any given case, and as a matter of fact, whether this has occurred so frequently that the terms in question cannot be regarded as standard, and if on any occasion a party has substantially modified its prepared terms, it is a question of fact whether those terms have been so altered that they must be regarded as not having been employed on that occasion."

The judge then concluded that the two contracts in question had been made on McAlpine's written standard terms of business. The two contracts had been made in December 1994 and November 1985. Between January 1983 and November 1985 McAlpine had entered into 15 other contracts of the relevant type. Seven had used the relevant terms (with some deviations from the norm), six had been made on the other party's terms and twice the JCT Standard Form had been used.

Even if it is accepted that the question of pattern of use of a set of terms and variation of the terms themselves must be considered as matters of fact and degree in deciding if the contract was made on the basis of "written standard terms", there are still matters which would seem to require decision as a matter of law. One question is whether a standard form which is common throughout a particular trade, and has been devised by a third party, such as a trade association, should fall within s 3. Can it be regarded as the written standard terms of business of the relevant party? Certainly, the Contractor's Plant Association model conditions were assumed to be the written standard terms of the relevant party in *Cox Plant Hire (London) Ltd* v *Dialbola* (1983) 21 December, Lexis, and *USA* v *ARC Construction Ltd* (1991) 8 May, Lexis. It was considered in *British Fermentation Products* v *Compair Reavell* [1999] 2 All ER (Comm) 389 whether a contract made on the basis of the Institute of Mechanical Engineers Model Form General Conditions of Contract Form C could constitute the defendant's written standard terms of business. There was, however, no proof of the manner in which the terms were used by the defendant and the judge made the point that if s 3 could apply to "model forms drafted by an outside body", there would need to be proof of their adoption by the relevant party as his, or her, standard terms, "either by practice or by express statement". It is contended that the better view is that, subject to such adoption, the 1977 Act should extend to such contracts. A difficult borderline might otherwise be generated. Some model standard terms will be arrived at by consultation with representatives of both sides of those involved in the transaction to which the terms relate and may not carry the same risk of one-sided terms as some other standard form contracts. However, such factors can be considered in the application of the "requirement of reasonableness" and as the Law Commission pointed out in relation to such model standard terms:

> "They are not drafted with any particular transaction between particular parties in mind and are often entered into without much, if any thought being given to the wisdom of the standard terms in the individual circumstances." (Law Com No 69, para 152).

(ii) The instant case

If the relevant party has "written standard terms of business", the question is whether they were used in the instant case. In *McCrone* Lord Dunpark indicated that for the instant case to have been made on the relevant party's standard terms, they should have been used "without material variation". However, it should not be too easy to argue that the relevant party's standard terms have been sufficiently departed from to take the contract outside of the scope of s 3. It must be a question of degree whether the variation in terms is such that the parties are not contracting on the "standard terms". This should be assessed not only by looking at the number of terms which have been varied, but also at which of the terms have been varied. Some terms are inherently dependent upon the particular contract, whilst changes to others would be a strong indicator that the relevant party's standard terms had ceased to be used as such. "In many contracts there may be negotiations as to, for example, quality or price but none as to the crucial exempting terms" (*St Alban's City and District Council* v *International Computers Ltd* [1995] FSR 686, Scott Baker J at p 706). Nevertheless, the contract as a whole must be considered. In *Watford Electronics* v *Sanderson* [2000] 2 All ER (Comm) 984 the situation was viewed as not taken outside of s 3 by an amendment which was seen as "narrow and insubstantial" when "considered against the totality of the standard conditions which otherwise remained unamended" (para 113).

There is some suggestion that factors other than the pattern of usage may be relevant in considering whether the instant contract was made on the relevant party's "written standard terms". In *Salvage Association* v *CAP Financial Services Ltd* [1995] FSR 654 (at p 672) HH Judge Thayne Forbes (Off Ref) listed factors which he thought should be taken into account in deciding if a contract was made on the proferens written standard terms of business:

"(i)   the degree to which the 'standard terms' are considered by the other party as part of the process of agreeing the terms of the contract.

(ii)   the degree to which the 'standard terms' are imposed on the other party by the party putting them forward.

(iii) the relative bargaining power of the parties.

(iv) the degree to which the party putting forward the 'standard terms' is prepared to entertain negotiations with regard to the terms of the contract generally and the standard terms in particular.

(v)   the extent and nature of any agreed alterations to the 'standard terms' made as a result of the negotiations between the parties."

The final factor would be relevant to a simple comparison of the contract made, with the relevant standard terms. The other factors indicated would require a very different approach to the question of whether the parties dealt on the relevant "written standard terms". They would require a detailed examination of the contracting process. It would be argued, for example, that the proferens did have "written standard terms" but that they had merely provided the starting point for negotiations, and that the other party had an opportunity to influence the final contract terms, but chose to accept the terms originally put forward by the relevant party. However, it should be emphasised that a finding that the contract was made on the relevant party's "written standard terms of business" does not result in the automatic negation of any clause. If the contract falls within the scope of s 3 then certain terms are rendered ineffective if they fail to satisfy the requirement of reasonableness. The type of factors identified in (i) to (iv) above are addressed when the requirement of reasonableness is applied and it is more appropriate that they be considered at that point when all the factors relevant to the requirement of reasonableness can be looked at. It might be argued to be more helpful to business if the scope of s 3 is narrowed at this point, so that fewer contracts between businesses are subject to the uncertainties of the application of the requirement of reasonableness. However, narrowing the scope of s 3 by considering the first four factors indicated above, would introduce the same type of uncertainty at the earlier stage. A less complex test at the earlier stage may well create less uncertainty overall.

Written terms

A question arises in relation to the situation which occurs when terms are incorporated by a "consistent course of dealing". Offer and acceptance often occur orally in such cases. Are a set of "standard terms" then incorporated as written terms? To answer the question in the context of s 3, we need to consider the basic mechanism for incorporation by a course of dealing. The mechanism is that, although there is no specific reference to standard terms in making a particular contract, the past dealings between the parties are such that, in the absence of any contrary indication, those terms are taken to have been included in the offer and acceptance (see page 153). They should be regarded as incorporated as "written" terms if they have been embodied in a written document in the past. An analogy can be made with incorporation by reference. The terms are incorporated as terms recorded in the written standard document in which they previously appeared.

The final question to be considered here relates to contracts made using computers. Such contracts could be made using a structured system of Electronic Data Interchange or simply via e-mail or on the Internet. In either case, standard terms may well have been offered by one party, to the other, by electronic means. They may simply remain in electronic form and be viewed on a computer screen (visual display unit). There is no definition of writing in the 1977 Act but, in general, writing "includes typing, printing, lithography, photography and other modes of representing words in a visible form" (Sch 1 Interpretation Act 1978). Although the words appear on the VDU, they are actually represented, and recorded, by electrically charged particles, and it must be open to doubt whether this will suffice to constitute "*written* standard terms of business". In fact, on this reasoning, it must also be open to doubt whether the terms would be regarded as written even if printed out by the party to whom these terms are offered — although it might be regarded as sufficient for the purposes of s 3 if the relevant party kept a master, paper copy of his, or her, standard terms. Again, there would be some analogy with incorporation by reference. (Macdonald and Poyton (2000) Web LJ — http://webjcli.ncl.ac.uk/2000/issue3/macdonald3.html)

The Unfair Terms in Consumer Contracts Regulations 1999 apply the test of "unfairness" to terms which have not been "individually negotiated" Normally, they will be "standard terms". There is no requirement that they be written (see page 224).

Section 3(2)(a)

In relation to contracts where one party "deals as consumer or on the other's written standard terms of business", s 3(2)(a) prevents that "other" party from restricting or excluding his liability for breach of contract by the use of any contract terms except in so far as that term satisfies the requirement of reasonableness. This is a very wide provision. It relates to the situation where there is a breach and the party in breach is claiming that the relevant term excludes or restricts his liability for breach. That term will be effective only "in so far as [it] satisfies the requirement of reasonableness". There is an overlap with the Unfair Terms in Consumer Contracts Regulations 1999.

Section 3(2)(b) — exclusion clauses "in disguise"

Under s 3(2)(b), a person contracting on his own "written standard terms of business" or contracting with someone who "deals as consumer" cannot by reference to any contract term "claim to be entitled—

(i) to render a contractual performance substantially different from that which was reasonably expected of him, or
(ii) in respect of the whole or any part of his contractual obligation, to render no performance at all,

except in so far as ... the contract term satisfies the requirement of reasonableness".

This is less straightforward than s 3(2)(a). It applies to situations where there is apparently no breach. Section 3(2)(b) is an attempt to deal with, what can be termed, exclusion clauses "in disguise".

The point was made above (see page 136) that there is a problem with the definition of exclusion clauses. An exclusion clause may be rewritten so that it is, in form, part of the definition of the obligation. This has led to the argument that an exclusion clause is not a distinct type of clause at all (Coote, *Exception Clauses*, 1964). However, the Unfair Contract Terms Act 1977 assumes that an exclusion clause is a distinct type of clause. On that basis, the Act recognizes that an exclusion clause can take the form of part of the definition of the obligation and still be an exclusion clause. Its form is then perceived as a possible means of evading provisions dealing with exclusion clauses. Section 3(2)(b) is one of the parts of the Act designed to bring exclusion clauses "in disguise" within its operation. The Law Commission, in considering the proposed Act to deal with exclusion clauses, recognized that what mattered about such clauses was not their form but their nature, the mischief they created. It was said (para 146, Law Com Rep No 69 (1975)):

"We do not propose to define exemption clauses in general terms; we regard this expression not as a legal term of art but as a convenient label for a number of provisions which may be mischievous in broadly the same way. Their mischief is that they deprive or may deprive the person against whom they are invoked ... *of rights which the promisee reasonably believed the promisor had conferred on him.*" (emphasis added)

Section 3(2)(b) is a result of this recognition that it is not the form of a clause that matters but its nature. It deals with the "mischief" of clauses which deprive the promisee of rights which he reasonably believed the promisor had conferred on him.

The reaction to the above might be to ask how the promisee's reasonable expectations can differ from the actual obligations embodied in the contract. The answer to this is the artificial way in which terms can be incorporated and the difficulty of understanding a long standard form document can present a danger that "the relatively unsophisticated or unwary party will not realise what or how little he has been promised, although the legal scope and effect of the contract may be perfectly clear to a lawyer" (Law Com Rep No 69 (1975) para 145). In other words the contracting process is so artificial that, as long as the reasonable person is not taken to be a lawyer, the expectations of the parties, as reasonable people, may differ from the obligations which lawyers would find in the contract (but see Coote, *Exception Clauses* (1964) Chapter 10).

Section 3(2)(b)(i) encompasses, for example, what have been seen as "trap" provisions — "cases in which the application of small print provisions would enable a party to perform a contract in a substantially different manner from that which could reasonably have been expected from a perusal of its primary terms" (*Liberty Life Insurance Co* v *Sheikh* [1985] *The Times* 25 June, *per* Kerr LJ). Another situation which may fall within s 3(2)(b) is where one term apparently states what the proferens' performance is to be, but another confers on the proferens a discretion as to that performance. It may be recognized as reasonable for the other party to expect that discretion to be exercised within narrow bounds, and for s 3(2)(b)(i) to apply if it is not. In relation to a contract for the supply of a service by British Telecom, which contained a clause stating that BT could terminate the contract on one month's notice, Sir Thomas Bingham MR said: "If a customer reasonably expects a service to continue until BT has substantial reason to terminate it, it seems to me at least arguable that a clause purporting to authorise BT to terminate without reason purports to permit partial or different performance from that which the customer expected" (*Timeload Ltd* v *British Telecommunications plc* [1995] EMLR 459).

The claimed extent of a discretion was an element in an example, given by the Law Commission, of the type of case which might now fall within s 3(2)(b). The clause was also relatively obscurely positioned. The case was that of *Anglo-Continental Holidays* v *Typaldos (London) Ltd* [1967] 2 Lloyds Rep 61 and the facts were:

> The plaintiff travel agent booked cabins for clients on the defendant's ship Atlantica for a Mediterranean cruise commencing on 12 August. On 2 August the defendant notified the plaintiff that the clients could not be accommodated on the Atlantica but had been booked on the Angelika. The Atlantica was a large ship with two swimming pools. The Angelika was a "small old crate". The itinerary of the Angelika differed from that of the Atlantica. The latter would have spent two days in Haifa allowing time for trips further into Israel. The former was to spend only eight hours in Haifa. The two days in Haifa would have been the climax of the trip for the plaintiff's clients as they were a Jewish group. Printed on the back of the defendant's handbook for travel agents was a clause which said "Steamers, Sailing Dates, Rates and Itineraries are subject to change without prior notice".

On being informed of the change of ship and itinerary, the plaintiff cancelled the arrangements and claimed damages for breach. The defendant sought to rely upon the clause on the back of the handbook. The Court of Appeal held that the clause could not assist the defendant who was liable for breach. The clause could not be used to alter the substance of the transaction. It had to be limited so that effect could be given to the main object of the contract.

In *Anglo-Continental Holidays* v *Typaldos (London) Ltd* the court recognized that the clause, as it appeared, was not in keeping with the "substance" and the "main object" of the contract. Effect was given to the "substance" of the contract by construction of the contract (see also *Sze Hai Tong Bank Ltd* v *Rambler Cycle Co Ltd* [1959] AC 576 and *Glynn* v *Margetson & Co* [1893] AC 351 — page 173). Similar facts to *Typaldos* might now be dealt with under s 3(2)(b) as the defendant was claiming to render a performance substantially different from that which was reasonably expected. The case emphasises the artificial nature of standard terms. The court was willing to recognize that the terms specific to the particular contract might well reflect its substance better than the standard terms used by one party in many contracts. A similar approach would now provide work for s 3(2)(b)(i). (Note also that in the consumer context, an unduly wide discretion may be unfair under the Unfair Terms in Consumer Contracts Regulations 1999 — see p 241.)

Three final points need to be made in relation to s 3(2)(b). The first is to emphasise that it contains a recognition both of the difficulty of distinguishing between the actual contract terms and the party's reasonable expectations and, also, the uncertainty such an exercise could create. It subjects to the requirement of reasonableness only those clauses on which one party seeks to rely to render a performance "*substantially* different from that which was reasonably expected". The assessment is a broad one. The second point to be noted is that before s 3(2)(b) is applied there is, apparently, no breach. There is no apparent breach because one party is claiming that a specific term prevents whatever he has done, or not done, from being a breach. Section 3(2)(b) subjects that term to the requirement of reasonableness. If the term does not satisfy the requirement of reasonableness, then it is ineffective and there is a breach. Finally, the point should be made that as the 1999 Regulations on Unfair Terms in Consumer Contracts do not merely apply to a particular type of term, such as exemption clauses, then to a very large extent, they do not raise the type of difficulty which s 3(2)(b) is needed to meet — evasion by the form of the clause.

(For further discussion of s 3(2)(b), see Yates, *Exclusion Clauses in Contracts* (2nd ed, 1982) pp 88–94. See also Macdonald (1992) 12 LS 277; Macdonald, *Exemption Clauses and Unfair Terms* (1999) Butterworths.)

3. Goods (ss 6 and 7)

Section 6 deals with exemption clauses relating to the implied terms in contracts for the sale or hire purchase of goods. Section 7 makes analogous provision for contracts where possession or ownership of goods passes and the contract is not one of sale or hire purchase. In relation to these sections it is often important to determine whether the exemption clause is being used against a person who deals as a consumer.

Section 6(1)(a) provides that liability for breach of the terms implied by s 12 Sale of Goods Act 1979 cannot be excluded or restricted. The terms implied by s 12 relate to title to the goods. Note that it is irrelevant whether it is sought to use the exemption clause against someone who deals as consumer. It should also be noted that the exemption clause is automatically ineffective. There is no need to consider whether it satisfies the requirement of reasonableness. Section 6(1)(b) makes the same provision for the terms implied into contracts of hire purchase.

Section 6(2)(a) precludes attempts to exclude or restrict liability for breach of the terms implied by ss 13–15 Sale of Goods Act 1979 where that attempt is being made against a person who deals as consumer. The terms implied by ss 13–15 relate to the conformity of the goods with description and sample, and their fitness for purpose and satisfactory quality. Note that the requirement of reasonableness is again irrelevant. Any exemption clause is automatically ineffective. Section 6(2)(b) makes the same provision for contracts of hire purchase.

Section 6(3) deals with exemption clauses relating to the same implied terms as s 6(2), but it covers the cases where the person against whom it is sought to use the exemption clause does *not* deal as consumer. Section 6(3) differs from s 6(2) in the effect it has on exemption clauses. It does not make exemption clauses automatically ineffective. Exclusion or restriction of the implied terms is possible in so far as the exemption clause satisfies the requirement of reasonableness.

The difference between subss (2) and (3) means that the person seeking to rely upon the exemption clause will often argue that the clause is not being used against someone who "deals as consumer". If it can be established that the buyer did not "deal as consumer", there is a possibility that the exemption clause is effective, depending upon the "requirement of reasonableness". If the buyer dealt as consumer, the exemption clause will be ineffective, no matter how reasonable it is. In *Peter Symmons & Co v Cook* [1981] NLJ 758 (Lexis):

> Mr Cook was a motor car dealer. In 1978 he sold to the plaintiffs, a firm of surveyors, a 1964 Silver Cloud Mark III Rolls Royce. The car proved to be unmerchantable and not reasonably fit for its purpose, ie the seller was in breach of the terms implied by s 14 Sale of Goods Act 1893 (now 1979). The seller wished to rely upon an exemption clause to protect him from this breach.

The court had to consider whether the plaintiff purchasers dealt as consumers. It was held that the plaintiffs had dealt as consumers and that meant that the exemption clause was automatically ineffective under s 6(2). In order to bring the case within s 6(3) Mr Cook had argued that the purchase had been made in the course of a business. Had he been successful, s 6(3) would have given him the opportunity to argue that the exemption clause was effective because it was reasonable.

Section 6(4) states that the liabilities referred to in s 6 "are not only the business liabilities defined by s 1(3), but include those arising under any contract of sale of goods or hire purchase agreement". This is not as great an extension as at first it might appear to be. The terms as to quality and fitness for purpose implied by s 14 Sale of Goods Act 1979 are implied only if the seller sells the goods "in the course of a business". In addition, someone can only use the more extensive protection available to consumers where the person with whom he is contracting does so "in the course of a business". It is not possible for one party to deal as consumer, within the definition in s 12, unless the other party contracts in the course of a business.

Section 7 makes similar provision for contracts under which possession or ownership of goods passes, but which are not contracts of sale or hire purchase. The sort of contracts covered are contracts of hire or contracts for work and materials. (See Supply of Goods and Services Act 1982 in relation to the implied terms.)

4. Indemnities by consumers (s 4)

Section 4 deals with contract terms under which a consumer is to indemnify another party in respect of liability that may be incurred by the other for negligence or breach of contract. The indemnity will be ineffective except in so far as it satisfies the requirement of reasonableness. This applies whether the person to be indemnified by the term is a party to the contract or not, and also whether his liability is vicarious or direct. It does not matter whether the liability is to the person dealing as a consumer or to someone else. Section 4 makes no provisions for indemnity clauses between business people. It relates only to the situation where someone dealing as a consumer is providing the indemnity (see page 194).

One question which should briefly be considered is whether an indemnity clause could also fall within the ambit of one of the other active sections, s 2, for example, if it related to negligence, or s 3, if it related to breach. The question is important because s 4 may have less impact upon a clause than another section would. As we have seen, s 2 makes some clauses automatically ineffective without the need to consider whether the clause is reasonable. The approach indicated by the courts has been to distinguish the two situations in which an indemnity may operate. It may operate "reflexively" and as an insurance, ie it may operate when the liability in question is to the other party (reflexive) and when it is to a third party (insurance). The approach of the courts is that the clause is one which also excludes or restricts liability when it operates reflexively (*Phillips Products Ltd* v *Hyland* [1987] 2 All ER 620) but not when it operates as an insurance (*Thompson* v *Lohan* [1987] 2 All ER 631; *Jones* v *Northampton Borough Council* [1990] The Independent 25 May). The argument is that, in the latter case, the clause does not exclude or restrict liability because the injured party is unaffected by it. The injured party will recover whether the clause is effective or not, as the only effect of the clause is to determine which of the two parties to whom the clause is relevant will ultimately have to pay for that recovery. This can be illustrated by *Thompson* v *Lohan*. In that case the defendant hired an excavator and driver to H for use in H's quarry. The hire was on the terms of the Contractor's Plant Association, including Condition 8, a clause which acted as an indemnity clause. The driver was negligent and the excavator was involved in an accident which resulted in the death of the plaintiff's husband. The plaintiff successfully claimed damages for her husband's death from the defendant in tort. The defendant claimed to rely upon his standard form contract to recover the damages from H. *Inter alia* H argued that Condition 8 did not have that result because it excluded or restricted liability and was rendered ineffective by s 2(1) Unfair Contract Terms Act 1977. The court held that Condition 8 was effective and that s 2 did not apply to it as, from the victim's perspective, there was no exclusion or restriction of liability. It was said that the Act was not concerned with the way in which the contracting parties chose to allocate liability between themselves if the victim was not affected. (See Adams & Brownsword [1988] JBL 146, Macdonald, *Exemption Clauses and Unfair Terms* (1999) Butterworths pp 101–102.)

5. "Guarantee" of consumer goods (s 5)

Section 5 relates to the situation where a manufacturer or distributor of goods tries to use a particular method of excluding or restricting his liability for loss or damage arising from goods proving defective, while in consumer use, due to his negligence. The particular method of exclusion or restriction precluded by s 5 is that of the "guarantee" which purports to promise or assure the consumer that "defects will be made good by complete or partial replacement, or by repair, monetary compensation or otherwise" (s 5(2)(b)) whilst at the same time removing liability for other loss or damage — ie the exclusion or restriction of liability is "hidden" in a clause which gives the appearance of being beneficial to the user of the goods.

Section 5(1) states:

"In the case of goods ordinarily supplied for private use or consumption, where loss or damage

(a) arises from goods proving defective while in consumer use; and
(b) results from the negligence of a person concerned in the manufacture or distribution of the goods,

liability for the loss or damage cannot be excluded or restricted by reference to any contract term or notice contained in or operating by reference to a guarantee of the goods".

Note that this does not apply as between parties to a contract under or in pursuance of which possession or ownership of goods passes (s 5(3)). This means that it does not apply between seller and buyer. (As between seller and buyer s 6 can be used or, as negligence is involved, s 2.)

Goods are "in consumer use" when a person is using them, or has them in his possession for use, otherwise than exclusively for the purposes of a business (s 5(2)(a)). This differs from the definition of "deals as consumer" in s 12.

6. Two contracts (s 10)

Section 10 of the Unfair Contract Terms Act 1977 deals with the situation where there are two contracts and a clause in the second affecting rights arising under the first. Section 10 states:

"A person is not bound by any contract term prejudicing or taking away rights of his which arise under, or in connection with the performance of, another contract, so far as those rights extend to the enforcement of another's liability which this Part of this Act prevents that other from excluding or restricting."

The drafting of this section is somewhat obscure. It does not reflect the style generally adopted in the Act as it does not refer to the exclusion or restriction of liabilities, or even rights, but rather to "prejudicing or taking away rights". One major problem with the borderlines of the section has been resolved by *Tudor Grange Holdings Ltd* v *Citibank* [1991] 4 All ER 1 in which it was held that the section did not apply to an agreement settling a contractual dispute. More generally, Browne-Wilkinson V-C did not think that s 10 dealt with the situation where both contracts were between the same parties. He gave an example of the type of contract which he thought s 10 was designed to cover. He said (at p 13):

"Under contract 1, the supplier (S) contracts to supply a customer (C) with a product. Contract 1 contains no exemption clause. However, C enters into a servicing contract, contract 2, with another party (X). Under contract 2, C is precluded from exercising certain of his rights against S under contract 1. In such a case s 10 operates to preclude X from enforcing contract 2 against C so as to prevent C enforcing his rights against S under contract 1."

It would seem to provide an opportunity for evasion of the Act if that section is confined to the situation where both contracts are not with the same parties. However, what must be borne in mind is that Browne-Wilkinson V-C's view that s 10 is so confined was accompanied by his further view that ss 2 and 3 were themselves wide enough to encompass a clause in a second contract between the parties to the original contract. He said (at p 13):

"Under ss 2 and 3 there is no express requirement that the contract term excluding or restricting S's liability to C has to be contained in the same contract as that giving rise to S's liability to C."

This must certainly be borne in mind if *Tudor Grange* is cited in relation to the proposition that s 10 deals only with a second contract made with a third party to the original contract. However, it would seem very doubtful that s 10 does not cover the situation where both contracts are between the same parties. The provision in the Scottish part of the Act which deals with the situation where there are two contracts has not been seen as so restricted (*Chapman* v *Aberdeen Construction Group plc* [1991] IRLR 505). There is nothing in the wording of s 10 to indicate such a limitation, and any such limitation would seem to be open to abuse.

Note should also be taken of the general approach which Browne-Wilkinson V-C indicated to the scope of s 10. He considered the marginal note to s 10 which reads "Evasion by means of secondary contract" and he thought that indicated that the section did not cover the type of situation before the court. He did not consider a contract to settle a dispute arising from the performance of an earlier contract to be an "evasion" of the provisions of the Act. In addition, he did not regard a contract to settle a dispute as a "secondary" contract. This would indicate a general approach to s 10 which requires consideration of whether a clause is an "evasion" of the Act and whether the contract containing it is to be regarded as a "secondary" contract. (See Macdonald [1994] JBL 441.)

7. Conclusion

Consideration of the above should already have led to the conclusion that the active sections are not discrete. They overlap, and more than one section may be applicable to a given situation. All the possibilities must be considered. The requirements of the different sections vary, and one may be easier to use than another. Section 2 will require proof of negligence, but it may be possible to establish a breach and the applicability of s 3 on the basis of strict liability. The active sections also vary in their effect upon an exemption clause. Section 3 subjects to the requirement of reasonableness those exemption clauses to which it applies. If the circumstances are such that s 6(2) would also apply to the clause in question, then that subsection renders the clause ineffective whether it is "reasonable" or not.

C. Definitions

1. "Deals as consumer" (s 12)[3]

Section 12(1) states:

"A party to a contract 'deals as consumer' in relation to another party if—

(a) he neither makes the contract in the course of a business nor holds himself out as doing so; and

(b) the other party does make the contract in the course of a business; and

(c) in the case of a contract governed by the law of sale of goods or hire purchase, or by section 7 of this Act, the goods passing under or in pursuance of the contract are of a type ordinarily supplied for private use or consumption."

It is important to note the burden of proof in s 12(3). It is "for those claiming that a party does not deal as a consumer to show that he does not".

(a) "In the course of a business"

The key to determining whether someone "deals as consumer" under the definition in s 12 is the question of when a contract is made "in the course of a business". Under s 12(1), if someone is to "deal as consumer", they must not contract in the course of a business (s 12(1)(a)), and the other party must contract in the course of a business (s 12(1)(b)). The Court of Appeal had to consider the meaning of "in the course of a business" in the context of s 12 in *R & B Customs Brokers Co Ltd* v *United Dominions Trust* [1988] 1 All ER 847. Consideration will be given to the line taken in that case. It can, however, be subject to considerable criticism and the issue of its appropriateness will also be addressed below.

In *R & B Customs Brokers Co Ltd* v *United Dominions Trust* [1988] 1 All ER 847 the facts were:

> The plaintiff company, R & B Customs Brokers, carried on the business of a freight forwarding agent. Using the defendant finance house, the plaintiff company traded in a Volvo for a Colt Shogun car. The car was for the business and personal use of its directors and sole shareholders, Mr & Mrs Bell. It was discovered that the car roof leaked and the leak could not be cured. The upholstery became "sodden with water, mouldy and evil smelling". The car was not "reasonably fit for the buyer's purpose" and would be in breach of a term implied by s 14 Sale of Goods Act 1979 if such a term was part of the contract. There was an exemption clause purporting to exclude any such implied term unless the buyer dealt as a consumer within the definition in s 12 Unfair Contract Terms Act 1977.

The Court of Appeal concluded that the defendants were liable for breach of the implied term. The plaintiff company had not made the purchase "in the course of a business" and had dealt as a consumer. Dillon LJ stated (at p 854):

> "there are some transactions which are clearly integral parts of the business concerned, and these should be held to have been carried out in the course of those businesses; this would cover, apart from much else, the instance of a one off adventure in the nature of trade where the transaction itself would constitute a trade or business. There are other transactions, however, such as the purchase of the car in the present case, which are at the highest only incidental to the carrying on of the relevant business; here a degree of regularity is required before it can be said that they are an integral part of the business carried on and so entered into in the course of that business."

This identifies a test to be used when it needs to be established whether someone makes a contract in the course of a business. Leaving aside, for the moment, the question of one off adventures in the nature of trade, the question is basically whether the transaction was an integral part of the business in itself or, if it was merely incidental to the business, whether such transactions occurred with sufficient regularity to have been made "in the course of a business". In the instant case, the purchase of a car was not integral to the business of freight forwarding agents and the car was only the second or third so acquired by R & B and the acquisition was not a sufficiently regularly occurring incidental transaction. Further guidance on the test can be obtained from cases interpreting the phrase "in the course of a business" in the context of the Trade Descriptions Act 1968. The Court of Appeal in *R & B Customs Brokers* adopted the interpretation of "in the course of a business" in the cases decided under the 1968 Act.

It should be noted that under the 1999 Regulations on Unfair Terms in Consumer Contracts, the definition of "consumer" is confined to "natural" persons and so cannot encompass a company.

(b) The test

Leaving aside "one-off" adventures in the nature of trade, for the moment, under the approach taken in *R & B Customs Brokers,* there are two ways in which a transaction may be made in the course of a business. It may be:

(i) an integral part of the business in itself, or
(ii) merely incidental to the business in itself, but occurring with sufficient regularity.

The first point to note is that a very restrictive view is taken of those transactions which are "integral" to a party's business. Only those transactions which are the basis of the business qualify. This is illustrated by the case of *Davies* v *Sumner* [1984] 3 All ER 831. In that case:

> Mr Davies was a self-employed courier. Using his own car he transported films, video tapes and other material for HTV between Mold and Cardiff. When he had done 100,000 miles in the car he decided to purchase another one. His first car went to the garage in part exchange. At the time of the sale the odometer on that car showed 18,100 miles. Prior to purchasing that first car Mr Davies had rented a car for a few months and used that in his business.

The applicabilty of s 1 Trade Descriptions Act 1968 hinged upon whether the false trade description, the odometer reading, had been applied to the car "in the course of a business". The House of Lords concluded that Mr Davies had not acted "in the course of a business". There was no pattern of such transactions, and the sale of a car was not integral to the business of a courier. Similarly, the sale of a car by a taxi business is not integral to that business (*Devlin* v *Hall* [1990] RTR 320). Nor is the sale of his boat by a fisherman. It "is the transaction and not the goods which must be integral to the business" (*Stevenson* v *Rogers* [1999] 1 All ER 613 at p 626).

The alternative way in which a transaction may be "in the course of a business" is if, although incidental, it is regularly occurring. The two or three transactions in *R & B Customs Brokers,* were not sufficient to turn an incidental transaction into one made in the course of a business. The sale of a car by a hire car business was "in the course of a business" when the business had a fleet of twenty-four cars and there was a practice of selling a car after it had been owned for about two years (*Havering LBC* v *Stevenson* [1970] 3 All ER 609). It has not been specifically referred to the courts, but "regularity" would also seem to involve some element of frequency.

As has been indicated, the effects of this test, and criticism of it will be considered below, after two further points have been addressed.

(c) "One-off" adventures in the nature of trade

Unless the transaction is integral to the business, the basic requirement for a transaction to be "in the course of a business" is that it should be one occurring with sufficient regularity. However, as was indicated above, the possibility has also been perceived to exist of a one-off adventure in the nature of trade. The question will then be whether the particular transaction itself has sufficient "flavour" of "trading" and the point could be made that this is not a separate category but a specific example of a transaction "integral" to the business — in this case, the transaction is the business. However, the question of "one-off" adventures in the nature of trade has arisen in the context of revenue law where the profits from certain "one-off" transactions have been held to be taxable as income from a trade. For example, the purchase and resale of one million toilet rolls (*Rutledge* v *IRC* (1929) 14 TC 490) or 44 million yards of parachute silk (*Martin* v *Lowry* [1927] AC 312) were held to be trading on the basis that the quantities purchased meant that private use could not have been intended. There may be an analogy to be made with the tax cases but, in the context of s 12 Unfair Contract Terms Act 1977, s 12(1)(c) should be noted. Section 12(1)(c) imposes an additional requirement for a person to be dealing as a consumer where the agreement in question is a sale of goods or hire purchase contract or one covered by s 7 of the Act. In relation to such contracts the person in question cannot be dealing as a consumer unless the goods "are of a type ordinarily supplied for private use or consumption". A question arises as to what amounts to a "type" of goods ie is a "type" of goods merely "a toilet roll" or can quantity be taken into account? Can it be asserted that one million toilet rolls are not a "type" of goods ordinarily supplied for private use or consumption despite the fact that one toilet roll would be? If quantity can be taken into account under s 12(1)(c), when considering the "type" of goods, it would be irrelevant whether transactions similiar to those in the above tax cases also amounted to "one-off" adventures in the nature of trade for the purposes of s 12. The seller or buyer would not be dealing as a consumer in any event because of s 12(1)(c).

(d) Holding out as dealing in the course of business

It should be noted that a person may preclude himself, or herself, from "dealing as a consumer" by holding himself, or herself, out as dealing in the course of a business, although he, or she, is not actually so dealing. For example, does a person hold himself out as dealing in the course of a business if he claims a trade discount? The comment of Dillon LJ in *R & B Customs Brokers* would limit the cases where this additional factor will prevent someone from "dealing as a consumer". He said (at p 853):

> "In the present case there was no holding out beyond the mere fact that the contract and finance application were made in the company's corporate name and in the finance application the section headed 'Business Details' was filled

in to the extent of giving the nature of the company's business as that of shipping brokers, giving the number of years trading and the number of employees, and giving the names and addresses of the directors."

Such a limited approach is in keeping with the interpretation being put upon "in the course of a business". Basically it will require someone to hold out that the transaction in question is an integral part of his, or her, business in itself, or that it is incidental to that business but that it is also a transaction which he, or she, regularly undertakes. The point has been made that the basic *R & B Customs Brokers* approach is open to criticism. What should be noted here is that whatever the approach taken to the interpretation of "in the course of a business", it must be reflected in that taken to the question of whether people hold themselves out as contracting "in the course of a business".

(e) Criticism — alternative approach

The approach taken in *R & B Customs Brokers* can be criticised. The first point to be made is that the approach is inappropriate because the phrase "in the course of a business" occurs in both s 12(1)(a) and (b). The impact of this, in the light of the *R & B* approach should be considered. The narrow approach taken to the meaning of "in the course of a business" in *R & B Customs Brokers* enabled the greater protection provided by the Unfair Contract Terms Act 1977 to purchasers who deal as consumers to be extended in one direction. It allowed merely incidental, and not regularly occurring, business purchases to gain that protection. However, although at first sight extending the protection provided by the 1977 Act, the approach taken to the meaning of "in the course of a business" by the Court of Appeal in *R & B Customs Brokers* is inappropriately restrictive of it. It is inappropriately restrictive because of the use of the phrase "in the course of a business" in both s 12(1)(a) and s 12(1)(b) and this point can be most easily made by the use of a simple example. Suppose that there was nothing wrong with the car when R & B bought it, but that it did have the relevant defects when sold by R & B to a purchaser, X, who clearly had no business connections. On the basis of the approach taken in *R & B Customs Brokers,* X would not be dealing as consumer in making the purchase. Clearly, X would not have bought in the course of a business, but that only fulfils the requirement in s 12(1)(a). In order for X to have dealt as consumer, it is also required by s 12(1)(b) that the seller must have sold "in the course of a business" and it is equally clear that that would not have been the case (the sale would not have been integral to the seller's business and there would have been no sufficient regularity). In *R & B Customs Brokers* in extending the protection afforded to those who deal as consumers to the type of purchase by a business there considered, the Court of Appeal took more appropriate cases outside of the scope of that protection. An approach which allowed incidental transactions by a business, whether regularly occurring or not, to be regarded as made "in the course of a business" would not lead to this result.

The second point to be made here is on the wording of the phrase "in the course of a business". It can be argued that the words of s 12(1) themselves show that the line taken in *R & B Customs Brokers* is inappropriate. The reference in s 12 is to transactions "in the course of *a* business" and not to those "in the course of business". "The former suggests things done by and for a business, while the latter suggest acts limited to the kind of business in which a person is engaged" (Kidner (1987) NILQ 46 at p 53). Transactions which are merely incidental to the relevant party's business could be construed as having been made "in the course of a business" without the need to establish any regularity in their occurrence. In fact, the phrase could be construed even more widely than that, to mean any transaction by a business.

A further point should be made here not in relation to the use of the phrase in s 12, but in relation to its use elsewhere in the Unfair Contract Terms Act 1977. It was noted above that basically the operation of the Act is restricted to "business liability" and the most significant part of this is liability arising from things done or to be done "in the course of a business" (s 1). There is considerable impetus to give the same meaning to the same phrase used in different sections of the same Act. It would unduly curtail the operation of the Act if its scope was limited by the approach taken to "in the course of a business" in *R & B Customs Brokers.*

Some support for a wider approach to the phrase "in the course of a business" can be found in the judgment of Scott Baker J in *St Albans City and District Council* v *International Computers Ltd* [1995] FSR 686 (see also Nourse LJ [1996] 4 All ER 481 at p 490. But see *Peter Symmonds & Co* v *Cook* [1981] NLJ 758, Lexis). He concluded, *obiter,* that the Council did not deal as consumer in purchasing a computer system because it had contracted "in the course of a business". He decided that it had so contracted simply on the basis of the statement in s 14 that "business includes ... the activities of any ... local or public authority". He did not consider the relationship which the purchase of a computer bore to the main activities of the local authority. In other words there was no attempt to apply the approach taken in *R & B Customs Brokers* in this context (see also *Lease Mangement Services Ltd* v *Purnell Secretarial Services* [1994] 13 Tr LR 337 at p 344). The judge's approach is not in keeping with that taken in *R & B Customs Brokers.* It would be in keeping with an approach which allowed even transactions incidental to a relevant party's business to be construed as having been made "in the course of a business".

Further, and significant, support for a wider approach to the interpretation of "in the course of a business" can be found outside the context of the Unfair Contract Terms Act 1977 in the case of *Stevenson* v *Rogers* [1999] 1 All ER 613. There the Court of Appeal had to consider the meaning of "in the course of a business" in the context of the Sale of Goods Act 1979, s 14(2), where it limits the statutory implication of a term as to the quality of the goods to sales where sellers are acting "in the course of a business". The facts were:

> The defendant had been a fisherman for some twenty years. He sold his boat, the *Jelle,* to the plaintiff in April 1988. He had previously owned and sold one other boat, the *Dolly Mopp.* The plaintiff claimed that the *Jelle* did not comply with the quality term implied by the Sale of Goods Act 1979, s 14(2). However, a requirement that goods be of the requisite quality was only implied by the section if the sale was made "in the course of a business". The meaning to be given to the phrase "in the course of a business" came to be considered by the Court of Appeal as a preliminary matter.

At first instance, the judge had followed the meaning given to "in the course of a business" under the Unfair Contract Terms Act 1977 and the Trade

Descriptions Act 1968 and held that the fisherman had not sold in the course of a business — the sale not being integral to his business or regularly occurring. However, the Court of Appeal in *Stevenson* v *Rogers* held that the judge had not applied the correct test in determining whether the sale was "in the course of a business" within the Sale of Goods Act 1979, s 14(2). The phrase was used to ensure that "every buyer from a business seller should have a right ... to receive goods of" the relevant quality. The obligation was to be imposed on "every trade seller no matter whether he is or is not habitually dealing in goods of the type sold". Potter LJ made the comment (at p 623) that the phrase was there to:

> "distinguish between a sale made in the course of a seller's business and a purely private sale of goods outside the confines of the business (if any) carried on by the seller."

It can be contended that such an approach would similarly be a more appropriate approach to the use of the phrase "in the course of a business" under the Unfair Contract Terms Act 1977, than that currently taken.

It can be contended that the broader approach taken to the meaning of "in the course of a business" in *Stevenson* v *Rogers* reflects the more natural meaning of the words used. The point can also be made, that in *R & B Customs Brokers* the Court of Appeal was adopting the approach taken under the Trade Descriptions Act 1968. That Act and the Unfair Contract Terms Act 1977 may broadly share a purpose of consumer protection, but it must not be lost sight of that the 1968 Act involves criminal offences. It is appropriate to narrowly construe a provision which sets the limits of criminal liability. There is no similar impetus to narrow construction when what is in question is a statute which will impact upon civil liability. There are far better reasons for bringing the Unfair Contract Terms Act 1977 into line with the Sale of Goods Act 1979, than for construing either of them in the same way as an Act imposing criminal liability. The approach in *Stevenson* v *Rogers* is also one which would allow the same interpretation to be given to "in the course of a business" in both s 12 and s 1 of the Unfair Contract Terms Act 1977 without unduly curtailing the Act's operation.

2.   The requirement of reasonableness (s 11)[4]

The active sections often render a clause ineffective except in so far as it satisfies the requirement of reasonableness. Meaning is given to that requirement in s 11, with guidelines in Sch 2.

There was a predecessor to the Unfair Contract Terms Act 1977 test of reasonableness in the Supply of Goods (Implied Terms) Act 1973. This was preserved, for contracts made between 18 May 1973 and 1 February 1978, by s 55 Sale of Goods Act 1979 (originally Sale of Goods Act 1893). Some of the cases referred to below were decided under this predecessor to the Unfair Contract Terms Act 1977, and some differences between the two tests of reasonableness must be noted to assess the significance of those cases today.

Section 11(5) places the burden of proof upon the person claiming that the contract term satisfies the requirement of reasonableness.

The EC Directive/Regulations apply a test of "fairness" (see page 229).

(a) Timing — Assessing the whole clause

Section 11(1) states:

> "In relation to a contract term, the requirement of reasonableness . . . is that the term shall have been a fair and reasonable one to be included having regard to the circumstances which were, or ought reasonably to have been, known to or in the contemplation of the parties when the contract was made."

The reasonableness of the clause is to be assessed on the basis of the circumstances known to or contemplated by, or which should have been known to or contemplated by, the parties at the time of contracting. The particular breach is not directly relevant. It can be relevant only to the extent that it was one of the possibilities the parties contemplated, or should have contemplated, at the time of contracting. Assessing the reasonableness of the clause in relation to the circumstances at the time of contracting should assist contract planning. A clause should not be rendered unreasonable because it appears unreasonable in the light of unforeseeable events which occurred once the contract had been made, although courts always have to live with the temptation of hindsight.

It was s 11(1), and the question of timing, which the Court of Appeal focused on in *Stewart Gill Ltd* v *Horatio Myer & Co Ltd* [1992] 2 All ER 257 in deciding that the reasonableness of a clause must be assessed as a whole and not merely the part of the clause being relied upon in the instant case[5]. In that case:

> The defendants had contracted with the plaintiffs for the supply and installation of an overhead conveyor system for a price of £266,400. The defendants were to pay in stages, and it was the last 10 per cent which gave rise to the dispute. The plaintiffs were asking for summary judgment for the remaining 10 per cent of the price. The defendants contended that summary judgment should not be given as the plaintiffs had committed certain breaches which gave rise to claims which could be set off against the unpaid 10 per cent of the price. The plaintiffs relied upon clause 12.4 of their standard form contract to meet the defendants' contention. Clause 12.4 stated:
>
> > "the Customer shall not be entitled to withhold payment of any amount due to the Company under the contract by reason of any payment set off counterclaim allegation of incorrect or defective goods or for any other reason whatsoever which the Customer may allege excuses him from performing his obligations hereunder".
>
> At first instance the plaintiffs' application for summary judgment was refused.

The clause was not in the form of a simple exclusion or restriction of liability but the Court of Appeal concluded that the clause was brought within s 3 Unfair Contract Terms Act 1977 by s 13(1)(b), and so its effectiveness depended upon whether it satisfied the requirement of reasonableness (see page 195). Although of the view that the exclusion of the right of set off — the part of the clause relied upon in the instant case — might be reasonable, the court did not view the clause as a whole as reasonable. It was not viewed as reasonable that the defendants should not be entitled to withhold payment to the plaintiffs by reason of any "credit" owing by the plaintiffs to the defendants or by reason of any payment made by the defendants to the plaintiffs (eg an over-payment under some other contract).

The Court of Appeal concluded that they must assess the clause as a whole in *Gill* v *Myer* because of s 11(1). The "time-frame" of assessment required by s 11(1) meant that the actual events in relation to which the clause would be used could not be taken into account and, on that basis, the court concluded that the whole clause had to be assessed. After considering s 11(1), Stuart-Smith LJ said (at p 262):

> "Although the question of reasonableness is primarily one for the court when the contract term is challenged, it seems to me that the parties must also be in a position to judge this at the time the contract is made. If this is so, I find it difficult to see how such an appreciation can be made if the customer has to guess whether some, and if so which, part of the term will alone be relied upon."

The point can be made that there may be a pattern of dealing or known trade practice which is such that the parties can reasonably contemplate that the clause will not be used in certain circumstances. Such an argument might be raised to try to establish that the clause was not unreasonable, despite its apparent width, because it would not be used to its full extent. There is some indication that the courts may be willing to take account of the reasonably contemplated use of a clause to determine its reasonableness, but where such contemplation was used in the instant case, it was used to show that the clause was unreasonable. The simplest point to be made from *Gill* v *Myer* is that draftsmen might be advised to include several narrow exemption clauses rather than one wide clause, such as that above, so that at least some of their exemptions may survive.

Finally, it should be noted here that the time at which reasonableness is assessed is one of the differences between the reasonableness test under the Unfair Contract Terms Act 1977 and its predecessor in, what became, s 55 Sale of Goods Act 1979. Under the previous legislation the question was whether it was fair and reasonable to allow reliance upon the term, and the question of reasonableness thus fell to be judged in the light of the breach and its consequences. Although cases decided under s 55 will provide some guidance on the operation of the reasonableness test in s 11 Unfair Contract Terms Act 1977, this difference in timing will affect the current relevance of some factors in those earlier cases. The test of unfairness in the EC Directive/Regulations uses the same "time frame" as the 1977 Act. The assessment of unfairness is made on the basis of the circumstances at the time of contracting (see page 230).

(b) Guidelines

Schedule 2 contains guidelines for the application of the requirement of reasonableness. The factors in Sch 2 are:

> "(a) the strength of the bargaining position of the parties relative to each other, taking into account (among other things) alternative means by which the customer's requirements could have been met;
>
> (b) whether the customer received an inducement to agree to the term, or in accepting it had an opportunity of entering into a similar contract with other persons, but without having to accept a similar term;

(c) whether the customer knew or ought reasonably to have known of the existence and extent of the term (having regard, among other things, to any custom of the trade and any previous course of dealing between the parties);

(d) where the term excludes or restricts any relevant liability if some condition is not complied with, whether it was reasonable at the time of the contract to expect that compliance with that condition would be practicable;

(e) whether the goods were manufactured, processed or adapted to the special order of the customer."

By s 11(2) the above guidelines are applicable when the contract is one covered by s 6 or s 7 Unfair Contract Terms Act 1977 but, even in that context, they are not exhaustive. Outside ss 6 and 7, the guidelines will not apply by "legislative prescription" but the factors set out in the guidelines are still likely to be factually relevant to the reasonableness of an exemption clause (see eg *Singer Co (UK) Ltd* v *Tees and Hartlepool Port Authority* [1988] 2 Lloyd's Rep 164 at p 169; *Stewart Gill Ltd* v *Horatio Myer & Co Ltd* [1992] 2 All ER 257 at p 262; *Schenkers* v *Overland Shoes* [1998] 1 Lloyd's LR 498 at p 505). In *Phillips Products Ltd* v *Hyland* [1987] 2 All ER 620 the Court of Appeal thought that the judge at first instance had been wrong to assume that the case did not fall within s 7 but found that, in any event, that did not affect the way in which the decision on reasonableness had been taken. Those factors from Sch 2 which were relevant to the case had been taken into account, not because they were within the statutory guidelines, but simply because they were factually relevant (at p 628).

(c) Limitation of liability to a specified sum

Section 11(4) makes two factors particularly relevant to the question of the reasonableness of a clause which purports to limit liability to a specified sum. When someone tries to use such a clause, regard is to be had to:

"(a) the resource which he could expect to be available to him for the purpose of meeting the liability should it arise; and

(b) how far it was open to him to cover himself by insurance."

The cases show that the availability and cost of insurance are important factors generally, not only in relation to clauses limiting liability (see page 206).

In the context of s 11(4), it should not be thought that when the factors in that subsection point towards the clause being unreasonable that this necessarily decides the issue. All the relevant factors present must be taken into account and this may lead to a different conclusion. In *Singer Co (UK) Ltd* v *Tees and Hartlepool Port Authority* [1988] 2 Lloyd's Rep 164 the limitation clause was found to be reasonable despite the fact that the factors in s 11(4) indicated otherwise. In that case:

Singer Co were shutting down their UK operations and shipping their machinery overseas. The port authority took delivery of a piece of Singer's machinery for the purpose of loading it on to a ship. In the course of loading, it was dropped and badly damaged. Singer claimed damages from the port authority. The port authority sought to rely upon exemption clauses in its standard terms, stating:

"24. The Authority will not be responsible for any loss or damage . . . sustained by goods . . . during any service performed by them except for injury or damage arising from the proven negligence of their servants . . .

26. . . . the total liability of the authority for any . . . damage shall not exceed the value of the goods and shall be limited to a sum of £800 per tonne of the gross weight of the whole consignment".

Clause 24 served to reverse the burden of proof in relation to the liability for negligence of bailees; as Singer Co could not prove that the damage had occurred through negligence, the authority was *prima facie* not liable, subject to whether or not the clause satisfied the requirement of reasonableness. Steyn J found clause 24 to be reasonable and, the point to be emphasised here, he arrived *obiter* at the same conclusion in relation to the limitation of liability in clause 26. A number of factors indicated that clause 24 was reasonable. It did not attempt to remove liability for negligence, merely to reverse the burden of proof. The parties were not of unequal bargaining power. The port authority's standard terms were approved by the authority's board of directors, on which users of the port were well represented. The standard terms were widely distributed and readily available. Both parties could have insured but it was probably cheaper for Singer to do so. Most important were the day-to-day problems faced by the authority in the running of the port. These indicated that clause 24 was reasonable and also clause 26. The problems were that the authority had a minimal knowledge of, and little control over, the nature of the cargoes and it frequently had to load cargoes which were badly packaged or labelled. In addition, the reasonableness of clause 26 was indicated by the fact that there was an option to contract with or without the clause, the price being increased if the clause was not used. These factors made the limitation of liability in clause 26 reasonable despite the fact that s 11(4) would have indicated otherwise. The port authority had sufficient resources to meet such a claim and could have insured. Section 11(4) was not "virtually decisive" of the question of reasonableness. The other factors present had to be considered.

More generally it has been indicated that when liability is limited to a specific sum, that sum has to be justified in order to satisfy the requirement of reasonableness. In *The Salvage Association* v *CAP Financial Services* [1995] FSR 654 it was seen as relevant to ask whether the sum related to the turnover or insurance of the party seeking to rely on it, the contract price, or the uninsurable risk to which the other party is exposed. In *St Albans City and District Council* v *International Computers Ltd* [1995] FSR 686, Scott Baker J said:

"There are some types of agreement where ordinary risks fall within a particular sum, and there may be good reasons for limiting liability to that sum and leaving the purchaser to carry any additional risk".

In relation to standard terms it may be easier to establish that a monetary limit is reasonable if it is regularly reviewed (*Singer Co (UK) Ltd* v *Tees and Hartlepool Port Authority* [1988] 2 Lloyd's Rep 164).

Overseas Medical Supplies Ltd v *Orient Transport Services Ltd* [1999] 1 All ER (Comm) 981 raises the issue of the use of a single limitation clause in relation to different types of liability. The plaintiff suppliers of medical equipment, employed the defendants as freight forwarders to transport equipment to and from a trade exhibition. The defendants were specialists in dealing with that type of contract. The defendants' terms included a clause requiring the plaintiff to insure, either through the defendants themselves or independently, for loss or damage to the equipment, and another clause limited the defendant's liability to £600. The plaintiff opted to insure through the defendants — there had been no realistic possibility that they would do otherwise, it being far easier for the defendants to do so, due to their general work in the area. The equipment was lost on the return journey from the exhibition, at a cost to the plaintiff of some £8,500. The defendants had failed to effect the insurance requested by the plaintiff. The limitation was held unreasonable, and ineffective, under the 1977 Act because it not only covered liability for loss or damage to the equipment being transported but also for the defendant's failure to insure — leaving the plaintiff without any worthwhile recompense for their loss had it been effective. More broadly, the point was made as to the unreasonableness of limitation clauses covering very different types of loss. The point was made (at para 21) that whereas a "broad brush approach to limitation of liability will be reasonable" in relation to "certain package services", the position of the defendants in the instant case:

"was that of trading organisation which, under a single contract had agreed to combine at least two activities or functions in respect of which the nature of the work undertaken, the incidence of risk as between the parties, and the effect of a breach of duty by the appellants were all of a different character, yet were to be treated without distinction as subject to a single limitation of liability of only £600".

Such an approach was unreasonable.

(d) Inequality of bargaining power

Inequality of bargaining power is referred to in para (a) of the guidelines in Sch 2. It is one of the most basic factors to be considered in relation to the question of the reasonableness of an exemption clause. It is to be assessed on a broad basis.

"It can scarcely have been the intention of Parliament that a clause in a ship repairer's standard terms would be fair and reasonable one week — when the yard had no work and was willing to make concessions if asked — but unfair and unreasonable the following week, when the yard was busy. Relative bargaining power must surely be judged by somewhat broader considerations" (*Stag Line Ltd* v *Tyne Ship Repair Group Ltd; (The Zinnia)* [1984] 2 Lloyd's Rep 211 *per* Staughten J at p 222).

It will be relevant to ask whether the customer could have gone elsewhere to contract for the required goods or services. However, in "relation to the question of equality of the bargaining position, the court will have regard not only to the question of whether the customer was obliged to use the services of the supplier, but also the question of how far it would have been practicable and convenient to go elsewhere" (*Overseas Medical Supplies* v *Orient Transport Services* [1999] 1 All ER (Comm) 981 (para 3)). Standard terms, used throughout a particular trade, may indicate that one side of a common transaction is always in a better bargaining position than the other but this is not necessarily so. Whether standard terms throughout a trade indicate inequality of bargaining power will depend upon how the standard terms were arrived at. For example, in *RW Green* v *Cade Bros Farms* [1978] 1 Lloyd's Rep 602 (see below) the standard form contract, containing the exemption clause, was used throughout the trade by sellers of seed potatoes but the standard form had been arrived at after discussions between the National Association of Seed Potato merchants and the National Farmers' Union. It had not simply been imposed by the seedsmen upon their purchasers. The use of a standard form did not indicate inequality of bargaining power. (See also *Singer Co (UK) Ltd* v *Tees and Hartlepool Port Authority* [1988] 2 Lloyd's Rep 164; *George Mitchell Ltd* v *Finney Lock Seeds Ltd* [1983] 2 AC 803; *Schenkers Ltd* v *Overland Shoes* [1998] 1 Lloyd's LR 498.)

(e) Insurance

As we have seen, the possibility of obtaining insurance to cover a potential liability is made specifically relevant to the reasonableness of a limitation clause by s 11(4). It is also a factor which the courts have indicated as being of general significance. The reasonableness of the risk allocation in the exemption clause is assessed against the possibilities open to either party to insure against it (*Flamar Interocean Ltd* v *Denmac Ltd* [1990] 1 Lloyd's Rep 434).

In *Photo Production Ltd* v *Securicor Ltd* [1980] AC 827 the Unfair Contract Terms Act 1977 was not applicable because of the date when the events occurred, but the House of Lords commented upon the reasonableness of the exemption clause in general terms. In that case:

> Securicor had contracted to provide a security patrol of Photo Production's factory. One of Securicor's employees, Musgrove, whilst carrying out a patrol of the factory, decided one night to start a fire, and the factory burnt down. The question was whether Securicor was liable for the destruction of the factory. Securicor wished to rely upon an exemption clause.

The main issue was that of the construction of the clause. However, having held that the clause was appropriately worded to cover the events which had occurred, the House of Lords also considered, *obiter*, whether the clause was reasonable; it thought that it was. The contract was one between two businesses of equal bargaining power. The risk of fire damage had been allocated to the party who could most appropriately insure against it. Photo Production had to insure their factory against fire damage generally. Securicor might not have been able to obtain the appropriate insurance and, even if it had, paying for insurance cover would have increased Securicor's costs and prevented the provision of the security service at the cheap rate given to Photo Production.

It should be emphasised that what must be asked is not merely whether a party could have insured but also at what cost (see also *Singer Co (UK) Ltd* v *Tees and Hartlepool Port Authority* [1988] 2 Lloyd's Rep 164 at p 169). *George Mitchell Ltd* v *Finney Lock Seeds Ltd* [1983] 2 AC 803 contrasts with the *Photo Production* case. In *Mitchell* v *Finney Lock Seeds* a case decided under s 55 Sale of Goods Act 1979, the person seeking to rely upon the clause could have insured without materially increasing his prices, and this was one factor which led the court to conclude that the exemption clause was unreasonable. *Mitchell* v *Finney Lock Seeds* concerned the sale of cabbage seed. The seed should have been of a variety of winter cabbage but what was negligently supplied was autumn cabbage seed of an inferior quality. The plants produced were very poor, without hearts. The entire crop was useless and had to be ploughed in. The farmers sought to claim for their lost year's production (about £61,000). Finney Lock claimed to rely upon a clause which limited their liability to the cost of the seed (about £200). In deciding that it was not fair and reasonable to allow reliance on the clause, the court indicated that it was relevant that the sellers could have insured against the risk of crop failure caused by supplying the wrong seed and such insurance would not have led to a significant increase in the price of their seed.

There were other relevant factors in *Mitchell* v *Finney Lock Seeds*. Most importantly, Finney Lock's practice had been to settle those claims that they thought were justifiable for sums in excess of the amount indicated by the exemption clause, and they had even attempted to settle the claim before the court. This last factor was looked upon by the court as determining the issue before it. It took it to indicate that Finney Lock themselves did not regard the clause as one on which it was fair and reasonable to rely. Further consideration is given to this last factor below (see page 211), where the need to treat it with some care is discussed.

It is clear that exemption clauses may be employed to circumvent the need to pay for insurance against the risk of having to pay damages. As in *Securicor*, this may be regarded as a reasonable course to have taken. Y may be in a better position to insure than X and if X does not have to bear the cost of insurance he may offer Y a better contract price. However, an exemption clause may still be regarded as unreasonable even where its ineffectiveness will mean that the person who sought to rely upon the clause will have to insure in the future and increase his contract price accordingly. Such increased costs may be preferable to the consequences which would follow if the exemption clause were to be effective. This point is illustrated by *Smith* v *Eric S Bush* [1989] 2 All ER 514:

> Mrs Smith wished to purchase a house. In order to do so she applied to a building society for a mortgage. The building society instructed a firm of valuers, Eric S Bush, to report on and value the property. Mrs Smith paid the building society a fee and signed an application form which stated that the society would provide her with a copy of the mortgage valuation. The form contained a disclaimer to the effect that neither the society nor its valuer warranted that the valuation would be accurate and that the valuation would be supplied without any acceptance of responsibility. When Mrs Smith received the valuation, it too contained the disclaimer. The valuation stated that no essential repairs were required and valued the house at £16,500. Relying upon the report and without obtaining an independent survey, Mrs Smith purchased the house for £18,000, £3,500 coming from the mortgage. The valuers had been negligent in their inspection of the house and had failed to notice the lack of support for a chimney which fell through the roof eighteen months later, causing considerable damage.

Mrs Smith claimed damages from the valuers in tort because of their negligent valuation. The House of Lords found that a duty of care was owed to Mrs Smith by the valuers and considered the disclaimer. Its reasonableness fell to be considered under s 2(2) Unfair Contract Terms Act 1977. That section deals with non-contractual notices purporting to exclude liability in tort as well as contractual exemption clauses, and it is the House of Lords decision on the reasonableness of the clause which is of interest here. The court noted that, although it was open to someone purchasing a house to commission a full survey, the purchaser in this case had relied upon the mortgage valuation rather than arranging for her own survey to be carried out, and such reliance was common practice in house purchases. Purchasers often could not afford to pay for the valuation and a separate survey. Those factors indicated that the disclaimer was not reasonable. The court also considered the practical consequences if the disclaimer was effective. It would mean one individual would bear the loss involved, and that would be likely to cause hardship. Individuals could find themselves with an uninhabitable dwelling and a mortgage still to be paid on it. If the disclaimer was ineffective, leaving the valuer with the consequences of his negligence, it would merely result in him increasing his insurance cover. The cost of increased insurance would be borne by a small price increase to all his clients, and the whole of the risk of his negligence would not fall on one unfortunate house purchaser. In this case the likely increase of valuers' fees to meet their new insurance premiums was a preferable, and more reasonable, outcome to that which would follow if the disclaimer was effective (see also *St Albans City and District Council* v *International Computers Ltd* [1995] FSR 686, and this point was affirmed in the Court of Appeal [1996] 4 All ER 481).

(f) Availability of alternatives

Paragraph (b) of Sch 2 deals with the availability of an alternative form of contract, without the exemption clause in question, and this is also a factor which has been prominent in the case law. *Woodman* v *Phototrade Processing Ltd* (1981) (unreported but see (1981) 131 NLJ 935 and Miller & Harvey, *Consumer and Trading Law Cases and Materials* (1985) p 245) illustrates this factor:

> Mr Woodman had taken photographs at his friends' wedding. He had intended to give them the photographs as a wedding present. There was no other photographer present. He took his film into a shop which acted as an agent for Phototrade Processing Ltd (PTP). On the counter in the shop was a sign containing an exemption clause limiting PTP's liability to replacement of lost films with new ones. PTP negligently lost Mr Woodman's film.

Mr Woodman claimed damages in excess of the cost of a replacement film because of the distress caused by the loss (see page 469). The question was whether the exemption clause was effective to prevent this from being successful. As negligence was involved, s 2(2) Unfair Contract Terms Act 1977 rendered the clause ineffective except in so far as it satisfied the requirement of reasonableness. It was argued that the clause was reasonable because it enabled PTP to operate a cheap mass production service. The judge considered such a service to be good enough for the majority of photographers whose pictures were not valuable. He also thought that the majority might complain if they had to pay a higher rate in order to protect the interest of the minority whose pictures were of greater value. However there was no choice for the minority who required greater care to be taken with their photographs. In addition, the code of practice of the photographic industry, as agreed with the Office of Fair Trading, recognized the possibility of a two tier system of liability for photographic processors. This code envisaged the customer being offered the choice of a cheaper service and very limited liability for the processor or a more expensive service with the processor accepting greater liability. PTP did not offer their customers a more expensive/greater liability alternative service and this was taken as decisively indicating that the exemption was unreasonable. (See also *Singer Co (UK) Ltd* v *Tees and Hartlepool Port Authority* [1988] 2 Lloyd's Rep 164 at p 170.)

In *RW Green Ltd* v *Cade Bros Farms* [1978] 1 Lloyd's Rep 602 the availability of more expensive seed potatoes which would be more likely to be healthy indicated that the exemption clause was reasonable in relation to the purchase of cheaper seed potatoes. In that case:

> Seedsmen, RW Green, sold twenty tons of King Edward seed potatoes to a farmer on the standard terms of the National Association of Seed Potato merchants. The potatoes were infected with a virus which was undetectable until the crop started to grow. The standard terms contained an exemption clause which stated that any claim had to be notified to the sellers within three days of delivery and which also limited liability to the cost of the seed.

When RW Green claimed the price of the seed, the farmers counterclaimed for their lost profit on the crop (about £6,000). The counterclaim depended upon whether the exemption clause passed the reasonableness test in the predecessor to the Unfair Contract Terms Act 1977 (see p 202). It was decided that it was not fair and reasonable to allow reliance upon the three day time limit as the virus could not be detected until the crop started to grow. In contrast, the limitation of liability to the cost of the seed (£634) passed the reasonableness test. The parties were of equal bargaining power. The standard terms were the result of discussions between the seedsmen's association and the National Farmers' Union. This counterbalanced the fact that the same terms were used throughout the trade and the farmers could not have made such a purchase without the exemption clause being a part of the contract. The reasonableness of the limitation was also indicated by the fact that those standard terms had been used for about twenty years and the parties had dealt together for five or six years so that they both should have known of the exemption clause. More specifically, the fact that the farmers had the alternative of purchasing certified seed at a higher price indicated that limiting liability to a specified sum was reasonable. Certified seed would have come from a crop which had been inspected for signs of virus the previous year and purchasing such seed would have provided "a very real safeguard" against the risk of obtaining infected seed. The farmer had chosen to buy cheaper seed with a higher risk of the virus being present in it. (It should be remembered that it has been held that, under the 1977 Act, the court will not hold part of a clause reasonable — *Stewart Gill Ltd* v *Horatio Myer & Co Ltd* [1992] 2 All ER 257.)

It is clear that the availability of an alternative is important to the reasonableness of the exemption clause. However it must be borne in mind that not all alternatives will render the exemption clause reasonable. The reality of the alternative must be borne in mind. In *Smith* v *Eric S Bush* [1989] 2 All ER 514 (see above) it will be recalled that the House of Lords had to consider the reasonableness, under the Unfair Contract Terms Act 1977, of the disclaimer of liability by a valuer in relation to a mortgage valuation of a dwelling house. The purchaser could have obtained her own survey but the court considered the reality of this possible alternative. It was recognized that most purchasers of dwelling houses relied on the valuation carried out for the building society. It was regarded as impracticable and too expensive for such purchasers to obtain a separate survey. The purchaser had to pay for the valuation for the mortgage, and often could not afford to pay again for a survey. The possibility of a separate survey was not an alternative which rendered reasonable the disclaimer of liability on the mortgage valuation. In addition, the reality of the alternative will also be considered from another perspective. If a condition "works in such a way as to leave little time to put such option into effect this may effectively eliminate the option as a factor indicating reasonableness" (*Overseas Medical* v *Orient Transport* [1999] 1 All ER (Comm) 981 at 987). The person seeking to rely on an exemption clause cannot simply use a clause stating that he, or she, has an alternative available if there is no intention to make such alternative contracts (*Overseas Medical* v *Orient Transport* [1999] 1 All ER (Comm) 981).

(g) Knowledge/consent

Guideline (c) in Sch 2 refers to the factor of knowledge, ie whether there was, or should have been, knowledge of the exemption clause on the part of the person against whom the clause is being used. Such knowledge, actual or constructive, could indicate that the clause is reasonable. More broadly, there is the factor of whether the injured party should be taken to have consented to the clause.

In *Stevenson* v *Nationwide Building Society* [1984] EG Dig 934 the situation was very similar to that in *Smith* v *Eric S Bush* [1989] 2 All ER 514 except that the person purchasing the property was himself an estate agent. He had "trade" knowledge of the house purchasing process and the disclaimer of liability for a negligent valuation was considered reasonable. It was said (at p 935):

> "When I bear in mind that the person affected by the disclaimer is someone well familiar with the possibility of obtaining a survey, and also familiar with the difference between a building society valuation and a survey and their different costs, it seems to me perfectly reasonable to allow the building society, in effect to say to him that if he chooses the cheaper alternative he must accept that the society will not be responsible for the content to him."

However, it should be emphasised that the whole picture must be considered. Even actual knowledge of the clause may not indicate that the clause is reasonable if there is inequality of bargaining power. In such circumstances the clause may have been knowingly accepted on the basis that there was no realistic alternative (*Phillips Products Ltd* v *Hyland* [1987] 2 All ER 620 at p 629).

The question of knowledge will often be a matter of whether the relevant party should have known of the proferens' terms, rather than actual knowledge. It should be emphasised that when the reasonableness of a contract term is under consideration, the question of "knowledge" is looked at "in circumstances where *ex hypothesi* the term has been validly incorporated in the contract" (*AEG (UK) Ltd* v *Logic Resources Ltd* [1996] CLC 265 at p 274) but factors similar to those looked at in relation to incorporation of contract terms will nevertheless be examined. It has been said that "it is necessary, in order to assess reasonableness, to consider to what extent the party has actually consented to the clause" (*AEG* at p 279), but this is to make the test too subjective. It should be a question not simply of actual knowledge but of what the reasonable person should have known. The difference between this assessment and that made in relation to incorporation is that the artificiality with which the facts are often clothed by the rules on incorporation should be avoided.

Trade practice and a long course of dealing between the parties indicated knowledge of the clause and pointed to its reasonableness in *RW Green Ltd* v *Cade Bros Farms* [1978] 1 Lloyd's Rep 602. Similarly, in *Singer Co (UK) Ltd* v *Tees and Hartlepool Port Authority* [1988] 2 Lloyd's Rep 164 an indicator of the reasonableness of the clause was the wide distribution and ready availability of the port authority's standard terms (see also *Schenkers* v *Overland Shoes* [1998] 1 Lloyd's LR 498 at 507). Also relevant to the question of actual or constructive knowledge of a clause is its legibility and intelligibility. In *Stag Line Ltd* v *Tyne Ship Repair Group Ltd; (The Zinnia)* [1984] 2 Lloyd's Rep 211 Staughten J commented (*obiter* at p 222) that he was inclined to find the exemption clauses unreasonable because the print was so small that it was barely legible and also because "the draftsmanship was so convoluted and prolix that one almost need[ed] an LL.B. to understand them". Similarly, it indicated the unreasonableness of the clause in *Overseas Medical* v *Orient Transport* [1999] 1 All ER (Comm) 981 that there was "insufficient clarity in the conditions to bring home to the plaintiffs the effect of" the clause (para 20). However, it can again be emphasised that despite some similarities with the common law rules on incorporation, this aspect of the test of the reasonableness of an exemption clause allows account to be taken of the artificial way in which a clause may be incorporated into a contract. As was seen above, incorporation by notice or signature has little to do with any real agreement to the terms and may be a very artificial process.

(h) The width of the clause

The width of the clause may be relevant to its reasonableness under the Unfair Contract Terms Act 1977. For example, it may be easier to find that an exemption clause is reasonable if it has been construed as applying only to non-negligent breaches (see *Stag Line Ltd* v *Tyne Ship Repair Group Ltd; (The Zinnia)* [1984] 2 Lloyd's Rep 211 at p 223). It should be emphasised that s 11(1) requires the reasonableness of the clause to be assessed on what was known or contemplated, or what should have been known or contemplated, by the parties at the time of contracting. The fact that the working of the exemption clause might be perfectly reasonable in relation to the specific breach which has occurred does not mean that the clause will pass the reasonableness test. The clause may be unreasonable because of the breaches which it potentially covers. On this basis the wider the clause the greater the possibility of its being considered unreasonable[6]. In fact, as indicated above, it should also be emphasised here that the Court of Appeal in *Stewart Gill* v *Horatio Myer* (see page 190) refused to split the reasonable and unreasonable parts of a clause, and the whole clause was rendered ineffective by the 1977 Act. (See also the discussion of *Overseas Medical Supplies* v *Orient Transport Services* [1999] 1 All ER (Comm) 981 in relation to the unreasonableness of a clause limiting different types of liability to a single sum " p 204.)

(i) Settlement of past claims

In *George Mitchell Ltd* v *Finney Lock Seeds Ltd* [1983] 2 AC 803 the "decisive factor" in the House of Lords' conclusion that the exemption clause was unreasonable was the seed sellers' past practice. In the past they had settled claims which they regarded as justifiable for sums in excess of the limit set by the exemption clause. The sellers had even attempted to negotiate a settlement in the instant case. This "decisive factor" needs to be given further consideration. First, it is necessary to consider whether any account of it should be taken in applying the test in s 11 Unfair Contract Terms Act 1977. Second, once it is decided that it is a potentially relevant factor, it should be asked what conclusions should be drawn from it in relation to that test of reasonableness.

It should be remembered that the reasonableness of the exemption clause in *Mitchell* v *Finney Lock Seeds* fell to be determined under what is now s 55 Sale of Goods Act 1979 rather than under s 11 Unfair Contract Terms Act 1977. It must be emphasised again that the test under s 55 is whether it is fair and reasonable to allow reliance on the clause. As that test relates to reliance, the events after formation of the contract were relevant to the question of reasonableness. Under s 55 the fact of an attempted settlement in the particular case could come within the range of factors to be considered. Equally, because of the difference in the test in s 11 Unfair Contract Terms Act 1977, any attempted settlement of the particular case cannot be relevant to "reasonableness" under that Act. Section 11 looks to the time at which the contract was made. However, there was a past practice of settling claims in *Mitchell* v *Finney Lock Seeds* and it seems that this past practice should have been one of the factors contemplated by the parties at the time of contracting. If the past practice has been such that the parties should have contemplated it at the time of contracting, it would be possible to take account of such past settlements under the s 11 test of reasonableness. Such a factor has been considered in coming to a decision on the application of s 11. In *Rees Hough Ltd* v *Redland Reinforced Plastics Ltd* [1985] 2 Con LR 109 the parties' past practice of settling claims rather than relying upon the exemption clause was regarded as the most important factor against the clause, and it was decided that the clause did not satisfy the requirement of reasonableness in s 11 Unfair Contract Terms Act 1977 (but see *Stewart Gill Ltd* v *Horatio Myer & Co Ltd* [1992] 2 All ER 257 — see page 201).

Under s 11 Unfair Contract Terms Act 1977, it is possible to consider a past practice of settling claims rather than relying upon the exemption clause, but what is its relevance? In *Mitchell* v *Finney Lock Seeds* [1983] 2 AC 803 such practice was taken to indicate that the sellers themselves did not regard it as reasonable to rely upon the clause (at p 817). It can be contended that such a conclusion will often not be appropriate. Business people often may not take a legalistic view and seek to enforce strict contractual rights because they do not wish to endanger their business relationship with the other party. Negotiation and settlement are more conducive to the continuance of relationships than a legal battle. The business community in which the parties operate may even regard the use of legal action as an inappropriate way to settle disputes[7]. In *Schenkers* v *Overland Shoes* [1998] 1 Lloyd's LR 498 the Court of Appeal distinguished *Mitchell* v *Finney Lock* on its facts and refused to accept the argument that non-reliance on the clause in past transactions showed that it was unreasonable. Pill LJ said (at p 508):

"In the present circumstances, I see little merit in the defendant's argument that the clause had not in practice been relied upon. The give and take practised by the parties in the course of substantial dealings ... was admirable and conducive to a good business relationship but did not prevent the plaintiffs, when a dispute arose, relying upon the terms agreed."

(j) Conditions placed on claims

Guideline (d) relates to exclusion or restriction of liability unless a condition is complied with. This relates to the situation where one party seeks to use an exemption clause to place a condition upon his liability. For example, he may state that the other party must notify him of any claim within a specified time (eg *RW Green* v *Cade Bros Farms* [1978] 1 Lloyd's Rep 602). The test of reasonableness in s 11 Unfair Contract Terms Act 1977 requires some consideration in relation to such restrictions.

The facts which can be taken into account under s 11 in looking at conditions on claims should be considered. In *RW Green* v *Cade Bros Farms* the exemption clause was in two parts. The first stated that any claim had to be notified to the sellers within three days of delivery of the seed potatoes. The second part limited any claim to the contract price of the seed potatoes. It will be recalled that although the second part of the exemption clause was found to be reasonable, the time limit was not. The time limit was not reasonable because the problem with the potatoes was a viral infection which could be detected only after the crop started to grow. Obviously that would be outside the three day limit. That case was decided under the previous test of reasonableness. It should be emphasised that under s 11 the reasonableness of the time limit cannot be assessed in relation to the particular breach which occurred. The possibility of the potatoes being defective because of such a virus can be considered only to the extent that it was, or should have been, contemplated by the parties at the time of contracting.

If the condition is one which will, within the contemplation of the parties, lead to capricious results, that may indicate that the exemption is unreasonable. For example, if a clause in a ship repair contract requires the return of the ship to the repairer's yard for any defect to be remedied this may be unreasonable because it is capricious. "The apportionment of risk is made to depend upon where a casualty happens to occur, and whether the owner happens to find it convenient and economic to return his vessel to the yard" (*Stag Line Ltd* v *Tyne Ship Repair Group Ltd; (The Zinnia)* [1984] 2 Lloyd's Rep 211 at p 223).

(k) Negligence

One factor relevant to holding the exemption clause unreasonable in *Mitchell* v *Finney Lock Seeds Ltd* [1983] 2 AC 803 was the fact that the breach involved negligence. Again the point should be made that s 11 does not allow the actual breach to be taken into account in considering whether the clause is reasonable, merely the potential for it (*Rees Hough Ltd* v *Redland Reinforced Plastics Ltd* [1985] 2 Con LR 109). The point can also be made that, in the consumer context, the Director General of Fair Trading clearly views clauses attempting to exclude or restrict liability for negligence as generally unfair under the 1999 Regulations on Unfair Terms in Consumer Contracts (see eg OFT Bulletin 3 at pp 30, 54; OFT Bulletin 4 at p 65).

(l) Customer's detailed specifications

Paragraph (e) in Schedule 2 specifically makes relevant to the requirement of reasonableness "whether the goods were manufactured, processed or adapted to the special order of the customer".

In *Edmund Murray Ltd* v *BSP International Foundations Ltd* (1993) 33 Con LR 1 the sellers manufactured a drilling rig for the buyers. The contract contained detailed specifications as to the technical standards which the rig was required to meet, and it was made clear exactly how the buyers wished to use the rig. Against that background, the court considered it unreasonable for the sellers to restrict their liability to replacement of defective parts.

(m) Appeals and precedent

The courts have given some consideration to the approach to be taken to an appeal from a decision on the requirement of reasonableness in s 11 Unfair Contract Terms Act 1977. In *George Mitchell Ltd* v *Finney Lock Seeds Ltd* Lord Bridge, with whom the other members of the court agreed, said in relation to the test of reasonableness under s 11 (and s 55 Sale of Goods Act 1979):

> "There will sometimes be room for a legitimate difference of opinion as to what the answer should be, where it will be impossible to say that one view is demonstrably wrong and the other demonstrably right. It must follow . . . that, when asked to review such a decision on appeal, the appellate court should treat the original decision with the utmost respect and refrain from interference with it unless satisfied that it proceeded upon some erroneous principle or was plainly and obviously wrong" (at p 816).

This indicates that decisions on the requirement of reasonableness will often provide very limited guidance for the future. Another judge might have weighed the factors in the same case differently, come to the opposite conclusion, and still not be overturned on appeal. *Phillips Products Ltd* v *Hyland* [1987] 2 All ER 620 provides an example of the way this approach to appeals works. In that case, the court was concerned with a standard form, widely used by those in the business of hiring out plant. Despite the fact that the Court of Appeal took a different view from the trial judge on several of the factors relevant to the issue of reasonableness, it declined to overrule his decision. It accepted the approach to appeals indicated in *Mitchell* v *Finney Lock Seeds Ltd.* In keeping with this, the Court of Appeal emphasised that it was considering the reasonableness of the clause in the particular contract between the particular parties. The contract was made on the basis of a widely used standard form but the court indicated that its decision did not mean that the exemption clause was to be taken to be unreasonable in every transaction in which the standard form was used. The decision on reasonableness related to the instant case. Even in relation to a standard form contract, this must follow from the adoption of the above approach to appeals.

This approach to appeals inevitably creates uncertainty as to what is required for an exemption clause to pass the reasonableness test in s 11 Unfair Contract Terms Act 1977. This presents some hindrance to contract planning. It is difficult for a person in business to decide whether to pay for insurance and increase his costs, and contract price, if there is uncertainty concerning the efficacy of the exemption clause which he had designed to obviate the need for insurance.

However, in some cases of standard forms, the factors indicating that the clause is unreasonable may be present so often when the form is used that a case may be widely relevant to the issue of reasonableness. The House of Lords decision in *Smith* v *Eric S Bush* [1989] 2 All ER 514 is such a case. The House of Lords thought its decision on the reasonableness of the disclaimer in the mortgage valuation to be of general application to the purchase, via a mortgage, of a dwelling house of "modest value". It was in relation to such transactions that it was known that purchasers did not usually obtain their own survey but relied on the mortgage valuation. Lord Griffiths said (at p 532):

> "It must, however, be remembered that this is the sale of a dwelling house of modest value in which it is widely recognized by surveyors that purchasers are in fact relying on their care and skill. *It will obviously be of general application in broadly similar circumstances.* But I expressly reserve my position in respect of quite different types of property for mortgage purposes, such as industrial property, large blocks of flats or very expensive houses. In such cases it may be that the general expectation of the behaviour of the purchaser is quite different" (emphasis added).

3. Exemption clauses (s 13)

The active sections frequently refer to clauses which "exclude or restrict" liability. A fairly narrow interpretation could have been given to that phrase and such an interpretation would have limited the clauses falling within the operation of the Act. Section 13 makes it clear that the Act is not so restricted. Section 13(1) states:

> "To the extent that this Part of this Act prevents the exclusion or restriction of any liability it also prevents—
> (a) making the liability or its enforcement subject to restrictive or onerous conditions;
> (b) excluding or restricting any right or remedy in respect of the liability, or subjecting a person to any prejudice in consequence of his pursuing any such right or remedy;
> (c) excluding or restricting rules of evidence or procedure;
>
> and (to that extent) sections 2 and 5 to 7 also prevent excluding or restricting liability by reference to terms and notices which exclude or restrict the relevant obligation or duty".

Paragraphs (a) to (c) ensure that clauses which have the effect of excluding or restricting liability, but in a slightly round-about way, are dealt with as if they limited or excluded liability more simply (see eg *Stewart Gill Ltd* v *Horatio Myer & Co Ltd* [1992] 2 All ER 257). For example, (a) covers a clause stating that any claim must be made within a certain time period, and (b) covers a clause which allows recovery of damages but which purports to remove any right to terminate the contract for breach. A clause stating that signature was proof that the goods delivered met the requirements of the contract falls within (c). It is the last part of s 13 which presents difficulties and requires further consideration.

It has already been seen that s 3(2)(b) deals with exclusion clauses in the form of part of the definition of the obligation. The last part of s 13(1) is similarly a provision to prevent evasion of the Act by exclusion clauses in "disguise". Section 13(1) ensures that some clauses which, in form, define the obligation will be identified as exclusion clauses, in nature, for the purposes of ss 2, 5, 6 and 7 Unfair Contract Terms Act 1977. The difficulty is that it does not indicate how to determine which clauses are to be treated in this way. We need to consider how the limits of the operation of s 13(1) are to be set.

We have already seen that a clause in the form of an exclusion of liability could have been drafted instead as a clause in the form of part of the definition of the obligations (see page 136). Both forms of clause mark out the boundaries within which a legal remedy is available. A clause in the form of an exclusion of liability does that by removing the legal remedies for breach of what would be, but for the clause, an obligation. A clause in the form of part of the definition of the obligations simply states the obligations. The problem presented by the last part of s 13(1) is to determine which clauses in the form of part of the definition of the obligation it requires to be treated in the same way as clauses in the form of exclusions of liability. The lack of any clarification of this in the Act means that there is a conceptual hole at the centre of the Unfair Contract Terms Act 1977.

The House of Lords considered the coverage of the final part of s 13(1) in *Smith* v *Eric S Bush (a firm)* [1989] 2 All ER 514. The case was considered above in the context of the court's conclusion that the surveyor's disclaimer of his tortious liability for negligence did not satisfy the requirement of reasonableness applied by s 2(2) of the Act. The point to be considered here is the surveyor's prior argument that the disclaimer was not subject to s 2(2) because it did not exclude or restrict the surveyor's liability but rather prevented the duty of care from arising. The House of Lords did not agree with that contention. It was concluded that the disclaimer fell within the relevant part of s 13(1) and so was brought within s 2(2). Lord Griffiths arrived at that conclusion by applying the "but for" test. He said (at p 530):

> "the existence of the common law duty of care ... is to be judged by considering whether it would exist 'but for' the notice ..."

In other words, the approach taken was simply to ask whether there would be an obligation in the absence of the clause. If there was, then the clause was to be regarded as excluding it and within the relevant part of s 13(1). This reflects the approach indicated by the Court of Appeal in *Phillips Products Ltd* v *Hyland* [1987] 2 All ER 620 where, in the contractual context, in considering whether there had been a breach of an obligation to take reasonable care, Slade LJ said (at p 625):

> "the court has to leave out of account at this stage the contract term which is relied on by the defence as defeating the plaintiff's claim for breach of such obligation or duty."

The "but for" test would also seem to be indicated by *Johnstone* v *Bloomsbury Health Authority* [1991] 2 All ER 293. The case concerned the contract of employment of a junior hospital doctor. The contract provided that he should work for 40 hours a week and be on call for up to a further 48 hours a week. It was the express term concerning the hours on call which was at the centre of the dispute. The doctor claimed that his health had been damaged by the long hours which he had worked, and he argued that the health authority was in breach of an implied term that it had a duty to take care not to foreseeably damage his health. The Court of Appeal was asked to strike out his action but his claim survived. A term will not be implied in the face of an express contradictory term but the majority of the court thought that the express term did not contradict the implied term contended for, but merely set the limits within which the health authority should exercise its discretion in relation to the "on call hours". However, the point of interest here is that all three members of the court agreed that, if the express term prevented the implication, then that express term would be regarded as a clause falling within the final part of s 13(1) and would thus be rendered ineffective by s 2(1) Unfair Contract Terms Act 1977.

The idea of using the Unfair Contract Terms Act 1977 in the way in which the court envisaged in *Johnstone* v *Bloomsbury Health Authority* illustrates how wide the compass of the Act would be under the application of the "but for" test. It would seem to render subject to the Act any express term contradicting a term which would, in the absence of the clause, be implied into a contract falling within the Act (provided that the liability existing in the absence of the clause is appropriate to bring the clause within one of the relevant "active sections"). "But for" the clause the implication would be made. In addition, the "but for" test would seem to make it impossible for the parties to define an obligation to take due care by stating it widely and then qualifying it, without its being subject to s 2 of the Act. However, perhaps the width of the "but for" test is most forcefully illustrated by reference to the terms implied by the Sale of Goods Act 1979. In relation to a sale to someone dealing as consumer, s 6(2) of the 1977 Act prevents the exclusion or restriction of the terms implied by ss 13–15 of the 1979 Act. If the sale is not to someone who deals as consumer then, under s 6(3) such a clause is effective only if it satisfies the requirement of reasonableness. The point to be made here is that the "but for" test would seem to make subject to the 1977 Act any clause which was merely intended to show that the transaction was not one in which it was appropriate to imply the term in question. For example, a clause indicating that "sale" goods were simply sold as seen and not "by description" would be subject to the Act as a clause in the absence of which s 13(1) of the 1979 Act would imply a term that the goods should correspond with their description. It seems inappropriate for it to be concluded that the Unfair Contract Terms Act 1977 should apply to all such clauses, particularly when it is borne in mind that if the sale is to a consumer the seller cannot even argue that his clause should survive the application of the Act because it is reasonable (contrast *Cavendish Woodhouse* v *Marley* (1984) 82 LGR 376 and *Hughes* v *Hall* [1981] RTR 430).

The "but for" test is very mechanical, which means that it is easy to apply. It does not require reference to any such matter as the parties' view of the role of the clause in question (which is relevant to distinguish a penalty clause and a liquidated damages clause — see page 487), which would inevitably introduce an element of uncertainty. However, that ease of application is paid for by a lack of discrimination. The "but for" test seems to be too wide, bringing clauses inappropriately within the Act.

It can be contended that an exclusion clause can be identified "in nature" by looking to the origin of the obligations in question. In contract, for the most part, the terms and the obligations stem from the intention of the parties and it may be argued that the nature of a clause can be ascertained by looking at the extension of that intention to the point of performance and looking at the parties' reasonable expectations of performance. A clause is then an exclusion clause "in nature" if it means that the parties' reasonable expectations of performance are greater than the performance actually required by the contract. It has already been indicated above how the artificiality of the contracting process can result in the parties' reasonable expectations of performance differing from the performance actually required by the contract (see page 188). The "expectations test" is a matter of looking at the expectations created by the facts rather than simply following the dictates of the legal rules on incorporation and construction. Of course, any test based upon the parties' reasonable expectations will be far less certain and easy to apply than a mechanical "but for" test, but it could provide a more discriminating test for the application of the final part of s 13(1). (For a full discussion of the "expectations test" and its application see Macdonald (1992) 12 LS 277; Macdonald, *Exemption Clauses and Unfair Terms* (1999) Butterworths.) The final point to make here is that this type of problem should largely be avoided under the Regulations on Unfair Terms in Consumer Contracts, provided that an appropriate approach is taken to identifying the core terms — the Regulations are not limited in their application to a specific type of term such as exemption clauses.

Footnotes

(1) Section 149 Road Traffic Act 1988, s 29 Public Passenger Vehicles Act 1981, and the Carriage of Goods by Sea Act 1971 provide examples of legislation to deal with exemption clauses in particular situations.

(2) Although Schedule 1 would preclude it from the operation of the Act.

(3) See Kidner (1987) 38 NILQ 46; Brown [1988] JBL 386; Pearce [1989] LMCLQ 371.

(4) Adams & Brownsword, *The Unfair Contract Terms Act 1977: A Decade of Discretion* (1988) 104 LQR 94.

(5) Peel (1993) 56 MLR 98, Brown & Chandler (1993) 109 LQR 41.

(6) See *Howard Marine and Dredging Co Ltd* v *A Ogden & Sons (Excavations) Ltd* [1978] QB 574 and Lord Denning MR's discussion of the contrasting provision in what is now s 55 Sale of Goods Act 1979, the predecessor to s 11 Unfair Contract Terms Act 1977.

(7) See Macauley, *Non-Contractual Relations in Business,* (1963) 28 Am Soc Rev 55; Beale and Dugdale, *Contracts between Businessmen: Planning and Use of Contractual Remedies,* (1975) 2 Br J Law and Soc 45. For discussion of this factor in relation to the requirement of reasonableness see Adams and Brownsword (1988) 104 LQR 94.

Chapter 11

Unfair Terms in Consumer Contracts Regulations 1999

1. Introduction

(a) Significance

The Unfair Terms in Consumer Contracts Regulations 1999 (SI 1999 No 2083)[1] came into force on 1 October 1999, replacing the 1994 Regulations of the same name (SI 1994 No 3159). They apply a test of "fairness" to non-individually negotiated terms in contracts between consumers and sellers or suppliers, and they are of considerable significance. It has been said (Pat Edwards, Legal Director OFT, 'The Challenge of The Regulations' in OFT Bulletin No 4 on Unfair Contract Terms, p 19):

> ". . . that cherished principle [of freedom of contract], instilled in the course of academic studies and practice had, of course, been much under attack well before 1995 in its application to some aspects of consumer contracts. But nothing had hitherto actually turned on its head, as the Directive does, the general duty of the lawyer to draft wholly and exclusively in the interests of the client, in whatever language is adapted to preserve and enhance the client's legal position . . . Now in order properly to serve their clients, legal advisers must have a wider perspective than taking into account *only* those client's interests, while at the same time using plain intelligible language of a kind which has never featured prominently in time-honoured legal precedents."

Obviously, it is the fairness test which requires a change in outlook in relation to consumer contracts. However, it is the enforcement regime which makes the Regulations of great significance. The Regulations can be used by an individual consumer in dispute with a particular seller or supplier but the most important enforcement mechanism is a more general one. The 1994 Regulations gave the Director General of Fair Trading power to apply for injunctions to prevent the continued use of unfair terms in general use and, under the 1999 Regulations, that power is extended to other "qualifying bodies", as set out in Sch 1, including the Consumers' Association[2]. So far the Director General has achieved the removal or modification of many terms in standard form consumer contracts – mostly by negotiation rather than having to resort to litigation – and that can be seen in the Bulletins published by the Office of Fair Trading (OFT) to show how complaints about terms have been dealt with. Such an enforcement mechanism is important in the consumer context because consumers do not generally litigate and often do not know their rights. The

Director General has even encountered terms which would have been automatically ineffective under the 1977 Act (eg Bulletin 3 at 1.2). Any terms which cannot have the effect they may appear to the consumer to have may be used to intimidate the consumer (Bulletin 3 at 4.4), but they cannot have that impact or even simply mislead the consumer as to his, or her, rights if the Director General or a "qualifying body" ensures their removal from the contract documents encountered by the consumer.

(b) EC background

The Regulations are the implementation of the EC Directive on Unfair Terms in Consumer Contracts (93/13/EEC (1993) OJ L 95/29). Prior to Maastrict there was no EC treaty provision for consumer protection as such. The Unfair Terms Directive was made under Article 100 A on the basis that it is concerned with the establishment of the internal market. The idea being that a community-wide provision for the removal of unfair terms from consumer contracts will facilitate the establishment of the internal market by giving consumers the confidence to contract outside their own states, thus increasing choice and facilitating competition (recital 5).

However, the approach taken in the Directive is that it merely provides a minimum level of consumer protection, leaving member states free to provide more extensive protection through their own national laws, such as the Unfair Contract Terms Act 1977. This approach creates a degree of tension, with the aim of preventing distortions of the market through different levels of consumer protection in different member states (recital 2).

As has been indicated, the Directive was implemented here by regulations — initially the Unfair Terms in Consumer Contracts Regulations 1994 (SI 1994 No 3159). (The Directive required implementation by 31 December 1994 but the Regulations only came into force on 1 July 1995). The 1999 Regulations have now replaced those of 1994, extending the enforcement powers of the Director General of Fair Trading to other "qualifying bodies" and otherwise having the effect of moving the language of the Regulations even closer to that of the original Directive, rather than trying to produce the effect required by the Directive in terms more familiar, or anyway more intelligible, to English lawyers. In considering the Regulations, their genesis in an EC measure must be borne in mind. The need to ensure the implementation of the Directive may influence their interpretation and some of the terms used in the Regulations may need a European interpretation through the ECJ.

(c) Basic scope of the Regulations

As has been indicated, basically the Regulations apply a fairness test to terms in contracts between "consumers" and "sellers or suppliers", which have not been "individually negotiated" and any unfair term does not bind the consumer. The test of unfairness requires that, contrary to the requirement of good faith, there should be a significant imbalance in the rights and obligations of the parties to the detriment of the consumer. In addition, Sch 2 contains a "grey list" of terms which may be regarded as unfair. Under the 1994 Regulations certain contracts were specifically excluded from their scope — contracts "relating to" employment, succession rights, rights under family law, or the incorporation and organisation of companies or partnerships (Sch 1). This specific exclusion does not form part of the 1999 Regulations but the earlier exclusion was a reflection of the recitals to the Directive and may therefore impact upon whether a contract is regarded as being between a "consumer" and a "seller or supplier". More importantly, even when the contract is one to which the Regulations apply, certain "core" terms are excluded from being the subject matter of the fairness test, provided they are in plain intelligible language and this will be considered further below (see p 225). In addition, reg 4(2) makes it clear that the Regulations do not encompass "contractual terms which reflect –

(a) mandatory statutory or regulatory provisions (including such provisions under the law of any Member State or in Community legislation having effect in the United Kingdom without further enactment);

(b) the provisions or principles of international conventions to which the Member States or Community are party."

If the reflection of the statutory or regulatory provisions or the convention is not a sufficiently accurate one, there may be scope for the application of the 1999 Regulations. The OFT considered the second of the above exclusions in looking at the standard terms of a ferry company in the light of the Athens Convention, but viewed the exemption clauses in the contract as falling within the scope of the Regulations as they went beyond the Athens Convention, excluding liability which it merely allowed to be limited (OFT Bulletin 1, Stena Line Ltd pp 28–29). The recitals to the Directive require Member States to ensure that unfair terms are not included in the statutory or regulatory provisions of national law and the Director General of Fair Trading advises on that (OFT Bulletin 1, 2.1).

(d) Contrasts with the Unfair Contract Terms Act 1977

Several obvious contrasts with the Unfair Contract Terms Act 1977 can be indicated at this point. Firstly, the 1977 Act is basically restricted to terms which "exclude or restrict liability" (but see s 3(2)(b) and s 13 — pp 188, 215). Although there is an exclusion of "core terms" from being the subject matter of the fairness test, there is no such limitation of the Regulations to a specific type of term. Provided that an appropriate approach is taken to the scope of the "core" exclusion, the Regulations largely avoid the conceptual problems posed by the 1977 Act of labelling terms as being of a specific type (ie ones excluding or restricting liability). Secondly, the Regulations are restricted to contracts between "consumers" and "sellers or suppliers" and the 1977 Act not only takes a broader approach to who "deals as consumer" than that taken to who will be a "consumer" under the Regulations but, as we have seen, the Act also extends to some contracts between businesses. Thirdly, we have also seen that in many of the situations in which it is applicable, the Act applies the "requirement of reasonableness", and while they may have elements in common, it should by no means be assumed that the fairness test under the Regulations is the same. The tests are set out in different terminology and apply in different contexts and to different types of terms. In addition, the 1977 Act has a small "black list" of terms which are automatically ineffective and there is no equivalent list under the Regulations. The final point of comparison to be made here is in the area of enforcement. The Regulations can be used in a dispute between a particular consumer and a particular seller or supplier. Similarly, the 1977 Act applies in relation to the specific contract between the parties to a dispute and the Act is merely a weapon for the use of one of those parties. However, that is all the Act does. In contrast, and most significantly, as has already been indicated, under the Regulations, the Director General of Fair Trading, and now also the qualifying bodies (Sch 1), are given powers to try to prevent the continued use of unfair terms which are in general use. There is, nevertheless, a large area of overlap between the scope of the Regulations and the 1977 Act and no attempt has yet been made to deal with this by legislation. There will be many cases in which the possible application of both the 1977 Act and the Regulations will need to be considered.

(e) Scope of the chapter

As has been indicated, the Regulations basically provide for a "fairness" test to be applied to non-individually negotiated terms in contracts between "consumers" and "sellers or suppliers", with "core" terms, themselves, not being subjected to that test. Detailed consideration should now be given to:

- the meaning of "consumer";
- the meaning of "seller or supplier";
- the fairness test;
- the "core" exclusion;
- the requirement of "plain intelligible language" and interpretation;
- enforcement;

and other matters.

2. "Consumer"

Regulation 3(1) states:

> "'consumer' means any natural person who, in contracts covered by these Regulations, is acting for purposes which are outside his trade, business or profession".

One major difference between this definition and the approach taken to the interpretation of "deals as consumer" under the 1977 Act can immediately be noted. Regulation 3 expressly limits the definition of "consumer" to a "natural person", but we have already seen that a company may, in appropriate circumstances, "deal as consumer" under the 1977 Act (see eg *R & B Customs Brokers Co Ltd* v *United Dominion Trust* [1988] 1 All ER 847). The stated limitation of the Directive, and the Regulations, to consumers as "natural persons" indicates that a technical approach to the situations in which the protection of the "consumer" classification is required, rather than one considering whether a small business might equally need that protection, and it seems likely that the courts will take a restrictive view of when somone is acting "for purposes which are outside his trade, business or profession" and so as a "consumer".

3. "Seller or supplier"

Regulation 3 states:

> "'seller or supplier' means any natural or legal person who, in contracts covered by these Regulations, is acting for purposes relating to his trade, business or profession, whether publicly or privately owned".

"Person" here refers to a natural or legal person and obviously includes companies. The reference to "purposes relating to his business" would also seem to indicate a broad approach to applying the label of "seller or supplier". Certainly "related to" does not seem to indicate that a strong connection with the business is required. It would not, for example, seem to be restricted to transactions integral to the business or even to incidental ones which occur regularly[3].

The OFT has made the point that clubs wholly controlled by their members "arguably" do not fall within the Regulations, "since it may not be possible to distinguish consumers from suppliers". Obviously, that exclusion from the Regulations does not arise "in the case of a club which is run for profit by a commercial venture", but the OFT had to consider a hybrid situation (OFT Bulletin 5 at 18 (American Golf (UK) Ltd)). However, as "in its capacity as general manager" the company controlled "certain aspects of the running of the club, including the financial and other terms of the membership agreement, the view was taken that such terms were therefore subject to the Regulations".

The final point to be made here is as to the removal of a restriction included in the definitions of "seller or supplier" in the 1994 version of the Regulations. Those Regulations had imported into the definitions of seller and supplier the requirements that a seller be a "seller of goods" and that a supplier be a "supplier of goods or services". Thus appearing to exclude, for example, contracts relating to land. The definitions of "seller" and "supplier" in the Directive do not contain the express requirement that the seller be a seller of "goods" and that the supplier be a supplier of "goods or services". The restriction was included in the 1994 Regulations on the basis of the references in the recitals to, for example, "the seller of goods or the supplier of services" (eg recitals 2, 5, 6, 7) and was always open to question. It was contended that appropriate implementation of the Directive required regulations which covered contracts concerned with land (Bright & Bright, "Unfair Terms in Land Contracts" (1995) 111 LQR 655 at p 659). However, the references to "goods and services" have been removed from the definition of seller or supplier which is now included in the 1999 Regulations. The Regulations may be applied in relation to contracts dealing with land if they are between a consumer and a seller or supplier — eg the commercial letting of properties to consumers.

4. Terms not individually negotiated

Subject to certain exclusions, the Regulations apply to any term in a contract between a consumer and a seller and supplier which "has not been individually negotiated" (reg 5(1)). The draft directive had contained no such restriction and its application to individually negotiated terms was criticised as a "drastic restriction of the autonomy of the individual" (Brandner & Ulmer (1991) CML Rev 647 at p 652). The restriction of the Directive itself to terms which have not been individually negotiated may be seen as basically limiting the protection provided to the consumer to the situation in which the consumer needs assistance because of the way in which the contract was made (procedural unfairness). Most such terms will be contained in standard form contracts and, if they read standard form contracts, consumers do not generally comprehend them sufficiently to be able to negotiate on them or, even if the terms in question are read and understood, the consumers' lack of bargaining power means that they cannot effectively negotiate on the terms (see Collins (1994) OJLS 229 at p 239).

However, we should now consider when a term will not have been "individually negotiated". The burden of proving that a term was individually negotiated lies with the seller or supplier claiming that it was (reg 5(4)). Guidance as to which terms are not individually negotiated is provided by reg 5(2) which states:

> "a term shall always be regarded as not having been individually negotiated where it has been drafted in advance and the consumer has therefore not been able to influence the substance of the term".

Obviously, the reference to any term which has not been "individually negotiated" is wider in its scope than the references in the 1977 Act to "written standard terms of business" (see p 183). There is no requirement here that the terms be "written" although, obviously it will only be in rare situations that that is not the case (but see the discussion of the application of the 1977 Act in the context of contracts made on the web or by e-mail and terms incorporated by a course of dealing — see p 187). More importantly, the Regulations seem capable of encompassing terms which are either specific to the particular contract or, although not merely used for one contract, do not constitute the relevant party's "standard terms of business". Such terms may be "drafted in advance" with the consumer "unable to influence" their substance. Of course, the Regulations will most obviously apply in cases where a standard form contract has been used. However, this still leaves numerous questions in relation to when a term will be "not individually negotiated".

Even in relation to unchanged standard terms there is some scope for argument that they were "individually negotiated". For example, the seller or supplier might argue that although the term was drafted in advance, the consumer did have an opportunity to influence its substance and that it is not therefore a term which would "always be regarded as not individually negotiated". In other words, the seller or supplier might argue that he had standard terms but that they were merely the starting point in contractual negotiations and the consumer did have an opportunity to influence them but chose to accept them. It seems unlikely that such an argument would meet with success and certainly it seems likely that the courts would give close scrutiny to the alleged "negotiations". Variations of that type of situation could also occur. For example, a seller or supplier might commence the contracting process with very harsh terms and always ensure that some of them are varied, to a standard format, during the course of contracting with any particular consumer. He might then claim that the altered term or terms were "individually negotiated", although he seems unlikely to succeed if he has used standard variations — and again any claim that negotiation had occurred would be carefully considered. Another variation of this type of situation might be one in which the consumer is offered a choice of two or more sets of standard terms (Bragg [1994] Consum LJ 29). If the term in question varies according to the different sets of terms, but is standard in its particular set, could the seller or supplier maintain that it was "individually negotiated"? Offering such a choice has become one way of indicating the reasonableness of a clause excluding or restricting liability under the Unfair Contract Terms Act 1977 — and the term might be found to be fair — but it seems unlikely that it would avoid the application of the unfairness test on the basis that it had been "individually negotiated" (see eg *George Mitchell* v *Finney Lock Seeds* [1983] 1 All ER 108; *R W Green Ltd* v *Cade Bros Farm* [1978] 1 Lloyd's Rep 602). It seems unlikely that a court would often be convinced that a consumer had influenced the substance of a term which had been drafted in advance.

5. The "core" exclusion

Under the Regulations, the fairness test is only applied to what may be regarded as, in some sense, the "subsidiary" terms of the contract, although it will also apply to other terms if they are not in plain, intelligible language. This is because the "core" terms cannot form the subject matter of the fairness test, provided that they are in "plain intelligible language". Regulation 6(2) states:

"In so far as it is in plain intelligible language, the assessment of fairness of a term shall not relate–

(a) to the definition of the main subject matter of the contract, or
(b) to the adequacy of the price or remuneration, as against the goods or services supplied in exchange".

This is derived from equally obscure provisions in the Directive (see Art 4(2) and recital 19)[(4)]. The label "core" term has become common in relation to terms falling within the scope of this exclusion from the application of the fairness test — nevertheless it has been emphasised that the label should not be allowed to substitute for the actual exemption stated in the Regulations. In *Director General of Fair Trading* v *First National Bank* [2000] 1 All ER (Comm) 371 the Court of Appeal stated (at para 25):

"The test in respect of the relevant term is not whether it can be called a 'core term' but whether it falls within one or both of paras (a) and (b) of [the regulation]".

Basically Regulation 6(2) would seem to provide that, if they are in "plain intelligible language", terms defining the main subject matter of the contract, or stating the price, should not be the subject matter of the fairness test. The OFT has said (OFT Bulletin 4, at p 21):

"We can take no action against certain kinds of terms the most significant being those describing the main subject matter of the contract or setting the price to be paid for it — provided they are in plain intelligible language."

This "core exclusion" involves some preservation of the basic principle that the courts will not inquire into adequacy of consideration (see p 53), but it is subject to the limitation that the "core" terms must be in "plain intelligible language", if they are to escape the application of the test — in any event, despite the wording of Reg 6(2), recital 19 would seem to make it clear that "core" terms should, nevertheless, be taken into account in assessing whether other terms are fair (see n 4).

Prima facie the "core" exclusion could be very wide and restrictive of the operation of the Regulations. Certainly, a wide approach to the core would seem to be suggested by the example given in recital 19 (see n 4) where the "core" of an insurance contract is seen as those terms which "define or circumscribe the insured risk ... since these restrictions are taken into account in calculating the premium paid by the customer". It could be argued that the price is related to all the other terms of the contract. However, consideration should be given to the approach being taken to the "core" exclusion in various contexts.

In *Director General of Fair Trading* v *First National Bank* [2000] 1 All ER (Comm) 371 one of the arguments facing the Court of Appeal was that the term they were being asked to address was outside the scope of the fairness test because it was "core". The case was concerned with a standard form consumer credit agreement. The term in question dealt with the continuation of the contractual rate of interest after judgment for default. In the absence of that provision, interest would have ceased to be payable under the contract as such. The difficulty with such a term particularly arises in the situation in which courts make orders for payment of the sum due in instalments which have been worked out in relation to the debtor's ability to pay. The Court of Appeal outlined the complaints received by the Director General (at para 18):

"Borrowers complained of unfairness in that they found themselves liable to the bank for amounts beyond those provided for in the judgments against them. They in particular complained that when an order for payment by instalments is made, sometimes after offers for repayments by instalments in accordance with what the borrowers could afford have been accepted by the bank, compliance with that order might nevertheless leave the borrowers in debt. The accrual of interest at the contractual rate might mean that the amount of what is owed to the bank substantially increases even if the debtor duly pays the instalments fixed by the court. Borrowers were not always aware of the effect of the relevant term when they entered the agreements and the attention of the court, when the bank obtained judgment and the court was considering a time order, was not drawn to the relevant term ...".

The Court of Appeal was faced with the initial argument that the term was "core" and two points should be noted. Firstly, the more specific point that the line was taken that "realistically" the term could not be said (para 25):

"to concern the adequacy of remuneration, relating as it does only to the case where the borrower is in default and then merely providing for the continuation of the contractual rate after judgment".

Secondly, the broader point should also be noted — the court indicated that too wide an approach should not be taken to the "core" exclusion. It was stated that (para 25):

"if the bank was right, almost any provision containing part of the bargain would be capable of falling within the reach of [the "core" exclusion]. There is nothing in the Directive to require so wide an interpretation."

The narrower point made in the *First National Bank* might be seen as indicating that a payment to be made after default will not be treated as "core". However, that was not the line taken by the Northern Ireland court in *Kindlance* v *Murphy* (12 December 1997, Lexis) where one of the terms which the court was asked to consider provided that mortgage payments were at a "concessionary rate" as long as the borrower paid promptly but if he failed to pay on time the much higher "standard rate" became payable. The court considered the term to be "core" as it "concern[ed] the adequacy of price and remuneration". However, a very different line has been taken by the Director General of Fair Trading. When considering the question of clauses providing for the rate of interest to be paid by a debtor to be increased when payment was not made on time, the OFT took the view that the term stating the higher rate was not "core". It was said that (OFT *Non Status Lending – Guidelines for Lenders and Brokers* (revised November 1997) OFT 192):

> "a term providing for a higher rate of interest on default cannot be a core term . . . regardless of how the term is drafted and whether the higher rate of interest is expressed to be the ordinary rate. The term providing for the higher rate of interest is in substance a term making provision for payment of compensation upon a breach of an obligation and not, therefore a core term".

In the context of the Regulations, the OFT was dismissing one of a number of fine distinctions, based on the form of clauses, which means that the law relating to penalty clauses can be easily avoided. English law will not enforce penalty clauses — clauses which set an amount of money to be paid on breach which are "stipulated as *in terrorem* of the offending party" to coerce performance, rather than a genuine pre-estimate of loss (*Dunlop Pneumatic Tyre Co* v *New Garage and Motor Co* [1915] AC 79 — see p 487 below). A clause providing a positive incentive to perform will not fall within the scope of the penalty rules. In the context of the type of "dual interest" rate schemes referred to above, if a clause simply states that a higher rate is to be paid on default then the rules as to penalties apply. If the clause states that the debtor is entitled to a discounted rate for prompt payment and only pays the "standard" rate if he, or she, does not qualify for that discount through not making timely payments the penalty rules will not apply. The approach of the court in *Kindlance* v *Murphy* carries this formalistic distinction over into the use of the Regulations. The line taken by the OFT does not and is to be preferred. It is in keeping with the "grey list" identifying terms by reference to their "object or effect" rather than their form (see p 236). It should also be noted that, in the light of the OFT's views, the City Mortgage Corporation agreed with the Director General to stop using dual interest rate clauses (OFT Bulletin 5 at pp 8–9) and a term allowing for a discounted rate — as long as prompt payment was made — was assumed to be subject to the fairness test by HH Judge Elystan Morgan in *Falco Finance Ltd* v *Michael Gough* [1998] Tr L Rep 526.

However, it should be considered whether there are any further indications of the content of the "core". As has been indicated, *Director General of Fair Trading* v *First National Bank* might be seen as indicating that clauses dealing with payments to be made after breach are not to be regarded as "core". This type of approach might be taken further to argue that clauses allowing for variation from the initially stated performance might not be regarded as "core". Such an approach would allow the fairness test to be applied to the type of term encountered in the *Anglo Continental Holidays* v *Typaldos (London) Ltd* [1967] 2 Ll Rep 61 case (see p 189). In that case, the clause in the holiday contract stated "Steamers, Sailing Dates, Rates and Itineraries are subject to change without notice". Such a clause could be seen as part of the definition of the main subject matter of the contract as that is, technically, what it helps to set the boundaries of. (There is no assistance to be gained, in this context, from the approach to interpretation which has been taken to such clauses ie that they should be read as confined by the main object of the contract. Such an approach to construction limits their legal effects but also assists in the argument that they are part of the definition of the main subject matter of the contract). However, as indicated the line could be taken that clauses giving rights to vary the initially agreed performance should not be regarded as part of the definition of the main subject matter of the contract. Certainly the OFT seems to be assuming that such terms are subject to the fairness test (see OFT Bulletins eg Bulletin 1, cases 1 and 2) and the grey list could be seen as encompassing many such terms (eg para 1(k)).

However, whilst it may be that the "core" does not include terms dealing with payments after breach or more broadly with terms allowing for variation of the initially stated performance, it should be asked whether a more general approach to determining the scope of the "core" can be found. It may be that what is required is an approach which, objectively, takes account of the parties' view of the terms. This can be illustrated in the context of exclusion clauses. Such clauses give rise to a familiar argument that, whatever their form, exclusion clauses are part of the definition of the obligations (see p 136). However, the point could be made that exclusion clauses appear in the grey list (eg paras 1(a) and 1(b)) and certainly it is envisaged that some exclusion clauses should not be binding on the consumer after being subjected to the fairness test. Recital 5 says:

"acquirers of goods and services should be protected against the abuse of power by the seller or supplier, in particular against one-sided standard contracts and the unfair exclusion of essential rights in contracts".

This envisages that an "exclusion of essential rights" will not fall within the "core" exclusion and seems to invite a distinction to be made between exclusion clauses and definitional terms. It was indicated in the context of the Unfair Contract Terms Act 1977 that exclusion clauses could be distinguished from definitional terms by considering, objectively, their impact upon the parties' perceptions of the contractual performance, provided that was judged absent the artificialities which may be present in the contracting process through the manner of a term's incorporation or drafting (see p 217). It may be that the same type of approach is required here (although it does not appear to be the kind of approach indicated by the insurance contract example provided in recital 19 (see n 4), which seems to require a more technical line, simply based upon the words of the contract). Certainly, some of the comments made by the OFT could be seen as indicating an approach to establishing the core which considered, objectively, the consumer's perceptions of the clause, absent such artificialities. For example, the OFT had to consider a complaint by a consumer about an exclusion of liability under a mechanical breakdown insurance. The term excluded liability unless the vehicle received a partial service every 3,000 miles and it appeared only on a sticker on the back of the policy. It was said of reg 3(2) of the 1994 Regulations, which then provided for the core exclusion:

"Regulation 3(2) provides that terms which define the subject matter of the contract cannot be assessed for fairness, provided they are in plain intelligible language. The conditions of a warranty are likely to come within this exemption unless they have not been properly drawn to the consumer's attention. In our view, this exemption does not apply to terms which are hidden from the consumer's view or if he has no chance to get to know the terms."

In addition, the OFT has said (OFT Bulletin 2, para 2.25. See also Bulletin 1 at para 1.15):

"In our view, it would be difficult to claim that any term was a core term unless it was central to how consumers perceived the bargain. A supplier would surely find it hard to sustain the argument that a contract's main subject matter was defined by a term which a consumer had been given no real chance to see and read before signing . . .".

However, although in the end, the two approaches may not be too far divorced in the results they achieve in many cases, it would seem that the OFT's approach is not directly to regard the consumer's perceptions, objectively determined, as establishing the "core". Rather it would seem that they focus on the limit upon the "core" exclusion — that it applies only to terms in "plain intelligible language" — and view another factor which is highly relevant to establishing, objectively, the consumers' or the parties' perceptions, as grafted onto that limitation. The OFT treats a requirement that terms be sufficiently drawn to the consumer's attention as present if they are to escape the application of the fairness test, importing an additional, and related, proviso alongside that of "plain intelligible language". The OFT has said (Bulletin 4 at p 21):

"We can take no action against certain kinds of terms, the most significant of which being those defining the main subject matter of the contract or setting the price to be paid for it — provided they are in plain intelligible language. That proviso is critical. Recital 20 of the Directive links it with another — logically indispensable if it is to have any meaningful effect — that the consumer should actually be given an opportunity to examine all the terms. We consider that requirement helps define the 'core terms' exemption too."

Insufficiently drawing terms to the consumer's attention seems to have been viewed as both putting the expiry date of gift vouchers outside the "core" exclusion and indicating their unfairness (OFT Bulletin 6 at 49 (Kingfisher plc)).

6. Unfair terms

The Unfair Contract Terms Act 1977 subjects certain clauses, which exclude or restrict liability, to the "requirement of reasonableness". In relation to contracts between consumers and sellers or suppliers, the Regulations subject non-individually negotiated terms more generally to the test of "fairness" (see Beale (1989) CLP 197, Collins (1994) 14 OJLS 229). This receives some explanation in Regulation 5(1) — a term is regarded as unfair if:

"contrary to the requirement of good faith, it causes a significant imbalance in the parties' rights and obligations arising under the contract to the detriment of the consumer".

It may often be helpful to break this down into constituent elements and in the Court of Appeal in *Director General of Fair Trading* v *First National Bank* [2000] 1 All ER (Comm) 371 it was said that (para 26):

"Three elements in the test in the Regulations of unfairness may be noted, viz: (1) an absence of good faith; (2) a significant imbalance in the parties' rights and obligations under the contract; and (3) detriment to the consumer".

It would seem though that the second and third of these naturally run together and that there are basically two elements requiring further detailed discussion:

(i) significant imbalance in the parties' rights and obligations to the detriment of the consumer;
(ii) the requirement of good faith.

It may be that the reaction to this identification of the two elements leads to a *prima facie* inference that they reflect substantive unfairness and procedural unfairness ie that "significant imbalance" is concerned with substantive unfairness (basically unfairness in the content of the contractual rights and obligations) and that "good faith" is concerned with procedural unfairness (unfairness in the way in which the contract was made such as the lack of any realistic opportunity for the consumer to become acquainted with the terms). Whilst that may be in large measure accurate, the interaction and overlap between the two elements must be considered and that will also be addressed in the discussion below.

However, before the elements identified above are considered further, two preliminary points should first be made in relation to the fairness test. First, there is a list in Sch 2 of terms which "may be unfair" (the "grey list" — see below p 235). The list is of limited substantive effect — it does not even shift the burden of proof, in relation to the fairness test, to the seller or supplier —ie there is no requirement that sellers or suppliers disprove the unfairness of the terms falling within the list. It may, nevertheless, provide very useful guidance as to which terms will be regarded as unfair and has certainly been so treated by the Director General of Fair Trading (see the OFT Bulletins on Unfair Terms in Consumer Contracts where most of the terms regarded as unfair are classified by reference to the grey list).

The second point to be made here on fairness is concerned with the factors identified as relevant to the test and, particularly, the identification of the "time frame" of the assessment as that of the making of the contract. Regulation 6(1) states:

"Without prejudice to regulation 12, the unfairness of a contractual term shall be assessed taking into account the nature of the goods or services for which the contract was concluded and by referring, as at the time of the conclusion of the contract, to all the circumstances attending the conclusion of the contract and to all other terms of the contract or of another contract on which it is dependent."

With its reference to the "time frame" of the conclusion of the contract, this provision is more aptly drafted to deal with the situation where the Regulations are used by a specific consumer in relation to a particular contract, rather than the more general assessment of the fairness of standard terms, which is the concern of the Director General of Fair Trading (and the qualifying bodies), and, as can be seen, the 1999 Regulations specifically state that regulation 6(1) is "without prejudice" to that more general assessment allowed for under regulation 12. Regulation 6(1) is similar to that provision dealing with the requirement of reasonableness in the Unfair Contract Terms Act 1977 (s 11(1)), which is only applied in the context of a particular contract. In applying the fairness test, all the other terms of the contract, including any "core terms" which cannot themselves be the subject matter of the fairness test, and all the circumstances attending the conclusion of the contract, are relevant — as are the terms of other, "dependent", contracts (compare s 10 of UCTA 1977). Obviously, in dealing with the more general test, which is the concern of the Director General of Fair Trading (and the qualifying bodies), and not simply that applied in the context of one particular transaction, such matters must be considered at an abstract and generalised level. It may be that what should be considered are the circumstances normally surrounding the conclusion of the standard form contract in question. However, the "time frame" of the assessment of fairness means that, in relation to neither the particular contract, nor the more general question, is an actual breach, or the actual operation of a contract, of any relevance. The OFT has taken the line that (Bulletin 3, p 7):

> "The test of unfairness takes note of how a term *could* be used. If a term is so widely drafted that it could be used in such a way as to cause consumer detriment, then it is open to challenge. The OFT cannot regard such a term as fair solely on the basis of protestations that it is not in practice used unfairly."

Similarly, under the Unfair Contract Terms Act 1977, an exemption clause may operate reasonably in relation to the breach which has occurred, but fail to satisfy the requirement of reasonableness because of its potential coverage (*Stewart Gill Ltd* v *Horatio Myer & Co Ltd* [1992] 2 All ER 257, see p 201).

(a) Significant imbalance

There is no explanation of the meaning to be given to "significant imbalance" in the Regulations and it is not unproblematic. The point should be made that the reference is to *"significant* imbalance" and the imbalance should not be judged too finely. It should also be remembered that whether the test is being applied to a particular case (against the background of the time of the making of the contract) or more generally in relation to the powers of the Director General (or a qualifying body), what is in question is not proof that a significant imbalance of rights and obligations has led to actual detriment to the consumer in the operation of the contract. The OFT has acknowledged that it is the terms' potential for unfairness which is considered (OFT Bulletin 1 at 1.2).

Consideration of significant imbalance could focus on the parties' rights and obligations in a contract, whether at the particular or general level, weighing those rights and obligations as a whole, to see if, across the board, there is a significant imbalance between those of the consumer and the seller or supplier, to the detriment of the consumer. To carry out such a weighing is obviously a complex and time-consuming task, and it can be doubted whether it will often be productive, as it has been suggested that the basic problem in relation to standard form contracts is usually not that of exploitation but of unfair surprise, due to artificiality of drafting and incorporation, so that harsh terms are usually offset by a lower price, which they have been inserted to achieve

(Beale "Unfair Contracts in Britain and Europe" (1989) CLP 197 at 200–201). On that basis, such an imbalance test was rejected when the French legislature considered proposals in relation to what became the *Loi Scrivener* of 1978 (Beale *op cit*).

However, the "imbalance test" might be used to look at the term in question, and simply ask if there is any corresponding right provided for the other party. This approach is suggested by the "grey list". Paragraph 1(d) of the grey list of terms in Sch 2, provides, for example, for terms having the "object or effect of":

> "permitting the seller or supplier to retain sums paid by the consumer where the latter decides not to conclude or perform the contract, without providing for the consumer to receive compensation of an equivalent amount from the seller or supplier where the latter is the party cancelling the contract".

Such an approach seems more appropriate in relation to some types of terms than others. It does not seem particularly apt in relation to exemption clauses as, for example, in the case of a clause excluding liability for consequential loss — "since in the nature of things the seller cannot suffer consequential loss the exclusion" cannot be balanced by a term mirroring it (Beale *Unfair Contracts in Britain and Europe* (1989) CLP 197 at 204–205). Nevertheless, the OFT have indicated an approach which is something of a combination of this approach and the one previously indicated. The OFT has said:

> "When a term looks in itself unfair, we need to establish first that there is no balancing provision — which we interpret as one which: first is as potentially detrimental to the supplier as the term in question is to the consumer; and secondly is obviously linked to it, so that the two, on a common sense view, tend to cancel each other out. The commonest example is provided by cancellation rights, which we accept are fair if the consumer enjoys equally extensive rights — always assuming that in the circumstances, the right to cancel is of equal benefit. We also look of course at the rest of the contract for any qualifying proviso that would tend to remove the possibility of detriment in the term under suspicion, rather than balancing it."

In addition, something of this type of approach has also been indicated by the Court of Appeal in *Director General of Fair Trading* v *First National Bank* [2000] 1 All ER (Comm) 371. The court said (para 35):

> "In our view the relevant term . . . does cause a significant imbalance in the rights and obligations of the parties by allowing the bank to obtain interest after judgment in circumstances when it would not obtain interest [under legislation] . . . and no specific benefit to compensate the borrower is provided, and it operates to the detriment of the consumer who has to pay interest."

We can see here the idea of significant imbalance caused because there is no balancing term, but another element should also be noted. The *prima facie* reason for seeing the term as "unfair" and looking for a balancing term is because the term causes a departure from the more beneficial situation in which the consumer would otherwise have been (ie not paying the contract interest after judgment) in the absence of the term. Something of this had already been suggested by the OFT in the light of the "grey list" (in Sch 2 of the 1999 Regulations).

"[Schedule 2] shows that an imbalance is created where a term goes beyond what the law would allow or require if the contract was silent. All the examples of terms in the schedule tend either (i) to exclude liability in circumstances where it would otherwise arise, or (ii) permit what would otherwise not be possible under the ordinary rules of contract." (*ABTA Travel Law Seminar* — A talk by Ray Woolley, Head, Unfair Contract Terms Unit, Office of Fair Trading, 25 March 1999 — http://www.oft.gov.uk/html/research/sp-arch/sp13-99.htm)

In relation to attempts to use a term to exclude negligence liability for personal injury or death the OFT has indicated that "it would be difficult to conceive of circumstances in which [such a term] would be fair" (Bulletin 3 at 1.2).

(b) The requirement of good faith

For a term to be unfair the "significant imbalance" it generates must be "contrary to the requirement of good faith". The reference to good faith is not one which is familiar to lawyers in England and Wales, but is more familiar in civil law systems. In *Interfoto Picture Library Ltd* v *Stilletto Visual Programmes Ltd* [1989] QB 433 Bingham LJ said (at p 439):

"In many civil law systems . . . [good faith] does not simply mean that they should not deceive each other, a principle which any legal system must recognise; its effect is perhaps most aptly conveyed by such metaphysical colloquialisms as 'playing fair', 'coming clean' or 'putting one's cards face up on the table'. It is in essence a principle of fair and open dealing."

It can be suggested that there is a strongly procedural impetus to good faith in this context, regulating "unfair surprise" for the consumer, and that was referred to by the Court of Appeal in *Director General of Fair Trading* v *First National Bank* [2000] 1 All ER 371 (para 29):

"the good faith element seeks to promote fair and open dealing, and to prevent unfair surprise and the absence of real choice. A term to which the consumer's attention is not specifically drawn but which may operate in a way in which the consumer might not reasonably expect and to his disadvantage may offend the requirement of good faith."

In the instant case the Court of Appeal concluded that the relevant term did "create unfair surprise" and so did not "satisfy the test of good faith" (para 25). Certainly "good faith" seems capable of encompassing procedural issues such as the fact that a term is not in "plain intelligible language", for example, or that the manner of its incorporation did not provide the consumer with any realistic opportunity to become acquainted with the term. Nevertheless, it should be noted that there may be some interaction with the significant imbalance part of the fairness test — it would seem that it may be relevant to a surprise being "unfair". In addition, the point has been made that Germany has made extensive use of a test of good faith and that "test does not seem to be purely procedural" (Beale, 'The Directive on Unfair Terms in Consumer Contracts' in *Good Faith and Fault in Contract Law,* Beatson & Freidman (eds) (1995) at 244). There may be cases in which the "imbalance" is such that in itself it is sufficient to show a lack of good faith, no matter how clearly set out the term is (Beale *op cit*). The recitals to the Directive may hold the key to another element of good faith which provides the explanation for this. Recital 16 states:

> "Whereas in making an assessment of good faith, particular regard shall be had to the strength of bargaining position of the parties, whether the consumer had an inducement to agree to the term and whether the goods or services were sold or supplied to the special order of the consumer; whereas the requirement of good faith may be satisfied by the seller or supplier where he deals fairly and equitably with the other party whose legitimate interests he has to take into account."

There is some emphasis here on the final factor referred to and it can be suggested that the significant element of good faith, going beyond the purely procedural, is that the seller or supplier must sufficiently take account of the interests of the consumer — rather than merely his, or her, own. In fact, although the other factors have an apparent familiarity from their relevance to the "requirement of reasonableness" under the Unfair Contract Terms Act 1977, it can be suggested that in the context of good faith, their relevance may be seen to be as indicators of whether or not the seller or supplier took sufficient notice of the legitimate interests of the consumer. It is possible to argue that there is some suggestion of this in *Director General of Fair Trading* v *First National Bank* (para 35) where, in the context of good faith, the comment was made:

> "The Bank, with its strong bargaining position as against the relatively weak position of the consumer, has not adequately considered the consumer's interests . . .".

There may be some cases where the significant imbalance is itself indicative of the absence of good faith, in the sense that a sufficient significant imbalance may show that the seller or supplier took insufficient account of the interests of the consumer. The Court of Appeal has said that "the element of significant imbalance would appear to overlap substantially with that of the absence of good faith" (*Director General of Fair Trading* v *First National Bank* [2000] 1 All ER (Comm) 371, para 30).

One further area needs to be considered in relation to the fairness test — an area where there may again be an overlap between the lack of good faith and significant imbalance. Clearly, the Director General of Fair Trading regards artificiality of incorporation or obscurity of drafting as very significant when the question of the fairness of a term arises (see below p 243). In addition, para 1(i) of the grey list of terms which may be unfair (Sch 2 of the Regulations) applies to terms which have the "object or effect" of "irrevocably binding the consumer to terms with which he had no real opportunity of becoming acquainted before the conclusion of the contract". Under that element of the grey list, terms incorporating others by reference might be seen as unfair if the terms referred to were insufficiently accessible (see p 147). However, whilst it seems clear that a term which is very artificially incorporated or obscurely drafted will, because of those factors, in themselves, fail the good faith requirement of fairness, it is not immediately obvious that there will be a significant imbalance in the parties' rights and obligations, which is also required if the term is to be found to be unfair. Nevertheless, the point to be made is that artificiality of incorporation or obscurity of incorporation could, in themselves, generate a "significant imbalance". The example might be considered of a clause requiring notification of any defects within a specified time. "If the consumer is not aware of such a term, it will work to cause significant imbalance to the detriment of the consumer even though the substance of the term is not unfair. This weaves together matters of substance and procedure" (Bright (2000) 20 LS 331 at p 348). The idea is that the consumer will not be able to use the contract rights fully because he, or she, does not know about them, and they are then imbalanced. There is, however, a further point to be considered in relation to this argument. How can there be a significant imbalance in the parties' contract rights when they are as such balanced and the imbalance only lies in one party's failure to avail themselves of them fully? The same type of question arises in the context of misleading terms and can be addressed in that context.

As has been indicated, a question arises in relation to the unfairness of certain types of misleading terms — terms which appear to have an effect other than that which they actually do. The point has been made that (OFT Bulletin 3, at p 12):

"The OFT normally objects to clauses which reflect the general contractual position concerning damages for breach of contract but in a misleading way. Contracts sometimes give the impression that, if they are cancelled by the consumer, the company can recover all the profit it would have made. In law the supplier actually has a duty to mitigate . . .".

Here, the point is that it must be questioned as to how a term which does not actually affect the rights of either party to damages can cause a significant imbalance in their rights and obligations. The very objection to such a term is that it is misleading as to actual contractual rights. However, the OFT has simply assumed that such terms can be regarded as unfair because they are misleading. It can be suggested that a purposive approach is required by the Directive and certainly in relation to the question of the creation of a "significant imbalance in the rights and obligations of the parties" the terms, or clauses, could be regarded as distorting the rights which the consumer believes he, or she, has and thus creating an imbalance in the rights and obligations which will be, effectively usable under the contract. It may be that that should be regarded as sufficient for the unfairness test (Macdonald (1999) 58 CLJ 413).

(c) The list and types of unfair terms

As has already been mentioned, Sch 2 contains a list of terms which may be regarded as unfair (reg 5(5)). The list is set out below, but a few preliminary points should first be made. After the list has been set out consideration will be given to some types of unfair term.

The list has a relatively insignificant technical status, not even reversing the burden of proof in the fairness test. It has, nevertheless, been seen as of considerable significance. The OFT has said (OFT Bulletin 4 at p 22):

"It is the most authoritative guide to what fairness entails. It is not a "black list" but the exact shade of grey is debatable. Our view is that if a term appears in the list it is under substantial suspicion, but that correspondence with an item in the list cannot of itself determine the issue of unfairness."

This not only indicates the importance of the list as a guide to which terms will be unfair, but also emphasises that ultimately it is the fairness test in reg 5(1) — set out above — which must determine the issue. The list is not exhaustive. "Exclusion from the [grey list] cannot be seen as forming any sort of 'white list'. Any standard term will be seen as being unfair whether or not it appears in ... the list, if it fails the test in" reg 5 (OFT Bulletin 5 at p 10). The list is drafted in terms which would make it unsuitable as a "black list" as the boundaries of the terms falling within it are not fixed with certainty. This arises from two factors. Firstly, the terms referred to in the list are stated by reference to their "object or effect", so that its content is not based simply on form. Secondly, the list often contains factors of assessment. Para 1(b), covering exemption clauses, for example, refers to terms which have the object or effect of "*inappropriately* excluding or limiting the rights of the consumer ..." (emphasis added). However, the need to make such an assessment, to ascertain if a term falls within the scope of para 1(b), should strengthen the argument that it is unfair, if it clearly does. Whilst the fact that terms are identified by their object, or effect, makes the compass of the list less certain, it does have a positive benefit. It helps to avoid difficult questions as to the classification of clauses. A term may be "under suspicion" even if it does not look like a term on the list, "if it is calculated to affect consumers in the same way as anything on the list" (OFT Bulletin 5 at p 10). In other words, this formulation of the grey list terms, helps to avoid the type of questions which arise in relation to identifying exemption clauses and the appropriate coverage of the active sections of the Unfair Contract Terms Act 1977. Such difficulties are avoided more generally because the application of the fairness test is not restricted to a certain type of clause — such as one excluding or restricting liability. Of course, the extent to which such classification problems are not encountered depends upon the approach taken to identifying terms falling within the "core exclusion". An appropriate approach to classifying "core" terms will mean that such problems are largely avoided (see p 225). The grey list itself should now be considered.

SCHEDULE 2

INDICATIVE AND NON-EXHAUSTIVE LIST OF TERMS WHICH MAY BE REGARDED AS UNFAIR

1 Terms which have the object or effect of—

  (a) excluding or limiting the legal liability of a seller or supplier in the event of the death of a consumer or personal injury to the latter resulting from an act or omission of that seller or supplier;

  (b) inappropriately excluding or limiting the legal rights of the consumer vis-à-vis the seller or supplier or another party in the event of total or partial non-performance or inadequate performance by the seller or supplier of any of the contractual obligations, including the option of offsetting a debt owed to the seller or supplier against any claim which the consumer may have against him;

  (c) making an agreement binding on the consumer whereas provision of services by the seller or supplier is subject to a condition whose realisation depends on his own will alone;

  (d) permitting the seller or supplier to retain sums paid by the consumer where the latter decides not to conclude or perform the contract, without providing for the consumer to receive compensation of an equivalent amount from the seller or supplier where the latter is the party cancelling the contract;

  (e) requiring any consumer who fails to fulfil his obligation to pay a disproportionately high sum in compensation;

(f) authorising the seller or supplier to dissolve the contract on a discretionary basis where the same facility is not granted to the consumer, or permitting the seller or supplier to retain the sums paid for services not yet supplied by him where it is the seller or supplier himself who dissolves the contract;

(g) enabling the seller or supplier to terminate a contract of indeterminate duration without reasonable notice except where there are serious grounds for doing so;

(h) automatically extending a contract of fixed duration where the consumer does not indicate otherwise, when the deadline fixed for the consumer to express his desire not to extend the contract is unreasonably early;

(i) irrevocably binding the consumer to terms with which he had no real opportunity of becoming acquainted before the conclusion of the contract;

(j) enabling the seller or supplier to alter the terms of the contract unilaterally without a valid reason which is specified in the contract;

(k) enabling the seller or supplier to alter unilaterally without a valid reason any characteristics of the product or service to be provided;

(l) providing for the price of goods to be determined at the time of delivery or allowing a seller of goods or supplier of services to increase their price without in both cases giving the consumer the corresponding right to cancel the contract if the final price is too high in relation to the price agreed when the contract was concluded;

(m) giving the seller or supplier the right to determine whether the goods or services supplied are in conformity with the contract, or giving him the exclusive right to interpret any term of the contract;

(n) limiting the seller's or supplier's obligation to respect commitments undertaken by his agents or making his commitments subject to compliance with a particular formality;

(o) obliging the consumer to fulfil all his obligations where the seller or supplier does not perform his;

(p) giving the seller or supplier the possibility of transferring his rights and obligations under the contract, where this may serve to reduce the guarantees for the consumer, without the latter's agreement;

(q) excluding or hindering the consumer's right to take legal action or exercise any other legal remedy, particularly by requiring the consumer to take disputes exclusively to arbitration not covered by legal provisions, unduly restricting the evidence available to him or imposing on him a burden of proof which, according to the applicable law, should lie with another party to the contract.

2 Scope of paragraphs 1(g), (j) and (l)

(a) Paragraph 1(g) is without hindrance to terms by which a supplier of financial services reserves the right to terminate unilaterally a contract of indeterminate duration without notice where there is a valid reason, provided that the supplier is required to inform the other contracting party or parties thereof immediately.

(b) Paragraph 1(j) is without hindrance to terms under which a supplier of financial services reserves the right to alter the rate of interest payable by the consumer or due to the latter, or the amount of other charges for financial services without notice where there is a valid reason, provided that the supplier is required to inform the other contracting party or parties thereof at the earliest opportunity and that the latter are free to dissolve the contract immediately.

Paragraph 1(j) is also without hindrance to terms under which a seller or supplier reserves the right to alter unilaterally the conditions of a contract of indeterminate duration, provided that he is required to inform the consumer with reasonable notice and that the consumer is free to dissolve the contract.

(c) Paragraphs 1(g), (j) and (l) do not apply to:
— transactions in transferable securities, financial instruments and other products or services where the price is linked to fluctuations in a stock exchange quotation or index or a financial market rate that the seller or supplier does not control;

    — contracts for the purchase or sale of foreign currency, traveller's cheques or international money orders denominated in foreign currency.

(d) Paragraph 1(1) is without hindrance to price indexation clauses, where lawful, provided that the method by which prices vary is explicitly described.

Certain groupings of types of terms can be identified in the list. Paragraphs 1 (a), (b) and (q) of the list, for example, clearly encompass exemption clauses and will overlap with the Unfair Contract Terms Act 1977. There are, in addition, other paragraphs which will cover clauses not in the form of exemptions but which would, nevertheless, fall within the Act — in some cases brought within it by s 3(2)(b) or s 13 — eg paras 1 (j), (k), (m), (n). There are also paragraphs which will encompass clauses falling within the common law rules dealing with penalty clauses or which raise related issues (paras 1 (d) and (e) — see p 494). In addition, several of the paragraphs can be identified as relating to clauses conferring an inappropriate discretion on the seller or supplier in relation to performance (eg paras 1 (j), (k), (l)). (For a full consideration of the paragraphs of the list see Macdonald *Exemption Clauses and Unfair Terms* (1999) Butterworths pp 202–228.)

(d) Exemption clauses

Several paragraphs of the grey list, as has been mentioned, clearly relate to exemption clauses (paras 1 (a), (b), (q)) and others will also overlap with the application of the Unfair Contract Terms Act 1977. Section 2(1) of the Unfair Contract Terms Act 1977 "black lists" (ie renders automatically ineffective) terms excluding or restricting liability for negligently caused death or personal injury. Nevertheless, the Director General of Fair Trading has still encountered clauses purporting to have that effect (OFT Bulletin 3 at 1.2) and the superiority of the enforcement mechanism under the Regulations has already been referred to (see 219). Such clauses are only "grey listed" in the Regulations (para 1 (a)) but the OFT has said that "it would be difficult to conceive of circumstances in which [such a clause] would not be unfair" (OFT Bulletin 3 at 1.2. See eg Bulletin 1, cases 2, 7, 23). In addition, the Director General obviously views exemption clauses dealing with other negligently caused loss or damage as generally unfair in the consumer context and some clauses have been redrafted to make it clear that they do not extend to liability for negligence (eg OFT Bulletin 3 at pp 30, 54, Bulletin 4 at p 65). Some consideration can be given to the factors which have proved important in determining "reasonableness" under the 1977 Act — they may prove helpful in identifying unfairness under the Regulations. However, in making any such analogies care must be taken in moving from the business to business contracts, which have often been the context for consideration of the "requirement of reasonableness" under the 1977 Act, to the consumer contracts which fall to be addressed under the Regulations. Some comparisons, nevertheless, may prove helpful.

Under the 1977 Act, insurance has been identified as a key element in relation to the "requirement of reasonableness". It has been relevant to ask which party was in the best position to insure, the cost of insurance, whether the placement of that cost has been reflected in the price charged, and the overall impact of the clause (see 206). Such factors may also be relevant in relation to the fairness test — a redrafted clause by a security firm stated (OFT Bulletin 4 (Chubb Alarms Ltd)):

"Our liability under this agreement — We do not know the value of the contents of your premises. You do (or should) know the value of the contents in your premises. Since the loss or damage you might suffer will probably be more than the amounts we can reasonably charge you, and because we are giving you the chance to discuss and agree different amounts from those set out in the following paragraphs of this clause, we will limit out liability to those amounts (unless we agree in writing to change those limits)."

Consideration will need to be given to the most appropriate party to insure and also to the likelihood of the consumer understanding the need to insure. In addition, even if such understanding is likely to be present, the likelihood of insurance cover being taken out, may be relevant. There may be unfairness if, by using a term placing the need to insure on the consumer, the supplier reduces the price slightly for all consumers, but at a risk of placing very significant risk on the small number of consumers for whom it may materialise and who may well not have insured (see Beale "The Directive on Unfair Terms in Consumer Contracts" in *Good Faith and Fault in Contract Law*, Beatson & Freidman (eds) (1995) at p 243. For an example, in the context of the Unfair Contract Terms Act 1977 see *Smith* v *Eric S Bush* [1990] 1 AC 831 — see p 207).

Again, in the context of the Unfair Contract Terms Act 1977, the availability, or otherwise, of an alternative contract has been a significant indicator of whether an exemption clause satisfies the requirement of reasonableness. In the situation where a cheap photographic developing service was provided on the basis of an extensive exemption clause, the clause was, nevertheless, held not to satisfy the Act's requirement of reasonableness against the background of an industry practice that an alternative service should also be offered — one involving a higher price and the potential for greater liability (*Woodman* v *Phototrade Processing* (1981) 131 NLJ 935, Lexis). In contrast, limiting liability in relation to the sale of seed potatoes, was seen as reasonable when the farmer had been given a choice of paying a higher price for seed involving less risk of disease (*RW Green Ltd* v *Cade Bros Farms* [1978] 1 Lloyd's Rep 602). However, under the Act, the reality of the alternative has been considered so that the existence of a safer alternative, which most consumers could not afford, was not viewed as rendering an exemption clause reasonable (*Smith* v *Eric S Bush* [1990] 1 AC 831). Similar factors might be considered under the Regulations. A realistic choice, properly drawn to the consumer's attention, might be seen as relevant to the question of good faith. The provision of such an alternative could be seen as indicating a seller or supplier who takes account of the interests of the consumer. In addition, such an alternative could also be relevant to the question of "significant imbalance" — the alternatives might draw attention to the balancing elements in the different contracts eg restricted liability/cheaper price.

As has been indicated, problems can arise under the Act in determining if a clause is to be treated as one "excluding or restricting" liability (see p 215). One context for that problem is the question of clauses relating to the terms implied by ss 13–15 of the Sale of Goods Act 1979. When the buyer "deals as consumer", attempts to exclude or restrict liability for breach of those terms are automatically ineffective under s 6(2), Unfair Contract Terms Act 1977. Sellers may seek to use clauses which are not in the form of exemption clauses but which attempt to show that the circumstances of the sale do not give rise to the relevant implied term, for example:

"It is the customers' responsibility to make sure they have tried goods before delivery and that they are fit for the purpose for which they are intended." (OFT Bulletin 5 at p 55.)

Questions can arise as to the appropriate treatment of clauses taking this approach — ie whether they fall within the scope of the 1977 Act. See further Macdonald *Exemption Clauses and Unfair Terms*, Butterworths (1999) at pp 126–130). That contrasts with the Regulations. Provided an appropriate approach is taken as to what constitutes a "core term" (see p 225), such difficulties are avoided under the Regulations. The fairness test is applied without the need to categorise terms as exemption clauses (see eg OFT Bulletin 1 (Humberside Caravans), Bulletin 3 (GP Care Supplies), Bulletin 4 (Caledonia Motor Group), Bulletin 3 (Richline Ltd). See Further Macdonald *op cit* at pp 204–207).

(e) Penalty and related clauses

Paragraphs 1 (d) and (e) of Sch 2 of the Regulations overlap with the rules dealing with penalty and related clauses. Parties to a contract may specify that upon a particular breach occurring the breaching party is to pay a specified sum in damages. If the clause is a genuine liquidated damages clause it will be enforceable — it will have been beneficial in providing certainty for the parties. However, if it is not "a genuine pre-estimate of loss" but a sum set *in terrorem* of the breaching party to compel performance, it will be classified as a penalty clause and the injured party will only be able to recover to the extent of their actual loss (*Dunlop Pneumatic Tyre Co* v *New Garage Motor Co* [1915] AC 79. See further p 487 below). However, the application of the penalty clause rule is very dependent upon the form of the clause. Basically it only applies to clauses under which a specified payment is to be made on a breach occurring. This has led to frequent evasion of the rule through a clause having the same effect as a penalty clause but drafted in a different form, for example, clauses requiring deposits, acceleration clauses providing for a sum which was to be payable in instalments over time to immediately be due in full, and clauses providing for a reduced payment upon timely performance and a higher "standard rate" if a payment is late (see p 490 below and p 226 above). Avoidance could also be achieved if the event triggering the payment was labelled as a variation of performance, rather than a breach, and that led Lord Denning to comment in *Bridge* v *Campbell Discount* [1962] 1 All ER 385 (at p 399):

"Let no one mistake the injustice of this. It means that equity commits itself to this absurd paradox; it will grant relief to a man who breaks his contract but will penalise the man who keeps it."

Such anomalies were due to the dependence upon the form of the clause to determine the application of the rule. The common law has now mitigated the problem in relation to deposits — allowing the recovery of "unreasonable deposits" (*Workers Trust and Merchant Bank* v *Dojap Investments Ltd* [1993] 2 All ER 370). However, in the consumer context, provided that an appropriate approach is taken to identifying "core" terms (see p 225), the Regulations are a greater mitigation of the problematic borderline for the application of the penalty rule, because their application is not dependent upon the form of a clause (see further Macdonald *Exemption Clauses and Unfair Terms*, Butterworths (1999) at pp 211–216).

(f) Seller/supplier's discretion

Several of the paragraphs of the "grey list" refer to clauses conferring a discretion on the seller or supplier as to the performance of the contract (eg paras 1 (f), (g), (j), (k), (l)). Some discretion may be appropriate but it will have to be set within limited boundaries to be considered fair under the Regulations. For example, a roadside breakdown service originally used a clause which stated (OFT Bulletin 3, Britannia Rescue Services):

"We may cancel membership at any time by sending seven days' notice by recorded delivery to your last known address and in such event you will receive a pro rata refund of your subscription, unless the service has been used."

The OFT viewed that as "potentially unfair . . . since it allowed [the business] to cancel contracts on a discretionary basis and thus to get out of a bad bargain" (Bulletin 3 at p 26). The clause was redrafted to allow the business to cancel in limited circumstances, where the service might be seen as being used inappropriately:

"If excessive use of the service has occurred through failure to seek permanent repair following any temporary repair effected by an agent or due to lack of routine vehicle maintenance, we may cancel membership by sending seven days' notice by recorded delivery to your last known address."

Another example is provided by the contract of a supplier and installer of kitchens. In that contract, a clause was seen as "of questionable fairness" in the light of para 1(k) (OFT Bulletin 1 (Moben Kitchens)). The original clause stated:

"If, for any reason, the Company is unable to supply a particular item of furniture or a particular appliance, the Company will notify the Customer. The Company will normally replace it with an item of equivalent or superior standard and value."

The clause was revised to state:

"If, for any reason beyond the Company's control, the Company is unable to supply a particular item of furniture or a particular appliance, the Company will notify the Customer. With the agreement of the Customer the Company will replace it with an item of superior standard and value."

The revised clause was seen as an "improvement" as it specified that the substitution must be for reasons "beyond the company's reasonable control" and required the consumer's consent to the change.

Some clauses providing a seller or supplier with a wide discretion as to performance would fall within the scope of the Unfair Contract Terms Act 1977 — in particular s 3(2)(b)(i) (see p 188 above). Again the applicability of the Regulations is likely to be less problematic than that of the 1977 Act.

7. Plain, intelligible language — interpreting the terms

The concept of "plain intelligible language" is important to the operation of the Regulations. A "core" term is only exempt from the fairness test if it is in plain, intelligible language (reg 6(2). (See p 225.) Regulation 7(1) may give rise to the contention that there is a requirement that terms be in plain, intelligible language, although it will be argued that the better view is that whether terms are so drafted merely impacts upon the fairness test. In addition, there is a rule of interpretation in reg 7(2) to deal with the situation in which there is "doubt about the meaning of a written term". The "core" exemption was addressed above. Here consideration must be given to what constitutes "plain intelligible language", whether there is a requirement that contracts be drafted in such language, and the interpretation rule in the Regulations.

(a) Meaning

To determine if a term is in "plain intelligible language", it must be asked to whom should the language used in a term be plain and intelligible. What is needed is that a standard be set and that requires an objective approach, which could be put in terms of the "ordinary consumer". Certainly, the OFT takes the view that it should be "the ordinary consumer without legal advice" (Bulletin 3, at p 19) — although that begs the question as to the linguistic ability of the ordinary consumer. The absence of legal advice is specified as "consumers would rarely consider there was any necessity for them to seek legal advice before entering into most types of contract" (Bulletin 2, 2.12). A different approach might be suggested where a contract is of a type in relation to which legal advice is normally obtained. (On the problem of "plain English" see M Clarke "Freedom of Information in Commercial Disputes" in *Freedom of Expression and Freedom of Information* Beatson and Cripps eds pp 377–379.)

Some specific factors can be identified if terms are to be in "plain intelligible language". It may be inappropriate, in particular, to use a contract drafted to be used with other commercial parties when contracting with a consumer (eg OFT Bulletin 5 at p 29 (Emmanuel Spence Ltd)). In a contract with a consumer there should be an avoidance of technical legal terminology such as "consequential loss", "time is of the essence", and "force majeure", but if it is unavoidable it should be explained (OFT Bulletin 3 at p 19, Bulletin 2, 2.19). "Plain intelligible language" may not merely be a matter of the words used but also the style of the document — long sentences and frequent cross-referencing do not assist ready intelligibility (OFT Bulletin 2, 2.19). It has been suggested that long documents may be improved if "accompanied by summaries of their main points" (OFT Bulletin 4 at p 22), but care will have to be taken with any such summaries if they are not to mislead. (A misleading summary might be argued to constitute a misrepresentation of the full contract terms — compare *Curtis* v *Chemical Cleaning and Dyeing Co* [1951] 1 KB 805 — see p 141).

In some cases, particularly with longer and more complex sets of terms, there may be some scope for difficulties with the language of the terms to be ameliorated by opportunities given to the consumer to digest and understand them. Information packs, dispatched to consumers before the contract is made, may be of assistance to the seller or supplier when the fairness of a term is questioned, as may the provision of a "cooling-off period" after the contract is made, providing the consumer with an opportunity to withdraw, without penalty, after time for digestion and consideration of the terms (OFT Bulletin 3, 13.2). Such mitigating factors would seem not to affect the question of whether a term is plain and intelligible, but may, nevertheless, impact upon its fairness.

The question can also be raised as to whether it will always be sufficient if the only language in which the contract is expressed is English. A supplier may know, or be in a situation where he, or she, should be aware that the consumer is not, or the relevant group of consumers are not, competent in English. Certainly, in such a case, even if the question of "plain intelligible language" was not affected as such, it would seem that there would be an impact upon the fairness test and, in particular, the element of good faith.

(b) Requirement?

The questions which must now be addressed are whether there is a requirement that terms be drafted in plain, intelligible language, and further, whether there is also a requirement that the consumer be given an opportunity to examine all the terms. The starting point for any contention as to the existence of such requirements is Recital 20 of the Directive, which states:

"Whereas contracts should be drafted in plain, intelligible language, the consumer should actually be given an opportunity to examine all the terms and, if in doubt, the interpretation most favourable to the consumer shall prevail."

Much of that recital is reflected in Article 5 and reg 7, which states:

"(1) A seller or supplier shall ensure that any written term of a contract is expressed in plain, intelligible language.
(2) If there is doubt about the meaning of a written term, the interpretation which is most favourable to the consumer shall prevail but this rule shall not apply in proceedings brought under regulation 12."

The first point to note is that neither Article 5, nor reg 7, embody the reference — which is to be found in recital 20 — to the need for the consumer to be provided with an "opportunity to examine all the terms", although para 1(i) of the grey list does refer to terms which have the object or effect of "irrevocably binding the consumer to terms with which he has no real opportunity of becoming acquainted before the conclusion of the contract". Both Article 5, and reg 7, do refer to the need for "plain intelligible language" in mandatory terms, but without expressly specifying any penalty for a failure to draft contracts in compliance with such a "requirement", beyond that inherent in the application of the Directives'/Regulations' rule of construction. However, there are comments in the OFT Bulletins which would seem to indicate that there is a requirement that "plain intelligible language" must be used and, in addition, that the consumer should be given an opportunity to examine all the terms. For example, in the second Bulletin it was said:

"The message sent by the Regulations is clear enough. The use of small print and obscure language (so often found together) is fatal — if not counter productive — and should be jettisoned".

Similarly, in the first Bulletin:

"The use of unreadable small print in consumer contracts is surprisingly common, but it is pointless and counter productive. Illegible print and obscure wording can, by themselves, make terms unenforceable because the Regulations require the consumer to be given an opportunity to examine all the terms before he is bound by them".

What is now reg 7 was seen as the "starting point" which "merely underlines one aspect of the general requirement of the Regulations — and the underlying EC Unfair Contract Terms Directive to which the Regulations give effect — that consumers have a right to know and understand the terms of their contracts" (Bulletin 2, 2.2).

However, the strength of any argument that there is a requirement that the consumer should actually be given an opportunity to examine all the terms must be doubted. The mandatory tones of Article 5 and reg 7 strengthen the contention that there is a requirement that contracts be in plain, intelligible language. Even in that situation, however, the existence of any requirement as such must also be doubted. The absence of any penalty for failing to draft in plain, intelligible language, would seem to be fatal to any contention that there is any requirement to that effect (but see De Moor (1995) 3 European Review of Private Law 257 at pp 262–263). The alternative view is that lack of clarity in the language of contract terms, or artificiality in the manner in which terms are incorporated, are factors relevant to the application of the fairness test and, in particular, that element of it which focuses on whether the supplier was acting in good faith. There are, nevertheless, indications that the Director General does view plain, intelligible language as a requirement, with the "penalty" lying in a term being found unfair. The OFT has said (OFT Bulletin 4 at p 22):

> "In the Director General's firm view, any term may be found to be unfair by reason of not being in plain intelligible language ... Breach of this requirement can harm consumers by misleading or confusing them."

Obviously, the argument that there is a requirement that contracts be drafted in plain, intelligible language is stronger than that in relation to a requirement of an opportunity for consumers to examine the terms. The references to the former extend into the body of the Directive, whilst the latter is only to be found in that form in the recitals. (On unfairness generated by obscure drafting or incorporation see above pp 234–235.)

(c) Interpretation

Consideration of interpretation under the regulations requires reg 7(2) to be addressed. It states:

> "If there is doubt about the meaning of a written term, the interpretation which is most favourable to the consumer shall prevail but this rule shall not apply in proceedings brought under regulation 12."

The reference to "regulation 12" is to the situation in which consideration is being given to terms drawn up for general use — ie where such terms are being considered by the Director General or a "qualifying body" and an injunction may be applied for. In other words, the rule of construction in reg 7(2) is concerned with the application of the Regulations in the context of a particular dispute between a consumer and a seller or supplier and separate consideration must be given to intepretation in relation to a dispute between particular parties and in the more general context.

In the context of particular contracts, the rule of construction in reg 7(2) may simply be viewed as a version of the familiar common law *contra proferentem* rule that any ambiguity in a clause will be construed against the person putting it forward (see p 161). It can, however, be suggested that in considering, under reg 7(2), which interpretation is "most favourable to the consumer", the impact of the fairness test should be borne in mind. In relation to an exemption clause, for example, it may be that the interpretation "most favourable to the consumer", absent any consideration of the fairness test, would result in a narrowing of the scope of the term, so that it would then be viewed as fair. In contrast, a wider construction might lead to its categorisation as unfair, with the effect that it would not bind the consumer. The wider construction could be viewed as that "most favourable to the consumer" if the impact of the fairness test is borne in mind. It can be suggested that the rule of construction in reg 7(2) may require consideration of the interaction of any particular interpretation and the fairness test.

As has been indicated, in interpreting contracts under the Regulations, a distinction must be drawn between the particular contract and the more general consideration of a set of standard terms drawn up for general use. In that general assessment, it would seem that the fairness of the terms should simply be assessed on the basis of the interpretation which is least likely to lead to the terms' classification as fair, although, in giving a meaning to a term, the lack of clarity in its drafting should not be forgotten as at least a factor indicative of unfairness in its own right.

8. Enforcement

Consideration of enforcement under the Regulations requires this issue to be addressed both in relation to a particular dispute and at a more general level. As with the 1977 Act, the Regulations may simply be used by a consumer to attack a particular term (or terms) in a particular contract between the consumer and the seller or supplier. If the term is unfair it is not binding on the consumer (reg 8(1)). The contract continues to bind the parties "if it is capable of continuing in existence without the unfair term" (reg 8(2)). The consumer may receive some assistance from the court. In cases C–240/98 to C–244/98 (*Oceano Grupo Editorial SA* v *Quintero*) the European Court of Justice has taken the line that a consumer does not have to raise the issue of the unfairness of a term under the legislation implementing the Directive on Unfair Terms in order for a court to find that a term is unfair and so not binding on the consumer. The court stated (para 26):

> "The aim of Article 6 of the Directive, which requires Member States to lay down that unfair terms are not binding on the consumer, would not be achieved if the consumer were himself obliged to raise the unfair nature of such terms. In disputes where the amounts involved are often limited, the lawyer's fees may be higher than the amount at stake, which may deter the consumer from contesting the application of an unfair term. While it is the case that, in a number of Member States, procedural rules enable individuals to defend themselves in such proceedings, there is a real risk that the consumer particularly because of ignorance of the law, will not challenge the term pleaded against him on the grounds that it is unfair. It follows that effective protection of the consumer may be attained only if the national court acknowledges that it has power to evaluate terms of this kind of its own motion."

The argument that the court should be able to raise the issue of the unfairness of a term under the appropriate legislation, was further strengthened by reference to Article 7 which requires enforcement to prevent the continued use of unfair terms at the more general level. The ECJ took the view that in the light of the requirement of enforcement at the general level it was "inconceivable" that in a particular case a court could not "set aside application of the relevant term solely because the consumer [had] not raised the fact that it is unfair" (para 28).

However, as has been indicated, there is also a more general level of enforcement to be considered under the Regulations. The Directive required there to be a means of preventing the continued use of an unfair term in general. Article 7(1) requires Member States to provide "effective means to prevent the continued use of unfair terms" and Article 7(2) states that such "means" should include "provisions whereby persons or organisations having a legitimate interest under national law in protecting consumers may take action ... before the courts ... for a decision as to whether contractual terms drawn up for general use are unfair ...". The requirements of Article 7 have been addressed in the Regulations by the powers given to the Director General of Fair Trading and the qualifying bodies. The Director General of Fair Trading has to consider any complaint made to him that a term drawn up for "general use" is unfair unless the complaint is "frivolous or vexatious" or "a qualifying body has notified the Director General that it agrees to consider the complaint" (reg 10(1)). The Director General may bring proceedings for an injunction "against any person appearing" to him "to be using, or recommending the use of, an unfair term drawn up for general use in contracts concluded with consumers" (reg 12). However, the Director General of Fair Trading may decide not to pursue an injunction and he is, under reg 10(3), entitled to have regard to any undertakings as to the continued use of such terms in contracts with consumers. It should also be noted that if an injunction is sought it may relate not only to the particular term, but also "to any similar term, or a term having like effect, used or recommended for use by any person". Similar powers are conferred on the qualifying bodies. To avoid overlapping actions, a qualifying body must give the Director General at least fourteen days notice of its application for an injunction, unless the Director General consents to its applying within a shorter period (reg 12(2)). Regulation 12 is quite wide in its scope, allowing for injunctions to be obtained not only against those who use the term in question but also those who recommend its use and this might cover, for example, a trade association which recommends a set of standard terms to its members, including the term in question. The scope of the injunction is also extended beyond the particular term to similar terms or terms having like effect. Obviously some such extension had to be included if any such injunction was not to be largely fruitless and easily avoided by simple redrafting. It may, however, raise difficult questions as to when a term is similar, or of like effect, to the term in question.

The final point should be made that the provisions dealing with the assessment of the unfairness of a term are not specifically drafted to deal with the assessment of a term "drawn up for general use" in the abstract, divorced from an individual contract. This is particularly clear in reg 6(1) with it's reference to, for example, "the time of conclusion of the contract" as the circumstances providing the basis for the assessment of unfairness. This is obviously inappropriate to the more general assessment and, indeed reg 6(1) is stated to be "without prejudice to regulation 12", which provides for the more general level of enforcement. However, it says nothing about how the assessment is to be made at the more general level. It would seem that the questions of "significant imbalance" and "the requirement of good faith" will need to be addressed by considering what the position is, in general, for the parties for whom the term in question is "in general use". This may well require the position of only one, or a number of specific, sellers or suppliers, to be considered but the other side of the contract would seem to need to be addressed through consideration of something like "the average consumer of the goods or services in question". That would seem to be the case even where the term is brought to the attention of the Director General in relation to a particular contract between a particular seller or supplier. Such an approach is required simply by the extension of the remedy beyond the particular case.

Footnotes

(1) See generally Macdonald *Exemption Clauses and Unfair Terms* (1999) Butterworths, Ch 4, Beale [1989] CLP 229, Duffy [1993] JBL 67, Dean [1993] 56 MLR 581, Collins (1994) 14 OJLS 229, Reich (1992) 14 Syd LR 23, Goyens [1992] CML Rev 71, Hondius (1994) 7 JCL 34, Brandt & Ulmer (1991) CML Rev 647, Bragg [1994] Consum LJ 29, Willett [1994] Consum LJ 114, Macdonald [1994] JBL 441, Harrison *Good Faith in Sales* (1997), Beale in *Good Faith and Fault in Contract Law* (1995) Beatson & Friedmann (eds), Brownsword, Howells & Wilhelmsonn in *Aspects of Unfairness in Contracts* (1996) Willett (ed), Bright & Bright (1995) 111 LQR 655, De Moor (1995) 3 European Review of Private Law, Bright (2000) 20 LS 331, Whittaker (2000) 116 LQR 95.

(2) The list in Sch 1 covers in Part One (as amended by The Unfair Terms in Consumer Contracts (Amendment) Regulations 2001 (SI 2001 No 1186)):
   1. The Information Commissioner
   2. The Gas and Electricity Markets Authority
   3. The Director General of Electricity Supply for Northern Ireland
   4. The Director General of Gas for Northern Ireland
   5. The Director General of Telecommunications
   6. The Director General of Water Services
   7. The Rail Regulator
   8. Every weights and measures authority in Great Britain
   9. The Department of Enterprise, Trade and Investment in Northern Ireland
   10. The Financial Services Authority
       And in Part Two:
   11. The Consumers' Association.

(3) It has been suggested, however, that the French version of the Directive has some "connotation of the 'usual course of business'" here — see Harrison *Good Faith in Sales* (1997) at 19.13.

(4) Article 4(2) states:
"Assessment of the Unfair nature of terms shall relate neither to the definition of the main subject matter of the contract nor to the adequacy of price and remuneration on the one hand, as against the services or goods supplied in exchange, on the other in so far as those terms are in plain intelligible language."

In addition, Recital 19 states:
"Whereas, for the purposes of this Directive, assessment of unfair character shall not be made of terms which describe the main subject matter of the contract nor the quality/price ratio of the goods or services supplied; whereas the main subject matter of the contract and the price/quality ratio may nevertheless be taken into account in assessing the fairness ofother terms; whereas it follows, *inter alia*, that in insurance contracts, the terms which clearly define or circumscribe the insured risk and the insurer's liability shall not be subject to such assessment since these restrictions are taken into account in calculating the premium paid by the consumer".

Chapter 12

Mistake

1. Introduction

There is much dispute about the scope and content of a chapter on the subject of mistake in the law of contract[1]. For this reason the reader will perhaps find more variety in the treatment of this topic than in any other area of contract law. One, or both, of the parties to a contract may enter into it under some misunderstanding or mistake. For example, S agrees to sell his car to B for £2,000. Unknown to both parties, the car, whilst parked in the street, has been totally wrecked by a bus colliding with it, shortly before the contract was made. This is traditionally known as "common mistake"; both parties are under the same misapprehension. Alternatively, S offers to sell his "surfing equipment" to B, who accepts. S intends to sell his surf-board, but B thinks the offer relates to S's wind surf-board. In this instance, where the parties are at cross-purposes, it is described as a case of "mutual mistake".

In contrast to the above examples, in which both parties are mistaken, there is also the category of "unilateral mistake". This occurs when one party enters into a contract under some mistake, but the other party is aware of this. For example, A intends to contract with B, but later discovers that the other party to the apparent agreement is, in fact, C. In cases of unilateral mistake, there is normally some misrepresentation or fraud involved and this leads us to an important point. The subject of mistake in contract law cannot be easily divided off from other related subjects. So where parties are at cross-purposes, or where one party enters into a contract having mistaken the identity of the other party, these types of mistake relate to the formation of contracts; that is, have the parties reached a binding agreement? In short, such instances may be described as "agreement mistakes".

Where the parties are both mistaken about the same fact, such as a contract for the sale of goods which no longer exist, there is no dispute about agreement. These cases involve the issue of "performability". This subject raises fundamental questions about the extent of contractual obligations. In other words, are contractual obligations absolute or can a party escape liability if he is unable to perform through no fault of his own? As some writers have observed, the subjects of performability and the extent of contractual obligations suggest a close connection between mistake in the law of contract and the doctrine of frustration (see Chapter 20). In the hypothetical instance given earlier, if the car, which was the subject of the agreement, was destroyed immediately after the contract was concluded (through no fault of either party) would the parties be discharged from the contract? (For an interesting case which shows the sometimes arbitrary distinction between mistake and frustration, see *Amalgamated Investment & Property Co Ltd* v *John Walker & Sons Ltd* [1976] 3 All ER 509.)

Although there are, traditionally, various sub-divisions of mistake in the law of contract, the subject can be more helpfully divided into two broad categories: mistake relating to agreement, and mistake relating to the performability of the contract. The subject of mistake cannot be entirely separated from a number of related issues in the law of contract, as we have seen, but it is consistent with decisions of the courts and with the opinion of the majority of writers on the subject, to devote a separate chapter to this area of law. This is not to imply, however, that the case law and the traditional approach to the subject are not open to criticism.

2. Narrow view of mistake in contract law

The word "mistake" has a narrower meaning in contract law than it does in everyday language. Parties will not be easily discharged from their contractual undertakings simply because they entered into the contract under some mistake or misunderstanding, or made a bad bargain (see *Clarion Ltd and others* v *National Provident Institution* [2000] 2 All ER 265). In the interests of certainty and commercial convenience, parties are bound by their apparent agreements. It will be remembered that the law takes a predominantly objective view of agreement. It is not, in general, the subjective intention of the parties with which the law is concerned, but rather, what can be inferred from their conduct[2]. This principle is well illustrated in *Centrovincial Estates plc* v *Merchant Investors Assurance Co Ltd* [1983] Com LR 158:

> P had let several floors of an office building to the Food, Drink and Tobacco Training Board who underlet one floor to D at a rent of £68,320 per year. Under a rent review clause, it was provided that the rent paid by D should be increased at a later date (25 December 1982) to the current market rental value. On 22 June 1982 (by which date the Board was thinking of a surrender to P of the lease), a firm of solicitors wrote to D, on behalf of P and the Board, inviting D to agree to a figure of £65,000 per year as the correct rental value at the review date. D accepted this proposal the following day. On 28 June, a partner in the firm of solicitors telephoned D to say that the letter of 22 June contained an error and that P had intended to propose a rent of £126,000 per year. D refused to agree to this corrected proposal and claimed that there was a binding contract concluded by the two letters of 22 and 23 June. P claimed that the parties had failed to reach agreement on the current rental value and that the matter should be referred to an independent surveyor, as provided for in the rent review clause. In other words, it was denied by P that the exchange of letters had resulted in a binding agreement. P argued that there was no meeting of the minds due to the error.

The Court of Appeal rejected P's contention and explained, *obiter*, the correct approach to such a mistake, stating:

> "It was contrary to the well established principles in contract law to suggest that the offeror under a bilateral contract could withdraw an unambiguous offer, after it had been accepted in the manner contemplated by the offer,

merely because he had made a mistake which the offeree neither knew nor could reasonably have known at the time when he accepted it."

Thus the law tends to uphold apparent agreements, even if one or both of the parties would not have entered into the contract if the true facts had been realised. Mistake, at common law, operates within strict limits. Where it is applicable, it operates in an inflexible way so as to render the whole transaction void from the start (*ab initio*). For example, if A sells goods to B and the contract is rendered void due to the doctrine of mistake, and B sells the goods to C, a *bona fide* purchaser for value, the goods can be recovered by A. This may cause hardship to C and will appear unfair, so the doctrine of mistake at common law cannot be invoked lightly. (As we shall see, more flexible results can be achieved where mistake is recognized by equity.)

3. Agreement mistake

(a) Mistake as to identity

A difficult problem arises where S intends to sell goods to Y, but later discovers that the other party to the apparent agreement is, in fact, X. This situation is usually described as one of unilateral mistake: only one party is mistaken, as a result of some fraudulent misrepresentation by the other. In a typical example of this sort of case, S will have parted with goods in return for a cheque which turns out to be worthless. A contract can be set aside for such a fraudulent misrepresentation, but X, the "rogue" (to use the time honoured description), will normally have resold the goods to someone else (B) before the contract can be avoided by S.

What is the legal effect of such a mistake? The difficulty lies in deciding which of either S or B owns the goods. As long as B is a *bona fide* purchaser for value, and not a party to the rogue's fraud, there are two innocent people claiming ownership. Both have been duped by the rogue, who has often disappeared by the time the fraud is discovered. The legal action which usually follows is in the law of tort, that is, S sues B for conversion in an attempt to recover the property.

To succeed in such a claim, S must show that there was no contract between himself and the rogue; that any apparent agreement was negatived by the mistake as to identity induced by the fraud. If S can show there was no contract whatsoever with the rogue, then title to the goods does not pass to the rogue and therefore B does not acquire title (ownership) from the rogue. Under s 21(1) Sale of Goods Act 1979 it is stated that where goods are sold by a person who is not their owner, and who does not have the owner's consent or authority to do so, the person buying from him will not (generally) acquire title to the goods. Thus S will attempt to prove that the apparent agreement with the rogue was void as a result of a mistake as to identity. As a consequence, an innocent purchaser buying from the rogue will not become the owner of the property.

On the other hand, B will assert that there was a valid contract between S and the rogue, which was merely voidable for fraud. If this view is accepted, then the rogue has a voidable title to the goods and if the contract has not been avoided (set aside) at the time when B purchases the goods from the rogue, B will acquire title to them. (See s 23 Sale of Goods Act 1979.) The law has the difficult choice between protecting the owners of property and upholding commercial transactions in the interests of certainty. It might be thought that some apportionment of the loss, between the two innocent parties, would provide the fairest solution to the problem — this suggestion is considered later. It must be emphasised that it is no comfort to either S or B to know that they have a remedy against the rogue, for he will normally have disappeared. If he is found, he probably has no money with which to compensate the injured parties.

(b) Identity or attributes?

Despite the fact that S has been tricked by the rogue into parting with the property, it can be recovered from a *bona fide* purchaser for value (B) only if S can show that he did not intend to deal with the rogue. The rogue must also be aware of S's mistake. But it may be difficult to say whether S's mistake is truly one as to the "identity" of the person he is dealing with, or simply as to that person's "attributes". This fine distinction, and its practical importance, are well illustrated in the cases which follow. In the famous case of *Cundy* v *Lindsay* (1878) 3 App Cas 459:

> Lindsay & Co (P) were linen manufacturers, who received an order for a large quantity of handkerchiefs from a rogue named Alfred Blenkarn. Blenkarn had business premises in the same street as a reputable company, Blenkiron & Co, and he signed his letters to P in such a way that the name of his firm looked like "Blenkiron" rather than "Blenkarn". P knew Blenkiron & Co to be a reputable business, and sent the handkerchiefs to the rogue thinking that they were dealing with Blenkiron & Co (the invoices were headed "Messrs. Blenkiron and Co., London"). Before Blenkarn's fraud was discovered — he was later convicted of obtaining goods by deception — he sold 250 dozen handkerchiefs to Cundy (D), an innocent purchaser. P sued D for the return of the goods.

In order to succeed, Lindsay & Co had to show that there was no contract between themselves and the rogue, Blenkarn. For if no contract existed, Blenkarn did not have title to the goods, and therefore none could be acquired by Cundy. In contrast, if there was a valid contract between P and the rogue, which was merely voidable for fraud, then title would pass to D as a *bona fide* purchaser for value. It was decided by the House of Lords that there was no contract between Lindsay and the rogue, as they intended to deal not with him, but with the respectable firm of Blenkiron & Co. The identity of the person they were dealing with was crucial to the plaintiffs and there was clearly an important mistake in this respect. This mistake was known to the rogue. Lord Cairns stated (at p 465):

> "Of [Blenkarn] they knew nothing, and of him they never thought. With him they never intended to deal. Their minds never, even for an instant of time rested upon him, and as between him and them there was no consensus of mind which could lead to any agreement or any contract whatever. As between him and them there was merely the one side to a contract, where, in order to produce a contract, two sides would be required".

It must be remembered that the decision in *Cundy* v *Lindsay* protects the original owner of the property but places the loss (and considerable hardship) on the innocent purchaser for value. For this reason, its scope is very narrow and cases of this type can be regarded as exceptional. The mistake must be one of identity, where the identity of the other is regarded by the mistaken party as crucial at the time the contract is made. (For a recent case on this point, where *Cundy* v *Lindsay* was distinguished, see *Citibank NA* v *Brown Shipley and Co Ltd* [1991] 2 All ER 690, *per* Waller J at pp 699 and 702.) An interesting contrast is provided by *King's Norton Metal Co* v *Edridge, Merrett & Co* (1897) 14 TLR 98:

> King's Norton Metal (P), who were metal manufacturers, received a letter from "Hallam & Co." in Sheffield, ordering brass rivet wire. The letterhead on the order gave the appearance of a large and thriving company, depicting a large factory and listing a number of overseas depots. The goods were despatched to "Hallam & Co." but were never paid for. In fact, the impressive looking "Hallam & Co." was the fictitious creation of a rogue named Wallis. Before the fraud was discovered, Wallis had sold the goods to Edridge & Co (D), who bought the metal in good faith. P sued D to recover damages for the conversion of these goods. In order to succeed, it had to be established that there was no contract between P and Wallis.

The Court of Appeal held that the contract was not void, on the ground of mistake, but was merely voidable for fraud. Accordingly, title (albeit voidable) passed to Wallis, and D acquired a good title from him. P had intended to contract with the writer of the letter. Wallis and Hallam & Co were, in fact, the same "person" and therefore King's Norton Metal were not mistaken as to the identity of the person with whom they entered into a contract. They were mistaken only as to the creditworthiness or attributes of the person with whom they were dealing.

This distinction between a person's identity and his attributes is clearly a fine one. Some critics claim that the distinction is spurious. (Lord Denning described it as "a distinction without a difference" in *Lewis* v *Averay* [1972] 1 QB 198.) A person's name, as well as being the most important guide as to his identity, may also be one of his attributes. If a party to a contract gives a false name, and the other party regards the identity of the person he is dealing with as crucial, is this a mistake as to identity or as to attributes?

It is possible to distinguish the cases of *Cundy* v *Lindsay* and *King's Norton Metal* v *Edridge*. In the former, there was a reputable company called Blenkiron & Co, of whom the plaintiff company had heard and with whom they clearly thought they were dealing. In the latter case, there was no "Hallam & Co.", it being merely the fictitious creation of the rogue, Wallis. Had there actually been a company called Hallam & Co, and had this company been known by reputation to the plaintiffs, then presumably the case would have been decided differently. But it is questionable whether the rights of an innocent purchaser for value, buying from the rogue, should depend on this rather tenuous distinction.

It is probably true to say that there will be very few cases today where a person could successfully claim that his apparent contract with another is void due to a mistake as to the other's identity. The reason for stating this rather tentatively is due to the unsatisfactory and inconsistent nature of the case law on this subject (see below). But, in policy terms, it is a question as to which of the two innocent parties should bear the loss; it seems wholly wrong that the *bona fide* purchaser for value should suffer. The original owner of the goods can always take more care before parting with goods on credit, but there is little that an innocent purchaser from the rogue can do. Also, it serves the interest of commercial certainty if contracts are upheld despite the mistake made by the original owner in parting with the goods to the rogue. It seems correct that there should be a heavy burden to be discharged by the owner to show that he took reasonable steps to check the identity of the person he was dealing with. He must also regard that person's identity as crucial, a requirement which was discussed in *Citibank NA* v *Brown Shipley & Co Ltd* [1991] 2 All ER 690. The facts were:

> By telephone, a rogue tricked a bank (the "issuing bank") into preparing a banker's draft drawn on a client company's account, of which the rogue claimed (fraudulently) to be a signatory. The banker's draft was made in favour of another bank (the "receiving bank") which, labouring under the same deception, had innocently agreed to supply large amounts of foreign currency to the rogue. The issuing bank handed the draft to the rogue, mistakenly believing him to be a messenger for the *bona fide* company. In return he gave the bank a forged letter which purported to confirm the company's earlier telephone instructions. The rogue then presented the draft to the receiving bank which, after checking with the issuing bank that the draft was authentic, paid the money directly to the rogue. The receiving bank was then paid by the issuing bank on presentation of the draft. On discovering the fraud, the issuing bank sought to recover the value of the draft as damages in conversion by claiming that title in the draft had never passed to the receiving bank. In other words, it claimed that the rogue had never acquired good title to the draft and, therefore, neither had the receiving bank.

The issuing bank's claim was dismissed by Waller J, who held that the receiving bank did not convert the draft by presenting it for payment. He stated that the delivery of the authorised banker's draft from one bank to the other established a contract between the two banks. The fact that this delivery was brought about by the rogue did not affect the formation of a contract. (The rogue was merely a "conduit pipe" through whom title did not need to pass.) Thus the rogue's identity was not to be regarded as of fundamental importance in this situation. The judge stated (at pp 699–700):

> "So far as authority is concerned, it will usually be very difficult for A to establish that it was of crucial importance to him who actually physically transported the draft to B. In this case, for example, delivery might have been done by post; it might have been done by one or other of the banks' messengers; it might have been done by some other messenger. It so happened that in this case that [*sic*] it was done by someone thought to be the customer or his messenger, but that was not of crucial importance. That being so, the authority, as it seems to me, albeit induced by fraud, would not be void; the authority would be actual, even if voidable."

Waller J went on to state (at p 700) that in this area of law "each case rests on its own facts". It is likely that the judge, in finding against the issuing bank, thought that it (rather than the receiving bank) was in a better position to protect itself against the risk of dealing with a rogue.

(c) Parties dealing face to face

These issues have also arisen in a series of cases in which the parties were dealing face to face with each other. Where someone receives a letter ordering goods, it is possible to imagine, as a result of some deception, how they could be mistaken as to the identity of the person placing the order (although it must be acknowledged that the seller has time to check the identity of this person). But when the contract is made *inter praesentes* it might seem difficult for the seller to claim that he did not intend to contract with the person who was physically present (eg in a shop), but with some other person who was not present. In *Phillips* v *Brooks Ltd* [1919] 2 KB 243:

> A man named North called in person at P's shop and asked to look at some jewellery, eventually selecting some pearls and a ring. He then made out a cheque for the total amount and stated: "You see who I am, I am Sir George Bullough" and he gave an address in St James' Square. P had heard of Sir George Bullough and checked the address in a directory. Being satisfied, P allowed the man to take away the ring, without the cheque (which was worthless) being cleared. North pledged the ring for £350 to the defendants, a firm of pawnbrokers, who were totally unaware of North's fraudulent conduct. P sued the pawnbrokers for the return of the ring, or alternatively, its value, claiming that he intended to contract only with Sir George and not the man who came into his shop.

In the High Court, Horridge J rejected this argument and found in favour of the defendants. There was not a mistake as to identity so as to render the contract void. There was a passing of property and the defendants acquired a good title to the ring. But would it not be fair to say that the jeweller thought he was dealing with Sir George? He certainly hoped that he was doing so, but he did take the risk that the man was not Sir George. The jeweller did not make a careful check on his customer's identity. Horridge J (at p 246) was surely correct in concluding that "although [P] believed the person to whom he was handing the ring was Sir George Bullough, he in fact contracted to sell and deliver it to the person who came into his shop".

When the parties deal with each other face to face, there is a strong presumption that the seller intends to contract with the person who is physically present, and not the person that the rogue is purporting to be. Another way of expressing this point is to say that the mistake is not as to identity at all but as to the attributes of the person the seller is dealing with. In the majority of these cases the owner of the goods parts with them on credit or in return for a worthless cheque. What concerns the seller, then, is the creditworthiness of the person he is dealing with. Despite this correct statement of the law in *Phillips* v *Brooks Ltd*, the law became confused by some of the cases that were decided later. For example, in *Lake* v *Simmons* [1927] AC 487:

> A jeweller (P) was induced by a woman, who came into his shop, into letting her have possession of two pearl necklets on approval. She fraudulently represented that she was the wife of a person of some substance (namely that she was "Mrs Van der Borgh"), and that she wanted the necklets for the purpose of showing them to her husband, and to a purely fictitious person, for their approval with a view to purchase by them. She then disposed of the necklets for her own benefit. P claimed on his insurance for loss of the necklets by theft or dishonesty; but his policy excluded liability where the loss was incurred as a result of the dishonesty of a customer to whom the goods had been entrusted by the jeweller.

It was held that P's loss was covered by the insurance and that the exclusion clause did not defeat his claim. But the reasoning employed by the House of Lords is open to serious criticism. It was argued that P did not intend to deal with the woman who came into his shop and that there was no genuine consent by P to her obtaining possession of them (see Viscount Haldane's speech at pp 500–501). The woman was not "a customer" within the meaning of the exclusion clause, as P did not regard *her* as his customer, but rather he thought of the two men, to whom she claimed she would show the necklets, as his possible customers! Their lordships concluded that there was no contract between P and the woman with whom he dealt face to face due to a mistake as to her identity. (This is discussed further in the case of *Citibank NA* v *Brown Shipley & Co Ltd* [1991] 2 All ER 690 — see above.)

Another heavily criticised case, the facts of which are similar to *Phillips* v *Brooks Ltd*, is *Ingram* v *Little* [1961] 1 QB 31:

> Elsie and Hilda Ingram were joint owners of a car, which they advertised for sale. A man, falsely calling himself "Hutchinson", came to look at it and have a trial run. He then offered £717 to the ladies for their car, which they were willing to accept. However, he produced a cheque book to pay for the car, and it was then stated by Elsie Ingram that under no circumstances would they accept a cheque and that the proposed deal was off. The man told them he was PGM Hutchinson, of Stanstead House, Caterham, and that he had business interests in Guildford. Hilda Ingram checked in the directory that there was indeed a PGM Hutchinson residing at that address. The ladies then accepted the man's cheque in exchange for their car. The man was not PGM Hutchinson and the cheque was dishonoured. The rogue, in the meantime, had sold the car to the innocent defendant (D). The ladies now sought to recover the car, or its value, from D.

The Court of Appeal decided that the apparent contract between the plaintiffs and the man who called at their house was void due to the mistake as to identity. The car still belonged to the ladies and D did not acquire good title from the rogue. The majority argued (with Lord Devlin dissenting) that although the identity of the man would have been unimportant as long as he had paid cash for the car, it became of crucial importance once the man wished to pay by cheque. The ladies refused to accept a cheque initially and they verified that there was a PGM Hutchinson listed at that address in the telephone directory. Therefore, their "offer" was not addressed to the man who was in their presence, but to the real PGM Hutchinson (whom they had never met).

It is submitted that, in certain exceptional circumstances, it might be possible to argue that an offer was not made to the person identified by sight and hearing, but *Ingram* v *Little* is some way from coming within this category. (The court's decision might have been more defensible if the ladies had gone to Stanstead House to deal with the genuine Hutchinson and then been deceived on the premises by someone falsely pretending to be that person[3].) It is difficult to escape the conclusion that the court allowed its sympathy for the ladies to cloud its judgment of the issues. In his dissenting speech, Lord Devlin correctly pointed out that what should have concerned the ladies was the creditworthiness of the person they were dealing with and not his identity. He stated (at p 68):

> "The fact that [the rogue] gave P.G.M. Hutchinson's address in the directory was no proof that he was P.G.M. Hutchinson; and if he had been, that fact alone was no proof that his cheque would be met. Identity, therefore, did not really matter."

It can hardly be claimed that the plaintiffs took reasonable steps to check the identity of the person with whom they were dealing. But, more fundamentally, it can be argued that the material mistake in *Ingram* v *Little* was as to the man's attributes and not as to his identity. (This is not to deny that the ladies thought the man's identity was important.) In fact, there is little to distinguish the case from the earlier decision in *Phillips* v *Brooks*, which emphasised the need to protect the innocent purchaser for value who buys the goods from the rogue. *Ingram* v *Little* was perhaps too concerned with protecting the original owner of the goods. This is the dilemma which faces judges in cases of this sort. It has been cogently argued that the law should permit some division of the loss between the two innocent parties in such proportion as is just in all the circumstances (see Lord Devlin's comments in *Ingram* v *Little*). This solution did not find favour with the Law Reform Committee in 1966[4]. However, the Committee did recommend that "where goods are sold under a mistake as to the buyer's identity, the contract should, so far as third parties are concerned, be voidable and not void".

In practice, this is the result that will probably be arrived at today in most cases of mistake as to identity. This conclusion is supported by *Lewis* v *Averay* [1972] 1 QB 198, the most recent decision on the point. The facts, which closely resembled *Ingram* v *Little*, were as follows:

> Lewis offered his car for sale at £450. A man arranged to see the car, tested it and expressed interest in buying it. The man told Lewis that he was Richard Greene, a famous film and television actor[5], and he wrote a cheque for the agreed price of £450, signed RA Green. As the purchaser wished to take away the car immediately, Lewis requested some means of identification, and was shown an admission pass to Pinewood Studios in the name of Richard A Green, which bore the man's photograph. Lewis permitted the man to take the car and log book in exchange for the cheque. In fact the cheque had been taken from a stolen cheque book and was worthless; the man was not Richard Greene, the famous actor. The rogue sold the car to an innocent buyer, Averay, for £200. Lewis sued Averay for conversion.

The Court of Appeal did not allow Lewis to recover the car or its value, deciding that Averay acquired a good title to it. Lewis intended to deal with the man who called to see the car. Although the contract was voidable for fraud, Lewis was unable to recover the property from someone who bought in good faith from the rogue for value. The court disagreed with *Ingram* v *Little*, preferring to base its decision on *Phillips* v *Brooks*. It is respectfully submitted that this is the correct conclusion to have reached. It has been argued that *Ingram* v *Little* is distinguishable on the ground that in that case the ladies would not conclude the agreement until they had looked in the telephone directory. But this is, to say the least, a tenuous argument. It is unlikely that *Ingram* v *Little* would be followed if substantially similar facts were to occur today.

(d) Mistake as to the terms or subject matter of a contract

Most of the cases considered in this section are instances of mutual mistake where the parties are at cross-purposes as to the terms or subject matter of the contract. Once again, the issue is that there is no genuine agreement, despite appearances. Before looking at these decisions, a further case of unilateral mistake should be noted. In *Hartog* v *Colin & Shields* [1939] 3 All ER 566:

> D contracted to sell to P three thousand Argentine hare skins. But by mistake he offered to sell them at a certain rate per "pound" (weight), instead of per "piece".

The price stated by D was extremely low — the price per piece was about one third of that per pound. The negotiations leading up to the sale had been on the basis of the price per piece, and this was the accepted custom within the trade. P purported to accept this offer and sued D for non-delivery.

It was held that there was no contract. The apparent agreement was negatived as P must surely have known that D's offer was made due to a mistake. ("The plaintiff could not reasonably have supposed that the offer contained the offeror's real intention": *per* Singleton J at p 568.) It is interesting to contrast this decision with the case of *Centrovincial Estates* v *Merchant Investors Assurance Co Ltd*, which was considered earlier. In that case the offeror was bound by his apparent agreement with the defendant despite offering to rent premises to D for £65,000 per year, rather than at the intended rent of £126,000. The important distinction seems to be that in the *Centrovincial* case the offeree (D) did not know, and could not reasonably have known, of the mistake at the time of acceptance.

Generally, parties are bound by their apparent agreements in the interests of certainty and commercial convenience. As we have seen, the law takes a predominantly objective view of agreement. It is not, usually, the subjective intention of the parties with which the law is concerned[6], but rather, what can be inferred from their conduct: "In contracts you do not look into the actual intent in a man's mind. You look at what he said and did" (*per* Lord Denning in *Storer* v *Manchester City Council* [1974] 3 All ER 824 at p 828). If one party makes an offer, as in the *Centrovincial* case, that can be understood in only one reasonable way, and the other party understands and accepts the offer in that reasonable way, there will normally be a binding agreement even if the offeror intended some different meaning. There will also be a heavy burden falling on the party alleging a mistake to disprove the existence of a contract.

It is necessary to assess the extent of the objective principle, particularly in relation to parties at cross-purposes — for example where one party intends to sell one thing and the other party intends to buy something different; or one party intends to contract on one set of terms and the other intends to deal on a different set of terms. In this type of situation (known as mutual mistake) the parties are mistaken as to each other's intention. In *Raffles* v *Wichelhaus* (1864) 2 H & C 906, the facts were:

> D agreed to buy from P a cargo of 125 bales of Surat cotton "to arrive ex Peerless from Bombay". In fact, there were two ships called "Peerless" and both sailed from Bombay. D meant the "Peerless" which sailed in October, and P meant the "Peerless" which sailed in December. D refused to accept the cotton sent on the ship which sailed in December. P claimed that he was ready to deliver the goods which were shipped on the vessel named in the agreement and from the agreed port, and that D was liable for refusing to accept or pay for the goods.

It was accepted by the court that D was not liable due to the ambiguity inherent in the agreement. In fact, the court (for procedural reasons) did not have to decide whether there was a contract, but the most plausible inference from the decision is that there was no contract. It is possible that there was an agreement to ship the cotton on the "October Peerless", but this is unlikely. Once it emerged that there were two ships of the same name, both due to sail from Bombay, it is impossible to say that the parties reached a genuine agreement. In terms of the objective approach, a reasonable person would not conclude that agreement had been reached.

A more difficult case involving ambiguity in an apparent agreement is *Scriven Bros* v *Hindley & Co* [1913] 3 KB 564, in which the facts were as follows:

> P instructed an auctioneer to sell a number of bales of hemp and of tow by auction. (Tow is the coarse and broken part of flax or hemp.) The goods were described in the auctioneer's catalogue as a certain number of bales in two separate lots, with the same shipping mark, without disclosing the difference in the commodities; ie it failed to state that one lot contained tow, not hemp. Before the sale, samples of the hemp and tow were available for inspection in a showroom. On the floor of the room the catalogue numbers of the lots of hemp and tow were marked in chalk opposite the respective samples. Having previously examined the hemp, and (mistakenly) believing both lots to contain hemp, D's manager did not inspect the samples which were on view. At the auction D's buyer, thinking that he was bidding for hemp, made an excessively high bid for the lot containing tow! His bid was successful. Expert witnesses stated that it was very unusual for Russian tow and Russian hemp to be landed from the same ship under the same shipping mark. P brought an action to recover the price.

Put simply, P intended to sell one thing, whilst D intended to buy something else. Neither was aware of the other party's misapprehension. It was held that there was no contract of sale as the parties had not reached agreement as to the subject matter of the proposed sale. This decision might seem rather favourable to the defendants, permitting them to escape a bad bargain. But the decision is probably sound. If we ask whether a reasonable person, taking an overview of the situation, would conclude that an agreement between the parties had been reached, the answer would probably be negative. Due to the ambiguities in the circumstances under which the auction took place, it is difficult to conclude that there was a contract for the sale of tow. But for the potentially misleading nature of the auction catalogue, however, the outcome of the case would surely have been different.

Interesting issues are raised by the famous case of *Smith* v *Hughes* (1871) LR 6 QB 597, but whether it can be accurately described as one of mutual mistake is debatable due to the disputed facts of the case. First, the facts:

> A farmer (P) offered to sell the manager of D, a race horse trainer, a quantity of oats and showed him a sample. The manager wrote to P accepting the offer. When the first delivery of oats was made, D discovered that the oats were "green" (ie that season's oats) and of no use to him. He claimed that he thought he was buying "old" oats and he refused to pay for that delivery or any subsequent delivery. P, who knew that the oats were new, refused to take them back and sued D for the price. There was a dispute as to what was said in the exchange between P and D's manager; D claimed that P had described them as "good old oats", whereas P denied using the word "old". After a finding in favour of D at the trial, P appealed.

If the word "old" had, in fact, been used then the finding for D was clearly correct. But if the word "old" had not been used by the parties, then the situation was more complex. It was this problem that was dealt with by the appeal court. If D's manager believed the oats to be old and P was aware of his belief, without doing anything to encourage it (simply offering his goods and exhibiting his sample), was there a contract? As Cockburn CJ stated (at p 603):

> "The question is whether, under such circumstances, the passive acquiescence of the seller in the self-deception of the buyer will entitle the latter to avoid the contract. I am of the opinion that it will not."

In ordering a new trial the court agreed with his lordship's conclusion. Assuming that the word "old" was not used by the parties, D received the goods which he contracted to buy and which corresponded with the sample inspected by D's manager, and therefore he was bound by the contract. To quote Lord Cockburn once again (at p 603):

> "Here the defendant agreed to buy a specific parcel of oats. The oats were what they were sold as, namely, good oats according to the sample. The buyer persuaded himself they were old oats, when they were not so; but the seller neither said nor did anything to contribute to his deception. He has himself to blame. The question is not what a man of scrupulous morality or nice honour would do under such circumstances".

(e) Agreement mistake in equity

It is correct that the law should take a narrow view of mistake. This approach upholds the need to be able to rely on the apparent intention of the party with whom you are dealing, in the interests of certainty and commercial convenience. However, the equitable jurisdiction of the courts permits a more flexible approach[7]: a contract may be upheld as valid but, in the interests of justice, the court may still grant relief against the consequences of mistake. The most practical form of equitable relief is the discretion of the court to refuse specific performance even in cases where the contract is valid at law. In the case of *Malins* v *Freeman* (1837) 2 Keen 25, for example, the defendant (due to his late arrival) mistakenly made a bid for one property at an auction thinking that he was bidding for another. The mistake was due to the defendant's own carelessness and the contract was clearly valid (contrast *Scriven Bros* v *Hindley*, above). Although the plaintiff could have claimed damages, the court refused to order specific performance against the defendant. (Also, see *Wood* v *Scarth* (1855) 2 K & J 33 and (1858) 1 F & F 293 for a further illustration of this flexible approach.) The court may exercise its discretion so as to avoid hardship to a defendant[8] and it "will not be active in assisting one party to an agreement, who has always his remedy in damages, to take advantage of the mistake of the other so as to involve him in serious and unforeseen consequences" (*Stewart* v *Kennedy* (1890) 15 App Cas 75 at p 105, *per* Lord Macnaghten).

In the interest of certainty, and to prevent fraud, the court will not allow a defendant to escape the performance of a contract simply because he made a mistake. In *Tamplin* v *James* (1879) 15 Ch D 215 the facts were:

> A certain inn, "The Ship", and adjoining shop were to be sold by auction. The defendant knew the property for sale and he knew that certain gardens, which were hardly separated from the property to be sold, were occupied along with the inn and the shop. However, the gardens did not belong to the vendor and this was clear from the plans which were on display in the sale-room. The defendant did not look at the plans or at the particulars of sale, and he bought the land in the mistaken belief that he was buying the gardens along with the inn and shop.

The Court of Appeal ordered specific performance. There was no misrepresentation by the vendor; nor was there any ambiguity in the terms of the contract. (For an interesting contrast, see *Denny* v *Hancock* (1870) LR 6 Ch App 1, in which the vendor's plan of the property for sale was potentially misleading.) In the absence of these factors, a court will be justified in refusing specific performance only where "hardship amounting to injustice" (*per* James LJ at p 221) would be inflicted on the defendant by holding him to the agreement and where it would be unreasonable to do so. But in *Tamplin* v *James* it was the defendant's own carelessness that led to his mistake and he bought the property which he intended to purchase; it was simply less extensive than he thought. It was not unreasonable or unjust for the court to hold him to his contract and grant the plaintiff specific performance.

Another equitable remedy which may be granted at the discretion of the court is that of rectification. The purpose here is to grant relief in relation to mistakes made in the recording of agreements. For instance, where A and B reach agreement on a certain set of terms and then a written agreement between them is subsequently drawn up which, by mistake, does not accurately reflect those terms, the court may rectify the document. In other words, the document is amended so as accurately to reflect either the terms agreed by A and B, or their prior common intention (see *Joscelyne* v *Nissen* [1970] 2 QB 86). The equitable remedy of rectification will not, generally, be available in cases of unilateral mistake (although exceptionally it may be; see *Roberts & Co Ltd* v *Leicestershire County Council* [1961] Ch 555). It is usually only where the document does not reflect the intention of both A and B that a claim for rectification will be granted. In the case of *Riverlate Properties Ltd* v *Paul* [1975] Ch 133, the facts were as follows:

> P, a landlord, granted a lease of a maisonette for 99 years to D at a price of £6,500, with a yearly ground rent of £25. It was P's intention that D should pay half the cost of structural and exterior repairs. But owing to a drafting error in the draft lease sent to D's solicitor, the lease which was executed did not reflect P's intention in this respect. Neither D nor her solicitor was aware of the mistake, and it was D's understanding that she was not responsible for these repairs. P's claim was to have the contract set aside, or, alternatively, rectified so as to include D's liability for sharing the cost of external repairs.

P's claim was rejected by both the trial and appeal courts. This is surely correct as it would be contrary to the objective approach to agreement if a party could go back on an offer which he reasonably appears to have made and which has been accepted by the other party without any knowledge of the offeror's mistake. The matter was dealt with emphatically by Russell LJ (at pp 140–141):

> "What is there in principle, or in authority, binding on this court, which requires a person who has acquired a leasehold interest on terms on which he intended to obtain it, and who thought when he obtained it that the lessor intended him to obtain it on those terms, either to lose the leasehold interest, or, if he wished to keep it, to submit to keep it only on the terms which the lessor meant to impose but did not? In point of principle, we cannot find that this should be so. If reference be made to principles of equity, it operates on conscience. If conscience is clear at the time of the transaction, why should equity disrupt the transaction?"

But if one party is aware of the other's mistake and, by keeping quiet, unfairly derives some benefit from the error, there can be no objection to rectification in a case of unilateral mistake (see *Thomas Bates & Son Ltd* v *Wyndham's (Lingerie) Ltd* [1981] 1 All ER 1077). Moreover, rectification may be available where one party is mistaken and the other both intends and *suspects* this, and behaves unconscionably so as to encourage the error (*per* Stuart-Smith LJ in *Commission for the New Towns* v *Cooper (GB) Ltd* [1995] 2 All ER 929, and discussed in *Templiss Properties Ltd* v *Dean Hyams* [1999] EGCS 60). However, rectification will not be granted merely because one party has driven a hard bargain in the negotiations and the other party has not been sufficiently alert to the possible consequences of a particular provision of the agreement (see *Oceanic Village Ltd* v *Shirayama Shokusan Co Ltd and others* [1999] EGCS 83). For a court to rectify on the ground of unilateral mistake, there needs to be clear evidence that the defendant has acted unconscionably and unfairly.

4. Common mistake

(a) Performability mistake (or "initial impossibility")

Where performability mistake is at issue, there is no dispute between the parties about the existence of an agreement. This type of mistake, often referred to as "common mistake", arises where the parties share the same misapprehension about some underlying fact which renders the contract impossible to perform or devoid of purpose, and one party maintains that the agreement is nullified by the mistake. For example, A contracts to sell his bicycle to B, but unknown to both parties, the bicycle was wrecked beyond repair five minutes before their agreement. What is the legal position in cases of this type? Does such a mistake render the contract void as a matter of law; or could the seller be liable for failing to supply the bicycle as promised; or could the buyer be liable for the price of the bicycle?

It is true that problems of performability mistake are far from common in practice. But an analysis of them is crucial to an understanding of contract law, as it provides an important insight into the strength of contractual obligations. The general rule of contractual obligation is that a party is bound to perform the contract or else to provide a remedy for its breach. How strict is this rule? When will a party be excused from performance on the ground of "impossibility"?

(b) Mistake as to existence of subject matter

Usually this type of mistake has involved contracts for non-existent goods but, exceptionally, other factual situations can arise. For example, in *Galloway* v *Galloway* (1914) 30 Times LR 531, a man (D) and woman (P) entered into a separation deed by which D agreed to pay P the weekly amount of £1 for the support of their three children. D discovered that, contrary to his mistaken assumption, his first wife was not dead! Thus the separation agreement between D and P was based on their common, but erroneous, assumption that they were in fact married to one another. D fell behind with his payments under the agreement and argued that the contract should be set aside. Ridley J held that there was no doubt that the agreement between the parties was void due to a common mistake of fact which was material to the existence of an agreement. (The case deals only with the validity of the agreement; presumably D was still under a legal duty to provide for the children.)

A more important line of cases deals with goods which have ceased to exist, physically or commercially, at the time the parties entered into a contract. In the leading case of *Couturier* v *Hastie* (1856) 5 HL Cas 673:

> There was a contract for the sale of a cargo of corn — of "fair average quality when shipped" — which was thought to be in transit between Salonika and London. Unknown to the contracting parties, the corn had become badly overheated and had been sold at Tunis (by the master of the ship) shortly before the contract was made. The seller contended that the buyer was still liable for the price of the corn; namely, that the buyer had purchased an interest in a "maritime adventure" (including risks), represented by the shipping documents and insurance. The buyer argued that the contract was for the sale and purchase of goods, not for the sale of goods or the documents representing them, and therefore denied liability for the price.

Here we have an interesting dispute about the true interpretation, or construction, of the agreement between the parties. The House of Lords decided that the purchaser was not liable to pay for the corn. In an important speech, Lord Cranworth LC stated (at pp 681–682):

> "[T]he whole question turns upon the construction of the contract . . . looking to the contract itself alone, it appears to me clearly that what the parties contemplated . . . was that there was an existing something to be sold and bought . . . The contract plainly imports that there was something which was to be sold at the time of the contract, and something to be purchased".

In other words the contract was not void *automatically* because the goods no longer existed at the time of the contract. It was a question of construction: what did the parties contract about? Because the House of Lords interpreted the contract as one for the purchase of specific goods (and not the documents representing them as an alternative), the purchaser was not liable. It was never decided whether the seller would have been liable if an action for non-delivery of the goods had been brought by the purchaser against him. It is submitted that the seller would be liable in these circumstances only if, as a matter of construction, he assumed the risk of the goods' non-existence. This would perhaps be fairly unusual, but such a situation is well illustrated in the Australian High Court case of *McRae* v *Commonwealth Disposals Commission* (1951) 84 CLR 377. The facts were:

> The Commonwealth Disposals Commission (D) invited tenders "for the purchase of an oil tanker lying on Jourmand Reef . . . the vessel is said to contain oil". P's tender of £285 was accepted by the defendant Commission. P went to much expense in preparing for a salvage expedition only to discover, on arrival at the designated area, that there was no tanker to be found. (Nor was there any place known as "Jourmand Reef").

The court held that this was not an example of a contract nullified by mistake. The defendants had made an implied promise that there was a tanker at a particular location. As there was no such tanker, this was a breach of contract and P was entitled to damages[9]. The court was clearly of the opinion that *Couturier* v *Hastie* did not establish a rule of law that a contract is void for mistake where the goods do not exist at the time the contract is made. It was stated (at pp 406–407):

> "The truth is that the question whether the contract was void, or the vendor excused from performance by reason of the non-existence of the supposed subject matter, did not arise in *Couturier* v *Hastie*. It would have arisen if the

purchaser had suffered loss through non-delivery of the corn and had sued the vendor for damages. If it had so arisen, we think that the real question would have been whether the contract was subject to an implied condition precedent that the goods were in existence".

The decision in the case of *McRae* is certainly in keeping with the approach taken in *Couturier* v *Hastie*. However, *Couturier* v *Hastie* has received an interpretation in English law that perhaps is inconsistent with what was actually stated by the House of Lords in that case. Despite the fact that it was stressed that "the whole question turns upon the construction of the contract", the decision led to the belief that in cases of non-existent goods the "contract" will be void. This interpretation was encapsulated in s 6 Sale of Goods Act 1893 which purported to give effect to the decision in *Couturier* v *Hastie*. Section 6 of the Act (now the 1979 Act) provides that:

"Where there is a contract for the sale of specific goods, and the goods without the knowledge of the seller have perished at the time when the contract is made, the contract is void".

This raises a number of interesting issues. It appears to state as a rule of law something which was held to be a question of construction at common law. As such it produces a more rigid approach than that favoured by the Australian High Court in *McRae*. This can be illustrated by *Barrow, Lane & Ballard Ltd* v *Phillips & Co Ltd* [1929] 1 KB 574, in which the facts were that P sold to D 700 bags of nuts, but at the time of making the contract there were not 700 bags in existence. In fact, there were only 591 bags; the remaining 109 having been stolen or misdirected (due to the actions of a third party). P claimed the price of the bags which were still in existence, but Wright J rejected this argument and held the contract to be void for mistake as to the existence of goods. This was stated as a matter of law under s 6 Sale of Goods Act. Apparently it made no difference that only some of the goods did not exist and that more than three-quarters of the bags were still there. Wright J stated (at p 583):

"A contract for a parcel of 700 bags is something different from a contract for 591 bags, and the position appears to me to be in no way different from what it would have been if the whole 700 bags had ceased to exist"[10].

It is possible to distinguish *McRae* from the other cases we have considered on the basis that s 6 refers to goods that "have perished" at the time of the contract, whereas in *McRae* the goods never existed[11]. But there is no reason, in principle, why this should make any material difference and perhaps the wording of the Act is merely fortuitous. It might be pointed out that this discussion is rather academic; that in the modern age of instantaneous methods of communication, it is unlikely that there will be many problems relating to non-existent goods. But it might also be cogently argued that in view of these modern developments, it would be more realistic to hold that the seller of specific goods is usually understood to have promised that the goods exist[12].

(c) Mistake as to "quality" of subject matter

In the cases which we have just considered, it is easy to understand why an apparent contract may be a nullity due to the non-existence of the subject matter. The contract may be emptied of all its content and, unless any other construction is possible, it may be regarded as void. But outside this category of cases involving non-existent goods, there are few clear instances of a contract being held void on the grounds of common mistake. Here we are concerned with cases where the parties are both mistaken as to some fundamental fact (such as the "quality" of the thing contracted for) and whether an apparent contract can be nullified on these grounds. If the courts are willing to declare a contract void for this reason, there is perhaps an independent doctrine of common mistake recognized by the common law. However, the existing case law is rather unclear on this point, being open to more than one interpretation. Where a court is not prepared to declare a contract void at common law on the basis of some important mistake as to "quality", it may nevertheless exercise equitable jurisdiction by declaring the contract voidable because of the mistake; that is, the contract may be set aside and terms may be imposed on the parties.

It is difficult to assess whether there is a general doctrine of common mistake capable of rendering a contract void *ab initio*, despite a recent judicial pronouncement on the subject which suggests that there is (see *Associated Japanese Bank (International)* v *Crédit du Nord SA* [1988] 3 All ER 902). It must be remembered that the courts will not permit a party to escape his contractual undertakings simply because he made what turned out to be a bad bargain. But what if, for example, a person sells something at a tiny fraction of its true commercial value because both parties are mistaken as to its quality or its nature? Or, to pose a further question, if the subject matter lacks some essential quality which the parties thought it possessed, can it be argued that the object of the contract is impossible to achieve?

The leading case of *Bell* v *Lever Bros* [1932] AC 161 is difficult to interpret but it illustrates the limitations of any general doctrine of common mistake. Generally, a mistake as to quality of the thing contracted for will not make a contract void at common law. In *Bell* v *Lever Bros* the facts were:

> Lever Bros employed the appellants, Bell and Snelling, as chairman and vice-chairman (respectively) of the Niger Company — a company controlled by Lever Bros. Before the expiry of their five-year contracts, Lever Bros wished to terminate Bell's and Snelling's contracts, and under a further agreement Lever Bros promised to pay the men compensation of £30,000 and £20,000 respectively. After payment of the compensation, Lever Bros discovered that Bell and Snelling had committed certain breaches of duty, during their employment, which would have entitled their employers to dismiss them without compensation. (In the course of their employment the men had secretly engaged in speculative transactions in cocoa on their own account.) It was found as a matter of fact that Bell and Snelling had forgotten about their breaches of duty at the time of entering into the compensation agreements with Lever Bros. Therefore, it was not a case either of fraud or of unilateral mistake. Lever Bros tried to recover the £50,000 on the ground that the compensation agreements with the two men were void due to common mistake.

Put simply, Lever Bros paid a total of £50,000 to terminate the contracts of two men that they could have dismissed for nothing. The trial judge and the Court of Appeal held that the compensation agreements were void due to a fundamental mistake. The House of Lords reversed this decision with the majority holding that the contracts were valid and binding. It is worth considering the important and controversial words of one of the majority, Lord Atkin (at pp 223–224), in some detail. He stated:

"Is an agreement to terminate a broken contract different in kind from an agreement to terminate an unbroken contract, assuming that the breach has given the one party the right to declare the contract at an end? I feel the weight of the plaintiff's contention that a contract immediately determinable is a different thing from a contract for an unexpired term, and that the difference in kind can be illustrated by the immense price of release from the longer contract as compared with the shorter ... But, on the whole, I have come to the conclusion that it would be wrong to decide that an agreement to terminate a definite specified contract is void if it turns out that the agreement had already been broken and could have been terminated otherwise. The contract released is the identical contract in both cases, and the party paying for release gets exactly what he bargains for. It seems immaterial that he could have got the same result in another way, or that if he had known of the true facts he would not have entered into the bargain."

Although it is difficult to agree that Lever Bros got "exactly" what they bargained for, it must be accepted that it was in the company's interest, because of a corporate merger, to terminate the men's service contracts. Moreover, the compensation was a reward (at least in part) for the good work that the two men had done during their employment and it ensured their co-operation in carrying through the amalgamation. It might be contended that the value of this service was unaffected by the breach of contract committed by the two men. On the other hand, it might be argued that the basis of the compensation agreement was the termination of valid service contracts and that, accordingly, there was a common mistake as to a fundamental fact.

We have seen that a mistake as to the existence of the subject matter of an agreement can render the agreement void. But, in view of the actual decision in *Bell* v *Lever Bros*, are there any circumstances in which the courts will declare a contract void due to some fundamental mistake as to the quality of the thing contracted for? A narrow view, evident in some parts of the judgments given in *Lever Bros*, is that an agreement will be nullified only where the identity of the subject matter is in effect destroyed by the mistaken assumption; ie "does the state of the new facts destroy the identity of the subject matter as it was in the original state of facts?" (*per* Lord Atkin, *ibid*, p 227). In such a (rare) event, therefore, the mistake would be analogous to cases of non-existent goods and would nullify agreement.

A slightly wider view of the law, also expressed by Lord Atkin (at p 218), is that a common mistake will render a contract void where both parties are mistaken "as to the existence of some quality which makes the thing without the quality essentially different from the thing as it was believed to be"[13]. This view of common mistake was approved in the case of *Associated Japanese Bank (International)* v *Crédit du Nord SA* [1988] 3 All ER 902 (which is discussed below). In this case Steyn J stated, *obiter* (at p 913), that this wider interpretation of *Bell* v *Lever Bros* is to be preferred. The test to be applied is that the mistake must render the subject matter of the contract essentially and radically different from the subject matter which the parties believed to exist.

However, there is still a distinct impression that much of this debate is merely abstract theorising. If we look at the decision in *Bell v Lever Bros*, and the decisions that have followed, it is hard to establish a doctrine of common mistake at common law which will render an apparent contract void for mistake as to quality of the thing contracted for. (For cases which lend some support to the existence of such a doctrine, see *Scott v Coulson* [1903] 2 Ch 249 at p 252, and also *Nicholson and Venn v Smith-Marriott* (1947) 177 LT 189)[14]. The doctrine is said to exist in theory, but in practice it is difficult to find examples of cases decided on this basis alone. This is not surprising in view of the outcome of *Lever Bros*. The company paid £50,000 to dismiss two men that it could have dismissed for nothing. If this was not sufficiently fundamental to come within a doctrine of common mistake, it is reasonable to question the existence of such a doctrine.

A further illustration of the strict view of mistake at common law is the case of *Leaf v International Galleries* [1950] 2 KB 86. The facts were as follows:

> In 1944 the defendants sold a picture, entitled "Salisbury Cathedral", to P for £85. The defendants represented that it was the work of John Constable. But when P tried to sell the painting, five years later, he discovered that it had not been painted by Constable. P sought rescission of the contract and repayment of £85 on the basis of the defendants' innocent misrepresentation. (P did not claim damages for breach of condition or warranty.)

The Court of Appeal held that P was not entitled to rescind the contract despite the defendants' innocent misrepresentation. In the opinion of Lord Denning, P had ample opportunity to examine the picture in the first few days after buying it, and as he had not rejected the painting within a reasonable period after its purchase, he lost the right to rescind. (For an interesting modern case on this point, see *Peco Arts v Hazlitt Gallery* [1983] 3 All ER 193.) In his lordship's opinion, a claim for damages for breach of contract might have succeeded but P did not bring such a claim before the court. (But see *Harlingdon and Leinster Enterprises Ltd v Christopher Hull Fine Art Ltd* [1990] 1 All ER 737.) Lord Denning also stated (at p 89):

> "There was a mistake about the quality of the subject-matter, because both parties believed the picture to be a Constable, and that mistake was in one sense essential or fundamental. Such a mistake, however, does not avoid the contract. There was no mistake about the subject-matter of the sale. It was a specific picture of 'Salisbury Cathedral'. The parties were agreed in the same terms on the same subject-matter, and that is sufficient to make a contract".

When a person buys the work of a famous artist it is, perhaps, rather perverse to suggest that he or she is buying merely "a painting" (eg of Salisbury Cathedral). There are two possible interpretations of *Leaf* in relation to common mistake. On the one hand it could be argued that the relatively low price of the painting suggests a slightly speculative venture which includes the risk that the painting of Salisbury Cathedral was not "a Constable" — in which case there is clearly no fundamental mistake. On the other hand, and more plausibly, it can be asserted that the parties contracted for the sale of "a Constable" and therefore there was a mistake as to an essential quality of the subject matter. However it appears that even such an important mistake will not nullify the contract.

Lord Denning's statement (above) suggests therefore that a contract will rarely, if ever, be void as a result of a common mistake as to some essential quality of the thing contracted for. Lord Denning's opinion echoes that of Lord Atkin in *Bell v Lever Bros* (see [1932] AC 161 at p 224), in which the latter considered an example with facts similar to those which actually occurred in *Leaf* v *International Galleries*. The apparent injustice suffered by the plaintiff in *Leaf* v *International Galleries* is overshadowed by the fact that, in the words of Lord Atkin (at p 224), it is of "paramount importance that contracts should be observed".

But in the more recent case of *Associated Japanese Bank (International)* v *Crédit du Nord SA* [1988] 3 All ER 902 support was given for the existence of a doctrine of common mistake as to quality rendering a contract void *ab initio* at common law. It was not, in fact, necessary to decide the case on this particular basis, but Steyn J was at pains to explain the nature and scope of such a doctrine. The facts were:

> The plaintiff bank (P) bought four specific micro textile compression packaging machines from Mr Jack Bennett (B) and then leased them back to him. B received £1,021,000 from P under the transaction. As a condition of the transaction, B's obligations under the "leaseback" agreement were guaranteed by the defendant bank (D). At all times both banks believed that the four machines existed and were in B's possession. In fact, when B fell behind with his payments under the lease, it was discovered that the machines did not exist! (The transaction was a fraud perpetrated by B.) B was found to be bankrupt and therefore P's claim against him under the lease was fruitless. P sued the defendant bank on the guarantee.

In dismissing P's claim, Steyn J held that, on its construction, the guarantee was subject to an express condition precedent that there was a lease in respect of four existing machines. This was because both banks were informed and believed that the machines existed. (In any case, the learned judge thought that there was an implied condition precedent that the machines existed and so P's claim would have failed for this reason.)

Steyn J went on to explain, *obiter* (at pp 912–913), the principles relevant to common mistake as to quality of the subject matter: the law will normally uphold apparent contracts; the doctrine of mistake can be relied on only in unexpected and "wholly exceptional" circumstances. It must be a mistake of both parties relating to facts as they existed at the time of contracting. A party seeking to rely on a common mistake must have had reasonable grounds for entertaining the belief on which the mistake was based. Applying the *dicta* of Lords Atkin and Thankerton in *Bell* v *Lever Bros*, the learned judge stated that the mistake must render the subject matter of the contract "essentially and radically different from that which the parties believed to exist".

Applying these principles to the facts of the case, he concluded (at p 913) that "the stringent test of common law mistake is satisfied; the guarantee is void *ab initio*". For both parties, the guarantee of obligations under a lease with machines that did not exist, was essentially and radically different from a guarantee of a lease with four machines that both parties thought were in existence at the time of contracting[15].

(d) Common mistake in equity

If the question of mistake as to quality is raised by one of the parties, the first task of the court will be to see (as a matter of construction) if either of the parties to the contract bears the risk of the relevant mistake. (For example, in *William Sindall plc* v *Cambridgeshire County Council* [1994] 1 WLR 1016, P argued that a contract to buy D's land should be rescinded for mistake when P discovered that a sewer ran across the land. The Court of Appeal, however, rejected P's argument as it was held that the agreement between the parties allocated the risk of this kind of mistake to P.) If the contract is silent on this point, then the doctrine of mistake may be considered[16]. If the case does not come within the strict definition of common law mistake as to quality, which will render the contract void *ab initio*, the court may nevertheless exercise equitable jurisdiction and set the contract aside on terms. Mistake in equity is not so strictly circumscribed as common law mistake and the remedies are more flexible.

The opinion has been expressed by some writers and judges, most notably by Lord Denning (see *Solle* v *Butcher* [1950] 1 KB 671 at p 691), that a common mistake, even of a fundamental nature, does not make the contract void at common law, but merely liable to be set aside in equity. (Also see his lordship's statement to the same effect in *Frederick Rose Ltd* v *William Pim Jnr Ltd* [1953] 2 QB 450 at pp 459–460.) However, this is inconsistent with what was stated in *Bell* v *Lever Bros* and with the most recent judicial pronouncements. It appears, therefore, that we have to accept the coexistence of mistake at law and mistake in equity. In the words of Steyn J in *Associated Japanese Bank (International)* v *Crédit du Nord SA* [1988] 3 All ER 902 at p 912:

> "[A] narrow doctrine of common law mistake (as enunciated in *Bell* v *Lever Bros*), supplemented by the more flexible doctrine of mistake in equity (as developed in *Solle* v *Butcher* and later cases), seems ... to be an entirely sensible and satisfactory state of the law."

If a party raises the issue of mistake at common law, the court will consider this in the light of the principles which we looked at in the previous section. If the case comes within the very narrow definition, then it will be void and the equitable jurisdiction will be irrelevant. But such cases are exceptional. In the interest of upholding apparent contracts, the court will normally decide that the contract is valid, despite a mistake as to the quality of the subject matter. So where the contract is held to be valid, the court may still have to decide on the question of mistake in equity. In *Solle* v *Butcher* [1950] 1 KB 671 the facts were:

> In 1947, D took a long lease of a building, which had previously been converted into five flats, with the intention of carrying out repairs caused by war damage and substantial alterations to the property. Although the flats were empty in 1947, one of them (Flat No 1) had been let before the war to a tenant at a rent of £140 per year. P and D were partners in an estate agents' business and they discussed the rent that could be charged for the flats once the improvements had been carried out. D relied on P in calculating the rents that could be charged, and P told D that he could charge £250 per year for the flat in question (Flat No 1), and that the rent was not controlled by the Rent Restriction Acts (as the flat had been altered extensively). In September 1947, D let Flat No 1 to P for seven years at an annual rent of £250; both parties were satisfied that the earlier rent of £140 did not apply as the "standard rent". In other words they entered into the contract under the mistaken impression that the flat was not controlled by the Rent Restriction Acts. In fact the maximum rent that could be charged was £140 and this could not be increased during the contractual tenancy (due to the relevant legislation) once the lease was executed. After nearly two years, P sought a declaration that the standard rent of the flat was

£140 and he tried to claim the amount that he had already overpaid to D under the lease. The trial court found that the standard rent was £140 per year. The defendant counterclaimed for rescission of the lease on the basis of common mistake of fact.

It was decided by the Court of Appeal that the contract was not void *ab initio*, once again illustrating the narrow view of common mistake at law. However, the court exercised its equitable jurisdiction and ordered rescission of the lease, but on the terms that would enable P "to choose either to stay on at the proper rent [ie £250 per year] or to go out" (*per* Lord Denning at pp 696–697). In so doing, the court illustrated the flexibility of the equitable approach[17]. Not only did it relieve one party from the hardship caused by the mistake, but it also did justice to the other party. A further illustration of this approach is provided by *Grist* v *Bailey* [1967] Ch 532:

> The defendant, Mrs Minnie Bailey, agreed to sell to the plaintiff, Frank Grist, a freehold house for £850, "subject to the existing tenancy thereof". At the time of contracting, both parties thought that the house was occupied by a protected tenant (under the Rent Acts) who was entitled to remain in the house, and the price reflected their belief. In fact, they were incorrect; the tenant left the house without making any claim to protection. The true value of the house with vacant possession was £2,250. Mrs Bailey refused to complete the contract and an action for specific performance was brought by the plaintiff. The defendant argued that the contract should be set aside on the ground of common mistake.

Goff J held that the common mistake as to the nature of the tenancy affecting the property was not sufficient to render the contract void at common law. (This is surely correct for the subject matter was not fundamentally or essentially affected by the mistake.) But the considerable undervaluing of the house, due to the mistake, would have caused considerable hardship to the defendant. For this reason the judge upheld the defendant's claim for rescission. The contract was set aside in equity on the terms that the plaintiff was to have the option of entering into a fresh contract to buy the house at a proper vacant possession price.

It might be objected that the decision seems rather indulgent towards the vendor who made a bad bargain (which could presumably have been avoided if greater care had been exercised), and that it conflicts with the requirement of certainty in commercial dealings. But it would have been extremely harsh to refuse to grant relief to the defendant in view of the material mistake. The case is a good example of the flexible approach in equity. A less satisfactory use of equity can be seen in *Magee* v *Pennine Insurance Co Ltd* [1969] 2 QB 507, where the facts were:

> In 1961, P bought a car for his eighteen-year-old son to drive. P, who could not drive, signed a proposal form to insure the car with the defendant company, but the details of the form were completed by the person at the garage from whom he bought the car. Although there was no dishonesty on P's part, the information supplied on the form contained certain innocent misrepresentations. For example, it stated incorrectly that P held a provisional licence and that he and an elder son (who had a full licence) would drive the car as well as the younger son. (In signing the form, P promised that the information it contained was true and that this declaration was to be the basis of a contract of insurance with the defendant company.) The insurance policy on the car (and its replacement) was duly issued and renewed each year. In 1965, the younger son had a serious accident in the car which resulted in a claim on the insurance. P claimed £600 under the policy as the value of the car,

but he was offered £385 in settlement of his claim and he accepted this offer. On discovery of P's misrepresentations, the defendants refused to pay him £385 under the compromise agreement. P brought an action for this sum.

In the Court of Appeal, Lord Denning (at p 514) accepted that this was a case of common mistake as "both parties thought that the contract was good and binding". However, he reiterated his opinion that a common mistake, even on a fundamental matter, does not make a contract void at law, but makes it liable to be set aside in equity. It was held (with Winn LJ dissenting) that the contract, despite being valid at law, would be set aside in equity. It was thought that it would be unfair to hold the insurance company to an agreement based on an invalid insurance policy. But it can be objected that justice was done to one party only. No terms were imposed by the court. The decision meant that P had paid insurance premiums for a number of years on an invalid policy and had totally wasted his money. It is submitted that the decision was too advantageous to the defendants. (*Quaere:* should P have been able to recover his premiums if the contract was to be set aside?)

It is interesting that in *Magee*, a case which closely resembles the facts of *Bell v Lever Bros*, the contract was set aside — whereas in *Bell v Lever Bros* the company was unable to recover its money from its ex-employees. Attempts have been made to distinguish between these two closely analogous cases by arguing that in *Bell v Lever Bros* the money had already been paid to the men before discovery of the mistake, whilst in *Magee v Pennine Insurance Co* the money had not been paid at the time the mistake was discovered. This may suggest therefore that it was not inequitable to set the agreement aside in *Magee*, but that it might have been if the company had already paid out the £385 under the compromise agreement. However, there is nothing in the judgment to indicate that this was the basis of the decision.

In truth, it is difficult to find any material difference between the facts of these two cases. The difference in outcome reflects, perhaps, the extent of the development of an equitable approach to common mistake since the time of the *Bell v Lever Bros* decision. Because of the narrow view of mistake at common law, it has been necessary to allow a more flexible and discretionary approach to mistake in equity. It could be argued that this tends to negate the very purpose of the strict approach at common law: the need to uphold apparent contracts in the interest of certainty. But, whatever the scope of an independent doctrine of common mistake at law (and this is still a matter for debate), there can be little objection to the exercise of equitable jurisdiction by a court in setting aside a contract on the ground of common mistake if this serves the interests of justice[18].

The extent of this power to set a contract aside in equity is difficult to delineate. In Lord Denning's opinion, as expressed in *Solle v Butcher* [1950] 1 KB 671 at p 693:

"A contract is . . . liable to be set aside if the parties were under a common misapprehension either as to facts or as to their relative and respective rights, provided that the misapprehension was fundamental and that the party seeking to set it aside was not himself at fault."

This is probably too restrictive a view of the equitable approach for two reasons. First, in *Grist v Bailey* the mistake was probably not "fundamental", but it was certainly material. This should suffice if justice requires the granting of equitable relief[19]. Secondly, "fault" is difficult to define in this context and therefore this limitation is unhelpful. Where a party alleging mistake is the sole cause of the common misapprehension, it might be proper to refuse equitable relief (for example, see *The Lloydiana* [1983] 2 Lloyd's Rep 313). But in less obvious circumstances, the notion of "fault" may not be determinative of the issue. In *Grist* v *Bailey* it could be argued that the vendor could have established the status of the tenant before reaching agreement to sell her house; and in *Magee* v *Pennine Insurance Co* the defendants could have checked the validity of the policy before reaching a compromise agreement with the plaintiff. It appears that the cases cannot be explained simply on the basis of the conduct of the parties and their respective degrees of fault.

5. Documents signed by mistake

Generally the law takes a strict view of signed documents. In the absence of fraud or misrepresentation, a person who signs a document is bound by this, regardless of whether he has read or understood what he is signing (see *L'Estrange* v *Graucob* [1934] 2 KB 394). This is a further illustration of the law's objective approach to agreement[20]. The signer of a document will, of course, be able to rescind a contract induced by the fraud of the other contracting party. But this will be of no avail if a *bona fide* third party has acquired rights under the contract, for value, before it is avoided. (The document in question may also bring the signer into a contractual relationship with someone other than the fraudulent person.) The only defence which is then of any assistance to the signer is to claim that the contract is void altogether and not merely voidable for fraud. This involves relying on the argument that his mind did not accompany the signing of the document and pleading *non est factum* ("it is not my deed").

This particular defence, as its name suggests, originated to protect a person who executed a deed after it had been incorrectly read over to him. It was a necessary development in an age when many people could not read. For example, in *Thoroughgood's Case* (1582) 2 Co Rep 9a:

> Thoroughgood (P), who could not read, was owed rent by a tenant. The tenant drew up a deed which was incorrectly read over to P by someone posing as a helpful bystander. Instead of merely releasing the tenant from his arrears of rent as he supposed, P in fact signed away his rights to the property. The tenant sold the land to an innocent purchaser; P sued in trespass for recovery of his land.

Thoroughgood succeeded in his action. He was not bound by his deed because it was misrepresented to him and he could not read it. In the context of its time, this was a fair and sensible exception to the general rule that deeds were regarded as absolutely binding. But, later, the defence of *non est factum* was extended to cover written documents not under seal, and to cases where the signer was not illiterate (see *Foster* v *Mackinnon* (1869) LR 4 CP 704 at p 711). These developments were much more contentious, even though the defence did not cover a person who was simply negligent.

As the basis for the defence of *non est factum* is a lack of intent on the part of the signer, the result of a successful plea is that the contract is a complete nullity (ie void). In the interest of commercial certainty, and in view of the fact that most people today are able to read, the use of this plea should be strictly limited. Otherwise it can cause injustice to third parties. This restrictive approach was supported by the House of Lords in *Saunders* v *Anglia Building Society* (sometimes referred to as *Gallie* v *Lee*) [1971] AC 1004, which is the leading case on the scope of *non est factum* today. The facts were:

> Mrs Gallie (P) was a widow, aged seventy-eight, who gave the deeds of her house to her nephew so that he (together with a business associate named Lee) could raise money by using the house as security. She stipulated that she should continue to live in the house until she died. Lee and her nephew asked P to sign a document which she was unable to read as she had broken her glasses. Lee told her, dishonestly, that it was a deed of gift to her nephew. In fact, it was a document (drawn up by a dishonest clerk) which transferred the house by sale to Lee for the price of £3,000. Lee failed to pay P any of the money; instead, he mortgaged the house to a building society for his own benefit, and nothing was paid by him to the nephew. Lee defaulted on the mortgage instalments and the building society claimed possession of the house. P sued Lee and the building society, seeking a declaration that the document that she signed was void on the ground of *non est factum*. Her claim was that she had not intended to sell the house to Lee, but rather she had intended to make a gift to her nephew.

The case is a good illustration of how a third party's rights may become involved where someone has mistakenly signed a document. The House of Lords (affirming the Court of Appeal's decision) held that the defence of *non est factum* could not be relied on by P in these circumstances. This was because, in the opinion of the judges, the document that she signed was not radically or totally different in character from the one that she thought she was signing. She intended that her nephew should be able to raise money by using the house as security, and it can be argued that this would have still been achieved under the document that she actually signed, but for Lee's dishonesty[21]. So this is the first limitation on the use of *non est factum* as a means of nullifying an apparent agreement.

The second limitation, and a further reason for P's claim being rejected, is that a party cannot rely on the defence where he or she has acted carelessly. The plea originated, as we have seen, to protect those who could not read, at a time when illiteracy was widespread. Despite the subsequent development of the doctrine to cover a wider group of people, it is surely correct that someone who has been careless should not be able to rely on it as a means of escape from a document that they have signed. Otherwise it would be difficult for anyone to have confidence in the validity of a signature on a document and this would be extremely inconvenient in commercial matters. A person who has broken his glasses can usually delay signing a document until they have been repaired. Mrs Gallie was, regrettably, careless and the decision was therefore correct.

This point is also illustrated in *United Dominions Trust Ltd* v *Western* [1976] 1 QB 513, where D agreed to buy a car from dealers on hire purchase. In addition to the payment of a deposit, D signed a blank copy of a finance company's (P's) standard form agreement and left the dealers to fill in the relevant details. When the form was forwarded by the dealers to the finance company it contained inaccuracies about the price of the vehicle and the size of deposit paid by D. The plaintiff company accepted the figures as correct and that the signed document formed a contract between themselves and D. D later found out that the figures did not represent what he agreed with the dealers but he took no action to remedy the mistake. He paid no instalments under the agreement and the plaintiffs claimed £750, which was the incorrect price stated on the form signed by D. The Court of Appeal found in favour of the plaintiffs. It is clear that where a person signs a blank form and leaves someone else to fill in the details, he cannot argue that he failed to consent to the figures that are inserted. The signer of a blank document is careless, and no sensible distinction can be made between this situation and that where a person carelessly signs a completed document[22].

We have seen the ways in which the scope of the defence of *non est factum* has been curtailed by decisions of the courts[23]. But, assuming that the signer has not been careless[24] (presumably to be judged by the standards of that person), and that the document signed was radically different from that which it was supposed to be, what types of people can rely on the plea? Those who have signed as a result of some deception will be able to; so too will those who are unable to understand the meaning of a document through no fault of their own, without having it explained to them, "whether that be from defective education, illness or innate incapacity" (*per* Lord Reid in *Saunders* v *Anglia Building Society* [1971] AC 1004 at p 1016).

The defence was successfully relied on in the case of *Lloyds Bank plc* v *Waterhouse* ([1990] The Independent 27 February). This involved an illiterate defendant who signed a bank guarantee of his son's debt without either reading the document or indicating that he was unable to read it. However, he had done his best, by asking questions, to ascertain the nature and extent of his liability, and the bank's employees had misrepresented the nature of the document to him. The Court of Appeal allowed the defendant's appeal; various reasons were given to support this decision, including the negligent misrepresentation of the bank. Woolf LJ did not deem it necessary to decide the issue of *non est factum*, but Purchas LJ had no doubts that the defence was successfully established by the defendant. He explained that the defendant's illiteracy was clearly a disability; that the signed document was different from that which he thought he was signing; and that the defendant was not careless, having "energetically investigated the ambit of the guarantee from the outset".

It might be safer though, to regard the case as decided on the basis of negligent misrepresentation, rather than *non est factum*. It is surely questionable whether the defendant exercised proper care for his own protection. It might also be questioned whether the document actually signed by the defendant was radically or fundamentally different in character from the one that he thought he was signing.

Footnotes

(1) For example, see CJ Slade, *Myth of Mistake in the English Law of Contract*, 70 LQR 385; and P Atiyah, *Introduction to the Law of Contract*, 5th ed, ch 12.
(2) For a detailed discussion of intention in the law of contract, see A De Moor (1990) 106 LQR 632.
(3) Consider *Hardman* v *Booth* (1863) 1 H & C 803, which Pearce LJ, in *Ingram* v *Little*, accepted was a clearer case of there being no contract than *Ingram* v *Little* itself.
(4) See 12th Report, *Transfer of Title to Chattels*, Cmnd 2958, 1966.
(5) He was best known for his starring role in the television series "Robin Hood".
(6) But see De Moor, note (2) above, for a more detailed examination of the issue.

(7)   It does not, however, extend to relieving a party from a contract simply because he or she made a bad bargain. So a mistake as to the commercial consequences of an agreement, as opposed to its subject matter or terms, will not be sufficient: see *Clarion Ltd and others* v *National Provident Institution* [2000] 2 All ER 265.

(8)   For an interesting modern example of this, see *Patel* v *Ali* [1984] Ch 283.

(9)   The damages awarded would include compensation for the money spent in reliance on the defendants' promise; that is, in equipping a salvage expedition.

(10) Had the contract been severable — that is, an agreement for a number of separate lots which were to be paid for separately — then presumably the decision would have been different. The buyer would have been liable for the price of the remaining bags of nuts.

(11) A discussion of the meaning of "perish" under the Sale of Goods Act is beyond the scope of this book. Briefly, it may be noted that some minor deterioration of goods will not amount to "perishing". However, goods may perish in a commercial sense, even though they physically still exist, when there is sufficient deterioration: see *Asfar* v *Blundell* [1896] 1 QB 123.

(12) See Atiyah, *Introduction to the Law of Contract*, 5th ed, p 222.

(13) Alternatively, in Lord Thankerton's words (at p 235), the mistake must "relate to something which both must necessarily have accepted in their minds as an essential and integral element of the subject matter".

(14) In a USA case, *Sherwood* v *Walker* (1887) 33 NW 919, a contract for the sale of a cow believed by both parties to be barren, was held to be void when it was discovered to be with calf and worth considerably more than the price agreed by the parties.

(15) For an interesting discussion of Steyn J's approach, see J C Smith, *Contracts — Mistake, Frustration and Implied Terms* (1994) 110 LQR 400.

(16) See *Sheikh Bros* v *Ochsner* [1957] AC 136 where a contract was held void after first deciding that neither party assumed the risk that the contract would be impossible to perform.

(17) For a more recent example, see *AL and S Nutt* v *PE and Y Read*, TLR, 3 December 1999.

(18) It should be noted, however, that just as a claim for rescission for misrepresentation may be lost (eg for lapse of time), a claim to have the contract set aside for mistake may be defeated for the same reasons.

(19) For a recent attempt to explain what is meant by a "fundamental" mistake, both at common law and in equity, see *William Sindall Plc* v *Cambridgeshire County Council* [1994] 1 WLR 1016.

(20) For a critical view, see JR Spencer [1973] CLJ 104.

(21) Although this argument appears to overlook the fact that Mrs Gallie stipulated that she was to remain in occupation of the house during her lifetime.

(22) Also note that the plea of *non est factum* is not open to a person who signs a document in the belief that it is "just a form", having no precise idea as to its nature; see *Gillman* v *Gillman* (1946) 174 LT 272.

(23) The restrictive approach of the courts is further illustrated by the case of *Norwich and Peterborough Building Society* v *Steed (No 2)* [1993] 1 All ER 330.

(24) For a recent discussion, see *AL Factors Ltd* v *Pamela Morgan*, LTL, 5 July 1999.

Chapter 13

Misrepresentation

1. Introduction

An operative misrepresentation (ie one which has legal effect) is basically a false statement of existing or past fact made by one party to the contract to the other, before, or at the time of, contracting, on which that other party relied in contracting. (Whether there is also a requirement that the misrepresentation should be material is considered below (see page 287).)

The person to whom a misrepresentation, or alleged misrepresentation, is made is referred to as the representee. The person making the misrepresentation, or alleged misrepresentation, is the representor.

Much discussion may occur before a contract is made. In the course of that discussion one party may make a statement to the other which subsequently proves to be untrue. The other party will feel aggrieved if he, or she, relied upon that statement in entering into the contract. What can be done? If that statement became a term of the contract, or of a collateral contract, then there is a breach of contract and the injured party can take action accordingly (see Chapter 21). If it did not become a term, there is no possibility of a remedy for breach. However, a remedy may lie for misrepresentation and this means that, when a dispute arises over a pre-contractual statement which has proved to be false, the injured party will often raise two arguments:

   (i) that the statement became a term; and
   (ii) that the statement was an operative misrepresentation.

Misrepresentation is divided into different types; the classification is particularly important when the representee wishes to claim damages for the misrepresentation. Until the 1960s the classification was only twofold. Misrepresentations were either fraudulent or innocent (ie not fraudulent). There was no reason to separate negligent from wholly innocent misrepresentations because damages were available only for fraudulent misrepresentations (through the tort of deceit), and rescission was available for all misrepresentations. Because of the availability of damages we now differentiate four types of misrepresentation:

   (i) fraudulent misrepresentation — damages available under the tort of deceit;

  (ii) a misrepresentation which is also a negligent misstatement, so that the damages are available for the tort of negligent misstatement;

 (iii) a misrepresentation for which damages are available under s 2(1) Misrepresentation Act 1967 (ie the misrepresentor cannot prove that he, or she, believed the truth of what was misrepresented, and that there were reasonable grounds for doing so, up until the time the contract was made);

 (iv) innocent misrepresentation, ie misrepresentations not falling within the above categories. No damages are available for innocent misrepresentation, as such, but s 2(2) allows the court to award damages in lieu of rescission where the misrepresentation is non-fraudulent.

The second and third categories are often both referred to as negligent misrepresentations. Obviously, within the third category the label is inapposite to the extent that it is not tortious negligence which is in question and it is for the misrepresentor to establish his belief and its reasonableness. Nevertheless, as the action under s 2(1) is based upon the absence of reasonable belief — despite the fact that the absence of reasonable grounds for belief is not proven but merely not disproved — negligent misrepresentation is a more apt label than innocent misrepresentation for the third category (but see *Royscott Trust Ltd* v *Rogerson* [1991] 3 All ER 294 *per* Balcombe LJ).

However, even when the common law was providing damages only for fraudulent misrepresentation, equity allowed rescission for all misrepresentations. If rescission occurs, the parties return to their pre-contractual positions. Rescission is the carrying into effect of the decision to treat a voidable contract as if it had never been made. It is a radical remedy and there are bars on its availability.

The topic of misrepresentation is difficult because of the involvement of the common law, equity and statute (the Misrepresentation Act 1967). It is additionally complicated by the need frequently to refer to the law of tort, although it is the contractual aspects which are concentrated on here.

2.   What constitutes an operative misrepresentation?

As was stated above, an operative misrepresentation is, basically, a false statement of existing or past fact made by one party to the contract to the other, before, or at the time of, contracting, which induces the other party to contract. (Whether the misrepresentation must also be material is considered below (see page 287).)

As we shall see, the term "statement" can be misleading because, although there is no general duty to disclose relevant facts in pre-contract negotiations, there are some circumstances in which a misrepresentation is found to have occurred because of something which the representor has omitted to say or write. In addition it is possible to base a misrepresentation on physical appearance rather than on an oral or written statement.

There are two basic points to be considered when asking what constitutes an operative misrepresentation: (i) which "statements" are capable of being misrepresentations, and (ii) under what circumstances is the appropriate sort of "statement" operative, ie under what circumstances does it have legal effect as a misrepresentation? In simple terms, the first of these requirements is for a false statement of existing or past fact. For that statement then to constitute an operative misrepresentation it must have been relied upon by the person to whom it was made in contracting with the person who made it. (It will be considered below whether in addition, it must relate to a matter which would have influenced a reasonable person in making the decision to contract (at p 287).)

(a) The misrepresentation

In order for there to be a misrepresentation there must be a false statement of existing or past fact. Statements of opinion, intention or law will not suffice, in themselves, but they must be given careful consideration. A statement of fact may often be found where initially there appears to be only a statement of opinion, intention or law.

Statements of intention

A statement of intention cannot, in itself, constitute a misrepresentation. A statement of fact is required. However, a statement of intention carries with it an implied statement of fact as to the state of mind of the representor. If someone falsely states their intention, then they have falsely misrepresented the fact that they hold that intention. In *Edgington* v *Fitzmaurice* (1885) 29 Ch D 459 Bowen LJ said (at p 483):

> "The state of a man's mind is as much a fact as the state of his digestion. It is true that it is very difficult to prove what the state of a man's mind at a particular time is, but if it can be ascertained it is as much a fact as anything else. A misrepresentation as to the state of a man's mind is, therefore, a misstatement of fact."

This is illustrated by the facts of *Edgington*:

> The directors of a company issued a prospectus inviting subscriptions for debentures, ie they were seeking to raise money. The prospectus stated that it was intended to use the money obtained to make improvements in the company by altering its buildings, purchasing horses and vans, and developing the trade of the company. The real intention was to use the money obtained to pay off existing debts of the company.

It was held that a fact had been misrepresented because there was no intention to use the money in the manner stated.

Statements of opinion

In *Bisset* v *Wilkinson* [1927] AC 177 it was held that there was no misrepresentation. The statement made was only a statement of opinion and not fact. In that case:

> Mr Bisset wished to sell a piece of land in New Zealand. He told Mr Wilkinson that the land would support 2,000 sheep. No one had previously used the parcel of land in question as a sheep farm. Mr Wilkinson purchased the land. It failed to support 2,000 sheep.

The Privy Council held that the statement as to the capacity of the land did not constitute a misrepresentation. As that parcel of land had not previously been used for sheep farming, it was purely a statement of opinion and not one of fact.

Where an opinion is stated which is not held, however, the same reasoning applies as that used in *Edgington* v *Fitzmaurice*. A misrepresentation of the representor's state of mind would have occurred (*Bisset* at p 182). In such a situation, where there is a straightfoward lie as to the opinion held by the representor, it is obvious where the misstated fact can be found but, even in the absence of such fraud, the line between opinion and fact is not as distinct as might at first be thought. The opinions of experts, or those in the best position to have ascertained the truth of the matter, create obvious difficulties when it is sought to distinguish opinion and fact. An opinion given by such a person is likely to be treated as a statement of fact and, often quite reasonably, relied upon. In such circumstances the courts have endeavoured to find that statements of fact have been made.

A misrepresentation was found in *Smith* v *Land and House Property Corporation* (1884) 28 Ch D 7. The facts were as follows:

> The plaintiff put a hotel up for sale. The particulars stated that it was "let to Mr F. Fleck (a most desirable tenant), at a rental of £400 per annum, for an unexpired term of twenty-seven and a half years". Mr Fleck was not a desirable tenant; he had not been paying his rent on time, and it was in arrears.

The court held that the statement as to Mr Fleck's suitability as a tenant was not merely a statement of opinion. The landlord was in a much better position than anyone else to know what sort of a tenant there was on the property. There was an implied misrepresentation. Bowen LJ said (at p 15):

> "if the facts are not equally known to both sides, then a statement of opinion by the one who knows the facts best involves very often a statement of a material fact, for he impliedly states that he knows facts which justify his opinion."

The misrepresentation provided an answer to the plaintiff's claim for specific performance of the sale contract and the defendants were able to rescind. (See also *Credit Lyonnais Bank Nederland* v *Export Credits Guarantee Dept* [1996] CLC 11. But see *Economides* v *Commercial Union Assurance Co plc* [1997] 3 All ER 636, cf Bennett (1998) 61 MLR 886.)

Whether there were facts making Mr Fleck an undesirable tenant is a matter of opinion. In *Brown* v *Raphael* [1958] 1 Ch 636 it was made clear that, in this type of case, the fact which is being misrepresented is that the representor had reasonable grounds for his opinion or belief. Such a representation, that an opinion is based on reasonable grounds, will be found to have been made where the person stating his, or her, opinion is in a better position than the other party to know, or to find out, the truth. *Brown* v *Raphael* concerned the sale of a reversion. Its value depended upon the tax position of the person with the life interest. The buyer could not ascertain this and had to depend upon the statement of the seller indicating that the tax position was favourable. The question was whether this was a misrepresentation or merely a statement of opinion. It was held that it was a misrepresentation. One party knew the facts far better than the other could know them. The opinion on the tax position carried with it the implied statement of fact that the seller had reasonable grounds for that belief. There was a misrepresentation as the seller had no such grounds.

The above argument should also apply in cases where the facts are accessible to either party but one party is an expert and he, or she, states an opinion on a matter within that area of expertise. The expert will impliedly state that he, or she, has reasonable grounds for that opinion. If the expert has not considered the question at all, or been negligent in coming to a conclusion, then it should be possible to find a misrepresentation. In *Esso Petroleum Co Ltd* v *Mardon* [1976] QB 801, an expert's assessment of the potential sales by a new petrol station was made negligently, without due consideration of all the facts. It was decided that there was a breach of an implied term that the expert would take due care in his assessment and also that there was a claim in tort for negligent misstatement. The point to note here is the court's obvious willingness to find a statement of fact in the statement of opinion by an expert, although the case was not decided on the basis of misrepresentation.

There is no difficulty in following the construction of the argument that a fact has been misstated in the above type of case, where there has apparently been only a statement of opinion. It is nevertheless somewhat artificial, and the impetus behind the court's acceptance of the argument is worth considering. It may well be that the court's willingness to find statements of fact in such circumstances is based upon the reasonableness of the representee's reliance upon the stated opinion (see *Chitty on Contracts* 28th ed (1999) vol 1, para 6–010). In *Bisset* v *Wilkinson* [1927] AC 177, in deciding that there was merely a statement of opinion and no misrepresentation, the court emphasised that it was known to both sides that the particular parcel of land had not been used as a sheep farm before. Neither side was in a better position than the other to judge the capacity of the land, and the purchaser knew that there was no reason to place particular reliance upon the vendor's opinion of that capacity (but see *Avon Ins* v *Swire Fraser* [2000] 1 All ER (Comm) 573 at p 581).

Statements of law

A statement of law cannot constitute a misrepresentation but this is limited in its effect. A statement of law will often be a statement of opinion and may then carry with it a statement of fact in the manner indicated above. There are also statements which appear to be statements of law but which are not classified as such. A statement of foreign law is treated as a statement of fact (*André et Cie SA* v *Ets Michel Blanc & Fils* [1977] 2 Lloyd's Rep 166) as is a statement of private rights, as distinct from the general law (*Cooper* v *Phibbs* (1867) LR 2 HL 149).

No general duty to disclose

The law does not impose any general duty on a contracting party to disclose relevant facts to the other party and, in general, silence does not constitute a misrepresentation. In most cases the law allows a party to profit from his superior knowledge. It is possible to view this as economically efficient for otherwise the incentive to acquire information would be removed (Kronman, *Mistake, Disclosure, Information and the Law of Contracts* (1978) 7 JLS 1). It is also the case that the lack of a general duty to disclose prevents the problems, and uncertainties, which would arise in determining what information should fall within the duty. However, there are exceptions to the general rule, which are considered below.

Turner v Green [1895] 2 Ch 205 provides an example of the operation of the general rule. In that case:

> Turner and Green were engaged in a legal dispute. Turner's solicitor, Fowler, reached a settlement with Green on behalf of his client. Before concluding that agreement, Fowler did not reveal to Green that other proceedings had taken place which made the settlement disadvantageous to Green.

When Turner claimed specific enforcement of the agreement, Green tried to rely upon the non-disclosure to resist the claim. The court held that mere non-disclosure of a material fact could not provide a basis for rescission or a denial of specific performance. It did not constitute a misrepresentation (see also *Keates v Cadogan* (1851) 10 CB 591; *Fletcher v Krell* (1872) 42 LJQB 55).

Partial non-disclosure

The situation is different if there is not complete silence on a particular matter which is being dealt with, but partial disclosure. This occurs where what has been stated is literally true but misleading because of other facts which have been omitted. In *Notts Patent Brick and Tile Co v Butler* (1886) 16 QBD 778:

> Butler wished to sell a piece of land which was subject to several restrictive covenants one of which precluded its use as a brickyard. The plaintiff company, which manufactured bricks, wished to purchase the land to use in its business. The company inquired of Butler's solicitor whether the land was subject to any restrictive covenants. The solicitor stated that he was not aware of any but did not add that he had not inspected the relevant documents. The company contracted to purchase the land and paid a deposit.

The solicitor's reply had been literally true but was misleading because he did not add that he had not inspected the relevant documents. There had been a misrepresentation which entitled the purchaser to rescind the contract and recover the deposit. The same line was taken in *Dimmock v Hallett* (1866) 2 Ch App 21 where an estate was for sale. One of the farms on it was described as let to a certain tenant at £290 per year. It was not stated that the tenant had paid only £1 for the three months he leased the farm before his year's occupation, nor was it stated that he had left the farm and no new tenant had been found for it, even at a lower rent. What had been said was literally true but, without the additional details, it constituted a misrepresentation. (See also *Atlantic Lines & Navigation Co Inc v Hallam Ltd; (The Lucy)* [1983] 1 Lloyd's Rep 188 (see page 286).)

Change of circumstances

A statement of fact may be made which is true at the time it is made, but which has ceased to be true before the contract, which it has induced, is concluded. Under these circumstances, if the person making the representation knows of the change in the facts, there will be a misrepresentation if he fails to disclose it. In *With v O'Flanagan* [1936] Ch 575:

O'Flanagan wished to sell his medical practice. In January he told With that the practice brought in about £2,000 a year. The contract for the sale of the practice was made in May. In the intervening months O'Flanagan was unwell and the practice became practically worthless. In the three weeks before the sale the takings of the practice averaged only £5 a week.

The change in the facts should have been revealed and failure to do so meant that the contract could be rescinded (see also *Davies* v *London and Provincial Marine Insurance Co* (1878) 8 Ch D 469; *Reynell* v *Sprye* (1852) 1 De GM & G 660 at p 708; *Shelley* v *United Artists Corporation* [1990] 16 EG 73. But see *Thomas Witter Ltd* v *TBP Industries Ltd* [1996] 2 All ER 573). Two possible ways in which the misrepresentation could be occurring were identified. First, the misrepresentation could be the silence itself on the basis that the initial statement had given rise to a duty to disclose the changes. Secondly, the misrepresentation could merely lie in the initial statement which is then seen as a continuing representation which becomes a misrepresentation with the change in the facts (*With* at pp 583–4, *per* Lord Wright MR). Whether there is a statement which can be regarded as a continuing representation and eventually a misrepresentation, or whether it is the silence itself which forms the basis of the right to rescind, is relevant to the question of whether or not the Misrepresentation Act 1967 can apply to the above situation. That Act applies where a misrepresentation is *made* and this is inapt to cover the situation where it is silence as such which is being dealt with (*Banque Financière de la Cité SA* v *Westgate Insurance Co* [1989] 2 All ER 952 (CA), [1990] 2 All ER 947 (HL)). The continuing representations approach is indicated in *Spice Girls* v *Aprilia*, 24 February 2000, Smith-Bernal transcript, *The Times*, 5 April 2000.

The situation becomes more difficult where a statement of intention has been made and that intention has changed before the contract is concluded. In *Traill* v *Baring* (1864) 4 DJ & S 318:

An insurer wished to lessen his risk on a very large policy by contracting with other insurers for them to take part of the risk. The first insurer told the prospective second insurer that he intended to keep part of the risk. The second insurer contracted for part of the risk but by the time that this contract was made the first insurer's intention had changed. The rest of the risk was contracted out to other insurers. This change of intention was not communicated to the second insurer before the contract was made.

There was a misrepresentation because of the failure to communicate the change in intention. Turner LJ said:

"if a person makes a representation by which he induces another to take a particular course, and the circumstances are afterwards altered to the knowledge of the party making the representation . . . and are so altered that the alteration of circumstances may affect the course of conduct which may be pursued by the party to whom the representation is made, it is the imperative duty of the party who has made the representation to communicate . . . the alteration of those circumstances."

However, this case must be treated with some care. There is nothing to indicate that the court thought that the view it was taking was not of general application, but two points should be noted before the case is accepted as indicating that the approach in *With* v *O'Flanagan* [1936] Ch 575 applies to a change of intention. First, the court did not make any reference to the statement being one of intention rather than fact. Secondly, although the court gave no indication that it was dealing with a special type of contract, the case was concerned with a contract of insurance. Contracts of insurance are contracts *uberrimae fidei* and, in relation to such contracts, the mere non-disclosure of material facts itself gives rise to the right to rescind (see below). As a case of general authority, *Traill* v *Baring* should be treated with circumspection. A changed intention led to a different approach in *Wales* v *Wadham* [1977] 1 WLR 199 (Phillips 40 MLR 599). In that case:

> Mr and Mrs Wales' marriage had broken down. In contemplation of divorce Mr Wales offered his wife £13,000 from his share of the sale of the matrimonial home. The payment was intended as a substitute for periodic maintenance payments. Periodic payments to an ex-wife cease upon her remarriage. It would not have been beneficial to Mr Wales to make a lump sum payment instead of periodic payments if Mrs Wales was likely to remarry soon after the divorce. Mr Wales' offer of £13,000 was made on the basis that she had stated that it was not her intention to remarry. However, after that statement was made, but before the agreement was signed, she decided to marry Mr Wadham. She did not reveal this to Mr Wales as she did not want Mr Wadham to become involved in the divorce.

The Court of Appeal held that the agreement could not be rescinded on the basis of this non-disclosure. A change of intention was distinguished from a change in the facts.

However, it was noted above that a statement of intention carries with it a statement of fact as to the state of mind of the person making the statement. The facts, in the form of Mrs Wales' state of mind, had changed before the contract was made. When analysed in this way the situation appears to be directly analogous to that in *With* v *O'Flanagan*, and the different result in *Wales* v *Wadham* can be questioned[1]. (But see *Avon Ins* v *Swire Fraser* [2000] 1 All ER (Comm) 573 at 578–581.)

Fiduciary or confidential relationships

Where there is a fiduciary relationship, such as where the parties are principal and agent (*Armstrong* v *Jackson* [1917] 2 KB 822), there will be a duty to disclose material facts. However, more than mere disclosure will be required if the relationship is one giving rise to the presumption of undue influence, such as solicitor and client or trustee and beneficiary. Such transactions may well be set aside unless the "weaker party" has received independent advice (on undue influence see page 324).

Contracts uberrimae fidei

In relation to contracts *uberrimae fidei* (contracts of the utmost good faith) a duty to disclose material facts is imposed. In such contracts one party is usually in a far better position than the other to know or ascertain the relevant facts. Contracts of insurance form the main type of contracts *uberrimae fidei*. Contracts relating to family settlements are also contracts *uberrimae fidei* (eg *Gordon* v *Gordon* (1821) 3 Swan 400).

Other contracts are related to contracts *uberrimae fidei* and require more limited disclosure, eg a surety contract. Statute now contains a requirement of disclosure in relation to company prospectuses and provides a remedy in damages where this has not occurred[2].

Misrepresentation by conduct — implied misrepresentation

A misrepresentation may stem from conduct. There are examples from the criminal law, which supply analogies in the context of misrepresentation. In *R v Barnard* (1837) 7 C&P 784 the defendant wore the cap and gown of a university student to persuade an Oxford bootmaker to supply him with bootstraps. This form of dress was held to amount to a false pretence. A more up to date example is provided by the idea that in merely sitting down in a restaurant and ordering a meal there is an implied representation that the person concerned has the funds to pay for the meal (*Ray* v *Sempers* [1974] AC 370). In *R* v *Charles* [1977] AC 177 it was held that the use of a cheque card carries with it a representation that the user has the bank's authority to use the card. In the context of misrepresentation itself, there was a misrepresentation by conduct, an implied misrepresentation, by the Spice Girls (as Spice Girls Ltd) in the making of a contract with Aprilia for the promotion of Aprilia's new scooters — to be known as 'Spice Sonic Scooters'. On 4 May 1998, the original five Spice Girls, including Geri Halliwell, participated in a commercial advertising shoot, and two days later contracted with Aprilia in relation to the use of that material and other promotion of Aprilia's scooters for a period up to March 1999. The band had known on 25 April 1998 that Geri Halliwell intended to leave in September 1998 at the end of a US tour. Arden J concluded that, 'Given that the benefits of the commercial shoot could not be enjoyed by Aprilia if one of the Spice Girls left the group before March 1999, participation in the shoot ... carried with it a representation by conduct that SGL did not know, and had no reasonable ground to believe, that any of the Spice Girls had an existing declared intention to leave the group before that date' (*Spice Girls Ltd* v *Aprilia World Service BV*, 24 February 2000, Smith-Bernal transcript, *The Times*, 5 April 2000). The factors indicative of an implied misrepresentation were considered more broadly in *Geest plc* v *Fyffes plc* [1999] 1 All ER (Comm) 672 in the context of a contract under which a guarantee or indemnity was provided by a "surety" to a "beneficiary". It was said that in considering whether there was an implied misrepresentation "a helpful test is whether, having regard to the beneficiary's conduct in such circumstances, a reasonable potential surety would naturally assume that the true state of facts did not exist and that, had it existed, he would in all the circumstances have been informed of it" (at p 683). Although the court's comments were put in the context of a contract of indemnity or guarantee, it was clear that they were intended to apply to contracts more generally. In the instant case, no implied misrepresentation was found. The situation was one in which the commercial practice was for the negotiations to proceed within an elaborate regime of disclosure by the beneficiary in response to specific requests for information by the surety so that the surety was not entitled to make assumptions about an issue on which information had not been requested.

(b) When is a misrepresentation operative?

The parties to the contract

The person making the misrepresentation must become a party to the contract with the person to whom it was made (eg *Hasan* v *Wilson* [1977] 1 Lloyd's

Rep 431 at p 431) although agency can of course be as relevant here as elsewhere.

Reliance

In order for a misrepresentation to be operative, it must have been relied upon. It must have induced the contract. No remedy lay for a misrepresentation, in *Smith* v *Chadwick* (1884) 9 App Cas 187, which had played no part in the plaintiff's decision to contract. There the prospectus of a company had contained the false statement that a certain person of local importance, a Mr Grieve, was one of the directors. The plaintiff purchased shares in the company on the faith of the prospectus but he had never heard of Grieve and he admitted that Grieve's name in the prospectus had not influenced him. The misrepresentation that Grieve was a director could not provide a basis for a claim in damages for fraud as it had not been relied upon.

The requirement of reliance means that there are certain situations where there cannot be an operative misrepresentation. For example, there cannot be an operative misrepresentation where the misrepresentation is not known about or the truth is known. Similarly, there will not be an operative misrepresentation where the representee decides not to rely upon the representor's statement but upon his own investigation of the facts.

Horsfall v *Thomas* (1862) 1 H & C 90 provides an example of a case where the misrepresentation was not known to the person whom it was meant to mislead. That case concerned the sale of a defective gun. The defect, a soft spot in the metal, was concealed by a metal plug but this did not constitute an operative misrepresentation. The gun had not been examined by the buyer and the metal plug could not have affected his judgement. Bramwell LJ said (at p 99):

> "If the plug, which it was said was put in to conceal the defect, had never been there, his position would have been the same; for as he did not examine the gun or form any opinion as to whether it was sound, its condition did not affect him."

(See also *Re Northumberland and Durham District Banking Co, ex parte Bigge* (1859) 28 LJ Ch 50.)

The situation may be that the misrepresentation is not operative because, although it was known to the representee, it was not relied upon because the representee chose to rely upon his own investigation of the facts stated. In *Attwood* v *Small* (1838) 6 Cl & Fin 232:

> Attwood was selling a mine. He made exaggerated and untrue statements as to its earning capacity. Before agreeing to buy the mine, Small sent his own experts to assess the mine's capacity. They concurred in Attwood's assessment.

When the true situation was discovered the purchaser claimed to rescind for misrepresentation. The House of Lords held that the action for rescission failed. The purchaser had relied upon his own experts rather than the vendor.

A misrepresentation cannot be held to have induced a contract where the representee knew it to be untrue before the contract was made. However, the misrepresentation will still be effective, provided it was relied upon, if there was merely an opportunity to discover the truth and that opportunity was not taken. In *Redgrave* v *Hurd* (1881) 20 Ch D 1:

> Mr Redgrave, a Birmingham solicitor, wished to sell his practice. Mr Hurd wished to establish himself in practice as a solicitor and agreed to make the purchase. Before Mr Hurd agreed, Mr Redgrave told him that the practice brought in £300–£400 a year. Mr Hurd was given an opportunity to examine the accounts but did not do so. Had he done so they would have revealed that the business was worth only about £200 a year.

The misrepresentation meant that Mr Hurd could rescind. The mere opportunity to discover the truth did not prevent rescission, provided the representee had relied upon the misrepresentation. (See also page 296 in relation to a claim for reduction of damages on the basis of the representee's contributory negligence.)

Degree of reliance

Consideration now needs to be given to the degree of reliance required if a misrepresentation is to be operative. It would seem that a distinction may need to be drawn between fraudulent and non-fraudulent misrepresentations.

The first point to note is that it is clear that the misrepresentation need not have been the sole factor inducing the contract in order for it be operative. In *Edgington* v *Fitzmaurice* (1885) 29 Ch D 459:

> Rev. Edgington was induced to take debentures in a company. He made the decision partly because of a misrepresentation in the prospectus (see above p 277) and partly because of his own mistaken belief that the debenture holders would have a charge on the company's leasehold property. Rev. Edgington admitted that he would not have become a debenture holder in the absence of his mistaken belief.

Rev. Edgington was able to claim damages for deceit despite his mixed motives. It was not necessary to show that the misrepresentation was the sole cause of his contracting. But what is the level of reliance required in order for the misrepresentation to be operative? This problem was commented on by the privy council in *Barton* v *Armstrong* [1976] AC 104. In that case the Privy Council had to deal with a claim that a contract was voidable for duress and the counter argument that the contract was valid because it would have been made even if the threats had not been uttered. Nevertheless, the situation in relation to misrepresentation was considered. It was said (at pp 118–119):

> "Had Armstrong made a fraudulent misrepresentation to Barton for the purpose of inducing him to execute the deed ... the answer to the problem would have been clear. If it were established that Barton did not allow the representation to affect his judgment then he could not make it a ground for relief even though the representation was designed ... to affect his judgment. If on the other hand Barton relied on the misrepresentation Armstrong could not have defeated his claim to relief by showing that there were other more weighty causes which contributed to his decision to execute the deed ... Their Lordships think that the same rule should apply in cases of duress and that if Armstrong's threats were a reason for Barton's executing the deed he is entitled to relief even though he might well have entered into the contract if Armstrong had uttered no threats to induce him to do so."

The Privy Council clearly envisaged that a misrepresentation could still be operative even though the contract might have been concluded had it not been made ie they were not applying the "but for" test.

It may appear somewhat odd, at first, that a misrepresentation can be operative even where the contract might have been made without the presence of the misrepresentation and not to require the "but for" test ie that "but for" the misrepresentation the contract would not have been made on those terms. However, such an approach can be seen as reflecting the complexities of the decision making process and it becomes more explicable if that is viewed as a weighing process. On this basis, it could be contended that if the misrepresentation went into the scales on the side favouring the making of the contract then it can be taken to have been relied upon.

However, the context of the above approach must be considered. In *Barton* v *Armstrong* the Privy Council had to deal with a case of duress by threats of physical violence. It was a case in which they would have wanted to place as few restrictions as possible in the way of a successful claim of duress. Similarly when they made their analogy with misrepresentation, the court referred to "fraud" rather than using the more general term, "misrepresentation", and fraud is the type of misrepresentation where there is the most reason for the court to intervene. The "but for" test may have a significant role to play outside of the context of fraud (or duress to the person). Certainly, there is an indication that the "but for" test has been considered in the context of non-fraudulent misrepresentation as, for example, in *Atlantic Lines & Navigation Co Inc* v *Hallam Ltd (The "Lucy")* [1983] 1 Lloyd's Rep 188. In that case:

> Atlantic had chartered a ship, the "Lucy", and wished to sub-charter it. There were restrictions in the charter on the places that the "Lucy" could go. Atlantic showed Hallam a document which did not contain all the restrictions on the voyages the "Lucy" could make but Hallam thought that it was a complete list of such restrictions. Hallam made a sub-charter for the "Lucy".

Hallam sought to rescind their sub-charter of the "Lucy" on the basis that the restrictions on the ship's voyages, in the charter between Atlantic and its owners, were more extensive than they had been represented to be and there had been an innocent misrepresentation. Mustill J accepted that the disclosure of some restrictions but not of others could amount to a misrepresentation but denied that it was operative as there had been no reliance by Hallam. He found "that the question of trading outside limits had no material influence on Hallam's conduct of negotiations". However, he also stated that, even if Hallam felt any concern regarding that question, they had failed to satisfy him "that they would have declined to enter into the sub-charter at all, or would have done so only at a lower rate of hire" had they known the truth. At least in relation to innocent misrepresentation, Mustill J was treating the test of reliance as the question whether the contract would have been made in the absence of the misrepresentation ie applying the "but for" test.

However, even if the "but for" test is generally applicable outside of the context of fraudulent misrepresentation (or, in the context of duress, of duress to the person), the complexity of the decision-making process means that it cannot provide an absolute requirement even in that context. Its uniform application could involve the conclusion that a decision had no cause. That would be the case, for example, if a decision was based on a number of factors and it could not be said that the removal of any one single factor would have resulted in the decision not being reached. Something of this was recognised where no fraud was in question, but merely negligence, in *JEB Fasteners Ltd v Marks Bloom & Co (a firm)* [1983] 1 All ER 583. Donaldson LJ said (at p 588):

> "In real life decisions are made on the basis of a complex of assumptions of fact. Some of these may be fundamental to the validity of the decision. 'But for' that assumption, the decision would not be made. Others may be important factors in reaching the decision and collectively, but not individually, fundamental to its validity. Yet others may be subsidiary factors which support or encourage the taking of the decision. If these latter assumptions are falsified in the event, whether individually or collectively, this will be a cause for disappointment to the decision-taker, but will not affect the essential validity of his decision in the sense that if the truth had been known or suspected before the decision was taken, the same decision would still have been made."

More plainly, in the context of economic duress, it has been recognised that "there may ... be cases where a common sense relaxation, even of a but for requirement is necessary, for example in the event of an agreement induced by two concurrent causes ... so that it could not be said that, but for either, the agreement would not have been made" (*Huyton SA* v *Peter Cremer GmbH* [1999] CLC 230, Mance J at p 250). The "but for" test may be generally applicable at least outside of the context of fraud (or in the duress context, of duress to the person) but at least in some cases a more flexible approach must be recognised. In *Avon Ins* v *Swire Fraser* [2000] 1 All ER (Comm) 573, having referred to the *JEB Fasteners* case, Rix J took the view (at p 580) that he derived from the case:

> "the distinction between a factor which is observed or considered by the plaintiff, or even supports or encourages his decision, and a factor which is sufficiently important to be called a real and substantial part of what induced him to contract."

Materiality

General statements as to the requirements of a misrepresentation are often found to include materiality (eg *Pan Atlantic Ins Co Ltd* v *Pine Top Ins Co* [1994] 3 All ER 581) ie that the misrepresentation must have been one which would have induced the reasonable person to contract. Such a requirement is obviously necessary where silence as such can give rise to the right to rescind, for example, in relation to a contract *uberrimae fidei*, such as a contract of insurance. In that type of situation the question of materiality must be referred to in order to determine which facts must be disclosed (see s 20(2) of the The Marine Insurance Act 1906). However, whilst a requirement of materiality has been contended for outside those cases (Treitel *The Law of Contract* 10th ed pp 311–312) its existence has also been disputed, with materiality merely seen as of evidential value in raising a factual presumption as to the actual reliance by the representee (eg Goff & Jones *The Law of Restitution* 5th ed at p 272. See *obiter Museprime* v *Adhill* [1990] 2 EGLR 196). It is not disputed that there is no requirement of materiality where the misrepresentation was fraudulent. The fraudulent misrepresentor cannot rely upon a claim that his misrepresentation was not such as to have induced the reasonable person to contract (*Smith* v *Kay* (1859) 7 HLC 750). In addition, it is suggested that "at least where the representor knows or ought to know that the representee is likely to act on the misrepresentation, relief will not be denied because a reasonable man would not have been influenced by it" (*Chitty on Contracts* 28th ed para 6–040). The real area of dispute would seem to lie in relation to other negligent and purely innocent misrepresentations, with innocent misrepresentations raising the strongest case for a requirement of materiality before the misrepresentee will have a remedy. There may be some indication of a need for a requirement of materiality in the recent case of *Avon Ins* v *Swire Fraser* [2000] 1 All ER (Comm) 573 in the approach taken to the question of when a statement is untrue, introducing into that context the concept of inducement of the reasonable person. In that case the claim was based on s 2(1) of the Misrepresentation Act 1967 (so the representee did not have to establish negligence, but merely the existence of a misrepresentation, leaving it to the representor to disprove negligence — see p 293) and the court took the line that the inaccuracy of some incorrect representations is not sufficiently significant for them to be regarded as untrue and misrepresentations. Rix J said (at p 579):

> "a representation may be true without being entirely correct, provided that it is substantially correct and the difference between what is represented and what is actually correct would not have been likely to induce a reasonable person in the position of the claimants to enter into the contract".

3. Damages and types of misrepresentation

Rescission may be thought of as the primary remedy for misrepresentation. It is a very radical remedy and, unlike damages, it is available for all types of misrepresentation. Nevertheless, damages will be considered first. It is principally in the context of damages that it is necessary to distinguish the different types of misrepresentation, and it is convenient to classify misrepresentations when considering the issue of damages. The various types of misrepresentation are classified according to the state of mind of the misrepresentor.

It is of course possible to claim damages and to rescind the contract. For example, in *F & H Entertainments Ltd* v *Leisure Enterprises Ltd* (1970) 240 EG 445 the plaintiffs were able both to rescind and to recover damages under s 2(1) Misrepresentation Act 1967. However, the courts will always strive to prevent a "double recovery" and no damages should be available to cover a loss which has effectively been wiped out by rescission.

The types of misrepresentation which we must consider are:

(a) fraudulent misrepresentations (damages are available through the tort of deceit);
(b) misrepresentations which are also negligent misstatements (damages are available through the tort of negligent misstatement);
(c) misrepresentations coming within s 2(1) Misrepresentation Act 1967;
(d) wholly innocent misrepresentations, ie misrepresentations not coming within any of the above categories.

(a) Fraudulent misrepresentations

Fraud was defined by Lord Herschell in *Derry* v *Peek* (1889) 14 App Cas 337. He said (at p 374):

"fraud is proved when it is shown that a false misrepresentation has been made, (1) knowingly, or (2) without belief in its truth, or (3) recklessly, careless whether it be true or false."

The essence of fraud is a lack of belief in the truth of the statement made. Despite the reference to carelessness, there is no fraud if the misrepresentor believes his statement to be true. Negligence and fraud are clearly distinct. In *Derry* v *Peek*:

The directors of a company issued a prospectus stating that it had the right to operate trams driven by steam power. The respondent purchased shares in the company on the faith of that statement. The company had the right to operate horse-drawn trams only. The use of steam-powered trams was conditional upon the company obtaining the consent of the Board of Trade. That consent was not given and the company was wound up.

The respondent sued the directors for damages in deceit. The trial judge had found that the directors honestly believed that their statements were true and, on that basis, the House of Lords found that there was no fraud and the action failed.

The treatment of the representor's misunderstanding of his own representation emphasises that fraud is distinct from negligence and requires an absence of belief in the truth of the statement made. If the representor understood his representation in a different sense from the representee, the representor's belief in the truth of his representation, and his fraud, will be tested against his understanding of his representation. In *Akerhielm* v *De Mare* [1959] AC 789:

Mr De Mare bought shares in Dantile Ltd. He had done so after Baron Akerhielm had informed him that "about one third of the capital has already been subscribed in Denmark". In fact some of this one third had been issued fully paid to persons resident in Kenya for services rendered in Denmark in connection with the formation of the company. The company failed.

Mr De Mare claimed that Baron Akerhielm had been fraudulent in his representation that one third of the capital had been subscribed in Denmark. The Privy Council said that, although the representation had to be construed in such a way that it was false, there was no fraud. The judge at first instance, in the Supreme Court of Kenya, had found that Baron Akerhielm had understood his statement in a sense in which he believed it to be true and, on this basis, the Privy Council found that there was no fraud. Lord Jenkins said (at p 805):

"The question is not whether the defendant in any given case honestly believed the representation to be true in the sense assigned to it by the court on an objective consideration of its truth or falsity, but whether he honestly believed the representation to be true in the sense in which he understood it, albeit erroneously, when it was made."

(See also *Gross* v *Lewis Hillman* [1970] Ch 445 at p 459.)

The same approach should be taken in relation to the situation of partial non-disclosure considered above (see page 221). If what the representor says is literally true, but misleading because of what is omitted, whether this involves fraud should depend upon the way in which it is viewed by the person making the representation. Fraud should be found only if he believed it would, or intended it to, mislead and this is the approach adopted by the courts. In *Jewson & Sons Ltd* v *Arcos Ltd* (1933) 47 Lloyd's L Rep 93:

> In 1930 the market for Russian timber in the UK had become very difficult. Jewson, timber sellers, did not wish to buy it at one price only to discover that it was being sold to their competitors at a lower price, enabling them to undercut Jewson. From 14 May, Arcos were negotiating with Jewson to sell Russian timber to them. Arcos told Jewson of a scheme they had devised to encourage sales by reducing the uncertainty of the market. The scheme was based on a standard contract and a standard price which would be kept to until 1 January 1931. Details of the scheme were issued on 28 May. Jewson contracted on the basis of the standard contract. It subsequently became known that, on 23 May, whilst negotiating with Jewson, Arcos had contracted with Hillas, a competitor of Jewson, to sell timber to Hillas at a price lower than the standard price.

At first instance Jewson were awarded damages for fraudulent misrepresentation and the Court of Appeal upheld that decision. It was true that the standard terms and price were used from 28 May but, by not revealing the lower price sale to Hillas, Arcos had misled Jewson into thinking that they had not sold below that price since 14 May. Arcos were fraudulent because they had intended to mislead Jewson by merely showing them the standard contract and not revealing the sale to Hillas (see *R* v *Kylsant* [1932] 1 KB 442).

If the appropriate state of mind is present, the motive is not relevant to the question of fraud. It is irrelevant that there was no intention to cheat anyone or cause any loss by the untrue statement (*Polhill* v *Walter* (1832) 3 B & Ad 114). There is no requirement of "dishonesty" in the criminal law sense (*Standard Chartered Bank* v *Pakistan National Shipping Corp (No 2)* [2000] 1 All ER (Comm) 1, para 27).

Damages are available for a fraudulent misrepresentation by taking action in tort for deceit. Damages are measured according to tort principles, rather than contractual principles (*Doyle* v *Olby (Ironmongers) Ltd* [1969] 2 QB 158; *Smith Kline & French Laboratories Ltd* v *Long* [1989] 1 WLR 1 at p 6). In tort the aim is to give damages which will put the party back in the position he was in before the tort occurred (reliance loss). In the situation we are concerned with, tort damages will attempt to restore the representee to the position he would have been in had the misrepresentation not been made. They are not awarded to put him in the position he would have been in had the misrepresentation been true; that would be like awarding the contractual measure of damages. If we were dealing with an action for breach of contract, the aim of damages would be to put the injured party in the position he would have been in had the contract been fulfilled, ie contract damages can cover the injured party's expectation loss, the benefit he would have derived from completion of the contract (see page 459).

However, in a sense it would oversimplify matters to say that contract damages can encompass lost profit whilst tort damages cannot. An action for damages for deceit (or under s 2(1) Misrepresentation Act 1967, or for negligent misstatement) can encompass a claim for the "opportunity cost" of reliance on the misrepresentation, ie the representee cannot recover the profit he would have made had the misrepresentation been true (the contract measure of damages) but he can recover for the profit he might have made had he not relied upon the misrepresentation and used his resources in another way. In *East* v *Maurer* [1991] 2 All ER 733, where the representee bought a hairdressing business on the basis of a fraudulent misrepresentation, the damages did not cover the profit he would have made had the misrepresentation been true. But a sum was awarded for the profit which the representee might have made had he purchased a different hairdressing business in the area. A further example of tortious damages covering the "opportunity cost" can be provided by the situation where a loan of £10,000 has been made on the basis of a negligent misrepresentation. The tortious measure of damages cannot provide for recovery of the interest which would have been paid under the particular contract, but they can encompass damages for the loss of the use of the £10,000 whilst it was locked up in that contract (see *Swingcastle* v *Alastair Gibson* [1991] 2 All ER 353; see also *Clef Aquitaine* v *Laporte Materials* [2000] 3 All ER 493 for a further example in relation to fraud).

It seems unlikely that the action for deceit will be much used now. Where the action for damages under s 2(1) Misrepresentation Act 1967 is available that will generally be preferable. Under s 2(1) the representee does not have to establish fraud or even negligence. Under s 2(1) it is for the representor to establish his reasonable belief in the truth of what he misrepresented, if he is to escape liability. Even the common law action for damages for negligent misstatement will often be preferable to the action for deceit. That action requires the representee to prove only negligence, and not fraud, on the part of the representor. However, there are a few ways in which it may be beneficial to be suing for deceit rather than for negligent misstatement. The test of remoteness may be less of a hurdle in relation to damages for deceit than for negligent misstatement. The normal tort test of remoteness, used in relation to a claim based on negligence, is that of "reasonable foreseeability". In *Doyle* v *Olby* [1969] 2 QB 158 the Court of Appeal indicated that all that is required in an action for deceit is that the damage "flowed" from the deceit. Lord Denning said (at p 167):

> "the defendant is bound to make reparation for all the actual damages flowing from the fraudulent inducement ... it does not lie in the mouth of the fraudulent person to say that [the damage] could not reasonably have been foreseen."

(See also Winn LJ at p 168 and Sachs LJ at p 171; Treitel 32 MLR 556.)

This may prove very significant in terms of the damages which are recoverable (contrast *Smith New Court Securities Ltd* v *Scrimgeour Vickers (Asset Management) Ltd* [1996] 4 All ER 769 and *South Australia Asset Management Corporation* v *York Montague Ltd* [1996] 3 All ER 365). However, on the current state of the law, a claim for damages under s 2(1) may have the advantages of the claim for deceit which are denied in an action for negligent misstatement. In *Royscott Trust Ltd* v *Rogerson* [1991] 3 All ER 294 the Court of Appeal stated that the test for remoteness of damage under s 2(1) was the more lax test used in deceit, rather than the negligence test. The court came to that conclusion on the basis of the fiction of fraud in s 2(1) and, thus, on this reasoning any other advantages in the deceit action for damages could also apply to a damages claim under s 2(1). This must be questioned, however, and some divergence of approach has already been indicated in relation to the question of whether damages should be reduced for the injured party's contributory negligence (see *Alliance and Leicester Building Society* v *Edgestop Ltd* [1994] 2 All ER 38 and *Gran Gelato Ltd* v *Richcliff (Group) Ltd* [1992] 1 All ER 865 — see page 296). More broadly, this equation of the treatment of damages for fraud and under s 2(1) must be questioned in principle. Special treatment of fraud may be justified as deterrence and on the basis of morality. The same arguments do not apply when the misrepresentation falls under s 2(1) (see further below at page 295). In any event, even without the advantages associated with the action for fraud, the damages claim under s 2(1) is usually preferable to a claim based on negligent misstatement at common law. In general, the claim under s 2(1) is the best means of claiming damages for a misrepresentation.

(b) Negligent misstatements

The tort action for negligent misstatement was established in *Hedley Byrne & Co Ltd* v *Heller & Partners Ltd* [1964] AC 465. It requires not only proof of a lack of reasonable grounds for the representor's belief in the truth of what he asserted but also that he owed the representee a duty of care. In the context of negligent misstatement, this duty of care requires a "special relationship" to exist between the parties. (See *Caparo Industries* v *Dickman* [1990] 1 All ER 568.)

At one stage it was thought that, once a contract had been concluded between the parties, the tort action could not be used to claim damages for a negligent misstatement. However, in *Esso Petroleum Co Ltd* v *Mardon* [1976] QB 801 the Court of Appeal held that the making of the contract did not preclude the remedy in tort. The tort action is available in relation to appropriate misrepresentations.

As was indicated above, when damages are awarded in tort for negligent misstatement it will be on the tort basis of returning the injured party to the position he was in before the tort occurred (reliance loss). Unlike the contractual measure, it will not seek to put the injured party in the position he would have been in had the statement been true, ie he will not be awarded his expectation loss. However, as we have seen, the possibility exists of claiming tort damages to cover the "opportunity cost" of reliance on the misrepresentation, ie the loss of the opportunity to use elsewhere resources committed to the contract. (See *Swingcastle* v *Gibson* [1991] 2 All ER 353; *East* v *Maurer* [1991] 2 All ER 733.)

Note that, in an action for negligent misstatement, it is for the representee to prove that the representation was made negligently, and this contrasts with s 2(1).

(c) Section 2(1) Misrepresentation Act 1967

The Misrepresentation Act 1967 resulted from the tenth report of the Law Reform Committee in 1962 (Cmnd 1782) which recommended that damages should be available for negligent misrepresentation. By the time the report was followed by legislation, the courts had provided a damages remedy for negligent misstatement in *Hedley Byrne & Co Ltd* v *Heller & Partners Ltd*

[1964] AC 465. Nevertheless, the Act provides for damages in s 2(1) and it is the statutory remedy which deserves the greater consideration here.

Section 2(1) states:

> "Where a person has entered into a contract after a misrepresentation has been made to him by another party thereto and as a result thereof he has suffered loss, then, if the person making the misrepresentation would be liable to damages in respect thereof had the misrepresentation been made fraudulently, that person shall be so liable notwithstanding that the misrepresentation was not made fraudulently, unless he proves that he had reasonable grounds to believe and did believe up to the time the contract was made that the facts represented were true."

This deals with the situation where X falsely states a fact, Y enters into a contract in reliance upon it, and X cannot establish that he had reasonable grounds for believing that fact to be true. The reference to fraud imports the requirement that the "misrepresentation" should be a misrepresentation within the definition given above, ie a statement of existing or past fact. The reference to fraud also affects the calculation of damages under s 2(1) (see page 295).

Advantages/disadvantages of an action under s 2(1)

Section 2(1) reverses the burden of proof from that which applies under the tort action for negligent misstatement. This is very important. It makes an action under s 2(1) a much easier way to obtain damages than an action which relies upon liability in tort for negligent misstatement. Under s 2(1) the representee has only to establish that he entered into a contract in reliance upon a misrepresentation made by the other party to the contract, and that he suffered loss thereby. It will then be for the representor to prove that, until the time the contract was made, he had reasonable grounds for his belief in the truth of the representation. If he cannot establish the reasonableness of his belief, he will be liable in damages.

Section 2(1) has a further advantage over the tort action for negligent misstatement. It does not require a duty of care to have existed between the parties. It merely requires that the misrepresentation should have led to a contract between representor and representee.

The importance of the burden of proof in s 2(1), and of the lack of any requirement of a duty of care, are both illustrated by the case of *Howard Marine & Dredging Co Ltd v A Ogden & Sons (Excavations) Ltd* [1978] QB 574 (Sealy [1978] CLJ 229; Sills 96 LQR 15):

> Ogden wished to hire barges from Howard Marine. During the negotiations Howard Marine told Ogden that the carrying capacity of their barges was 1,600 tonnes. Ogden and Howard Marine concluded a contract of hire. Ogden used the barges, and the work for which they were required fell behind schedule. Ogden discovered that the true carrying capacity was only 1,055 tonnes and refused to continue paying the hire charge.

Howard Marine sued Ogden for the hire charge. Ogden counterclaimed under s 2(1), and in tort for negligent misstatement. In the Court of Appeal, Ogden succeeded by a majority decision. Shaw LJ and Bridge LJ found for Ogden under s 2(1) on the basis that Howard Marine had not shown that they had reasonable grounds for their belief that the capacity was 1,600 tonnes. Lord Denning MR dissented as he thought that Howard Marine had established that their belief was reasonable. The importance of the distinctions between s 2(1) and the tort action for negligent misstatement is revealed in the fact that Howard Marine would have won had Ogden had to rely upon the tort action for negligent misstatement. Neither Lord Denning MR nor Bridge LJ thought that Howard Marine had owed a duty of care to Ogden. That prevented Ogden from succeeding in the tort action for negligent misstatement. In addition, even if there had been a duty of care, Bridge LJ thought that there was no evidence to establish that Howard Marine had been negligent and breached that duty. Shaw LJ was alone in thinking that Ogden could succeed in an action in tort for damages for negligent misstatement. If Ogden had not been able to make a claim under s 2(1), they would have lost by a majority decision in the Court of Appeal, rather than winning by one[3].

However, s 2(1) can be used only where the negligent misrepresentation was made by one party to a contract to the other party before the contract was concluded. The tort claim for negligent misstatement is not linked to the making of a contract. For example, a claim can be made in tort, for negligent misstatement, against a third party to a contract. *Hedley Byrne & Co Ltd* v *Heller & Partners Ltd* itself concerned a claim against a third party. The tort claim could relate to a statement made during pre-contractual negotiations which did not lead to a contract. In addition, the lack of any requirement of the existence of a contract means that the action could be used if a contract had apparently been made but was found to be void for mistake. An action under s 2(1) is doubtful if the contract is void. It should also be noted that a claim in tort for negligent misstatement is not dependent upon there being a misrepresentation in the sense indicated above.

Assessment of damages under s 2(1)

As has been indicated, the basis for the calculation of damages differs in contract and tort. It is more appropriate that damages under s 2(1) should be assessed on the basis of the rules in tort rather than contract, because s 2(1) is not dealing with a legally enforceable promise. Where there is a promise in the form of a contract term, it is apt that the damages for its non-fulfilment, its breach, should attempt to put the injured party in the position he would have been in had the promise been fulfilled (ie to compensate for the expectation loss). Section 2(1) does not relate to contract terms and promises, but to mere representations. The injured party has entered into a contract in reliance upon the representation and suffered loss thereby, but he is not suing on a broken promise, a broken term, and damages covering expectation loss would be inappropriate. It is apt to adopt the tort approach to damages and undo the harm caused by the misrepresentation by putting the representee back in the position he was in before the misrepresentation (ie to compensate for the reliance loss).

Some of the earlier decisions dealing with damages under s 2(1) pointed towards the contract measure of damages (*Gosling* v *Anderson* [1972] EGD 709; *Jarvis* v *Swans Tours* [1973] 1 QB 233; *Watts* v *Spence* [1976] Ch 165) but it is now clear that it is the tort measure of damages which is used under s 2(1) (*Chesneau* v *Interhome Ltd* [1983] The Times 9 June, 134 NLJ 341 (Lexis); *Sharneyford Supplies* v *Edge* [1987] 2 WLR 363 at p 376 *per*

Balcombe LJ (CA), [1985] 1 All ER 976 *per* Mervyn Davies J; *Naughton* v *O'Callaghan* [1990] 3 All ER 191; *Royscott Trust Ltd* v *Rogerson* [1991] 3 All ER 294) and the reference to fraud in s 2(1) is seen as providing a basis for this. In *Chesneau* v *Interhome Ltd* counsel had argued that damages under s 2(1) should be assessed on the principles applied to damages in tort. Everleigh LJ said:

> "For myself, I think that that is probably correct . . . The subsection itself says: '. . . if the person making the misrepresentation would be liable to damages in respect thereof had the misrepresentation been made fraudulently, that person shall be so liable . . .'. By 'so liable' I take it to mean liable as he would be if the misrepresentation had been made fraudulently."

More recently the reference to fraud in s 2(1) has been taken still further, arguably beyond its proper bounds. In *Royscott Trust Ltd* v *Rogerson* [1991] 3 All ER 294, the Court of Appeal stated that damages under s 2(1) should be calculated as if they were damages for fraud, and applied the laxer remoteness test which is used in relation to deceit rather than that applied to negligent misstatement (see page 291). The court's conclusion was based upon the reference to fraud in s 2(1). *Royscott* concerned the hire purchase of a car (ie the dealer sells the car to the finance house, and the finance house contracts with the customer for its hire purchase). The car dealer and the customer misrepresented to the finance company that the customer was supplying a higher deposit than he was. They did so because the finance company did not undertake transactions unless the customer was supplying at least a 20 per cent deposit. The customer did not finish paying the instalments to the finance company before selling the car to a third party, who acquired good title to it. The finance house brought an action for damages under s 2(1) against the dealer. The Court of Appeal held that the loss through the sale of the car did not have to pass the remoteness test of reasonable foreseeability, which would be applied in the tort of negligent misstatement, but merely the laxer remoteness test applied to deceit. However, in dealing with a point relating to causation, the court also held that it was reasonably foreseeable that the customer would sell the car to a third party. The court's comments on the applicability of a remoteness test derived from deceit could be regarded as unnecessary to the decision.

The point should be made that the equation of s 2(1) and fraud is not easy to justify in principle and may be open to question in the future. In *Smith* v *Scrimgeour Vickers* [1996] 4 All ER 769, where the court was concerned with fraud, Lord Browne-Wilkinson made no comment as to the correctness of the decision in *Royscott* v *Rogerson*, but it is worth noting, in particular, Lord Steyn's consideration of the justification for the wider availability of damages for fraud than for negligence. He noted that deterrance may be in question and that "in the battle against fraud civil remedies can play a useful role". In addition, he noted "moral considerations". He said (at p 790):

> "That brings me to the question of policy whether there is a justification for differentiating between the extent of liability for civil wrongs depending on where in the sliding scale from strict liability to intentional wrongdoing the particular civil wrong fits in. It may be said that logical symmetry and a rule of not punishing wrongdoers by civil remedies may favour a uniform rule. On the other hand it is a rational and defensible strategy to impose wider liability on an

intentional wrongdoer. As Hart and Honore *Causation in the Law* (2nd ed, 1985) at p 304 observed: 'an innocent plaintiff may, not without reason, call on a morally reprehensible defendant to pay the whole of the loss he has caused'. The exclusion of heads of loss in the law of negligence, which reflects considerations of legal policy, does not necessarily avail the intentional wrongdoer."

Such arguments militate against the "fiction of fraud" in s 2(1) being used to justify damages being awarded in exactly the same way as if the misrepresentor had been fraudulent, rather than as merely indicating *a* tortious measure. (See also *Avon Ins* v *Swire Fraser* [2000] 1 All ER (Comm) 573 at pp 578–581.)

In addition, some divergence of approach between an action for deceit and an action under s 2(1) has been indicated in relation to the question of whether the injured party's damages will be reduced for contributory negligence (Oakley [1994] CLJ 219, Chandler & Higgins [1994] LMCLQ 326). The Law Reform (Contributory Negligence) Act 1945 applies where "any person suffers damage as the result partly of his own fault and partly of the fault of any other person". (Fault is defined in s 4 — see page 485.) Where that is the situation, the damages recoverable shall be reduced to such an extent as the court thinks just and equitable having regard to the claimant's share in responsibility for the damage. It has been held that this does not apply to an action based on deceit (*Alliance and Leicester Building Society* v *Edgestop Ltd* [1994] 2 All ER 38) even where the claimant has also been involved in fraud (*Standard Chartered Bank* v *Pakistan National Shipping Corp (No 3)* [2000] 2 All ER (Comm) 929), but is the same approach taken in relation to a claim based on s 2(1)? *Royscott* and the fiction of fraud indicates that it would be, but the analogy made in *Gran Gelato Ltd* v *Richcliff (Group) Ltd* [1992] 1 All ER 865 was with an action for negligent misstatement. Where there was concurrent liability in tort and under s 2(1), it was held that contributory negligence was applicable to the claim under s 2(1). In *Gran Gelato*, liability under s 2(1) Misrepresentation Act was seen as (at p 875) "essentially founded on negligence", and that being so it was seen as being "very odd if the defence of contributory negligence were not available as a defence to a claim under that Act". However, having decided that the 1945 Act applied, Nicholls V-C then concluded that it would not be "just and equitable" for there to be any reduction of the plaintiff's damages in the instant case. He said (at p 876):

"The essential feature of the present case is that Gran Gelato's claim, both at common law and under the 1967 Act, is based on misrepresentation. Richcliff intended, or is to be taken to have intended, that Gran Gelato should act in reliance on the accuracy of [its answers]. Gran Gelato did so act. In those circumstances it would need to be a very special case before carelessness by Gran Gelato, the representee, would make it just and equitable to reduce the damages payable . . . In principle, carelessness in not making other inquiries provides no answer to a claim when the plaintiff has done that which the representor intended he should do."

Thus damages were not reduced in that case and, on this reasoning, it would seem that there will only be limited cases in which reduction of damages will occur when a misrepresentation is involved. The reference to "carelessness in not making other inquiries" would cover situations like that in *Redgrave* v *Hurd* (1881) 20 Ch D 1, where the representee could have discovered the truth of the misrepresentation had he examined the accounts available to him. *Redgrave* dealt with whether or not the representee could rescind but, in *Gran Gelato*, Nicholls V-C referred to it in reaching the conclusion that there should be no diminution of the plaintiff's damages and indicated (at p 876) that he was following the approach there taken. (The question of the applicability of contributory negligence to a claim based on breach of contract is dealt with below — see page 485.)

Non-disclosure

Section 2(1) relates to misrepresentations which are "made". This language is inapt to cover silence, and it does not provide a right to damages where there is non-disclosure in circumstances where there is a duty to disclose. Section 2(1) does not apply to non-disclosure in contracts *uberrimae fidei*[(4)]. Given that, it is important whether cases like *With* v *O'Flanagan* [1936] Ch 575 are regarded as continuing representations based on the statements made, which become misrepresentations with the change in circumstances, or as cases where what has been said has given rise to a duty to disclose further information and it is the non-disclosure itself which constitutes the misrepresentation. If the former is taken to be the mechanism by which a misrepresentation occurs, damages should be available under s 2(1) in such cases (Hudson (1969) 85 LQR 524).

Damages in lieu of rescission (s 2(2))

Section 2(2) Misrepresentation Act 1967 is sometimes referred to as a statutory bar to rescission. In certain circumstances it permits the court to prevent rescission for non-fraudulent misrepresentation and award damages in lieu of rescission. This is considered further below in relation to rescission (see page 303).

(d) Innocent misrepresentation

Since the decision in *Hedley Byrne & Co Ltd* v *Heller & Partners Ltd* [1964] AC 465, and the Misrepresentation Act 1967, the category of innocent misrepresentations has ceased to encompass all non-fraudulent misrepresentations. Innocent misrepresentations are now simply those not covered by any of the above categories. There is no damages remedy as such for innocent misrepresentation, although damages may be awarded in lieu of rescission under s 2(2) Misrepresentation Act 1967 (see below, page 303).

4. Rescission

Although the common law allowed rescission where there was a fraudulent misrepresentation, it was equity which made it available for all types of misrepresentation. In addition, equity provided an action for rescission rather than merely recognizing the right and was far more flexible than the common law when the contract was no longer entirely executory (see below on the bar of *restitutio in integrum*).

A misrepresentation renders a contract voidable at the option of the representee. This means that the contract can be rescinded and, in this context, rescission "wipes out" the existence of the contract entirely and returns the parties to the positions they were in before the contract was made. It is rescission *ab initio* and must be distinguished from rescission for breach which merely puts an end to the contract for the future. When a contract is rescinded for breach, its past existence is not disturbed. One effect of this is that, although damages may be available for misrepresentation as well as rescission, it should not be possible to rescind for misrepresentation and claim damages for breach. Once the contract has been rescinded for misrepresentation, there is no contract in relation to which damages for breach could be claimed. Termination for breach does not prevent any claim for damages for breach — the contract is only ended for the future. Some confusion can be avoided if the term "rescission" is reserved for use in the context of voidable contracts, and "termination" is used to describe the situation when a contract is ended after a breach (see page 426).

Rescission may be a self-help remedy. It may be possible for the representee simply to tell the other party that he, or she, is electing to rescind. This is most obviously the case where the contract is still entirely executory and there has been no performance by either party. The right to rescind for misrepresentation will then serve to protect the representee if the representor tries to claim specific performance or sue for breach. Where the contract is not entirely executory, whether rescission requires the assistance of the court will depend on what has been done in performance of it. If, for example, the representee has received goods and handed over a cheque he may still be able simply to return the goods and stop the cheque. However, if restoring the position before the contract was made requires the co-operation of the representor it is likely that an appropriate order will have to be sought from the court. If, for example, the representor has received goods under the contract, the court may have to order their return. The situation is complicated where the subject matter of the contract has been altered in some way and this problem will be considered below, in relation to the bar upon rescission which occurs once the parties can no longer be returned to their pre-contract positions, ie once *restitutio in integrum* is impossible.

In appropriate circumstances rescission can be achieved simply by notifying the representor of the election to rescind. In general, it is also *necessary* to inform the representor of the election to rescind. Merely coming to that decision and providing some evidence of it is usually insufficient. However, it seems that there is no need to inform the representor of the decision to rescind where the representee has simply retaken the property which he transferred under the voidable contract (*In re Eastgate, ex parte Ward* [1905] 1 KB 465). There is another, and more doubtful, exception to the need for communication in the case of *Car and Universal Finance Ltd* v *Caldwell* [1965] 1 QB 525. In that case:

> A Jaguar car was purchased from its original owner, Mr Caldwell, by Mr Norris, "a rogue". Norris paid by cheque and, when this proved to be worthless, Mr Caldwell wished to rescind but Norris and the car had disappeared. Mr Caldwell informed the police and the Automobile Association of the fraud and asked them to trace the car. Norris sold the car to a motor dealer with knowledge of the fraud, but it was eventually sold on to an innocent third party.

The question of ownership between Mr Caldwell, the original owner, and the innocent third party depended upon whether Mr Caldwell had rescinded before the sale to that innocent third party (see below on the bar to rescission where there has been a purchase by a *bona fide* third party). Norris had disappeared after the original sale, preventing the owner from communicating his election to rescind. Nevertheless, the Court of Appeal found that rescission had occurred. In informing the AA and the police, Mr Caldwell had done all he reasonably could and he had clearly demonstrated his intention to rescind. In the circumstances that was sufficient. The "rogue", Norris, had intended to avoid actual communication of rescission when he had known that it would almost certainly be desired.

The decision in *Caldwell* is certainly beneficial to the original owner but it means that the loss falls on the innocent third party purchaser. The court seems to have given too little consideration to the fact that it was, in effect, being asked to determine which innocent party should bear the loss. In this situation one innocent party is bound to suffer a loss. Is it better that it falls on the party who was parting with money in return for goods, rather than on the party who was prepared to part with his goods in return for a cheque? The decision seems unfortunate and has been criticised. There is every reason to confine it as much as possible, and it will probably not operate outside the sphere of fraudulent misrepresentations[5].

(a) Indemnity

There is a money remedy which may be used alongside rescission to help to put the representee back in the position he was in before the contract was made. It is called an indemnity and it is available for all types of misrepresentation. It is a far more restricted money remedy than damages. It covers only the cost to the representee of the obligations created by his contract with the representor. Given its restricted nature, an indemnity is unlikely to be appropriate where damages can be claimed. Its limited scope is illustrated by *Whittington* v *Seale-Hayne* (1900) 82 LT 49:

> The Whittingtons were breeders and exhibitors of prize poultry and wished to lease premises to carry on their business. The defendant assured them that his premises were in a sanitary condition, and the Whittingtons leased them on the basis of this innocent misrepresentation. In fact the water supply was poisoned and Mr Cooper, the farm manager, fell ill and most of the poultry died. The local authority declared the premises unfit for habitation and required work to be done on the drains. Under the lease the Whittingtons had to pay for that work. The Whittingtons rescinded the contract and also sought an indemnity. They claimed the cost of the rates and the repairs to the drains. In addition, they also claimed for their lost profit, their lost stock, their expenses in setting up the land as a poultry farm and the medical bills of Mr Cooper, the farm manager.

The court held that only the rates and the repair bill could be covered by an indemnity. It could not extend beyond expenses which the lease had obliged the plaintiffs to incur. Using the land as a poultry farm was their choice. The lease did not require them to spend money in that way, and the expenses connected with it could not be covered by an indemnity[6]. Their lost profits were a claim totally out of keeping with the idea of an indemnity. A claim for lost profits belongs with a claim for breach of contract where the injured party will be given his expectation loss, ie he will be put in the position he would have been in had the contract been fulfilled.

(b) The bars to rescission

There are certain bars to rescission; once one of those bars comes into operation, the representee ceases to have the right to rescind the contract. He then has to be content with any remedy he may have in damages. The existence of a bar to rescission does not affect a claim to damages (*Production Technology Consultants Ltd* v *Bartlett* [1988] 1 EGLR 182). The common law bars can be listed:

(i) *restitutio in integrum* is impossible;
(ii) third party rights;
(iii) affirmation;
(iv) lapse of time.

In addition, the courts' power to stop the representee from rescinding and to award him damages in lieu of rescission under s 2(2) Misrepresentation Act 1967 is sometimes referred to as a statutory bar, and it is considered at (v) on page 303.

Section 1 Misrepresentation Act 1967 makes it clear that, if the misrepresentation has also become a term or if the contract has been performed, those facts are not, in themselves, bars to rescission. Of course, if one of the bars indicated above is present, that bar will prevent rescission.

(i) *Restitutio in integrum* is impossible

Rescission takes both parties back to the position they were in before the contract was made. What if the contract is not wholly executory, but has been acted upon, so that it is not simply a matter of the representee informing the representor of his, or her, election? The court may order the return of property or money in order to restore the parties to their pre-contractual positions. The difficulties arise if property has been destroyed or altered and it is impossible to return the parties to their pre-contractual position. Representees cannot claim to be restored to their pre-contractual position if they cannot restore to the representor the property which was handed over to him under the contract. Under such circumstances, rescission is said to be barred because *restitutio in integrum* is impossible. For example, where the representee bought shares in a partnership he could not rescind on discovering the truth of the misrepresentation. The partnership had become a limited liability company in the meantime. The shares in the company were different in nature and status from those in the partnership. The representee could not give back what the representor had before the contract, ie shares in a partnership (*Clarke* v *Dickson* (1858) EB & E 148).

However, in order for rescission to be possible, equity, unlike the common law, will not require that the parties be returned precisely to their pre-contractual positions. The courts:

"can take account of profits and make allowances for deterioration. And I think the practice has always been for a court of equity to give this relief whenever, by the exercise of its powers, it can do what is practically just, though it cannot restore the parties precisely to the position they were in before the contract" (*Erlanger* v *New Sombrero Phosphate Co* (1878) 3 App Cas 1218 at pp 1278–9).

Rescission, in equity, is possible on the basis of substantial restoration of the property and a payment to take account of the change. Where a company bought a phosphate mine and worked it, but did not exhaust it, the company was allowed to rescind on the basis that the mine could be substantially restored to the seller and the company would account to the seller for the profits obtained from working it (*Erlanger* v *New Sombrero Phosphate Co*).

No precise rules have been formulated for the point at which equity will regard *restitutio in integrum* as impossible. The factors to be weighed in determining whether that point has been reached do not simply include the degree of change which the property has undergone. The fault of the representor will be considered. In *Spence* v *Crawford* [1939] 3 All ER 271, Lord Wright said (at p 288):

"The court will be less ready to pull a transaction to pieces where the defendant is innocent, whereas in the case of fraud the court will exercise its jurisdiction to the full in order, if possible, to prevent the defendant from enjoying the benefits of his fraud at the expense of the innocent plaintiff."

In *Spence* v *Crawford* the court would not allow the fraudulent representor to rely upon changes in the property to prevent the representee from rescinding. In that case:

Crawford owned a substantial proportion of the shares in a certain company, and he fraudulently induced Spence to sell him his shares in that company. After the sale, the constitution of the company was changed. There was a reconstruction and enlargement of the share capital. The result of the change was that Crawford's holding was diminished as a proportion of the company's share capital. As part of the contract with Spence, Crawford had undertaken to relieve Spence of his guarantee of the company's overdraft. In accomplishing the release of Spence's guarantee Crawford had to undertake liability to the bank himself in relation to the company. The bank asked Crawford to sell some of his shares to maintain his liquidity. He made a loss of about £1,000 on the shares.

The question was whether the representee, Spence, could rescind after the change in the company's constitution and the sale, at the insistence of the bank, of some of Crawford's shares. These changes meant that rescission would leave Crawford, on the basis of his proportionate share holding, in a very much less powerful position, in relation to control of the company, than he had been before he had purchased the shares from Spence. Nevertheless, emphasising that the representor had been fraudulent, the court allowed rescission. Spence recovered his shares and the dividends received on them by Crawford. Crawford was repaid the purchase price plus interest, and a sum was allowed for the £1,000 he had lost. Of course, even where fraud is involved, there will come a point at which *restitutio in integrum* will be viewed as impossible, and rescission will be barred (eg *Hughes* v *Clewley; (The Siben) (No 2)* [1996] 1 Lloyd's Rep 35).

(ii) Third party rights — the *bona fide* third party purchaser

A contract is voidable for misrepresentation, and not void. We can illustrate the effect of this in relation to third party rights by reference to the sale of a car. Suppose that a "rogue" purchases a car by means of a fraudulent misrepresentation. The contract for the sale of the car is valid until rescinded. Whilst the contract is valid the rogue has a voidable title to the car. If the rogue sells it to a *bona fide* third party before the contract is rescinded, the third party acquires a valid title which the original owner cannot defeat. This is why, in *Car and Universal Finance* v *Caldwell* (see above), Mr Caldwell was so anxious to convince the court that he had rescinded his contract with the rogue, Norris, before Norris sold the car to a *bona fide* third party. In that case Mr Caldwell recovered the car because the court, somewhat anomalously, accepted that rescission had occurred without communication to the rogue.

Where rescission has not occurred in time to prevent its being barred by a third party's rights, the argument is often raised that the contract is void for mistake, rather than merely voidable for misrepresentation (eg *Lewis* v *Averay* [1972] 1 QB 198; *Phillips* v *Brooks* [1919] 2 KB 243). In the rare cases where this is successful, it means that the contract never existed at all and that there was nothing to rescind — the rogue had no title to pass on to the third party, and the third party will not be able to use the above argument to defeat the original owner's claim to the car (eg *Ingram* v *Little* [1961] 1 QB 31).

(iii) Affirmation

As soon as the representee has learnt of the falsity of the misrepresentation, he, or she, can elect to affirm the contract or rescind it. Once the representee has affirmed, the right to rescind is lost. Affirmation may be express or implied. The representee may actually tell the representor of the decision not to rescind for misrepresentation, or affirmation may be implied from an act inconsistent with the representee's having an intention to rescind. For example, the representee's continued use of the subject matter of the contract may amount to affirmation. Where a contract concerned the sale of shares the right to rescind for misrepresentation was lost through delay and through continuing to act as a shareholder by attending, and participating in, a shareholder's meeting (*Sharpley* v *Louth and East Coast Railway* (1876) 2 Ch D 663). An attempt to sell shares acquired on the basis of a misrepresentation may also constitute an affirmation (*Re Hop and Malt Exchange and Warehouse Co, ex parte Briggs* (1866) LR 1 Eq 483). Similarly, where a misrepresentation induced the representee to lease machines from the representor, continued use of machines leased from the representor was held to amount to affirmation in *United Shoe Machinery of Canada* v *Brunel* [1909] AC 330 (see also *Long* v *Lloyd* [1958] 1 WLR 753; Atiyah 22 MLR 76; Odgers [1958] CLJ 166).

The possibility of affirmation arises only after the representee knows of the truth of the misrepresentation. In addition, it seems that there can be no affirmation if the representor did not know of the right to rescind even though he, or she, had discovered the truth of the misrepresentation. In *Peyman* v *Lanjani* [1984] 3 All ER 703:

> Lanjani was the lessee of a restaurant. His title to the lease was defective as he had obtained the assignment of it to him by fraud. The fraud had involved M pretending to be Lanjani when dealing face to face with the landlord, as Lanjani was scruffy and spoke no English. Peyman agreed to purchase the lease from Lanjani. To obtain the landlord's consent to the assignment, Lanjani again called upon M to impersonate him. Peyman learnt of that impersonation and the earlier one which rendered Lanjani's title defective. Peyman had already become reluctant to continue with the sale but his solicitor, who was acting for both parties, advised him to continue. Before the landlord consented to an assignment to him, Peyman went into

possession of the restaurant and paid £10,000 to Lanjani. A month later, Peyman went to another solicitor and was told that he had a right to rescind because of Lanjani's defective title.

Peyman gave notice of his decision to rescind. At first instance it was held that going into possession and handing over payment, after he had discovered what had occurred, meant that he had affirmed and could no longer rescind. The Court of Appeal held that he had not lost his right to rescind. He had discovered the true facts, but he had acted without any knowledge that he had a legal right to rescind. (See also *Stevens & Cutting Ltd* v *Anderson* [1990] 1 EGLR 95 at p 97; *Compagnia Tirrena di Assicirazioni* v *Grand Union Insurance* [1991] 2 Lloyd's Rep 143.)

However, the Court of Appeal in *Peyman* v *Lanjani* also considered the question of the representor being misled by an apparent, but not actual, affirmation into detrimentally relying upon the apparent affirmation. If an apparent affirmation occurs, the representee may be estopped from denying that he has affirmed the contract. No estoppel was found in that case, but such an estoppel will arise if the representor has relied upon the apparent affirmation to his detriment and there was nothing to indicate to the representor that the representee was acting in ignorance either of the truth or the law (see also *Container Transport International Inc* v *Oceanus Mutual Underwriting Association (Bermuda)* [1984] 1 Lloyd's Rep 476).

(iv) Lapse of time

Lapse of time can constitute evidence of affirmation (*Clough* v *London and North Western Railway Co* (1871) LR 7 Ex 26 at p 35) but this relates to the situation where time has passed since the representee learnt the truth of the misrepresentation. Until the truth is known there can be no affirmation. However, in *Leaf* v *International Galleries* [1950] 2 KB 86 a five-year lapse between the making of the contract and the attempt to rescind barred rescission, although the representee attempted to rescind as soon as he discovered the truth. The lapse of time was held to constitute a bar in itself, at least in relation to an "innocent" misrepresentation. (The case was decided before any distinction was made between the different types of non-fraudulent misrepresentation, and it probably applies to all such misrepresentations.) In *Leaf*:

In 1944, International Galleries represented to Mr Leaf that a painting they had for sale was by John Constable. Mr Leaf bought it for £85. In 1949, when he tried to sell the painting at Christie's, Mr Leaf discovered that it was not a Constable.

Mr Leaf tried to rescind the contract and obtain the return of the £85 from International Galleries. The Court of Appeal held that rescission was barred by lapse of time. Jenkins LJ said (at p 92):

"Contracts such as this cannot be kept open and subject to the possibility of rescission indefinitely ... it behoves the purchaser either to verify or, as the case may be, to disprove the representation within a reasonable time".

(See also *Peco Arts* v *Hazlitt Gallery Ltd* [1983] 3 All ER 193 at pp 199–200.)

(v) Section 2(2) Misrepresentation Act 1967

As has already been indicated, s 2(2) is sometimes labelled as the statutory bar to rescission. It states that:

"where a person has entered into a contract after a misrepresentation has been made to him otherwise than fraudulently, and he would be entitled, by reason of the misrepresentation, to rescind the contract, then if it is claimed in any proceedings arising out of the contract, that the contract ought to be or has been rescinded, the court or arbitrator may declare the contract subsisting and award damages in lieu of rescission, if of the opinion that it would be equitable to do so having regard to the nature of the misrepresentation and the loss that would be caused by it if the contract were upheld, as well as to the loss that rescission would cause to the other party."

Rescission is a very radical remedy; before the enactment of s 2(2) it was the only remedy available for a wholly innocent misrepresentation. In relation to non-fraudulent misrepresentations, s 2(2) now gives the court a discretion to declare the contract subsisting and award damages in lieu of rescission where it "would be equitable to do so". This allows the court to substitute damages for rescission where the misrepresentation was fairly trivial and the radical nature of the remedy of rescission is not in keeping with the "wrong" on which it was founded. The subsection requires account to be taken of "the nature of the misrepresentation and the loss that would be caused by it if the contract were upheld, as well as the loss that rescission would cause to the other party". In other words, taking account of the nature of the misrepresentation, it is a matter of considering the effects on both parties of allowing rescission or awarding damages in lieu.

The exercise of the courts' discretion under s 2(2) was considered *obiter* in *William Sindall plc* v *Cambridgeshire County Council* [1994] 3 All ER 932. In that case:

The builders, William Sindall plc, had purchased a piece of land from the council, to develop it. After that transaction was concluded, it took eighteen months to obtain planning permission for their detailed development plans and during that time the market slumped and the market value of the land was reduced from over £5m to £2m. When the builders discovered a nine-inch sewer running through the land which had not been revealed by the council they claimed that they had contracted with the council on the basis of a misrepresentation. The council had stated that, to its knowledge, there were no such incumbrances on the land. The builders claimed that there was effectively nothing which could be done to deal with the problem created for their development by the drain and claimed to be able to rescind the contract. The drain problem was remediable at a cost of approximately £18,000. At first instance, a misrepresentation was found and rescission was not denied under s 2(2).

The Court of Appeal concluded that there was no misrepresentation but, *obiter*, considered how s 2(2) Misrepresentation Act 1967 would have been dealt with had an operative misrepresentation been found. There were three basic factors to consider (Evans LJ at p 959):

"the nature of the misrepresentation, the loss that would be caused by it (sc the misrepresentation) if the contract was upheld, and the loss that rescission would cause to the other party (sc the non-fraudulent author of the misrepresentation)."

In relation to the decision whether to prevent rescission, the court indicated that it would not have allowed the builders to make use of a relatively minor misrepresentation to rescind and so to escape from what had become a bad bargain because of a general fall in the value of land (which was not connected to the misrepresentation). However, the court also indicated how it would have measured damages in lieu of rescission under s 2(2). It took the line that just as rescission should not have been available to protect the builders from the slump in the market price of the land, s 2(2) also should not reallocate that market risk from the builders back to the council.

This dismisses any simple idea of calculating damages in lieu of rescission merely on the basis that they are given "in lieu of rescission", ie as if they were simply to put the representee in the position he, or she, would have been in, had rescission been allowed. Some of the comments of Evans LJ, at p 963 in particular, could be seen as indicating that the contract measure of damages should be used, but that would be even less appropriate than under s 2(1) (see above). It may be that the basic principle behind the calculation of damages under s 2(2) is that they should replace the remedy of rescission, but with account being taken of any "over compensation", which rescission would have provided — such as coverage of a drop in market value which is unconnected with the misrepresentation.

It should be noted that if the misrepresentation is not wholly innocent, the representee may be claiming damages as well as rescission. Section 2(3) deals with the possibility of a claim for damages under s 2(1) and the court also awarding damages under s 2(2). It aims to prevent a double recovery by providing that damages awarded under s 2(1) should take account of any damages awarded under s 2(2). The damages remedy in s 2(1) should cover only those losses not falling within damages in lieu of rescission under s 2(2).

Section 2(2) applies where the representee "would be entitled ... to rescind", and the question arises as to whether the court can still award damages in lieu of rescission if rescission itself would be prevented by one of the common law bars. In *Atlantic Lines & Navigation Co Inc v Hallam Ltd; (The Lucy)* [1983] 1 Lloyd's Rep 188 (see above, page 286), Mustill J accepted that a bar on rescission prevented the court awarding damages under s 2(2) but that was *obiter dictum*. In *Thomas Witter Ltd v TBP Industries Ltd* [1996] 2 All ER 573 Jacobs J found such an argument "unattractive" (at p 590). He said (at p 590):

> "The argument assumes that the Act is referring to the remedy of rescission though this is not clear. If it were only the remedy which is referred to then it would be difficult to understand the reference to 'has been rescinded' in the section. It seemed to me that the reference may well be to a claim by the representee that he was entitled to rescission, in which case it may be enough for the court to find that the agreement was rescissionable ..."

Jacobs J considered the speeches in the House of Commons at the time of the passing of the Act and found that "the Solicitor General told the House ... that damages could be awarded under s 2(2) where there was an impossibility of restitution". Jacobs J concluded that an award of damages under s 2(2) is not dependent upon an existing right to rescind, but only that such a right existed in the past. However, the point has been made that the legislative history of the provision is not as clear as Jacobs J indicated (Beale (1995) 111 LQR 385) and the more recent cases have also taken the line that the more literal interpretation of s 2(2) indicates that it does not make damages available if rescission is barred before the action comes to court (*Floods of Queenferry v Shand Construction* [2000] Build LR 81, *Government of Zanzibar v British*

Aerospace [2000] CLC 735). In addition, in *Government of Zanzibar* v *British Aerospace* the judge considered the legislative evolution of the provision. He pointed out that the Law Reform Committee had envisaged s 2(2) as providing a needed limit on the right to rescind which had otherwise been broadened by s 1 removing the previous bar which had existed once performance had been commenced or completed. He also pointed out that not only was the Solicitor General's statement, referred to by Jacob J in *Witter* (above), ambiguous but that it was an "ex tempore answer given a little after three o'clock in the morning" and that it "does not accord with" other statements during the passage of the Bill (at p 744). The point was made that, in introducing the Bill in the House of Lords, Lord Gardiner had said:

> "I now come to damages as an alternative to rescission. The Committee recommended that a discretionary power should be conferred on the court to award damages in lieu of ordering rescission where damages would afford adequate compensation to the victim of an innocent misrepresentation, whether it was made negligently or not. They thought that there were a number of cases where the remedy of rescission might be too drastic in the circumstances. This is the recommendation which is implemented by Clause 2(2)".

The judge saw s 2(2) as merely providing a means for the court to mitigate the effects of the right to rescind where it existed. He saw s 2(1) as providing the basic right to recover damages and that was subject to the representor not being able to prove belief, and reasonable grounds to believe, in the truth of what he, or she, had asserted (at p 743). However, the point can be made that the common law recognised the "wrong" and the need for a remedy even where the misrepresentation was wholly innocent. If it was not to cause hardship or injustice, such a powerful remedy had to be hedged around with restrictions relating to what happened after the events generating the right, but the mere fact that the bars are relevant to the question of the availability of rescission, as such, does not mean that they should be seen as relevant to the availability of a money remedy to deal with the recognised "wrong".

5.   Exemption clauses and misrepresentations[7]

Subject to the usual rules on incorporation and construction (see Chapter 9), an exemption clause may serve to exclude or restrict liability for non-fraudulent misrepresentation, but it has been held that such clauses are ineffective in relation to a fraudulent misrepresentation. In *S Pearson & Son Ltd* v *Dublin Corporation* [1907] AC 351 the plaintiffs contracted to construct sewage works for a price calculated in reliance upon a misrepresentation. The court held that liability for a fraudulent misrepresentation could not be affected by an exemption clause.

However, s 3 Misrepresentation Act 1967 (as substituted by s 8 Unfair Contract Terms Act 1977) now renders an exemption clause ineffective, in relation to all types of misrepresentation, if the representor cannot establish that the clause satisfies the requirement of reasonableness in s 11 Unfair Contract Terms Act 1977. Section 3 Misrepresentation Act 1967 now states:

> "If a contract contains a term which would exclude or restrict–

(a) any liability to which a party to a contract may be subject by reason of any misrepresentation made by him before the contract was made; or

(b) any remedy available to another party to the contract by reason of such a misrepresentation,

that term shall be of no effect except in so far as it satisfies the requirement of reasonableness as stated in section 11(1) of the Unfair Contract Terms Act 1977; and it is for those claiming that the term satisfies the requirement of reasonableness to show that it does."

Section 3 deals with terms which exclude or restrict liability, or a remedy, for misrepresentation. It renders such a term ineffective unless the representor can establish that it satisfies the requirement of reasonableness.

The scope of s 3 presents difficulties in relation to clauses which appear to try to prevent a statement from being a misrepresentation at all, rather than merely excluding or restricting the liability or the remedies available for a misrepresentation. It is a similar problem to that which has to be considered in deciding whether a clause should be regarded as an exclusion clause in substance and subject to the Unfair Contract Terms Act 1977, despite its form (see Chapter 10). One additional difficulty here is that the Misrepresentation Act 1967 has no equivalent to s 13 Unfair Contract Terms Act 1977 which specifically extends the clauses covered by the 1977 Act beyond those which are in the form of exclusions or restrictions of liability (see also s 3 Unfair Contract Terms Act 1977). To bring within s 3 Misrepresentation Act 1977 clauses which appear to prevent a misrepresentation occurring at all may require more judicial development than is required under the Unfair Contract Terms Act 1977.

In *Overbrooke Estates Ltd* v *Glencombe Properties Ltd* [1974] 3 All ER 511 Brightman J indicated a narrow approach to the question of which clauses are covered by s 3. In that case:

> The plaintiffs sold their property to the defendants through an auction. The catalogue for the auction had set out particulars of the property and the general conditions of sale. Those general conditions contained a clause stating that the auctioneers did not have any authority to make any representations in relation to the property. Before the auction the defendants had telephoned the auctioneers and obtained an assurance from them that the local authority had no plans in relation to the property. After contracting to purchase the property, the defendants discovered that it was within an area which was under consideration for slum clearance.

The plaintiffs claimed specific performance of the contract of sale and applied for summary judgment. The defendants resisted this on the basis that there had been a misrepresentation by the auctioneers, as the plaintiff's agents, as to the local authority's interest in the property. It was held that even if there had been a misrepresentation, which was doubted, it was not made by the plaintiffs. They had denied the auctioneers any authority to make a representation by the clause in the particulars of sale. In addition, and importantly here, it was held that the clause dealing with the auctioneers' authority did not fall within the ambit of s 3 Misrepresentation Act. It had been argued that, as the authority of the agent was a necessary ingredient of the contracting party's liability, a clause restricting the agent's authority was a clause restricting the liability of the contracting party and so it fell within s 3. Brightman J saw no room for this argument. It was necessary to look at any restrictions on the agent's authority before deciding if the plaintiff had made a misrepresentation through the agent. This shows an obvious unwillingness to look behind the form of a clause to see if, in substance, it excludes or restricts liability for misrepresentation. (See also *Collins* v *Howell-Jones* [1981] EGD 207.)

However, in *Cremdean Properties Ltd* v *Nash* [1977] EGD 63 the Court of Appeal took a broad approach to the scope of s 3 Misrepresentation Act 1967 and indicated that the substance of a clause should be examined, and not just its form. In that case:

> Nash contracted to sell to Cremdean Properties a block of properties in Bristol to be used as office space. The particulars of the properties had stated that the amount of office space available was 17,900 sq ft but it was actually much less. A footnote to the special conditions of sale contained the following clause:
>
> "[The vendor's estate agents] for themselves and the vendors . . . give notice that (a) These particulars are prepared for the convenience of an intending purchaser . . . and although they are believed to be correct their accuracy is not guaranteed and any error, omission or misdescription shall not annul the sale or be grounds on which compensation may be claimed and neither do they constitute any part of an offer of a contract, (b) Any intending purchaser . . . must satisfy himself by inspection or otherwise as to the correctness of each of the statements contained in these particulars."

Cremdean sought rescission of the contract, or damages in the alternative, on the basis of a misrepresentation as to the amount of office space in the property. As a preliminary issue the effect of the footnote was considered. Nash argued that it prevented there being a representation at all, and that therefore it did not exclude or restrict liability and did not fall within s 3 Misrepresentation Act 1967. The Court of Appeal held that the footnote came within the ambit of s 3 Misrepresentation Act 1967 and that at the full trial of the action, the court would have to consider whether the footnote was "reasonable" in order to decide if it was effective to exclude liability. Of interest here is the court's rejection of the argument that the clause fell outside the ambit of s 3. Bridge LJ thought that the clause was inappropriately worded to bring about the situation where no representation had been made, but he also said (at pp 71–72):

> "if the ingenuity of a draftsman could devise language which would have that effect, I am extremely doubtful whether the court would allow it to operate so as to defeat s 3. Supposing the vendor included a clause . . . in some such terms as 'notwithstanding any statement of fact included in these particulars the vendor shall be conclusively deemed to have made no representation within the meaning of the Misrepresentation Act 1967', I should have thought that *that was only a form of words the intended and actual effect of which was to exclude or restrict liability*, and I should not have thought that the courts would have been ready to allow such ingenuity in forms of language to defeat the plain purpose at which s 3 is aimed" (emphasis added).

Scarman LJ similarly thought that the footnote was subject to s 3. He considered the argument that the footnote qualified the statement on the office space by removing from it any representation that its content was accurate, ie the argument that, with the footnote present, the statement was merely one of belief. Scarman LJ said (at p 72):

"Humpty Dumpty would have fallen for this argument. If we were to fall for it, the Misrepresentation Act would be dashed to pieces which not all the King's Lawyers could put together again."

Buckley LJ agreed with both Bridge and Scarman LJJ.

It should be noted that Bridge LJ acknowledged that the problem is one of form and substance but his example of a clause which would fall within the ambit of s 3, despite being an attempt to prevent there being a misrepresentation at all, is very obvious. A clause which simply attempted to "deem" a statement to be something other than what it actually is leaves little room for doubt as to its purpose. This leaves open to doubt how far Bridge LJ would have been prepared to go in searching for the substance of a clause behind its form. This doubt is the greater because Bridge LJ also approved the approach of the court in *Overbrooke Estates Ltd* v *Glencombe Properties Ltd* [1974] 3 All ER 511. If the acknowledgment of substance was restricted to such situations, form would fail to be the determining factor in only the most obvious of cases. However, the more sweeping approach of Scarman LJ indicates a more extensive search for substance, as does the fact that the court viewed the last part of the clause, which told the purchaser not to rely on the particulars but to check them for himself, as merely relevant to the question of whether or not there was actual reliance. (See also *South Western General Properties* v *Marton* (1983) 2 TLR 14; *William Sindall plc* v *Cambridgeshire CC* [1994] 3 All ER 932 at pp 948, 951.)

In keeping with the above approach to those clauses which state that there should be no reliance on the part of the representee, is the line taken in *Thomas Witter Ltd* v *TBP Industries Ltd* [1996] 2 All ER 573 in relation to a clause which sought to deny that there was reliance. The second sentence of the clause in question stated:

"the purchaser acknowledges that it has not been induced to enter into this agreement by any representation or warranty other than the statements contained in or referred to in schedule 6".

Whether a statement, other than those in schedule 6, had been relied upon, and "induced" the contract is a matter of fact. That fact, as such, could not be changed by a contractual promise (although the contract term might affect how difficult it was to prove such "other" reliance) and that was the line taken by Jacobs J (at p 596). In other words, the clause was simply ineffective if another, inducing, representation could be established. However, he also was of the view that even if the clause was somehow effective to impact upon the misrepresentation issue, it would fall within the scope of s 3 and be subject to the "requirement of reasonableness".

Some additional support for a broad approach to the use of s 3 Misrepresentation Act 1967 can be gleaned from the line taken by the House of Lords in *Smith* v *Eric S Bush* [1989] 2 All ER 514 on the ambit of the Unfair Contract Terms Act 1977. In *Smith* v *Bush* the valuer's disclaimer of responsibility to the house purchaser, in relation to his valuation of the property for the building society, was held to come within the Unfair Contract Terms Act 1977. The court did not accept that the disclaimer simply related to whether a duty of care was owed to the house purchaser by the valuer and, as such, did not fall within s 2 Unfair Contract Terms Act 1977 as an exclusion or restriction of liability for negligence. However, in relation to the Unfair Contract Terms Act 1977 the courts are assisted in looking beyond the form of a clause, to its substance, by s 13 of that Act — there is no equivalent to that section in the Misrepresentation Act 1967.

The Misrepresentation Act 1967 has no equivalent to the list of contracts excluded from the operation of the Unfair Contract Terms Act 1977 (see page 182), and the clause might be subject to the requirement of reasonableness under s 3 although it falls within a contract of a type excluded from the operation of the 1977 Act.

Some consideration must also be given here to the 1999 Regulations on Unfair Terms in Consumer Contracts (see generally Chapter 11). They relate to contracts between sellers or suppliers and consumers and, with the exception of "core terms" in plain, intelligible language, they apply a test of fairness to all non-individually negotiated terms and unfair terms do not bind the consumer. An unfair term is one which, "contrary to the requirement of good faith" causes "a significant imbalance in the parties' rights and obligations arising under the contract, to the detriment of the consumer" (reg 5(1)). Given that definition of "unfair term" it can be questioned whether an exemption clause dealing with misrepresentation can ever be "unfair", as it can be contended that such a term does not affect the parties' "rights and obligations *under the contract*" (emphasis added) and cannot cause the required "significant imbalance". However, in misleading the representee consumer as to some matter relevant to the contract, a misrepresentation may have led to the making of a contract in relation to which the rights and obligations of the parties are significantly imbalanced. A clause removing, or limiting, the ability of the representee consumer to take action in relation to the misrepresentation, may be a term helping to maintain that imbalance and, in a sense, to be a cause of its continuance. It is possible to argue that an exemption clause dealing with misrepresentation could be found to be an unfair term under the Regulations. It might be argued that it is largely irrelevant whether that is so, because such exemptions will be subject to the test of reasonableness by s 3 of the Misrepresentation Act 1967. However, it should be remembered that, under the Regulations, the Director General of Fair Trading, and the "qualifying bodies", have powers to prevent the continued use of unfair terms drawn up for general use (reg 12). The 1999 Regulations can prevent consumers encountering what would be unfair exemption clauses, and being misled by them as to their rights. In addition, as the scope of the Regulations is not confined to terms which "exclude or restrict liability", they do not give rise to the difficult question as to whether the term is preventing the misrepresentation from occurring rather than removing liability.

Footnotes

(1) On the specific point of an agreement embodied in a consent order, *Jenkins* v *Livesey* [1985] AC 424 makes it clear that statute required disclosure (s 25 Matrimonial Causes Act 1973, replaced by s 3 Matrimonial and Family Proceedings Act 1984).

(2) Financial Services Act 1986.

(3) Taylor (1982) 45 MLR 139; Cartwright [1987] Conv 243.

(4) *Banque Financière de la Cité SA* v *Westgate (UK) Insurance Co* [1989] 2 All ER 952 (CA) — see note (2) above.

(5) See Law Reform Committee, 12th Rep, 1966, Cmnd 2958, para 16. In *Newtons of Wembley Ltd* v *Williams* [1965] 1 QB 560, where there was a direct sale from the rogue to the innocent third party, the innocent third party was held to acquire good title under s 9 Factors Act 1889. This limits the effect of Caldwell and makes an anomalous distinction between an innocent first purchaser directly from "the rogue" and subsequent purchasers further down the chain.

(6) *Adams* v *Newbigging* (1886) 34 Ch D 582 *per* Bowen LJ, but see the judgments of Cotton and Fry LJJ.

(7) See further Macdonald, *Exemption Clauses and Unfair Terms* (1999) Butterworths, Chapter 6.

Chapter 14

Duress and undue influence

1. Introduction

Duress and undue influence relate to the situation where one party has distorted the other's decision to contract; either duress or undue influence will render a contract voidable. Both duress and undue influence relate to the unacceptable situation in which the contract was formed.

The question of the general effect of "unconscionability" on a contract is considered in Chapter 16.

A. Duress

1. Introduction

If someone makes a contract whilst a gun is being held to his head, it is obvious that the contract should not be enforced. English law regards the contract as voidable (see *Barton* v *Armstrong* [1976] AC 104), because the person threatened had to make the decision whether to contract in unacceptable circumstances.

Threats to the person are the obvious form of duress. It is only in comparatively recent years that English law has clearly recognized any other type of duress as capable of making a contract voidable (or grounding a restitutionary action). Even the legal effect of duress to goods was far from certain[1]. However, *obiter*, in *The Siboen and The Sibotre (Occidental Worldwide Investment Corporation* v *Skibs A/S Avanti)* [1976] 1 Lloyd's Rep 293, Mocatta J recognized that a contract could be voidable because economic duress had been present when it was made and that is now an accepted principle. "Economic" duress simply refers to the fact that it is the economic interest of the individual which is being threatened, and, if the law will react to threats even to that interest, it can be said that there is a general principle in English law that duress will render a contract voidable. The law is now prepared to look at a very wide range of threats in deciding if the decision to contract was made in unacceptable circumstances.

An example of a case where economic duress was found will indicate the type of situation in which the plea of duress is commonly raised. In *Atlas Express* v *Kafco (Importers and Distributors) Ltd* [1989] 1 All ER 641:

> Kafco, a small company which imported and distributed basketware, had made a contract to supply Woolworths. Kafco needed to contract with a carrier for delivery to Woolworths. They concluded a contract with Atlas Express. Once the contract with Atlas had commenced, Atlas realised that they had miscalculated and that the rates specified in the contract made it a "bad deal" from their point of view. Atlas told Kafco that they would cease to make the deliveries unless the contract pricing was changed. Kafco was heavily dependent upon the contract with Woolworths and knew that a failure to deliver the baskets would lead to its loss and an action for breach by Woolworths. At that time it was not possible for Kafco to find another carrier and Kafco felt that Atlas had them "over a barrel". Kafco agreed to the new contract, at the rates demanded by Atlas, but made it clear that they felt that they were acting under duress.

Atlas Express sued Kafco for non-payment of the new rate of carriage. Tucker J held that they could not succeed. The agreement to the new rates, in the new contract, had been made while Kafco were subject to economic duress. In any event, there had been no consideration for the new agreement.

Atlas Express v *Kafco* illustrates the situation in which a claim of duress will now often arise. The parties have made a contract but, either because of miscalculation or because of a change in circumstances, one party wishes to increase the contract price. He tells the other party that, unless the price is renegotiated, he will not perform. The question is whether any new agreement will be voidable for economic duress. That question has become all the more important because the decision in *Williams* v *Roffey Bros & Nicholls (Contractors) Ltd* [1990] 1 All ER 512 (see page 59) has thrown the emphasis in such cases upon duress rather than consideration. As the important point in such cases would seem to be whether the agreement was made improperly, in unacceptable circumstances, rather than whether some "technical" consideration can be found, this is a welcome development. However, it does make duress of great significance. We need to consider when the courts will find that a contract was made under duress and is voidable.

The language of the courts

Before considering the test for duress, the language used by the courts in relation to duress should be examined. At times, the courts have given the appearance of stating a clear test for duress whilst using language which, on closer examination, is obscure in its meaning. In particular, care must be taken with the use of terms such as "voluntariness" and "consent", and references to the "overborne will"[2]. This use of language is superficially attractive. It seems to provide the perfect basis for interfering with an apparently valid contract. If the person claiming duress was acting involuntarily, if he did not consent, then his agreement to the contract can be labelled as merely apparent and dismissed. However, in considering whether he truly consented, in the sense of whether his agreement was given voluntarily, the test is not being used as it would be if the question was whether his actions were unwilled, as they would be if he were in a state of automatism. It is clear that truly unwilled actions, in the sense of automatism, are not what is being considered by the courts in relation to duress. This was acknowledged by the House of Lords in *DPP for Northern*

Ireland v *Lynch* [1975] AC 653 in the context of a plea of duress in the criminal law. Atiyah has pointed out that the reasoning on that point should not be regarded as restricted to the criminal law ((1982) 98 LQR 197). When a person under duress agrees to contract because of the other party's threat, he does not do so "involuntarily", because his will has been "overborne", but rather because he chooses to, albeit only because it is the least unattractive of the alternatives before him. There is nothing to be gained from considering the reality of the consent of the person claiming duress. It is always "real". It is not a question of someone being made an "offer he could not refuse", merely of an offer which he was given very powerful reasons for accepting. In other words there is no simple factual test of whether the person claiming duress has ceased to act "voluntarily". The real question in relation to duress is whether the decision to contract was made in unacceptable circumstances (*Dimskal Shipping Co SA* v *International Transport Workers' Federation; (The Evia Luck)* [1991] 4 All ER 871 at p 878).

2. The test for the existence of duress

Despite the language used by the courts, the test for duress is not a simple factual one of establishing whether the "will" of the person threatened was "overborne" or whether he was acting "involuntarily". It is a more complex process, involving consideration of the circumstances in which he decided to contract and whether the other party had introduced an unacceptable element into those circumstances. There are two factors involved in this *(Enimont Overseas* v *Rojugotanker Zadar (The Olib)* [1991] 2 Lloyd's Rep 108 at p 114):

    (i) the illegitimacy of the threat; and
    (ii) the lack of a reasonable alternative to agreeing, for the person threatened.

However, where what is threatened is a crime, rather than merely a civil wrong, it seems that only stage (i) of the test will apply. It is inapposite, in the circumstances of a threatened criminal offence, to ask if the person threatened had a reasonable alternative to agreeing (see below, page 322). A further possible exception to the need for stage (ii), as stated here, is also considered below (see page 321).

(i)   Illegitimacy of the threat

It was established in *Universe Tankships Inc. of Monrovia* v *International Transport Workers' Federation and Laughton* [1983] AC 366 that the threat must be "illegitimate"[3]. The boundaries of this require consideration. In that case:

> A Liberian corporation owned a ship under a flag of convenience. When the ship docked at Milford Haven, the ITF blacked it to try to get improved conditions for the crew. To extract their vessel from port the owners paid various sums, including a "contribution" to the ITF welfare fund. Once the ship was clear the owners tried to recover that sum as money paid under economic duress.

The ITF conceded that the money could be recovered on the basis of economic duress unless the pressure used could be regarded as legitimate. The Trade Union and Labour Relations Act 1974 would have conferred immunity, in tort, on ITF's actions, provided that ITF were acting in furtherance of a trade dispute. The court did not think that applicability, or non-applicability, of the statutorily conferred tort immunity automatically decided the question of whether what had occurred could amount to duress in a different area of the law. In any event, the immunity related to tort and the court was faced with a restitutionary claim to recover the money paid. The court said that it was a matter of public policy whether such actions were "illegitimate" and could amount to duress. The trade union legislation provided the court with clear guidance as to what that public policy should be. In the instant case the dispute did not come within the protection of the legislation, even in relation to a tort action, and on the basis of that guidance, public policy indicated that the blacking was "illegitimate" and constituted duress (see also *Dimskal Shipping Co SA* v *International Transport Workers' Federation; (The Evia Luck)* [1991] 4 All ER 871).

However, in the absence of special circumstances, it seems that the threat of any unlawful act will be illegitimate. In this context, an act is unlawful not only if it is criminal but also if it is a civil wrong, eg a tort or a breach of contract. Another possibility is that the act threatened may not be unlawful, but the threat itself may be (blackmail, for example). The extension of what will amount to an illegitimate threat, beyond what is unlawful, is open to question. Any extension of duress beyond the area of threats which are unlawful, in themselves, or to do unlawful acts, will be infringing upon freedom of contract without the obvious justification of "unlawfulness". It may be seen as the policing of contracts on the basis of inequality of bargaining power. Duress, even when confined to the unlawful, may be seen as rendering a contract voidable on the basis of inequality of bargaining power, but in an obviously restricted way. Other areas of the law indicate the unacceptability of the way in which the person making the threat has increased his bargaining power. Certainly there are indications against any generalised doctrine of relief against inequality of bargaining power (see *Pao On* v *Lau Yiu Long* [1980] AC 614 at p 634; *National Westminster Bank* v *Morgan* [1985] 1 All ER 821 at p 830).

However, in *CTN Cash and Carry Ltd* v *Gallaher* [1994] 4 All ER 714 the Court of Appeal took the view that it is possible, in principle, for duress to be based on a lawful threat, but, on the facts of the particular case, no duress was found. In that case:

> The plaintiff company ran a cash and carry business. The defendant supplied them with cigarettes (and was the only possible supplier of some brands) on a regular basis, on credit terms, but each transaction was covered by a separate contract. A dispute arose between them and the defendants refused to continue to supply the plaintiffs on credit unless they paid the sum which the defendants were asserting was due to them. The plaintiffs claimed that the sum was not due but paid the defendants in order to continue to trade with them on credit terms. The plaintiffs sued to recover the sum paid on the basis that it had been paid under economic duress.

The defendants' threat was not unlawful. It did not involve a threatened tort or breach of contract, as it merely related to the terms of potential future contracts. On this basis, the Court of Appeal rejected the plaintiffs' claim. The court did indicate, however, that it was not impossible, in principle, for duress to be found without an unlawful threat — and the court pointed out some factors relevant to such a conclusion. The court emphasised that the instant

315

case did not concern a "protected relationship" and did not concern transactions between a supplier and a consumer. Rather the dispute arose out of "arms length commercial dealings between two trading companies" (at p 717). The court acknowledged that the defendants were the sole distributors of certain brands of cigarette and therefore were, in a sense, in a monopolistic position, but took the view that:

> "The control of monopolies is ... a matter for Parliament. Moreover the common law does not recognise the doctrine of inequality of bargaining power in commercial dealings" (Steyn LJ at p 717).

On that basis, the fact that the defendants were in a monopoly could not "by itself convert what [was] not duress into duress". In addition, the court also emphasised that the defendants were *bona fide*. They believed that they were entitled to the money which they demanded. Steyn LJ concluded (at p 719):

> "Outside the field of protected relationships, and in a purely commercial context, it might be a relatively rare case in which 'lawful act duress' can be established. And it might be particularly difficult to establish duress if the defendant *bona fide* considered that his demand was valid. In this complex and changing branch of the law I deliberately refrain from saying 'never'. But as the law stands I am satisfied that the defendants' conduct in this case did not amount to duress."

The factors which the court emphasised as relevant to a decision on duress by a lawful threat were the context (ie whether the relationship between the parties was a "protected one" or between consumer and supplier) and also the *bona fides* of the party making the threat. There was no explanation given of which relationships between the parties would be "protected ones" but some vulnerability or inequality beyond the norm would seem to be required (see presumed undue influence — page 326). However, the court also put the question of duress by a lawful threat in the context of the policies involved. Steyn LJ said (at p 719):

> "We are asked to extend the categories of duress of which the law will take cognisance. That is not necessarily objectionable, but it seems to me that an extension capable of covering the present case, involving 'lawful act duress' in a commercial context in pursuit of a *bona fide* claim, would be a radical one with far-reaching implications. It would introduce a substantial element of uncertainty in the commercial bargaining process. Moreover, it will enable *bona fide* settled accounts to be reopened when parties to commercial dealings fall out. The aim of commercial law ought to be to encourage fair dealings between the parties. But it is a mistake for the law to set its sights too highly when the critical inquiry is not whether the conduct is lawful but whether it is morally or socially unacceptable."

It has already been indicated that the question of determining when a contract has been made in "unacceptable circumstances" is highly problematical if it was made because of a lawful threat. The question of reopening compromises is considered below. (See also *Alf Vaughan & Co Ltd* v *Royscot Trust plc* [1999] 1 All ER (Comm) 856).

(ii)   Lack of a reasonable alternative[4]

Consideration of a second requirement for a finding of duress is necessary where what is threatened is not a criminal offence (see below, page 322 in relation to the situation in which the threat involves a criminal offence).

The Privy Council considered the question of duress in *Pao On* v *Lau Yiu Long* [1980] AC 614. In that case:

> Shares in the Shing On company were being sold by the plaintiffs, P, to the Fu Chip company to be paid for with shares in Fu Chip. There was some concern that, if P chose to dispose too rapidly of those Fu Chip shares, it would adversely affect the value of Fu Chip shares in general. P agreed to retain 60 per cent of the shares for a year. In return, the defendants, D, the family owning most of the Fu Chip shares, agreed to buy the shares after a year at a set price. Fu Chip shares were expected to rise in value and P realised that they had probably made a bad bargain with D. P told D that unless the agreement between them was changed, to one of indemnity, P would not carry out the main contract for the transfer of the shares in Shing On to Fu Chip. D was concerned that news of a problem with the Shing On sale would affect public confidence in Fu Chip. It was agreed to change the contract with P to one of indemnity. Unexpectedly the shares in Fu Chip slumped in value and, when P asked for the indemnity to be performed, D argued that it was voidable for economic duress.

Lord Scarman, delivering the judgment of the court, recognized that economic duress could render a contract voidable in appropriate cases. He said that for duress to be found there must have been "a coercion of the will which vitiates consent" and D's agreement must have been "involuntary" (at p 636). Of greater interest is the list of factors which he regarded as relevant indicators of duress. He said (at p 635):

> "It is material to enquire whether the person alleged to have been coerced did or did not protest; whether at the time he was allegedly coerced into making the contract, he did or did not have an alternative course open to him such as an adequate legal remedy; whether he was independently advised; and whether after entering the contract he took steps to avoid it."

Lord Scarman thought all those matters relevant to determine whether the person alleging duress "acted voluntarily or not". The important factor is that of the availability of an alternative, to agreeing, for the person threatened. It has come to the fore in subsequent cases; and, on closer examination, it is more than a pointer towards duress — it is generally the second element in the test for duress. In *Pao On* D knew that P had no answer to a claim for specific performance. There was an alternative open to him in the form of "an adequate legal remedy". It was decided that there was no duress, merely "commercial pressure" (at p 635).

The question of the alternatives open to the person threatened was again considered when the House of Lords came to look at the question of economic duress in *Universe Tankships Inc of Monrovia* v *International Transport Workers' Federation* [1983] AC 366. Although, in that case, duress was conceded if the ITF's acts were illegitimate (see above), the discussion of it is, nevertheless, of value. After referring to the "compulsion of the will of the victim", Lord Scarman said (at p 400):

> "There must be pressure, the practical effect of which is compulsion or the absence of choice. . . The classic case of duress is, however. . . the victim's intentional submission arising from the realisation that there is no practical choice open to him."

Lord Scarman's "classic case" helps to identify the true general limitation upon economic duress. This second part of the test is generally that of the sufficiency of the alternative courses of action open to the person claiming duress in the light of the other party's threat. The "classic case" is inconsistent with the idea that the test of voluntariness refers to the situation where someone truly acts without will, as an automaton. It would be inconsistent to look for such lack of will and, at the same time, to acknowledge that the person concerned chose between alternatives. The explanation of this inconsistency is partly linguistic and partly due to the superficial justification for the court's interference with the parties' agreement which is provided by a test which appears to be based upon a lack of willed action.

Speaking of duress in terms of involuntariness, or lack of consent, and sometimes even putting in a reference to the will being coerced, tends to create an impression of someone acting without will. The idea that the person under duress is acting without will seemingly provides a justification for the courts' interference with an apparently valid agreement. However, although it is obvious that in looking at questions of duress the court is not considering situations in which someone has been acting without will, this does not make it wholly unacceptable to put the test in terms of voluntariness. The test of "voluntariness" does not merely serve to provide the courts with an apparent justification for their actions. The test of voluntariness is also an effective test when it is thought of in terms of everyday speech. In everyday speech the test of voluntariness is converted into the question of whether the person threatened had "no choice", and this, in turn, is understood as meaning "did he have a 'practical' or 'reasonable' alternative?" As long as the question of voluntariness is understood in everyday terms, as a question of the sufficiency of alternatives, it indicates a workable test of economic duress.

Some recognition of the true test is to be found in *B & S Contracts and Design Ltd* v *Victor Green Publications Ltd* [1984] ICR 419:

> B & S had agreed to erect stands for VG at Olympia to be used for a trade exhibition. B & S intended to use employees who were to be made redundant as soon as they had erected the stands, and they refused to work unless given £9,000 severance pay. B & S paid £4,500 but told VG to pay the rest, in addition to the contract price. It was clear that B & S would not be able to perform the contract unless those employees went back to work. If the stands were not erected, it would have had "disastrous consequences" for VG and the exhibitors, and payment of the money was VG's only means of ensuring that the stands were erected.

It was held that VG had acted under duress. Griffiths LJ thought that the threatened breach placed VG (at p 426):

> "in the position envisaged by Lord Scarman in . . . *Pao On* v *Lau Yiu Long* in which they were faced with no alternative course of action but to pay the sum demanded of them. "

Of course, it is not accurate to say that VG had "no alternative" available. VG could have refused to pay and then sued for breach of contract. However, such an alternative was too damaging to VG. Griffiths LJ said that not having the stands "would have clearly caused grave damage to [VG's] reputation and. . . might have exposed them to very heavy claims from the exhibitors" (at p 426). To speak of "no alternative" is clearly to mean that the alternatives available to VG were not sufficiently acceptable. It is merely to say, in everyday language, that VG had no "reasonable alternative", although the language actually used carries with it something of the flavour of the "lack of will situation", with its seemingly obvious justification for the court's interference. The fact that the contract was made in unacceptable circumstances provides a justification for the court to interfere with an apparently valid contract, but it is a less obvious justification. In addition, this true justification more obviously requires the court to draw limits for its intervention.

The reality of the test as a consideration of alternatives was recognized in the judgment of Kerr LJ. He said (at p 428) that a threat to break a contract will constitute duress if:

"the consequences of a refusal would be serious and immediate so that there is no reasonable alternative open such as legal redress. . .".

This recognizes that such a general limitation upon duress is an assessment of the acceptability of the alternatives open to the person claiming duress, and the test used by Kerr LJ is that of a "reasonable" alternative. (See also *North Ocean Shipping Co Ltd* v *Hyundai Construction Co Ltd; (The Atlantic Baron)* [1978] 3 All ER 1170 at p 1182 (see page 324).)

The question of the availability of a reasonable alternative was again raised in *Vantage Navigation Corp* v *Suhail and Saud Bahwan Building Materials; (The Alev)* [1989] 1 Lloyd's Rep 138, although there were also references to whether consent was "overborne" and "coercion of the will". In that case:

The plaintiffs, P, owned a ship and had made a bad choice of charterer. The charterer had run into financial difficulties and was no longer paying hire for the vessel but, as freight prepaid bills of lading had been issued to the cargo owners, the shipowners were still bound to carry the cargo to its destination. P knew that they were obliged to continue to carry the cargo but they nevertheless decided to attempt to extract an agreement from the defendant cargo owners, D, to pay further for the service which P were already bound to provide. D were well aware that, under such circumstances, shipowners sometimes simply dump the cargo at a convenient port or even sell it in the exercise of some pretended lien. D made a new agreement with P, but made it clear that they were acting under protest and on the basis that they would not otherwise receive their cargo. When P sought to enforce the agreement, D contended that it was voidable for economic duress.

Hobhouse J considered the principle of economic duress to be well established, and he thought that (at p 145):

"The consent of [D] was overborne. There was a coercion of their will. They neither in law nor in fact entered into the agreement voluntarily."

Here again we have the type of language which can serve to create the illusion that economic duress concerns the situation where the person threatened is acting without will, but Hobhouse J also quoted (at p 145) that part of Lord Scarman's judgment in the *ITF* case which refers to the "classic case of duress", ie the situation where the person claiming duress intentionally submits because he realises that he has no "practical alternative". In addition, it was in the light of the judgment of Kerr LJ in *B & S Contracts* (see above) that Hobhouse J considered whether there was a "reasonable alternative" (at pp 146 and 147) open to D and decided there was not. Being deprived of the cargo was "seriously disruptive" of D's business and the "legal remedies [were] inadequate to meet [D's] legitimate commercial needs" (at p 147). Despite the linguistic difficulties, the courts are accepting the test of the availability of a reasonable alternative (see also *The Olib (Enimont Overseas* v *Rojugotanker*

Zader) [1991] 2 Lloyd's Rep 108 at p 114 — "practical alternative"). However, the opinion has been voiced that:

"It is not necessary to go as far as to say that it is an inflexible ... essential ingredient of economic duress that there should be no, or no practical alternative course open for the innocent party" (*Huyton SA* v *Peter Cremer GmbH & Co* [1999] CLC 230 at p 252).

It will be considered below as to whether in exceptional cases, there maybe economic duress despite the presence of a reasonable alternative ie whether there is an alternative second stage test in exceptional circumstances.

What constitutes a reasonable alternative?

What should be looked at when establishing whether there was a reasonable alternative to agreeing, for the person threatened? We can take X as the person claiming duress, and Y as the person alleged to have made the threat, and consider the situation where Y threatened to break his contract with X unless X increased the amount to be paid to Y. Basically, the test looks at whether, instead of giving in to Y's demands, X had a reasonable alternative open to him, whether legal or practical. Where the damage which Y's breach will do to X is small, it may be a reasonable alternative simply to be able to claim damages. If the consequences of non-performance by Y are more serious so that the only reasonable option for X, other than simply agreeing to Y's demand, is to find a substitute for Y's performance, then unless the cost of the substituted performance is small, X will need not only a substitute for the performance itself but also sufficient damages to pay for it. In such a case there is both a legal and a practical side to the reasonableness of the alternative. The question becomes almost entirely legal if the only sufficient alternative open to X, instead of agreeing to Y's demand, is to force Y to perform. In such circumstances, the availability of a sufficient alternative for X will hinge upon whether he can obtain an order for specific performance with sufficient speed. All these factors are relevant to the question of whether or not there are sufficient alternatives open to X, rather than agreeing to Y's demands.

Criticism of the reasonable alternatives test — an alternative?

It has been suggested that the reasonable alternatives test is too uncertain and merely a vehicle for the court to exercise "inarticulate discretion" (Birks [1990] LMCLQ 342 at p 347). Certainly, the degree to which the reality of the alternatives available is examined may vary from case to case. In *Hennessy* v *Craigmyle & Co* [1986] ICR 461 the court seems to have given little thought to the reality of the alternative available to the person claiming duress. Its mere existence seems to have sufficed to defeat the claim of duress. A possible different approach is not to concentrate upon the person claiming duress but instead to look at whether the person making the threat did so with bad faith or malice (Birks, *op cit* at p 346). This serves to distinguish the "honest" contractor, overtaken by changing circumstances and asking for a new contract to help him in a difficult situation, from one who seeks to take advantage of, and profit by, the other party's dependence upon their existing contractual commitment to each other. However, there is little evidence of such an approach at present (although see *D & C Builders* v *Rees* [1966] 1 QB 617) and it, too, seems to be a fairly imprecise test. Its possible strength lies in the satisfaction of the instinct to look for fault. However, although any such search for malice or bad faith should not displace the alternatives test on any general basis, the use of a "bad faith" test must be given some further consideration in two contexts — firstly, where the illegitimate threat is a civil wrong (eg a tort or a breach of contract) and, secondly, where it is not a civil wrong.

Firstly, if a test of bad faith were to displace the alternatives test in the situation where a civil wrong has been "threatened", the innocent party could be left without any effective means to protect the right which would have been infringed had the threat been carried out. The innocent party could find him, or herself, in the situation where he, or she, had no reasonable alternative to agreeing (and so had no effective legal remedy at that point) and no remedy for the duress, as such, because no bad faith was involved in the threat. The innocent party should not be left without any effective means of protecting the rights which were threatened. However, it has been said that:

"Even in cases where the pressure relied on is an actual or threatened breach of duty, it seems to me better not to exclude the possibility that the state of mind of the person applying such pressure may in some circumstances be significant" (*Huyton SA* v *Peter Cremer* [1999] CLC 230 at p 251).

It can be contended that the alternatives test should be displaced by a test of bad faith in a particular situation and where a particular meaning is given to bad faith. The particular situation is where although the injured party does have a reasonable alternative, they perceive themselves as being without one. In that situation the reasonable person would have had an effective means of protecting their rights but the particular individual's perceptions prevent them from doing so. It is contended that they should be allowed to rely upon their own perceptions of the lack of a reasonable alternative where it has, in a sense, been exploited by the other party, ie where the other party intended that to occur, or was reckless (subjectively) as to it occurring. An analogy can be made with the clear acceptance that a fraudulent misrepresentor cannot rely upon a claim that the misrepresentation was not such as to have induced the reasonable person to contract (*Smith* v *Kay* (1859) 7 HLC 750 — see page 388). In addition, some support for this point might be gained from *Huyton* v *Peter Cremer* [1999] CLC 230, where Mance J envisaged the misconceptions of the innocent party as relevant if the other party was in some sense responsible for them. More generally, the requirement of the lack of a reasonable alternative must be insisted upon to protect compromises (see 322).

The second situation to be considered here is where the threat is not otherwise unlawful — neither what is threatened, or the threat itself, constitute a civil or a criminal wrong. The point was made above that bad faith may be relevant in this context and here it may provide a cumulative test with the absence of a reasonable alternative (see page 315). "That good or bad faith may be particularly relevant when considering whether a case might represent a rare example of 'lawful act duress' is not difficult to accept" (*Huyton SA* v *Peter Cremer* [1999] CLC 230 at p 251).

Why have a two stage test when a legal wrong has been threatened?

If what is threatened is a legal wrong, in the civil sense, then why should not that, in itself, be sufficient for a claim of duress? Why, in addition, require the lack of a reasonable alternative course of action for the person threatened? Leaving aside, for the moment, a threat which is unlawful in the criminal sense and dealing purely with civil wrongs, let us consider the impetus behind the alternatives test. The limitation of a claim of duress by the alternatives test is a balancing of the competing needs of protection of the original legal position of the person claiming duress and the enforceability of compromises (see Beatson [1974] CLJ 97). If economic duress could be claimed successfully after any unlawful threat, it would undermine the security of any transaction caused by one party's announcement of his intention to, for example, breach his contract. The law has an interest in ensuring that many such transactions are regarded as binding, although they are founded on a wrong. First, the functioning of the legal system depends upon such "compromises" being made. Not all such disputes could be litigated without overloading the legal system. Secondly, if the parties can reach agreement themselves then it may increase their chances of being able to continue to do business with one another, both throughout that transaction and in the future. Thirdly, it must be remembered that, although we are dealing with the situation where the person making the threat is threatening something unlawful, for example to breach a contract, the threat may have been made under a mistaken belief that it is not unlawful. He may believe himself entitled to whatever it is he is demanding from the other party. To make such "compromises" worthwhile, they must be transactions which cannot easily be reopened. The alternatives test draws a line (see the comments of Steyn LJ in *CTN Cash and Carry Ltd* v *Gallaher Ltd* [1994] 4 All ER 714 — see above, page 315).

However, a completely different approach could be taken:

> "Suppose, for example, that great importance were attached to encouraging responsibility in bidding for contracts. It might be said that the interest of the customer and the interest of competitors of the bidder concur in requiring this priority. Competitors have a grievance if an irresponsible bidder takes the business by bidding too low, confident of later renegotiation. The customer has an interest in knowing that a bid is something better than the beginning of negotiations. If discipline in the process of bidding were expressly the priority... duress would easily be found" (Birks *op cit* at pp 345–346).

If the maintenance of initial rights, rather than the encouragement of compromises, was taken as the priority then there would be no place for the alternatives test. If a threat was unlawful, even in the civil law sense, that would be sufficient. However, the alternatives test achieves a balance between these competing interests. It promotes compromises, but not at the expense of a party who did not have an effective legal remedy when the threat to his rights was made. By definition, at that time he had no "reasonable alternative" open to him, and that encompasses the lack of an effective legal remedy. A very significant inroad would be made upon the protection of compromises if "bad faith" or "malice" was regarded as a sufficient reason for recognizing duress generally, rather than merely exceptionally, even though a reasonable alternative had been available. It would not, however, be to the extent of always protecting initial rights. That would only occur if the mere presence of an unlawful threat, without more, was sufficient to constitute duress.

A different approach is required where what has been threatened is a criminal offence. The alternatives test in such a situation is inappropriate, as it is derived from cases where the threats have been of civil wrongs. There is no indication of it in *Barton* v *Armstrong* [1976] AC 104 where the threats were of physical violence. Where a criminal offence is involved, the law has no interest in the protection of a compromise. In relation to crimes, the sole question concerning the existence of duress seems to be that of legitimacy — ie once it is established that what was threatened was an offence, the existence of duress is confirmed.

3. Is the duress operative?

Once the presence of duress is established, the question of whether it was operative must be asked. There may be positive reasons why the person threatened agreed to the new contract. He might have made the agreement even without the existence of the threat. The fresh consideration offered for making the new contract might be more than purely technical. The person claiming duress may have decided to agree because he does not wish to destroy a longstanding business relationship. This might particularly be the case where, although the other party has, for example, threatened a breach, he did not realise that it was a breach. Even without a long-term business relationship, the person threatened might decide that he should not stand upon his full legal rights. This might be the case where the other party realises that what he is threatening is, for example, a breach, but his side of the contract has been so affected by changed circumstances that performance would be very damaging to him. The person threatened may think that he should assist the other party on this occasion as part of the give and take of commercial life.

The question which must be asked is the degree to which the "threat" must have induced the contract in order for it to be operative. Similar points could be made here as in relation to the question of the degree of reliance required for a misrepresentation to be operative (see page 285). Following *Barton* v *Armstrong* [1976] AC 104 it would seem that in cases of threats to the person it is sufficient if the threat can be viewed as "a" cause of the contract — and the "but for" test need not be satisfied. However, outside of that type of duress, it has been said that "the minimum basic test of subjective causation in economic duress" ought to be a "but for" test (*Huyton SA* v *Peter Cremer* [1999] CLC 230 at p 250). One exceptional situation where the "but for" test should not be required is where there are two concurrent causes of the decision to contract, neither in themselves sufficient, so that if the "but for" test was applied, the contract would be found to have no cause. In that situation a "common sense relaxation, even of a but for requirement is necessary" (*Huyton SA* v *Peter Cremer* [1999] CLC 230 at p 250).

It should finally be noted that whether or not economic duress is found has been seen as a matter of whether an illegitimate threat is present or not and, if there is found to be an illegitimate threat, that the threat was a "significant cause" of the contract (*The Evia Luck* [1992] 2 AC 152 at p 165). The question of "significant cause" was seen as encompassing not only the issue considered here but also the alternatives test set out above.

4. Rescission

It was made clear in relation to misrepresentation that the right to rescind a voidable contract may be lost (see page 299), and the same applies here. In *The*

Atlantic Baron (North Ocean Shipping v *Hyundai Construction Co Ltd)* [1978] 3 All ER 1170 a contract had been made for the building of a ship. When the dollar was devalued the builders threatened to cease work unless the price was increased to take account of that. There was no legal basis to the builders' claim but the purchasers agreed to it. They had already chartered out the ship to Shell and would not have been able to obtain a suitable alternative. Mocatta J found that the agreement to pay the increased price was made under duress but the purchasers could not rely upon it. They were found to have affirmed the contract. By the time the final payments had to be made the market had changed to such an extent that the purchasers could have refused to pay the increase without any risk of non-delivery, but they made no protest. The ship was delivered in November 1974. No indication of any intention to claim duress was given until the end of July 1975 (see Burrows, *The Law of Restitution* (1993) at p 168).

B. Undue influence

1. Introduction

Whilst the common law delayed in developing duress beyond duress to the person, equity provided a more extensive remedy through undue influence. In many cases what equity was asked to do was to enable the person claiming undue influence to recover a gift to a "spiritual adviser" (eg *Allcard* v *Skinner* (1887) 36 Ch D 145). However, undue influence can also be found in cases where consideration is present and it will render a contract voidable. The modern cases are more usually concerned with contracts. Undue influence is about the situation in which one party's decision making has been undermined, where judgment has been abdicated, in areas relevant to the transaction in question.

There are two types of undue influence to consider — actual and presumed. These were labelled as types 1 and 2 by the House of Lords in *Barclays Bank* v *O'Brien* [1993] 4 All ER 417 (at p 423). Type 2, presumed undue influence, came into being because the courts were asked to deal with "insidious forms of spiritual tyranny" and "protect persons from the exercise of such influence under circumstances which render proof of it impossible" (*Allcard* v *Skinner* at pp 183–4). The presumption of undue influence arises when an appropriate relationship exists between the parties. In addition it is necessary to make a sub-division within presumed undue influence into types 2A and 2B. The presumption may arise automatically from the type of relationship (2A), or it may be necessary to establish that the specific relationship between the particular parties is such as to give rise to the presumption (2B). In relation to both types of presumed undue influence, consideration will need to be given to the additional requirement for relief, that there should be "manifest disadvantage" to the person alleging undue influence. Where the presumption operates, what is being presumed is that the potential for undue influence existing in the relationship of the parties did cause the particular gift or contract in question (Birkes & Chin Nyuk Yin 'On the Nature of Undue Influence' in *Good Faith and Fault in Contract Law* Beatson & Friedmann (eds)).

The presumption may be rebutted by showing that the transaction was entered into "only after full, free and informed thought about it" (*Zamet* v *Hyman*

[1961] 3 All ER 933 at p 938). This was explained in *Inche Noriah* v *Shaik Allie Bin Omar* [1929] AC 127 (at p 135) in the context of a gift, but the point is more generally applicable:

> "It is necessary for the donee to prove that the gift was the result of the free exercise of independent will. The most obvious way to prove this is by establishing that the gift was made after the nature of the transaction had been fully explained to the donor by some independent and qualified person so completely as to satisfy the Court that the donor was acting independently of any influence from the donee and with full appreciation of what he was doing . . .".

There may be occasions when a transaction is so disadvantageous that no one taking due account of proper advice could enter into it. In those circumstances, the fact that independent advice has been given will not rebut the presumption (see *Credit Lyonnais* v *Burch* [1997] 1 All ER 144).

As with misrepresentation, and irrespective of whether the undue influence is actual or presumed, the right to rescind may be lost, eg by affirmation[5].

Below, we consider the following:

- actual undue influence (type 1);
- presumed undue influence — from the type of relationship (type 2A);
- presumed undue influence — from the specific relationship (type 2B);
- manifest disadvantage;
- third parties affected by undue influence.

2. Actual undue influence

Actual undue influence is about the situation where one party enters into a transaction, or makes a gift, because of the influence of another. The relevant party has not exercised his, or her, own decision-making powers because of the trust and confidence he, or she, places in the other or because of the relationship between them of dependency and ascendency or dominion.

Actual undue influence was present between husband and wife in *Bank of Credit and Commerce International SA* v *Aboody* [1989] 1 QB 923. In that case the question arose as to whether the wife had been under the undue influence of the husband when executing guarantees, and charges on the matrimonial home, relating to loans by the bank to the husband's business. The facts were:

> Mrs Aboody was born an Iraqi Jew, and was educated in Baghdad in a very traditional way. In 1946, at the age of seventeen, she married Mr Aboody. It was an arranged marriage, and he was twenty years older than she was. In 1949 they came to England. Mr Aboody went into business and, on the retirement of his brother, Mrs Aboody became nominally a director and secretary of Eratex Ltd, the family business. She did not understand the business. It was routine for her to sign whatever her husband asked her to sign in relation to Eratex Ltd. She distinguished between signing documents presented by her husband, and those presented by a stranger. She stated that if a stranger asked for her signature she would read the document, but she trusted her husband to be acting for the good of the business. In relation to the last transaction, a charge, the bank's solicitor tried to ensure that she

had independent advice. However, when a solicitor tried to discuss it with her, at the bank, she was already resolved to sign, having been told by her husband that the solicitor was merely to witness her signature. In the middle of the solicitor's attempt to advise her, Mr Aboody burst into the room in a state of agitation, and Mrs Aboody was reduced to tears.

In the Court of Appeal actual undue influence was conceded in relation to the last transaction, but the court also found that there was actual undue influence in relation to the previous transactions. The court found that Mr Aboody had asked Mrs Aboody to sign the documents and he had used his influence to ensure that she did so without any discussion or consideration of the risks. He deliberately prevented her from giving proper detached consideration to her independent interests in transactions which involved substantial risk to those interests. It did not matter that Mr Aboody had not acted with any malign intent to cause detriment to his wife. There was actual undue influence in the making of the guarantees and the charges.

3.   Presumed undue influence — from the type of relationship

There are certain well established types of relationship which give rise to the presumption of undue influence automatically:

"There are several well defined relationships, such as parent and child, superior and member of a sisterhood, doctor and patient, and solicitor and client to which the presumption is, as it were, presumed to apply unless the contrary is proved. In such relationships it would seem that you only have to look at the relative status of the parties in order to presume that the requisite degree of trust and confidence is there" (*Goldsworthy* v *Brickell* [1987] 1 All ER 853, *per* Nourse LJ at p 865).

When one of these relationships exists the presumption arises automatically, without any investigation of the relationship between the particular parties in the specific case. It should be noted that the relationship of husband and wife is not one of those encompassed within the automatic presumption[6].

4.   Presumed undue influence — from the specific relationship

Discussion of the requirements of a relationship giving rise to the presumption has been quite limited. There is a tendency merely to rely upon labelling a relationship as "confidential" or "fiduciary" if the presumption is to arise. What is required is a relationship in which one party has surrendered relevant decision making. Most commonly, what is in question is a relationship of trust and confidence — the type of trust and confidence which leads one party, A, to rely upon the other party, B, to act in his, A's interests, rather than B's own interests. It is reliance upon, and trust in, disinterested advice.

In *Lloyds Bank* v *Bundy* [1974] 3 All ER 757 the presumption was found to arise, and the situation was distinguished from the trust whch can exist in a business relationship between parties dealing at arm's length. In that case, the facts were as follows:

Mr Bundy charged his home to guarantee his son's business debts to the bank. Both father and son used the same bank. The father's relationship with the bank was longstanding, and he relied upon it for advice. When the assistant manager brought the charge to Mr Bundy's home to be signed he realised that Mr Bundy looked to him for advice. The assistant manager not only explained the legal effect of the charge but also discussed the situation of the son's company. Mr Bundy "was seeking and being given advice on the viability of the company as a factor to be taken into account" in his decision to sign the charge. The charge was not to enable the son to borrow more money from the bank but merely to secure his existing loans. The execution of the charge meant that the bank was not demanding repayment immediately, but it did not guarantee a period within which it would not do so. Very little was gained by Mr Bundy, or his son, in return for the execution of the charge but the bank gained security for existing debts. The assistant manager had not perceived any conflict of interest and had not advised Mr Bundy to obtain independent advice.

When the bank claimed possession of Mr Bundy's home, he argued that the charge should be set aside for undue influence. The Court of Appeal concluded that Mr Bundy's reliance upon the bank to give general advice on the wisdom of the transaction raised the presumption of undue influence and, in the absence of independent advice for Mr Bundy, it was not rebutted. Sir Eric Sachs considered the type of relationship in which the presumption arises (at p 767):

"Such cases tend to arise where someone relies on the guidance or advice of another, where the other is aware of that reliance and where the person on whom reliance is placed obtains, or may well obtain, a benefit from the transaction or has some other interest in it being concluded. In addition there must of course be shown to exist a vital element which in this judgement will be referred to as confidentiality. It is this element which is so impossible to define and which is a matter for the judgement of the court on the facts of any particular case. . . It imports some quality beyond that inherent in the confidence that can well exist between trustworthy persons who in business affairs deal with each other at arm's length. It is one of the features of this element that once it exists, influence naturally grows out of it."

Despite his reluctance to regard the "vital element" of "confidentiality" as definable, Sir Eric Sachs' distinction between the situation in which undue influence may be presumed, and that of business dealings at arm's length between trustworthy persons, makes it clear that he is referring to the situation where one party is expected to give disinterested advice to the other. The question is: Is the person concerned trusted to the extent that he is relied upon to act in the interests of the other party, and not his own? It is that degree of trust, reliance, or confidence, which gives rise to the possibility of undue influence and the need for the presumption.

The relationship of banker and customer was again considered in *National Westminster Bank plc* v *Morgan* [1985] 1 All ER 821, and the House of Lords distinguished the case from *Bundy*. In *Morgan*, the facts were as follows:

A husband and wife were in danger of losing their home because the building society was seeking possession for non-payment of the mortgage. The bank agreed to a refinancing of the house purchase on the basis of a bridging loan to cover the few weeks until the husband expected to have the money. His business was then looking prosperous, although it had been through hard times. However, the bank required a charge on the house for the loan. The bank manager called at the house to obtain the wife's signature on the legal charge. He mistakenly assured the wife that the charge would not extend to her husband's business liabilities to the bank. In fact the charge was sufficiently widely worded to cover those business liabilities, but it was not the intention of the bank that it should be so used and it never was so used. The husband died and the bank sought possession of the house.

The wife did not raise the issue of innocent misrepresentation but merely claimed that the charge should be set aside for undue influence. The House of Lords held that the relationship did not raise the presumption. The manager had explained the charge to her but the wife had not looked to the manager for general advice on the wisdom of the transaction. She executed the charge because that was how she and her husband planned to preserve the family home, and she knew that it was the only way to do so. In *Bundy* the bank had discussed with Mr Bundy the position of his son's business. In addition, the House of Lords held that the court could not act, on the basis of presumed undue influence, in relation to a transaction where there was no manifest disadvantage to the person claiming undue influence. There was no such manifest disadvantage in the instant case. It was a normal commercial loan taken to preserve the family home (see page 330 for the requirement of manifest disadvantage).

We should give brief consideration to the use by Lord Scarman (with whom the rest of the court agreed) of the term "dominating influence" to indicate the situation in which the presumption of undue influence arises. The context of this reference must be made clear. The House of Lords was keen to establish the requirement of manifest disadvantage, and the reference to a "dominating influence" was merely an echo of the terminology used in *Poosathurai* v *Kannappa Chettiar* [1919] LR 47 (Ind App). That case was referred to not for its description of the relationship necessary to give rise to the presumption, but because it was helpful in establishing the requirement of manifest disadvantage (*Morgan* at p 829). It was a Privy Council decision from India and the use there of the term "domination" followed from the reference to "a person in the position to dominate the will of another" in the Indian Contract Act 1872. Although the presumption should arise where one party's domination over another is such that the other has abdicated relevant decision making, it should not be thought that Lord Scarman's terminology indicates that a dominating influence is necessary before the presumption of undue influence will arise under English law.

The lack of a requirement of "dominating influence" was made clear in *Goldsworthy* v *Brickell* [1987] 1 All ER 853, where the Court of Appeal explained the context of the reference in *Morgan* (at pp 868–9). In *Goldsworthy*, the facts were as follows:

Mr Goldsworthy owned a farm which from 1970 to 1976 he had run with his son as his sole employee. He had little faith in his son's abilities, relations between them were strained, and the farm was in a run-down condition. The son did not live in the farmhouse with his father. From the end of 1976 Mr Brickell, a neighbouring farmer, gave Mr Goldsworthy help and advice in the running of his farm. Mr Brickell's employees worked on Mr Goldsworthy's farm at no cost to him. One of Mr Brickell's female employees cleaned Mr Goldsworthy's house and did his shopping for him. Mr Goldsworthy's reliance upon Mr Brickell and his employees was such that by early 1977 Mr Brickell was effectively managing Mr

Goldsworthy's farm. In April 1977, Mr Goldsworthy, who was then eighty-five, whilst keeping the right to live on the farm, granted Mr Brickell a tenancy of his farm with an option to purchase it on his death. Both were on terms very disadvantageous to Mr Goldsworthy.

The Court of Appeal set aside the tenancy agreement. The relationship between Mr Brickell and Mr Goldsworthy was sufficient to raise the presumption of undue influence. The court made it clear that the relationship was sufficient to support the presumption even though it fell short of domination. It was enough that the appropriate trust and confidence existed between the parties.

The case also contains further indication that the essence of the "trust and confidence" relationship which will give rise to the presumption is that of reliance, not merely upon someone's judgement, but also upon their advice being totally disinterested, ie not tainted by their own interests. Nourse LJ explained why the relationships of solicitor and client, and doctor and patient, are regarded as automatically giving rise to the presumption. He said (at p 868):

"doctors and solicitors are trusted and confided in by their patients and clients to give them conscientious and disinterested advice on matters which profoundly affect, in the one case their physical and mental and, in the other, their material wellbeing. It is natural to presume that out of trust and confidence grows influence".

He also explained why the banker-customer relationship is not one which ordinarily gives rise to the presumption:

"a banker, being a person having a pre-existing and conflicting interest in any loan transaction with a customer, cannot ordinarily be trusted and confided in so as to come under a duty to take care of the customer and give him disinterested advice".

Again the emphasis is upon it being the expectation of disinterested advice which is looked for to give rise to the presumption (see also *Elton John* v *James* [1991] FSR 397 at pp 449–451).

Although it seems necessary to identify the type of trust and confidence giving rise to the presumption, Lord Scarman's warning in *Morgan* [1985] 1 All ER 821 must be borne in mind. He said (at p 877):

"There is no precisely defined law setting the limits to the equitable jurisdiction of a court to relieve against undue influence. This is the world of doctrine, not of neat and tidy rules. . .".

The final point to be made here is that it may be relevant to consider the disadvantageous nature of the transaction in deciding whether the circumstances are sufficient to generate the presumption of undue influence. In *Credit Lyonnais* v *Burch* [1997] 1 All ER 144, Millett LJ said (at p 154):

"The mere fact that a transaction is improvident or manifestly disadvantageous to one party is not sufficient by itself to give rise to a presumption that it has been obtained by the exercise of undue influence; but where it is obtained by a party between whom and the complainant there is a relationship like that of employer and junior employee which is easily capable of developing into a relationship of trust and confidence, the nature of the transaction may be sufficient to justify the inference that such a development had taken place; and where the transaction is so extravagantly improvident that it is virtually inexplicable on any other basis, the inference will readily be drawn."

As will be seen, the improvident nature of a transaction is also relevant to the question of whether a third party has been affected by contructive notice of undue influence between others (see page 334).

5. Manifest disadvantage

(a) When is it required?

In *National Westminster Bank plc* v *Morgan* [1985] 1 All ER 821 the House of Lords stated that no presumption of undue influence, on which the courts would act, would arise unless the transaction was one in which there was a manifest disadvantage to the party claiming undue influence. There were parts of Lord Scarman's judgment which could be seen as indicating that manifest disadvantage was required even in relation to actual undue influence (eg at p 828) and that was the line taken by the Court of Appeal in *Aboody* (above). However, the House of Lords in *CIBC Mortgages plc* v *Pitt* [1993] 4 All ER 433 made it clear that such an approach was wrong and that any requirement of manifest disadvantage was confined to cases of presumed undue influence and did not apply to cases in which actual undue influence had been established. Lord Browne-Wilkinson, with whom the other members of the court agreed, said (at p 439):

"Whatever the merits of requiring a complainant to show manifest disadvantage in order to raise ... a presumption of undue influence, in my judgment there is no logic in imposing such a requirement where actual undue influence has been exercised and proved ... The effect of the wrongdoer's conduct is to prevent the wronged party from bringing a free will and properly informed mind to bear on the proposed transaction which accordingly must be set aside in equity as a matter of justice."

However, following the decision in *CIBC Mortgages plc* v *Pitt*, it has been questioned whether the requirement of manifest disadvantage will be maintained even in relation to cases of presumed undue influence. In that case, Lord Browne-Wilkinson stated that "the exact limits of the decision in *Morgan* may have to be considered in the future" (at p 439). In *Morgan* the line had been taken that the presumption was a matter of dealing with the situation in which one person "victimised", or took advantage of, another. That led to the need to show manifest disadvantage to establish "victimization" (*National Westminster Bank plc* v *Morgan* [1985] 1 All ER 821 at pp 826–829). However, there are indications in *Pitt* that, contrary to *Morgan,* the presumption of undue influence is based on the public policy of dealing with the potential for the abuse of certain types of relationship. Of course, if presumed undue influence is concerned with the mere potential for abuse then there need be no requirement of manifest disadvantage. Something of this has been acknowledged recently by the Court of Appeal in *Barclays Bank plc* v *Coleman and another* [2000] 1 All ER 385. The requirement of manifest disadvantage was seen as "an original creation of their Lordships House" in *Morgan* (at p 399) and the court recognised that whilst it was currently bound to hold that there was such a requirement, "the House of Lords have signalled that it may not continue to be a necessary ingredient indefinitely" (at p 400). Under those circumstances, the court had "no disposition to enlarge its significance" and took a narrow view of what manifest disadvantage required.

There is every reason to suggest that the House of Lords may remove manifest disadvantage as a requirement when the opportunity arises. Until that occurs, the lower courts may take the course of developing the meaning of manifest disadvantage to diminish its significance. Of course, if the requirement is removed, the disadvantage of a transaction may still have evidential value in establishing that the relationship is one which should give rise to the presumption (see page 329). It should, however, be acknowledged that "manifest disadvantage" could be maintained as a requirement for the presumption of undue influence to arise even if undue influence is not perceived as based on "victimization". It could be maintained merely as a pragmatic limit upon the cases in which a transaction will be set aside on the basis of undue influence (Birks & Chin Nyuk Yin 'The Nature of Undue Influence' in *Good Faith and Fault in Contract Law* Beatson & Friedmann (eds) at p 82).

(b) What constitutes manifest disadvantage?

Manifest disadvantage must be assessed in the light of the circumstances which were known to, or which should have been known to, the parties at the time the transaction was entered into (*Aboody* at p 965). In *Aboody* it was emphasised that the disadvantage must be "manifest" and so could not be a disadvantage which emerged only "after a fine and close examination of the facts", but must be such that "it would have been obvious as such to any independent and reasonable person who considered the transaction at the time with knowledge of all the relevant facts" (at p 965). More recently, in *Coleman* where the court was indicating that manifest disadvantage might be ripe for review by the House of Lords in relation to cases of presumed undue influence, it was indicated that it should not be seen as too significant a hurdle to a finding of presumed undue influence. Nourse LJ, with the other members of the court agreeing, said (at p 400):

> "To some judges 'manifest' seems to have connoted substance, not appearance. But ... it means 'clear and obvious'. So there must be a disadvantage and it must be clear and obvious. But that does not mean that it must be large or even medium-sized. Provided it is clear and obvious and more than de minimis, the disadvantage may be small."

Some examples of the courts' application of the requirement should be looked at. That there may, recently, have been some change in emphasis should be borne in mind.

In *Aboody* the transactions were the giving of guarantees and the execution of charges; under those circumstances the question of whether manifest disadvantage was present was seen as a weighing process. There is always a risk that a guarantee might be called upon or a charge enforced. The question was one of weighing that risk against the benefit gained by the person giving the guarantee or executing the charge. In the particular case, there were substantial potential liabilities and the possible loss of the family home. However, that was balanced against the fact that Mrs Aboody's actions gave some hope of survival to the family business, which was the sole or principal means of support of Mr and Mrs Aboody. The Court of Appeal saw no sufficient reason for disagreeing with the judge's conclusion that no manifest disadvantage was present. Similarly, in *Morgan* no manifest disadvantage was considered to be present. The wife was taking a risk that executing the charge might result in the bank claiming the matrimonial home. However, at that point, executing the charge was the only way to prevent the building society from claiming the Morgans' home immediately.

Even outside the context of guarantees and charges, determining whether there is a manifest disadvantage may be seen as a question of weighing the advantages and disadvantages of the transaction in question. In *Cheese* v *Thomas* [1994] 1 All ER 35:

> The 88 year old plaintiff agreed to buy a house with his great-nephew, the defendant. The house cost £83,000, of which the plaintiff supplied £43,000 from the sale of his flat in Peacehaven, Sussex where he had lived with his brother who had died. The house was in Hayes, Middlesex, where he had lived previously, and where his wife and daughter were buried. The defendant took out a mortgage to cover the remaining £40,000. The house was purchased solely in the name of the defendant but it was agreed that the plaintiff would reside there, alone, for the rest of his life. The defendant failed to keep up the mortgage payments and the plaintiff sought to withdraw from the transaction and recover his £43,000.

The first issue for the court was whether the transaction could be set aside on the basis of undue influence. The great-nephew conceded that the relationship was such as to give rise to the presumption of undue influence. The Court of Appeal considered whether there was manifest disadvantage. In return for his £43,000 the plaintiff had received the right to live in a house which he could not himself afford to buy, and the house was in an area in which he wished to live. However, he had used all his capital in the transaction. If he wished to move again, he could not compel the defendant to sell the house or return any of his money. In addition, there was the important factor that he would be in jeopardy if the defendant failed to maintain the mortgage payments. The court concluded that there was a manifest disadvantage. Sir Donald Nicholls V-C said (at p 39):

> "I agree with the judge that the transaction is properly to be described as manifestly, that is, clearly and obviously, disadvantageous to [the plaintiff]. He used all his money, and it was not an insignificant amount, in buying a right which was seriously insecure and which tied him to this particular house."

The distinction between this and a case like *Morgan* seems to lie in the need to take the degree of risk which the transaction entailed. In *Morgan* "the wife knew that there was no other way of saving the house" (at p 825). Under those circumstances, the transaction merely involved trading a certainty of losing the house for a chance to save it. Even a slim chance of saving it was seen as indicating that there was no manifest disadvantage. Of course, there could be cases in which the cost of that "chance" would be so high as to entail a manifest disadvantage, but there was no indication that that level of cost had been reached in *Morgan* (although the situation might have been otherwise had the charge been treated as covering the husband's business liabilities). In contrast, there was no indication of a similar degree of necessity for the transaction in *Cheese* v *Thomas* and that meant that the risks involved in the transaction, such as the defendant failing to make the mortgage payments, outweighed the advantages and there was a manifest disadvantage.

It should be emphasised that any weighing by the courts of the benefits and disadvantages of a transaction is unlikely to be an accurate economic assessment with, for example, the possibility of keeping a matrimonial home being accurately converted into money terms. The courts carry out the sort of weighing process involved in assessing manifest disadvantage in a much more "rough and ready" and intuitive fashion. In any event, the costs involved in an accurate economic weighing process would be very high. Accurately translating an interest such as the possibility of keeping a matrimonial home into economic terms would be very costly. A great deal of information would have to be gathered to make such an assessment possible at all.

6. Undue influence and third parties

The question which now needs to be considered is when a third party will be affected by undue influence — actual or presumed. In the situation in which undue influence is often raised, its proven use or presumption will only be the first enquiry. This is because the problem is frequently that a wife, acting under the undue influence of her husband, has acted as a surety for a loan to the husband, or the husband's business, and secured it by a charge on the matrimonial home. Under such circumstances, if the transaction is to be set aside for undue influence, the bank (or other creditor), to which the surety was given, will have to be affected by the undue influence. The question then which needs to be considered here is: when will a third party to the undue influence be affected by it?

After a series of decisions by the lower courts, in *Barclays Bank plc* v *O'Brien* [1993] 4 All ER 417 (Lehane (1994) 110 LQR 166) the House of Lords had to consider the question of when third parties are affected by either undue influence or misrepresentation. The case was concerned with the surety, charged on the matrimonial home, which a wife had given in relation to the overdraft of her husband's business. She claimed that she had executed it whilst acting under the undue influence of her husband and that he had misrepresented the extent and duration of the borrowing covered by it. By the time the case reached the House of Lords, the claim was restricted to misrepresentation, but it is clear that the test of the impact upon the bank is the same whether the wife acted under undue influence or misrepresentation.

The House of Lords said that there were basically two ways in which a bank's surety could be affected by a husband's undue influence and a charge set aside. That would occur if either (i) the husband had acted as the bank's agent to obtain the execution of the charge, or (ii) the bank had actual or constructive notice of the facts giving rise to the wife's claim (at p 428). Although stated in relation to husband and wife, this is of general application and must be considered as such. The first possibility, involving a finding of an agency relationship between creditor and debtor, is unlikely to occur. It is "notice" which requires further consideration here and, in particular, "constructive notice". Basically, constructive notice occurs if the bank (or other creditor) knows of facts which put it on inquiry as to the possible existence of undue influence and it fails to make such inquiry or take such other steps as are reasonable to verify the situation (at p 429). Some immediate examples can be identified. If the relationship between the debtor and surety is one giving rise to a type 2A presumption of undue influence (ie a relationship from which the presumption of undue influence arises automatically) then normally the creditor should be "automatically ... on inquiry" (*Royal Bank of Scotland plc* v *Etridge (No 2)* [1998] 4 All ER 705 at p 719). Similarly, if the creditor knows facts about the actual relationship which would put it in the 2B category, that should also normally put the creditor automatically on inquiry. "Furthermore, where the transaction is so extravagantly improvident that it is difficult to explain in the absence of some impropriety, then the [creditor] may likewise be put on inquiry" (*Etridge (No 2)* [1998] 4 All ER 705 at p 719). However, the creditor would not normally be put on inquiry where the surety dealt with the creditor through a solicitor (*Etridge (No 2)* [1998] 4 All ER 705 at p 721 — the issue of a solicitor who is acting not only for the surety but also the debtor or the creditor is considered below). The relationship of husband and wife is not a type 2A relationship and guidance was given in *O'Brien* as to when a creditor dealing with husband and wife will be put on inquiry as to possibility of the husband's undue influence. Lord Browne-Wilkinson, with whom the other members of the court agreed, said ([1993] 4 All ER 417 at p 429):

> "A creditor is put on inquiry when a wife offers to stand surety for her husband's debts by the combination of two factors: (a) the transaction is on its face not to the financial advantage of the wife; and (b) there is a substantial risk in transactions of that kind that, in procuring the wife to act as surety, the husband has committed a legal or equitable wrong that entitles the wife to set aside the transaction."

So, in the central case "[t]he wife needs to show only that the bank knew that she was a wife living with her husband and that the transaction was not on its face to her financial advantage. The burden is then upon the bank to show that it took reasonable steps to satisfy itself that her consent was properly obtained" (*Barclays Bank plc* v *Boulter and another* [1999] 4 All ER 513 at p 519). However, in *O'Brien* itself, the House of Lords also recognised that their approach was of more general application and not solely confined to the husband and wife type of case. The factors identified in *O'Brien* need to be considered further, as does the question of what a creditor can do to prevent itself being fixed with constructive notice of undue influence. There is a need to strike a balance between vulnerable parties and lenders — the family home must not be stultified as an asset against which businesses can raise money.

(a) Transaction, on its face, not financially advantageous to the "wife"

In Lord Browne-Wilkinson's *dictum*, the factor referred to, is that the transaction is not financially advantageous to "the wife". However, as will be seen, the approach taken in *O'Brien* is not restricted to cases of undue influence between husbands and wives, but is of general application (see *(b)* below). Here the point to be made is that the transaction must be one which, to the third party creditor, did not appear financially beneficial to the party who claims to have entered into it because of undue influence. The disadvantage must appear on the face of the transaction — so that it is, or should be, apparent to the third party. Constructive notice of the wrong (undue influence/misrepresentation) was not found where what was involved was a mortgage of the family home and the mortgage application stated that it was to buy a holiday home, even though its purpose was, actually, to allow the husband to speculate on the stock exchange (*CIBC Mortgages* v *Pitt* [1993] 4 All ER 433); nor was there any constructive notice where the purpose of the mortgage was stated to be the purchase of shares in a family business, when the real reason was, in fact, the discharge of the husband's existing business debts (*Halifax Mortgages* v *Stepsky* [1996] 2 All ER 277). Where a wife has been asked to assist in relation to the finances of a business, the transaction will appear improvident on its face "if all that the lender knows is that the business is one in which the husband (but not the wife) has a direct financial interest" (*Bank of Scotland* v *Bennett*) [1999] 1 FCR 641 at p 648).

(b) Substantial risk in transactions of that kind that, in procuring the wife to act as surety, the husband has committed a legal or equitable wrong

The point has been made that this approach to when third parties will be affected by undue influence is not confined to the situation where that undue influence arises between husband and wife. It was indicated in *O'Brien* that the type of factors which could make undue influence a recognisable risk between husband and wife also applied in other circumstances of cohabitation. Lord Browne-Wilkinson said (at p 431):

"the same principles are applicable to all other cases where there is an emotional relationship between cohabitees. The 'tenderness' shown by the law to married women is not based on the marriage ceremony but reflects the underlying risk of one cohabitee exploiting the emotional involvement and trust of the other. Now that unmarried cohabitation, whether heterosexual or homosexual, is widespread in our society, the law should recognise this. Legal wives are not the only group which are now exposed to the emotional pressure of cohabitation. Therefore if, but only if, the creditor is aware that the surety is cohabiting with the principal debtor, in my judgment the same principles should apply to them as apply to husband and wife."

In addition, it is now clear that this approach applies even more generally. In *Massey* v *Midland Bank plc* [1995] 1 All ER 929 it was applied in the context of two parties who had never cohabited but who had enjoyed a long-standing stable sexual and emotional relationship and who, in fact, had two children. It was also applied in *Credit Lyonnais Bank Nederland NV* v *Burch* [1997] 1 All ER 144 where the bank knew that the security for the company's extended borrowing was being provided by a junior employee, who was not a shareholder or director, and who had no financial interest in the company. The relationship of employer and junior employee was viewed as "easily capable of developing into" one of "trust and confidence" (at p 154). The point has been made that:

"It should not be overlooked that a transaction which a wife or cohabitee might well consider (and be advised) was in her interest may be virtually inexplicable in the case of anyone else in the absence of undue influence." (*Royal Bank of Scotland* v *Etridge (No 2)* [1998] 4 All ER 705 at p 719.)

There is an interaction between the two factors identified in *O'Brien* and, as has already been indicated:

"where the transaction is so extravagantly improvident that it is difficult to explain in the absence of some impropriety, then the bank may . . . be put on inquiry" (*Etridge (No 2)* [1998] 4 All ER 705 at p 719).

What can the third party do to prevent itself being fixed with constructive notice?

The point has been made that a balance must be achieved between the protection of wives and other vulnerable parties and the need not to stultify the family home as an asset which can be used to raise money for the family business. There must be some certainty as to the steps which the creditor can take to prevent itself being affected by undue influence between debtor and surety. So, if the situation is one in which constructive notice of any undue influence would otherwise be found, how is the third party to avoid being affected by it? This was addressed in *O'Brien,* in relation to wives, but the point applies more generally. It was indicated that, if a bank is to avoid being fixed with constructive notice, it must take reasonable steps to satisfy itself that the agreement of the wife has been properly obtained (at p 429). To do that a bank can "reasonably be expected to take steps to bring home to the wife the risk she is running by standing as surety and to advise her to take independent advice". More concretely, guidelines were provided for the ordinary case. It was indicated that, in the ordinary case, the bank can avoid being found to have constructive notice of any undue influence (at pp 429–430):

> "if it insists that the wife attend a private meeting (in the absence of the husband) with a representative of the [bank] at which she is told of the extent of her liability as surety, warned of the risk she is running and urged to take independent legal advice".

Nothing of the sort had occurred in *O'Brien* and the bank had constructive notice of the husband's wrong. However, in the main, since *O'Brien*, it is not a procedure in keeping with the guidelines in that case that the court has had to consider. The situation commonly needing to be addressed is where the bank has required "the wife to obtain independent legal advice and provide written confirmation that she has done so" (*Etridge (No 2)* at p 720). The point has been made that, if the wife has actually received independent advice, the "objective of Lord Browne-Wilkinson's guidance [in *O'Brien*] has been achieved" and the bank will be able to rely upon a certificate from the solicitor that such advice has been given and that she appeared to understand it. That will generally be the case even if the solicitor is also acting for the other party or even for the bank "in a ministerial capacity". The position was summarised in *Royal Bank of Scotland* v *Etridge (No 2)* [1998] 4 All ER 705 at pp 721–722[7]:

> "When giving advice to the wife the solicitor is acting exclusively as her solicitor ... It makes no difference whether he is unconnected with the husband or the wife ... or is also the husband's solicitor ... or that he has agreed to act in a ministerial capacity as the bank's agent at completion ... Whoever introduces the solicitor to the wife and asks him to advise her, and whoever is responsible for his fees, the bank is entitled to expect the solicitor to regard himself as owing a duty to the wife alone when giving her advice...
>
> It follows that the bank is not fixed with imputed notice of what the solicitor learns in the course of advising the wife even if he is also the bank's solicitor. Such knowledge does not come to him in his capacity as the bank's solicitor...
>
> The bank is entitled to rely on the fact that the solicitor undertook the task of explaining the transaction to the wife as showing that he considered himself to

be sufficiently independent for this purpose ... The bank is not required to question the solicitor's independence, even if it knows that he is also the husband's solicitor...

While the bank is normally entitled to assume that a solicitor who is asked to advise the wife will discharge his duties fully and competently ... it cannot make any such assumption if it knows or ought to know that it is false ... If the bank is in possession of material information which is not available to the solicitor, or if the transaction is one into which no competent solicitor could properly advise the wife to enter, the availability of legal advice is insufficient to avoid the bank being fixed with constructive notice."

It may not be satisfactory if the bank invited the solicitors to obtain, from the husband, details of the underlying business transaction to which a loan and guarantee relates (*National Westminster* v *Kostopoulos* [2000] 1 FLR 815). However, if a solicitor is to advise the wife as to the giving of a charge to secure the liabilities of the husband and wife to the bank, "he may reasonably be expected to inform himself of the nature of those liabilities; and on learning that those liabilities are themselves liabilities under a guarantee for the company's indebtedness to the bank, to inform himself as to the company's financial position" (*Bank of Scotland* v *Bennet* [1999] 1 FCR 641 at p 671). There will be situations in which the bank cannot assume that it can rely upon the solicitor's consideration of the possibility that he should not advise the wife because of a conflict of interest and that none exists if he has advised her. Where the solicitor is also the company secretary and has played a major role in the company's quest for finance, the situation is regarded as outside the normal case in which the bank can rely upon the solicitor having satisfactorily considered the possibility of a conflict of interest. The bank could not rely upon his advice to the wife to prevent itself being fixed with constructive knowledge of undue influence (*National Westminster Bank* v *Breeds* (2001) 151 NLJ 170). In addition, advising the surety to obtain independent advice, or even having a certificate that she has received it, may not prevent the creditor being fixed with constructive notice if no solicitor could advise her to enter into the transaction. Advising that independent advice be obtained did not protect the third party from constructive notice in *Credit Lyonnais Bank Nederland NV* v *Burch* [1997] 1 All ER 144. In that case:

the security for the company's extended debts was provided by a junior employee on a "modest wage". She had no financial interest in the company. She provided a second charge on a small flat which was valued at £100,000 and which was subject to a mortgage of £30,000. She understood that the charge was unlimited in time and amount but she had no idea of the significance of that. She did not know that, on the figures at the time of the transaction, the company's failure could have exposed her to the loss of her home and a personal debt of £200,000 on top of that. It was "an extreme case. The transaction was not merely to the manifest disadvantage of Miss Burch; it was one which, in the traditional phrase 'shocks the conscience of the court'." (at p 152). If she had received independent advice, it would have been not to enter into the transaction.

It was clear that there was undue influence between employer and employee and, despite the fact that she had been advised to take independent advice, the bank could not enforce the security. Millett LJ made the general point that circumstances raised the suspicion of undue influence and the bank could not avoid being fixed with constructive notice unless two conditions were satisfied (at p 155):

(i) it must have taken reasonable steps to allay any such suspicion; and

(ii) the result of the steps which it took must be such as would reasonably allay any such suspicion.

In this particular case, the bank had done what it reasonably could, in urging Miss Burch to take independent advice, but the results of doing so could not allay its suspicion, or prevent there from being constructive notice, as any solicitor would have advised her not to enter the transaction. The fact that she went ahead with such a transaction added to the reasons to suspect undue influence.

In each case the various factors will need to be addressed. Here separate consideration has been given to the two issues identified in *O'Brien* as indicative of constructive notice for the creditor and also of the ways in which the creditor can prevent itself being fixed with such notice. However, it should be emphasised that what is in question is a weighing of all of the factors:

"Ultimately the issue is whether, at the time when value is given, and in the light of all the information in the bank's possession, including its knowledge of the state of account, the relationship of the parties, and the availability of legal advice for the wife, there is still a risk that the wife has entered into the transaction as a result of her husband's . . . undue influence." (*Etridge (No 2)* at p 722, para 50.)

Footnotes

(1) Contrast *Skeate* v *Beale* (1841) 11 A & E 983 and *Astley* v *Reynolds* (1731) 2 Str 915; Beatson [1974] CLJ 97.

(2) For example, *North Ocean Shipping* v *Hyundai* [1978] 3 All ER 1170 at p 1183; *Pao On* v *Lau Yiu Long* [1980] AC 614 at p 636; *The Siboen and the Sibotre* [1976] 1 Lloyd's Rep 293 at p 335; *Hennessy* v *Craigmyle* [1986] ICR at p 468.

(3) Lord Diplock at p 384 and Lord Scarman at p 400. Carty & Evans [1983] JBL 218.

(4) Macdonald [1989] JBL 460.

(5) In *Allcard* v *Skinner* (1887) 36 Ch D 145, although undue influence was found, the court also held that the person influenced had lost the right to have her gift returned. She had delayed taking action for six years after she had left the "sisterhood" and the influence of her "spiritual adviser".

(6) *Bank of Montreal* v *Stuart* [1911] AC 120; *Midland Bank* v *Shephard* [1988] 3 All ER 17 at p 21; *National Westminster Bank* v *Morgan* [1985] 1 All ER 821 at p 826.

(7) The court derived this summary from:
Banco Exterior Internacional v *Mann and others* [1995] 1 All ER 936;
Barclays Bank plc v *Thomson* [1997] 4 All ER 816;
Midland Bank plc v *Serter* [1995] 3 FCR 711;
Massey v *Midland Bank plc* [1995] 1 All ER 929;
Halifax Mortgage Services Ltd v *Stepsky and another* [1996] 2 All ER 277;
Credit Lyonnais Bank Nederland NV v *Burch* [1997] 1 All ER 144.

Chapter 15

Illegality

1. Introduction

An agreement may possess all the requisite elements of a valid contract, such as offer and acceptance and consideration, but it may nevertheless contravene a legal rule or be regarded as contrary to public policy. Such a contract can be regarded as "improper", or "illegal" in a very general sense, or, at least, tainted with illegality. Since there are many and disparate reasons for statutory and judicial intervention on the basis of illegality or impropriety, it is not always easy to categorise these reasons.

It is conventional to subdivide illegal contracts on the basis of the legal consequences of those contracts. Accordingly, contracts are described as being either "void" or "illegal". The problem with such a classification is that there is no general agreement as to which category each type of improper contract falls into. Such a division also fails to reflect the fact that the nature of the illegality which may taint a contract can vary considerably in its seriousness[1]. It is also possible to classify the different types of illegality according to either the nature of the objectionable conduct, or the source of the rule which invalidates it. None of the attempts at classification is wholly convincing.

It must be emphasised that the traditional approach to the subject is of only limited value as an analytical device. However, for the purpose of clear exposition, it is proposed to adhere to the now favoured distinction between void and illegal contracts. But first, a warning: the following sections are not intended as an exhaustive list of all the different types of illegality. Furthermore, the detailed discussion is focused on those areas of greater commercial and practical significance, particularly in relation to restraint of trade.

A. Void contracts

A variety of contracts are rendered void as a result of some statutory provision. One obvious example is a wagering contract, which is rendered void by s 18 Gaming Act 1845, which states:

> "All contracts or agreements, whether by parole or in writing, by way of gaming or wagering, shall be null and void; and no suit shall be brought or

maintained in any court of law or equity for recovering any sum of money or valuable thing alleged to be won upon any wager, or which shall have been deposited in the hands of any person to abide the event on which any wager shall have been made . . .".

It should be emphasised that this provision does not declare such a contract to be illegal, but simply void; that is, no rights are conferred on either party[2]. A wagering contract is a bet between two parties concerning some existing fact, or the outcome of some event, such as a race. It will not be a wager unless each party has a chance of winning or losing (see *Ellesmere (Earl of)* v *Wallace* [1929] 2 Ch 1). Also, the parties must have no other financial interest in the subject matter of the contract other than the amount wagered. As no definition of a wagering contract was provided by the Gaming Acts of 1845 and 1892, the discussion of this matter in *Morgan Grenfell & Co Ltd* v *Welwyn Hatfield DC (Islington London BC, third party)* [1995] 1 All ER 1, *per* Hobhouse J at pp 7–10, is instructive. In this case it was held that an interest rate swap contract, entered into between the plaintiff bank and the defendant local authority, was not a wagering contract. Although such agreements have, at least potentially, a speculative character, in this instance it was a commercial and financial transaction to which the law would give effect. This was the normal presumption in such a case, which would have been rebutted only if the purpose of both parties to the agreement was to wager (in which case it would have been an invalid agreement).

1.   Contracts in restraint of trade

A contract in restraint of trade is one by which a person promises another that his future freedom to trade, or to conduct his profession, with whomsoever he wishes, will be curtailed in some way. The restriction may be geographical, for instance covering a particular town or area, and usually it will also cover a specific period of time. The basic rule is that such restraints are *prima facie* void, but they may become valid if they can be justified as being reasonable between the parties and not inimical to the public interest.

The doctrine of restraint of trade is largely associated with two particular classes of agreement. (The ambit of the doctrine and its application to other types of agreement are considered later.) These are (i) an agreement by a person selling the "goodwill" of a business that he will not start another business in direct competition with the buyer; and (ii) an agreement between employer and employee by which the latter promises that he will not, on leaving his present employment, work for a rival of his employer, or start a business in competition with his employer. There are two major reasons for the legal regulation of such contracts. First, it is thought to be in the public interest that competition should not be unnecessarily restricted. Secondly, without such a doctrine, one party could exploit the weaker bargaining position of the other in an unfair manner[3]. (For an interesting example, see *Schroeder Music Publishing Co* v *Macaulay* [1974] 3 All ER 616.)

Although restraint of trade agreements appear to be anti-competitive, it should be pointed out that they can serve more desirable purposes. For example, where the goodwill of a business is being sold, the purchaser will wish to protect his legitimate interest in receiving value for the price that he has paid.

If the seller were permitted to set up a rival business immediately in direct competition with the purchaser, then potential purchasers would in future be deterred from buying businesses. In turn, this would affect a future vendor as he would not receive full value for the business that he has built up. Also, in the case of employers, they should be able to protect themselves, in a reasonable way, from employees going to work for rival firms and taking with them secret or confidential information, or the customers or clientele of their former employer. These are illustrations of how restraint of trade agreements may indeed be reasonable and commercially necessary. On the other hand, it must be ensured that the restraint imposed by such an agreement is not wider in scope than it need be to achieve its intended purpose.

A useful starting point for our discussion of agreements in restraint of trade is the case of *Nordenfelt* v *Maxim Nordenfelt Guns and Ammunition Co Ltd* [1894] AC 535. The facts were as follows:

> N was a manufacturer and inventor of guns and ammunition. Although his customers were fairly few his trade was worldwide. He sold his business to a company for £287,500 and he entered into an agreement restricting his future commercial activities. When the company was amalgamated with another, two years later, N's agreement to the restraint of his activities was repeated in a contract of service he entered into with the amalgamated (respondent) company. (It was accepted by the court that the covenant N entered into with the respondents could be regarded as a covenant made on the occasion of selling a business and could therefore be assessed according to the principles relating to such a case.) The restriction was that N should not, for a period of twenty-five years, "engage except on behalf of the company either directly or indirectly in the trade or business of a manufacturer of guns . . .or ammunition, . . . (or in any business competing or liable to compete in any way with that for the time being carried on by the company)".

The latter part of the covenant, contained within the brackets, was clearly too wide in its scope as it extended to all competing businesses. But this clause was severable from the rest of the agreement. The question for the House of Lords to decide was whether the rest of the covenant was too wide or whether it was a reasonable restriction on N's future activities. Although the restraint was not restricted to any particular geographical area, their lordships dismissed N's appeal and held that the covenant was necessary for the protection of the respondents' commercial interests. As the company's trade was worldwide, a commensurate restraint was reasonable. The restraint was upheld as valid. In a famous statement, Lord MacNaghten explained (at p 565) the basic approach to such cases in the following authoritative way:

> "The public have an interest in every person's carrying on his trade freely: so has the individual. All interference with individual liberty of action in trading, and all restraints of trade of themselves, if there is nothing more, are contrary to public policy, and therefore void. That is the general rule. But there are exceptions: restraints of trade and interference with individual liberty of action may be justified by the special circumstances of a particular case. It is a sufficient justification, and indeed it is the only justification, if the restriction is reasonable — reasonable, that is, in reference to the interests of the parties concerned and reasonable in reference to the interests of the public, so framed and so guarded as to afford adequate protection to the party in whose favour it is imposed, while at the same time it is in no way injurious to the public"[4].

It should be appreciated that the facts of *Nordenfelt* were unusual. Most restraints need to be narrower in both duration and geographical area in order to be valid. But the judgments in the case still provide a useful foundation for our study of contracts in restraint of trade. The judicial approach involves a balancing of interests between an individual's freedom to carry on his chosen trade or profession without restraint, and the protection of certain legitimate commercial interests of those buying the goodwill of a business, or of employers. It is not in the public interest for restraint of trade agreements to operate simply to reduce competition, and for this reason there is a presumption that such agreements are void. But if the purchaser of a business or an employer can show that he is trying to protect a genuine proprietary interest, and that the clause in question is both reasonable and not contrary to the public interest, then it may be adjudged as valid. The courts are better placed to judge the reasonableness of an agreement as between the two parties than they are the question of the public interest.

(a) Sale of a business

The *Nordenfelt* case (above) is a good illustration of a valid restraint contained in a contract for the sale of a business. The purchaser gave value for the goodwill by paying a fair amount for the vendor's business. It was reasonable, as between the contracting parties, that the purchaser's proprietary interest was to be protected by restricting the vendor's freedom to trade in the same goods in the future. The courts are more willing to uphold restraints in contracts for the sale of a business than they are in contracts between employer and employee. In contracts of service there is more likely to be an inequality of bargaining strength between the parties; restrictions on an employee's future activities may well be unconscionable. In addition, it may be difficult for an employer to claim that he is protecting a genuine proprietary interest rather than merely guarding against future competition.

For a restraint to be valid, in an agreement to sell a business, the first requirement is that there is a genuine sale of a business from one party to the other (see *Vancouver Malt and Sake Brewing Co Ltd* v *Vancouver Breweries Co Ltd* [1934] AC 181). Without this there will be no transfer of an intangible asset, namely the goodwill, from the vendor to the purchaser. Secondly, the clause must not be too wide in its scope. The restraint will not be valid if it purports to confer protection on the purchaser that goes beyond the actual business sold by the vendor. For example, in *British Reinforced Concrete Engineering Co Ltd* v *Scheff* [1921] 2 Ch 563, the facts were:

> The plaintiff company manufactured and sold "BRC" road reinforcements throughout the country. The defendant had a smaller, more local business, selling "Loop" road reinforcements, but he was not involved in manufacturing these products. The plaintiff company bought the defendant's business, and the defendant covenanted that he would not enter into competition with them (either in business or in the employment of a rival) in the manufacture or sale of road reinforcements. The defendant was later employed by a road reinforcement company and was sued by the plaintiff company for breach of his agreement with them.

The court held that the restraint of trade clause in the sale of the business was too wide, and was void. The clause sought to restrain the defendant in general terms from competing with the plaintiff company. The plaintiffs were entitled to the protection of their proprietary interest in the defendant's business, which they had just bought, but they were not entitled to protection in respect of their wider business interests. The defendant's business was concerned with the sale, not the manufacture, of a particular type of road reinforcement. It was not reasonable to restrict the defendant's future activities in such an extensive way.

Restraints may be unreasonable because they purport to cover too long a period or too wide an area. It must be emphasised that *Nordenfelt* was unusual — the clientele of the business sold was small in number, but spread throughout the world. An unusually extensive restraint, in both time and area, was adjudged to be reasonable in the circumstances. What amounts to a reasonable period of time for a restraint to operate will, naturally, depend on the nature of the business being sold. A purchaser of a business who pays for the goodwill is entitled to contract for the benefit of protection against competition for a limited period. This period can be long enough to allow for the goodwill or "know-how", which has been bought, to be fully transferred to the purchaser. But it should not be excessive in either time or area[5].

Nordenfelt illustrates the fact that if part of the restraint clause is too wide, but the remainder of it is reasonable, the court may sever the offending part from the rest of the clause, which may then be upheld. The extent of the court's power, and its willingness, to do this is considered later. But a further example of this approach can be found in *Goldsoll* v *Goldman* [1915] 1 Ch 292:

> The plaintiff (P) and the defendant (D) each carried on a similar business as a dealer in imitation jewellery in London. In order to avoid competition, D sold his business to P and agreed that he would not, for a period of two years, "either solely or jointly with or as agent or employee for any other person or persons or company directly or indirectly carry on or be engaged concerned or interested in or render services... to the business of a vendor of or dealer in real or imitation jewellery in... London, or any part of the UK, Ireland, the Isle of Man, France, United States, Russia, or Spain...". P sought an injunction when D committed breaches of the agreement.

The Court of Appeal held that the agreement was too wide in area, but that the unreasonable parts of the restraint were capable of being severed from the rest of it. Accordingly, D's promise not to carry on business in the UK and the Isle of Man was a reasonable restraint and therefore enforceable against him. The commercial activities covered by the covenant (namely, "real or imitation jewellery") were also too wide, but it was reasonable to restrain the defendant from dealing in imitation jewellery. Thus the court undertook a certain amount of re-writing of the agreement for the parties in order to reduce the excessive restraint to one of reasonable scope. It should be added that the court may be less willing to apply the idea of severance in cases between employer and employee (see *Attwood* v *Lamont* [1920] 3 KB 571, discussed below) as there is less likely to be parity in terms of the bargaining strength of the parties. In the sale of a business, the court will wish to ensure that the purchaser does receive value for the price paid for the goodwill.

(b) Restraints in a contract of employment

A restraint of trade in a contract of employment is *prima facie* void. It will be valid only if it protects a genuine proprietary interest of the employer, such as trade secrets or freedom from solicitation of his customers, and so long as it is a reasonable restraint, and not against the public interest. The clause will not be valid if it merely attempts to protect the employer from competition. Obviously, an employee may gain experience and expertise in the course of his employment which may equip him to be a future competitor of his employer. The employer cannot prevent this. It is in the public interest that employees acquire skills and are able to use them and pass them on to others. However, an employee would have an unfair advantage in his future activities if he were able to utilise confidential or secret information obtained from his employer. He may also be able to gain a personal knowledge of, and influence over, his employer's customers. In these situations, it is appropriate that an employer is able to restrain his employee's future activities in order to protect his proprietary interests. (For a useful discussion, see Lord Parker's judgment in *Herbert Morris v Saxelby* [1916] 1 AC 688 at p 709. Also see Lord Atkinson's speech in the same case at p 704.)

Trade secrets and confidential information[6]

It is not always easy to distinguish between those situations where an employee has access to highly confidential information and those where he has simply developed an expertise or skill during the course of his employment. (For a recent discussion, see *FSS Travel & Leisure Systems Ltd v Johnson* (1998) IRLR 382.) The employer is entitled to protect himself in the former situation, but not the latter (see Lord Atkinson's judgment in *Herbert Morris Ltd v Saxelby* [1916] 1 AC 688 at pp 704–705). So the first question to be decided is "what constitutes trade secrets?" This was the issue in *Forster & Sons Ltd v Suggett* (1918) 35 TLR 87, where the facts were:

> The plaintiff company (P) and the defendant (D) entered into an agreement under which D was to be employed as works engineer at P's works and was not to divulge any trade secret during his employment or afterwards. The company made glass bottles and glass making machinery. There was also a covenant in D's contract which prevented him, at the end of his employment with P, from going to work in the United Kingdom for a rival glass making firm or being involved in glass bottle manufacture, for a period of five years. In the course of his employment with the plaintiff company, D had been instructed in certain confidential methods which were of economic value. D wished to be released from his promise and the company sought an injunction to enforce the agreed restraint.

Sargant J granted an injunction to the company to restrain D from divulging any trade secrets or manufacturing processes to potential rivals of the plaintiff company. He did not think that the restraint was unreasonable in the circumstances of the case. The time restraint of five years was upheld. The fact that the restraint covered the whole of the United Kingdom was also reasonable. But it must be emphasised that much depends on the particular circumstances of the case in deciding whether a restraint is reasonable. In other cases, a five year restraint covering the whole country may well be unreasonable.

In some cases the courts have experienced greater difficulty in deciding whether an employee is in a position to pass on trade secrets to one of his employer's rivals. In *Saxelby* (see above), the plaintiffs were the leading manufacturers of hoisting machinery in the United Kingdom and the defendant was employed by them as a draughtsman under a contract which restrained him, on leaving the company, from working in the same field for a period of seven years. The House of Lords held that the covenant was void as a result of being too wide; seven years was too long a period. But some doubts were also expressed as to whether the defendant was in a position to pass on trade secrets. The same issue was discussed (and *Saxelby* was distinguished) in *Commercial Plastics Ltd* v *Vincent* [1965] 1 QB 623. The facts were:

> The plaintiff company (CP) were manufacturers of thin PVC calendered plastic sheeting, a rapidly developing section of the plastics industry, in which new discoveries were being frequently made. CP had five principal UK competitors, with whom they shared most of the market, but CP's pre-eminence was in the field of manufacturing thin PVC calendered sheeting for adhesive tape. This was a particularly difficult process and CP had spent considerable amounts of money, time and effort on research into this process. As a result, they had a very large share of this particular market. CP employed Vincent (V), a plastics technologist, to co-ordinate research and development in the production of thin PVC calendered sheeting for adhesive tape. His work gave V access to the company's mixing specifications recorded in code, but it was not possible for him to remember these details without the help of documents. It was a condition of V's employment that he would not seek employment with any of CP's rivals in the PVC calendered sheeting field for one year after leaving CP's employment. V wanted to disregard this condition and CP sought an injunction.

CP's action failed because the clause in restraint of trade was too wide. The clause was worldwide, whereas CP did not require protection outside the UK. Moreover, it extended to their competitors in the whole PVC calendering field, when CP required protection from V only in relation to competitors in the plastics/adhesive tape industry. Accordingly, the Court of Appeal thought that the clause was unreasonable and therefore void. The court expressed some regret at this finding, as it thought that a suitably drafted restraint would have been enforceable against V. However, it was decided that severance of the offending parts of the clause was not possible in this case as the restraint was contained in just one provision which was too wide.

It is relevant to note that, in spite of the decision in *Commercial Plastics* v *Vincent*, the court was of the opinion that the plaintiff company did have confidential information which it was entitled, by a suitably worded covenant, to restrain the defendant from divulging (*per* Pearson LJ, delivering the judgment of the court, at p 642). Given the circumstances of the case this must surely be correct; there was identifiable objective knowledge which could be regarded as the employer's "trade secrets". The outcome of the case was, therefore, unfortunate. But similar issues were raised by the later case of *Littlewoods Organisation Ltd* v *Harris* [1978] 1 All ER 1026. The facts were as follows:

> Littlewoods ran a retail chain store business and a mail order business in the United Kingdom. Their main competitor in the mail order field was Great Universal Stores Ltd (GUS) which had a large number of subsidiaries carrying on various businesses throughout the world. Littlewoods and GUS, between them, enjoyed two-thirds of the mail order trade in the United Kingdom. Littlewoods' mail order business centred around a twice yearly catalogue. These catalogues required considerable advance planning and business skill, especially in relation to the price, quantity and type of goods which were to be sold. Paul Harris was employed by Littlewoods and, having been rapidly promoted due to his considerable ability, he became executive director of their mail order business. As such he was responsible for planning and compiling Littlewoods' catalogues. A clause in his contract restrained Harris' future activities by providing that, in the event of the determination of his

contract, he should not at any time within twelve months enter into a contract of service with GUS Ltd or any of its subsidiary companies, or be involved in the trading or business of GUS or its subsidiaries. Harris resigned from his job with Littlewoods, informing them that he had accepted an offer of employment from GUS. Littlewoods sought an assurance from him that he did not intend to infringe the restraint clause by going to work for GUS within twelve months of leaving their employment. Harris refused to give this, and Littlewoods sought an injunction.

There was no doubt that Harris knew a great deal about Littlewoods' mail order sales trends, the percentage and identity of the returns, sources of manufacture, findings of market research, and the company's plans for the foreseeable future. But did this amount to confidential information which they were entitled to protect by a covenant in restraint of trade? The Court of Appeal held that the plaintiffs were entitled to the protection of a reasonable covenant restraining Harris from going to work for a rival in the mail order business within a limited period of leaving their employment. (Also see *Rock Refrigeration Ltd* v *Jones and another* [1997] 1 All ER 1.)

In *Littlewoods*, Lord Denning considered at some length the question of an employer's protection of confidential information. He explained the difficulty of drawing a line between information which is confidential and that which is not. Where information is of a type that an employee can carry it away in his head, it is particularly hard to prove a breach of a covenant which restrains an employee from divulging confidential information. In practice, the only effective restraint is to stipulate that an employee must not work for a rival firm for a limited (and reasonable) period of time. His lordship concluded (at p 1034):

"It seems to me . . . [that] this really was a case where Littlewoods had a great deal of confidential information which Paul Harris had acquired in the course of his service with them and which they were entitled to protect by a reasonable covenant against his going away and taking it to their rivals in trade . . . [ie GUS]."

There was the further question in *Littlewoods* of whether the restraint on Harris was too wide. (See *Commercial Plastics* v *Vincent*, above, where the facts were very similar.) The covenant prevented Harris from being concerned in businesses of GUS and its subsidiaries. Yet these businesses were extremely varied and worldwide; whereas Littlewoods' interests were restricted to the United Kingdom and to only two commercial areas. Was the fact that the clause was too widely drawn fatal to its enforceability against Harris? Lord Denning was critical of the outcome of *Commercial Plastics* and he explained the need to construe the restraint clause in relation to its intended purpose. Such a clause should not be rendered ineffective simply because of unskilful drafting and the inclusion of words that were too wide in scope. He argued (at p 1035) that a court is able to limit a wide restraint so as to ensure that the clause is reasonable and enforceable. In the present case, he stated that the clause should be restricted to the United Kingdom and to the mail order business, but that an injunction would be granted to Littlewoods. Thus the restraint was enforceable.

So far, we have considered cases where the employer has stipulated some restraint on an employee in a contract of service. A slightly different situation occurred in *Kores Manufacturing Co Ltd* v *Kolok Manufacturing Co Ltd*

[1959] Ch 108, where two companies agreed that neither would, without the other's consent, employ a person who had worked for the other company during the previous five years. Both companies were involved in the manufacture of similar products involving chemical processes. An action was brought by one of the companies against the other to enforce the agreement by restraining the defendants from employing a former employee of the plaintiffs.

The Court of Appeal held that the agreement did not satisfy the essential requirement for a restraint of trade to be enforceable, as it was unreasonable in the circumstances. If either company had tried to enforce a similar restraint contained in a covenant given by an employee they would not have succeeded. This was because the companies were merely trying to prevent competition and were not protecting a genuine proprietary interest. Furthermore, the agreement between the companies failed to distinguish between employees who were in possession of trade secrets and those who were not (and were not even likely to be): "The five year ban was equally applicable to an unskilled manual labourer who had been for a single day in the employment of the plaintiffs, and to a chief chemist with many years' service" (*per* Jenkins LJ at p 124). It did not make any difference that the parties dealt on equal terms in reaching their restraint of trade agreement. It was still open to the court to hold that the restraint was both unreasonable and too wide. It also appears to be contrary to the public interest for the labour force to be restricted in such a way.

Clauses restraining solicitation of customers

An employer is entitled to protect his trade connections, otherwise it would be possible for a former employee to entice away his customers. A distinction must be made, however, between an employee who has acquired some influence over his employer's customers, and one who merely has knowledge of such customers. Obviously much will depend on the type of business in question and the type of work carried out by the employee. But if the employee has enjoyed a position in which customers have relied on his individual skill or judgement, and are likely to take their trade to him if he starts his own business, or goes to work elsewhere, then the employer is entitled to reasonable protection from this potential loss of trading connection.

In *Fitch v Dewes* [1921] 2 AC 158, a restraint was held by the House of Lords to be enforceable against a solicitor's managing clerk. Whilst working in Tamworth, he had agreed with his employer that he would not practise within seven miles of Tamworth town hall, after leaving his employment. This covenant was enforceable, despite the fact that the restriction was of unlimited duration. It was adjudged reasonable, given the nature of the profession concerned. The defendant would have acquired an influence over his employer's clientele and a limited time restraint would not have afforded the required protection to the employer. However, in other circumstances, a restraint may well be void for covering too wide an area or too long a period. In many trades, an employee's influence over his ex-employer's clients or customers will diminish as time passes. (Also see *M & S Drapers v Reynolds* [1957] 1 WLR 9.)

Restraints against damaging an employer's trading connection are not limited to particular professions or to senior personnel (although greater protection may be reasonable against senior employees). For example, in *Marion White Ltd* v *Francis* [1972] 1 WLR 1423, the defendant, Ann Francis, worked as a hairdresser in the plaintiff's salon. She covenanted not to work as a hairdresser, for twelve months after leaving P's salon, within a half mile radius of P's premises. On her dismissal, Ann Francis went to work at a salon merely 150 yards from P's premises. It was held that the covenant was not too wide in those particular circumstances and was enforceable. (In fact, a declaration was granted to P. An injunction was not possible as the time limit in the covenant had elapsed by the time the case was resolved.)

The scope of restraint clauses and severance

We have seen that clauses in restraint of trade, in employment contracts, have been enforceable even where the restraint was unlimited in time (as in *Fitch* v *Dewes*) or covered the whole country (see *Forster* v *Suggett*, above). However, the restraint must not be unreasonably wide in area or long in duration; what is reasonable will depend on the circumstances of the case and the business in question. The restraint must be to protect the employer's business and not simply to inconvenience the employee. In *Mason* v *Provident Clothing & Supply Co Ltd* [1913] AC 724, for example:

> Provident Clothing Limited employed Mason as a local canvasser in its Islington branch in London. His job was to obtain members and collect their instalments; he had no duties outside his assigned district. Mason covenanted not to enter into similar employment within twenty-five miles of London for a period of three years.

The House of Lords, allowing Mason's appeal, held that the clause covered an area which was much greater than was reasonably required for the protection of his former employers. Provident Clothing were entitled to protect themselves against the danger of a former employee canvassing or collecting for a rival firm in the district in which he had been employed. But the restraint which the company was trying to enforce was too wide. The possibility of enforcing a more limited (and reasonable) restraint was considered by the court. It was stated that this could be done where severance was possible, and where the excessive part of the clause was merely technical, or of trivial importance, and not part of the main substance of the clause. Their lordships did not favour such an approach where the employer, having deliberately framed a clause in unreasonably wide terms, now asked the court in effect to re-write the clause to make it reasonable and enforceable. In the circumstances of the case, this was undoubtedly a fair conclusion. (But contrast *T Lucas & Co Ltd* v *Mitchell* [1974] Ch 129.) In the *Mason* case, the company's argument was dealt with convincingly by Lord Moulton:

> "It is evident that those who drafted this covenant aimed at making it a penal rather than a protective covenant, and that they hoped by means of it to paralyse the earning capacities of the man if and when he left their service, and were not thinking of what would be a reasonable protection to their business, and having so acted they must take the consequences".

The question of severance was also considered in *Attwood* v *Lamont* [1920] 3 KB 571. The facts were:

> The plaintiff, Harry Attwood, owned a general outfitter's business, which comprised several departments. James Lamont was employed by Attwood as head

of the tailoring department, but he was not directly concerned with any of the other departments. In his employment contract he had bound himself, after the termination of his contract, not to be involved in "the trade or business of a tailor, dressmaker, general draper, milliner, hatter, haberdasher, gentlemen's, ladies' or children's outfitter, at any place within a radius of ten miles of the employer's place of business" in Kidderminster. Lamont left Attwood's and started his own business outside the ten mile radius. He did business with several of his former employer's customers, however, and took orders from them within the ten mile radius. Attwood sought an injunction to restrain Lamont from disregarding the covenant. Lamont claimed that the clause was too wide in its terms to be reasonable.

Although the clause was wider than was reasonably necessary for the protection of Attwood's business, the Divisional Court had been willing to permit severance; that is, to reject the illegal part of the clause and to enforce the part relating to the tailoring business. However, the Court of Appeal held that not only was the covenant too wide, but that it was also not susceptible to severance. It would have been possible, by deleting the offending words in the clause, to reduce its scope to reasonable proportions, but the Court of Appeal refused to do so. Although the court would not have been re-writing the agreement for the parties, it would have radically altered the scope and purpose of that agreement to have permitted severance. Moreover, their lordships thought that there were strong public policy grounds for refusing severance so that employers would be encouraged to keep such restraint clauses within the bounds of reasonableness. Otherwise employers could impose unreasonably wide restraints in employment contracts and then rely on the court, through the process of severance, to give effect to part of the offending clause.

Severance will be permitted in certain instances, but it is not very clear what the requirements are. We have seen earlier in *Goldsoll* v *Goldman* that, although a covenant was too wide in both the area and the commercial activity to be covered, the court permitted severance of the offending parts and enforced the remainder which was then a reasonable restraint. (Also see *Kall Kwik Printing (UK) Ltd* v *Rush (Frank Clarence)* [1996] FSR 114.) But it should be remembered that in *Goldsoll* the covenant was between the vendor and purchaser of a business. In this context, the policy grounds for refusing severance are not so strong. The court is happy to permit the purchaser to get full value for the price he has paid for the proprietary interest in the business. But, in relation to covenants between employer and employee, a court may be more reluctant to enforce a restraint of trade clause.

A good example of the differing views about the ability of a court in effect to re-write a restraint clause for the parties can be seen in *Littlewoods Organisation* v *Harris* [1978] 1 All ER 1026. It will be recalled that Harris' agreement with Littlewoods prevented him from going to work, within twelve months, for their main mail order rival (GUS) or its subsidiaries. Although Littlewoods' interests were limited to the United Kingdom and to two commercial areas, the clause was worldwide in scope and not restricted to the mail order business. Lord Denning argued that unskilful drafting should not prevent the clause from being construed more narrowly so as to limit its scope to preventing Harris from working for GUS' mail order business in the United Kingdom. Megaw LJ shared Lord Denning's view and insisted (at p 1043) that, in using the principles of construction available to the court to limit the scope of the clause, he was not re-writing the covenant. However, there was a strong dissenting judgment from Browne LJ. He stated (at p 1046):

> "With all deference to Lord Denning MR and Megaw LJ, I think this is re-writing the clause, and re-writing it so as to make enforceable that which would otherwise be unenforceable . . . I think that is something which this court cannot do. I do not think that severance has any relevance to this part of the contract."

Although the outcome of the *Littlewoods* case is obviously defensible, it must be acknowledged that this dissenting judgment is a valid criticism of the majority's approach. Severance permits the illegal part of a covenant to be separated from the rest, by deleting it, leaving the remainder in force. In theory at least, it does not permit a re-writing of the covenant for the parties. (For a recent illustration of this distinction, see *Scully UK Ltd* v *Anthony Lee* (1998) IRLR 259.) The majority in *Littlewoods* thought that the principles of construction enabled the court to restrict the scope of an unreasonably wide clause, but this approach comes very close to a re-writing of the agreement by the court[7].

Restraints protecting other interests

Restraint clauses may also be used in circumstances which do not fit neatly into the categories that we have just considered. For example, in *Eastham* v *Newcastle United Football Club Ltd* [1964] Ch 413, the facts were:

> The plaintiff, George Eastham, was a highly rated footballer who played for Newcastle United, the defendant club. Under the rules (at that time) of the Football Association and the Football League, his employment with the club was subject to a retain and transfer system. This system prevented a player who was employed by one club from being employed by another. His transfer to another club could be effected only with the consent of both clubs. Eastham wanted to join another club, Arsenal, and sought a declaration against his present club and the football authorities.

It is clear that the defendant club was not using the restraint clause, namely the retain and transfer system, to protect either of the two established proprietary interests (discussed above). But this did not automatically mean that the club had no further interests capable of protection (see Wilberforce J's comments at p 432). However, it was decided that, on the facts of the case, the retain and transfer system was invalid and was unnecessary for the protection of the club's proprietary interests. Eastham was granted a declaration not only against his employer, but also against the football authorities whose rules led to the unjustifiable restraint on his freedom of employment. (The rules relating to the transfer system were altered as a result of this case.) But the case does, at least, suggest that the interests that can be protected are not strictly limited.

In other instances a covenant may be used to restrict a person's commercial freedom even though the parties are not, strictly speaking, bound by a contract of employment. A good example is provided by *Schroeder Music Publishing Co Ltd* v *Macaulay* [1974] 3 All ER 616. The facts were as follows:

> Tony Macaulay, a young and unknown song writer, entered into an agreement with the defendant music publishing company, whereby the defendants engaged his exclusive services. Under this agreement, Macaulay gave the company the copyright of all his compositions for the next five years (with a further five year option), and in return was to receive royalty payments. The company could end the

contract by giving Macaulay one month's written notice, but there was no corresponding provision to allow Macaulay to do the same. The company was not even under any obligation to publish any of Macaulay's songs. Although this agreement was not a contract of employment as such, Macaulay sought a declaration that it was contrary to public policy, as being in unreasonable restraint of trade, and void. The company argued that the doctrine of restraint of trade was inapplicable to its standard form agreement.

The House of Lords held that the restrictions in the agreement between Macaulay and the publishing company were not fair and reasonable in that they combined a lack of obligation on the company's part, with a total commitment on the part of Macaulay. If the company chose not to publish his work, for instance, he would be unable to earn his living as a song writer. Thus the contract was in unreasonable restraint of trade and Macaulay was entitled to a declaration[8]. Lord Reid stated (at p 622):

"Any contract by which a person engages to give his exclusive services to another for a period necessarily involves extensive restriction during that period of the common law right to exercise any lawful activity he chooses in such manner as he thinks best. Normally the doctrine of restraint of trade has no application to such restrictions: they require no justification. But if contractual restrictions appear to be unnecessary or to be reasonably capable of enforcement in an oppressive manner, then they must be justified before they can be enforced".

Similar issues arose more recently in *Silvertone Records* v *Mountfield* [1993] EMLR 152, which concerned a dispute between a record company and the members of a pop group in relation to their recording and publishing contracts. The agreements (made when the group was comparatively unknown) gave the company, *inter alia*, the option of the group's services for six further periods beyond the duration of the original contract. The group claimed that the agreements were one-sided and represented an unreasonable restraint of trade. The company claimed that it had been made clear to the group that the agreements were a package and that the group members had waived their objections to it. Accordingly, the company sought a declaration that the agreements were enforceable against the group. Humphries J held that the whole agreement was objectionable, as there was a large inequality of bargaining power between the parties at the time it was entered into. (In a situation like this one, it was held to be a restraint of trade if a performer was prevented from reaching the public with his work for a prolonged period.) The judge stated that the members of the group had not waived their objections to the enforceability of the agreements. (Also see *Zang Tumb Tuum Records* v *Johnson* [1993] EMLR 61 for a further example of a one-sided and unenforceable contract between a record company and a pop group.)

(c) Are the categories of restraint closed?

The two main types of contract in which restraint clauses are *prima facie* unenforceable are those between employer and employee, and those between the buyer and seller of a business. Does the doctrine also apply to other types of agreement or are the categories of restraint of trade closed? This issue has arisen in relation to "solus" trading agreements, eg where garage proprietors agree with an oil company not to sell the products of rival companies. Such arrangements can benefit both parties, as the garage or filling station operator may receive a rebate on the price of petrol or a loan (at favourable rates) to help with the development of his business. The advantage to the oil company is obvious. This type of agreement was the subject of the important case of *Esso Petroleum Co Ltd* v *Harper's Garage (Stourport) Ltd* [1968] AC 269. The facts were:

> H owned two garages (H1 and H2) which were both subject to solus agreements with Esso. Under the terms of these agreements H agreed to buy all his petrol from Esso and, in turn, H was to receive a small rebate on the price of petrol. The agreement in relation to H1 was for four and a half years; it stipulated that H should buy Esso's petrol and no other and it laid down certain other conditions. In relation to H2, there was a similar solus agreement, but in addition Esso had a mortgage over the premises to secure a sum of £7,000 lent to H. The H2 agreement was for the duration of the mortgage repayments, ie twenty-one years. The mortgage provisions also stipulated that H was to buy his petrol exclusively from Esso. H later started to sell another brand of petrol, and Esso sought an injunction to prevent him from doing so. Were the ties in the agreements in restraint of trade and unenforceable?

The House of Lords held that both agreements were within the scope of the restraint of trade doctrine. (*Per* Lord Reid: "In the present case the respondents before they made this agreement were entitled to use this land in any lawful way they chose, and by making this agreement they agreed to restrict their right by giving up their right to sell there petrol not supplied by the appellants".) This meant that the agreements would not be enforced by the court unless they were reasonable. Their lordships held that the restriction on H1 was reasonable, but that the restriction relating to H2 was not. The principal reason for distinguishing between the two agreements was the difference in their respective lengths. A restriction lasting twenty-one years was an unreasonable one in the circumstances (but contrast *Alec Lobb Garages Ltd* v *Total Oil (Great Britain) Ltd* [1985] 1 WLR 173). The restriction should not have been longer than was reasonably necessary to protect the legitimate interests of the oil company, that is, to maintain a stable system of distribution. A much shorter restriction would have sufficed to achieve this end.

(d) Further regulation of restraint of trade

We have seen that contracts in restraint of trade are unenforceable, unless the restriction is reasonable as between the parties to the agreement and is not against the public interest. The courts have been more adept at judging the first of these requirements than the second. Consideration of the public interest necessitates more wide-ranging enquiry than the courts have traditionally been prepared to undertake. (For a classic example, see *Mogul SS Co Ltd* v *McGregor, Gow & Co Ltd* [1892] AC 25.) Whereas the reasonableness of a restraint clause from the point of view of the parties will be fully explored in court by the litigants, the public interest will not be directly represented. Judges may be better equipped, by both outlook and training, to weigh the relative interests of the parties to an agreement than to consider the broader economic issues raised by restraint agreements.

Although there has been some recent indication of a greater willingness to take account of the public interest in restraint of trade cases[9], the failure of judges to do so in the past is one of the factors which inhibited the development of a comprehensive common law doctrine to regulate anti-competitive behaviour. Other factors include the uncertainty about the ambit of the common law doctrine of restraint of trade, and its inability (until recently) to protect third parties who were adversely affected. For these reasons, competition policy has been delineated largely by legislative provisions, which have been substantially changed by the recent Competition Act 1998. It is not appropriate in a book on the general principles of contract law to enter into a detailed discussion of these legislative provisions; those requiring further information should consult a specialist work on UK competition law[10].

2. Other contracts void at common law on grounds of public policy

(a) Contracts to oust the jurisdiction of the courts

We have seen in Chapter 6 that it is possible for the parties to an agreement to stipulate that their agreement shall not be legally enforceable. Thus in *Jones* v *Vernons Pools* [1938] 2 All ER 626 it was a condition of entry that the arrangements of the "football pool" were binding in honour only: a so-called "gentlemen's agreement". The company could not be sued successfully by the plaintiff as the agreement carried with it no legal obligations on either side, and conferred no legal rights. (Also see *Rose and Frank Co* v *JR Crompton & Bros Ltd* [1925] AC 445.) It is not, however, open to the parties to a contract to stipulate that their agreement will have legal consequences but will not be susceptible to the supervision of the courts.

An agreement which purports to prevent the parties to it from submitting questions of law to the courts is contrary to public policy and void. (Only the offending part of the agreement is void; the rest of the contract may be valid and enforceable.) Contractual freedom is, therefore, limited in this way as it is thought to be in the public interest that parties should not be free to oust the jurisdiction of the courts.

The parties may, however, provide that no cause of action will arise until an arbitrator has made an award. This type of arbitration clause is not regarded as contrary to public policy. This was established in *Scott* v *Avery* (1855) 5 HLC 811, where a contract between a shipowner and the underwriters made it clear that no action should be brought against the insurers until the arbitrators had dealt with any dispute arising between the parties. It was held that it is permissible for the parties to agree that no right of action shall accrue until an arbitrator has decided on any difference which may arise between them. Lord Campbell (at p 851) explained the matter as follows:

"... What pretence can there be for saying that there is anything contrary to public policy in allowing parties to contract, that they shall not be liable to any action until their liability has been ascertained by a domestic and private tribunal, upon which they themselves agree? Can the public be injured by it? It seems to me that it would be a most inexpedient encroachment upon the liberty of the subject if he were not allowed to enter into such a contract."

The important point is that such an arbitration clause does not oust the jurisdiction of the courts. Within our legal system there will always tend to be a conflict between two distinct approaches to dispute settling: that is, the "ideal" principle of justice which wants justice no matter what the cost, and the "pragmatic" principle which seeks to limit litigation and its concomitant costs. Although it is the right of the citizen to have his or her legal position decided by the ordinary courts, it is desirable that many disputes should first be heard by an arbitrator. There has to be some compromise between these two approaches, so it is permissible for contracting parties to provide that any disagreement that arises will be referred to arbitration.

The general rule, that an agreement which purports to oust the jurisdiction of the courts is void, is well illustrated in *Baker* v *Jones* [1954] 1 WLR 1005. The facts were:

> An association, which controlled the sport of weightlifting in the United Kingdom, by its rules vested the government of the association in a central council consisting of the officers and a number of members. The association empowered its central council to be the sole interpreters of the rules and to act on behalf of the association regarding any matter not dealt with by the rules. In all circumstances, the decision of the council was to be regarded as final. As a result of disagreements between the members, two libel actions were brought against certain officers and council members. The central council authorised the payment of two sums of £100 to solicitors, out of the association's funds, towards the defendants' legal costs. A member of the association challenged this decision of the council by seeking a declaration that this use of the association's funds was improper.

Lynskey J held that the provision in the rules giving the central council the sole right to interpret the rules was contrary to public policy and void. (It should also be noted that there was no power under the association's rules for the central council to authorise the use of funds for the proposed purpose.) The contract in these circumstances was contained in the association's rules, so the relationship between its various members was indeed contractual. The judge explained (at p 1010) that although, in theory, the parties to a contract may make any contract that they like, this is subject to certain limitations imposed by public policy. One of these limitations is that the jurisdiction of the courts cannot be ousted by the agreement of the parties. He cited with approval the statement of Lord Denning in *Lee* v *Showmen's Guild of Great Britain* [1952] 2 QB 329 at p 342:

> "If parties should seek, by agreement, to take the law out of the hands of the courts and put it into the hands of a private tribunal, without any recourse at all to the courts in case of error of law, then the agreement is to that extent contrary to public policy and void".

A further example of a situation where an agreement to oust the jurisdiction of the courts may arise is that of a maintenance agreement between husband and wife. As part of a separation agreement, a husband may promise his wife an allowance in exchange for which she agrees not to apply to the courts for maintenance. This issue arose in *Hyman* v *Hyman* [1929] AC 601, where it was held that a wife cannot, by her own agreement, preclude herself from invoking the jurisdiction of the court. (Also see *Sutton* v *Sutton* [1984] 1 All ER 168.) The main disadvantage of this common law rule was that if the husband did not pay the promised allowance, his wife was not able to sue him to enforce payment. But under the present statutory provisions (see s 34 Matrimonial Causes Act 1973), a wife can successfully sue her husband, if the agreement is written, to enforce payment of the promised allowance.

(b) Contracts undermining the status of marriage

In the public interest, the law seeks to uphold the sanctity of marriage. Accordingly, certain types of agreement which tend to undermine or damage the institution of marriage are invalidated. One example of this is a contract which purports to restrict a person's freedom to marry whomsoever he wishes. In *Lowe* v *Peers* (1768) 4 Burr 2225, for instance, a man promised the plaintiff, under seal, that he would not marry any other person except her. He stated that if he broke this promise to her, he would pay her £2,000. His promise was held to be void, as it restricted his freedom of choice without there being any reciprocal promise from the plaintiff. (Until the abolition of an action for breach of promise in 1970, a couple's engagement to marry — involving reciprocal promises — was a valid contract. This was not the situation in *Lowe* v *Peers*, where the parties did not directly promise to marry each other.)

Another type of agreement which is thought to undermine the status of marriage is the so-called "marriage brokage" contract: ie an agreement for reward for the procurement of marriage. Such agreements are regarded as contrary to public policy and therefore void. The rather outmoded reasoning behind this rule is that these agreements tend to promote unsuitable marriages and for this reason are harmful to the public! (Given the current rate of matrimonial breakdown, such a moral stance might appear particularly quaint.) The invalidity of such agreements appears to extend to those between matrimonial agencies and their clients where the latter are introduced to a number of people of the opposite sex with a view to marriage. In *Hermann* v *Charlesworth* [1905] 2 KB 123, the facts were:

> Miss Hermann saw an advertisement in the defendant's paper, *The Matrimonial Post and Fashionable Marriage Advertiser*, and later signed an agreement with the defendant in the following terms: "In consideration of being introduced to or put in correspondence with a gentleman through the influence of the proprietor of the paper entitled 'The Matrimonial Post and Fashionable Marriage Advertiser', and in the event of a marriage taking place between such gentleman and myself, I hereby agree to pay to the said proprietor the sum of £250 on the date of my said marriage". Miss Charlesworth also paid the defendant a "special client's fee" of £52. She was introduced to several men by the defendant, who also interviewed and wrote to others on her behalf, but no marriage or engagement followed. She sued the defendant to recover back the £52.

The Court of Appeal held that it made no difference that the agreement was not intended to bring about Miss Charlesworth's marriage with a particular individual. It was still to be regarded as a marriage brokage agreement despite the fact that she was introduced to a number of men and therefore had some degree of choice. It was decided that the transaction in this case came within the rule which invalidates marriage brokage contracts. Accordingly, the plaintiff was entitled to recover back the money paid under this contract, even though the defendant had brought about introductions and incurred expense in doing so.

B. Illegal contracts

It should be borne in mind that the distinction between illegal and void contracts is not universally accepted. The terminology employed both by academics and the courts is far from consistent. The distinction is maintained here largely for expository purposes and it is conceded that other categorisations are equally acceptable. A contract may be improper for a such a variety of reasons, ranging from the serious to the trivial, that the subject does not always lend itself to analysis by categorisation. But whereas the vitiating aspect of a "void" contract (as described above) will be apparent on the face of the agreement, the "illegal" contract may or may not be improper at face value. If the vitiating aspect is not apparent on the surface, the agreement may be rendered unlawful by some ulterior purpose of one or both of the parties[11].

What follows is by no means an exhaustive guide to the subject of illegality. It should be seen more as a series of examples of where the issues of illegality or impropriety have been raised and how they have been dealt with by the courts.

1. Contracts to commit an unlawful act

If the purpose of an agreement between the parties is to commit a crime, or a tort, or a fraud against another party then it can be said that such a contract is illegal and unenforceable. It is not surprising that the courts refuse to assist those whose purpose is to achieve an unlawful or an illegal end. Even where an agreement is of a type which is commonly made in certain commercial contexts, it will still be unenforceable if it is based on an unlawful transaction. For example, if a shipowner carries X's goods and, in return for a promise of an indemnity from X, certifies that the goods are shipped "in good condition", despite his knowledge that they are not, he would not be able to enforce the indemnity. The purpose of such an arrangement is to defraud a third party, and the fact that such a practice is widespread does not excuse the unlawful nature of the agreement (see *Brown Jenkinson & Co Ltd* v *Percy Dalton Ltd* [1957] 2 QB 621).

The situation becomes more complex where there is a lawful contract between the parties, but it is performed by one of them in an unlawful manner, for example, in breach of a statutory provision. The party who is in breach of the law may be unable to enforce any claim (eg to recover the price of goods) as a result of his own illegal performance. (See *Anderson* v *Daniel* [1924] 1 KB 138.) Of course, this principle will not apply to the innocent party under the transaction unless in some way he participated in the other party's illegal performance. (This subject is discussed in more detail later.) However, even the guilty party may be able to enforce the contract in some circumstances. Much may depend on the purpose of the statute in question. In *St John Shipping Corporation* v *Joseph Rank Ltd* [1956] 3 All ER 683, for example:

> Under a contract of carriage, the plaintiffs conveyed a cargo of wheat from America to England in their ship which was overloaded and thus contravened the Merchant Shipping (Safety and Load Line Conventions) Act 1932. A fine of £1,200 was imposed on the master of the ship in respect of this offence, but the freight earned by the excess wheat carried was £2,295. The defendants, who were to receive about one third of the cargo of wheat, paid part of the freight for their share, but withheld £2,000 of the agreed sum in view of the overloading. (It should be noted that the wheat was delivered safely to them.) The plaintiffs claimed the balance of the freight and the defendants argued that the contract was unenforceable by the plaintiffs by reason of illegality.

Devlin J explained that, although a contract which is entered into with the object of committing an illegal act is unenforceable, this principle was not applicable in the present case. He stated (at p 687) that "whether or not the overloading was deliberate when it was done, there is no proof that it was contemplated when the contract of carriage was made". Accordingly, the judge held that the plaintiffs were entitled to the balance of the freight; they were not barred from recovering it by the fact that the overloading was a crime. It is important to note that the statutory provision in question did not make the contract of carriage unlawful, it merely penalised overloading. As this infringement of the legislation was not contemplated by the contract, there was nothing to prevent even the guilty party from enforcing that contract. The goods were safely delivered and no part of the claim for freight could be identified clearly as being the excess illegally earned. The purpose of the Act was achieved by the fine imposed on the master of the ship for the offence. (Also see *Hughes and others* v *Asset Managers plc* [1995] 3 All ER 669).

Devlin J's remarks in *St John Shipping Corporation* v *Joseph Rank Ltd* were applied in *Shaw* v *Groom* [1970] 1 All ER 702. In this case a landlord failed to provide his tenant with a rent book in contravention of the relevant landlord and tenant legislation. The Court of Appeal held that this omission did not disentitle the landlord from recovering the rent of the premises from the tenant. The purpose of the legislation was not to preclude the landlord from recovering rent, but merely to penalise him for the breach of the statutory provision. This is a sensible approach in view of the scope and purpose of the statute. If this purpose is to be achieved by the imposition of a fine on the offender, it may well be unfair and unnecessary to go further and make the contract unenforceable by the party who is in breach of the law. Otherwise even a minor transgression by the offender might excuse the "innocent" party from performing his contractual obligations.

In contrast to the unlawful performance of an otherwise lawful contract, we should also consider a contract which is illegal in itself. For example, in *Re Mahmoud and Ispahani* [1921] 2 KB 716 the plaintiff, who had a licence to sell linseed oil, sold some to the defendant in contravention of the Seed, Oils and Fats Order 1919. This statute made it an offence to buy or sell linseed oil without a licence; the defendant was unlicensed — he had induced the plaintiff to sell him the oil by a fraudulent representation that he was licensed. The defendant later refused to accept delivery of the oil and was sued for damages by the plaintiff. The Court of Appeal held that the plaintiff's claim failed because of the illegality of the contract. Despite the fact that the plaintiff was the innocent party, the legislation specifically prohibited any sale of oil to unlicensed persons.

2. Contracts promoting sexual immorality

An agreement which tends to promote sexual immorality may well be found to be illegal as a principle of common law. This is certainly the case where the agreement in some way involves or encourages prostitution. In the rather old case of *Pearce* v *Brooks* (1866) LR 1 Ex 213 for instance, the plaintiff agreed to hire a horse and carriage to a prostitute, knowing that it would be used, in some way, to assist her in her enterprise. It was held that the plaintiff could not recover the hire charge when the defendant refused to pay it. Lord Pollock explained (at p 218):

> "I have always considered it as settled law that any person who contributes to the performance of an illegal act by supplying a thing with the knowledge that it is going to be used for that purpose, cannot recover the price of the thing so supplied ... Nor can any distinction be made between an illegal and an immoral purpose; the rule which is applicable to the matter is *ex turpi causa non oritur actio*, and whether it is an immoral or an illegal purpose in which the plaintiff has participated, it comes equally within the terms of that maxim, and the effect is the same; no cause of action can arise out of either the one or the other".

Such a conclusion may not be surprising, but it is debatable how widely the notion of "sexual immorality" should be interpreted. The attitude of society to such questions is constantly changing and behaviour that is regarded as shocking to one generation may not seem so outrageous to a later generation. (For example, see *Armhouse Lee Ltd* v *Chappell, The Times*, 7 August 1996.) However, the statement of Lord Pollock was applied in *Upfill* v *Wright* [1911] 1 KB 506, where the facts were:

> P, through his agent, let a flat in London to D, an unmarried woman. The agent knew that D was the mistress of a certain man and he assumed that the rent would be paid as a result of her being a "kept woman"; that is, it would come from the man whose mistress she was. Eventually, P's agent gave D notice to quit. D failed to pay the rent for the last half year of the tenancy. P sued for the rent which was still owed to him.

It was held that P was not entitled to recover the rent because the flat was let for an immoral purpose. The reasoning put forward by the Divisional Court might strike us today as rather absurd. Darling J stated (at pp 510–512):

> "The flat was let to the defendant for the purpose of enabling her to receive visits of the man whose mistress she was and to commit fornication with him there ... That fornication is sinful and immoral is clear ... I am of the opinion that this flat was let for an immoral purpose and the fact that the rent was to arise out of the letting made it clear that the landlord participated in the illegal or immoral act and in the immoral gains of the defendant. Therefore the case comes within the rule that out of a forbidden act no cause of action can arise."

It is questionable whether the law would feel the need today to protect public morality in such a zealous way. For example, the cohabitation of men and women outside marriage has become much more widespread and acceptable in modern times and the courts today are more reluctant to invoke this area of public policy. In certain cases involving an unmarried woman's contractual rights over the home jointly occupied by the cohabitees, the court has not raised the question of the immorality of the couple's arrangements. In *Tanner* v *Tanner* [1975] 1 WLR 1346, for instance, P decided to buy a house to provide a home for D and her twin daughters. P was the father of the twins. P bought the house on a mortgage and D gave up her rent controlled flat and moved into the house with the children. Three years later, P wanted to evict D, who now refused to move out of the house. The Court of Appeal held that D had a contractual licence to reside in the house with her children so long as the children were of school age and they required the accommodation.

3. Contracts prejudicial to the interests of the state

This is a very general heading and is susceptible to a number of interpretations. One obvious instance is a trading contract concluded in time of war between someone in the United Kingdom and a foreign enemy. Such an agreement is, not surprisingly, illegal. If the contract pre-dates the outbreak of hostilities it will still be dissolved, but rights and obligations which existed before the outbreak of war may be enforced after its conclusion.

There is also a prohibition against contracts which tend to injure the United Kingdom's friendly relations with another state (that is, one with which we are not at war). If an agreement promotes action which is inimical to a friendly foreign country it will be regarded as unlawful and unenforceable by our courts (see *De Wutz* v *Hendricks* (1824) 2 Bing 314). An interesting example of the application of this prohibition is provided by *Regazzoni* v *KC Sethia Ltd* [1957] 3 All ER 286. The facts were as follows:

> An ordinance issued by the government of India prohibited the taking of goods out of India if they were destined for any part of South Africa, or were intended to be taken to South Africa despite being initially destined for another country. An English company, KC Sethia Ltd, agreed to sell and deliver to Polissino Regazzoni 500,000 bags of jute. To the knowledge of both contracting parties the jute was to be shipped from India to Genoa so that it might there be resold to a South African buying agency in contravention of the Indian ordinance. Sethia failed to deliver the jute and Regazzoni claimed damages in an English court for breach of contract. Sethia defended the action by claiming that the contract was, to Regazzoni's knowledge, an illegal contract and therefore unenforceable as its breach of the Indian ordinance was harmful to the interests of the state.

The House of Lords held that, as a matter of public policy, the contract was unenforceable in England. Its performance would have involved, as the parties were well aware, doing an act in a friendly foreign country which violated the law of that country. Lord Reid explained the reasoning of the court as follows (at p 293):

> "The real question is one of public policy in English law; but, in considering this question, we must have in mind the background of ... the comity of nations. This is not a case of a contract being made in good faith but one party thereafter finding that he cannot perform his part of the contract without committing a breach of foreign law in the territory of the foreign country. If this contract is held to be unenforceable it should, in my opinion, be because from the beginning the contract was tainted so that the courts of this country will not assist either party to enforce it[12]."

It was stressed by Lord Reid (at pp 294–295) that in deciding that the contract was unenforceable for breach of Indian law, the court was not necessarily implying its approval of that particular law. On the other hand, there was no express disapproval of that law. But, in a different situation, if our courts regarded a particular foreign law as positively distasteful for some reason, they might not refuse to enforce a contract which was in breach of such a law.

4. Contracts prejudicial to the administration of justice

Under this heading we can include agreements to interfere with or suppress a prosecution. The validity of such an agreement may, however, depend upon the nature of the unlawful act which raised the possibility of the criminal proceedings. If the harm caused by the act was of an essentially private nature (such as criminal libel or common assault) then an agreement not to prosecute might well be permissible. On the other hand, it would not be valid to agree to suppress a prosecution for an act which was more overtly injurious to the public interest — in any case, it is a substantive crime to conceal an arrestable offence. It should also be noted that an agreement to interfere with the due course of a criminal investigation or prosecution might well be unlawful on the ground that it constitutes an attempt or conspiracy to pervert the course of justice. In *R* v *Andrews* [1973] QB 422, for example:

> D witnessed a traffic accident between a motor car and a moped, as a result of which criminal proceedings against the car driver were contemplated. D invited the car driver to pay him to give false evidence at the prospective prosecution, and the driver offered him a sum of money but no bargain was in fact struck. D was convicted on a charge of inciting the motorist to pervert the course of justice.

The Court of Appeal dismissed the defendant's appeal against the conviction. It stated that to produce false evidence in order to mislead the court and to pervert the course of justice was a substantive offence; that inciting someone to act in this way was also an offence and therefore the conviction was justified. The case was concerned with the defendant's culpability rather than the question of illegality of contracts, but it is obvious that had the defendant and the motorist reached an agreement, it would have been both illegal and unenforceable on the ground of public policy.

Another example of agreements which may be prejudicial to the administration of justice are those between a husband and wife where they collude in order to facilitate divorce proceedings. Whether such collusion invalidates an agreement today will depend on whether or not it is a corrupt agreement, ie one that is designed to practise a deception on the court[13].

5. Contracts promoting corruption in public life

It would be contrary to the public interest if public offices or honours could be bought and sold. Such practices encourage corruption and result in the public not being served by the most able public officials. Consequently, agreements for the sale or purchase of such offices are unlawful. A good example of the scope of this principle is provided by *Parkinson* v *College of Ambulance Ltd and Harrison* [1925] 2 KB 1. The facts were:

> Colonel Parkinson was told by Harrison, the secretary of the defendant charity, that the charity would arrange for him to be granted a knighthood if he made a substantial donation. Harrison had told Parkinson of the charity's royal patronage. Parkinson paid £3,000 to the College of Ambulance on the understanding that he would receive a knighthood and he also promised further payment to the charity in the future. When Parkinson did not receive a knighthood and realised that he had been duped, he brought an action against the charity to recover back the money that he had paid.

Lush J held that as the contract was for the purchase of a title, it was contrary to public policy and was an illegal contract. Despite the fact that the plaintiff had been defrauded, he knew that he was entering into an improper agreement and he could not recover back the money he had paid to the charity; nor could he recover damages from the charity or its secretary.

C. The effects of impropriety and illegality

We have seen that there are numerous types of impropriety which can affect a contract and that these involve varying degrees of unlawfulness. For this reason it is difficult to generalise about their consequences. We have considered the effects of impropriety on some types of contract in earlier parts of this chapter. What follows is intended only as an outline of some of the main principles that have been developed by the courts for dealing with problems of impropriety.

1. Void contracts

In the case of contracts that are void due to some statutory provision, such as wagering contracts, it is necessary to look closely at the particular statute in question to assess the effects of impropriety. In contracts void at common law on the grounds of public policy, it will be remembered that it may be possible to separate the offending part of the agreement from the rest of it. For example, where an agreement purports to prevent the parties to it from submitting questions of law to the courts, although such a clause will be void, the rest of the contract may be enforceable.

In the section on contracts in restraint of trade, we considered the doctrine of severance. This permits the unreasonable part of a clause or covenant to be separated from the rest of it, by deleting it, leaving the remainder in force. For example, in *Goldsoll* v *Goldman* [1915] 1 Ch 292, the restraint imposed on the vendor of a jewellery business was too wide in the geographical area that it purported to cover. However, the Court of Appeal held that the unreasonable parts of the restraint were capable of being severed from the rest of it. The restraint that was permitted by the court was the one covering the United Kingdom, as this was reasonable in the circumstances. It should be borne in mind that courts may be less willing to apply the idea of severance in cases between employer and employee as the parties are unlikely to possess equal bargaining strength.

A party to an agreement which is void for being contrary to public policy may have paid money to the other party under that "contract". It seems likely that the party who has paid the money will be able to recover it from the other. For example, in *Hermann* v *Charlesworth* [1905] 2 KB 123, the plaintiff paid a special client's fee of £52 to the defendant under a so-called "marriage brokage" contract. Despite being introduced to several men by the defendant, the plaintiff did not become engaged or married to any of them. The Court of Appeal decided that this contract was invalid as it was contrary to public policy to enforce marriage brokage contracts. Yet the plaintiff was entitled to recover back the money paid under the contract, even though the defendant had brought about the introductions as promised. It should be noted that some of the reasoning employed by their lordships in this case was far from convincing.

2. Illegal contracts

It is difficult to generalise about the effects of illegality, as much depends upon the circumstances of each case, such as the nature of the illegality in question, and the state of mind of the contracting parties. Although we have concentrated, so far, on contracts which are illegal at common law on the grounds of public policy, it must be emphasised that the making of certain agreements may also be prohibited by statute. It is an instructive starting point to consider certain cases involving illegality arising out of a statutory prohibition. In *Re Mahmoud and Ispahani* [1921] 2 KB 716 (discussed earlier), the facts were that P sold linseed oil to D, in contravention of a statutory provision. P was misled by D into thinking that D possessed a licence to deal in linseed oil, when in fact he had no such licence. Subsequently, D refused to accept delivery of the oil and claimed that the contract was illegal. P claimed damages.

The Court of Appeal held that as D was unlicensed, the contract in question was prohibited by the Seed, Oils and Fats Order of 1919 and was, therefore, illegal. Despite the innocence of the plaintiff, his claim was unsuccessful. The statutory prohibition was in the public interest and no claim could be made under the contract. It seems that the state of mind of the parties did not make any difference to the outcome where there was such an unequivocal statutory prohibition of this type of contract. Their agreement was illegal from the outset. This can be contrasted with a situation where an innocent party sues on a contract which is not *ex facie* illegal, but which is performed by the other party in an illegal manner. For example, in *Archbold's (Freightage) Ltd* v *Spanglett Ltd* [1961] 1 All ER 417:

> The defendants agreed to carry a load of whisky by road, from Leeds to London, for Archbold's. Archbold's were unaware that the vehicle to be used by the defendants did not have the correct licence in order to comply with s 1(1) Road and Rail Traffic Act 1933. The defendants, however, were aware of this fact. Somewhere on the route to London the goods were stolen as a result of the negligence of the defendants' driver. The defendants argued that they were not liable for damages because the contract was illegal by reason of the Road and Rail Traffic Act.

It was held that Archbold's were not debarred from recovering damages by the illegality of the defendants' use of their vehicle. Archbold's were innocent, but that fact had not helped the plaintiff in *Mahmoud's* case (above). The reason why *Mahmoud* was distinguishable from the present case was due to the nature of the statutory prohibition. In *Mahmoud*, the contract of sale to an unlicensed person was expressly forbidden. (Also see *J Dennis and Co Ltd* v *Munn* [1949] 2 KB 327.) Whereas in *Archbold's* the carriage of Archbold's whisky was not as such prohibited. The legislation in question merely regulated the manner in which carriers should transport goods. The contract was not, therefore, expressly forbidden by the statute and the plaintiffs were entitled to damages. It is worth noting that if both parties to the contract had known that the vehicle did not have an appropriate licence, the contract would have been unenforceable, as they would have known that it could not be carried out without breaking the law.

It must be emphasised that it is important to look at the language, scope and purpose of the relevant statute in considering the effects of any illegality arising out of the contravention of its provisions. (For example, see *Hughes and others* v *Asset Managers plc* [1995] 3 All ER 669.) In certain circumstances, it may even be possible for an "illegal" contract to be enforced by both the innocent and the guilty party. If we reconsider the case of *St John Shipping Corporation* v *Joseph Rank Ltd* [1956] 3 All ER 683, where the plaintiffs carried a cargo of wheat from America to England in an overloaded ship, the question arose whether they could sue for the balance of freight owing to them under the contract of carriage. The plaintiffs had infringed the Merchant Shipping Act 1932 and the master of the ship was, accordingly, fined. But it was held that this did not prevent them from recovering the freight from the defendants. The relevant statutory provision did not intend to make such a contract of carriage unlawful, it simply aimed to penalise overloading. Thus the purpose of the statute was achieved adequately by the imposition of a fine on the master of the ship. In reaching this conclusion, Devlin J had to contend with the following observation of Lord Atkin in *Beresford* v *Royal Insurance Co Ltd* [1938] 2 All ER 602 at p 605:

> "... No system of jurisprudence can with reason include amongst the rights which it enforces rights directly resulting to the person asserting them from the crime of that person."

Devlin J explained that the relevant prohibition in *St John Shipping* imposed a penalty under the criminal law which was designed to deprive the offender of the benefits of his crime. This being so, it would be unfair if the civil law imposed a further penalty by denying the plaintiffs the freight which was owed under the contract. He added (at p 693) that "it would be curious, too, if in a case in which the magistrates had thought fit to impose only a nominal fine their decision could in effect be overridden in a civil action".

The fact that the guilty party was not prevented from succeeding in the above case serves as a useful warning that general rules about the effects of illegality are difficult to detect. This is inevitable in view of the differing degrees of seriousness which can arise in illegality cases. It is unlikely that the courts will apply a consistent set of rules regardless of how they view the impropriety in question. An interesting contrast to *St John Shipping* is provided by *Ashmore, Benson, Pease & Co* v *AV Dawson Ltd* [1973] 2 All ER 856. The facts were:

> Ashmores wished to have a twenty-five ton "tube-bank", which they had manufactured, transported from their works to a port for shipment. Ashmores' transport manager arranged for Dawsons, a small road haulage firm, to carry the tube-bank. He was also present when it was loaded on to one of Dawsons' vehicles, and he was familiar with the statutory regulations governing the transporting of loads on vehicles. Dawsons overloaded their vehicle in contravention of s 64(2) Road Traffic Act 1960, but Ashmores' manager raised no objection to their use of an inappropriate vehicle — the goods should have been carried on a "low loader", but Dawsons did not have one. On the journey to the port, the vehicle toppled over, causing over £2,000 of damage to the tube-bank. Ashmores brought an action for damages against Dawsons.

At the trial the plaintiffs gained judgment as the contract was lawful when made. But the Court of Appeal held that even if the contract was lawful at its inception, its performance was unlawful. Ashmores, through their manager, had participated in the illegality since he had permitted the excessive loading of the vehicle. As a result of this participation, the plaintiffs were debarred from claiming damages in respect of the accident which occurred.

3. Some general principles

Despite the hazards of attempting to deduce general principles from the decided cases on illegality, a few principles relating to the effects of illegality are summarised briefly in the sections which follow. Unless otherwise stated, these principles refer to contracts which are illegal at the outset.

(a) An illegal contract is unenforceable by either party

It is generally accepted that where both parties participate equally in a transaction which is illegal in itself, then neither can enforce the agreement against the other. In a famous statement in *Holman* v *Johnson* (1775) 1 Cowp 341 at p 343, Lord Mansfield stated that "no court will lend its aid to a man who founds his cause of action upon an immoral or an illegal act". This is a principle based on public policy and, as a result (somewhat oddly), it may enable the defendant to rely on the illegality or the immorality as a means of escaping liability under an agreement. It will be remembered in *Pearce* v *Brooks* (1866) LR 1 Ex 213, that the plaintiff who hired a carriage to a prostitute, in the knowledge that it would in some way assist with her occupation, was unable to recover the hire charge when the defendant refused to pay. No cause of action could arise out of an illegal transaction of this type to which the plaintiff had contributed. (But see *Howard* v *Shirlstar Container Transport* [1990] 1 WLR 1292, in which the plaintiff was permitted to benefit from his illegal act — a breach of Nigerian air traffic control regulations — as such an outcome was held not to be an affront to public conscience.)

A slightly different problem arises where both parties are aware of a prohibition, but one of them can be regarded as more blameworthy than the other. If the purpose of the prohibition in question is to protect the public, the court may still decide that even the less culpable party is unable to enforce the illegal agreement. For example, in *Mohamed* v *Alaga & Co (a firm)* [1999] 3 All ER 699, M claimed that he had an agreement with the defendant solicitors, under which he would introduce Somali asylum seekers to the solicitors and assist the solicitors (as a translator) in preparing their clients' cases. In return, the solicitors were to pay him a share of any fees received from the Legal Aid Board for acting on behalf of these clients. M's claim to enforce the agreement, which was contrary to Rule 7 of the Solicitors' Practice Rules 1990, was rejected by the Court of Appeal as it was an attempt to enforce an illegal contract. The court reached this conclusion despite the fact that the prohibition in question was imposed on solicitors, and it was they who faced professional penalties for breach of the rules. It was held that the public interest would not be protected if a non-solicitor could enforce such an agreement. However, the Court of Appeal held that M could succeed with his claim for a reasonable price for the work he carried out at the solicitors' request. The court thought that it was relevant here that, if the alleged agreement had been made, M's conduct was less blameworthy than that of the solicitors. (See the comments of Lord Bingham CJ at p 707).

(b) Money or property transferred is not recoverable

A further general principle relates to property which is transferred under an illegal transaction. For example, in *Parkinson* v *College of Ambulance Ltd and Harrison* [1925] 2 KB 1 the plaintiff gave money to the defendant charity after receiving assurances from its secretary that it could arrange a knighthood for him. Having failed to receive the promised honour, the plaintiff tried to recover his money. Due to the illegality of the transaction, it was held that he was not entitled to the return of his money despite having been defrauded. There can be little surprise at such a result, for this seems to follow logically from the principle considered above. Both parties were equally involved in a transaction, which was illegal in itself, and therefore neither could enforce the agreement against the other.

But a slightly different problem occurred in *Belvoir Finance Co Ltd* v *Stapleton* [1971] 1 QB 210. The facts were as follows:

> The plaintiff finance company (BF) were supplied with cars by a dealer which they, in turn, let on hire-purchase terms to the Belgravia Car (BC) hire company. All three parties were (to their knowledge) involved in an illegal transaction, as the contracts of sale and of hire were in breach of certain statutory regulations. BC fraudulently sold the cars to innocent buyers and then went into liquidation. BF sued the defendant, who was an assistant manager of BC and who had actually sold the cars, in conversion. His defence to this action was based on the argument that BF could not recover because of their own participation in the illegal transactions. For their part, BF needed to show that they were the owners of the cars at the time of the defendant's fraudulent disposal of them.

The Court of Appeal held, perhaps surprisingly, that the defendant was liable. It appeared to be prepared to overlook the illegality of the original contract under which BF bought the cars from the dealer, and it found that the cars belonged to the finance company. This conclusion was reached in spite of the fact that the cars had never been delivered to BF — the cars went directly from the dealer to the car hire company. In allowing the plaintiffs to recover damages against the defendant it does seem that, despite protestations to the contrary (at p 218), the Court of Appeal enforced an illegal contract.

Exceptions

It should be noted that there are exceptions to the general rule that money or other property transferred under an illegal transaction cannot be recovered. For example, if a party can make out his case quite independently of the illegal contract (that is, based on some lawful ground), then he will be able to recover back his money or property because, in so doing, he is not forced to rely on the illegality in question. (See *Amar Singh* v *Kulubya* [1964] AC 142 for a neat illustration of this point.) For another, rather questionable, example it is instructive to consider *Bowmakers Ltd* v *Barnet Instruments Ltd* [1945] KB 65. The facts were:

> The plaintiff company, Bowmakers, supplied certain machine tools to the defendants, Barnet Ltd, under three hire-purchase contracts. These contracts were illegal (or at least this was assumed by the court), as they were in breach of war-time ministerial regulations. The defendants, having failed to make all the hire-purchase payments which were due under the contracts, sold the tools which they had acquired under two of the contracts. In addition, they refused to return the remaining tools, which they held under the third contract, to the plaintiffs. The defendants argued that the plaintiffs had no remedy against them, because of the illegality of the three agreements.

The Court of Appeal held that the plaintiffs' action for conversion (of all the goods) was successful despite the illegality of the transactions. It was argued that the plaintiffs' action did not rely on the illegal hire-purchase contracts, but on the independent cause of action that they were the owners of the goods. This certainly explains why the plaintiffs' action could succeed in relation to the goods which were sold by the defendants, but it is far from convincing in relation to the goods which were merely retained. In respect of these goods, which were not sold by the defendants, the court was surely allowing the plaintiffs to succeed in an action which was based on an illegal transaction. The plaintiffs' right to recovery of these goods was clearly based on the defendants' failure to make the payments that were agreed under an illegal hire-purchase contract. It might be argued, by way of defence of the court's decision, that it would have been unfair if the defendants had been able to hide behind the mere breach of a ministerial order as a means of escaping liability[14].

The *Bowmakers* v *Barnet* approach was followed more recently by the House of Lords in *Tinsley* v *Milligan* [1993] 3 All ER 65, where the facts were:

> Two women, T and M, lived together in a house for which they jointly provided the money to buy. They agreed for the house to be in T's name only, so that M could make false claims for social security payments (from which they both benefited). They later quarrelled, and T claimed possession of the house. M argued that T held the house on trust for both of them in equal shares, but was her claim barred by her own illegal conduct?

The House of Lords, by a narrow majority, upheld the Court of Appeal's decision — that T held the property on trust for both of the parties in equal shares — but it relied on different reasoning. The majority held that M did not need to rely on the illegality to support her claim. She needed only to show that she had contributed to the purchase price of the house and that there was an understanding between the parties that the house was jointly owned: ie that there was a resulting trust. In reaching their decision, the majority applied the principle established in *Bowmakers* v *Barnet*, enabling M's claim to succeed on what appear to be rather technical grounds. The judgment seems to take little account of the illegality of the plaintiff's conduct. (*Quaere*: Would a claimant whose conduct involved more serious offences than M's be allowed to succeed under similar circumstances — on a technicality — or would the court be forced to consider the public policy issues involved? See Lord Goff's dissenting views in *Tinsley* v *Milligan* at p 79.)

The approach of the House of Lords has been criticised[15], and perhaps the judgment of the Court of Appeal in *Tinsley* v *Milligan* is to be preferred. The Court of Appeal was prepared to assess the conduct of M to see whether it was so serious as to merit the penalty which would be incurred by the loss of her interest in the house; and, if it was not, whether the public conscience would be affronted by the success of her claim. It can be appreciated why the House of Lords had reservations about this more discretionary approach, with the uncertainty which would inevitably accompany it. But it is submitted that the *Bowmakers* v *Barnet* principle (as interpreted by the House of Lords in *Tinsley* v *Milligan*) is far from satisfactory, as it relies too heavily on procedural or technical issues and makes little reference to policy or justice[16].

Similar issues were raised in the recent case of *Tribe* v *Tribe* [1995] 4 All ER 236. In this case, P owned 459 out of 500 shares in a family company and he was the tenant of two leasehold properties which the company occupied as licensee. The landlord of the properties claimed against P for repairs and, if the claims were successful, P was faced with having to sell the company. In order to prevent this, P transferred his shares to one of his sons (D), a director of the company. It was never intended that the proposed price for the transfer should actually be paid and, indeed, D did not pay. Eventually, after satisfactory resolution of the disputes over the lease, P wanted to revert to the position which had existed before he was faced with claims for repair. However, D now refused to transfer the shares back to P, and P took action to recover them. The judge found that the illegal purpose of the transfer (ie to deceive P's creditors into thinking he was no longer the owner of the shares) had not been carried into effect in any way. As the claims over repairs were resolved, no deception of creditors was needed by P. The judge upheld P's claim for return of the shares and the Court of Appeal dismissed D's appeal. It appears that it was sufficient for P to withdraw voluntarily from the illegal transaction when it was no longer necessary, without any need to repent his illegal purpose (*per* Millet LJ in the Court of Appeal).

Another exception to the general rule about the irrecoverability of property transferred under an illegal contract is where the parties are not *in pari delicto* — ie where they are not equally guilty. In certain circumstances it may be possible for the court to allow the less culpable party to recover property that he has transferred to the other, more guilty party. If, for example, one party has entered into an unlawful agreement, having been defrauded by the other (or as a result of oppression), it is eminently sensible that the "victim" should not be debarred from recovering property which has been transferred. It may not always be quite so easy, however, to decide whether one party is more culpable than the other. In *Kiriri Cotton Ltd v Dewani* [1960] AC 192, for example:

> KC Ltd let a flat in Uganda for a term of seven years to Dewani, who paid a premium of Shs 10,000. Although neither party realised they were breaking the law, the taking of a premium was, in fact, a breach of a government ordinance. This ordinance did not make any express provision that an illegal premium was recoverable by the tenant (in contrast to the analogous legislation in England). Dewani brought an action to recover the premium.

The Privy Council held that the premium was recoverable by the tenant, despite the lack of an express provision in the ordinance permitting this. It was clear that the statute was aimed at protecting a particular class of person from another, namely prospective tenants from landlords. So although both parties were unaware that they were breaking the law, the court was of the opinion that the duty of observing the law fell more heavily on the landlord than the tenant. Thus, despite appearances to the contrary, they were not *in pari delicto*. (Of course, some statutes make express provision to achieve this effect, in which case there is no need to rely on the common law principle.) The approach of the law was summed up by Lord Mansfield, in *Browning v Morris* (1778) 2 Cowp 790 at p 792, in the following way:

> "But, where contracts or transactions are prohibited by positive statutes, for the sake of protecting one set of men from another set of men; the one, from their situation and condition, being liable to be oppressed or imposed upon by the other; there, the parties are not *in pari delicto*; and in furtherance of these statutes, the person injured, after the transaction is finished and completed, may bring his action and defeat the contract".

The scope of this principle was discussed in *Green v Portsmouth Stadium Ltd* [1953] 2 QB 190. The facts were:

> Frederick Green, a bookmaker, claimed that he had been overcharged by the defendants over a period of years, contrary to the provisions of s 13(1) Betting and Lotteries Act 1934. The defendants owned the Portsmouth Stadium greyhound racing track. Green alleged that although the highest charge which the defendants were authorised to make under s 13(1) was 11s 3d, he had been charged £2 each time he went on to the course. He now claimed from the defendants the excess fees which he had paid to them. He based his argument on the fact that he was not *in pari delicto* with the defendants and sought to rely on the *dictum* of Lord Mansfield.

The Court of Appeal held that the plaintiff was not able to recover the amounts that he had been overcharged by the defendants as the obligation imposed by the relevant statute was enforceable only by criminal proceedings. (The Act did not expressly provide for the recovery of any overcharge — it stated only that the person responsible for it was guilty of an offence.) This reasoning is not entirely convincing, but the court went on to reject Green's argument that he was not *in pari delicto* with the defendants. Lord Hodson (at p 197) observed that the plaintiff had not proved that he was less guilty. He stated that, as far as the evidence went, Green seemed to have been "as much a party to breaking [the law]" as the defendants.

A further exception to the general rule is where a party repents or withdraws before the contract has been substantially performed. (Also see *Tribe v Tribe* [1995] 4 All ER 236, discussed earlier.) So where a party takes proceedings before the illegal purpose has been achieved, he may be allowed to recover property which he has transferred under the contract (for example, see *Taylor v Bowers* (1876) 1 QBD 291). But this raises the obvious problem of deciding whether the repentance has taken place at an early enough stage to allow recovery. How will a court decide whether matters have progressed too far? The first requirement, if the plaintiff is to succeed, is to show that it is a genuine case of repentance — ie, that he has chosen to abandon the illegal purpose. If he has no choice in the matter due to the other party's failure to perform, he will not be allowed to recover (see *Bigos v Bousted* [1951] 1 All ER 92). The second requirement relates to the time at which the repentance takes place in relation to the progress of the illegal purpose (see *Ouston v Zurowski*[17]). Where the illegal purpose has been accomplished it is obvious that recovery will not be allowed. But it also appears that even where the illegal agreement has been only partly performed, recovery will not be permitted if the illegal purpose has been substantially achieved. For example, in *Kearley v Thomson* (1890) 24 QBD 742:

> The defendant firm of solicitors was to act on behalf of a petitioning creditor against a bankrupt named Clarke. The plaintiff, a friend of Clarke's, agreed to pay the defendants their costs, in return for which they would neither appear at the public examination of Clarke, nor oppose his order of discharge. The solicitors, on receiving the promised payment, did not appear at Clarke's public examination, in accordance with their illegal agreement with the plaintiff. But the plaintiff changed his mind before any application was made for the bankrupt's discharge, and he tried to recover the money which he had paid to the defendants.

It was held by the Court of Appeal that he could not recover the money. The illegality of the agreement was that it was aimed at interfering with the course of justice. As this purpose had already been substantially achieved, the repentance came too late. In the words of Fry LJ (at p 747):

> "[W]here there has been a partial carrying into effect of an illegal purpose in a substantial manner, it is impossible, though there remains something not performed, that the money paid under that illegal contract can be recovered back."

(c) Related transactions between the parties

The parties to an illegal contract may also enter into a subsequent agreement which is based on the illegal transaction. In this case, the later agreement will also be tainted by the illegal purpose of the original contract. So if one party owes another money under an illegal contract, and he gives some security in respect of the money which is due, this will be unenforceable against him by the other party. In *Fisher* v *Bridges* (1854) 3 E & B 642, for example, P agreed to sell, and subsequently conveyed, land to D for a purpose which was illegal. The defendant still owed some money to P under the transaction and he executed a deed by which he promised payment of the outstanding sum. It was held that such a deed was unenforceable as it was tainted by the illegality of the main transaction. This is hardly surprising, for if the law refuses to enforce the original contract, it follows that any subsequent agreement which springs from this should be treated in the same way.

A separate issue (not to be confused with the above rule) is where the courts allow one party a remedy against the other, despite the illegality of their contract, under a "collateral" contract. We have seen, in other areas of contract law, how this device is sometimes used by the courts to enable a fair solution to be reached when it would otherwise be precluded by some substantive principle of law. Here it is used so as to enable the innocent party to sue the guilty party under an illegal transaction without relying on the transaction itself. An instructive case is *Strongman (1945) Ltd* v *Sincock* [1955] 2 QB 525:

> The plaintiff building company contracted with the defendant, an architect, to modernise some houses. An appropriate licence was required from the Ministry of Works so that the refurbishment did not contravene statutory regulations; without such a licence the contract was illegal. The defendant promised the plaintiffs, before the contract was made, that he would take responsibility for securing the necessary licences. The plaintiffs carried out work which exceeded £6,000 in value. But the defendant had obtained licences for only £2,150. The defendant paid only £2,900 to the builders and he argued that the performance of the contract was illegal. The builders sued for the unpaid sum.

The Court of Appeal held that, despite the illegality of the main transaction, the builders could succeed on the basis of the collateral promise made by the defendant that he would obtain the necessary licences for the work. Presumably it was thought that the work was carried out by the builders on the understanding that he had in fact done as he promised. Although the conclusion reached by the court was desirable, there is, in truth, some difficulty in distinguishing this case from *Re Mahmoud and Ispahani* [1921] 2 KB 716 (discussed earlier). It should be added that this judicial device will be used to assist the "innocent" party in very limited circumstances.

4. Illegal performance of lawful contracts

A contract may not be unlawful in itself, but one of the parties to the agreement may perform the contract in an illegal manner, without the other knowing of this. This was basically the situation in *Archbold's (Freightage) Ltd v Spanglett Ltd* [1961] 1 All ER 417 where, it will be remembered, the illegality of the defendants' use of their vehicle did not debar the plaintiffs from recovering damages. Archbold's were innocent of any knowledge of the illegality and the contract (for the carriage of goods by road) was not illegal in itself. Of course, the guilty party will normally be in a different position, and will not be able to sue successfully as a result of his illegal performance. If both parties participate in the illegal performance of the contract, then it is likely that both will find themselves without a remedy (see *Ashmore, Benson, Pease & Co* v *A V Dawson Ltd* [1973] 2 All ER 856).

The contrast between the positions of the innocent and the guilty party is well illustrated by *Marles* v *Philip Trant & Sons Ltd* [1954] 1 QB 29:

> The plaintiff, a farmer, bought wheat from the defendant seed merchants. The defendants believed the goods to be "spring" wheat (having bought them under that misdescription from a third party) and they were described as such to the plaintiff. In fact, it was not "spring" wheat which they sold to the farmer. The performance of the contract was illegal due to the fact that the defendants were in breach of a statute for failing to deliver an invoice with the goods. Did the illegality affect the plaintiff's right to damages?

It was held that the contract was not illegal in itself, but only in the manner of its performance. The farmer was the innocent party and he was, therefore, not prevented from succeeding in his action for damages.

5. Proposals for reform

It is clear from the previous sections that the courts are not always consistent in their application of the principles relating to the enforcement of illegal agreements, resulting in a body of case law which is far from satisfactory. The House of Lords' decision in *Tinsley* v *Milligan* (see earlier discussion) illustrates the way in which technical legal arguments may lead to an avoidance of the consideration of wider issues of policy and justice. Furthermore, a recurring problem faced by the court is how to signify its disapproval of an illegal agreement without allowing one party to be unjustly enriched or advantaged at the expense of the other. (See the discussion, above, of *Mohamed* v *Alaga & Co (a firm)* [1999] 3 All ER 699.)

A recent Law Commission Consultation Paper[18] concluded that there is a need for legislative reform of this area of law and it has recommended, provisionally, that the existing rules relating to the effects of illegality should be replaced by a discretion[19]. Such a discretion would enable a court to decide whether to enforce an illegal agreement, to recognise that property rights have been transferred or created by it, or to hold that benefits conferred under the agreement are recoverable[20]. However, the Law Commission favoured a structured discretion, in the interests of greater certainty and to provide guidance to the courts. It provisionally recommended that, in the exercise of its discretion, the court should have regard to:

"(i) the seriousness of the illegality involved;
(ii) the knowledge and intention of the party seeking to enforce the illegal transaction, seeking the recognition of legal or equitable rights under it, or seeking to recover benefits conferred under it;

(iii) whether refusing to allow standard rights and remedies would deter illegality;

(iv) whether refusing to allow standard rights and remedies would further the purpose of the rule which renders the transaction illegal; and

(v) whether refusing to allow standard rights and remedies would be proportionate to the illegality involved."[21]

Footnotes

(1) See Treitel, *Law of Contract*, 10th ed, p 393.

(2) Although the winner cannot sue the loser, the loser cannot recover his money if he does pay up.

(3) The relevance of the respective bargaining strengths of the parties was illustrated recently in *Dawnay Day & Co Ltd* v *Frederick de Braconier d'Alphen and others* [1998] ICR 1068.

(4) The agreement was not contrary to the public interest as it strengthened the position of an English company in its manufacturing of guns to be sold worldwide!

(5) Also see EC Article 85(2).

(6) For a discussion of the relevance of the distinction between these terms, see *Faccenda Chicken Ltd* v *Fowler* [1987] Ch 117. Here it was explained that an employee, after his employment has terminated, may use confidential information unless this is expressly forbidden. However, he is not entitled to use or disclose "trade secrets", either during or after his employment, regardless of whether there is an express stipulation to this effect. (Presumably, a trade secret is something of a highly confidential nature.) The ambit of any implied term, imposing restrictions on an employee after the employment comes to an end, was considered recently in *Peter Brooks* v *Olyslager Oms (UK) Ltd* [1998] IRLR 590.

(7) Lord Denning stated at p 1037: "I think that limiting words ought to be read into the clause so as to limit it to the part of the business for which Littlewoods are reasonably entitled to protection".

(8) The case is also of considerable interest on the subject of unconscionability and is discussed further in Chapter 16.

(9) For instance, see *Esso Petroleum Ltd* v *Harper's Garage Ltd* [1968] AC 269 and *Schroeder Music Publishing* v *Macaulay* [1974] 3 All ER 616.

(10) For example, see S Singleton, *Competition Act 1998*, 1999 Blackstone Press.

(11) This distinction is well explained in Smith and Thomas, *Casebook on Contract* 11th ed, p 684.

(12) Also see *United City Merchants* v *Royal Bank of Canada* [1981] 3 All ER 142 in which *dicta* of Viscount Simonds and Lord Reid in *Regazzoni* were applied.

(13) See *Nash* v *Nash* [1965] 1 All ER 480.

(14) Also see *Saunders* v *Edwards* [1987] 1 WLR 1116.

(15) For example, see Enonchong, *Illegality: The Fading Flame of Public Policy* (1994) 14 OJLS 295.

(16) For another recent case raising similar issues, see *Skilton* v *Sullivan* [1994] The Times 25 March.

(17) *Ouston* v *Zurowski* [1985] 5 WWR 169. In this Canadian case one party was entitled to recover under an illegal contract because he repented before performance of the contract; that is, by not carrying into effect the illegal purpose (a "pyramid" scheme) in a substantial manner before abandoning the scheme.

(18) Law Commission Consultation Paper No 154, 1999, *Illegal Transactions: The Effect of Illegality on Contracts and Trusts*.

(19) *Ibid*, para 9.1.

(20) *Ibid*, para 1.18 and paras 7.2 to 7.26.

(21) *Ibid*, para 1.19 and paras 7.27 to 7.43. Note that this proposed discretion would not apply where there are express statutory provisions relating to the effect of illegality on a transaction.

Chapter 16

Unconscionability and unfairness

1. Introduction

The law of contract has to tread a delicate path between two distinct and often opposing ideas. On the one hand, the law supports the freedom on the part of the individual to enter into a contract of his choosing without unnecessary judicial or statutory interference. On the other, the law does not wish to see one party to a contract take unfair advantage of the other by virtue of either his own superior bargaining strength, or the other's weakness. It is often stated that our law does not possess a general doctrine of "unconscionability" or "unfairness" and that such a doctrine would be injurious to the requirement of predictability and certainty. As we have seen in earlier chapters, the law seeks stability in matters of commercial activity, and it does not favour general doctrines which offer too wide a basis for judicial interference with the bargains reached by the parties[1]. The "classical" view of contract law has fostered the idea of freedom of contract and the law has taken an essentially objective view of agreement. In other words, it is not primarily concerned with the fairness of exchange between the parties so long as they have, to outward appearances, reached agreement. It is not for the courts to intervene simply because one party has made a poor bargain. To this extent it is true to say that (formally) the law of contract has not been concerned, traditionally, with the substantive fairness of a transaction.

The law is, of course, concerned with procedural fairness. Therefore, a contract may be set aside for such reasons as fraud, misrepresentation, duress, or undue influence. This approach has been likened to the conduct of a game in that the law ensures that the rules are fair but it does not try to interfere with the outcome (or result) once the basic rules of fairness have been followed. This may well represent the theory behind the law, but it is difficult to accept that it is a fair reflection of legal reality. For, in reality, judges have not been reluctant to use a variety of techniques at their disposal to ensure a fair outcome when one party appears to have exploited some unfair advantage, particularly when there is a considerable disparity in economic strength between the parties. (For example, see *Silvertone Records* v *Mountfield* [1993] EMLR 152, which is discussed on page 351.) We should not be misled by what judges say they are doing. It is what they actually do which is important.

In practice, in order to achieve a fair result, a judge may rely on equitable doctrines, or on techniques of construction and interpretation of contracts; he may imply terms, or he may refuse certain remedies. It is misleading to argue that issues of unconscionability or unfairness will form no part of judicial thinking when contemplating the use of such powers and doctrines. Judges may even make overt reference to the issue of unconscionability as a factor in reaching a particular conclusion (for example, see *Backhouse* v *Backhouse* [1978] 1 All ER 1158; *Cresswell* v *Potter* [1978] 1 WLR 255; *Watkin* v *Watson-Smith* [1986] The Times 3 July; *Boustany* v *Pigott* [1993] EGCS 85; and *Commission for the New Towns* v *Cooper (GB) Ltd* [1995] 2 All ER 929). It has been well said that "despite lip service to the notion of absolute freedom of contract, relief is every day given against agreements that are unfair, inequitable, unreasonable, or oppressive"[2]. This vigilance on the part of judges using their common law and equitable powers helps to ensure that freedom of contract and "objectivity" are not seriously abused.

Such intervention is, of its very nature, both piecemeal and unpredictable. In some areas where the problem of unfairness was especially pressing, such as in relation to the use of unfair exemption clauses, judicial attempts at "policing" have been augmented and largely superseded by statutory change. Thus the Unfair Contract Terms Act 1977 represented a significant move towards controlling the fairness of certain types of contractual terms and, more recently, the EC Directive on Unfair Terms in Consumer Contracts was introduced to regulate unfair terms in non-negotiated contracts between consumers and businesses (see earlier discussion in Chapters 10 and 11). But such statutory developments, whilst very important in themselves, have not brought to an end the need for common law and equitable principles which promote fairness and prevent unconscionable bargains.

This introduction would not be complete without a warning about judicial pronouncements on the existence, or absence, of some general principle relating to unconscionable contracts. Our law of contract stresses certainty and stability, so it tends to discourage statements of general (and uncertain) application to the effect that the courts have a wide power to "police" agreements on the ground of unconscionability. (This is in contrast to such general statements as are contained in the United States' Uniform Commercial Code, section 2–302.) Although attempts have been made to assert a general principle of substantive fairness, most notably by Lord Denning in *Lloyds Bank Ltd* v *Bundy* [1974] 3 All ER 757 (at p 765), these have tended to encounter opposition from other senior judges. So Lord Denning's assertion of such a principle was criticised in the House of Lords by Lord Scarman in *National Westminster Bank plc* v *Morgan* [1985] 1 All ER 821 at p 830. Their conflicting opinions are discussed in more detail later.

It would be wrong, however, if the cool reception given to Lord Denning's view by Lord Scarman were to be regarded as the final word on the subject. The law cannot pursue the goals of certainty and flexibility simultaneously, as they will often be in opposition to one another. The law goes through periods in its history when the need for certainty and predictability appear to dominate judicial thought. But it is also true that such periods of "formal" justice are followed by periods of greater flexibility and discretion. It may well be that Lord Scarman's assertion in *Morgan*, that the imposition of restrictions on freedom of contract is best left to Parliament, will prove too stultifying and will, in turn, incur the displeasure of other judges.

2.   Examples of judicial intervention to prevent unfairness

It is perhaps surprising that so important a question as whether a contract must meet a general requirement of fairness has not been dealt with more authoritatively by the courts. The reason for so few statements of general principle is that the courts appreciate the difficulty of formulating such a doctrine and prefer to leave their undoubted powers fairly vague. What follows in this section is a brief account of some (but by no means all) of the areas in which questions of unfairness and unconscionability have influenced the courts.

We saw in Chapter 4 that the courts are not supposed to be concerned with the adequacy of consideration so long as the consideration is "sufficient" in a legal sense. The theory is that it is not for the courts to make bargains for the parties who are free to agree to whatever exchange they wish, no matter how one-sided, so long as there is no procedural unfairness (such as fraud or duress). This may be a perfectly reasonable approach where the parties, knowing of the technical requirement of consideration, agree to some nominal consideration; or where the apparent inadequacy of the consideration is offset by some other benefit which the parties were presumably aware of when contracting (see *Mountford* v *Scott* [1975] Ch 258). It is also true to say that the courts will not intervene simply because someone has paid a higher price for goods than they need have done; the courts are not regarded as the appropriate place for controlling prices or fair exchange. But the fact that the courts are not concerned (formally) with the adequacy of the consideration does not mean that they will take no interest in a case where the exchange between the parties is extremely unfair. The courts share the ordinary person's intuitive dislike of injustice and judges will use whatever techniques are available to avoid an unconscionable result[(3)]. For example, in *Boustany* v *Pigott* [1993] EGCS 85, P (who was elderly) granted B a renewal of a lease on terms which were very favourable to B. It appeared that B took advantage of P in a number of ways, before and at the time of the agreement, and with full knowledge that her behaviour was unconscionable. The Privy Council set aside the lease because of B's unconscionable conduct. It was held that B had clearly abused her position in relation to P, by exploiting her incapacity.

A good illustration of judicial flexibility is provided by *Backhouse* v *Backhouse* [1978] 1 All ER 1158, where the facts were:

> A husband (H) and wife (W) bought a house in their joint names with the help of a mortgage. W left the matrimonial home and went to live with another man. H persuaded his wife to sign an agreement which transferred the house into his sole name. Although no duress was used, H did not advise his wife to seek independent legal advice. In exchange for signing the document of transfer W received only a release from her liability under the mortgage. (She signed because of a sense of guilt towards H.) The couple were divorced and both of them remarried. As a result of an increase in property values, the house was soon worth much more than when they bought it. W applied, *inter alia*, for a lump sum order and a property transfer order in respect of the former matrimonial home.

This is a very interesting case. In a strict (or objective) sense, the contract was freely entered into, as there was no duress by the husband. It is not, therefore, a case of procedural unfairness. The exchange also met the technical requirement of consideration provided by both parties. But looking at the case from a more realistic point of view it is immediately obvious that the whole transaction was extremely unfair. Due to a sense of guilt, or emotional strain, the wife entered into an agreement (without legal advice) from which she derived very little material value. The indemnity against liability on the mortgage was virtually worthless in practice as the value of the house was rising considerably. If the Family Division of the High Court had adopted the traditional view, there could be little reason for granting the wife relief from her very bad bargain. However, Balcombe J held that having regard to the wife's contribution to the purchase of the house, it would be repugnant to justice to deprive her of all interest in it. Accordingly, she was granted a share in the capital asset (the house) which she had helped to create, but she was not to benefit from any increase in value in the house occurring after her departure. The husband was ordered to pay her a lump sum of £3,500.

In *Backhouse* v *Backhouse* the judge specifically asked whether the agreement was unconscionable. (He also referred to the similar case of *Cresswell* v *Potter* [1978] 1 WLR 225 where an agreement between a husband and wife was set aside, largely on the basis of its unconscionability.) In answering this question the judge was prepared to consider the inadequacy of the consideration and subjective factors about the parties. For example, although the wife was in no sense "ignorant" — she was in fact an intelligent woman — she was not independently advised about the importance of the transaction. The judge continued (at pp 1165–1166):

> "[The wife] was given no value for her transfer, merely the release from her liability on the mortgage, and she received no independent advice. . . When a marriage has broken down, both parties are liable to be in an emotional state. The party remaining in the matrimonial home, as the husband did in this case, has an advantage."

Despite the general rule about the courts' lack of interest in the adequacy of the consideration, there are other well known examples of the courts intervening for this very reason. However, it is fair to state that some of these decisions can also be rationalised on other grounds which do less violence to traditional theory. But this should not disguise the fact that they are directly concerned with questions of unfair exchange. In *Lloyds Bank Ltd* v *Bundy* [1974] 3 All ER 757:

> Herbert Bundy was an elderly farmer. His only financial asset was his farmhouse. His son, Michael, ran a company which had run into financial difficulty; its account at Lloyds Bank was overdrawn. Herbert Bundy, who also banked at Lloyds, guaranteed his son's company's overdraft by charging his house to the bank. The son's plant-hire business deteriorated further, and the bank was not prepared to maintain Michael Bundy's overdraft without additional security. The new assistant bank manager, together with Michael Bundy, went to see Herbert Bundy to explain that the bank's financial support of the son's company would be withdrawn unless he was prepared to extend his guarantee of the son's overdraft. In effect, the old man would have to increase the charge on his farmhouse to £11,000, which was slightly more than its value, in return for which the bank merely promised not to withdraw the son's overdraft facilities for the time being. The bank manager gave Herbert Bundy a partial explanation of what was wrong with the son's company but was unable to go into detail. Herbert Bundy, who was not independently advised at the meeting, signed the relevant documents there and then. Six months later the bank withdrew its support of the company, which was still in trouble, and proceeded to enforce the charge and guarantee against Herbert Bundy. The bank sought to evict the old man from his farmhouse.

The Court of Appeal set aside the guarantee and charge signed by Herbert Bundy, allowing his appeal against the trial judge's decision. Although his colleagues preferred to base their decision on the narrower ground of undue influence, Lord Denning asserted a much wider principle to justify a finding in favour of Herbert Bundy. The general principle which he outlined is considered later, together with the views of his critics, but it is significant that he referred specifically (at p 765) to the fact that "the consideration moving from the bank was grossly inadequate". He observed that although the agreement conferred a considerable benefit on the bank, there was a marked absence of corresponding benefit to either the old man or his son's company: "All that the company gained was a short respite from impending doom". In short, it was an unconscionable agreement.

A further illustration of judicial intervention on the basis of an unfair exchange between the parties can be found in *Staffordshire Area Health Authority* v *South Staffordshire Waterworks Co* [1978] 3 All ER 769. In this case the court permitted a contract for the supply of water, which appeared to be of indefinite duration, to be terminated by reasonable notice given by the party that was supplying the water at one-fifteenth of its value. In reaching this conclusion, and in seeming to depart from what the parties had actually agreed, the court was clearly influenced by the fact that the agreement, made in 1929, bound the defendants to supply water at what had become an obviously uneconomic rate. Whatever the merits or demerits of the decision, it shows that the courts will not always be impotent when faced with a very uneven exchange between the parties.

Similarly, in *Schroeder Music Publishing Co Ltd* v *Macaulay* [1974] 3 All ER 616, the House of Lords held an agreement to be unenforceable, as an unreasonable restraint of trade, when a music publishing company engaged the exclusive services of a young song writer. The plaintiff gave the company the copyright of all his compositions for the next five years, but on terms that were wholly disadvantageous to himself. The restrictions in the agreement combined a lack of obligation on the company's part with a total commitment on the plaintiff's part. In reaching their conclusion, the judges were clearly mindful of the inadequacy of the consideration provided by the company. Lord Diplock went further than the other judges by observing that what was in issue was not some nineteenth century economic theory about the public interest in freedom of trade, but "the protection of those whose bargaining power is weak against being forced by those whose bargaining power is stronger to enter into bargains that are unconscionable" (at p 623). (For recent cases raising similar issues, see *Silvertone Records* v *Mountfield* [1993] EMLR 152 and *Zang Tumb Tuum Records* v *Johnson* [1993] EMLR 61.)

Although the restraint of trade doctrine is traditionally discussed in terms of the public interest (see Chapter 15), it is evident that the issue of fairness will frequently be influential in courts' decisions on this subject. The requirement that the restraint clause must be reasonable between the parties gives a judge the opportunity to assess the unconscionability of a particular agreement. Obviously the fairness of the exchange — ie the adequacy or generosity of the consideration — may determine whether a particular restraint is reasonable in the circumstances. Therefore, if one party has agreed not to compete with the other, but has received little material advantage in return for such an undertaking, then the court may be more disposed towards holding the restraint to be unreasonable and unenforceable. To take a different example, an agreement might appear fair but may be capable of operating in an unfair or oppressive way. In *Shell UK* v *Lostock Garage Ltd* [1977] 1 All ER 481, for instance, the facts were as follows:

> L Ltd was a small garage which was tied to Shell under the terms of a solus agreement made in 1955. This required L to sell only Shell's petrol. The agreement, which could be terminated by twelve months' notice, worked well until the oil crisis in the mid-1970s, when there occurred a petrol "price war". L had to compete with four neighbouring garages — two were Shell garages and two were "free". The two garages not tied to Shell cut their prices and Shell then introduced a support scheme which effectively subsidised the other two garages. L's garage was excluded from the scheme and was forced to trade at a loss, since it was unable to compete with the neighbouring garages. To meet the competition, L obtained petrol from another supplier, M. Shell threatened M with proceedings for inducing breach of contract and M stopped supplying L, which was then forced to resume taking its petrol from Shell. In the resulting legal action, L claimed that it was no longer tied to Shell under the solus agreement. Shell brought an action against L claiming, *inter alia*, damages for breach by L of the agreement because L took petrol from another supplier. L defended this claim by arguing that the agreement was unenforceable as being an unreasonable restraint of trade; alternatively, that the agreement was subject to an implied term by Shell that they would not discriminate against L in favour of competing and neighbouring garages.

The case gave rise to widely differing judicial views about the relevant issues, and it is not possible to consider all aspects of the decision here. It was held by the majority that Shell were not in breach of the solus agreement by operating the support scheme, there being no implied term that Shell should not discriminate against L. But Shell's claim for an injunction restraining L from breaking the tie provision was refused, with a variety of reasons being offered by the judges. For example, it would not have been just or equitable to grant Shell an injunction restraining L from breaking the tie provision whilst Shell were operating the support scheme and excluding L from it, as the scheme operated to L's prejudice. Therefore Shell could not enforce the tie provision whilst the support scheme was operating.

Although the case gave rise to technical issues relating to implied terms and the restraint of trade doctrine, it is difficult to separate these issues from questions of fairness, especially in relation to the appropriate remedies. This is particularly evident in the judgment of Lord Denning (at p 490):

> "[The tie] appeared superficially to be fair and reasonable at the time of the contract ... but, at the end of 1975, Shell started to subsidise two neighbouring Shell garages to such an extent that they were able to, and did, undercut Lostock ... To insist on the tie in these circumstances ... was most unfair and unreasonable. So much that I think the courts should decline to enforce it. At any rate, they should not enforce it so long as Shell operated their support scheme to the prejudice of Lostock".

A further example of the relevance of unconscionable behaviour can be found in *Foley* v *Classique Coaches* [1934] 2 KB 1. P agreed to sell a piece of land to D, but this contract was conditional upon D (who ran a motor coach business) entering into a separate agreement under which P would supply all of D's petrol "at a price to be agreed by the parties... from time to time". An arbitration clause in the "petrol" contract provided for the resolution of any disputes which might arise in the performance of the petrol agreement. After the conveyance of the land, D bought petrol from P for three years but then tried to argue that he was not bound because the agreement was too uncertain and that, furthermore, it was an unreasonable restraint of trade. The Court of Appeal rejected D's arguments and held that there was a binding contract. Scrutton LJ was clearly influenced by D's conduct which appeared to have been unconscionable. It would have been unfair to allow D to escape from his contractual obligation to buy P's petrol, having obtained a good deal on the purchase of the land in the first place. Scrutton LJ stated (at p 7) that he was glad to decide the case in P's favour as he did "not regard [D's] contention as an honest one".

The discretion of a court to grant the equitable remedy of rectification in cases of mistake in the recording of agreements may also be influenced by the unconscionable behaviour of one of the parties (see Chapter 12). In *Commission for the New Towns* v *Cooper (GB) Ltd* [1995] 2 All ER 929 the unconscionable conduct of the defendant was a vital issue in the Court of Appeal holding that rectification can be granted in cases of unilateral mistake.

Another area of contract law where the courts have taken a close interest in questions of fairness is in relation to the use of exemption or exclusion clauses. This topic has been discussed in detail in Chapters 9 and 10, but a few brief points need to be made here. It will be remembered that a party will use an exemption clause to exclude or limit his liability for, *inter alia*, breach of contract. This may be an entirely reasonable practice between two equal parties and it may simply be a means of allocating risk and indicating which of them should take out insurance cover. By limiting liability, one party may be able to provide cheaper services as a result, and for this reason the other party may choose to contract with him. Thus the amount of the consideration requested may be a relevant factor in deciding on the liability of the party relying on an exclusion clause, that is, in assessing the reasonableness of the clause in question. For a good example, see *Photo Production Ltd* v *Securicor Transport Ltd* [1980] AC 827. (The test of reasonableness contained in the Unfair Contract Terms Act 1977 will be discussed later.)

But there are other commercial situations where the use of exemption clauses is not so acceptable. This is particularly so in standard form contracts where the stronger party is seeking, in effect, to impose his terms on the weaker one. When such a practice involves a business relying on an exclusion clause against a consumer, it is easy to appreciate why this gave rise to much concern in the courts. For if the theory of contract law was based on contracts being freely entered into by the parties, as equals, this was clear proof that commercial reality was not in accord with legal theory. Because of the traditional approach of our law, which viewed contracts as bargains made by the parties and did not permit the courts to intervene and re-write agreements for them, there was no general rule at common law that an exemption clause was required to be fair. But, as we saw in Chapter 9, the courts developed a number of techniques to restrict the unconscionable use and enforcement of such clauses. In particular, techniques of construction were developed by judges so as to restrict the scope of an exclusion clause by finding that it did not cover the breach which had occurred.

Issues of substantive fairness clearly arise when considering the incorporation of an exclusion clause by notice. The general rule is that for a clause (contained in an unsigned document, for example) to be incorporated into a contract, X must give reasonably sufficient notice of it to Y (see *Parker* v *South Eastern Railway Co Ltd* [1877] 2 CPD 416). In theory, if such notice is given by X, then Y will be taken to have assented to the clause. But this approach says nothing about the fairness of the particular clause in question. Judges are reluctant, however, to permit an unusual or very unfair clause to be incorporated by X unless he makes a greater effort than is normally required to bring it to the attention of Y. As a matter of logic, if reasonably sufficient notice has been given, the content of the clause should make no difference to the question of incorporation. But the law does not always follow the dictates of logic; in the interests of preventing unfair or unconscionable contracts, some judges have been prepared to blur the distinction between procedural and substantive justice. In *Thornton* v *Shoe Lane Parking* [1971] 2 QB 163, for instance:

> P drove up to the entrance to D's car park where there was a notice: "All cars parked at owner's risk". P received a ticket from a machine at the entrance and drove in. P was injured, partly due to D's negligence, when he returned to the car park to collect his car. D attempted to escape liability by relying on an exemption clause displayed on a sign inside the car park and referred to on the ticket received by P at the entrance to the car park. This sign purported to exclude liability for injury to customers. Was this clause incorporated into the contract?

The Court of Appeal held that D was liable. The ticket arrived too late to incorporate any additional terms into the contract. It was significant that the term displayed at the entrance differed from the more unusual one inside the car park. A term which sought to exclude liability for injury to customers was more far-reaching and potentially unfair. It is hardly surprising that the judges had difficulty in separating the issues of reasonable notice and substantive fairness. Lord Denning thought that the clause was an example of the type of thing which he had considered in an earlier case, *Spurling* v *Bradshaw* [1956] 1 WLR 461 at p 466, namely an unreasonable clause, which therefore required a greater amount of notice to be incorporated. Megaw LJ (at p 172) also considered that the clause required additional notice, but he thought that it was only unusual clauses which should be treated in this way.

Since the enactment of the Unfair Contract Terms Act 1977 it might be contended that the interventionist approach of the courts, as exemplified by cases like *Thornton*, will not be so necessary. The courts will now be able to rely on the appropriate provisions of this statute to deal with unfair and unreasonable exemption clauses. But this should not obscure the general point which is being made here that the courts, faced with unjust or unconscionable agreements (or terms), may use whatever techniques they possess to prevent an unfair outcome. So we see the approach employed in *Thornton* being followed in *Interfoto Picture Library* v *Stiletto Visual Programmes* [1988] 1 All ER 348. Briefly, the facts were:

> Interfoto supplied forty-seven photographic slides on hire to an advertising agency, Stiletto, who required the slides for a presentation to a client. A delivery note, containing certain conditions, was sent to Stiletto together with the slides. One of these conditions (no 2) stated that a holding fee of £5 per slide per day would be charged for any slide kept for longer than fourteen days. Stiletto failed to return the slides within this two week period and, in reliance on condition 2, the plaintiffs claimed more than £3,500 from Stiletto. It should be noted that the holding fee

charged by the plaintiffs greatly exceeded that charged by other comparable agencies.

The Court of Appeal held that, as condition 2 in the delivery note was unusual and unreasonable, Interfoto had not given Stiletto sufficient notice to incorporate this clause into the contract. Accordingly, the defendants were not liable for the amount claimed by the plaintiffs, who instead were entitled to a *quantum meruit* of £3.50 per slide per week. This is a clear example of direct interference with freedom of contract in order to prevent an unfair result. If the holding fee had been more moderate and reasonable, there would presumably have been sufficient notice. It is difficult to escape the conclusion that, despite discussion about what amounts to reasonable notice of a contractual term, the court was effectively re-writing the agreement for the parties to achieve a fairer outcome than they had themselves provided for.

Other examples could be taken from the development of the common law in relation to exclusion clauses, but many of these have been discussed in detail in Chapter 9. It is worth remembering the way in which the courts developed the vague notion of "fundamental breach" as a weapon against the unconscionable use of exclusion clauses. Such a breach of contract was one that was so fundamental as to deprive the party in breach of the benefits of his exclusion clause (for example, see *Karsales (Harrow) Ltd* v *Wallis* [1956] 1 WLR 936). To be truly effective in policing exclusion clauses, it was necessary for the principle of fundamental breach to be given the status of a rule of law. The Court of Appeal persisted with such an approach (see *Harbutt's Plasticine Ltd* v *Wayne Tank & Pump Co Ltd* [1970] 1 QB 477), despite a ruling to the contrary by the House of Lords in *Suisse Atlantique Société d'Armement Maritime SA* v *NV Rotterdamsche Kolen Centrale* [1967] 1 AC 361. Due to the introduction of the Unfair Contract Terms Act 1977, this particular form of common law intervention is no longer strictly necessary, but it still provides a powerful example of the reluctance of judges to sit by and watch one party to a contract take unconscionable advantage of the other[4].

3.   A general doctrine of unconscionability?

In a commercial context, between parties who contract on an equal footing, the classical (or laissez-faire) approach has the obvious advantage of certainty and the courts will be wary of introducing a general discretion to relieve against hardship. This is well illustrated in the recent case of *Union Eagle Ltd* v *Golden Achievement Ltd* [1997] 2 All ER 215. The case involved a written contract in which the appellant purchaser (P) agreed to buy a flat in Hong Kong from the respondent vendor (V) and paid a 10 per cent deposit to V. It was a term of the agreement that completion was to be effected before 5.00 pm on 30 September 1991, and that time was of the essence in this respect. The agreement provided that P would forfeit the deposit in the event of failure to comply with any term or condition of the contract. P was ten minutes late in attempting to complete the transaction and was told by V that the contract would be rescinded and the deposit forfeited. P's action for specific performance was dismissed by the Hong Kong Court of Appeal, but P appealed to the Privy Council, arguing that P was entitled to relief against forfeiture of the deposit. The Privy Council dismissed the appeal. It stated that it was important to uphold V's right to rescind, in view of P's breach of an essential condition as to time. This right to rescind allowed V to know his position with certainty and that he was entitled to resell the flat. In delivering the judgment of the court, Lord Hoffmann (at p 218) rejected the suggestion that there was an unlimited discretion to relieve against hardship by imposing a fair solution in this type of case. The stipulation as to time was of great importance and P was, regrettably, late. The court held that it was irrelevant that he was only slightly late. Lord Hoffmann stated (at p 218):

> "The principle that equity will restrain the enforcement of legal rights when it would be unconscionable to insist upon them has an attractive breadth. But the reasons why the courts have rejected such generalisations are founded not merely upon authority ... but also upon practical considerations of business. These are, in summary, that in many forms of transaction it is of great importance that if something happens for which the contract has made express provision, the parties should know with certainty that the terms of the contract will be enforced. The existence of an undefined discretion to refuse to enforce the contract on the ground that this would be 'unconscionable' is sufficient to create uncertainty".

The above case illustrates the traditional view that a gerenal doctrine of unconscionability is undesirable as its precise scope would be difficult to formulate and it would be inimical to certainty and stability in a commercial context. It would also acknowledge that freedom of contract could be strictly limited in the interest of substantive justice. But the problem with the absence of any general principle is that the law (including equity) has developed a series of unrelated rules and doctrines for dealing with problems of unfairness. This can lead to either a "stretching" of such rules to cover a particular instance of injustice, or it can lead to powerlessness where such elasticity is simply not possible. This can create indefensible anomalies.

There is also a danger that the rules and doctrines are too inflexible for dealing with the particular situations in question. To take the example of exclusion clauses, discussed above; there are instances where the use of a very wide exclusion clause is acceptable in the commercial context in which it occurs (where both parties are, for example, of equal bargaining strength). A "rule" such as that of fundamental breach was too inflexible a method of dealing with such clauses. It operated (as rules do) in an all-or-nothing way and was capable of striking down both the legitimate and the unreasonable use of exclusion clauses. The same criticism can also be made of other rules developed by the courts to deal with unfairness in contracts[5]. A more general principle would not be open to this particular criticism, as its application would be much more sensitive to the particular context of each case.

Can the diverse methods by which judges have conferred protection on weaker parties be seen as strands which together form a composite doctrine capable of dealing more generally with unconscionability or inequality of bargaining power? In *Lloyds Bank Ltd* v *Bundy* (discussed above), Lord Denning was keen to postulate such a general principle. He made a connection between the (hitherto) distinct areas of duress, unconscionable transactions, undue influence, undue pressure and salvage agreements. He stated (at p 763) that despite the fact that our law does not, in general, interfere with freedom of contract, nevertheless:

> "There are cases in our books in which the courts will set aside a contract, or a transfer of property, when the parties have not met on equal terms, when the

one is so strong in bargaining power and the other so weak that, as a matter of common fairness, it is not right that the strong should be allowed to push the weaker to the wall. Hitherto those exceptional cases have been treated each as a separate category in itself. But I think the time has come when we should seek to find a principle to unite them. I put on one side contracts or transactions which are voidable for fraud or misrepresentation or mistake. All those are governed by settled principles. I go only to those where there has been inequality of bargaining power, such as to merit the intervention of the court".

This approach shows a willingness to break down doctrinal barriers in the interest of a more interventionist role for the courts. He went on (at p 765) to propose the following general principle:

"Gathering all together, I would suggest that through all these instances there runs a single thread. They rest on 'inequality of bargaining power'. By virtue of it, the English law gives relief to one who, without independent advice, enters into a contract on terms which are very unfair or transfers property for a consideration which is grossly inadequate, when his bargaining power is grievously impaired by reason of his own needs or desires, or by his own ignorance or infirmity, coupled with undue influences or pressures brought to bear on him by or for the benefit of the other. When I use the word 'undue' I do not mean to suggest that the principle depends on proof of any wrongdoing".

Although the Court of Appeal was unanimous in allowing Mr Bundy's appeal, the other two judges did not find it necessary to base their judgments on such a wide principle as that suggested by Lord Denning. The novelty of the Denning principle was his emphasis on the need to protect the weaker party where there was a clear disparity in bargaining strength between the parties. Thus it was the vulnerability of the weaker party that was stressed rather than any procedural unfairness. It is possible to reduce the significance of Lord Denning's principle by insisting that it was merely *obiter* (see Lord Scarman in *National Westminster Bank* v *Morgan* [1985] 1 All ER 821 at p 830), but it is still an influential opinion. It certainly offered great potential for development. But what was particularly worrying to commentators on the Denning principle was the possibility of the phrase "inequality of bargaining power" being used, in the future, as a more general justification for judicial intervention. In other words, it offered the opportunity for future development of an unpredictable nature.

It should not be thought that Lord Denning's was a lone voice. In *Schroeder Music Publishing Co* v *Macaulay* [1974] 3 All ER 616 it was not necessary to go beyond the restraint of trade doctrine to release the young song-writer from his contract with a music publishing company. But Lord Diplock went further (at p 623):

"Because this can be classed as a contract in restraint of trade the restrictions that [Macaulay] accepted fell within one of those limited categories of contractual promises in respect of which the courts still retain the power to relieve the promisor of his legal duty to fulfil them. In order to determine whether this case is one in which that power ought to be exercised, what your lordships have been doing has been to assess the relative bargaining power of the publisher and the song-writer at the time the contract was made and to decide whether the publisher had used his superior bargaining power to exact from the song-writer promises that were unfairly onerous to him".

Thus his lordship stressed that the important consideration for the court was the protection of the weaker or vulnerable party against being forced by a much stronger party to enter into an unconscionable agreement. The important question to be answered, according to Lord Diplock, is: "was the bargain fair?" (at p 623). In deciding that it was not fair, the court took into account the fact that the terms of the contract had not been the subject of negotiation between the parties; on the contrary, they had been dictated by the publishing company, who had been able to do this as a result of greatly superior bargaining power. (For a more recent example, see *Silvertone Records* v *Mountfield* [1993] EMLR 152.)

The danger with terms like inequality of bargaining power, and unconscionability, is that they can become rather trite through indiscriminate use. The latter term certainly lacks precision and the former, by itself, offers too wide a basis for intervention. Inequality of bargaining power is inherent in a great number of commercial transactions, but obviously not all of these are to be regarded as unfair. What matters is the use (or misuse) to which such disparity is put: there must be some unconscionable conduct or behaviour. (This point was well made by the Privy Council in the recent case of *Boustany* v *Pigott* [1993] EGCS 85, discussed above.) So if one party seeks to exploit a vastly superior bargaining strength by saying, in effect, to the other party: "take it or leave it", then this is an unconscionable agreement. But if a weaker party enters into an agreement without the stronger party subjecting them to pressure, then this is unlikely to be unconscionable. The case of *Alec Lobb Garages Ltd* v *Total Oil (Great Britain) Ltd* [1985] 1 All ER 303 provides a useful basis for a discussion of these issues. The facts were:

> The plaintiff company, Alec Lobb Ltd, owned premises from which it ran a garage and filling station. (The company comprised a mother and son who were the shareholders and directors.) The company was in serious financial difficulties. It was not possible for the plaintiffs to approach any other petrol company for finance, as they were already "tied" to the defendants under a previous loan agreement. Further negotiations took place between the plaintiffs and the defendants during the course of which the plaintiffs were independently advised by solicitors and accountants. The defendants agreed to put further capital into the plaintiff company by means of a lease and lease-back transaction. This consisted of a lease of the garage to the defendants for 51 years in return for the payment of a fair premium of £35,000 and an immediate lease-back of the premises to the son, personally, for a term of 21 years at a rent of £2,250. This underlease to the son also contained a petrol "tie"; he was to buy his petrol exclusively from the defendants. The transaction did not succeed in rescuing the plaintiff company from its lack of working capital. Nearly ten years after making this agreement, the plaintiffs sought to have the transaction set aside on the grounds, *inter alia*, that the bargain was harsh and unconscionable or, alternatively, that the "tie" covenant was void as being an unreasonable restraint of trade.

Of interest to our present discussion is the first of these two grounds, but it may be stated briefly that the Court of Appeal held that the petrol supply restraint was not unreasonable in view of all the circumstances. (It is worth noting that the adequacy of the consideration was one of the factors that the court took into account in reaching this conclusion.) The court went on to state that where one party had acted oppressively, coercively or extortionately towards the other, such a transaction would be set aside. An agreement was not rendered unconscionable merely because the parties to it were of unequal bargaining strength and the stronger party had not shown that the terms were fair and reasonable. Furthermore, a contract was not unconscionable merely because a party was forced to enter into it from economic necessity. It was important, on the facts of *Alec Lobb*, that no pressure had been exerted on the plaintiffs by the defendant oil company. The plaintiffs had received independent advice (which they had disregarded) and they had sought the defendants' assistance to escape their financial difficulties. The fact that the plaintiffs had little realistic alternative, and that they made a bad bargain, was not sufficient to render the defendants' conduct unconscionable.

This is a sensible restriction on the application of the terms "inequality of bargaining power" and "unconscionability"; that is, the former does not, by itself, prove the existence of the latter. (Also see *Burmah Oil Co Ltd* v *Governor of the Bank of England* (1981) 125 SJ 528.) It is the unfair or coercive exploitation of the superior bargaining strength of one party against the other which is the true reason for judicial intervention. This was not present in the instant case. But it should also be pointed out that Lord Denning's statement in *Lloyds Bank Ltd* v *Bundy* [1974] 3 All ER 757, at p 765, makes this restriction abundantly clear. He did not state that inequality of bargaining strength alone constitutes a sufficient ground for interfering with freedom of contract. So, in *Alec Lobb*, the fact that the plaintiffs received both independent advice and adequate consideration makes the case clearly distinguishable from *Bundy*. This point was well made by Dillon LJ (at p 313):

"Inequality of bargaining power must anyhow be a relative concept. It is seldom in any negotiation that the bargaining powers of the parties are absolutely equal. Any individual wanting to borrow money from a bank, building society or other financial institution. . . will have virtually no bargaining power; he will have to take or leave the terms offered to him. . . But Lord Denning did not envisage that any contract entered into in such circumstances would, without more, be reviewed by the courts by the objective criterion of what was reasonable. The courts would only interfere in exceptional cases where as a matter of common fairness it was not right that the strong should be allowed to push the weak to the wall. The concepts of unconscionable conduct and of the exercise by the stronger of coercive power are thus brought in, and in the present case they are negatived by the [findings of fact]."

It could be argued that Lord Denning's general principle thus received a restrictive interpretation in *Alec Lobb*. It was subjected to harsher treatment, however, in *National Westminster Bank plc* v *Morgan* [1985] 1 All ER 821. It will be remembered that the case concerned the relationship between banker and client. A husband and wife were in financial difficulty and the building society was seeking possession of their home for non-payment of the mortgage. The bank agreed to a bridging loan to cover a short period until the husband's business improved, but in return the bank required a charge on the house as security for the loan. The bank manager called at the house in order to obtain the wife's signature on the legal charge, and he mistakenly assured the wife that the charge would not extend to the husband's business liabilities to the bank. The charge was, in fact, sufficiently wide in scope to cover such liabilities, but the bank had no intention of using it for this purpose. The wife received no independent legal advice before signing the charge. The husband died and the bank sought possession of the house. The wife's claim that the charge should be set aside for undue influence was rejected by the House of Lords. It was held that there was no manifest disadvantage to the wife; the transaction involved a normal commercial loan for the purpose of preserving the family home. (Subsequent developments in this area of law are fully explained in Chapter 14).

Lord Scarman, in his judgment in *Morgan* (at p 830), made specific reference to Lord Denning's general principle. Lord Scarman observed that the principle (which he rather misleadingly referred to as being simply dependent on "inequality of bargaining power") was not the ground for the majority's decision in *Bundy*. He continued:

> "Nor has counsel for the wife sought to rely on Lord Denning's general principle; and, in my view, he was right not to do so. . . The fact of an unequal bargain will, of course, be a relevant feature in some cases of undue influence. But it can never become an appropriate basis of principle of [this] doctrine. . . I question whether there is any need in the modern law to erect a general principle of relief against inequality of bargaining power. Parliament has undertaken the task (and it is essentially a legislative task) of enacting such restrictions on freedom of contract as are in its judgement necessary to relieve against the mischief. . . I doubt whether the courts should assume the burden of formulating further restrictions".

Thus the House of Lords issued its rebuke to Lord Denning for venturing to construct a more general principle of unconscionability. A number of observations need to be made about Lord Scarman's speech. By his own concession, the wife's counsel in *Morgan* did not try to rely on the Denning principle. If this had been attempted, it would have been immediately obvious that the Denning principle did not apply to instances of mere inequality of bargaining power. In *Bundy*, his lordship was at pains to make it clear that in order to invoke the principle there must be an agreement on very unfair or one-sided terms, at a time of "grievously impaired" bargaining power for the disadvantaged party, "coupled with undue influences or pressures brought to bear on him by or for the benefit of the other". The absence of independent legal advice is also a relevant factor.

It should also be recognized that, although they deserve close attention, Lord Scarman's remarks about the Denning principle were *obiter*. They do not preclude reconsideration of the issue by a future court. Another prong of Lord Scarman's attack on the Denning principle is worthy of comment. He argued that the task of restricting freedom of contract, in order to give relief against inequality of bargaining power, is "essentially a legislative task". Therefore, he "questioned" the need for a general principle such as that asserted by Lord Denning in *Bundy*. Lord Scarman gave examples of statutory intervention and although, rather surprisingly, he did not mention the Unfair Contract Terms Act 1977 (see below), this is the most obvious example of what he had in mind. It cannot be denied that Parliament is capable of making substantial inroads into the principle of freedom of contract, but does this mean that the Denning approach is otiose?

There is certainly no logical justification for such a conclusion. Lord Scarman's view is presumably based on the reasoning that the creation of statutory exceptions to the principle of freedom of contract is proof of the absence of any general common law power of intervention on the basis of substantive unfairness. Yet as one commentator shrewdly observed on an earlier occasion[6]:

"Legislation, like judicial decisions, reflects the needs of a society, and the fact that the need for control of agreements has become so pressing in particular cases as to prompt legislative intervention argues. . . in favour, rather than against the need for general control".

In other words, a general principle could coexist with specific statutory intervention. Under existing legislation, judges will be called upon to play an important role in deciding whether a particular clause (eg under the Unfair Contract Terms Act) is reasonable. It should also be borne in mind that even the considerable protection given by this and other legislation against unfair contract terms does not cover all situations where substantive unfairness may arise. There may still be a place for a principle of general application which is not dependent on any specific statutory provision. Where issues of unfairness are dealt with by statute, the principle would have less significance. But in areas where no such protection has been conferred by Parliament, the principle would be most useful.

There is also something appealing about the notion of "unconscionability" as a basis for intervention rather than merely a statutory requirement of "reasonableness" (such as that contained in the Unfair Contract Terms Act). Although the two words may be regarded by some as synonymous, the criterion of reasonableness suggests objective standards of fairness, whilst "unconscionability" refers to something which is offensive to the dictates of conscience. It is submitted that this is a more subjective concept. This is both its strength and weakness. It permits a considerable degree of judicial flexibility in the interest of substantive justice, but this is achieved at the expense of certainty and stability. In matters of contract law in particular, our judges tend to favour consistency and certainty.

In recent times, some commentators[7] have advocated the development of the concept of good faith in contractual dealings — a concept which is familiar to the civil law systems of many European countries. (It should be noted that the "requirement of good faith" is referred to in the Unfair Terms in Consumer Contracts Regulations 1999 in establishing a test of unfairness. This is discussed further in Chapter 11). There has been support for the development of the concept of good faith in countries such as Canada and Australia[8]; and in *Interfoto Picture Library Ltd* v *Stiletto Visual Programmes Ltd* [1989] QB 433 (at p 439), Bingham LJ described the concept as essentially "a principle of fair and open dealing".

A major difficulty with the concept is that it could lead to much uncertainty in our law. It is significant that the House of Lords in *Walford* v *Miles* [1992] 1 All ER 453 did not support the idea of a duty to negotiate in good faith, which was regarded as impracticable. However, proponents of a general concept argue that the law already recognises a requirement of good faith and fair dealing in a number of situations and that the development of a more general principle could lead to a more coherent and consistent approach by the courts[9]. A further problem arises in attempting to define the concept of good faith and to establish its precise relationship to the ideas of unconscionability and unfairness, which were discussed earlier.

4. Examples of legislative intervention

It is not proposed to summarise all the relevant statutory provisions here. Parliament has made innumerable interventions to "police" particular types of agreement in the interests of fairness and, in particular, to protect consumers and weaker parties. For instance, s 137(1) Consumer Credit Act 1974 permits a court, in the case of an extortionate credit bargain, to "reopen the credit agreement so as to do justice between the parties". Section 138(1) states that a credit bargain is extortionate if it:

"(a) requires the debtor or a relative of his to make payments. . . which are grossly exorbitant, or
(b) otherwise grossly contravenes ordinary principles of fair dealing".

A number of factors can be considered in assessing whether a credit agreement is extortionate, including the personal circumstances of the debtor. These include his age, experience, business capacity and state of health, and the degree to which he was under financial pressure at the time of making the agreement[10]. Moreover, where a debtor (or any surety) alleges that a credit agreement is extortionate "it is for the creditor to prove the contrary" (s 171(7)). Wide powers are conferred on a court if it decides to reopen a credit agreement so as to relieve the debtor from payment of any sum in excess of what is fairly due and reasonable. It may, for example, "set aside the whole or part of any obligation imposed on the debtor or a surety by the credit bargain", or it may "require the creditor to repay the whole or part of any sum paid" under the agreement. A court is also empowered to alter the terms of the credit agreement. (See s 139(2).)

This legislation provides a good example of the wide discretion that can be given to courts to regulate particular types of agreement which are especially capable of giving rise to harsh and unconscionable terms. The Act refers to subjective factors in relation to the weaker party and it uses concepts such as "extortionate" credit agreements and agreements which "grossly" contravene ordinary principles of fair dealing. It is concerned with substantive as well as procedural justice. It has been suggested (above) that rather than seeing such provisions as exceptions to the general rule about freedom of contract, they might instead be viewed as part of a more general movement towards the protection of weaker parties.

A notable statutory inroad into the principle of freedom of contract is the Unfair Contract Terms Act 1977. In contrast to the more recent EC Directive on Unfair Terms in Consumer Contracts (discussed in detail in Chapter 11), the 1977 Act does not deal with unfair terms in general. It is concerned with exclusion clauses. In certain situations (for example, s 2(1) which deals with exclusion clauses concerning actions in negligence for death or personal injury), an exemption clause is rendered ineffective by the Act without any consideration of its reasonableness. In others, its provisions subject the clause to a "requirement of reasonableness" test. Despite the technicality of its provisions, the overriding purpose of the legislation is to "police" objectionable and unfair exclusion clauses. Section 11 states that in relation to a contract term, the requirement of reasonableness is that "the term shall have been a fair and reasonable one to be included having regard to the circumstances which were, or ought reasonably to have been, known to or in the contemplation of the parties when the contract was made".

All contract terms which are subject to the "requirement of reasonableness" are governed by the above statutory provision (s 11(1)). Certain terms (under ss 6 and 7) are also subject to Sch 2 to the Act which gives guidelines for the application of the reasonableness test. Under these guidelines the court must pay particular regard to five factors, including the relative bargaining strengths of the parties, and whether the customer knew or ought reasonably to have known of the existence and extent of the term. (Outside ss 6 and 7, the guidelines are still likely to be factually relevant to the reasonableness of an exclusion clause: see *Singer Co (UK) Ltd* v *Tees and Hartlepool Port Authority* [1988] 2 Lloyd's Rep 164 at p 169.)

The express reference in the Act to inequality of bargaining power (in Sch 2(a)) is not surprising. It is obviously an important factor in considering the reasonableness of an exclusion clause. But the point may be made once again that there may well be advantages if such statutory provisions were regarded as coexistent with a broad common law principle of unconscionability or unfairness. It would permit the courts to develop more consistent standards throughout the law of contract, rather than considering such ideas only under specific statutory provisions. It would become a more integrated part of judicial reasoning and education, and it would also avoid the problem of what to do in situations which are not expressly covered by statutory protection. On the other hand, it is fair to say that some commentators view further inroads into the principle of freedom of contract as unwarranted and undesirable. They are content to leave such matters to Parliament. Some economic theorists have even asked whether the statutory protection under the Unfair Contract Terms Act goes too far[11].

5. Other jurisdictions: the United States example

Our judges have tended to avoid the formulation of a general principle of unconscionability or unfairness in the law of contract. Intervention on these grounds takes place either under express statutory provisions or under (sometimes) technical and discrete doctrines. This approach is defended, as we have seen, on the basis that a more general principle would lead to uncertainty and unpredictability. There is, of course, the competing argument that the recognition of a general principle might, in the long run, lead to greater rationality in the law and the development of criteria that would offer a useful guide for future transactions.

What of the experience in other jurisdictions where a more general principle has been adopted either by the courts or by statute? An interesting example is that of the United States' Uniform Commercial Code ("UCC")[12]. Although American contract law is largely based on common law, the UCC is of considerable importance as it has been adopted by virtually all the states. The Code contains nine articles, but it is Article 2 (on the sale of goods) which has the largest impact on general principles of US contract law. Moreover, the US courts have consulted Article 2 for guidance beyond sale of goods transactions. The Code was accompanied by official comments which were produced (as was the Code) by the Permanent Editorial Board. These comments were intended as an aid to interpretation and uniformity of approach and they have proved valuable to the courts. Probably it is true to say that no other section has aroused greater interest than the provision on unconscionability (UCC s 2–302), which states:

(1) If the court as a matter of law finds the contract or any clause of the contract to have been unconscionable at the time it was made the court may refuse to enforce the contract, or it may enforce the remainder of the contract without the unconscionable clause, or it may so limit the application of any unconscionable clause as to avoid any unconscionable result.

(2) When it is claimed or appears to the court that the contract or any clause thereof may be unconscionable the parties shall be afforded a reasonable opportunity to present evidence as to its commercial setting, purpose and effect to aid the court in making the determination.

The official comment (see above) helps to explain the purpose of s 2–302. It was enacted so as to allow the courts to take action against unconscionable contracts or clauses. Formerly, this task had been accomplished by the manipulation of technical doctrines, such as adverse construction, but the purpose of s 2–302 is to enable a court to go directly to the issue of unconscionability and to "make a conclusion of law" on this ground. The basic test envisaged by the official commentators is whether the terms are so one-sided as to be unconscionable in the light of the general commercial background to the contract. The commentators add that "the principle is one of the prevention of oppression and unfair surprise and not of disturbance of allocation of risks because of superior bargaining power."

Thus s 2–302 was produced in order to give the courts power openly to "police" unconscionable provisions without resort to technical and covert methods. It has been accepted by the American courts as applying beyond its immediate statutory context (ie sale of goods) and has been incorporated into the general law of contract. It is interesting that the section confers wide discretion on a court. Its powers relate to situations where either the whole agreement or any clause of the contract is unconscionable. This is in direct contrast to the English statutory approach which has concentrated on unfair contract terms rather than whole agreements. The court also has some flexibility in dealing with the unconscionability in question. It may refuse to enforce the contract, or it may enforce the contract without the unconscionable clause. A further alternative is for the court to restrict the scope of such a clause so as to avoid an unfair result. It seems that a court can, to some extent, re-write an agreement for the parties, even though such a power is not expressly conferred by the enactment.

It is also interesting to note the use of the word "unconscionability" as opposed to the reference in United Kingdom law to "reasonableness". The latter term fits comfortably into a model of contract law which takes an objective view of agreement. If contracting parties were all rational and experienced bargainers, then such a term would be unobjectionable. But if this were the case, intervention would be far less necessary. Unfortunately, but inevitably, many contracting parties are not "reasonable"; they may be of low intelligence, inexperienced, or whatever. The strength of a test of unconscionability is that it permits the court to focus on more subjective questions, namely the particular inadequacies or susceptibilities of the weaker party. It can be argued that this is a more realistic approach.

Footnotes

(1) For a recent illustration, see *Union Eagle Ltd* v *Golden Achievement Ltd* [1997] 2 All ER 215 (and the comments of Lord Hoffmann at p 218).

(2) S Waddams, *Unconscionability in Contracts* (1976) 39 Mod LR 369 at p 390.

(3) In *Watkin* v *Watson-Smith* [1986] The Times 3 July a contract for the sale of a house at a serious undervalue was set aside on the grounds of mistake. The judge held that he would have set the contract aside as an unconscionable bargain, had it been necessary to do so. (In this case it was the old age and lack of judgement of the vendor, together with his desire for a quick sale, which produced the unconscionable agreement.)

(4) Also see the rules relating to forfeitures and penalties; see Waddams, *loc cit*, note (2), pp 370–375.

(5) For example, in relation to mortgages and penalty clauses.

(6) Waddams, *loc cit*, note (2), p 390.

(7) For example, see A F Mason, "Contract, Good Faith and Equitable Standards in Fair Dealing" (2000) 116 LQR 66.

(8) Mason, *ibid*, refers to a judgment of Finn J, in *Hughes Aircraft Systems International* v *Air Services Australia* (1997) 146 ALR 1 at pp 36–37.

(9) Mason, *ibid*, p 94.

(10) See s 138(a) and (b).

(11) For an interesting discussion, see P S Atiyah, *Introduction to the Law of Contract*, 5th ed, pp 308–312.

(12) For a useful discussion of the concept of unconscionability in United States law, see J Calamari and J Perillo, *Contracts*, 3rd ed, pp 397–409. Also of interest is S Deutch, *Unfair Contracts — The Doctrine of Unconscionability*, 1977.

Chapter 17

Capacity

An adult of sound mind has full contractual capacity, although he may still be able to claim that the contract is not enforceable on some other basis — undue influence, for example. The law recognizes the general incapacity to contract of minors and the mentally incapacitated. It also recognizes that it is desirable for there to be some degree of binding obligation in relation to some contracts to enable those persons to procure certain essentials.

The question of contractual capacity also needs to be briefly considered in the context of companies.

Incapacity raises a tension in the law between the need to protect someone who is incapacitated (or, in the case of a company, its shareholders) and the desire not to treat too harshly the person dealing fairly with the incapacitated person.

1. Minors

An individual is a minor until the age of eighteen. The basic rule of the incapacity of minors became of much less significance once the relevant age was reduced to eighteen from twenty-one by s 1 Family Law Reform Act 1969. (The earlier law referred to infants, but minors is now the preferred terminology.) The basic rule is that a minor is not bound by any contract which he makes, although the person contracting with him will be. However, upon attaining his majority a minor may ratify a contract which is otherwise not binding upon him. In addition, there are certain contracts which have some legal effect upon the minor despite his general lack of capacity. He is bound by contracts for necessaries, and employment and analogous contracts. There are also four types of contract, referred to as "voidable contracts", which are binding upon the minor until repudiated by him before he reaches majority or within a reasonable time of doing so.

(a) Necessaries

Contracts to provide minors with "necessaries" form the main exception to the general lack of capacity to contract. A minor will have to pay a reasonable price for a "necessary" if the contract is generally beneficial to him. It is for the party claiming to have contracted with the minor to establish that the contract is a contract for necessaries (*Nash* v *Inman* [1908] KB 1, see below).

Necessaries include goods and services. To some extent it is obvious what can be considered to constitute necessaries: contracts to provide food, drink, clothing, and education, are within this category. In *Chapple* v *Cooper* (1844) 13 M & W 252 it was held that a contract made by a minor for the burial of her deceased husband was a contract for necessaries. However, whether the contract is for necessaries is not decided on the objective basis of the requirements for living of an entirely abstract, reasonable, minor. The test is relative; it is dependent upon the age and social situation of the particular minor:

> "Things necessary are those without which an individual cannot reasonably exist. In the first place, food, raiment, lodging and the like. About these there is no doubt. Again as the proper cultivation of the mind is as expedient as the support of the body, instruction in art or trade, or intellectual moral and religious information may be necessary also ... Then the classes being established, the subject matter and extent of the contract may vary according to the state and condition of the infant himself. His clothes may be fine or coarse according to his rank; his education may vary according to the station he is to fill ... But in all these cases it must be made out that the class itself is one in which the things furnished are essential to the existence and reasonable advantage and comfort of the infant contractor. Thus articles of mere luxury are always excluded, though luxurious articles of utility are in some cases allowed" (*Chapple* v *Cooper per* Alderson B at p 258).

In relation to the sale of goods this relativity of requirements is reflected in s 3(3) Sale of Goods Act 1979 which states that "necessaries means goods suitable to the condition in life of the minor ... and to his actual requirements at the time of sale and delivery". Examples of this relative approach to necessaries can be found in *Peters* v *Fleming* (1840) 6 M & W 42 and in *Clyde Cycle Co* v *Hargreaves* (1898) 78 LT 296. In *Peters* v *Fleming* the minor was an undergraduate whose father was "a gentleman of fortune and a Member of Parliament", and in those circumstances a breast pin and a watch chain were considered to be necessaries. In *Clyde Cycle Co* v *Hargreaves* (1898) 78 LT 296, a racing bike was seen as a necessary. In that case:

> Mr Hargreaves was a young man of nineteen apprenticed to a scientific instrument maker and earning 21s a week. He lived with his parents. The bicycle cost £12 10s. Hargreaves used the bicycle for racing and won several prizes. He occasionally used it on the road; a roadster bike of similar quality with the usual accessories would have cost slightly more.

The court thought that had Mr Hargreaves purchased a horse the contract could not have been one for necessaries but, as the use of bicycles was common in his neighbourhood by someone in his position, the bicycle could be considered to be a necessary.

It is clear that the question of whether a contract is for necessaries is not an abstract test, even within the limits of the minor's social circumstances. It is dependent upon the minor's needs at the time of the contract. What might be a necessary one week may not be the next, if the particular need has been satisfied in the meantime. This is so even where the person contracting with the minor is unaware that his needs have been satisfied by another source (*Barnes & Co* v *Toye* (1884) 13 QBD 410). The burden of proof rests with the party claiming that the contract was for necessaries. In *Nash* v *Inman* [1908] KB 1 a contract for the purchase of clothes, including eleven waistcoats, was held not to be a contract for necessaries, even for a Cambridge undergraduate. The minor's father had given evidence that he had been well supplied with suitable clothing when going up to Cambridge. The supplier did not produce any evidence to show that that was not the case.

The person contracting with a minor to supply necessaries cannot rely upon that fact if the contract terms are harsh or onerous and the contract, as a whole, is not beneficial to the minor. In *Fawcett* v *Smethurst* (1914) 84 LJKB 473 a minor made a contract for the hire of a car. Under the circumstances it was capable of being a contract for a necessary. The minor crashed the car without any fault on his part. The owner tried to allege that the minor was liable. He claimed that it had been a term of the contract that the car was entirely at the minor's risk. The court did not accept that there was any such term, but held that, if there was, it would have prevented the contract from being enforceable against a minor. Even a contract for necessaries cannot be enforced unless it is generally beneficial to the minor. Such an onerous term as that discussed in *Fawcett* would have removed the contract from the "generally beneficial" category (see also *Flower* v *London and North Western Railway Co* [1894] 2 QB 65).

Even in relation to necessaries, the minor does not have to pay the contract price but merely a reasonable price. If the contract is for the sale of goods, that is stated by s 3(2) Sale of Goods Act 1979 which says, "Where necessaries are sold and delivered to a minor . . . he must pay a reasonable price for them". The requirement of payment of a reasonable price, rather than the contract price, leads to the suggestion that the minor's obligation is not a matter of contract at all but simply an obligation founded on the benefit which he has received. On that basis, there would be no liability for the minor on a purely executory contract. (The suggestion is reinforced by the reference in s 3(2) Sale of Goods Act 1979 to necessaries "sold and delivered".) In *Nash* v *Inman*, Buckley LJ regarded it as a matter of contract but Fletcher Moulton LJ saw the action as based upon what the minor had received, rather than upon the agreement itself. He said (at p 8):

"Its real foundation is an obligation which the law imposes on the infant to make a fair payment in respect of needs satisfied".

This suggests that enforcement of payment against the minor is a matter of restitution rather than contract, and Fletcher Moulton LJ's approach precludes any claim against a minor on an executory contract. However, a minor had to pay damages on such a contract in *Roberts* v *Gray* [1913] 1 KB 520. In that case:

The minor, Gray, was to join Roberts on a world tour playing billiards. Roberts was a noted professional billiard player. Gray was to learn from him. Roberts was to pay all the expenses and to be reimbursed out of money made on the tour. Roberts incurred expenses in making arrangements for the tour. When, the contract was still largely executory, they fell out over the type of billiard ball to be used. Gray refused to continue with the contract.

The court held that Roberts could recover damages in the usual way. The contract was regarded as relating to the minor's education, and therefore as a contract for necessaries. The fact that it was largely executory did not prevent Roberts' recovery. Hamilton LJ said (at p 530):

"I am unable to appreciate why a contract in itself binding, because it is a contract for necessaries not qualified by unreasonable terms, can cease to be binding merely because it is still executory".

(b) Employment contracts

It is obviously a good idea that a minor should not be prevented from earning a living, if he is of an appropriate age to do so. On that basis, the courts have recognized the enforceability of contracts for the employment of minors and analogous contracts. This is subject to the qualification that the contract must, as a whole, be beneficial to the minor. In *Clements* v *London and North Western Railway Co* [1894] 2 QB 482:

The minor, Clements, was employed by the railway as a porter. Under the contract of employment, he had given up his right to claim for personal injury under the Employer's Liability Act 1880 but had, instead, acquired rights under an insurance scheme. Although, under the insurance scheme, the payments were generally lower, it did not require the injury to have resulted from the employer's negligence. Clements was injured and claimed under the 1880 Act.

It was held that the contract as a whole was beneficial to Clements. He was bound by it and could not claim under the 1880 Act.

In contrast, the contract was not generally beneficial to the minor, and was not binding, in *De Francesco* v *Barnum* (1890) 45 Ch D 430. In that case a girl contracted with Signor De Francesco to be taught to dance. The contract bound her to him for seven years. During that time he did not have to maintain her, or pay her, unless he obtained engagements for her, and then the rate of pay was very low. She was not to obtain engagements for herself, or marry, without his consent. Signor De Francesco could terminate the contract at any time. The contract was held not to be binding on the girl. Its terms were unreasonable and not for her benefit. In general, in considering whether the contract is beneficial as a whole, the specific terms will be compared with the usual terms in the particular type of employment (*De Francesco* v *Barnum* at p 442; *Sir W C Leng & Co Ltd* v *Andrews* [1909] 1 Ch 763 at p 769).

The courts have been prepared to find that contracts which are analogous to contracts of employment are effective (eg the sale by a writer or composer of the copyright in his works). Again the contract must be generally beneficial to the minor (*Chaplin* v *Leslie Frewin (Publishers) Ltd* [1966] Ch 71 — where the title of the book in question was *I Couldn't Smoke the Grass on my Father's Lawn*). In *Doyle* v *White City Stadium Ltd and British Boxing Board of Control* [1935] 1 KB 110 Jack Doyle, a minor who was a professional boxer, had been granted a licence by the British Boxing Board of Control. Such a licence was necessary for someone to earn his living as a professional boxer. For the fight in question, the Board deprived him of his purse for breach of its rules. It was held that it was able to do so. The contract for the licence was analogous to a contract of employment and, on the whole, the rules were beneficial to the minor.

Although contracts of employment and analogous contracts are binding on a minor, a trading contract made by a minor is not. If a minor has a business, a contract made in the course of that business is not considered enforceable. In *Mercantile Union Guarantee Corp* v *Ball* [1937] 2 KB 498, a twenty year old minor, with a haulage business, was not bound by a contract for the hire purchase of a lorry for his business. The contract was not considered to be of a type which could be enforced against a minor and, in any event, the terms were not beneficial to him. Trading contracts may be seen as presenting a risk to the minor which is not present in a contract of employment (*Whywall* v *Campion* (1738) 2 Str 1083 — "the law will not suffer him to trade, which may be his undoing").

(c) Voidable contracts

There are four types of contract, commonly referred to collectively as "voidable contracts", which bind both parties unless the minor repudiates them. The minor can repudiate before he attains majority or within a reasonable time thereafter (*Edwards* v *Carter* [1893] AC 360). The contracts are:

- contracts relating to an interest in land (a minor can no longer hold a legal estate in land — s 1(6) Law of Property Act 1925);
- marriage settlements (eg *Edwards* v *Carter*);
- the purchase of, or subscription for, shares (*Steinberg* v *Scala (Leeds) Ltd* [1923] 2 Ch 452);
- partnerships (eg *Goode* v *Harrison* (1821) 5 B & Ald 147).

These contracts will bind both parties unless the minor repudiates. The repudiation relieves the minor of future liabilities. The position is not clear as regards liabilities which have arisen but not been discharged (*North Western Railway* v *M'Michael* (1850) 5 Ex 114 at p 125; *Blake* v *Concannon* (1870) IR 4 CL 323). It has been held that any money already paid under one of these contracts which has subsequently been repudiated by the minor cannot be recovered unless there has been a total failure of consideration. In *Steinberg* v *Scala (Leeds) Ltd* [1923] 2 Ch 452 a minor was allotted shares in a company. Her later repudiation meant that she was not liable for future calls but she could not recover sums she had already paid. She had received the shares which she had contracted to receive and there was no total failure of consideration (*Corpe* v *Overton* (1833) 10 Bing 252). However, it has been argued that a requirement of total failure of consideration is inappropriate. The incapacity itself should furnish sufficient basis for restitution provided that *restitutio in integrum* is possible, ie provided that the other party can be restored to his original position (*Valentini* v *Canali* (1889) 24 QBD 166 — see Goff & Jones, *The Law of Restitution* (4th ed) at pp 528–530).

(d) Ratification

If a contract with a minor does not fall within one of the exceptional situations above, it is not binding upon the minor. It is binding upon the other party but the minor is unlikely to succeed in an action for specific performance, unless he has already performed his side of the agreement, because of the lack of mutuality (*Flight* v *Boland* (1824) 4 Russ 298 and see page 457). However, even if the contract is not within one of the special cases it may become binding upon a minor if he ratifies it, expressly or impliedly, upon attaining his majority. Ratification could occur at common law (*Williams* v *Moor* (1843) 11

M & W 256), and the repeal of s 2 Infants Relief Act 1874 by the Minors' Contracts Act 1987 means that it is, again, generally available.

Before ratification, the minor will not be bound. Again it would seem that recovery by the minor of any property transferred under the "contract" is possible only to the extent that an adult would be able to do so, eg if there has been a total failure of consideration. Again it has been argued that restitution should be available simply on the basis of the incapacity (see *(c)* above).

(e) Restitution — from the minor

A minor may have received property under a "contract" which is not binding upon him. Section 3 Minors' Contracts Act 1987 gives the court a discretion to order the return of the property, or property representing it, where it is "just and equitable" so to do. Section 3(2) preserves the restitutionary actions for the recovery of the property although the wording is rather obscure. The courts have tried to avoid effectively enforcing the contract through the restitutionary actions, and the statutory discretion should be exercised with that in mind (see, for example, *R Leslie Ltd* v *Shiell* [1914] 3 KB 607), but it may be argued that they have too readily seen incapacity as a defence in that way (see Burrows, *The Law of Restitution* (1993) at pp 450–460).

(f) Tort

A minor can be liable in tort, but a tortious action will not succeed where it would amount to enforcement of a contract by which the minor is not bound. In *R Leslie Ltd* v *Shiell* [1914] 3 KB 607 a minor obtained a loan by fraudulently misrepresenting his age. The creditor could not recover damages for deceit; otherwise the effect would have been that the court was enforcing a contract which was not binding on the minor.

It may be difficult to decide when the tort claim is sufficiently closely connected to the contract to prevent its success. In *Jennings* v *Rundall* (1799) 8 Term Rep 335 a minor who hired a horse, "to be moderately ridden", could not be liable in tort for the injury caused by his improper riding of it. He was not bound by the contract and the tort action was too closely linked to the contract. Lord Kenyon said, "If it were in the power of a plaintiff to convert that which arises out of a contract into a tort, there would be an end to that protection which the law affords to infants". However, in *Burnard* v *Haggis* (1863) 14 CBNS 45 the minor was liable in tort. He had hired a horse, and had been expressly told that the horse was not let out for jumping and that it was more expensive to hire a horse for jumping. The horse died from being impaled on a stake while trying to jump a fence. The minor was held liable in tort.

(g) Guarantees of contracts made by a minor

Section 2 Minors' Contracts Act 1987 makes it clear that a contract guaranteeing a contract made by a minor is not ineffective simply on the basis of the minors' lack of capacity in relation to the main contract.

2. Mental incapacity and intoxication

There are some individuals whose mental incapacity has reached the point where their property is subject to the control of the court under Part III Mental Health Act 1983. It seems that those individuals entirely lack capacity to contract, and any contract to which they are a party is ineffective. This was the approach taken to earlier legislation on the basis that, if the situation were otherwise, the court's control of the incapacitated person's property would be incomplete and ineffective (*Re Walker* [1905] 1 Ch 160; *Re Marshall* [1920] 1 Ch 284).

In any case of mental incapacity not covered by the 1983 Act, the position is that the contract is binding unless the person claiming incapacity can establish, first, that he did not understand what he was doing and, secondly, that the other party knew that to be the case. (A contract for necessaries will be binding even if such lack of understanding and knowledge of it can be established — see below.) In *Imperial Loan Co v Stone* [1892] 1 QB 599, Lord Esher said (at p 601):

> "When a person enters into a contract and afterwards alleges that he was so insane at the time that he did not know what he was doing, and proves the allegation, the contract is as binding on him, in every respect, whether it is executory or executed, as if he had been sane when he made it, unless he can prove further that the person with whom he contracted knew him to be so insane as not to be capable of understanding what he was about."

In *Hart v O'Connor* [1985] AC 1000 the Privy Council had to consider the line adopted by the New Zealand court. That court had taken the approach that knowledge of the incapacity by the other party was not required if the contract was "unfair". The Privy Council rejected that line, maintaining the requirement of knowledge in all cases, whatever the "fairness" of the contract. However, it should be remembered that undue influence (see Chapter 14) can be raised even if incapacity, as such, cannot be established. In addition, it should be noted that in one respect the individual incapacitated in this way is better placed than a minor. It would seem that the individual can rescind and, subject to the bars, recover his property without the need to establish total failure of consideration (see *O'Connor v Hart* [1984] 1 NZLR 754).

If the strict requirements for establishing incapacity are fulfilled, it should, nevertheless, be possible for ratification to take place if the mental incapacity ceases (*Mathews v Baxter* (1873) LR 8 Ex 132).

Contracts for necessaries are binding on the incapacitated person, provided it was intended that the necessaries were to be paid for (*Re Rhodes* (1889) 44 Ch D 94). Payment should be of a reasonable price. Contracts for necessary goods are dealt with by s 3(2) Sale of Goods Act 1979 which imposes an obligation to pay a reasonable price on the mentally incapacitated person.

The individual who becomes so intoxicated that he does not understand what he is doing seems to be treated in the same way as someone who lacks mental capacity. He will have to pay a reasonable price for necessaries (see s 3(2) Sale of Goods Act 1979). Other contracts will not be binding if he did not understand what he was doing and the other party knew that to be the case (*Gore v Gibson* (1843) 13 M & W 625; *Mathews v Baxter* (1873) LR 8 Ex 132).

3. Companies created under the Companies Acts

A company is a legal person, separate from its shareholders or directors. The question of a company's capacity to make a particular contract used to depend upon the objects of the company set out in its memorandum. If the contract was outside those objects, then it was *ultra vires* and void. Although designed to protect the shareholders and creditors of a company, the *ultra vires* rule caused difficulty and hardship for those contracting with a company. As regards outsiders to the company the *ultra vires* rule has now, effectively, been abolished and from their perspective the company will not lack capacity (s 35 Companies Act 1985 as amended by the Companies Act 1989). A company's capacity, and the question of *ultra vires*, will still be relevant to matters internal to the company. It will still be relevant when considering the relationship of shareholders and directors.

Chapter 18

Privity and third party rights

1. Introduction

The doctrine of privity of contract has been a long established, yet controversial, principle of English law. The Contracts (Rights of Third Parties) Act 1999 has led to important reform of the doctrine and it will be considered in detail later in the chapter. However, it is appropriate to start with an explanation of what is meant by the term privity of contract. It represents the principle that only a party to a contract can enforce rights, or have duties enforced against him, under that contract (for example, see *Price* v *Easton* (1833) 4 B & Ad 433). The doctrine was referred to briefly in Chapter 4, in connection with the rule that consideration must move from the promisee (see also section 7 of this chapter). A party to a contract is one to whom a promise is made and who, in exchange for the promise, gives consideration for it. The traditional view has been that a promisee who is promised some benefit, but gives nothing in return, cannot enforce the promise; similarly, that a beneficiary of a promise, who is not the promisee, and who provides no consideration, cannot sue on that promise. It is easy to understand why someone who is not a party to a contract should not have burdens imposed upon him and this facet of the doctrine has not been subject to criticism, nor has it been affected by the 1999 legislation. But the idea that a "stranger" to a contract should not be able to enforce a provision which was intended for his benefit has been much more controversial.

In *Tweddle* v *Atkinson* (1861) 1 B & S 393 two fathers, by an agreement, promised one another that they would each pay a sum of money to William Tweddle, the son of one of them, who was to marry the other's daughter. William Tweddle sued his father-in-law's executors to enforce this promise, as his father-in-law died without having paid the promised sum. Despite the fact that the contract was for his benefit, his action failed as he did not provide consideration for the promise. An alternative explanation for the decision is that William Tweddle was not a party to the contract and, therefore, he could not enforce any benefit under a contract to which he was a stranger.

The privity rule, despite its uncertain origins and its potential for unfairness, was even more firmly established in English law by the House of Lords in *Dunlop Pneumatic Tyre Co Ltd* v *Selfridge & Co Ltd* [1915] AC 847. The facts were as follows:

Dunlop sold some tyres to Dew & Co, on the terms that Dew & Co would not resell them for less than Dunlop's list prices, and that when Dew & Co resold them to trade buyers, they (Dew & Co) would insist on the same undertaking from the trade buyers. Dew & Co sold the tyres to Selfridge, who agreed to conform with this restriction and, in the event of breaking the agreement, to pay Dunlop £5 for each tyre sold (in breach of it). Selfridge later sold tyres to customers for less than the list price and Dunlop sued Selfridge for damages.

The House of Lords gave judgment for Selfridge and dismissed the action. Lord Haldane LC affirmed the doctrine of privity authoritatively, by stating (at p 853):

"... In the law of England certain principles are fundamental. One is that only a person who is a party to a contract can sue on it. Our law knows nothing of a *jus quaesitum tertio* arising by way of contract. Such a right may be conferred by way of property, as, for example, under a trust, but it cannot be conferred on a stranger to a contract as a right to enforce the contract *in personam*. A second principle is that if a person with whom a contract not under seal has been made is to be able to enforce it consideration must have been given by him to the promisor or to some other person at the promisor's request."

The doctrine, despite its evident unpopularity with the judiciary, survived and even developed (see *Scruttons Ltd* v *Midland Silicones Ltd* [1962] AC 446, discussed below). It has been subjected to the scrutiny of law reform bodies for more than sixty years. For example, in 1937 the Law Revision Committee recommended in its sixth Interim Report that a third party should be able to enforce a contractual promise received by another for his benefit[1]. In 1991, a Law Commission Consultation Paper supported the argument for reform of the privity rule, stating:

"Over 50 years ago, the Law Revision Committee recommended the abolition of the third party rule ... Nothing has happened since [its] Report to suggest that its recommendations were misguided. Indeed, the greater complexity of the law as further exceptions and circumventions have developed, and the experience of statutory reform elsewhere, reinforce its conclusions". (*Privity of Contract: Contracts for the Benefit of Third Parties*, Law Commission Consultation Paper No 121, 1991, at p 95.)

These arguments were supported by Steyn LJ's criticisms of the doctrine in *Darlington Borough Council* v *Wiltshier Northern Ltd* [1995] 1 WLR 68 at p 76 where he stated:

"The case for recognising a contract for the benefit of a third party is simple and straightforward. The autonomy of the will of the parties should be respected. The law of contract should give effect to the reasonable expectations of contracting parties. Principle certainly requires that a burden should not be imposed on a third party without his consent. But there is no doctrinal, logical or policy reason why the law should deny effectiveness to a contract for the benefit of a third party where that is the expressed intention of the parties."

The above statements, and many more like them from judges and academic critics, illustrated the unpopularity of the privity rule and the need for its reform[(2)]. Furthermore, English law was out of step with that of many European countries which do not prevent third parties from enforcing contractual provisions[(3)]. In addition to precluding the closer harmonization of the laws of European Union member states, the English doctrine of privity was capable of disappointing various reasonable commercial and consumer expectations. The resulting unfairness of a strict application of the doctrine necessitated a series of, often complex, exceptions to it (discussed later). Before examining the recent legislative reform, it is important to understand the ambit of the privity rule prior to the 1991 Act, as the common law doctrine was reformed, and not abolished, by the Act.

2. Further development of the doctrine

Despite challenges to its validity, the House of Lords affirmed the doctrine once again in *Scruttons Ltd* v *Midland Silicones Ltd* [1962] AC 446 (at pp 467 and 473). The scope of the doctrine was considered in a slightly different form in this case as the stranger to the contract was not suing to enforce a positive right, but instead was seeking the protection of a term of the contract as a defence to an action by one of the contracting parties under a separate cause of action. In other words, the case was concerned with whether a third party can use a term of a contract as a shield, despite not being able to use a term intended for his benefit as a sword. The facts were:

> A drum containing chemicals was shipped from America to London. The bill of lading, under which it was shipped, limited to $500 (£179) per package the liability of the carrier in the event of loss, damage, or delay. Scruttons, who were the stevedores engaged by the carrier (under a separate contract), negligently dropped and damaged the drum whilst delivering it to the consignees, Midland Silicones. Midland Silicones sued Scruttons in tort, claiming the value of the lost contents (£593). Scruttons (the stevedores) argued that under the bill of lading their liability was limited to £179.

The House of Lords held that the stevedores were not entitled to rely on the limitation of liability contained in the bill of lading. Reference to the "carrier" in the bill of lading (which incorporated relevant American legislative provisions for the carriage of goods by sea) did not include the stevedores. Moreover, there was nothing in the bill of lading which implied that the parties to it intended the limitation of liability to extend to the stevedores. The court stated that, as it is a fundamental principle that only a party to a contract can take advantage of the provisions of that contract, the stevedores could not rely on a contract to which they were not a party in defending the action against them. It made no difference that the stevedores were attempting to use the contract as a shield and not as a sword. It was decided that the rule precluded a third party from taking an advantage from the contract (per Lord Reid at p 373), despite the inconvenience of this conclusion to the commercial world.

A party to a contract is a person to whom a promise is made, in return for which he provides consideration. If it could be shown, in circumstances like those of *Scruttons* v *Midland Silicones Ltd*, that the stevedore was a party to the contract and had provided consideration, he would then be able to rely on a clause in a bill of lading limiting the liability of the carrier. It did not matter that a rather strained and artificial interpretation of the facts was required to achieve this result. In *Scruttons* v *Midland Silicones Ltd*, one of the arguments advanced (unsuccessfully) by the stevedores was that they were the undisclosed principals of the carrier who acted as their agent and, therefore, the stevedores had a contractual relationship with the plaintiffs through the agency of the carrier. This contention was rejected by the court, but Lord Reid explained (at p 474) the conditions which would need to be satisfied for this agency argument to succeed. He stated, *inter alia*, that the bill of lading must make it clear that the stevedore is intended to be protected by its provisions which limit liability. The contract must also make it clear that the carrier, as well as contracting for these provisions on his own behalf, is also contracting as agent for the stevedore who will in turn be protected by the provisions. Moreover, the carrier would need the stevedore's authority to act in this way. Lastly, any difficulties about consideration moving from the stevedore would need to be overcome.

The matter was considered again in *New Zealand Shipping Co Ltd* v *Satterthwaite (AM) & Co* [1974] 1 All ER 1015, where the facts were similar to *Scruttons* v *Midland Silicones Ltd*:

> Cargo was shipped from Liverpool to the plaintiff (consignee) in New Zealand, under a bill of lading which conferred certain exemptions and immunities on the carrier. A clause in the bill of lading specifically provided that no servant or agent of the carrier (including independent contractors employed by the carrier) would be liable to the plaintiff for any loss or damage resulting from that person's negligence or default in carrying out the work. The clause also made it clear that the carrier was deemed to be acting as agent or trustee on behalf of those persons who were to be employed in handling the cargo, and that such persons were to be regarded as parties to the contract (ie the bill of lading). The defendants were stevedores in New Zealand, employed by the carrier (as independent contractors) to unload the cargo. The cargo was damaged as a result of the defendants' negligence whilst unloading. The plaintiff brought an action against the stevedores and argued that they could not rely on the exemptions and immunities contained in the bill of lading because they were not a party to the contract.

A majority of the Privy Council held that the stevedores were entitled to claim exemption from liability under the contract (see also *Port Jackson Stevedoring Pty* v *Salmond & Spraggon (Australia) Pty (The New York Star)* [1980] 3 All ER 257). It should be noted that, in contrast to *Scruttons* v *Midland Silicones Ltd*, the bill of lading provided that the exemptions of liability should apply to independent contractors such as stevedores. Applying Lord Reid's *dictum* in *Midland Silicones*, the court held that the exemption in the bill of lading was designed to cover the whole carriage of the goods by whomsoever it was performed. The solutions offered by the court to the problems of privity and consideration, whilst no doubt reflecting commercial realism and judicial ingenuity, were far from convincing from the perspective of legal doctrine.

The court held in *Satterthwaite* that the bill of lading was not simply a contract (or evidence of a contract) between the owners of the goods and the carrier. It also represented a contract between the owners and the stevedores, made through the carrier as agent. This was further explained by the idea of the owners making a unilateral offer, to those involved in unloading the goods, of exemption from liability in exchange for performing the requested services. The stevedores provided consideration by unloading the goods, despite the fact that they were already under an existing contractual obligation (owed to the carrier) to do precisely this. Although the stevedores were bound to unload the goods under a contract with the carrier, it will be remembered that the performance of an existing contractual duty owed to a third party can amount to good consideration (see Chapter 4). It was evident from Lord Wilberforce's judgment on behalf of the majority that he was determined to give effect to the clear purpose of a contractual document and not to allow this purpose to be defeated by technical difficulties. He explained the need for the law to take a practical approach to everyday commercial transactions, rather than to be confined by the technical and schematic rules of contract law.

There is no denying that this solution is commercially desirable — allowing the benefit of an exclusion clause, which is clearly intended to benefit a third party, to be relied on by that third party — but it is artificial and not entirely convincing. It was held that the stevedore entered into a contractual relationship with the owner (either shipper or consignee) by performance of the act of unloading which the owner requested in exchange for his promise. In other words, the contract is formed at a later date than the main contract (between the shipper and the carrier) — ie, when the stevedore performs the requested service. The decision in *New Zealand Shipping Co Ltd* v *Satterthwaite* was supported by the Privy Council case of *Port Jackson Stevedoring Pty* v *Salmond & Spraggon (Australia) Pty* [1980] 3 All ER 257, where the facts were similar to those of *Satterthwaite*. In *Port Jackson Stevedoring* the defendant stevedores, who were employed by the carrier, did not take proper care of a consignment of razor blades, which were stolen from a wharf after being unloaded by the stevedores from the ship. Once again, the court had to decide whether the defendants could rely on the defences and immunities contained in the bill of lading and the Privy Council held that they could do so. It was stated that all the parties concerned (that is, the shipper, the carrier and the stevedore) knew that this immunity was intended, and that the law should give effect to commercial practice in this respect.

This solution reflects commercial realism, but it was achieved only by some rather unconvincing reasoning, which was necessary to get round the doctrine of privity. It was also uncertain as to which cases the solution could be applied. (See, for example, *The Mahkutai* [1996] 3 All ER 502, in which the Privy Council held that the *Satterthwaite* approach should not be extended so as to apply to an exclusive jurisdiction clause in a bill of lading.) It is clear that a simpler and more predictable solution was required.

A further illustration of the practical problems caused by the doctrine, and of the need for rather artificial and technical solutions, is provided by the famous case of *Beswick* v *Beswick* [1968] AC 58. The facts were:

> John Beswick helped his uncle, Peter Beswick, who ran a coal merchant business. As Peter was in poor health, he agreed to let John have the business. In return, John was to pay a weekly sum of £6 10s to Peter and, after Peter's death, he was to pay £5 per week to Peter's widow. John made the agreed payments to Peter until the latter's death, but he made only one payment of £5 to Peter's widow and then refused to pay any more. Peter's widow sued John for the arrears under the agreement and asked for specific performance of the contract. She sued both in her capacity as administratrix of her husband's estate, and in her personal capacity.

The House of Lords held that, as she was not a party to the contract, the widow could not succeed in her own right. However, it was decided that she should be granted an order for specific performance as administratrix (personal representative) of her husband's estate. In this capacity there was no problem of privity, as she was suing on behalf of her deceased husband, whose rights she was entitled to enforce. In effect, she *was* able to enforce the defendant's promise for her own benefit and so the outcome was a fair one. But this was achieved only because she was administratrix of the estate; in her personal capacity, she would have been unable to enforce the defendant's promise due to the obstacle provided by the doctrine of privity.

3.   Reform of the law and the 1999 Act

As illustrated above, the privity doctrine was capable of disappointing reasonable contractual and commercial expectations. The fact that a series of ingenious (if contrived) devices were resorted to by the courts, together with a number of established common law and statutory exceptions to the doctrine, to avoid injustice in many cases, did not negate the case for reform. The various exceptions to, and evasions of, the basic rule merely served to demonstrate how impracticable and unpopular the doctrine of privity had become and this was reflected in the strictures of the judiciary. For example, in *Woodar Investment Development Ltd* v *Wimpey Construction UK Ltd* [1980] 1 All ER 571, Lord Scarman expressed the wish that the House of Lords would, in the future, "reconsider *Tweddle* v *Atkinson* and other cases which stand guard over this unjust rule". Despite critical remarks such as these, the judiciary (with the notable exception of Lord Denning) showed a disinclination to directly challenge the basic rule and to overturn the doctrine of privity. The courts were probably correct in insisting that such a fundamental change was, more appropriately, to be undertaken by Parliament.

The Law Commission considered the case for reform of the general rule which prevented a person from enforcing a right under a contract to which he is not a party (the "third party rule") in its report, *Privity of Contract: Contracts for the Benefit of Third Parties* (Law Com No 242, 1996, Cm 3329). This report supported the case for reform of the third party rule and stated that its recommendations would allow contracting parties to provide for enforceable third party rights without resort to the various evasions and exceptions which had developed to circumvent the privity rule. The report argued that this reform should be brought about in the form of detailed legislation, this strategy being favoured because of the certainty it would bring to the law. It observed that, despite the repeated criticism levelled at the privity doctrine in appellate cases, little progress had been made in actually overturning the third party rule. The legislative process offered the prospect of more detailed reform of the law and it was not dependent upon the vagaries of litigation.

The Contracts (Rights of Third Parties) Act 1999, based largely on the Law Commission's 1996 report (see above), brought about a significant reform of the doctrine of privity of contract[4]. The Act does not affect the existing exceptions to and circumventions of the doctrine, but it introduces an important new (and more general) exception into the law. The Act deals with the conferral of rights on third parties, but naturally it does not alter the rule which prevents liabilities being imposed on a third party. It must be emphasised that the doctrine of privity was not abolished by the Act; it creates a general and relatively simple exception to the doctrine. In doing so, the Act brings English law more closely into line with that of most of the other members of the

European Union and of many common law jurisdictions. The Act was passed on 11 November 1999, but it applies only to those contracts concluded on or after 11 May 2000 (ie six months after the new Act received the Royal Assent). However, the parties to a contract concluded during this six month period after the Act was passed may expressly provide for the Act to apply (see s 10(2) and (3)).

Conferring a third party right

Section 1(1) of the Act states that a "third party" is able to enforce a term of a contract in his own right if:

"(a) the contract expressly provides that he may, or

(b) subject to subsection (2), the term purports to confer a benefit on him."

Section 1(2) provides that subsection (1)(b) will not apply if, on the proper construction of the contract, "it appears that the parties did not intend the term to be enforceable by the third party". Although the third party does not have to be in existence when the contract is made, he or she must be expressly identified in the contract by name, or as a member of a class, or as answering a particular description (s 1(3)). Accordingly, a contractual provision might seek to benefit the future offspring of the contracting parties, or a company which is yet to be incorporated. References in the Act to a third party enforcing a contractual term are to be understood as including the right to rely on an exclusion or limitation clause; such references, therefore, are not restricted to a third party suing to enforce a positive right (s 1(6)). If a third party comes within the provisions of this new exception to the privity doctrine, he can exercise his right to enforce the contractual term in the same way as if he were a party to the contract, and the rules relating to damages, injunctions and specific performance apply equally to him (s 1(5)). However, any rights which are conferred on a third party are subject to any other relevant terms of the contract (s 1(4)); for example, where third party rights are created, the contracting parties might choose to limit those rights expressly by some other term of the contract.

What is the ambit of this new and wide-ranging exception to the doctrine of privity? The right of a third party, under s 1(1) (above), to enforce a term of a contract, is based on the intention of the contracting parties. This right may be conferred expressly by the contract, under the first limb, which is relatively straightforward. Alternatively, under the second limb, the third party may enforce a contractual term which purports to confer a benefit on him, subject to the proviso that this will not apply if, on a proper construction of the contract, the parties did not intend the term to be enforceable by the third party. The Law Commission used certain well-known past cases to illustrate the scope of the new third party right, especially in relation to the second limb of the test (Law Com No 242, *ibid*, paras 7.45–7.51). Applying the new law to *Beswick* v *Beswick* (discussed above), for example, the first limb of the test would not confer a right on the uncle's widow as there was no express provision to that effect in the contract. (Examples of such a provision would include words like "and C shall have the right to enforce the contract"; see Law Commission, *ibid,* para 7.10.) However, under the second limb, she would now almost certainly be able to enforce the nephew's promise in her own right. This is because the contract between the nephew and the uncle purported to confer a benefit on her and she was expressly identified in that contract. It is extremely unlikely that the presumption could be rebutted as the nephew would be unable to demonstrate that, on a proper construction, the contracting parties did not intend the term to be enforceable by her.

It might be questioned whether the second (and more complicated) limb was necessary, especially in view of its potential to introduce uncertainty into the law, and whether the first limb might have been better standing alone. However, the view of the Law Commission was that, on its own, the first limb would have been too restrictive an approach to reforming the law. This is because it would have failed to give rights to a third party in situations where, although no express right of enforceability had been conferred by the contracting parties, it had been intended that the third party should have such a right (Law Com No 242, 1996, para 7.11). Moreover, the Law Commission argued that with the inclusion of the "proviso" (ie, s 1(2)), the second limb represents a workable solution to the problem of giving effect to the contracting parties' intentions without the introduction of too much uncertainty into the law. It is possible that there may be problems for the courts in deciding whether on a "proper construction" the parties intended, on conferring a benefit on a third party, for it to be enforceable by the third party. But these problems are not insurmountable to judges used to taking an objective approach to contractual intention and, in the longer term, difficulties may be avoided by the more careful drafting of contracts by the parties. If the parties to a contract do not wish to confer an enforceable right on a third party, they should state this in clear terms, otherwise there may well be a strong presumption that the third party has the right to enforce the term in question.

Varying or cancelling the agreement

Where a third party has a right conferred on him under a contract, should the contracting parties have the freedom to vary, or even cancel, the third party's right? It could be argued that without such a freedom, there would be an unacceptable interference with the rights of the contracting parties, who would usually have the right to vary their agreement. However, the recognition of third party rights naturally involves some restriction on the contracting parties' freedom to modify the original contract, otherwise the reform of the third party rule (described above) would lack utility. The Law Commission sought to establish an appropriate test to determine the "crystallisation" of the third party's rights: ie the point beyond which the contracting parties would lose the right to vary or cancel the contract. It favoured a test of reliance or acceptance by recommending that: "the contracting parties' right to vary or cancel the contract or, as the case may be, the contractual provision should be lost once the third party has relied on it or has accepted it" (see Law Com No 242, 1996, para 9.26). However, it stated also that "the contracting parties may expressly reserve the right to vary or cancel the third party's right irrespective of reliance or acceptance by the third party" (*ibid,* 9.40). In other words, the Law Commission recommended a compromise between the conflicting interests referred to above, by allowing the contracting parties expressly to reserve the right to vary or cancel the right of the third party.

Accordingly, s 2(3) of the Act provides that the restriction on the right of the contracting parties to vary or cancel a third party's right, set out in s 2(1), is subject to any express term of the contract under which the contracting parties may, (a) by agreement rescind or vary the contract without the third party's consent, or (b) alter the circumstances for the third party's consent to be given from those set out in s 2(1). If the contracting parties do not include such an express provision in their agreement, their freedom to vary or cancel the third party's right is controlled by s 2(1). This states that where a third party has a right conferred on him (see s 1, above), the contracting parties are not permitted to agree to cancel or alter the agreement in such a way as to extinguish or alter the third party's right, without his consent if:

(a) the third party has communicated his assent (by words or conduct) to the term to the promisor,

(b) the promisor is aware that the third party has relied on the term, or

(c) the promisor can reasonably be expected to have foreseen that the third party would rely on the term and the third party has in fact relied on it.

Therefore, once a third party right has been conferred (under s 1), there are general restrictions (under s 2(1)) on the freedom of the contracting parties to vary or cancel their agreement subsequently, in the absence of any express provision in the contract (s 2(3)). In s 2(1), it should be noted that the word "reliance" is not restricted to where a third party has relied on the term to his detriment; the third party's conduct need not have left him in a worse position than before the promise was made. This distinction was made by the Law Commission, which defined reliance on a promise as "conduct induced by the belief (or expectation) that the promise will be performed or, at least, that one is legally entitled to performance of the promise" (*ibid*, para 9.14). This approach is consistent with one of the major reasons for reforming the privity doctrine; that is, that it can disappoint the reasonable expectations of the third party. If the third party has relied on the promise, this demonstrates that expectations have been created, even if no detriment has been suffered (see Law Com, *ibid*, para 9.19).

It should be noted that, under s 2(1), the promisor (ie the contracting party against whom the term is enforceable by the third party) actually has to be aware of the third party's reliance; or alternatively, can reasonably be expected to foresee that the third party would rely on the term and has in fact done so. Normally, where a promisor has contracted to confer a right on a third party, he should be aware that there is likely to be reliance on the contract by the third party. So, as a general rule, the promisor should check with the third party, where this is possible, before cancelling or varying the contractual provision in question. As an alternative to the reliance test, s 2(1) also provides a test of acceptance. The rationale is that where a third party communicates his assent effectively, this allows the promisor to know where he stands, and the third party should be able to enforce his right without having to show reliance (see Law Com, *ibid*, para 9.20). Therefore, to avoid any uncertainty, a third party may make certain of performance of the promise by communicating his assent to the promisor. It should be noted that communication in this context does not include the posting of a letter; the Act states that the assent may be by words or conduct, but if it is sent by post it will not be regarded as communicated until it is received by the promisor (s 2(2)(b)).

Defences

The Law Commission recommended that the right of the third party to enforce a term of the contract "should be subject to all defences and set-offs that would have been available to the promisor in an action by the promisee and which arise out of or in connection with the contract. . ." (Law Com No 242, para 10.12). Accordingly, s 3 of the Act deals with the defences available to a promisor where a claim is made by a third party in reliance on s 1. Section 3(2) provides that, subject to any express term of the contract to the contrary (s 3(5)), the promisor can rely on any defence or set-off which:

(a) arises from the contract and is relevant to the term in question, and

(b) would have been available to him if the action had been brought by the promisee (ie the party to the contract by whom the term is enforceable against the promisor).

In addition, the promisor is able to rely on (a) by way of defence or set-off any matter, and (b) by way of counterclaim any matter not arising from the contract, "that would have been available to him by way of defence or set-off or, as the case may be, by way of counterclaim against the third party if the third party had been a party to the contract"(s 3(4)).

Other provisions of the 1999 Act

Section 4 makes it clear that the conferral of an enforceable right on a third party does not affect the right of the promisee to enforce any contractual term (discussed later in this chapter). This section is consistent with the view expressed by the Law Commission (Law Com No 242, *ibid*, paras 11.3–11.4), which argued that the promisee (a contracting party who has provided consideration) should not lose the right to enforce a contractual right simply because the contract has conferred an enforceable right on a third party. It might be objected that this could raise the prospect of a double liability for the promisor; ie to pay damages to both the third party and the promisee for the same loss. Section 5 aims to prevent this by providing that, where a contractual term has conferred an enforceable right on a third party, and the promisee has recovered damages in respect of the third party's loss, then this will be taken into account in any proceedings brought by the third party. In other words, any sum awarded to the third party will be lowered appropriately to take account of the sum recovered by the promisee. This section does not deal explicitly with the reverse situation, in which the third party has already recovered damages from the promisor; but the logic of s 5 would suggest that, in such a case, there will be a similar restriction on the damages recoverable by the promisee. (However, in this situation, it is unlikely that the promisee will have suffered any loss and that is presumably why no express provision was included in the Act.)

Section 6 sets out the types of contract which do not fall within the ambit of the Act. For example, s 6(1) provides that s 1 does not confer a third party right "in the case of a contract on a bill of exchange, promissory note or other negotiable instrument". This exclusion follows the recommendation of the Law Commission (*ibid,* para 12.17), which was of the opinion that it would cause considerable uncertainty in the law if a more general third party right were created in relation to bills of exchange, promissory notes and other negotiable instruments, in addition to the one which is provided by the Bills of Exchange Act 1882. Under the 1882 Act, third party rights of enforceability are conferred only on holders of those instruments. If the 1999 Act had applied, it would have extended this right to third parties who were not holders and, in so doing, have undermined the policy of the 1882 Act and led to confusion.

The Law Commission recommended also that third party rights of enforceability should not be conferred in relation to contracts for the carriage of goods by sea, and contracts for the international carriage of goods by road, rail or air (*ibid*, para 12.6). Once again, the reasoning was that such a general right might be inconsistent with the policy of existing legislation, which is more attuned to the needs of a particular industry (such as shipping), and that the resulting conflict would produce uncertainty in the commercial world. (For the relevant legislation in relation to the carriage of goods by sea, see the Carriage of Goods by Sea Act 1992, s 2(1); contracts for the international carriage of goods by road or rail, or the carriage of cargo by air, are regulated by international conventions which are given force in English law by various implementing statutes). For this reason, s 6(5) of the 1999 Act states that no third party right of enforceability (under s 1) is conferred in relation to (a) contracts for the carriage of goods by sea, or (b) contracts for the carriage of goods by rail or road, or cargo by air. However, s 6(5) expressly states that this does not prevent a third party from enforcing exclusion or limitation of liability clauses in these two types of contract.

The 1999 Act confers no third party right in the case of any contract binding on any company and its members under s 14 of the Companies Act 1985 (see s 6(2)). Also, s 6(3) provides for the exclusion of employment contracts from the ambit of the new third party right. Accordingly, s 1 confers no third party right to enforce (a) any term of a contract against an employee, (b) any term of a worker's contract against a worker, or (c) any term of a relevant contract against an agency worker. This provision ensures that, for example, a customer of an employer will not be able to use the Act to bring an action against an employee for a breach of his or her contract of employment.

The Law Commission's aim was not to confer upon a third party the identical rights as would be enjoyed by a contracting party; for example, it did not support the argument in favour of amending the Unfair Contract Terms Act 1977 (see Chapter 10) so as to restrict the promisor's ability to exclude liability to third parties. The Commission argued that its test of enforceability was based on giving effect to the intentions of the parties to a contract to bestow legal rights on a third party, and that to apply the Unfair Contract Terms Act 1977 to claims by third parties "would cut across the essential basis" of the proposed reform (para 13.10). The Commission considered s 2(2) of the 1977 Act more specifically, which it felt needed to be the subject of an express provision. Therefore, it recommended that s 2(2) of the Unfair Contract Terms Act 1977 should not apply in respect of a claim by a third party under the new law. (It will be remembered that s 2(2) states that a person cannot limit or exclude liability for negligently caused loss or damage, other than personal injury or death, unless the contract term or notice in question satisfies the requirement of reasonableness.) Section 7(2) of the 1999 Act reflects the Law Commission's view by providing that s 2(2) of the Unfair Contract Terms Act 1977 will "not apply where the negligence consists of the breach of an obligation arising from a term of a contract and the person seeking to enforce it is a third party acting in reliance on section 1".

Finally, it should be noted that s 7(1) of the 1999 Act makes it clear that the new right of enforceability under s 1 "does not affect any right or remedy of a third party that exists or is available apart from this Act". This provision reflects the view of the Law Commission (*ibid*, paras 12.1–12.2), which argued for the retention of other existing statutory exceptions, and found "no merit" in attempting to abolish the common law exceptions to the doctrine. Moreover, it acknowledged that some of the common law exceptions give third parties more certain rights than those conferred under the new Act. But, the Commission observed that some of these common law exceptions to the doctrine "have developed through somewhat artificial and forced use of existing concepts" (para 12.1) and that such exceptions might "wither away", as a consequence of the new law, as they become redundant.

It is clear also, from s 4 (see above), that the conferral of an enforceable right on a third party does not affect the right of the promisee to enforce any contractual term and, in some instances, the promisee may be able to assist the third party. Therefore, it is necessary in this chapter to consider the other main exceptions to the privity doctrine, including a discussion of the right of the promisee to bring an action, although it should be emphasised that some of these exceptions will become less important as a consequence of the 1999 Act. (Also, it should be remembered that the new Act does not apply to all types of contract.)

4.   Other statutory exceptions

In contrast to the more general exception to the doctrine provided by the 1999 Act, there are other, narrower statutory exceptions which were introduced to avoid the commercial inconvenience caused by the privity rule. A good example is that of contracts of insurance, where various Acts confer rights on third parties. A car owner, for instance, may require insurance cover not only for his own use of his vehicle, but also for other people who drive his car with his permission. In theory, the contract of insurance which he takes out for the benefit of third parties would not be enforceable by them. However, to avoid this result, specific legislation was introduced to permit a third party to benefit from such an insurance policy. For example, s 148(7) Road Traffic Act 1988 states that a person issuing an insurance policy is liable to indemnify not just the person taking out the policy, but also the "the persons or classes of persons specified in the policy in respect of any liability which the policy purports to cover". In another statutory exception to the privity rule, it is provided that a person can effect an insurance on his or her life for the benefit of his or her spouse or children (see s 11 Married Women's Property Act 1882). Such a life insurance creates a trust in favour of the named beneficiaries, rather than becoming part of the insured person's estate.

For a fuller list of statutory exceptions, see the Law Commission's report (*ibid*, pp 31–35). It is worth noting, in this context, the Package Travel, Package Holidays and Package Tours Regulations 1992 (SI 1992 No 3288), which implemented Council Directive 90/314/EEC on package travel, package holidays and package tours. The problem for the consumer, posed by the doctrine of privity, was that the services comprising a package holiday may not be performed directly by the organiser or retailer with whom the contract was made. In order to get round this difficulty, the Regulations confer direct rights on consumers (see reg 2(2)) against the organiser or retailer with whom they contracted (see reg 15).

5.   Action brought by the promisee

The conferral of an enforceable right on a third party by the 1999 Act does not affect the right of a promisee to enforce any term of the contract (see s 4). As explained at the start of this chapter, a contract between A and B, under which A promises to confer some benefit on C, was not enforceable by C due to the privity doctrine. However, the promisee (B) is able to bring an action against A, as a party to a binding contract. One possible remedy for B is to seek an order for specific performance against A to force him to confer the promised benefit on C. An order for specific performance has the effect of ordering a contracting party to do what he has undertaken to do (see Chapter 21). If we return to the case of *Beswick* v *Beswick* [1968] AC 58 (discussed earlier), it was held that although the widow could not succeed in her own right, she should be granted an order for specific performance as administratrix of her husband's estate. In this capacity, as his personal representative, there was no problem of privity as she was suing on behalf of the promisee (her deceased husband), whose rights she was entitled to enforce. The contract in *Beswick* v *Beswick* was of a type that may be specifically enforced, but this would not have been the case if, for example, the contract had been for personal services — as such contracts are not normally specifically enforceable. The remedy of specific performance is not one which is widely available and such an order will not be made where damages are an adequate remedy. It could be argued that, as the 1999 Act has given the third party an enforceable right to claim damages in a case such as *Beswick* v *Beswick*, it is less likely that specific performance would be either sought by the promisee, or granted if similar facts occurred today.

Where the promisee sues for damages as a result of the promisor failing to confer a benefit on the third party, the question arises as to how such damages are to be assessed. Of course, the promisee can sue for his own loss (if he has suffered any) but, in general, he cannot recover damages for the loss of the third party. The promisee is not able to recover anything other than nominal damages where he has not suffered any direct loss. The rule was challenged in *Jackson* v *Horizon Holidays* [1975] 3 All ER 92, where the facts were:

> Mr Jackson (P) booked a holiday with the defendant company for himself, his wife, and his two small children. The price of the holiday (in Sri Lanka) was £1,200, which covered air fares and luxury hotel accommodation. When booking the holiday, P made various stipulations about the accommodation and meals that he and his family were to receive. He was assured that the hotel in question would be up to his expectation. In fact, P and his family were greatly dissatisfied with the hotel, its facilities, and the meals that were served. P brought an action against the defendants for breach of contract claiming damages, in respect of the disappointment and distress, for himself, his wife and his children. The defendants did not contest their liability, but they appealed against the amount of damages (£1,100) awarded by the deputy High Court judge.

The Court of Appeal dismissed the appeal and held that the damages awarded by the judge were not excessive. The majority stated that the amount would have been excessive if it had been awarded only for the loss suffered by Mr Jackson himself. (In this respect, the trial judge's decision was reversed by the majority in the Court of Appeal.) But, in these circumstances, where one party makes a contract for the benefit of himself and others, the court held that he should be able to claim on behalf of the whole party. Mr Jackson could, therefore, recover damages not only for his own dissatisfaction with the holiday, but also for that of his family. Lord Denning stated (at p 95):

"In this case it was a husband making a contract for the benefit of himself, his wife and children. Other cases readily come to mind. A host makes a contract with a restaurant for a dinner for himself and his friends . . . It would be a fiction to say that the contract was made by all the family, or all the guests . . . The real truth is that in each instance, the father, the host . . . was making a contract himself for the benefit of the whole party. In short, a contract by one for the benefit of third persons".

The approach adopted by the majority in *Jackson* v *Horizon Holidays* was potentially an attractive one, but it was based heavily on Lord Denning's view of what the law should be rather than on any convincing authority. This circumvention of the privity rule was not without its critics, and it is not surprising that the matter was considered once again by the House of Lords in *Woodar Investment Development Ltd* v *Wimpey Construction UK Ltd* [1980] 1 All ER 571. The facts were as follows:

A contract for the sale of fourteen acres of land for development, for a price of £850,000, included a provision that the purchasers should also pay, on completion, a further £150,000 to a third party who had no legal connection with the vendors. The contract gave the purchasers the right to rescind the contract if, before completion, a statutory authority "shall have commenced" to acquire the property by compulsory acquisition. In fact, compulsory purchase proceedings had been started for part of the property at the time the contract was completed, but it later became clear that there was a prospect of planning permission being granted for most of the land. Nevertheless, the purchasers wished to rescind the contract. The vendors claimed damages on the basis that the purchasers had wrongfully repudiated the contract. They included in their claim the loss suffered by the third party.

A majority of the House of Lords held that the purchasers had not wrongfully repudiated the contract and their appeal was allowed. The question of damages was not, therefore, relevant to the actual decision. But the court went on to consider the state of the law regarding the recovery of damages for the benefit of third parties and it disapproved of Lord Denning's broad statements in *Jackson* v *Horizon Holidays Ltd* [1975] 3 All ER 92 at pp 95–96. This does not mean that the actual decision in *Jackson* was incorrect, but the House of Lords would not endorse Lord Denning's interpretation of the relevant legal authorities. The actual decision in *Jackson* could still be supported on the basis that the plaintiff recovered solely for his own loss (see the rather terse judgment of James LJ in *Jackson,* at p 96), or alternatively, that the case belonged to a special type of contract (eg where a person contracts for a family holiday, or books a restaurant meal for a party) which requires "special treatment" (*per* Lords Wilberforce and Keith in *Woodar*, at p 576 and p 588 respectively).

However, in *Woodar* it was clear that the promisee (the vendors) would have suffered no loss in relation to the promisor's failure to pay the money to the third party. The House of Lords suggested that the vendors would not have been able to recover substantial damages for the third party's loss (see, for example, the statement of Lord Wilberforce at p 577). But, if the *Woodar* facts were to occur today, the third party would be able to claim the promised sum directly under the 1999 Act. This is because the contract purported to confer a benefit on the third party, who was expressly identified, and the promisor would surely not be able to rebut the presumption that the third party was intended to have an enforceable right.

In spite of the House of Lords' decision in *Woodar*, which rejected the idea that a contracting party could generally recover the third party's loss, later cases have considered this matter in different circumstances. For example, in *Linden Gardens Trust Ltd v Lenesta Sludge Disposals Ltd and others (and another appeal)* [1993] 3 All ER 417, the House of Lords considered whether a building owner can recover substantial damages for breach of a building contract, if he has parted with the property to a third party. In one appeal, a company (A) contracted with B for the removal of blue asbestos from its property. But, in breach of the agreement, not all the asbestos was removed by B, whilst A in the meantime had sold the property to C. A had attempted to assign its contractual rights to C, but this transaction was invalid and C was thus prevented from succeeding in its action against B for breach of contract. A was not in fact a party to the action in one appeal, but was in the other case which was considered at the same time by the House of Lords. Their lordships discussed whether A could recover anything other than nominal damages if it brought an action against B, as a result of the loss suffered by C. It was decided that A should be permitted to recover substantial damages as it was in the contemplation of both contracting parties that the property was likely to be bought by a third party before B's breach occurred, and that A should be regarded as having entered into the contract for C's benefit, as C's loss was foreseeable to B. (Their lordships relied on *Albacruz (Cargo Owners) v Albazero (Owners)*; *"The Albazero"* [1977] AC 774 *per* Lord Diplock at p 847.) Accordingly, A could recover for C's loss in these commercial circumstances, as C had no direct remedy. The *Linden Gardens* decision was then applied, and extended, by the Court of Appeal in *Darlington Borough Council v Wiltshier Northern Ltd* [1995] 1 WLR 68.

The actual outcomes of these cases are unexceptionable, with their avoidance of injustice — the disappearance of a substantial claim into a legal "black hole" — which would otherwise have resulted from a strict application of the rule restricting the promisee's right to recover damages in respect of a third party's loss. But it could be objected that the uncertainty in the law caused by differing interpretations of the scope of the general rule, and of the exceptions to it, is undesirable. It should be noted also that *Linden Gardens Trust* was distinguished in the House of Lords case of *Panatown Ltd v Alfred McAlpine Construction Ltd* [2000] 4 All ER 97, as on the facts of the latter case the third party had been given a direct cause of action against the contractor. In these circumstances, the necessity for the *Linden Gardens Trust* approach was not present, as the third party had a right to recover substantial damages by suing the contractor directly. Therefore, in arbitration proceedings brought by the claimant employer against the defendant contractor, seeking the recovery of substantial damages, a majority of the House of Lords decided against the employer and allowed the contractor's appeal. (The uncertainty over the ambit of the *Linden Gardens Trust* exception may well be resolved by a stricter adherence to the general rule in future, in view of the third party right which can now be conferred directly under the 1999 Act.)

Finally, there is another situation in which the promisee may be able to enforce a promise on behalf of a third party. This is where A makes a promise (expressly or impliedly) to B that he will not sue C. If an action is brought by A against C, B may be able to prevent A from succeeding with such an action. For example, in *Snelling* v *John G Snelling Ltd* [1972] 1 All ER 79, the facts were:

> Three brothers were co-directors of a family business, a building company. The business expanded, but disputes arose between the brothers and relations between them worsened. The three brothers made loans to the company to provide additional finance. The three of them contracted that in the event of any one of them voluntarily resigning his directorship, he would forfeit the money owed to him by the company. The agreement stated that if this occurred, the remaining directors could use the money, not for their personal benefit, but to repay a loan made to their business by a finance company. Three months later, Brian Snelling (the plaintiff) voluntarily resigned as a director and claimed payment from the defendant company of the sum which he had loaned to it. The company was joined by the other two brothers, Peter and Barrie, as co-defendants, who claimed that the sum due to the plaintiff had been forfeited by his resignation. Could the defendant company rely on a term in the agreement (between the brothers) which was for the company's benefit, when it was not a party to that agreement?

It was held by Ormrod J that the co-defendants, Peter and Barrie Snelling, were entitled to a declaration that the terms of the agreement were binding on Brian, the plaintiff. The company, on the other hand, was not a party to the agreement and could not, therefore, rely directly on its terms. However, the judge achieved a fair outcome by granting a declaration that the plaintiff was not able to call upon the defendant company to repay the loan and his action against the company was dismissed. The judge stated that this course of action was possible as the co-defendant brothers had made out a clear case and succeeded on their counterclaim; and because all the relevant parties were before the court, it would have been a proper case for a stay of all further proceedings. But as the judge thought that the plaintiff's claim had failed, he dismissed the claim rather than merely ordering a stay of further proceedings. In this way, the plaintiff was prevented from obtaining a judgment against the company in defiance of the clear agreement, made with his brothers, which was intended to put the family company on a secure business footing. It should be noted that the plaintiff did not actually promise not to sue the company, but such a promise was a necessary implication of the agreement which he made. (This decision can be contrasted with *Gore* v *Van der Lann* [1967] 2 QB 31.)

6. Circumventions of, and exceptions to, the doctrine

A number of devices and ingenious arguments have been used in the past to avoid the inconvenience or unfairness caused by a strict application of the privity doctrine. In view of the 1999 Act, such devices may be of less practical significance in the future, but they were not abolished by the new legislation (see s 7(1)) and, therefore, need to be considered in the sections which follow.

Collateral contracts

A good example of judicial ingenuity in avoiding the problem of privity is the use of the concept of a collateral contract. This concept was discussed in detail in Chapter 7; and it was considered also in Chapter 4, in relation to the practice of manufacturers of goods providing guarantees to the consumer, whose contract is with the retailer. The manufacturer is not, of course, a party to the main contract between the retailer and the consumer, and it might appear that such guarantees are unenforceable, as the consumer provides no consideration for the manufacturer's promise. In a rather artificial way, however, it could be argued that, where the consumer is invited to fill in a card or form and send it off to the manufacturer within a specified period, the performance of such an act by the consumer is an acceptance of the manufacturer's (unilateral) offer of a guarantee. Another way of examining such transactions is to say that the guarantee is the subject of a collateral contract, that is, one that exists alongside the main contract between the retailer and the consumer. The collateral contract represents a judicial device aimed at avoiding an unfair outcome which would otherwise be caused by an established rule of law. This is illustrated by the case *Shanklin Pier* v *Detel Products Ltd* [1951] 2 KB 854, where the facts were:

> The plaintiffs (the pier owners) employed contractors to paint their pier under a contract which enabled the plaintiffs to specify the paint to be used. The defendant company, wishing to secure the contract for supplying the paint, told the plaintiffs that their paint (known as DMU) would last for at least seven years. On the strength of this representation (or "guarantee"), the plaintiffs instructed the contractors to buy and use the defendants' paint for painting the pier. In fact, the paint was unsatisfactory and lasted for a mere three months! The plaintiffs brought an action against the defendants but they had to get round the problem that the paint was bought from the defendants by the contractors. Could the plaintiffs enforce the defendants' guarantee that the paint would last for at least seven years?

The court found in favour of the plaintiffs. Although the main contract was between the defendants and the contractors for the sale of the paint, there was also a collateral contract between the defendants and the plaintiffs which guaranteed the durability of the paint known as DMU. It must be presumed that the plaintiffs gave consideration for the defendants' guarantee of their paint by instructing the contractors to buy DMU rather than any other paint. (For a further, and more questionable, example of the use of the collateral contract device in relation to guarantees, see *Wells (Merstham) Ltd* v *Buckland Sand and Silica Co Ltd* [1965] 2 QB 170.) As the 1999 Act now permits an enforceable right to be conferred directly on a third party, there will be less need to use the collateral contract device to avoid the privity doctrine in future.

Trust of a promise

In affirming the common law rule of privity in *Dunlop Pneumatic Tyre Co* v *Selfridge* [1915] AC 847 (at p 853), Lord Haldane stated that although a third party cannot acquire rights by way of a contract, such a right may be conferred by way of property, for example, under a trust. The idea of a trust, as developed in equity, is that of B (the trustee) having rights over property (eg land or a fund), which he is bound by agreement with A, from whom he received the property, to exercise on behalf of C, the beneficiary. To put this another way, B holds the property on trust for the benefit of C. Under such an arrangement, C acquires an equitable interest in the property and he can enforce his rights against the trustee. When the trust is set up, C becomes the beneficial owner of the property and, accordingly, his rights are not a result merely of a promise in his or her favour.

The concept of a trust had some potential as a means of circumventing the privity rule. To take the familiar situation: A makes a promise to B, in exchange for consideration supplied by B, to confer some benefit on C. If it could be argued that B was a trustee for C, then C's rights would be enforceable. One difficulty is the limitation that, for there to be a valid trust, there must (*inter alia*) be property which is capable of being held on trust and in which the third party has an equitable interest. The question arose as to the circumstances in which the courts were prepared to find that a trust of a contractual right had been created. In other words, when could a promisee under a contract legitimately claim that he was a trustee of the benefit of that promise on behalf of a "stranger" to the contract? Initially the courts showed a willingness to rely on the trust idea in this way (see *Tomlinson* v *Gill* (1756) Amb 330; also *Gregory and Parker* v *Williams* (1817) 3 Mer 582; and *Lloyd's* v *Harper* (1880) 16 Ch D 290). The most well known example is *Les Affréteurs Réunis SA* v *Leopold Walford Ltd* [1919] AC 801, where the facts were:

> The appellants (the shipowners) entered into a contract to charter a ship to a company (the charterers) for a specific period. Under the contract, the appellants promised to pay a sum of money to the respondent brokers (Walford's) who had negotiated the contract. Clause 29 of the contract stated: "A commission of 3 per cent on the estimated gross amount of hire is due to Leopold Walford Ltd on signing this charter (ship lost or not lost)". The ship was requisitioned by the French government and the shipowners refused to pay any commission to Walford's. It should be noted that Walford's were not a party to the agreement, although Clause 29 was included for their benefit. Although the action was brought by Walford's, with the consent of the appellants it was treated as if the charterers had been added as plaintiffs.

The House of Lords held that Walford's were entitled to recover the commission from the shipowners. The charterers, who were the promisees, were able to enforce the appellants' promise made for the benefit of a third party. The charterers were trustees for Walford's, who were the beneficiaries of the promise. It was stated by Lord Birkenhead (at pp 806–807):

> "It appears to me that for convenience, and under long-established practice, the broker in such cases, in effect, nominates the charterer to contract on his behalf, influenced probably by the circumstance that there is always a contract between charterer and owner in which this stipulation, which is to enure to the benefit of the broker, may very conveniently be inserted. In these cases the broker, on ultimate analysis, appoints the charterer to contract on his behalf. I agree with the conclusion ... that in such cases charterers can sue as trustees on behalf of the broker".

This approach of implying a trust of a contractual right appeared to offer a convenient solution to a third party trying to enforce a promise made for his benefit. However, the solution raised certain difficulties. Principally, it was objected that the contracting parties will rarely, in fact, intend to create a trust. This is because if they do so, it would mean that they were not free to vary the terms of their agreement in the future, as this would interfere with the beneficiary's rights. As they are unlikely to intend such a restriction on their own contractual rights, it meant that the trust device was of limited utility. The courts now insist on clear evidence that the parties intended to create a trust, and this explains why the trust of a contractual right idea is of little value to third parties today. (For example, in *Vandepitte v Preferred Accident Insurance Corporation of New York* [1933] AC 70, the Privy Council held that there will be a trust only if it can be definitely proved that there was an intention to create one, and in this case no such intention to constitute a trust was proved.) The reluctance of the courts to imply a trust is further illustrated by *Re Schebsman* [1944] Ch 83. The facts were:

> Mr Schebsman was employed by both a Swiss company and its English subsidiary. On the termination of Schebsman's employment with the two companies, the English company agreed to pay him £5,500 in six annual instalments. The agreement also specified that the payments would be made to Schebsman's widow, if he died, and to his daughter, if his widow also died. During the period in which the payments were to be made to him by the company (and two years after the agreement was made), Schebsman was declared bankrupt and then he died. His trustee in bankruptcy sought a declaration that the outstanding sums still to be paid by the English company formed part of the debtor's (ie Schebsman's) estate; if this claim succeeded, the money payable by the company would have been available for Schebsman's creditors. The claim failed: the company was entitled to go ahead and make the agreed payments to Schebsman's widow.

The trustee in bankruptcy's appeal was dismissed by the Court of Appeal. The company was, in fact, willing to make the payments to the widow and such payment was held by the court to be due performance of the contract. (The court refused to imply a term into the agreement entitling the trustee in bankruptcy to intercept the sums which were to be paid to the wife and daughter). This had the effect of preventing the trustee in bankruptcy's claim. However, the court also made it clear that under the agreement between the company and Schebsman, the latter was neither a trustee nor an agent for his wife and daughter. Du Parcq LJ stated (at p 104) that unless the parties, by their language and by the circumstances of the case, show a clear intention to create a trust, the court should not be quick to imply such an intention. As the parties to the agreement in *Schebsman* would almost certainly have wished to retain their right at common law to vary the terms of that agreement, his lordship did not think that a trust had been created. (For instance, Schebsman might have wanted the money to be paid to someone other than his widow.)

Thus the courts are reluctant to "disregard the dividing line between the case of a trust and the simple case of a contract made between two persons for the benefit of a third" (*per* Lord Greene MR in *Re Schebsman* [1944] Ch 83 at p 89). (See also *Green v Russell* [1959] 2 QB 226 in which it was held that the mere intention, under a contract, to provide benefits for a third party was insufficient to create a trust.) For these reasons, it is clear that the idea of a trust of a contractual right is not a very useful means of evading the privity rule, although it is still theoretically available in cases which come within its narrow ambit. In view of the 1999 legislation offering a more straightforward method of conferring an enforceable right on a third party, it is unlikely that the trust argument will be of much practical significance in the future.

Assignment

The idea of assignment of contractual rights represents another limit on the doctrine of privity. A party to a contract may, in certain circumstances, assign (transfer) his existing contractual rights to a third party. For example, a creditor (A) may assign his rights against a debtor (B) to a third party (C). By means of such a transaction, C acquires rights against B, as a result of standing in the place of A. The consent of the debtor (B) to such an assignment is not required, although he must normally be notified of the transaction. It is argued that B is not at a disadvantage under this type of transaction, as the identity of the creditor usually does not matter to B. In its Consultation Paper on the doctrine of privity, the Law Commission stated that "the practical importance of assignment is considerable; the whole industry of debt collection and credit factoring depends upon it" (see Law Commission Paper 121, 1991, p 51).

Although the law generally permits the assignment of contractual rights, this is subject to the provisos that such transactions must not be unfair to the debtor, and they must not be contrary to the public interest. In particular, it should be noted that rights arising out of "personal" contracts are incapable of assignment. For example, where A employs B to perform certain services, it would be unfair to permit A to assign his contractual rights to C. So an employer is not entitled to transfer the benefit of his employee's services to a third party. In view of the willingness of the law to allow the assignment of existing contractual rights to a third party, it made the inflexibility of the privity doctrine, prior to 1999, difficult to understand. In the words of the Law Commission (Law Com 242, 1996, para 2.17): "If an immediate assignment is valid, there can hardly be fundamental objections to allowing the third party to sue without an assignment".

Agency

Another important limit on the ambit of the privity rule is provided by the doctrine of agency (discussed in detail in Chapter 23). Under the law of agency, when an agent (B) makes a contract with a third party (C) on behalf of his principal (A), this is treated by the law as if the principal had himself made the contract. A and C may sue one another for breach of that contract. However, this "exception" to the doctrine of privity is perhaps more apparent than real. The law is simply treating A and B as one person. The agent, acting on behalf of his principal, makes a contract between his principal and a third party.

However, the law goes further by permitting A to enforce a contract made on his behalf by B, despite the fact that C was unaware that B was acting on A's behalf. (Of course, A must prove that B did in fact have his authority to make the contract with C.) This idea of the "undisclosed principal" appears to be at variance with the doctrine of privity and it can, perhaps, be justified only on the basis of commercial convenience. The third party is contractually bound to a person with whom he did not intend to contract and of whose existence he was unaware.

Despite the obvious potential for evading the doctrine of privity through the idea of agency, the courts have been reluctant to imply an agency simply for this purpose. A person has to do more than merely claim that a contract was made on his behalf. For there to be an agency, one person has to acquire the authority to be the representative of another (see *Southern Water Authority* v *Carey* [1985] 2 All ER 1077). For example, an agent may have the express authority of his principal to act as his representative, or such authority may be implied as a result of the relationship between the parties. In either case, it is said that the agent has "actual" authority. Agency may also arise in other circumstances. For example, unless a third party is notified to the contrary, he is entitled to rely on an agent's "apparent" authority to represent another. So where A represents to C that he has given B authority to act as his representative, C is entitled to assume that B has the authority which he appears to have. (For a recent discussion of the scope of this doctrine, see *First Energy (UK) Ltd* v *Hungarian International Bank Ltd* [1993] BCLC 1409.)

The extent of the courts' willingness to accept an agency argument, as a means of circumventing the privity doctrine, was discussed at the start of this chapter in relation to attempts by third parties to rely on an exclusion clause. Here the issue is whether a third party can claim the benefit of an exclusion clause as a defence to an action by one of the contracting parties under a separate cause of action (usually negligence). It will be remembered that in *Scruttons Ltd* v *Midland Silicones Ltd* [1962] AC 446, the House of Lords held that the stevedores (third party) were not entitled to rely on the limitation of liability contained in the bill of lading, when sued in tort for their negligence in unloading the goods. The doctrine of privity prevented the stevedores from relying on a contract to which they were not a party in defending the action. The argument of the stevedores that they were the undisclosed principals of one of the contracting parties (the carrier), who acted as their agent, was also unsuccessful. Lord Reid set out (at p 474) the conditions which needed to be satisfied for the agency argument to succeed. He explained that the bill of lading must make it clear that the stevedore is intended to be protected by its provisions which limit liability. The bill of lading must make it clear that the carrier, as well as contracting for these provisions on his own behalf, is also contracting as an agent for the stevedore who will in turn be protected by the provisions. The carrier needs the stevedore's authority to act in this way, and any problems of consideration must be overcome.

Although the stevedores were unsuccessful with this agency argument in *Scruttons*, it will be recalled that the Privy Council, in *New Zealand Shipping Co Ltd* v *Satterthwaite* [1974] 1 All ER 1015, allowed the stevedores the protection of an exemption clause. In *Satterthwaite*, the court held (*inter alia*) that the bill of lading was not simply a contract between the owners of the goods and the carrier. It also represented a contract between the owners and the stevedores, made through the carrier as agent. (See also *Port Jackson Stevedoring Pty* v *Salmond & Spraggon (Australia) Pty* [1980] 3 All ER 257.) Despite the success of the agency argument in these cases, it provides a rather technical and uncertain solution to the problem. (For example, see *The Mahkutai* [1996] 3 All ER 502.) The courts naturally wish to take a practical approach to everyday commercial transactions, but a simpler solution is preferable to the one offered by the agency approach. A more convenient way of conferring such a benefit on a third party is now available under the new legislation (see earlier discussion). In the 1999 Act, references to a third party enforcing a contractual term are to be understood as including the right to rely on an exclusion or limitation clause (see s 1(6)).

7. Privity and the doctrine of consideration

In *Dunlop Pneumatic Tyre Co Ltd* v *Selfridge & Co Ltd* [1915] AC 847, Lord Haldane LC (at p 853) referred to the fundamental principles in English law that "only a person who is a party to a contract can sue on it . . . [and] that if a person with whom a contract not under seal has been made is to be able to enforce it consideration must have been given by him to the promisor or to some other person at the promisor's request". If we reconsider *Tweddle* v *Atkinson* (1861) 1 B & S 393 (discussed at the start of this chapter), the decision could be explained in terms of either lack of privity, or lack of consideration provided by the son-in-law. However, there has been much debate as to as to whether the privity doctrine is distinct and independent from the rule that consideration must move from the promisee, with academic opinion being quite divided on the subject[5].

The phrase "consideration must move from the promisee" is a little enigmatic, but it is generally accepted as meaning that a person can enforce a contractual promise only if he himself provided the consideration for that promise; ie consideration must have been provided by the claimant. When the phrase is understood in this sense, it is clear that it is not possible to "reform the privity doctrine while leaving untouched the rule that consideration must move from the promisee" (see Law Commission, *Privity of Contract: Contracts for the Benefit of Third Parties*, Law Com No 242, 1996, para 6.5), because the two doctrines are very closely linked. Accordingly, the Law Commission recommended that the legislation reforming the privity doctrine "should ensure that the rule that consideration must move from the promisee is reformed to the extent necessary to avoid nullifying [the] proposed reform of the doctrine of privity" (*ibid*, para 6.8). In the event, it was realised that a specific provision to this effect was unnecessary. It would be achieved by the central provision of the new law (ie s 1 of the 1999 Act) conferring a third party right to enforce a contractual term, as such a provision could only be interpreted as also reforming the rule that consideration must move from the promisee.

The Law Commission also addressed the wider policy implications, for the doctrine of consideration[6], of reforming the privity rule (*ibid*, paras 6.13–6.17). It was concerned, in particular, with the argument that a third party's right to enforce a contractual term puts him in a better position than a gratuitous promisee. However, by permitting an identified third party to enforce a contractual term, under s 1 of the 1999 Act, the law is giving effect to the intentions of the contracting parties, who have provided consideration; the bargain is being enforced, albeit by the third party. It can be argued that this situation is distinguishable from the one in which no consideration is given by a promisee in exchange for a promise (ie the gratuitous promisee); here, there is no bargain to be enforced, as no consideration was present.

The specific problem of whether a "joint promisee" who has provided none of the consideration under a contract can sue, is one which requires some discussion. Where a promise is made in favour of A and B, in circumstances where they can be regarded as joint promisees, but only A provides any consideration, can B enforce the promise? This problem was raised in the Australian case of *Coulls* v *Bagot's Executor and Trustee Co Ltd* [1967] ALR 385, where the facts were:

> Arthur Coulls agreed to give to the O'Neil Construction Co the sole right to quarry and remove stone from his land. The agreement continued: "O'Neil Construction Ltd agrees to pay at the rate of 3d per ton for all stone quarried and sold, also a fixed minimum royalty of £12 per week for a period of ten years with an option of another ten years [at the same rate]. . . I [Arthur Coulls] authorize the above Company to pay all money connected with this agreement to my wife, Doris Coulls

and myself, Arthur Coulls as joint tenants". This written agreement (not under seal) was signed by Arthur Coulls, Doris Coulls and O'Neil. After the death of Arthur Coulls, the O'Neil Company paid the royalty to Doris Coulls as agreed. The action involved a dispute between Arthur Coulls' executors and his wife as to who should receive the royalty payments.

It was held by a majority of the High Court of Australia that, after Arthur Coulls' death, the O'Neil Company was bound to pay the royalties to his estate and not to his wife. Three of the judges thought that Doris Coulls was not a party to the agreement and that the authority given by her husband to the company under the agreement, to make payments to her, lapsed on his death (ie she was not a promisee). It was thought significant that the husband had "authorised" payment to his wife; she was not entitled to payment in her own right. However, Barwick CJ and Windeyer J dissented, as they considered Doris Coulls to be a joint promisee. (The majority of the court were of the opinion that a joint promisee could sue even though he or she had provided no consideration.) In his judgment, Barwick CJ argued (at p 395) that the agreement was one in respect of which there was privity between the company and both the husband and wife, as joint promisees. Windeyer J (at p 403) thought that the promise of the company was to pay for the stone at the agreed rate, with "such payments to be made to the husband and wife jointly during their lives and thereafter to the survivor". Windeyer J went on to consider her apparent lack of consideration for the promise (at p 405):

"Still, it was said, no consideration moved from her. But that, I consider, mistakes the nature of a contract made with two or more persons jointly. The promise is made to them collectively. It must, of course, be supported by consideration, but that does not mean by considerations furnished by them separately. It means a consideration given on behalf of them all, and therefore moving from all of them. In such a case the promise of the promisor is not gratuitous: and, as between him and the joint promisees, it matters not how they were able to provide the price of his promise to them".

The Law Commission (*ibid*, para 6.10) argued that a joint promisee should have the right to sue despite not having provided the consideration. (See also *McEvoy* v *Belfast Banking Co Ltd* [1935] AC 24, *per* Lord Atkin, at p 43.) However, the Commission did not include such joint promisees within its reform proposals, for a variety of reasons which need not be considered here. It thought it preferable to leave the matter to the courts to develop "in the confident expectation" that, especially in view of the statutory reform of the privity doctrine, they will accept the joint promisee argument "so that a joint promisee who has not provided consideration will not be left without a basic right to enforce the contract" (at para 6.11).

8. Conclusion

The doctrine of privity has traditionally represented the principle that only a party to a contract can enforce a benefit, or have burdens imposed on him, under that contract. The restriction on a third party being able to enforce a provision which was intended for his benefit meant that the intentions of the contracting parties could be thwarted, and the reasonable expectations of the third party denied, by the doctrine. This necessitated a series of technical, and sometimes artificial, methods of evading the strict application of the privity rule. Also, a number of statutory exceptions were required to circumvent the doctrine in areas of commercial practice where its application was extremely inconvenient.

After repeated judicial and academic criticism over many years, and a detailed Law Commission report on the subject, the law was finally reformed by means of the important Contracts (Rights of Third Parties) Act 1999. However, the Act does not apply to all types of contract; nor does it directly affect the existing exceptions to and circumventions of the doctrine. It introduces a new, and more general, exception into the law, but the doctrine of privity was not abolished by the Act. The Law Commission (Law Com No 242, para 5.10) also expressed the view that the new Act should not be interpreted as preventing the future development of third party rights through the common law. (For example, see *London Drugs Ltd* v *Kuehne & Nagel International Ltd* (1992) 97 DLR (4th) 261, discussed in Chapter 9; for further discussion of the *London Drugs* case, and the role of the courts in making "incremental changes to the common law necessary to address emerging needs and values in society", see *Fraser River Pile and Dredge Ltd* v *Can-Drive Services Ltd* [2000] 1 Lloyd's Law Rep 199 (Supreme Court of Canada), *per* Iacobucci J, at pp 208–209.)

Finally, the aspect of the privity rule which states that a third party cannot have burdens imposed upon him by the contracting parties, has not been affected by the 1999 legislation. It should be noted, however, that certain contractual restrictions on the use of land are said to "run with the land" and can therefore burden people other than the original contracting parties. (The debate as to whether this principle has a wider application, beyond the boundaries of land law, requires no further elaboration here.)

Footnotes

(1) (1937) Cmnd 5449, at p 30. Para 48 states: "We therefore recommend that where a contract by its express terms purports to confer a benefit directly on a third party, the third party shall be entitled to enforce the provision in his own name, provided that the promisor shall be entitled to raise as against the third party any defence that would have been valid against the promisee. The rights of the third party shall be subject to cancellation of the contract by the mutual consent of the contracting parties at any time before the third party has adopted it either expressly or by conduct".

(2) See R Flannigan, "Privity — the End of an Era (Error)" (1987) 103 LQR 564.

(3) See Law Commission, *Privity of Contract: Contracts for the Benefit of Third Parties*, Law Com No 242, 1996, Cm 3329, at para 3.8.

(4) For further discussion of the Act, see M Dean, "Removing a Blot on the Landscape — the Reform of the Doctrine of Privity" [2000] JBL 143; P Kincaid, "Privity Reform in England" (2000) 116 LQR 43; and P Glover, "Contractual Rights for Third Parties" (1999) Law Soc Gaz 42.

(5) See Law Com No 242, footnote 3 above, at para 6.1.

(6) Also see C Mitchell, "Privity Reform and the Nature of Contractual Obligations" (1999) 19 Legal Studies, 229.

Chapter 19

Performance and breach

It is hardly surprising that much of what could be covered in a chapter dealing with performance and breach has already been discussed elsewhere. This chapter is largely a reminder of the relevant points to be considered.

1. Performance

(a) Discharge by performance and agreement

To begin with it is worth emphasising that, although we are often considering the situation where something has gone wrong with a contract, most contracts are performed without any problems arising. The usual way in which a party to a contract ceases to have any obligations under the contract is by doing what the contract requires. Where performance has been completed, and liability has ceased, the situation is referred to as discharge by performance.

What is required for performance of the contract will depend upon its express and implied terms and their construction (see Chapter 7). Often no fault will be required for a breach to occur, ie contractual obligations are often a matter of strict liability. For example, the terms implied by ss 12–15 Sale of Goods Act 1979, dealing with the title and, basically, the quality of the goods impose strict liability. They can be breached without any fault on the part of the seller. In contrast, terms requiring the exercise of a particular skill or expertise will normally require only that due care be taken in the exercise of the skill or expertise (see, for example, s 13 Supply of Goods and Services Act 1982; *Thake* v *Maurice* [1986] 1 All ER 497 — above page 93).

A breach will arise if there is disparity between what was promised and what has occurred, or not occurred, and there is no lawful excuse. The burden of proving that a breach has occurred lies on the party alleging that it has. Frustration (see Chapter 20) provides an example of "lawful excuse" for non-performance. It discharges both parties from further performance of the contract.

The parties themselves may have provided that the contract is to end upon the occurrence of a certain circumstance, a condition subsequent (see page 115). Alternatively, one party might be given an option to end the contract under certain circumstances. Those circumstances could include a breach by the other party which would not otherwise give rise to the right to terminate (ie the breach is not a breach of condition or a sufficiently serious breach of an innominate term). When that occurs, the damages awarded for the breach will not cover the loss of the rest of the contract, as they would do if the breach itself gave rise to the right to terminate (see page 130 and see *Financings Ltd v Baldock* [1963] 2 QB 104. But see also *Lombard North Central plc v Butterworth* [1987] 1 All ER 267).

The original contract may not provide for its termination but the parties may make a new agreement to end the original contract, ie a contract may be discharged by agreement. Any such fresh agreement raises the issue of consideration unless it is contained in a deed (see Chapter 4). There is no problem where it is decided to end a contract which is still executory, where both parties still have obligations to perform. The giving up of rights on each side will furnish the necessary consideration. The situation is more difficult where only one party still has to perform. That party should then supply fresh consideration for the agreement to end the original contract, but the recent decision in *Williams v Roffey Bros & Nicholls (Contractors) Ltd* [1990] 1 All ER 512 (see page 59), on what can constitute consideration, should be borne in mind — as should the possibilities of waiver or promissory estoppel (see Chapter 5). The same consideration problems arise where the parties agree to change their agreement, rather than end it. In addition, formality issues may arise where the original contract was one requiring formalities (Treitel, *The Law of Contract*, 10th ed, pp 170–173).

(b) Order of performance and independent obligations

The order of performance may be indicated by contingent conditions, ie where the performance of one party, A, is a condition precedent to the performance of the other party, B. In that situation, B does not have to perform until A has done so. An appropriate use of such contingent conditions can assist one party to encourage the other's performance (see page 116). However, if the obligations of the parties are independent, then non-performance by one party may not provide an excuse for the other's failure to perform. So, for example, the obligation of a tenant to pay rent is independent of the obligation of a landlord to repair (*Taylor v Webb* [1937] 2 KB 370) and the landlord's failure to repair does not entitle the tenant to withhold rent (see also *Liverpool City Council v Irwin* [1976] 2 All ER 39 — above page 104).

(c) Entire contracts

We have seen that there are certain contracts, called entire contracts, where partial performance by one party leaves him without any claim, under the contract, against the other party in relation to what he has done. When a sailor died before completion of the voyage, his widow was left without any claim for part of his wages for the voyage. The contract was entire and he was to be paid only on completion of the voyage (*Cutter v Powell* (1795) 6 Term Rep 320). However, the harshness of the "entire contracts" doctrine may be mitigated. It may, for example, be found that work done by one party has been adopted by the other party, who will have to pay for the value of the work done under a restitutionary action for *quantum meruit* (see Chapter 22). Thus in *Sumpter* v *Hedges* [1898] 1 QB 673 although Mr Hedges did not have to pay for the work which Mr Sumpter had done on the uncompleted houses, he did have to pay for the materials which Mr Sumpter had left on the site and which he (Mr Hedges) had made use of (see further page 133).

The greater mitigation of the "entire contracts" doctrine stems from the idea of "substantial performance". The incompletely performing party may be able to recover the sum due under the contract, less any damages payable as a result of the incomplete performance, if he has "substantially performed". So, for example, in *Hoenig* v *Isaacs* [1952] 2 All ER 176 Mr Hoenig was able to recover most of the £750 due under the contract in which he had agreed to decorate and furnish Mr Isaacs' flat, despite the fact that there were some defects in a bookcase and a wardrobe which would have cost about £55 to rectify. Mr Hoenig's substantial performance meant that he was not precluded entirely from recovering the contract price (see also *Bolton* v *Mahadeva* [1972] 2 All ER 1322 — see further page 134).

2. Breach

A breach of contract provides the injured party with a right to damages (see page 459), or he may be able to sue for the contract price (see page 496) if it has become due. On occasion equity may provide specific enforcement of the whole or part of the other party's obligations (see page 497). In addition, the question may arise of using a restitutionary remedy to recover sums paid or the value of goods or services supplied (see Chapter 22). Consideration may also need to be given to relief from forfeiture for the party in breach (see page 493).

However, one of the often disputed consequences of breach is that of the right to terminate the contract. When certain breaches occur, the injured party has a choice whether to terminate the contract.

(a) Termination for breach

An injured party has a right to damages for any breach (see page 459). However, we have also seen that the injured party occasionally also has the right to terminate the contract because of the other party's breach. So, for example, there is a right to terminate if there is a breach of condition or if there is a sufficiently serious breach of an innominate term (ie a breach which substantially deprives the injured party of all the benefit which he was intended to derive from the contract — *Hong Kong Fir Shipping Co Ltd* v *Kawasaki Kisen Kaisha Ltd* [1962] 2 QB 26, see above page 119). Such terms are labelled according to the intention of the parties at the time of contracting (*Bunge Corp* v *Tradax Export SA* [1981] 1 WLR 711 — see above page 117).

However, one party may repudiate the contract. He may indicate that he no longer intends to be bound by it, and that may be done in the context of an actual breach or an anticipatory breach (see below). The injured party will have the right to terminate where the other party gives "an intimation of an intention to abandon and altogether refuse performance of the contract . . . [or of] an intention no longer to be bound by the contract" (*Freeth* v *Burr* (1874) LR 9 CP 208 *per* Lord Coleridge at p 213). Determining whether the contract has been repudiated may be difficult. It can occur as a consequence of the party stating that he will not perform or, more problematically, by the parties' actions. For example, one party may allege that the other has rendered it impossible for him to perform the instant contract because that party has undertaken other obligations. It will then be a matter of finding whether those other obligations are "of such a nature or have such an effect that it can truly be said that the party in question has put it out of his power to perform" (*Toepfer International GmbH* v *Itex Itagrani Export SA* [1993] 1 Lloyd's Rep 360 at p 362). Another example of where difficulties arise is that of instalment contracts to be performed over a period of time. In *Decro-Wall International SA* v *Practitioners Marketing Ltd* [1971] 2 All ER 216, the facts were:

> The plaintiffs, a French manufacturing company, made a contract with the defendants giving the defendants the sole right to sell their products in the United Kingdom. The defendants undertook to develop the UK market for the plaintiffs' goods and were very successful in doing so. However, the defendants were obliged to pay for a batch of goods within ninety days of receiving it and they were often late in paying. Despite the successful market development by the defendants, the plaintiffs chose to terminate the contract for a late payment by the defendants. The plaintiffs never doubted that they would receive payment for goods delivered, even though it might often be late. The lateness of the payments caused them little damage.

The question for the Court of Appeal was "whether these past failures to pay on the due date, coupled with the likelihood of similar failures, constituted a repudiation of the contract" which entitled the plaintiffs to terminate. The Court of Appeal held that the termination had not been justified. The breaches which had occurred, and what was likely to happen in the future, did not go to the root of the contract.

The intention of the party in breach is relevant in this situation as it is in relation to an anticipatory breach; a mistake as to the requirements of the contract may be relevant here as with anticipatory breach, ie the party in breach may think that what he intends to do in the future will amount to performance whereas it will in fact amount to breach. There is difficulty with the court's treatment of such intention (see page 429).

When a breach occurs which could lead to termination, the injured party has a choice (*Decro-Wall International SA* v *Practitioners in Marketing Ltd* [1971] 2 All ER 216). He can terminate or he can decide to continue with the contract, to affirm it, in which case he is simply left with his remedy in damages.

Termination for breach is sometimes referred to as rescission of the contract, and this can be confusing. It is better to confine the use of the word rescission to the context of voidable contracts, for example where the contract has been made on the basis of a misrepresentation. In that context rescission is rescission *ab initio*; it is as if the contract had never existed. In the context of breach, rescission merely relates to the future.

> "[R]escission [for breach] is quite different from rescission *ab initio*, such as may arise for example in cases of mistake, fraud or lack of consent. In those cases the contract is treated in law as never having come into existence . . . In the cases of an accepted repudiatory breach the contract has come into existence but has been put an end to or discharged . . . acceptance of a repudiatory breach does not bring about rescission *ab initio*" (*Johnson* v *Agnew* [1979] 1 All ER 883 *per* Lord Wilberforce at p 889).

It is easier not to confuse the two situations if we refer to termination, rather than rescission, in relation to breach. What occurs on termination for breach can be more easily understood if we think of the contract in terms of primary and secondary obligations. The division is between the basic promised performance (primary obligations) and the obligations which arise on breach (secondary obligations). When X and Y have made a contract under which X is to build a wall for Y, and Y is to pay X for doing so, then the primary obligations relate to the building of the wall and the payment of money. When X refuses to build the wall, or builds a defective wall, there is a breach of X's primary obligations and the secondary obligation on X to pay damages arises. If the breach is merely a minor defect in the wall, Y will be able to claim damages from X for the breach and X and Y will still be liable to perform any further primary obligations. However, when X's breach is such as to entitle Y to terminate the contract, and he chooses to do so, the primary obligations cease, but damages are still calculated in relation to the promised performance. There is no question of the situation becoming one where the contract is treated as if it had never existed. In *Photo Production* v *Securicor Transport* [1980] 1 All ER 556 Lord Diplock analysed the situation, in relation to the unperformed obligations, in terms of primary and secondary obligations and made the continuing role of the contract clear. He said (at p 567):

> "[W]here such an election [to terminate] is made (a) there is substituted by implication of law for the primary obligations of the party in default which remain unperformed a secondary obligation to pay monetary compensation to the other party for the loss sustained by him in consequence of their non-performance in the future and (b) the unperformed primary obligations of that other party are discharged".

When there is a breach which gives rise to termination, the party in breach must pay damages for the immediate consequences of the breach and, in addition, for the loss caused by the non-performance of the rest of his primary obligations. In the secondary obligations the continued life of the contract is clear, as is the distinction between termination for breach and rescission *ab initio*.

A situation may arise in which one party claims to be able to terminate, because of the breach of the other, but he gives a reason which does not in fact justify termination. If, at the time of termination, there is another, unstated, reason which would justify that termination, then it can usually be relied upon by the party who is terminating to prevent his actions from themselves being a repudiatory breach. In *The Mihalis Angelos* [1971] 1 QB 164 the charterers had purported to cancel the charter on the basis of a *force majeure* clause. In fact, the charterers had no right to cancel on that basis. However, they were subsequently held not to be in breach because the owners had been in breach of a condition of the contract. That breach of condition had given the charterers the right to terminate when they had claimed to do so. It did not matter that they had not stated the correct justification for their termination at the time.

However, a party who initially states an invalid reason for terminating will not be able to rely upon an effective reason, which is only subsequently brought to the other party's attention, "if the point which was not taken could have been put right", ie where not stating the correct justification has prevented the other party from dealing with it (*Heisler* v *Anglo-Dal Ltd* [1954] 1 WLR 1273, at p 1278). It may also be that the party who claimed to be able to terminate will be estopped from asserting a true basis of termination, or will be taken to have waived it (*Glencore Grain* v *Lebanese Organisation for International Commerce* [1997] 4 All ER 514).

(b) Anticipatory breach

We now need to consider the question of anticipatory breach. This involves looking at the situation when X and Y have made a contract and, before the time for performance arrives, X declares that he no longer intends to perform. X is said to repudiate the contract and Y has the option to terminate the contract and claim damages at that point.

Anticipatory breach, therefore, refers to the situation, before the time for performance, when one party has indicated to the other that he does not intend to perform the contract. He may have done so expressly, or his actions may have shown that to be the situation. He may, for example, sell to Z the goods which the contract already requires him to deliver to Y. What is required is "an intimation of an intention to abandon and altogether to refuse performance of the contract ... [or of] an intention no longer to be bound by the contract" (*Freeth* v *Burr* (1874) LR 9 CP 208 *per* Lord Coleridge at p 213). This encompasses the situation where one party may wish to perform but his act or default has made it impossible for him to do so (*Universal Cargo Carriers Corporation* v *Citati* [1957] 2 QB 401). The "impossibility situation" then has to be distinguished from frustration which occurs when the impossibility is not self-induced (see page 449).

On the occurrence of X's anticipatory breach of his contract with Y, Y has a choice. Y can either keep the contract alive or he can accept X's repudiation and terminate it. If Y decides to keep the contract alive, he has no immediate right to damages. He will be able to claim damages only if X persists in his attitude and does not perform at the appointed time. In that case Y is simply suing for a breach because X has not performed at the time when performance became due. However, if Y accepts the repudiation and terminates the contract, he can sue for damages immediately, on the basis of X's anticipatory breach. Even if he does not accept the repudiation, and cannot therefore sue for damages at that point, he may still be granted, immediately, an order for specific performance compelling X to perform when performance becomes due (*Hasham* v *Zenab* [1960] AC 316). Termination, or acceptance of repudiation, does not require a particular form of communication.

> "An act of acceptance of a repudiation requires no particular form; a communication does not have to be couched in the language of acceptance. It is sufficient that the communication or conduct clearly and unequivocally conveys to the repudiating party that the aggrieved party is treating the contract as at an end." (*Vitol SA* v *Norelf Ltd* [1996] 3 All ER 193, *per* Lord Steyn at p 200.)

It is even possible for the injured or aggrieved party to be seen as having accepted a repudiatory breach, simply through not performing their further obligations under the contract, although a failure to act will often be equivocal (*Vitol SA* v *Norelf Ltd*).

Hochster v *De La Tour* (1853) 2 E & B 678 made it clear that damages can be claimed immediately on the basis of an accepted anticipatory breach, without any need to wait for the time of performance. In that case:

> In April 1852 the defendant made a contract with the plaintiff for the plaintiff to act as a courier for him from 1 June. On 11 May the defendant told the plaintiff that he had changed his mind, and that the plaintiff's services would not be required. On 22 May the plaintiff commenced an action against the defendant.

The court had to consider the defendant's claim that he could not be in breach of contract, and an action could not be commenced, before 1 June. The court rejected this and held that the plaintiff could sue successfully before the date for performance. A similar result was reached in *Frost* v *Knight* (1872) 7 LR Ex 111. In that case the defendant had promised the plaintiff that he would marry her when his father died. Subsequently the defendant broke off his engagement to the plaintiff. She took action while the defendant's father was still alive and was successful in her claim.

The basic requirement for an anticipatory breach is an intention not to perform. That is quite simple where one party is aware that what he intends will mean that the contract will be broken when it is time for performance. The situation is more complicated where one party mistakenly believes that what he intends is in keeping with the contractual requirements. However, even under those circumstances, what he intends to do is still a breach, and that was the line taken in *Federal Commerce and Navigation Co Ltd* v *Molena Alpha Inc* [1979] 1 All ER 307. In that case:

> The charterers and owners had made a time charter of a ship. The charterers deducted certain sums from their periodic hire payments. The owners disputed their right to do so and told the master not to issue freight pre-paid bills of lading. The owners thought that they were entitled to take that line. Effectively the charterers could not make use of the ship if such bills of lading could not be issued.

The charterers claimed that the owners' instructions to their ship's master amounted to a wrongful repudiation of the contract. The House of Lords found for the charterers, despite the fact that the owners had believed that they were acting within their rights and did not want to lose the charter.

Lord Wilberforce said (at p 315):

> "If a party's conduct is such as to amount to a threatened repudiatory breach, his subjective desire to maintain the contract cannot prevent the other party from drawing the consequences of his actions".

However, a different approach was adopted in *Woodar Investment Development Ltd* v *Wimpey Construction UK Ltd* [1980] 1 WLR 277:

> There was a contract for the sale of land. The contract stated that in certain circumstances the buyer, Wimpey, would be entitled to terminate. Wimpey honestly misconstrued the contract and wrongly thought that circumstances giving rise to the express right to terminate were present. Changes in the market made the contract uneconomic for Wimpey, and Wimpey wrongly claimed to be entitled to terminate. The seller, Woodar, argued that this amounted to a repudiation of the contract.

A majority of the House of Lords held that the seller, Woodar, could not claim damages for a repudiatory breach of contract. Their lordships felt that as Wimpey mistakenly believed that it was exercising a contractual right, it was seeking to act within the contract and not to repudiate it

More recently, the question of mistaken demands, which were actually in breach of contract, was considered by the Privy Council in *Vaswani* v *Italian Motors Ltd* [1996] 1 WLR 270. The case was concerned with a contract for the sale of a Ferrari Testarossa. A deposit was paid, but when the delivery time arrived, the sellers mistakenly demanded a higher price than that contracted for (the contract allowed for an increase in the price for some reasons but not others). There was a clause allowing for forfeit of the deposit if, when the car was ready for delivery, the buyer failed to pay the outstanding amount within seven days. When the buyer failed to make payment, the sellers forfeited the deposit. Attempting to apply both *Federal Commerce and Navigation Co Ltd* v *Molena Alpha Inc* and *Woodar Investment Development Ltd* v *Wimpey Construction UK Ltd*, the court held that the mistaken demand for a sum as payment was not, by itself, sufficient to amount to a repudiatory breach. Lord Woolf said (at p 276):

> "While therefore here the request for the payment of an excessive price would not in itself amount to a repudiation, if the conduct relied on went beyond the assertion of a genuinely held view of the effect of the contract the conduct could amount to repudiation. This is the position if the conduct is inconsistent with the continuance of the contract."

In the instant case the conduct was not seen as inconsistent with the continuance of the contract and, in the view of the court, was not repudiatory. This was explained further. It was said (at p 277):

> "In this case while the sellers did indicate to the buyer that he should pay a sum which was excessive or the deposit would be forfeited they never went so far as to indicate to the buyer that it would be purposeless to pay the correct sum required . . . All they had done was to put forward their calculation which had gone unchallenged. There was nothing to prevent the buyer paying the sum he calculated was due. Until he at least tendered the sum he considered was due the sellers were not required to deliver the vehicle . . . The sellers did not threaten a 'breach of the contract with serious consequences' as in *Federal Commerce and Navigation Co Ltd* v *Molena Alpha Inc*, and there was no conduct by them which was totally inconsistent with the continuance of the contract".

When an anticipatory breach occurs, the injured party may decide to keep the contract alive. What are the consequences of that decision? In *Avery* v *Bowden* (1856) 6 E & B 953, the court considered the situation where the innocent party had elected not to accept the defendant's repudiation of the contract. He had kept the contract alive in the hope that performance would ensue. In that case:

> The defendant had chartered the plaintiff's ship to load a cargo at Odessa within forty-five days. The ship was ready to load but the defendant repeatedly told the ship's captain that he could not obtain a cargo. Before the forty-five days were up, the Crimean war started and the contract was frustrated. The outbreak of war had made it illegal to load a cargo at an enemy port.

It was held that the plaintiff could not recover damages. In the first place the court did not think that what the defendant had done was sufficient to amount to a repudiatory breach. However, even if it had been sufficient, the plaintiff still did not have a cause of action. The court thought that such an anticipatory breach could not found a cause of action until it was accepted by the plaintiff. In this case the plaintiff had not accepted the repudiation. He had continued to ask for performance until war was declared and the contract was frustrated.

In *Avery* v *Bowden* the contract was kept alive only to be frustrated. However, keeping the contract alive may also provide the party who had evinced an intention to repudiate with an opportunity to terminate because of the other party's breach. If the contract is kept alive, it is kept alive for the benefit of both parties. The party who would have been the injured party, had he accepted the repudiation, may himself subsequently commit a breach and be liable for the consequences of so doing. In *Fercometal Sarl* v *Mediterranean Shipping Co SA* [1988] 2 All ER 742:

> A charterparty contained a clause enabling the charterer to cancel if the ship was not ready to load by 9 July. Before 9 July, the charterer wrongfully purported to cancel the charter. The owner could have accepted that purported termination as a repudiation but chose to continue with the contract. The ship was not ready to load on 9 July. The charterer claimed to cancel on the basis of the express provision for cancellation.

The House of Lords held that the charterer could take advantage of the express right to cancel. The owner had chosen to continue the contract, and that kept the contract alive for the benefit of both parties. The charterer's earlier conduct did not prevent the charterer from taking action on a subsequent breach by the owner. The earlier case of *Braithwaite* v *Foreign Hardwood Co Ltd* [1905] 2 KB 543 can no longer be regarded as establishing that if X repudiates a contract with Y, and Y does not accept the repudiation, Y is nevertheless excused his subsequent non-performance of his obligations. However, Y's non-performance of a particular obligation might not be actionable by X if X was estopped from such a claim, ie if X had indicated that he would no longer require Y to perform a particular obligation and Y had relied upon that in not making himself ready to perform.

The above cases illustrate the danger in deciding to keep the contract alive, rather than accepting the repudiation and terminating the contract. However, even where the repudiation is accepted, events which would inevitably have occurred before the time for performance may still be relevant to the question of damages. In *The Mihalis Angelos* [1971] 1 QB 164:

> There was a charterparty which stated that the ship was "expected ready to load" at Haiphong about 1 July. Clause 11 provided that if the ship was not ready to load by 20 July the charterers had an option to cancel the charterparty. The charterers purported to cancel on 17 July, and the owners accepted that as a repudiation of the contract.

It was held that, although it was clear on 17 July that the ship would not be ready to load by 20 July, the charterers could not exercise the option before 20 July. Nevertheless, the charterers had been entitled to cancel because the owners were in breach of condition. The owners had stated that the ship was "expected ready to load" on 1 July without having any reasonable grounds for such an expectation. The owners were in breach of a condition and, on that basis, the charterers could terminate the contract. However, the Court of Appeal also stated that, even had that not been the case, the owners would have recovered only nominal damages — and that is the important point in this context, ie had there been no breach of condition by the owners, the Court of

Appeal would have been prepared to award them only nominal damages for what would then have been a repudiatory breach by the charterers on 17 July. Only nominal damages would have been available because, on 17 July, it was inevitable that the ship would not arrive by 20 July and, on 20 July, the charterers would have been able to exercise the option to terminate the contract without breaching it. In other words the owners would not have received performance anyway, even had there been no breach on 17 July, and they would not have suffered a substantial loss through a repudiatory breach on 17 July. Lord Denning MR said (at p 196):

> "[T]he damages must be assessed by compensating the injured party for the loss he has suffered by the renunciation. One must take into account all contingencies which might have reduced or extinguished that loss ... the plaintiff must be compensated for such loss as he would have suffered had there been no renunciation ... Seeing that the charterers would, beyond doubt, have cancelled, I am clearly of the opinion that the shipowners suffered no loss and would be entitled at most to nominal damages".

(See also Megaw LJ at p 210 and Edmund Davies LJ at pp 202–203.)

There is a further difficult problem to be considered in the relationship between the injured party's choice in respect of the other party's anticipatory breach and the duty to mitigate. The duty to mitigate means that the injured party will not receive damages to cover any loss which the injured party would not have incurred had he behaved reasonably on breach. The problem is that if the injured party chooses not to accept the repudiation, then there is no breach at that point and no duty to mitigate. Of course, in most cases, the injured party will not be able to perform if the other party will not co-operate, but what of the exceptional cases? In exceptional cases the injured party will be able to perform without the co-operation of the other party and will then be able to put himself into the position where he can claim in debt for the money due under the contract, rather than having to sue for damages for breach. If the injured party can sue for the debt, he will not be concerned with the rules restricting recovery of damages, including the duty to mitigate. This can lead to the injured party claiming payment for an unwanted and "wasted" performance, which contrasts awkwardly with the mitigation rule's limitation on recovery. The point arises from the decision in *White and Carter (Councils) Ltd* v *McGregor* [1962] AC 413. In that case:

> The plaintiffs supplied litter bins to local councils and then made money by selling advertising on them. The defendants contracted for three years of advertisements of their garage business but, that same day, they repudiated the contract. The plaintiffs refused to accept the repudiation and went ahead with the advertisements.

Eventually the plaintiffs claimed the sum owed to them under the contract in return for their performance and, by a bare majority, the House of Lords allowed the claim. Obviously the plaintiffs could have simply accepted the repudiation and claimed damages at that point. Instead they chose to expend more money to carry out a performance which was no longer wanted. The case sits uneasily alongside the mitigation rule. However, Lord Reid suggested a qualification upon the injured party's right to choose not to accept the repudiation, to continue to perform, and to claim the sum due under the contract. He thought that if it could be shown that the injured party had "no legitimate interest" in performing, rather than accepting the repudiation and claiming damages, he ought not to be able to "saddle the other party with an additional burden with no benefit to himself" (at p 431). Support for Lord Reid's limitation can be found in the Court of Appeal in *The Puerto Buitrago (Attica Sea Carriers Corporation* v *Ferrostaal Poseidon Bulk Reederei GmbH* [1976] 1 Lloyd's Rep 250 where *White and Carter* v *McGregor* was distinguished. Lord Reid's approach was followed by Lloyd J in *The Alaskan Trader (Clea Shipping Corporation* v *Bulk Oil International)* [1984] 1 All ER 129. In that case:

> The charterers had repudiated a charterparty when the ship required repairs because of a serious problem with the engines. The owners would not accept the repudiation but repaired the ship and kept it ready, fully crewed, for the charterers for seven months until the end of the charter period.

The question then was whether the owners could recover the hire for that period. Lloyd J upheld the decision of the arbitrator that they could not. They had no legitimate interest in doing so rather than claiming damages. If a replacement charter could not be found, it would have been less costly if they had not kept the ship with a full crew, ready to sail, for that period. (See also *Stocznia Gdanska SA* v *Latvian Shipping Co* [1996] 2 Lloyd's Rep 132. But see *The Odenfeld (Gator Shipping Corp* v *Trans-Asiatic Occidental Shipping Establishment)* [1978] 2 Lloyd's Rep 357.)

Chapter 20

The doctrine of frustration

1. Introduction: initial and subsequent impossibility

After the parties have concluded a contract, events beyond their control may occur which "frustrate" the purpose of their agreement, or render it very difficult, or impossible, or even illegal, to perform. For example, where a hall which has been booked for the performance of a play is destroyed by fire, after the contract has been concluded, but before the date of performance of the play. Some writers have seen a close resemblance between this type of "subsequent impossibility" and the subject of common mistake (also referred to as "initial impossibility"). Indeed there are similarities between the two subjects. Both provide an important opportunity to define the strength of contractual obligations. How absolute are they? Under what circumstances will a party be excused from performing his contractual undertakings or from having to provide a remedy to the other? There are close similarities in some of the factual situations to which the two types of "impossibility" apply. (For example, contrast *Griffith* v *Brymer* (1903) 19 TLR 434 and *Krell* v *Henry* [1903] 2 KB 740. The former was decided on the basis of mistake and the latter on the basis of frustration.)

In certain circumstances, it may be a fine, almost tenuous, dividing line between these two different branches of contract law. In *Amalgamated Investment & Property Co Ltd* v *John Walker & Sons Ltd* [1976] 3 All ER 509, for example, the facts were:

> The defendants owned a commercial property which they advertised for sale as being suitable for occupation or redevelopment. In July 1973 the plaintiffs agreed, subject to contract, to buy the property for £1,710,000. The defendants knew that the plaintiffs' purpose in purchasing the property was to redevelop it and that they would require planning permission to do so. In their enquiries before entering into a binding contract, the plaintiffs asked the defendants whether the property was designated (ie, "listed") as a building of special architectural or historic interest. The defendants replied, on 14 August, that it was not. This was correct at the time. But in January 1973, unknown to the parties, officials at the Department of the Environment had included the property in a provisional list of buildings to be listed as being of architectural or historic interest. On 25 September, the parties signed the contract of sale. On 26 September, the Department of the Environment wrote to the defendants and informed them that the property had been included in the statutory list of buildings of special interest. (The list was given legal effect the following

day.) It transpired that the property had been unconditionally selected for inclusion in the list on 22 August. The value of the building without redevelopment potential was one and a half million pounds less than the contract price! The plaintiffs claimed rescission of the agreement on the basis of common mistake, or alternatively, they sought a declaration that the agreement was void or voidable and an order rescinding the agreement.

The plaintiffs' action was unsuccessful and specific performance was ordered against them. The case could not be treated as one of common mistake as the mistake did not exist at the time the contract was concluded. It was after the contract was made that the property was actually listed. (In the opinion of the court, the earlier inclusion of the property in the list of buildings of special interest was merely an administrative step towards listing.) The alternative argument put forward by the plaintiffs was that the contract was frustrated; that is, they had paid a high price for a property on the basis of its redevelopment potential and subsequently found that this objective was not possible to achieve. This contention was also rejected by the Court of Appeal as the plaintiffs were assumed to have taken the risk that the building may have been listed at some time after the contract was concluded. They were very unlucky that it was listed so soon after purchase but this was an inherent risk in the ownership of buildings (*per* Buckley J, at p 517). In other words, it was foreseeable that the obtaining of planning permission, which was crucial to the plaintiffs, might be thwarted by the listing of the building.

Although the plaintiffs' action failed, and they could claim neither common mistake nor frustration, the case is instructive with regard to the distinction between these two separate branches of contract law. The difference between initial and subsequent impossibility turned on the precise time at which the building was listed. Yet it is clear from the evidence that this "listing" was more of a process than a single decision or event. Is there any logical or practical reason why this factual situation should not be treated as one of mistake rather than one of frustration? (Of course, we do not know whether the plaintiffs would have succeeded even if the case had been treated as one of mistake.) The law seems rather rigid in its approach to these two related areas of impossibility when much may depend on a matter of days or even hours. The traditional justification for a rigid distinction between the two subjects is that mistake is concerned with the formation of contracts, whereas frustration deals with the discharge of contracts that have already been concluded. This explanation tends to ignore the difficulties posed by cases such as *Amalgamated Investment & Property Co Ltd v John Walker & Sons Ltd*.

2. Development of the doctrine of frustration

The doctrine of frustration is a means of dealing with situations where events occur, after the contract has been concluded, which render the agreement illegal, or impossible to perform, or even commercially sterile. The frustrating event must also not be the fault of either party or foreseeable. Of course, the parties might expressly provide for the consequences of a frustrating event by what is known as a *force majeure* clause. For example, a building contract might provide for what will happen in the event of a strike. In this way the parties themselves deal with the consequences of future events which might affect performance, and the doctrine of frustration will not apply. Certain types of agreement, for example export sales, shipping, building or engineering contracts, are particularly susceptible to disruption by unforeseen events. But, in the absence of express provision by the parties, the doctrine of frustration is a legal recognition of the fact that in some instances it is just to excuse a party from his contractual obligations.

Until a little over a hundred years ago, the law was reluctant to excuse a party his performance of a contract even in cases where supervening events rendered that performance difficult or impossible. The rationale of this rule was that a party could always make express provision for unforeseen events and, if he did not do so, he should be bound by his contractual obligations. This is known as the "absolute contracts" rule, which was clearly stated in the seventeenth century case of *Paradine* v *Jane* (1647) Aleyn 26. In this case, P brought an action against D for the rent due on a lease. D argued that he had been dispossessed of the land by force by an "alien born, enemy to the king and kingdom [who] had invaded the realm with an hostile army of men". D claimed that due to events beyond his control he had lost the profits from the land and, therefore, that he was not liable for the rent. This plea was rejected by the court. D had undertaken an obligation to pay rent under a contract and he was bound to fulfil this despite the supervening events. He could always have expressly covered this contingency in his contract with P.

This rigid approach has been mitigated, to some extent, by the gradual development of the doctrine of frustration. However, it must be emphasised that the doctrine operates within strict limits and does not provide an easy means of escape for those who have simply made a bad bargain (see *Amalgamated Investment & Property Co Ltd* v *John Walker & Sons Ltd* above). The famous case which marks the recognition of the doctrine is *Taylor* v *Caldwell* (1863) 3 B & S 826. The facts were as follows:

> On 27 May 1861, Taylor entered into a contract with Caldwell which gave T the use of the Surrey Gardens and music hall on four separate days later that summer. T was to use the premises for a series of four concerts, and for holding day and night fêtes on the days in question, and he was to pay £100 for each day. After the contract was concluded, but before the date of the first concert, the music hall was destroyed by fire. The fire was not the fault of either party and it made the performance of the concerts impossible. No express provision had been made by the parties to cover this contingency. T claimed damages for the money he had wasted in advertising the concerts.

It was held that the defendants were not liable and T's claim for damages did not succeed. This seems a fair decision but how did the court circumvent the general rule that in a contract to do a positive thing, a person must perform it or pay damages for failure to do so? Blackburn J stated that this rule applies only where the contract is not subject to any condition either express or implied. He continued (at p 833):

> "... [T]here are authorities which, as we think, establish the principle that where, from the nature of the contract, it appears that the parties must from the beginning have known that it could not be fulfilled unless when the time for the fulfilment of the contract arrived some particular specified thing continued to exist, so that, when entering into the contract, they must have contemplated such continuing existence as the foundation of what was to be done; there, in the absence of any express or implied warranty that the thing shall exist, the

contract is not to be construed as a positive contract, but as subject to an implied condition that the parties shall be excused in case, before breach, performance becomes impossible from the perishing of the thing without default of the contractor."

The judge held that the continued existence of the music hall was essential to the performance of the contract and the parties contracted on this basis. Although there was no express provision to this effect, the court implied one as a matter of construction. If the parties had thought about it when making the contract, they would have agreed to such a condition. In other words the doctrine of frustration, as established in *Taylor* v *Caldwell*, was based on an effort to give effect to the presumed intention of the parties.

The importance of the case is that it established the doctrine of frustration and made deep inroads into the notion of absolute contractual obligations. But, as we shall see, there is some debate about the theoretical basis of the doctrine. For example, in *Shell UK Ltd* v *Lostock Garage Ltd* [1977] 1 All ER 481 at p 487, Lord Denning stated (*obiter*) that "the legal effect of frustration does not depend on an implied term. It does not depend on the presumed intention of the parties, nor on what they would have answered, if asked, but simply on what the court itself declares to amount to a frustration". In other words, the court is imposing a fair solution, in the event of unforeseen circumstances, rather than giving effect to the presumed contractual intention of the parties.

Once the doctrine of frustration had been established, its scope had to be determined. *Taylor* v *Caldwell* dealt with the physical destruction of the subject matter of a contract, and its result was unexceptionable. Similarly, where a contract is made to do something which subsequently becomes illegal (eg trading with a country against which war is later declared), there is no difficulty in treating the contract as frustrated. But a more common and problematic type of case is where the commercial purpose of a contract is drastically affected by unforeseen events, whilst the performance of the contract remains physically and legally possible. A good example is the famous case of *Krell* v *Henry* [1903] 2 KB 740, where the facts were:

> Henry (D) agreed to hire a flat in Pall Mall from Krell (P) for the days of 26 and 27 June. These were the days that the coronation processions of Edward VII were to take place and the windows in the flat afforded good views of the procession route. D agreed in writing, on 20 June, to pay £75 for the exclusive use of the flat on the two days of the processions. The contract made no express reference to the coronation procession or to any other purpose. A deposit of £25 was paid by D at the time of contracting and the balance was to be paid the day before the processions took place. Due to the King's illness, the processions did not take place on the proposed days. Krell claimed £50 from Henry, who in turn counterclaimed for the return of the £25 which he had already paid under the contract.

The Court of Appeal decided that the contract was frustrated despite the fact that its performance was still physically possible. The doctrine is not strictly limited to "cases in which the event causing the impossibility of performance is the destruction or non-existence of some thing which is the subject-matter of the contract or of some condition or state of things expressly specified as a condition of it" (*per* Vaughan Williams LJ at p 749). Accordingly, the doctrine was applied in circumstances where some event, which must reasonably be regarded as the basis of the contract, failed to take place. The flat in Pall Mall could still have been used on the days in question, but the true purpose of the contract was frustrated by the postponement of the processions. Vaughan Williams LJ stated (at p 750):

"In my judgement, the use of the rooms was let and taken for the purpose of seeing the royal processions . . . It was a licence to use rooms for a particular purpose and none other. And in my judgement the taking place of those processions on the days proclaimed along the proclaimed route, which passed 56A, Pall Mall, was regarded by both contracting parties as the foundation of the contract. I think that it cannot reasonably be supposed to have been in the contemplation of the contracting parties, when the contract was made, that the coronation would not be held on the proclaimed days, or the processions not take place on those days along the proclaimed route; and I think that the words imposing on the defendant the obligation to accept and pay for the use of the rooms for the named days, although general and unconditional, were not used with reference to the possibility of the particular contingency which afterwards occurred."

This was a potentially far-reaching and controversial decision. It extended the doctrine to cases where the commercial object or purpose of the contract was frustrated. It raises problems as to what exactly is the "foundation" of a particular contract (for instance, contrast the decision in *Krell* v *Henry* with that in *Herne Bay Steam Boat Co* v *Hutton* [1903] 2 KB 683, below). Although the outcome of *Krell* v *Henry* seems fair, the courts have to be careful not to allow a party a convenient means of escape from a contract simply because it turns out to be a bad bargain. *Krell* v *Henry* represents, perhaps, the furthest development of the doctrine of frustration and subsequent cases have suggested a rather narrower view. It is unlikely that any further extension of this authority will be permitted by the courts[1].

3. A narrower interpretation of frustration

In *Krell* v *Henry* it was clear that the foundation of the contract was the taking place of the coronation processions on the planned dates. A suite of rooms in Pall Mall would not normally be hired on a daily basis and the high price clearly indicated that the contracting parties had a specific and common purpose or object in entering into the agreement. For these reasons, it was a very unusual case indeed. More typically, where a party hires or leases property from another it may be less obvious whether they share a common object. Their individual motives for contracting may be different and it may be difficult to say whether the common purpose is frustrated. The property which is to be hired may be susceptible to different types of use and enjoyment. Therefore, some restriction on the use of the subject matter of the contract, due to supervening events, will not necessarily result in the contract being discharged under the doctrine of frustration.

An interesting contrast to *Krell* v *Henry* is provided by *Herne Bay Steamboat Co* v *Hutton* [1903] 2 KB 683. The facts were that D agreed to hire the steamboat *Cynthia* from P for £250, on 28 and 29 June 1902, "for the purpose of viewing the naval review and for a day's cruise round the fleet". A deposit of £50 was paid in advance. The royal naval review, which was intended as part of the coronation festivities, was subsequently cancelled due to the King's illness. However, the fleet was still anchored at Spithead on 28 June. D did not use the *Cynthia* on either of the agreed days and P sued for the balance of the hire charge. It was held that P could recover the £200 from D and that the contract was not discharged on the ground of frustration.

At first sight it might be difficult to see why the case was decided differently from *Krell* v *Henry*. But on closer examination it is possible to distinguish it and to emphasise the limited application of *Krell* v *Henry*. It was held by the Court of Appeal, in *Herne Bay*, that the taking place of the royal review was not the foundation of the contract, despite the reference made to this event in the contract. It was still possible to cruise round the fleet and therefore the whole purpose of the contract was not frustrated. It is also significant that the contract was for the hire of a boat — something which is frequently hired for a variety of purposes, whereas in *Krell* v *Henry* it was highly unusual for rooms in Pall Mall to be let by the day. It seems that the contract in *Herne Bay* was for the hiring of a boat by D to make a certain voyage which it was still possible to make. The hirer had a particular object in mind, but this object was not the concern of P as owners of the boat. The contract was not physically impossible to perform, nor was the common purpose of both parties totally defeated. For these reasons the case can be distinguished from *Krell* v *Henry*, but it is clearly a very fine distinction.

The strict limits of the doctrine of frustration can be further illustrated by *Tsakiroglou & Co Ltd* v *Noblee Thorl GmbH* [1962] AC 93. The facts were as follows:

> The appellants contracted to sell groundnuts to the respondents at a price which included the carriage of the goods from the Sudan to Hamburg. Although no reference was made to this in the contract, it was assumed that shipment of the goods would be via the Suez Canal. The price of the nuts was calculated on this basis. After the contract was made, but before its performance, the Suez Canal was closed to commercial traffic due to political events. The alternative route, via the Cape of Good Hope, would have taken the appellants more than twice as long to ship the goods and would have doubled the cost of carriage. The appellants did not make the shipment and claimed that the contract had been frustrated by the closure of the Suez Canal.

The House of Lords rejected this argument. It was still possible to ship the goods, albeit at greater expense, and the contract was not discharged. The court refused to imply a term that the goods were to be shipped by the most direct route. The fact that the appellants had made what turned out to be a bad bargain did not by itself lead to the doctrine of frustration being applied. (The *John Walker* case, discussed earlier, is another vivid illustration of this point.) A court should not re-write the contract for the parties. The appellants were under a contractual obligation to ship the goods to Hamburg by any reasonable route that was available.

In *British Movietonews Ltd* v *London and District Cinemas* [1952] AC 166, another decision which shows the limited application of the doctrine, the contract in question related to the supply of films during the Second World War. The dispute occurred over the arrangements for termination of the contract. In 1943 a government order imposed certain restrictions on film supplies and, in a second agreement, the parties altered their termination arrangements until "such time as the Order is cancelled". It was presumably the parties' intention that this later (second) agreement should prevail only for the duration of wartime conditions.

The Court of Appeal was willing to hold that the contract was frustrated, when the Order continued after 1945 for reasons other than national safety, and to depart from the literal words of the agreement by giving effect to the presumed intentions of the parties. However, its decision was reversed by the House of Lords and the narrower approach to frustration was upheld. The House of Lords, as in *Tsakiroglou*, was not prepared to re-write the agreement for the contracting parties on the basis of what they were presumed to have intended at the time the contract was made. The parties were not to be discharged lightly from their contractual obligations despite the obvious hardship to one of them. In the words of Lord Simon (at p 185):

> "The parties to an executory contract are often faced, in the course of carrying it out, with a turn of events which they did not at all anticipate — a wholly abnormal rise or fall in prices, a sudden depreciation of currency, an unexpected obstacle to the execution, or the like. Yet this does not in itself affect the bargain which they have made".

It is well established that financial hardship alone is no reason for allowing a party to a contract to rely on the doctrine of frustration. A clear statement to this effect was made by the House of Lords in *Davis Contractors Ltd* v *Fareham UDC* [1956] AC 696. The facts were:

> Davis Contractors agreed to build seventy-eight houses for a local council, for the sum of £92,425, within an eight month period. Due to serious shortages of skilled labour and materials, the work took twenty-two months to complete and cost Davis Contractors approximately £18,000 more than they had estimated. The contractors argued that the contract with Fareham Council was frustrated due to the long delay which was the fault of neither party. They attempted to claim a larger sum than the agreed contract price as a fair reward for the services they had performed for the council (ie, they claimed on a *quantum meruit* basis).

The House of Lords rejected the argument of Davis Contractors; the contract was not frustrated. The parties had contracted for a specific number of houses which had now been built as agreed. There was no change in the basic obligations under the contract. Mere hardship or inconvenience to one of the contracting parties was not enough to frustrate a contract. Given the uncertainty in the supply of materials and labour at that time, the contractors could have made some express stipulation about this in the contract, yet they failed to do so. They were not allowed to escape from a bad bargain by simply arguing that the contract was frustrated. In Lord Radcliffe's words (at p 727), frustration could not be "lightly invoked as the dissolvent of a contract". (Also see a statement to this effect by Lord Roskill in *Pioneer Shipping* v *BTP Tioxide; (The Nema)* [1982] AC 724 at p 752.)

This narrow view of frustration adopted by the courts has meant that the doctrine will rarely succeed where performance of the contract is still possible but where it has merely become more difficult or disadvantageous for one of the parties to perform. Of course, where performance is actually prevented by supervening events beyond the control of the parties, a contract may be frustrated. For example, in *International Sea Tankers of Liberia Inc* v *Hemisphere Shipping Co of Hong Kong Ltd (The Wenjiang)* [1982] 2 All ER 437, a tanker which was chartered to carry a cargo of oil from Basrah, was trapped (like sixty other ships) on the Shatt-al-Arab river when war broke out in 1980 between Iran and Iraq. The parties agreed that in such circumstances the charterparty[2] was frustrated. The point of contention in this, and similar cases, was the precise date on which the contract was frustrated as this determined when the hire charge ceased to be payable by the charterers[3].

The important subject of who bears the loss when a contract is frustrated is dealt with in detail later. But it should be remembered that the parties may, and frequently do, include some express provision which deals with the allocation of risk in relation to supervening events. In this way the possible application of the doctrine of frustration is avoided by means of a relevant clause in the contract.

4. Scope of the doctrine

(a) Leases

It used to be argued that the doctrine of frustration could not apply to leases. This is because a lease is not simply a contract enabling a tenant to make use of the land in question; it creates a legal estate in the land. The argument ran that this legal estate survives despite supervening events which may prevent the use or enjoyment of the land (for example, see *London & Northern Estates Co v Schlesinger* [1916] 1 KB 20). This is a rather technical view which ignores the commercial reality of some leases, especially where the lease is short term and the tenant is concerned with the use of the land for a specific purpose rather than in the creation of any legal estate. After some judicial uncertainty on the subject (see *Cricklewood Property and Investment Trust Ltd v Leighton Investment Trust Ltd* [1945] AC 221), the leading case is now *National Carriers Ltd v Panalpina (Northern) Ltd* [1981] 1 All ER 161. The facts were as follows:

> The appellants had a ten-year lease of a warehouse from the respondents. After five and a half years of the lease, the local authority closed the only access road to the warehouse for a period of about eighteen months. This closure of the road prevented the appellants from using the warehouse for their business. As a result, the appellants stopped their payment of rent to the respondents and claimed that the lease was frustrated.

The House of Lords decided that the closure of the access road was not a sufficiently serious interruption to amount to a frustrating event. (This was in spite of the harm to the appellants' business caused by the closure.) There was still a further three years of the lease remaining when the road was opened again. The appellants were still liable for the rent under the lease. But although the frustration claim in fact failed, the House of Lords held that the doctrine is capable of applying to a lease. Their lordships could see no reason why, in principle, the doctrine should not apply to all types of contract. However, in practice, it will be quite rare for a lease to be frustrated. (*Quaere*: If the access road had been closed for most of the period of the lease, would the contract then have been frustrated in the *National Carriers* case?) It seems that the circumstances in which a lease will most likely be held to be frustrated are where the lease is short term and it is obvious that it is for a specific purpose. If that purpose is thwarted by supervening events beyond the control of both parties, the lease may well be frustrated.

(b) Illegality

The doctrine of frustration will apply in circumstances where the performance of a contract is contrary to some law passed after the contract is made. (If the illegality exists before the contract is made, the doctrine is not relevant — but see Chapter 15.) This is often described as a case of "supervening illegality". In such circumstances the contract is not impossible to perform, nor have the obligations under the contract (necessarily) been radically altered. It is more a question of public policy in ensuring that the law is not broken. For this reason it is not possible for the parties to exclude the operation of the doctrine, in relation to certain types of supervening illegality (such as trading with the enemy), by express agreement[4].

An obvious example of a contract's frustration due to supervening illegality is where its performance would involve trading with an enemy country at a time of war. In *Fibrosa Spolka Akcyjna* v *Fairbairn Lawson Combe Barbour Ltd* [1943] AC 32, which is discussed in detail later, there was a contract for the sale of machinery to a Polish company. The machinery was to be manufactured in England and delivered to Gdynia. Subsequently, Germany invaded Poland and occupied Gdynia. The contract was held to be frustrated despite a clause in the contract which expressly dealt with the consequences of delay due to "any cause whatsoever . . . including war". Trading with a country occupied by the enemy would have been contrary to the public interest. (For a further example of a contract frustrated by war, see *Avery* v *Bowden* (1856) 6 E & B 953.)

Other examples of supervening illegality are where new licensing regulations are introduced after the parties have contracted, or where restrictions on the import or export of certain goods are subsequently introduced. A problem may arise where the supervening illegality affects just part of the contract. In *Cricklewood Property and Investment Trust Ltd* v *Leighton Investment Trust Ltd* [1945] AC 221:

> In 1936, Cricklewood Property obtained a building lease for ninety-nine years for the purpose of building a shopping centre on a residential estate. With the outbreak of war in 1939, restrictions on the supply of building materials were introduced, and Cricklewood Property were unable to build on the land. As building on the land was a term of the lease, Cricklewood Property claimed that the contract was frustrated. The landlord, Leighton's Investment Ltd, brought an action for the rent. (Whether the doctrine of frustration can apply to a lease is discussed above and will not be considered here.)

It was decided that the contract was not frustrated and that Cricklewood Property were still liable for the rent under the lease. The reasoning was that it was a long lease, and ninety years of it were still unexpired. It was most unlikely that wartime regulations would last for a substantial part of the duration of the lease and there would be plenty of time for building once they had ended. There was no frustration, therefore, as the illegality did not destroy the main purpose of the lease. For a contrasting case, in which the main purpose of the contract was frustrated due to supervening illegality (restrictions on trading in timber), see *Denny, Mott & Dickson* v *James Fraser & Co* [1944] AC 265[5].

(c) Impossibility: destruction of subject matter

We have seen in *Taylor* v *Caldwell* a clear instance of "impossibility", namely the destruction of the subject matter of the contract. The contract was held to be frustrated by the fire which destroyed the music hall. The fire was not the fault of either party, nor was there any express stipulation to cover such a contingency. The main purpose of the contract was for the hirer of the hall to hold a series of concerts, and this became impossible as a result of the fire. It did not matter that the whole of the subject matter of the contract — which included the use of the Surrey Gardens — was not destroyed.

A similar approach can be seen in *Appleby* v *Myers* (1867) LR 2 CP 651, where P contracted to erect machinery on D's premises. When the work was well under way, but before it was completed, an accidental fire destroyed D's premises and the machinery that had been erected so far. P's claim to recover damages for the work already done and the cost of materials failed as the destruction of D's premises discharged both parties from their obligations under the contract. (The application of the Law Reform (Frustrated Contracts) Act 1943 to these facts is considered later.) The court's view was that the contract did not include an absolute undertaking by D that his premises would remain unaltered so as to permit P to complete the work contracted for. D had not assumed the risk of the accidental destruction of the premises. Of course, *Appleby* v *Myers* differs slightly from *Taylor* v *Caldwell* in that the premises were not the subject matter of the contract in *Appleby* v *Myers*. However, the existence of the premises was clearly essential for the performance of the contract and their destruction was rightly held to be a frustrating event.

Cases can occur where the subject matter of the contract is badly damaged by accident, but not totally destroyed. For example, in *Asfar* v *Blundell* [1896] 1 QB 123, a ship with a cargo of dates sank and was refloated after a few days. On arrival, it was found that the cargo was badly affected by the accident. It was held that the cargo owner was not liable to pay freight as the goods, in a commercial sense, had perished. It did not matter that the goods could still be put to some other commercial use, such as distillation into spirit; their nature had changed to such a degree that they could no longer be classified as dates. They were transformed into a "mass of pulpy matter impregnated with sewage and in a state of fermentation" (*per* Lord Esher at p 127)[6].

(d) Impossibility: sale of goods

Where a contract involves the sale of goods, we have to look at the particular rules relating to this subject in addition to the common law principles. A contract for the sale of goods may be frustrated for reasons that we have already considered, such as supervening illegality (see *Avery* v *Bowden* (1856) 6 E & B 953). But reference should also be made to the relevant provisions of the Sale of Goods Act 1979. Section 7 states that:

> "Where there is an agreement to sell specific goods, and subsequently the goods, without any fault on the part of the seller or buyer, perish before the risk passes to the buyer, the agreement is avoided".

So if S agrees to sell to B goods which are identified at the time the contract is made, and those goods subsequently perish before the risk passes to B, the contract is frustrated (or "avoided"). As with the common law, the contract will be frustrated only if neither of the parties is at fault. If the goods are not "specific", however, the section will not apply. If, for example, S agrees to supply B with 100 kg of "Golden Delicious" apples, but no particular source is specified, the contract will not be frustrated if the apples that S intended to use are subsequently destroyed. This is a contract for generic rather than for specific goods. S would be liable for non-delivery of the goods if he could not find another supply in order to fulfil his contractual obligations. (But contrast *Howell* v *Coupland* [1876] 1 QBD 258[7].)

Under a contract for the sale of goods it is well established (see s 20(1) Sale of Goods Act 1979) that risk passes with ownership. (The Act uses the word "property" to mean ownership.) Therefore, the risk of theft or damage to goods, unless otherwise agreed, falls on the owner, and not necessarily on the person who is in possession of them at the time. If the risk has passed to the buyer, and the goods are then damaged, the buyer will still be liable if he refuses to accept or pay for the goods. The contract will not be frustrated. If the property in the goods has not passed, and remains with the seller at the time of the loss or damage, the seller will have to carry out his contractual obligations unless the contract is frustrated.

(e) Impossibility: death or illness

Most commercial contracts do not require performance by a particular person and no other. Therefore, death or illness does not normally prevent performance of the contract. But where a contract is for some personal service, to be rendered by a party to the contract, the death or incapacity of that party will make performance impossible. In *Whincup* v *Hughes* (1871) LR 6 CP 78, for example, the plaintiff's son was apprenticed to a watchmaker for a six-year period at a premium of £25, but the watchmaker died after just one year. The contract, which was for a skilled and personal service, was obviously frustrated. However, at that time, P could not claim back any of the premium (for reasons which are explained later)[8]. In *Robinson* v *Davison* (1871) LR 6 Ex 269 a contract was held to be frustrated when a person who had been engaged to play the piano at a concert, on a particular day, was unable to do so because of illness. Also, in *Notcutt* v *Universal Equipment Co (London) Ltd* [1986] 1 WLR 641, a contract of employment was brought to an end, under the doctrine, as a result of the employee's chronic illness and his inability ever again to perform his contractual obligations. (For an interesting case, involving a slightly different set of facts, see *Shepherd* v *Jerrom* [1987] 1 QB 301.)

(f) Impossibility: due to unavailability

In some circumstances the subject matter of a contract, whilst still in existence, may simply not be available for the purpose that was contracted for. We have seen, in *The Wenjiang; (International Sea Tankers of Liberia Inc* v *Hemisphere Shipping Co of Hong Kong)* [1982] 2 All ER 437 for instance, how an oil tanker which was trapped on the Shatt-al-Arab river at the outbreak of war in 1980 was thus unavailable to fulfil a contract to carry oil from Basrah. In this, and in a number of similar cases, the charterparties were frustrated due to the unavailability of the subject matter. The dispute in these cases related to the precise date on which the contracts were frustrated. (A charterparty may also be frustrated where a ship is requisitioned for such a period as to substantially affect the obligations under the contract — see *Bank Line Ltd* v *Arthur Capel & Co* [1919] AC 435.)

In many cases the unavailability of the subject matter will only be temporary. If the contract specifies performance within a particular time, or on a certain date, then the unavailability of the subject matter at the crucial time will frustrate the contract (see *Robinson* v *Davison*, above). But it may not always be obvious whether there is a time limit on performance of the contract. In *Jackson* v *Union Marine Insurance Co Ltd* (1874) LR 10 CP 125 the facts were as follows:

> Jackson's ship was chartered to go, in January 1872, directly from Liverpool to Newport and there to load a cargo of iron rails to be shipped to San Francisco. Jackson took out insurance on the chartered freight for the voyage. On the way to Newport, on 2 January, the ship ran aground in Caernarfon Bay. It took a month to free the ship and a further six months for repairs to be carried out. Meanwhile, the charterers had chartered another ship as a replacement. Jackson claimed against the defendant insurance company for a total loss of the freight to be earned under the contract, by perils at sea. To succeed with such a claim, it was essential to decide whether the contract between Jackson and the charterer was frustrated, or whether he could have successfully sued the charterer for not loading the goods. In other words, did the charterer have the right to treat the contract with Jackson as discharged?

It was held that a voyage undertaken after the ship had been repaired would have been a very different adventure from the one which the parties had contracted for. A condition could be implied that the ship would arrive in Newport in time for the particular voyage. Its failure to do so within a reasonable time put an end to the contract. The long delay for repairs meant that the contract was frustrated: "The adventure was frustrated by perils of the seas, both parties were discharged, and a loading of cargo in August would have been a new adventure, a new agreement" (*per* Lord Bramwell at p 148).

The courts will sometimes have to decide whether a contract covering a lengthy period is frustrated by supervening events which cover part of that period. Typical examples of this include the effects of a strike on a shipping contract (see *The Nema; (Pioneer Shipping* v *BTP Tioxide)* [1982] AC 724), or the requisition of a commercial ship by the government at a time of war. Delay will frustrate a contract if it defeats the commercial venture, but this can be a difficult question to decide upon. In such instances the court must look at both the length of the contract and the length of the interference which causes the unavailability of the subject matter. It should be noted that the courts are supposed to judge the situation as at the date of the frustrating event and not with the benefit of hindsight. This can lead to odd results. For example, in *Tamplin Steamship Co Ltd* v *Anglo-Mexican Petroleum Products Co* [1916] 2 AC 397:

> A tanker was chartered from December 1912 for a five-year period. In February 1915, the vessel was requisitioned as a troop ship. The owners of the ship claimed that the contract was frustrated by this supervening event.

The House of Lords decided that the commercial object of the contract was not frustrated as, at the time of the event in question, it appeared likely that the ship would still be available to fulfil a substantial part of the contract after the war ended. As it turned out, the House of Lords was wrong in its assumption, because the war did not end until 1918. But the case illustrates the difficulty in judging the likely effect on a contract of some event which causes the temporary unavailability of the subject matter. (In contrast to the above case, see *Metropolitan Water Board* v *Dick, Kerr & Co* [1918] AC 119. A contract, made in 1914, to build a reservoir within six years, was interrupted in 1916 by a government Order, as a result of war. The contract was frustrated because the delay caused by the Order was likely to cause a radical change to the nature of the contract, if it was later resumed.)

(g) Impossibility: not just financial hardship

We have seen that the doctrine of frustration operates within strict limits. This is to prevent a party from trying to escape from a bad bargain on the grounds of financial hardship caused by subsequent events. The decision in *Krell* v *Henry* (discussed earlier) is not without its critics, but it was a very unusual case and probably correct in those particular circumstances. More typically, *Amalgamated Investment & Property Co Ltd* v *John Walker & Sons Ltd* illustrates the fact that financial hardship alone, suffered by one of the parties as a result of supervening events, will not normally frustrate a contract. It was stated by Lord Radcliffe in *Davis Contractors Ltd* v *Fareham UDC* [1956] AC 696 at p 729:

> ". . . [I]t is not hardship or inconvenience or material loss itself which calls the principle of frustration into play. There must be such a change in the significance of the obligation that the thing undertaken would, if performed, be a different thing from that contracted for."

In the example of *Tsakiroglou & Co Ltd* v *Noblee Thorl GmbH* [1962] AC 93 (see above), performance of the contract, for the shipment of groundnuts from the Sudan to Hamburg, was made much more difficult and expensive by the subsequent closure of the Suez Canal. It was still possible for the nuts to be shipped via the Cape of Good Hope, but this alternative route would have taken over twice as long and doubled the cost of carriage. The price of the shipment was calculated on the basis that the route would be via Suez, but the contract did not specify the route; nor did it specify a date for delivery. The House of Lords held that the contract was not frustrated. Performance of the contract was more difficult and expensive for the appellants, but it was not impossible. The court refused to imply a term that the goods were to be shipped by the customary and cheapest route. (Also see *The Eugenia (Ocean Tramp Tankers Corporation* v *V/O Sofracht)* [1964] 1 All ER 161.)

Tsakiroglou shows the reluctance of our courts to extend the doctrine to cover cases of impracticability or extreme financial hardship. (Contrast the United States' approach which has broadened the idea of impossibility to include extreme and unreasonable difficulty or expense to one of the parties.) But one case which offers some, albeit slender, support for a wider application of the doctrine is *Staffordshire Area Health Authority* v *South Staffordshire Waterworks Co* [1978] 3 All ER 769. The facts were:

> In 1929, the plaintiff hospital authority entered into a contract with the defendant water company which provided that "at all times hereafter" the hospital was to receive 5,000 gallons of water per day free, and all the additional water it needed at a rate of 7d (later agreed as 2.9p) per 1,000 gallons. This supply of water was in exchange for the hospital having given up its right to take water from its own nearby well. By 1975, the provision of water to the hospital at the agreed rate was clearly uneconomic; the normal rate charged by the defendants was 45p per 1,000 gallons. The company wrote to the hospital authority on 30 September 1975, giving

six months' notice of its intention to terminate the 1929 agreement. The company would still supply 5,000 gallons per day without charge, but the excess would be provided at the normal (economic) rates. The hospital refused to accept this notice and argued that the 1929 agreement was expressed as applying "at all times hereafter".

The Court of Appeal rejected the hospital authority's argument, and ruled that the defendant company's notice was effective. The majority did not rely on the doctrine of frustration, which explains why the case offers only slender authority for a wider interpretation of the doctrine on the grounds of financial hardship. The court simply decided that the contract could be brought to an end by giving reasonable notice. The judges did not think that the hospital should be permitted to go on receiving its water at one-fifteenth of the economic rate. But Lord Denning thought that the doctrine of frustration could cover this situation, and he stated (at p 775):

"... [W]e have to ask ourselves: what were the circumstances in which the contract was made? Does it apply in the least to the new situation which has developed? If events occur for which they have made no provision, and which were outside the realm of their speculations altogether, or of any reasonable persons sitting in their chairs, then the court itself must take a hand and hold that the contract ceases to bind. Such was the rule which I suggested long ago in *British Movietonews* v *London and District Cinemas Ltd* without success at that time ..."

Whatever the merits of Lord Denning's approach, he seems to have attracted little support from either fellow judges or learned writers. The major objection to his approach is that it widens the scope of the doctrine to an unacceptable degree. If it were to be applied to cases on the basis that the rate of inflation was beyond the contemplation of the parties, or of a reasonable person in their position, it might introduce uncertainty into various types of long-term commercial agreements, such as long leases and life insurance policies[9].

(h) Effect of express provision for frustrating event

The doctrine of frustration has developed as a means of dealing with subsequent, unforeseen events which render performance of a contract impossible, or illegal, or which fundamentally change the nature of the contractual obligations undertaken by the parties. However, the parties may make express provision dealing with certain supervening events and, in so doing, effectively preclude the operation of the doctrine. The original theory behind the doctrine, as explained in *Taylor* v *Caldwell*, was that it was based on an effort to give effect to the presumed intention of the parties. In other words, it could not operate if the parties had dealt with a particular contingency by express provision. (But see *Jackson* v *Union Marine Insurance Co*, below.)

One obvious exception, as we have seen, is that frustration on the ground that the contract involves trading with an enemy country cannot be excluded by express provision (see *Ertel Bieber & Co* v *Rio Tinto Co Ltd* [1918] AC 260). This is for reasons of public policy and is not exceptionable. But, generally, the parties may make express provision for other types of supervening event, such as strikes, closure of shipping routes, illness, floods, fires and other disasters.

Thus the parties can allocate the risk of such events as they see fit. They may, for example, expressly provide for an extension to the period of performance of the contractual obligations. They may further provide that should the interference with the contract continue beyond a specified period, then either party is entitled to terminate the contract. The parties can expressly decide that neither party is entitled to compensation in the event of these contingencies. Such forward planning is particularly useful for those involved in international trade, where the threat of disruption is more likely.

Although the doctrine of frustration is limited to supervening events which are not expressly provided for in the contract, the courts might interpret an express provision in such a way that the doctrine may still operate. In *Jackson* v *Union Marine Insurance Co Ltd* (1874) LR 10 CP 125 a contract for the hire of a ship stated that the vessel was to proceed with all possible speed (dangers and accidents of navigation excepted) from Liverpool to Newport, in order to load a cargo of iron for San Francisco. The ship ran aground, not far from Liverpool, and was delayed for eight months. It was held that, notwithstanding the express exception of dangers and accidents of navigation, the contract was frustrated. The words of exception appeared to cover the contingency which in fact occurred, but the court found a way of limiting their application because it clearly felt that a voyage undertaken after the repair to the ship would have been a different "adventure" altogether. Accordingly, the express provision was given a restrictive interpretation by the court; it would excuse the owner of the ship and protect him from an action for breach of contract, but it would not deprive the charterer of the right to treat his contractual undertakings as discharged. For a further example of a restrictive interpretation of an express provision, see *Metropolitan Water Board* v *Dick, Kerr & Co* [1918] AC 119.

(i) Frustration does not apply to foreseeable events

The doctrine of frustration does not generally apply to situations where the supervening event was foreseen or foreseeable. (Once again, trading with the enemy is an obvious exception for public policy reasons. Even if war was foreseeable, it would not prevent the doctrine from being applied.) If the parties foresee that a particular event might occur which may affect their performance of the contract, it will be assumed that they contracted in accordance with that risk. For example, in *Davis Contractors Ltd* v *Fareham UDC* [1956] AC 696, the House of Lords rejected the company's claim that the contract, for the construction of seventy-eight houses within a period of eight months for a fixed price, was frustrated by shortages of labour and materials which increased the cost of the work. The basic obligations under the agreement remained unchanged and financial hardship to one of the parties was not a sufficient reason for invoking the doctrine.

The *Davis Contractors* decision can be defended on the basis that the risk of increased costs, due to various shortages, was clearly foreseen by the company. It must therefore be assumed that it accepted that risk at the time of contracting. (The company had, in fact, sent a letter along with the original tender, stating that the tender was subject to the availability of adequate supplies of labour and building materials. This letter was not incorporated into the contract, nor was such a provision expressly included in the contract.) Lord Radcliffe stated (at p 731):

"Two things seem to me to prevent the application of the principle of frustration to this case. One is that the cause of the delay was not any new state of things which the parties could not reasonably be thought to have foreseen. On the contrary, the possibility of enough labour and materials not being available was before their eyes and could have been the subject of special contractual stipulation. It was not made so."[10]

(j) Frustration cannot be "self-induced"

The doctrine of frustration applies only in circumstances where the supervening event is beyond the control of the parties to the contract. It follows that, where the alleged frustrating event is caused by the deliberate act or decision of one of the parties, or by his negligence, the doctrine will not apply. Whichever theory lies behind the doctrine — whether it is based on the presumed contractual intention of the parties, or whether it is simply a fair solution imposed by the courts — it is not possible to justify its application to subsequent events which are "self-induced". An example of this rule is provided by *Ocean Tramp Tankers Corporation* v *V/O Sofracht; (The Eugenia)* [1964] 1 All ER 161, where the facts were:

> *The Eugenia* was let out to the charterers to go from Genoa to the Black Sea to load cargo, and thence to India to unload cargo. Having loaded, the ship proceeded on its route to India, which took it via Suez. In breach of contract, the charterers allowed the ship to enter a war zone. (The contract contained a "war clause" which prohibited the charterers from sailing the ship into a dangerous zone without the owner's permission.) The ship entered the Suez Canal and was trapped when the canal was closed. The charterers tried to rely on the detention of the ship as a frustrating event.

The Court of Appeal held that the charterers could not rely on the fact that the ship was trapped in the canal, as this was their own fault. They were in breach of contract by allowing the ship to enter a war zone and, therefore, the alleged frustrating event was self induced. A different case, illustrating the same basic rule, is *Maritime National Fish Ltd* v *Ocean Trawlers Ltd* [1935] AC 524 where:

> Maritime National Fish (MNF) chartered a steam trawler, fitted with an otter trawl, from Ocean Trawlers (OT). The parties expressly agreed that the trawler should be used only in the fishing industry. Both parties knew, at the time of the agreement, that it was illegal to use an otter trawl without a licence from the Canadian government. A few months after the contract was made, MNF applied for five licences for the five trawlers which they were operating, but they were granted only three by the government. MNF were, therefore, forced to name the three ships which they wished to license, and the three which they chose did not include the one chartered from OT. OT brought an action for the hire, and MNF argued that the contract was frustrated by the refusal of the government to grant more than three licences to them.

One of the reasons given by the Canadian appeal court for rejecting MNF's contention was that the risk of not obtaining a licence was foreseeable, and MNF could have insisted that some express provision be made for this contingency. Having failed to do so, MNF accepted the risk of not obtaining a licence to fish with OT's trawler. The Privy Council did not disagree with this ruling, but their lordships thought that it was unnecessary to hear detailed argument on this point. They held that the Canadian court's other reason for dismissing MNF's contention was correct and was a sufficient basis for dismissing MNF's appeal; namely, that the alleged frustrating event arose from the deliberate act or choice of MNF. The doctrine of frustration could not be relied upon where the supervening event in question was "self-induced". *Maritime National Fish* was applied more recently by the Court of Appeal in *J Lauritzen A/S* v *Wijsmuller BV (The Super Servant Two)* [1990] 1 Lloyd's Rep 1. The facts were:

> The defendants agreed to transport the plaintiffs' drilling rig from Japan to Rotterdam. The contract specified that the rig was to be delivered between 20 June and 20 August (in 1981) and was to be carried by what was described as the "transportation unit". This unit was defined as meaning either *Super Servant One* or *Super Servant Two*. Before performance of the contract was due, the defendants decided to use *Super Servant Two* for transporting the plaintiffs' rig, and they entered into contracts with other parties for which they planned to use *Super Servant One*. On 29 January 1981, *Super Servant Two* sank whilst being used on another job and, shortly afterwards, the defendants told the plaintiffs that they would not be carrying out their obligations under the contract, as *Super Servant One* was unavailable due to use in other contracts. Under a "without prejudice" agreement, the defendants eventually transported the plaintiffs' rig on a barge towed by a tug. The plaintiffs later claimed for the losses they had suffered.

The Court of Appeal held that the defendants could not rely on the doctrine of frustration as it was their own choice that they decided not to use *Super Servant One* for this purpose. The sinking of *Super Servant Two* did not bring the contract to an end automatically, as the defendants had an alternative. In other words, if it had been foreseen at the time of contracting that one of the vessels might become unavailable to transport the rig, the parties would not have been concerned as there was another vessel which could perform the same task. It would have been different if the defendants owned only one "transportation unit" and that had sunk through no fault of their own. Bingham LJ stated (at p 9):

> "The doctrine [of frustration] must avail a party who contracts to perform a contract of carriage with a vessel which, through no fault of his, no longer exists. But that is not this case. The contract [with the plaintiffs] did provide an alternative . . . [T]he present case does not fall within the very limited class of cases in which the law will relieve one party from an absolute promise he has chosen to make."

Similar issues were raised in the House of Lords in *Paal Wilson & Co A/S* v *Partenreederei Hannah Blumenthal; (The Hannah Blumenthal)* [1983] 1 All ER 34. The case concerned the sale of a ship under a contract which provided that any dispute arising out of the sale was to be settled by arbitration. Disputes arose about the vessel, and the buyers commenced arbitration proceedings. As originally agreed, both parties appointed an arbitrator, but a third arbitrator (as provided for in the contract) was never appointed. In all, there was a period of over seven years' delay in the arbitration. The question arose whether the arbitration agreement was frustrated as a result of the long delay which was the fault of both parties. The House of Lords held that, in such circumstances, the fact that the parties were under a mutual obligation to keep the arbitration process moving meant that neither party could rely on the delay of the other as a ground for claiming frustration of the agreement to arbitrate. Lord Brandon stated (at p 44):

> ". . . [T]here are two essential factors which must be present in order to frustrate a contract. The first essential factor is that there must be some outside

event or extraneous change of situation, not foreseen or provided for by the parties at the time of contracting, which either makes it impossible for the contract to be performed at all, or at least renders its performance something radically different from what the parties contemplated when they entered into it. The second essential factor is that the outside event or extraneous change of situation concerned, and the consequences of either in relation to the performance of the contract, must have occurred without either the fault or default of either party to the contract."[11]

However, if the "fault" of a party to a contract is merely of a minor nature, he may still be able to rely on the doctrine. It will be a question of degree as to whether the particular "fault" or "default" amounts to self-induced frustration. Where a person acts in a deliberate way (as in *The Eugenia*), or makes a deliberate choice (as in *Maritime National Fish*), so as to bring about the frustrating event, he will be precluded from relying on the doctrine. But, for example, would a contract for some personal performance be frustrated if the person concerned became incapacitated by his own carelessness — such as a professional acrobat who sustains injury on a private skiing expedition and, as a result, is unable to perform his act? This type of problem was acknowledged, without being resolved, in *Joseph Constantine Steamship Line Ltd* v *Imperial Smelting Corporation Ltd* [1941] 2 All ER 165 (*per* Viscount Simon LC at p 173). There seems to be no reason, in principle, why events brought about by a party's own negligence should not be regarded as self-induced and thus preclude the application of the doctrine.

It should be noted that, where self-induced frustration is alleged, the onus of proof falls on the party making the allegation. In *Joseph Constantine*, the owners of a steamship (*The Kingswood*) chartered the vessel to the respondents, to go to Australia and load a cargo there. Before the cargo was loaded, an explosion occurred in the boiler of the ship, preventing the contract from being carried out. The respondents sued the owners for damages and the owners claimed that the contract was frustrated by the explosion. The respondents argued that the onus of proof rested on the owners to show that the explosion was not their fault. The House of Lords held that the contract was frustrated. The cause of the explosion was not clear, but the respondents had failed to prove that the frustrating event was the owner's fault. The burden of proof was not on the owners to disprove negligence on their part.

5. Effects of the doctrine

So far in this chapter we have been concerned with the issue of whether a contract is frustrated. We must now consider the practical consequences that arise when the parties are discharged under the doctrine. Unless the law provides for a fair distribution of the loss resulting from the supervening event, it may not be satisfactory simply to hold that the contract is frustrated. For example, a party may have incurred considerable expenditure in reliance upon the contract before the frustrating event occurred. The common law rules governing this type of situation have now been improved upon by the Law Reform (Frustrated Contracts) Act 1943. Both are considered in turn below.

It is well settled that frustration automatically brings the contract to an end at the time of the frustrating event. (This is another reason why Lord Denning's judgment in *Staffordshire Area Health Authority* v *South Staffordshire Water-works Co* [1978] 3 All ER 769 is open to criticism[12].) This is in contrast to discharge by breach of contract where the innocent party can choose whether to treat the contract as repudiated. Moreover, a contract which is discharged by frustration is clearly different from one which is void for mistake. A frustrated contract is valid until the time of the supervening event but is automatically ended thereafter, whereas a contract void on the grounds of mistake is a complete nullity from the beginning. A clear statement about the legal effect of frustration on a contract can be found in *Hirji Mulji* v *Cheong Yue Steamship Co Ltd* [1926] AC 497, where the facts were:

> The respondent owners of a ship, *The Singaporean*, agreed by a charterparty of November 1916 to hire out their vessel to the appellants from 1 March 1917. The appellants agreed to use the ship for ten months from the date of delivery. Before 1 March 1917, the ship was requisitioned by the government and not released until February, 1919. When the ship was requisitioned, the owners, thinking that she would soon be released, asked the appellants if they were still willing to take up the charter (ie a little later). The appellants said that they would do so, but when the ship was finally released (later than expected) in February 1919, they refused to accept it. The owners argued that the appellants could not rely on the doctrine of frustration, despite the supervening event, as they had chosen to affirm the contract.

On appeal from the Supreme Court of Hong Kong, the Privy Council held that the contract was frustrated in 1917. This meant that the obligations under the contract were brought to an end immediately and automatically at the time of the frustrating event. The application of the doctrine did not rely upon the election of the parties. So even where the parties continue to treat the contract as subsisting for a period of time after the supervening event, the court may declare it to be frustrated. In reference to the delay caused by the requisitioning of the ship, Lord Sumner said (at p 501) that it was immaterial that the parties thought at first that the delay would not frustrate the contract. He went on (at pp 509–510) to explain that whereas repudiation (or rescission) for breach is "a right to treat the contract as at an end if [the victim] chooses", frustration operates independently of the choice of the parties. Frustration operates, he added, "irrespective of the individuals concerned, their temperaments and failings, their interest and circumstances".

As a consequence of the rule that a contract is valid until the time of the frustrating event, and is determined automatically thereafter, certain other rules were said to follow. The common law position was encapsulated in the slightly enigmatic expression that "the loss lies where it falls". For example, where money was paid under a contract which was later frustrated, it was not recoverable. This was because parties remained liable for contractual obligations which fell due before the supervening event. On the other hand, the parties escaped from performing those obligations which had not yet fallen due at the time of frustration. The potential for unfairness under this common law approach can best be understood by looking at the relevant decisions. In *Chandler* v *Webster* [1904] 1 KB 493 the facts were:

> The plaintiff contracted to hire a room in Pall Mall from the defendant for the purpose of watching the coronation procession on 26 June 1902. The price for the hire of the room was £141 15s and it was payable immediately. The plaintiff paid £100, but before he paid the balance the procession was cancelled due to the illness of the King. The plaintiff sought to recover back the money he had paid.

The Court of Appeal held that his claim could not succeed. Moreover, he was liable for the remaining £41 15s, as this obligation had fallen due before the frustrating event occurred. Despite receiving no actual benefit whatsoever, the plaintiff was still liable for the hire of the room. Lord Collins MR explained the justification for this outcome (at p 499):

"If the effect [of a frustrating event] were that the contract were wiped out altogether, no doubt the result would be that the money paid under it would have to be repaid as on a failure of consideration. But that is not the effect of the doctrine; it only releases the parties from further performance of the contract. Therefore the doctrine of failure of consideration does not apply".

The harsh results of this rule as laid down by *Chandler* v *Webster* were, not surprisingly, subjected to considerable criticism. The Law Revision Committee[13] suggested that the rule should be changed but, before any implementation of this Report took place, *Chandler* v *Webster* was overruled by the case of *Fibrosa Spolka Akcyjna* v *Fairbairn Lawson Combe Barbour Ltd* [1943] AC 32 ("the *Fibrosa* case"). The case involved a contract under which the respondents, an English company, were to manufacture certain machinery for the appellants, a Polish company, and deliver it to Gdynia. The appellants were to pay £4,800 for the machinery, a third of which (ie £1,600) was to be paid with the order. In fact, only £1,000 was paid with the order. Subsequently, Germany invaded Poland and occupied Gdynia. At this time, none of the machinery had been delivered. For reasons which we have considered earlier, the contract was frustrated and the appellants sued for the return of the £1,000.

The Court of Appeal followed the rule in *Chandler* v *Webster* and held that the money was irrecoverable. But the House of Lords decided that there had been a total failure of consideration and that the appellants were entitled to recover £1,000 from the respondents. Viscount Simon stated (at pp 46–47):

"To claim the return of money paid on the ground of total failure of consideration is not to vary the terms of the contract in any way. The claim arises not because the right to be repaid is one of the stipulated conditions of the contract, but because, in the circumstances that have happened, the law gives the remedy ... [I]t does not follow that because the plaintiff cannot sue 'on the contract' he cannot sue dehors [ie outside] the contract for the recovery of a payment in respect of which consideration has failed".[14]

The decision in the *Fibrosa* case was an improvement on the harshness of *Chandler* v *Webster*, but it was not a complete solution to the problem of money paid under a contract which was then frustrated. This was freely acknowledged by their lordships in the course of their judgments (see [1943] AC 32 at pp 49–50, 54–55, and 71–72). Recovery of money paid depended on there having been a total failure of consideration; the performance of just a part of the consideration would thus prevent such a claim from succeeding. (For example, consider *Whincup* v *Hughes* (1871) LR 6 CP 78.) So if the English company had delivered part of the machinery before the discharge of the contract, failure of consideration would not have been total, and the advance payment would have been irrecoverable.

Furthermore, the decision in the *Fibrosa* case made no allowance for the expenses which were incurred under the contract by the payee. In other words, it was not really a fair solution to both parties; it provided for the return of the prepayment, but it did not compensate the recipient for the expenditure that it had incurred whilst partially carrying out the contract. In the *Fibrosa* case itself, the £1,000 was recoverable, but the English company received nothing for the considerable amount of work it had done on the machinery before the frustrating event. The common law did not allow the apportionment of the prepaid sum in this situation. To deal with these obvious defects in the law, the Law Reform (Frustrated Contracts) Act 1943 was enacted soon after the *Fibrosa* case.

The Law Reform (Frustrated Contracts) Act 1943

(i) General

The Law Reform (Frustrated Contracts) Act 1943 ("the Act") was introduced in an attempt to provide for a fair solution between the parties when their contract has been frustrated. It aimed at preventing the unjust enrichment of either party to the contract at the expense of the other. It deals only with situations where contracts have "become impossible of performance or been otherwise frustrated" and the parties have consequently been discharged from further performance (s 1(1)). It should be noted that the Act does not lay down the general principles under which the doctrine will be invoked and this question is still dealt with under the common law rules that we have considered earlier in this chapter. Also, the parties may themselves have made express provision for the frustrating event which has occurred, in which case, under s 2(3), the court is to give effect to the parties' intentions and the Act is excluded by their contrary agreement.

The Act does not apply to all types of contract. Section 2(5) states that the Act is not applicable to the following:

(a) any charterparty, except a time charterparty . . ., or to any contract (other than a charterparty) for the carriage of goods by sea; or
(b) any contract of insurance . . . .
(c) any contract to which section 7 of the Sale of Goods Act (now 1979) applies, or to any other contract for the sale, or for the sale and delivery, of specific goods, where the contract is frustrated by reason of the fact that the goods have perished.

(ii) The main changes introduced by the Act

Section 1(2) provides that:

> "All sums paid or payable to any party in pursuance of the contract before the time when the parties were so discharged (in this Act referred to as 'the time of discharge') shall, in the case of sums so paid, be recoverable from him as money received by him for the use of the party by whom the sums were paid, and, in the case of sums so payable, cease to be so payable".

In other words, this subsection enacts that advance payments made in pursuance of the contract before the supervening event, are recoverable. This provision goes further than the *Fibrosa* case in that claims under s 1(2) are not restricted to cases where the consideration for the payment has totally failed. It also provides that money which is payable under the contract before the frustrating event, but not yet paid, ceases to be payable. Of course, there will be cases where the recipient of the advance payment has incurred expenses before the contract was frustrated. It may well be that the parties agreed on some advance payment for this very reason. If the whole sum is recoverable, on discharge, then this can be as unfair to the payee as the old rule in *Chandler v Webster* was to the payer. For this reason, the new provisions are subject to the following important proviso which is appended to s 1(2):

"Provided that, if the party to whom the sums were so paid or payable incurred expenses before the time of discharge in, or for the purpose of, the performance of the contract, the court may, if it considers it just to do so having regard to all the circumstances of the case, allow him to retain or, as the case may be, recover the whole or any part of the sums so paid or payable, not being an amount in excess of the expenses so incurred."

It should be emphasised that this award of expenses can be made only where an advance sum was either paid or payable before the frustrating event. Thus s 1(2) represents an improvement upon the common law decision in the *Fibrosa* case. In that case the English company had incurred considerable expenditure and received nothing in return. As we have seen, the common law did not permit the apportionment of an advance payment in circumstances such as these, and the legislature acted promptly in response to criticism of this lack of flexibility.

Under s 1(2), a party who has incurred expenses in the performance of the contract may be awarded his expenses up to a limit of the sums paid or payable to him under the contract before the frustrating event. Such an award will be made where the court "considers it just to do so having regard to all the circumstances of the case" — in other words, any award is at the discretion of the court. To return to the facts of the *Fibrosa* case, for example: the English company might, under the new provision, have been compensated for its expenses incurred before the supervening event. But, it will be remembered that only £1,600 was to be paid by the Polish company with the order for the machinery. Therefore that amount (£1,600) would be the maximum that could have been awarded to the English company for expenses. In considering an award for expenses, in circumstances such as those of the *Fibrosa* case, the court will take account of whether the goods are of any commercial value to the sellers. If they can be sold to another buyer, then the expenses incurred under the original contract (before frustration) will not have been wasted.

The recent case of *Gamerco SA v ICM/Fair Warning (Agency) Ltd and others* [1995] 1 WLR 1226 provides a rare judicial discussion of the application of s 1(2). The facts were that, in 1992, the plaintiff concert promoters (P) agreed to promote a pop group's (D's) concert at a football stadium in Madrid on a specific date, as part of that group's European tour. Shortly before the date of the concert, but after the contract was made by the parties, engineers discovered that the stadium was unsafe and its use was subsequently prohibited by the local authorities. Thus, P's permit to hold the concert was withdrawn and, as no other suitable venue was available at this time, the concert was cancelled. P had paid $412,500 to D in advance, and both parties had incurred some expenditure in preparing for the concert. The action involved P's claim to recover the advance payment under s 1(2) of the Act, and D's counterclaim for breach of contract by P for failing to secure the required permit for the performance.

The judge, Garland J, in the High Court held that the contract was frustrated due to the stadium being unsafe and its use for the concert being banned. D's counterclaim was unsuccessful as P was not required to ensure that the permit, once obtained, would remain in force. More significantly, it was decided to allow P's claim in its entirety, with the judge ordering the repayment of the whole sum paid in advance to D; ie there was no deduction (or "set off") to compensate D. The judge felt that, despite the fact that D had incurred some expenditure in advance of the proposed performance, justice would be done by making no deduction from the ordered repayment under the proviso. It seems that the precise nature of D's expenses was not very clear and the judge found it impossible to determine an accurate amount: "the best I can do is to accept that [D] did incur some expenses, but the extent of them is wholly unproven . . ." (per Garland J, at p 1235). Presumably, it was felt that P's expenses were heavier and more calculable than those of the defendant pop group.

Another important innovation introduced by the Act is contained in s 1(3), which states:

> "Where any party to the contract has, by reason of anything done by any other party thereto in, or for the purpose of, the performance of the contract, obtained a valuable benefit (other than a payment of money to which.. [section 1(2)] . . . applies) before the time of discharge, there shall be recoverable from him by the said other party such sum (if any), not exceeding the value of the said benefit to the party obtaining it, as the court considers just, having regard to all the circumstances of the case and, in particular—
>
> (a) the amount of any expenses incurred before the time of discharge by the benefited party in, or for the purpose of, the performance of the contract, including any sums paid or payable by him to any other party in pursuance of the contract and retained or recoverable by that party under . . . [section 1(2)], and
> (b) the effect, in relation to the said benefit, of the circumstances giving rise to the frustration of the contract."

Under the common law, a party escaped the performance of those obligations which had not yet fallen due at the time of frustration. So if (hypothetically), in the *Fibrosa* case, the contract had been for the English company to manufacture the machinery at a price of £4,800, to be paid on delivery, it would have received nothing when the contract was frustrated before completion of the work. This is supported by the case of *Appleby* v *Myers* (1867) LR 2 CP 651, where the plaintiff claimed damages for the work already done in erecting machinery on the defendant's premises before the contract was frustrated by an accidental fire which destroyed both the machinery and the premises. This claim was unsuccessful as the supervening event discharged both parties from their obligations under the contract and gave no cause of action to either of them. (The contract did not provide for any advance payment and the court interpreted the agreement as one for payment on completion of the work.)

The ponderously worded s 1(3) was introduced to improve upon the rather unjust position at common law. Where a party has obtained a "valuable benefit" under the contract, before the supervening event, the court may order him to pay a fair sum for it, having regard to all the circumstances. To return to the facts of *Appleby* v *Myers*, the court would now have to consider whether the defendants did in fact obtain a valuable benefit from the plaintiff's work. Before the fire took place, the machinery (albeit unfinished) possibly constituted a benefit; but, after the fire, such benefit as had been obtained, was rendered worthless to the defendant (see s 1(3)(b), above). It is, therefore, far from clear that the Act would improve the plaintiff's position in such a case. (*Quaere*: Should the court assess the value of the alleged benefit on the basis of how things stood immediately before the frustrating event?)

An illustration of the potential usefulness of s 1(3) is provided by the old case of *Cutter* v *Powell* (1795) 6 Term Rep 320. The second mate of a ship, the *Governor Parry*, was promised thirty guineas for the completion of a voyage from Kingston (Jamaica) to Liverpool. (The basic rate of pay per month was £4, but the contract in question provided for a much higher rate; this was payable only where the sailor served for the whole of the voyage.) The sailor died after seven weeks of the voyage and his widow (the executrix) claimed a proportion of his wages, on a *quantum meruit* basis, for the work he had done on the voyage before his death. The court rejected the widow's claim as the contract stipulated that the voyage had to be completed. This is sometimes referred to as the doctrine of strict performance.

It is possible that the outcome of *Cutter* v *Powell* would be different today under s 1(3) and that the widow could recover from the defendant for the valuable benefit which he had obtained from the sailor's labour (although the work would presumably be compensated at the basic rate only). But it is also possible that the Act would have been excluded by the contrary agreement of the parties, as provided for by s 2(3)[15]. This might depend on the construction of their agreement. Did they agree, for example, that there was to be no payment whatsoever unless the entire voyage was completed by the sailor?

The first major case to be decided on the 1943 Act was *BP Exploration Co (Libya) Ltd* v *Hunt (No 2)* [1982] 1 All ER 925. (The judgments of the Queen's Bench Division, the Court of Appeal, and the House of Lords can all be found under this reference.) The facts were as follows:

> Nelson Hunt had been granted an oil concession in Libya by the government of that country. He entered into an agreement with a large oil company, BP, to exploit the oil concession, as he lacked the resources to go ahead on his own. BP were to do the exploratory work, which they would finance, and in return they would get a half share of Hunt's concession. They also had to make certain "farm-in" payments to Hunt in cash and oil. As soon as the oil field became productive, BP were to receive half of all the oil produced from it, together with "reimbursement oil" (taken from Hunt's share) to meet the cost of the company's "farm-in" payments and to cover Hunt's share of the development expenses. Thus BP were to bear the principal risk of failure in their combined venture. After much expenditure, a large oil field was discovered, which became productive in 1967. But, in 1971, BP's half share in the concession was expropriated by the new Libyan government, following a revolution in that country. The same fate befell Hunt's half share in 1973. At the time of the frustrating event, BP had received about one-third of the reimbursement oil to which they were entitled. The company brought a claim under s 1(3) of the Act for an award of a just sum.

The claim was allowed by Robert Goff J and he awarded BP a just sum under s 1(3) of the Act. The precise calculation of the amount is a complex matter which will not be elaborated here. Hunt's appeals to both the Court of Appeal and the House of Lords were unsuccessful. The main judgment on the scope of s 1(3) is that of the trial judge. (In the House of Lords, their lordships dealt with fairly minor, technical issues.) Robert Goff J (at p 950) explained that Hunt's benefit was the increase in the value of the oil concession as a result of BP's work. It should be noted, however, that the value of this benefit was substantially reduced by the circumstances giving rise to the frustration of the contract, namely the expropriation of the parties' interests in the oil field.

Footnotes

(1) See *Maritime National Fish Co* v *Ocean Trawlers* [1935] AC 524, *per* Lord Wright at p 529.

(2) That is, a contract for the hire of a ship and the delivery of cargo.

(3) Also see *Kodros Shipping Corp of Monrovia* v *Empresa Cubana de Fletes; (The Evia)* [1982] 3 All ER 350.

(4) It will be remembered that, normally, the parties can avoid the operation of the doctrine by express stipulation in the contract relating to supervening events.

(5) See Lord MacMillan's statement in *Denny Mott* (at p 272): "It is plain that a contract to do what it has become illegal to do cannot be legally enforceable. There cannot be default in not doing what the law forbids to be done".

(6) Contrast the decision in *Horn* v *Minister of Food* [1948] 2 All ER 1036. Also see Brown (2000) LMCLQ 12.

(7) If, to take the same example, the sale of 100kg of "Golden Delicious" apples is stated to be "from the seller's existing stock" (which exceeds 100kg), and the entire stock is then destroyed before the property passes, the contract would probably be frustrated, even though the goods were not "specific". This would be in accordance with common law principles.

(8) The situation is now covered by s1(2) Law Reform (Frustrated Contracts) Act 1943.

(9) Surely the parties to the 1929 agreement in *Staffordshire Area Health Authority* would have been well aware of the realities of inflation? (Another case of interest in relation to the effects of inflation on a contract is *Wates Ltd* v *Greater London Council* (1983) 25 Build LR 1).

(10) Whether the doctrine can apply to events which were foreseen or contemplated by the parties is also discussed in *The Eugenia* [1964] 1 All ER 161.

(11) Also see Griffiths LJ's useful summary of the relevant authorities in his dissenting judgment in the Court of Appeal in the same case: [1982] 3 All ER 394 at pp 406–407.

(12) Lord Denning appears to argue (at p 777) that "mountainous inflation" resulted in the contract "ceasing to bind", and he states that the contract could be "determined by reasonable notice".

(13) 7th Interim Report, 1939, Cmnd 6009.

(14) The term "consideration" is used here in a different sense than we saw in Chapter 4. There it meant the promise given in exchange for some act or promise. Whereas in this context it denotes the actual performance of the promise. See the comments of Viscount Simon in the *Fibrosa* case [1943] AC 32).

(15) But consider *BP Exploration Co (Libya)* v *Hunt (No 2)* [1982] 1 All ER 925, where the House of Lords took a narrow view of s 2(3), refusing to hold that it defeated the plaintiff's claim for an award of a just sum.

Chapter 21

Remedies

1. Introduction

Although it is common to speak of "enforcing the contract", the primary remedy for breach of contract is not specific performance but damages. Specific performance is available only if damages are an inadequate remedy (see page 497). However, many disputes will be settled without the assistance of the courts[1]. The parties may reach an agreement which resolves their dispute. The contract itself may have been drafted to deal with difficulties. It might contain a liquidated damages clause (see page 487), stating how much is to be paid by one party in the event of a particular breach. The other party may then simply be able to deduct that sum from his contractual payments. In addition, the order of performance may have been fixed so that one party, X, can withhold his performance until the other party, Y, performs. Y then has an incentive to perform in order to trigger X's obligation (see page 116). In this context the right to terminate for breach should not be forgotten. The threat to exercise that right may induce the other party to comply with the contract, and the actual exercise of it enables the injured party to extract himself from the contract.

However, here we are concerned primarily with contractual damages and specific performance and injunctions.

A. Damages

1. Expectation loss

In general, the sum awarded for breach of contract will be calculated so as to compensate the injured party rather than to recover any profit made by the party in breach. So that generally, if the "injured" party has suffered no loss, the damages awarded will be nominal — merely marking the contractual right. However, the House of Lords has indicated that, very exceptionally, recovery of the profit of the party in breach is possible (*Attorney General* v *Blake* [2000] 4 All ER 385). This is dealt with below when restitution is considered. However, what must be emphasised here is the ordinary recovery of damages for breach of contract and compensating the injured party's loss.

The loss claimed will often relate to damage to the injured party's economic interest, such as the loss of profit, but it may also include personal injury or damage to property. In addition, in limited cases it will be possible to recover damages for mental distress occasioned by the breach (see page 469) and, more broadly, there has been some recognition that damages must be available to cover the "consumer surplus", the non-financial benefit which the injured party was to derive from the contract (see page 461). The "consumer surplus" is often the equivalent, in the consumer context, of the financial profit which commercial parties are to gain from the contract.

The basic principle behind an award of contractual damages is that the injured party should be put in the position he would have been in had the contract been performed. This was stated by Parke B in *Robinson* v *Harman* (1880) 5 App Cas 25. He said (at p 35):

"The rule of the common law is that where a party sustains a loss by reason of a breach of contract he is, so far as money can do it, to be placed in the same situation with respect to damages as if the contract had been performed."

Contractual damages are usually awarded in relation to the injured party's expectation loss — the loss of what he would have received had the contract been performed (but see Fuller & Perdue, 46 Yale LJ 52). This means that damages cover the profit which the injured party would have derived from the contractual performance. This can be simply explained by an example: X contracted with Y for the purchase of some goods from Y for £500 and, when the time came for delivery, Y refused to deliver. By that time the market price of the goods had risen to £600. X can claim £100, the profit he would have made on the contract. Had Y performed, X would have had goods worth £600 by the time of delivery (and it will cost him £100 more than the contract price to buy substitute goods in the market). £100 will put X in the position he would have been in had Y performed (see s 51 Sale of Goods Act 1979). In appropriate circumstances, however, instead of expectation loss the injured party may claim for his reliance loss (see page 465). There is also some scope for restitutionary recovery (see page 468).

Nominal damages are awarded where there is no loss. Such a situation should be distinguished from the case where the loss is difficult to quantify, for example where the injured party has been deprived of an opportunity of participating in the final round of a beauty competition (*Chaplin* v *Hicks* [1911] 2 KB 786). Under such circumstances, the court will not leave the injured party with nominal damages even though quantification is difficult. However, where the benefit to be derived from the contract, the expectation loss, is uncertain, it may be better for the injured party to claim for wasted expenditure, ie reliance loss (see below, page 465). Also see *McRae* v *Commonwealth Disposals Commission* (1951) 84 CLR 377; *Commonwealth of Australia* v *Amann Aviation Pty Ltd* (1991) 66 ALJR 123 (Treitel (1992) 108 LQR 226).

The measure of damages

Although it is simple to state the basic principle on which contractual damages are awarded, in some cases questions arise as to how that should be measured and converted into money terms. Here we shall briefly consider some of the cases in which there is a basic established measure of damages and also one area which has presented difficulties in recent years.

There are, of course, many situations in which an established rule for measuring damages can be followed. In the context of sale of goods, for example, the basic situations are covered by statute. Section 51(3) Sale of Goods Act 1979 provides a *prima facie* basis for calculating damages when the buyer fails to deliver. Section 51(3) states:

"Where there is an available market for the goods in question the measure of damages is *prima facie* to be ascertained by the difference between the contract price and the market or current price of the goods at the time or times when they ought to have been delivered or (if no time was fixed) at the time of refusal to deliver."

As has been indicated, where there is a market for the goods in question, this will put the buyer in the position he would have been in had the contract been performed. His damages cover the difference between the contract price and what he would have had to pay to buy substitute goods in the market when the seller breached. Of course, he might not have bought substitute goods on that day, but the duty to mitigate will normally confine his damages to that sum even where he delays purchasing and the market price rises further. The duty to mitigate, which is dealt with below, does not allow the injured party to recover damages for a loss which he could have avoided by behaving reasonably after the breach (see page 481 — see further below on the timing of the assessment of damages, page 464). In other words the injured party will normally be assumed to have taken the risk of any rise, or *fall*, in the market if he delays purchasing substitute goods, and he will also keep any benefit derived from his delay.

There is a similar *prima facie* rule for the situation in which the seller has delivered defective goods. Section 53(3) states that the *prima facie* loss is the "difference between the value of the goods at the time of delivery to the buyer and the value they would have had if they had" not been defective. This may provide an appropriate answer whether the goods are wanted for use or for resale.

However, even though an established means of calculating damages will often provide a quantification in a particular type of situation, the basic principle on which damages are awarded must always be borne in mind. The need for a reassertion of basic principle arose in a situation which has proved problematic in recent years — that of someone who contracts for work to be done on their property which will not add to its value but which will add to their enjoyment of their property. Such situations have raised difficulties in the calculation of damages where the builder does not carry out the work according to the contract terms. The defective performance makes no difference to the value of the property and the builder has contended that damages should merely be nominal, whereas the homeowner has argued that a substantial amount will need to be spent to cure the defect and that he, or she, should be awarded that "cost of cure". It seemed at one stage that the award of damages had to be based on one of these two sums, but, as we shall see, a reversion to basic principle has now shown that not to be the case.

The first case to consider is that of *Radford* v *De Froberville* [1977] 1 WLR 1262. In that case—

P had sold part of his land to D, D contracting to build a wall to separate her land from P's remaining land. This she failed to do. The wall would not have added to the value of P's property. P claimed the cost of building the wall on his side of the boundary.

Oliver J did not confine P's recovery to nominal damages. He awarded P the "cost of cure". He said (at p 1270):

> "*Pacta sunt servanda.* If he contracts for the supply of that which he thinks serves his interests — be they commercial, aesthetic or merely eccentric — then if that which is contracted for is not supplied by the other contracting party I do not see why, in principle, he should not be compensated by being provided with the cost of supplying it through someone else in a different way, subject to the proviso of course, that he is seeking compensation for a genuine loss and not merely using a technical breach to secure an uncovenanted profit."

The vital issue in such a case would seem to be to establish what the injured party's "genuine loss" is. That will depend upon what "interest" of the injured party the relevant contractual requirement served.

The difficulty in this area is that the injured party has contracted for a purpose which is not reflected in an objective market value. The injured party has contracted for the "consumer surplus" (ie "the excess utility or subjective value" which would have been obtained from the contractual performance — Harris, Ogus & Phillips, "Contract Remedies and the Consumer Surplus" (1979) 95 LQR 581 at p 582). If the difference which the contractual performance would have made to the objective value of the injured party's property is smaller than the "consumer surplus", then the injured party will be under-compensated if the injured party's recovery is restricted to that objective value (often nothing). In other words, damages ignoring the "consumer surplus" will not put the plaintiff in the position he, or she, would have been in had the contract been performed. It may then be appropriate for the plaintiff to recover the cost of cure, despite a nominal difference in value — as occurred in *Radford*. Certainly that will be the case if the "consumer surplus" is equal to, or greater than, the cost of cure. In that situation, the injured party will be mitigating his loss by curing the defect — the duty to mitigate means that the injured party will not recover a loss which he could have avoided by behaving reasonably after the breach (see page 481). However, the point should be emphasised that if the "consumer surplus" is less than the cost of cure, awarding the cost of cure over-compensates the plaintiff. In other words, where a "consumer surplus" is involved, it is not always appropriate to calculate the damages simply on the basis of either the cost of cure or the difference in value. If neither such sum is to be used as the basis of calculation, it must be admitted that the identification of the correct sum to award cannot be very accurate, but it is the only way to comply with basic principle and that was the conclusion reached in *Ruxley Electronics and Construction* v *Forsyth* [1995] 3 All ER 268.

In *Ruxley* v *Forsyth*—

> The plaintiff contracted with the defendant for the building of a swimming pool with a maximum depth of water of 7 ft 6 in. The plaintiff made it clear that the depth was important to him as he wanted to be able to dive and he needed that depth to feel safe to do so. The defendants built a pool with a maximum depth of 6 ft 9 in, and it was only 6 ft deep at the relevant point for diving. There was evidence that,

as constructed, the pool was safe for diving and the difference in the depth made no difference to the value. In order for the pool to be made to comply with the contract depth, it would have been necessary to rip out what had been installed and put in a new, deeper pool, at a cost of about £21,000. At first instance the plaintiff was awarded £2,500 general damages for loss of amenity and pleasure. The Court of Appeal (Dillon LJ dissenting) found that the appropriate measure was the cost of cure.

The Court of Appeal viewed the awarding of the cost of cure as the only means of placing the plaintiff in the position he would have been in had the contract been performed — ie in possession of a pool which he felt safe to dive into. Obviously, in awarding the cost of cure, the Court of Appeal in *Ruxley* was protecting a non-commercial interest of the plaintiff, but it was doing so inappropriately according to the House of Lords, which concluded that it was not restricted to awarding either the cost of cure or the difference in value, and that the plaintiff's "consumer surplus" should itself be valued. The House of Lords restored the award made at first instance.

In *Ruxley*, the House of Lords reasserted the basic principle that contractual damages should put the injured party in the position he, or she, would have been in had the contract been performed. Obviously, the Court of Appeal had also attempted to comply with basic principle but Lord Lloyd pointed out the basic fallacy in their reasoning. He stated the basic principle for the award of contractual damages and said (at p 282):

> "This does not mean that in every case of breach of contract the plaintiff can obtain the monetary equivalent of specific performance."

In other words, basic principle requires an injured party to receive the monetary equivalent of what he, or she, should have obtained from the contract. It does not mean that the injured party's expectations have to be fulfilled by providing the sum of money necessary to procure them through "curing" the defective performance (the Court of Appeal's conclusion). The basic principle which governs the award of contractual damages is about "ends" and not "means" (see also *Channel Island Ferries Ltd* v *Cenargo Navigation Ltd (The Rozel)* [1994] 2 Lloyd's Rep 161, *per* Phillips J at p 166, in a commercial context). In economic terms there is a substitute for the injured party's loss of the enjoyment of diving into a 7 ft 6 in swimming pool. The injured party might derive equal enjoyment from a holiday, costing far less than the cost of cure. The lost "end" — the lost pleasure — can be compensated in money terms without the need to furnish a sum which would provide it through the equivalent of the contractual "means". In other words, contrary to the view of the Court of Appeal, having decided that a nominal difference in value was not an appropriate award, there was an alternative to awarding the cost of cure — directly awarding a sum based on the lost consumer surplus.

In *Radford* and *Ruxley*, in deciding whether the "cost of cure" was an appropriate award, the courts referred to whether such an award was "reasonable" and this has received some emphasis. However, the duty to mitigate means that the injured party will not recover for a loss which he could have avoided by behaving reasonably on breach. A lost "consumer surplus" exceeding the cost of cure should be mitigated by behaving reasonably and "curing" the defendant's performance, and it is appropriate for the injured party to recover the cost of cure in damages. Similarly, if the cost of cure exceeds the "consumer surplus" it is in keeping with the duty to mitigate that the injured party should only recover the "consumer surplus" and not the larger cost of cure. It is contended that the references to reasonableness in *Radford* and *Ruxley* should be understood as reflections of the duty to mitigate.

In *Ruxley* Lord Mustill said (at p 277):

> "The law must cater for those occasions where the value of the promise exceeds the financial enhancement of his position which full performance will secure. This excess, often referred to in literature as the consumer surplus ... is usually incapable of precise valuation in terms of money, exactly because it represents a personal, subjective and non-monetary gain. Nevertheless, where it exists the law should recognize it."

If it does not recognize the consumer surplus, then the injured party may either be under-compensated or over-compensated. In fact this has, perhaps, been put even more broadly in terms of the need to recognize the injured party's "performance interest" if an inappropriate level of compensation is to be avoided (*Panatown Ltd* v *Alfred McAlpine Construction Ltd* [2000] 4 All ER 97, Lord Goff and Lord Millett). In *Radford* v *De Froberville* [1977] 1 WLR 1262 Oliver J awarded the cost of cure to compensate for a non-financial loss. He refused to accept that the injured party had to be left with nominal damages because the building of the wall would not affect the value of the property. Under the circumstances he regarded nominal damages, as (at p 1268):

> "a result so strange and so monstrously unjust that Mr Bumble's animadversion on the nature of law seems, by contrast, a restrained understatement".

In that case injustice could be avoided because the consumer surplus could be appropriately compensated for by an award of the cost of cure. However, in *Ruxley* the court had to deal with a situation in which awarding the cost of cure would have over-compensated the injured party and been unjust to the other party. It was necessary to recognize the possibility of directly compensating for a lost consumer surplus so that:

> "There is no need to remedy the injustice of awarding too little by unjustly awarding far too much." (*per* Lord Mustill at p 278).

Avoiding both forms of injustice requires damages to be generally available for a lost consumer surplus.

Fully complying with basic principle, and putting the injured party in the position they would have been in had the contract been performed, raises issues in relation to the limitations currently placed on the award of damages for mental distress. The availability of such damages will be returned to below (see page 469).

Time

Damages are usually assessed in accordance with the circumstances existing at the time of the breach. However, the time of breach can be displaced in appropriate circumstances[2]. Assessment at the time of the breach "is not an absolute rule; if to follow it would give rise to injustice, the court has power to fix such other date as may be appropriate in the circumstances" (*Johnson* v

Agnew [1979] 1 All ER 883 at p 896). The determination of the appropriateness of some other date should depend upon the rule as to mitigation of damages. The duty to mitigate means that the injured party will not be compensated for any loss which he could have avoided by taking reasonable steps after the breach. If the mitigation rule does not indicate that he should have acted to limit his loss immediately upon the breach occurring, then the time for the calculation of damages may similarly be delayed. In *Suleman* v *Shahsavari* [1989] 2 All ER 460 the duty to mitigate indicated that damages were not to be calculated in accordance with the circumstances at the time of the breach but at the time of judgment. In that case:

> Mr Suleman thought that he had contracted to buy a house. Unfortunately for him it was eventually decided that the solicitor of the vendor had not had authority to sign the contract of sale on the vendor's behalf. When there was no completion of the supposed contract of sale, Mr Suleman initially sought specific performance against the vendor. Specific performance was eventually denied and it was determined that the solicitor's lack of authority meant that there was no contract of sale. On that basis, Mr Suleman claimed damages from the vendor's solicitor for breach of warranty of his authority.

Mr Suleman succeeded in his action against the solicitor. The court had to determine the damages to be paid. The difference between the market price of the house and the "contract" price on the supposed date of completion of the sale was £9,500. The difference with reference to the date of judgment was £29,500. Mr Suleman was awarded £29,500 on the basis that it had been reasonable for him to delay seeking such damages while trying to claim specific performance against the vendors. His actions were not contrary to the duty to mitigate. Andrew Park QC (sitting as a deputy judge of the High Court) said (at p 463):

> "[Mr Suleman] has conducted himself entirely reasonably in seeking to obtain specific performance. . . He has been in no way dilatory over his claim and cannot be accused of having unreasonably failed to mitigate his damage."

2. Reliance loss

The basic principle on which contractual damages are awarded allows for the protection of the expectation interest, but there are cases in which the injured party may not attempt to claim the "profit" he should have derived from the contract, but merely the expenses he has incurred in reliance upon the contract. This is referred to as reliance loss, and a claim for reliance loss may well occur because the injured party finds it difficult to establish what profit, if any, he would have made on the contract. That was the situation in *Anglia Television* v *Reed* [1971] 3 All ER 690 when Robert Reed broke his contract with Anglia to be the leading man in a film to be made for television entitled *The Man in the Wood*. His breach meant that the film could not be made. Anglia sued for damages but did not claim for lost profit as they could "not say what their profit on this contract would have been if Mr Reed had come here and performed it". Anglia sued for their wasted expenditure and recovered it (see further below, page 468). Lord Denning MR said (at p 692):

> "a plaintiff in such a case as this has an election: he can either claim for his loss of profits; or for his wasted expenditure. But he must elect between them.

He cannot claim both. If he has not suffered any loss of profits — or if he cannot prove what his loss of profits would have been — he can claim in the alternative the expenditure which has been thrown away, that is, wasted, by reason of the breach".

Two points in that *dictum* deserve comment. First, we must look at the question of whether the injured party can always claim his reliance loss rather than his expectation loss. Secondly, some consideration needs to be given to whether there is a bar upon claiming both expectation and reliance loss.

The first point to consider is whether the injured party can always claim his reliance loss. The question becomes important if the contract is one on which the injured party would have made a loss, ie his expectation loss is less than his reliance loss because he made a bad bargain. The answer is that the injured party is free to make whichever claim he chooses, but he will not recover a greater sum in a reliance claim than he would have done if he had claimed his expectation loss. The basic contractual principle of putting the injured party in the position he would have been in had the contract been fulfilled is not overridden by the claim to reliance loss. This can be made more intelligible by consideration of two cases, *C & P Haulage* v *Middleton* [1983] 3 All ER 94 and *CCC Films (London) Ltd* v *Impact Quadrant Films Ltd* [1984] 3 All ER 298.

In *C & P Haulage* v *Middleton* [1983] 3 All ER 94:

Mr Middleton was a self-employed engineer. C & P granted him a six-monthly renewable licence to occupy certain premises. He spent money making the premises suitable for his work — a wall had to be built, a telephone moved and electricity laid on. It was an express term of the licence that fixtures put in by Mr Middleton were not to be removed at the expiry of the licence. Ten weeks before the end of a six month term, he was wrongfully ejected from the premises by C & P. As a temporary measure, he worked from home until well after the six month period would have expired.

Mr Middleton claimed the cost of the improvements he had made to the premises. The court held that C & P had been in breach of contract, in ejecting him from the premises before the expiry of the six month term, but he had not suffered any loss and was entitled only to nominal damages. He had not had to pay for other premises, as he had used his home, and he had not had to shut down his business and lost profits thereby. He would have lost the money spent on improving the premises even if C & P had waited until the end of the six months to eject him, and he could not succeed in a claim for that expenditure. The court was being asked to put Mr Middleton back in the position he would have been in had he not made the contract. The Court of Appeal refused to do that. Contract damages are to put the injured party in the position he would have been in had the contract been performed. He would have lost the money he spent if the licence had simply not been renewed at the end of the contract period, with no breach by C & P. Basically Mr Middleton had made a bad bargain and contract damages are not to compensate for that.

The line taken by the Court of Appeal in *C & P Haulage* v *Middleton* was followed by Hutchinson J in *CCC Films (London) Ltd* v *Impact Quadrant Films Ltd* [1984] 3 All ER 298 but in the latter case it was not obvious that what the court had to deal with was a bad bargain, and the judge had to consider the question of the burden of proof. In *CCC Films (London) Ltd* v *Impact Quadrant Films Ltd*:

> IQ owned the rights to certain films. IQ granted CCC a licence to exploit, distribute, and exhibit three films (*Dead of Night, Children Shouldn't Play with Dead Things* and *Blue Blood*). CCC paid IQ $12,000 for the licence. IQ delivered the films but they then undertook their safe delivery to Munich, to a potential purchaser who might help CCC exploit their licence. In breach of contract, IQ failed to insure the safe delivery of the films to Munich. CCC could not establish any lost profits from the breach but claimed the $12,000 from IQ as wasted expenditure. Neither party produced evidence of whether it would or would not have been possible for CCC to recoup that expenditure had the contract been performed.

Hutchinson J held that the injured party had an unfettered choice whether to claim for reliance or expectation loss. If he claimed for reliance loss then it was for the party in breach to establish that the injured party's expenditure would not have been recouped had the contract been performed, ie it was for the party in breach to establish that the injured party had made a bad bargain. In coming to this conclusion Hutchinson J quoted from, and adopted, the reasoning of Learned Hand CJ in *L Albert & Son* v *Armstrong Rubber Co* (1949) 178 F 2d at p 189. Hutchinson J quoted (at p 311):

> "In cases where the venture would have proved profitable to the promisee there is no reason why he should not recover his expenses. On the other hand, on those occasions in which the performance would not have covered the promisee's outlay, such a result imposes the risk of the promisee's contract upon the promisor. We cannot agree that the promisor's default in performance should under this guise make him an insurer of the promisee's venture; yet it does not follow that the breach should not throw upon him the duty of showing that the value of the performance would in fact have been less than the promisee's outlay. It is often very hard to learn what the value of the performance would have been; and it is a common expedient, and a just one, in such situations to put the peril of the answer upon the party who by his wrong has made the issue relevant to the rights of the other. On principle, therefore, the proper solution would seem to be that the promisee may recover this outlay in preparation for the performance, subject to the privilege of the promisor to reduce it by as much as he can show that the promisee would have lost, if the contract had been performed."

In the instant case CCC recovered. IQ could not establish that CCC would not have recouped the sum claimed had the contract been performed. (See also *Commonwealth of Australia* v *Amann Aviation Pty Ltd* (1991) 66 ALJR 123.) It may be, however, that this reversal of the normal burden of proof applies only where it is the breach which makes it impossible for the injured party to establish that performance of the contract would at least have allowed him, or her, to recoup expenditure (*Dataliner* v *Vehicle Builders and Repairers Assn* [1995] *The Independent* 30 August, Lexis).

The second point which should be considered is whether both expectation and reliance loss can be claimed. In order to consider that question, certain terminological problems need to be noted and avoided. In the above discussion the term "profit" has been used to encompass the entire sum which the injured party would have derived from the contractual performance, ie the gross profit. When used in this loose way, as it was for example in *Anglia Television* v

Reed, the terminology can lead to confusion. The term could be made more explicit by referring to the "gross" profit because it encompasses two elements: the net profit after deduction of expenses and the expenses. Once this terminological problem is recognized it helps to explain what should be meant when it is stated that it is not possible to recover for both lost profits and wasted expenditure (see Lord Denning MR above in *Anglia Television* v *Reed* and *Cullinane* v *British "Rema" Manufacturing Co Ltd* [1954] 1 QB 292). It certainly should not be possible to recover twice for the same loss and this must be the true limitation. If the claim for profits was, as it normally would be, a claim for the gross profits, then clearly the injured party could not recover both gross profit and expenses. If he could he would be recovering his expenses twice because, in addition to being recovered separately, the expenses would also be encompassed within the sum awarded for the lost gross profit. However, that should not prevent the success of claims to both net profit and expenses. If the injured party limited his claim for lost profits to his net profit, then he should additionally be able to claim his expenses. Together they would make up only the gross profit and the full extent of his loss. There would be no double recovery. Statements as to the mutual exclusion of claims for expectation and reliance loss must be viewed with caution against the background of the terminological difficulties. The basic prohibition must simply be against allowing the injured party to recover the same loss twice (see Macleod [1970] JBL 19).

Pre-contract expenditure

On a slightly different point it is necessary to give some further consideration to the damages awarded in *Anglia Television* v *Reed* [1971] 3 All ER 690. In that case the main part of the expenditure wasted had been incurred before the contract with Reed was concluded. Before contracting with Reed, Anglia Television had arranged a place to film and had employed a director, a designer and a stage manager. Under the contract Reed was to be available to Anglia between 9 September and 11 October. However, Reed's agent had double-booked him and on 3 September Anglia were informed that he would not be making their film. Anglia tried hard but could not find a substitute and they abandoned the proposed film. However, when Anglia sued, Reed argued that he was liable for only part of the expenditure that they were trying to recover. He claimed he was liable for only the £854.65 spent after he contracted with Anglia. The Court of Appeal awarded Anglia the whole £2,750 they were claiming, despite the fact that most of it was incurred before Reed contracted. Obviously the pre-contract expenditure had not been incurred in reliance on the contract, but it had been wasted because of such reliance and the court thought that it was simply a matter of whether or not the loss was too remote, and it held that it was not (on remoteness see page 474). Obviously, recovery of pre-contract expenditure should similarly be limited by the question of what the injured party would have recouped had the contract been performed.

3. Restitution

An outline of the law of restitution is provided in Chapter 22. The point to be made here is that, although it is more likely that a restitutionary remedy will be sought, and obtained, where, for example, questions of mistake or duress arise, there is some limited scope for restitutionary recovery where there has been a breach of contract.

The basis of restitutionary recovery is that the defendant has been unjustly enriched at the plaintiff's expense. There is a basic division between two types of situation in which the defendant's enrichment may be seen to be "at the plaintiff's expense". The first is unjust enrichment by subtraction where the defendant's enrichment derives directly from the plaintiff's loss ie the defendant's enrichment correlates to the plaintiff's loss. The second is unjust enrichment by wrong. In that type of case, the enrichment is said to be at the expense of the plaintiff purely in the sense that the defendant has gained through a wrong committed against the plaintiff — no loss by the plaintiff need be established (see page 519).

In relation to enrichment by subtraction, where there has been a breach, there are basically two types of situation to consider. (In relation to both, the breach will have led to the termination of the contract so that restitutionary recovery can be considered.) The first situation is where the claimant has made a money payment to the defendant. Generally, the enrichment is obvious in the handing over of a sum of money (see page 515). Recovery of the payment will be based on the claim that the reason for the payment has gone or, more technically, that there has been a "total failure of consideration" from the perspective of the claimant. ("Consideration" basically here refers to the performance and does not relate to the mere promise to perform.) The situation differs from recovery of reliance loss for breach where damages will be restricted in the case of a bad bargain. Here it is not relevant that restitutionary recovery will leave the claimant better off than if the contract had been performed. The basis of recovery is the defendant's enrichment, not the claimant's loss. Where the claimant has provided a service for the defendant, the "enrichment" of the defendant is less obvious (see page 515). Recovery of the value of the service has been seen as historically based upon free acceptance, but it is argued that it is properly to be seen as also based on failure of consideration. It is contentious whether the contract price should place a limit upon what can be recovered as the value of the services provided (see page 530).

As has been indicated, the second type of case in which the defendant can be regarded as enriched at the expense of the claimant is enrichment by wrong. The line has recently been taken by the House of Lords in *Attorney General* v *Blake* [2000] 4 All ER 385 that, in very exceptional cases, an accounting of profits may be ordered to allow the claimant recovery of the defendant's profit from his, or her, breach of contract (see page 535).

4. Damages for mental distress

The usual contractual damages claim will relate to damage to the injured party's economic interest but it may also cover personal injury or damage to property. However, with a limited exception, contract damages do not encompass damages for mental distress, ie damages for vexation, frustration, anxiety and disappointment. The basic restriction was established in *Addis* v *Gramophone Co Ltd* [1909] AC 488. In that case:

Mr Addis was employed as manager of G Co's business in Calcutta. His contract entitled him to six months' notice of dismissal. G Co gave him six months' notice but immediately appointed his successor and ensured that Mr Addis could no longer act as manager.

The manner of his dismissal injured Mr Addis' feelings but the House of Lords would not allow him to recover a sum in damages for that injury.

Briefly, after the decision in *Cox* v *Philips Industries* [1976] 1 WLR 638, it appeared that the courts might be in the process of distinguishing *Addis* out of existence, but *Cox* was overruled by the Court of Appeal in *Bliss* v *South East Thames Regional Health Authority* [1987] ICR 700 and claims for damages for mental distress must now be regarded as limited to certain types of contracts — contracts with appropriate "objects" or "purposes". In *Bliss*:

> The plaintiff was employed by the defendant authority as a consultant orthopaedic surgeon. The plaintiff's relationship with a colleague became very bad. In breach of contract, the defendant authority required the plaintiff to undergo a psychiatric examination. When he refused to comply he was suspended.

The defendant authority had repudiated the plaintiff's contract of employment and he accepted the repudiation and claimed damages. At first instance the award of damages to the plaintiff included a sum for mental distress. The Court of Appeal refused to allow recovery of such damages. The case was effectively one of wrongful dismissal and the court considered itself to be bound by the decision in *Addis* in relation to such a claim. However, Dillon LJ, with whom the other members of the court agreed, thought that, although the prohibition against damages for mental distress was a general one, there were limited exceptions. He said (at pp 717–718):

> "The general rule laid down by the House of Lords in *Addis* is that where damages fall to be assessed for breach of contract rather than in tort it is not permissible to award general damages for frustration, mental distress, injured feelings or annoyance occasioned by the breach. . . There are exceptions now recognized where the contract which has been broken was itself a contract to provide peace of mind or freedom from distress: see *Jarvis* v *Swans Tours Ltd* [1973] 1 QB 233 and *Heywood* v *Wellers* [1976] QB 446."

The basic restriction upon damages for mental distress, with its limited exception, was followed by the Court of Appeal in *Hayes* v *James & Charles Dodd* [1990] 2 All ER 815, although with some indication that further extension of the availability of such damages might occur. In that case:

> Mr and Mrs Hayes ran a motor repair business in London. They decided to expand and buy a motor repair business in Tenterden. The premises they eventually bought had only a narrow front access. Before they made the purchase they had been wrongly, and negligently, assured by the defendants, their solicitors, that there was a right of way at the rear giving good access to the garage. After they made the purchase the rear access was blocked. The premises could not be run successfully as a motor repair business with the narrow front access alone. The purchase had been made in 1982 but they were not able to dispose of all of the property until 1987.

Mr and Mrs Hayes suffered considerable financial difficulties because of the purchase and were awarded damages against the negligent solicitors for their financial losses. However, at first instance, they were also awarded damages for mental distress and that award was overturned by the Court of Appeal. The court held that it was not a case in which damages for mental distress could be awarded (see also *Alexander* v *Rolls Royce Motor Cars* [1996] RTR 95).

Staughton LJ thought that, "as a matter of policy", damages for mental distress were limited in contract. He quoted the restriction imposed by Dillon LJ in *Bliss* to contracts "to provide peace of mind or freedom from distress". However, he also considered that (at p 824):

"It may be that the class is somewhat wider than that. But it should not. . . include any case where the object of the contract was not comfort or pleasure, or the relief of discomfort, but simply carrying on a commercial activity with a view to profit."

The addition of contracts the object of which is to provide pleasure seems to be necessary to encompass the holiday contract in *Jarvis* v *Swans Tours* (see below), which was one of the cases Dillon LJ cited to justify his original statement of the exception. More recently, the same, restrictive approach to the availability of damages for mental distress was again reasserted by the Court of Appeal in *Watts* v *Morrow* [1991] 1 WLR 1421 (Furmston (1993) 6 JCL 64). The case was concerned with a survey of property which, in breach of contract, the defendant surveyor had performed negligently. The plaintiffs were busy people who wished to purchase a second home to relax in at weekends. The survey report indicated that the house they had decided upon had no major defects. That was inaccurate, and the plaintiffs had to expend considerable time and money in having it repaired. They recovered the difference between what they paid for the property and what it was worth because of the defects. They did not recover the larger sum which represented the cost of the repairs (see Dugdale (1992) 8 *Professional Negligence* 152 and see above, page 460). In addition, although, following *Perry* v *Sidney Phillips & Son* [1982] 3 All ER 705 (see below) they recovered for the mental distress consequent upon the physical inconvenience they had suffered, they did not recover more generally for their mental distress. Bingham LJ stated that such damages are not generally available. He said (at p 1445):

"A contract-breaker is not in general liable for any distress, frustration, anxiety, displeasure, vexation, tension or aggravation which his breach of contract may cause to the innocent party. This rule is not, I think, founded on the assumption that such reactions are not foreseeable, which they surely are or may be, but on considerations of policy."

It is worth emphasising the clear statement that the general non-availability of damages for mental distress is a matter of policy. There is also here, in the reference to foreseeability, a specific exclusion of any attempt to conceal that policy decision behind a contrived usage of the remoteness rule (see below). Bingham LJ stated the exception to the general unavailability of damages for mental distress. He said (at p 1445):

"But the rule is not absolute. Where the very object of a contract is to provide pleasure, relaxation, peace of mind or freedom from molestation, damages will be awarded if the fruit of the contract is not provided or if the contrary result is procured instead. If the law did not cater for this exceptional category of case it would be defective . . .".

This would seem to state the basic situation in English law. Damages for mental distress are not generally available in contract. They are exceptionally available where the object of the contract is to provide pleasure, relaxation, peace of mind or freedom from molestation. Although it is difficult to fit the case of *Ruxley* v *Forsyth* [1995] 3 All ER 268 (see above at page 462) into any of these categories, the perceived need to award the "consumer surplus" in that case, rather than either the difference in value or cost of cure, might have been seen as indicating the need to extend these exceptional categories — at the very least — but the courts have emphasised the restriction of damages for mental distress to those exceptional categories (eg *Farley* v *Skinner* [2000] 73 Con LR 70, *French* v *Barclays Bank* [1998] IRLR 646, *Knott* v *Bolton* (1995) 45 Con LR 127). There is an additional exception where the mental distress is consequent upon physical inconvenience.

As we have already noted, the courts have seen the general non-availability of damages as a matter of policy, but there has been no clear identification of what that policy is. However, in *Hayes* v *Dodd* Staughton LJ did say (at p 823):

> "Like the judge, I consider that the English courts should be wary of adopting what he called 'the United States practice of huge awards'. Damages awarded for negligence or want of skill, whether against professional men or anyone else, must provide fair compensation, but no more than that. And I would not view with enthusiasm the prospect that every shipowner in the Commercial Court, having successfully claimed for unpaid freight or demurrage, would be able to add a claim for mental distress suffered while he was waiting for his money."

Apart from the unlikelihood of an English court succumbing to the temptation of awarding "U.S.-style" damages, the point can be made that if mental distress has been occasioned by a breach then damages covering it would only amount to "fair compensation" in the sense that the award would simply be complying with a basic principle and putting the injured party in the position that that party would have been in had the contract been performed. In the light of that, the basis of Staughton LJ's statement would seem to be an apprehension that damages for mental distress will not be accurately calculated and will thereby not comply with a basic principle. The assessment of the sum of money which should be awarded in relation to this type of damage does pose obvious difficulties. The basis of the general non-availability of damages for mental distress would seem to be an assumption that the difficulties involved in that assessment, and the uncertainty that would generate, outweigh the benefits of making the mental distress caused by the breach the responsibility of the party in breach and complying with general principle (Macdonald (1994) 7 JCL 134).

A further restriction on damages for mental distress should also be noted, but it is one which is unlikely to be important as long as the generally restrictive approach indicated above is adhered to. It was emphasised in *Hayes* v *Dodd* that damages should not be awarded simply to cover the tension or frustration involved in a legal dispute. Staughton LJ pointed out that English law does not award damages simply for "wrongfully defending an action" (at p 823, see also Purchas LJ at p 827).

Examples

In considering the type of case in which an award of damages for mental distress is possible, it is worth considering those situations in which such damages have already been given by the courts. In *Jarvis* v *Swans Tours* [1973] 1 All ER 71 damages for lost enjoyment were awarded in relation to a contract for a holiday. In that case:

> Mr Jarvis booked a winter sports holiday with Swan. The holiday was described as a "house party". The brochure referred to afternoon tea and cakes and a yodeller evening and stated that ski-packs would be available. For the first week there were thirteen people there, but for the second week Mr Jarvis was the sole member of the "house party". The cakes for tea were merely crisps and dry nutcake. Full-sized skis were only available for two days. The yodeller evening turned out to consist of a local man coming to the hotel, in his work clothes, and quickly singing a few songs.

Mr Jarvis claimed damages for breach of contract as the holiday was not as promised in the brochure. At first instance he was merely awarded £31.72 as the difference in value between what he contracted for and what he got. The Court of Appeal awarded £125. It considered that he should be compensated for his lost enjoyment (see also *Jackson* v *Horizon Holidays Ltd* [1975] 3 All ER 92). A further example of a contract to provide pleasure is to be found in the Scottish case of *Diesen* v *Samson* 1971 SLT 49 (Sheriff Court Reports) where a bride was awarded damages for the injury caused to her feelings when the photographer she had booked failed to turn up to take photographs of her wedding.

In *Heywood* v *Wellers* [1976] 1 All ER 300, the purpose of the contract was to provide relief from anxiety. In that case:

> The plaintiff had employed solicitors to obtain an injunction to prevent a man from molesting her. The solicitors were negligent and he molested her further.

Damages for mental distress were awarded. The contract was not for a commercial purpose but to provide relief from distress, just as in *Jarvis* and *Diesen* v *Samson* the object of the contracts was to provide pleasure. In each case the mental distress arose from the breach itself and not from the ensuing litigation.

Mental distress consequent on physical inconvenience

In addition to the above cases, damages for mental distress can be recovered where it is a consequence of the physical inconvenience caused by the breach. In *Perry* v *Sidney Phillips & Son* [1982] 3 All ER 705:

> Ivan Perry purchased a house on the faith of a survey carried out by the defendant surveyors which stated that the house was in good order. After moving in, Mr Perry discovered that the roof leaked and was in poor condition and the septic tank was inefficient and "gave off an offensive odour". These defects caused him distress, worry, and inconvenience and his financial position was such that, with the defendant surveyors denying liability, he could not afford to have them fixed.

In addition to damages for the reduced value of the property, because of the defects, the Court of Appeal agreed with the judge at first instance that Mr Perry was entitled to damages for his mental distress. Kerr LJ said (at p 712):

> "So far as the question of damages for vexation and inconvenience is concerned, it should be noted that the deputy judge awarded these not for the tension or frustration of a person who is involved in a legal dispute in which the other party refuses to meet his liabilities. If he had done so it would have

been wrong, because such aggravation is experienced by almost all litigants. He awarded these damages because of the physical consequences of the breach, which were all foreseeable at the time."

(Staughton LJ, in referring to the case in *Hayes* v *James & Charles Dodd* [1990] 2 All ER 815 (at p 823), emphasised the physical consequences of the breach.)

An award of damages for mental distress is required in appropriate cases if the basic principle behind contract damages is to be fulfilled[3]. Without it there will be cases where the injured party will not be put in the position he would have been in had the contract been performed (Harris, Ogus & Phillips (1979) 95 LQR 581).

5. Remoteness of damages

There is a practical need for some restriction upon the liability of the party in breach for losses which he has caused. The sale of quite a cheap item may lead to very extensive liability if a defect in it causes a great deal of damage to the other party's property, particularly if the damage to that property affects the profits of that other party's business. Some limitation must be put upon the damage for which the party in breach can be liable. The rule as to remoteness of damage serves this purpose. It prevents recovery for a loss which is too remote.

The basic rule stems from the case of *Hadley* v *Baxendale* (1854) 9 Ex 341. In that case, the facts were as follows:

> The plaintiffs were millers. They owned and occupied the City Steam Mills, Gloucester. The crank shaft of their steam engine was broken so that the mill could not function. They arranged with the defendant carriers for the shaft to be taken to W Joyce & Co of Greenwich, who had agreed to make a new shaft, using the old one as a model. The defendant carriers broke their contract by delaying delivery. The new shaft was not received for several days after it should have been. The plaintiffs lost profits because of the delay in the return to work of the mill. The defendants argued that such loss of profits was too remote for them to be liable.

Alderson B set out the test for remoteness. He said (at p 355):

> "Where two parties have made a contract which one of them has broken the damages which the other party ought to receive in respect of such a breach of contract should be such as may fairly and reasonably be considered as either arising naturally, ie according to the usual course of things, from such breach of the contract itself, or such as may reasonably be supposed to have been in the contemplation of both parties at the time they made the contract as the probable result of the breach of it".

This is commonly known as the rule in *Hadley* v *Baxendale* and it can be broken down into two parts. The party in breach will be liable for losses either:

(a) arising naturally, ie according to the usual course of things; or
(b) such as may reasonably be supposed to have been in the contemplation of the parties, at the time they made the contract, as a probable result of the breach.

In effect, although the remoteness rule is often stated in this dual form, both parts relate to what the parties could reasonably contemplate as not unlikely to result from the breach (see *Heron II* below). The only difference between the two parts of the rule is the degree of knowledge attributable to the party in breach at the time of contracting. The first part of the rule deals with what any reasonable man should contemplate, because that is what would "usually" occur. The second part of the rule deals with the more extensive reasonable contemplation which should be produced by knowledge of special circumstances extending the plaintiff's loss beyond the "usual". In effect, the question almost inevitably is "what could have been contemplated by the party in breach, as a reasonable man?" The injured party should know of the special circumstances which may add to his losses on a breach occurring. In *Kpohraror* v *Woolwich Building Society* [1996] 4 All ER 119, Evans LJ said (at p 127):

> "The starting point for any application of *Hadley* v *Baxendale* is the extent of the shared knowledge of both parties when the contract was made (. . . including the possibility that knowledge of the defendant alone is enough). When that is established, it may often be the case that the first and second parts of the rule overlap, or at least that it is unnecessary to draw a clear line of demarcation between them".

In *Hadley* v *Baxendale*, the prolonged closure of the mill, and the loss of profits thereby, was not viewed as a "natural" result of the breach. It was thought that the millers might have had a spare crankshaft. In addition, such loss could not be brought within the second part of the rule. All that had been made known to the carriers at the time of contracting was that they were transporting a broken crank shaft for millers. They were given no special knowledge of the situation to bring the loss within their reasonable contemplation as a probable result of the breach. It was not made known that the millers did not possess a spare shaft.

Viewing the two parts of the rule as simply making up one rule was fully explained by Asquith LJ in *Victoria Laundry (Windsor) Ltd* v *Newman Industries Coulson & Co Ltd* [1949] 2 KB 528. In addition, the case well illustrates the difference between the "usual" type of loss and that for which additional knowledge, at the time of contracting, is required. In that case:

> Victoria Laundry wished to expand their business, and they ordered a larger boiler from Newman Industries. Delivery was to take place on 5 June. The boiler was damaged before delivery, and delivery was delayed until 8 November. Newman were aware of the nature of Victoria Laundry's business and had been informed that Victoria Laundry intended to put the boiler in use in the shortest possible time.

Victoria Laundry claimed for the profit they would have earned with the boiler in the time between 5 June and 8 November. In particular, Victoria Laundry claimed for the loss of, first, the extra laundry business they could have taken on, there being a shortage of laundries at the time, and, secondly, the loss of a number of highly lucrative dyeing contracts which they could and would have accepted from the Ministry of Supply. The Court of Appeal allowed recovery for the former but not the latter, although the court envisaged recovery of a sum to cover the loss of "ordinary" dyeing business.

Newman knew before contracting that Victoria Laundry were in the business of laundering and dyeing and that the boiler was wanted for immediate use in that business. They were supplying a boiler in accordance with strict technical specifications and could be taken to know more about the use or purposes to which boilers were put than the uninformed layman. They did not know whether the boiler was to replace a unit of equal or inferior capacity. The court thought that reasonable persons in their shoes must be taken to foresee that a laundry which wanted a boiler for immediate use, at a time when there was a shortage of laundry facilities, would be liable to suffer a loss if delivery was delayed for five months. That was the case whether they wanted the boiler to extend their business, maintain it, or to reduce a loss. In other words, Victoria Laundry could recover for the ordinary extra laundry business they would have taken on. They could not recover for the loss of the special dyeing contracts. In the absence of additional information, Newman could not foresee that loss as liable to result from the breach. No notice had been given of the possible, highly lucrative, dyeing contracts and their loss was too remote.

It was indicated above that the two parts of the rule in *Hadley* could be reformulated as a single rule, capable of encompassing the different levels of knowledge to be attributed, in different circumstances, to the parties. In delivering the judgment of the Court of Appeal in *Victoria Laundry*, Asquith LJ reformulated the rule in *Hadley* in this way. He restated it as entitling the injured party to recover such part of his loss "as was at the time of the contract reasonably foreseeable as liable to result from the breach", and this is reflected in the above discussion of the case. However, in *Heron II* (*Koufos* v *Czarnikow Ltd*) [1969] 1 AC 350 the House of Lords criticised the *Victoria Laundry* formulation. It was seen as not sufficiently indicating the degree of probability with which the loss must be foreseen. In particular, their lordships felt that the test of remoteness in contract must be kept distinct from the lesser requirement in tort. They thought that the tort test encompassed any type of damage which was reasonably foreseeable, even though it might happen only "in the most unusual case". The contract test required a loss to be reasonably foreseen with a much greater degree of probability. Lord Reid (at p 386) thought that there was a good reason for the difference:

"In contract, if one party wishes to protect himself against a risk which to the other party would appear unusual, he can direct the other party's attention to it before the contract is made".

(See also Lord Pearce at p 413, and Lord Upjohn at p 423.) In contrast, in tort the parties could be strangers.

To distinguish the two tests, their lordships favoured referring to "reasonable contemplation" in contract, rather than "reasonable foreseeability". In addition, there was much discussion of how the degree of probability necessary in contract should be expressed. It was seen as something less than an even chance but greater than what is required in tort. Various phrases were thought to encompass the requisite degree of probability — "not unlikely", "substantial probability", "likely", "liable to result", "serious possibility", "real danger". The extensive search for a way to express the requisite degree of probability is not very helpful. The main point to note is that the House of Lords wished to keep the contract and tort tests distinct, and required a higher degree of probability in contract than in tort (see below, page 478). This is made clear by referring to what can be reasonably contemplated as likely, or not unlikely, to result from the breach.

In *Heron II*, the facts were as follows:

A vessel was chartered to take a cargo of sugar from Constanza to Basrah, where there was a sugar market. It was the intention of the charterers to sell the sugar in the market immediately upon arrival there. In breach of contract the vessel arrived nine days late in Basrah. The market price had dropped in the intervening nine days and the charterers claimed the difference in the price from the owners of the ship.

The House of Lords held that the charterer was entitled to recover the difference in price of the sugar because of the nine day delay. The owner of the vessel had not known that the intention was to sell the sugar on arrival but he had known that there was a sugar market in Basrah. That being the case, he had to be taken to have realised that it was not unlikely that the sugar would be sold on arrival and he had to be taken to know that, in a market, prices fluctuate up and down from day to day. The charterer's loss was not too remote. It should have been contemplated as not unlikely to result from the delay.

The contract test for remoteness can be stated as being whether the loss was such that, at the time of contracting, the parties would have reasonably contemplated it as not unlikely to result from a breach. A number of general points must be emphasised in relation to this test before further consideration is given to the contract/tort distinction.

It should be emphasised that the parties need not have considered the possibility of a breach or its consequences at all. "Parties at the time of contracting contemplate not the breach of the contract but its performance". What matters is the conclusion of reasonable men, in the position of the parties, had they considered the question (*Victoria Laundry* at p 340). It should also be noted that the usual formulation of the rule refers to the contemplation of the parties and it must be emphasised that what might reasonably be contemplated by the injured party alone, because of his more extensive knowledge of any loss he might suffer, is irrelevant. The original two-part statement of the rule in *Hadley* emphasises that point. The remoteness test is really about what could be contemplated by the reasonable man in the position of the party in breach. However, as was made clear in *Victoria Laundry*, although the assessment is based on the reasonable man, what he may reasonably contemplate as not unlikely to result may be affected not only by actual knowledge of special circumstances but, more generally, by his position and the circumstances of the contract. If the party in breach is a businessman, then more may be taken to be within his reasonable contemplation as not unlikely to result, than if he is a consumer. In *Victoria Laundry* it was pointed out that the general knowledge of the business of those he contracts with may be taken to be more extensive in the case of a supplier than a carrier (distinguishing *Victoria Laundry* and *Hadley* v *Baxendale*). However, "it must always be a question of circumstances what one contracting party is presumed to know about the business activities of the other. No doubt the simpler the activity of the one, the more readily can it be inferred that the other would have reasonable knowledge thereof. However, when the activity of A involves complicated construction or manufacturing techniques, I see no reason why B who supplies a commodity that A intends to use in the course of those techniques should be assumed, merely because of the order for the commodity, to be aware of the details of all the techniques undertaken by A and the effect thereupon of any failure of or deficiency in that commodity." (*Balfour Beatty Construction (Scotland) Ltd* v *Scottish Power plc* 1994 SLT 807, Lord Jauncey at p 810).

(a) Contract/tort distinction and the type of loss

The contract/tort distinction emphasised by the House of Lords in *Heron II* must be returned to in the context of the judgments given by the Court of Appeal in *Parsons (H) (Livestock) Ltd* v *Uttley Ingham & Co Ltd* [1978] 1 All ER 525. In that case:

> Mr Parsons was a pig farmer. He ordered, from the defendants, a hopper to store pig nuts. The defendants were manufacturers of bulk food storage hoppers. The defendants knew the purpose for which the hopper was required. The contract described the hopper as "fitted with a ventilated top". The ventilator was sealed for transport to the pig farm and when the defendants installed the hopper they forgot to open the ventilator. The hopper was twenty-eight feet high, and it was not possible to see that the ventilator was closed from the ground. Because of the lack of ventilation some of the pig nuts stored in the hopper became mouldy. The farmer continued to feed them to the pigs until the pigs became ill. An outbreak of E Coli ensued and 254 pigs died.

The question was whether the defendants were liable, in damages, for the death of the pigs. The Court of Appeal held that they were, the losses were not too remote. Scarman LJ, with Orr LJ agreeing, found that the remoteness test from the *Heron II* was satisfied. The *degree* of loss did not have to come within the test, provided the *type* of loss did, and "no more than common sense was needed for them to appreciate that food affected by bad storage conditions might well cause illness in the pigs fed on it". This distinction, between extent of loss and type of loss, is not without difficulty. What constitutes a type of loss? Was the lost profit on the ordinary laundry business really a different type of loss from the lost profit on the highly lucrative dyeing contracts in *Victoria Laundry*? A distinction has, however, been made. In *Brown* v *KMR Services Ltd* [1995] 4 All ER 598 the losses of Lloyd's names were unforeseeable in their extent, due to the unanticipated size and frequency of the various disasters that occurred between 1987 and 1990. The agent who had misadvised them could not, however, claim that the losses were too remote. They were of the type which were clearly liable to result. The point to note in this context is the *dictum* of Stuart Smith LJ (at p 621):

> "I accept that difficulty in practice may arise in categorisation of loss into types or kinds, especially where financial loss is involved. But I do not see any difficulty in holding that loss of ordinary business profits is different in kind from that flowing from a particular contract which gives rise to very high profits, the existence of which is unknown to the contracting party who therefore does not accept the risk of such loss occurring."

Of course, losses will often stem from "particular contracts", but the point has also been made that:

> "loss of profits claimed by reference to an extravagant or unusual bargain are not of the same type as damages referable to bargains that are usual" (*North Sea Energy* v *PTT* [1997] 2 Lloyd's Rep 418 at 438).

In *Parsons* Lord Denning MR took an approach which was rather different from that of the majority, although it led him to the same conclusion. He thought that the test of remoteness should not depend on whether an action was brought in contract or tort. He thought that the "contract test" belonged with a loss of profits or economic loss, whether in contract or tort, and the lesser requirement of the "tort test" should be applied to all cases of physical injury or damage to property. Lord Denning MR thought that Mr Parsons could succeed because, although he was claiming in contract, his claim was for physical damage and the remoteness test was the lesser "tort test". On that basis, it was enough that the defendants could have foreseen a "slight possibility" that the pigs would be ill. Both Scarman and Orr LJJ thought that the authorities did not support this distinction between loss of profit and physical damage. However, on the difference in the remoteness test in tort and contract, Lord Scarman said (at p 535):

> "I agree with [Lord Denning] in thinking it absurd that the test for remoteness of damage should, in principle, differ according to the legal classification of the cause of action".

(See also *Brown* v *KMR Services Ltd* [1995] 4 All ER 598, *per* Hobhouse LJ at p 643; *Banque Bruxelles* v *Eagle Star* [1995] 2 All ER 769, *per* Bingham MR at p 481 (reversed on other grounds *sub nom South Australia Asset Corporation* v *York Montague* [1996] 3 All ER 365). And see *Henderson* v *Merrett Syndicates Ltd* [1994] 3 All ER 506.)

(b) Economic justification

It was indicated above that the rule restricting damages to losses which are not too remote was a matter of practical justice. It would be too harsh if the party in breach was liable for all the losses caused by his breach. In addition, the remoteness test has been perceived as economically efficient (Posner, *Economic Analysis of Law*, 2nd ed at pp 94–95). The remoteness rule:

> "induces the party with knowledge of the risk either to take any appropriate precautions himself or, if he believes that the other party might be the more efficient loss avoider, to disclose the risk to the other party and pay him to assume it".

(See also Harris, *Remedies in Contract and Tort* (1988) at pp 52–61.)

The remoteness rule therefore means that the party supplying goods or a service does not always have to increase his prices to protect himself against unusual losses by the other party if the supplier breaches. The other party has an incentive to protect himself until the situation reaches the point at which it is cheaper for him to inform the supplier and make a contract which is priced to take into account the risk of those losses.

(c) An additional requirement?

It has been suggested that the remoteness rule, as stated above, is not by itself a sufficient restriction on the liability of the party in breach for "unusual" losses. It has been suggested that practical justice requires more, so that the situation is such that the party in breach, as a reasonable man, can be taken to have accepted the risk of that loss. It is not clear that there is any such additional requirement but the reason for the debate can be explained by the posing of a problem:

> "[P] rings up his local taxi driver and books a taxi to drive him to the airport at 7am the next day. He tells the driver that it is most important as he is flying

to New York to sign a multi-million dollar contract. The taxi driver oversleeps, [P] misses his flight and loses his deal. Is the taxi driver liable?" (Beale, Bishop, Furmston, *Contract Cases and Materials* 2nd ed (1990) at p 478).

In *British Columbia Sawmill Co* v *Nettleship* (1868) LR 3 CP 499 a sawmill was being constructed in Vancouver. The defendant was a carrier delivering parts of the mill in boxes. He lost a box which contained a vital part, although he did not know that to be the case. The loss of that part delayed the operation of the mill, but the carrier was not liable for the loss of profit caused by the delay. In the course of his judgment Willes J said (at p 509):

"There must have been knowledge under such circumstances as would raise the presumption that he intended to make himself liable for the special consequences and that the person contracting with him believed, and had reasonable grounds for believing, that he intended to undertake such liability and unless there was a special payment it would be very difficult to get a jury to come to such a conclusion."

See also *Horne* v *Midland Railway* (1873) LR 8 CP 131.

It has been denied that there is any requirement of a term accepting liability for the "special circumstances" (*Heron II* [1969] AC 350, at pp 421–422). However, it still seems open to doubt whether there is any such requirement falling short of a term[4].

6. Causation

The party in breach will not be liable for the injured party's loss if his breach is not regarded as a sufficient cause of it. It has to be an effective cause (*County Ltd* v *Girozentrale Securities* [1996] 3 All ER 834).

Problems arise from intervening acts and events. In *Monarch Steamship Co* v *A/B Karlshamns Oljefabriker* [1949] AC 196 the defendants contracted to carry goods for the plaintiffs from Manchuria to Sweden. In breach of contract, sailing was delayed. The ship did not reach Sweden before the outbreak of the Second World War. The ship was stopped and the plaintiffs incurred extra expense as a result of the goods continuing the voyage in a neutral ship. The defendants argued that they were not liable for the expense because it was not due to their breach but to the outbreak of war. It was held that the outbreak of war was not an intervening cause which broke the chain of causation. At the time of contracting, it had been foreseeable that delay might result in such problems being encountered. The situation would have been different had the plaintiffs' loss been caused by the ship being struck by a typhoon. That might happen at any time and the loss would not then have been regarded as caused by the defendants' delay (at p 215).

An intervening act will not break the chain of causation where it is an act which the party in breach is under an obligation to guard against. It is an implied term of the contract between banker and customer that the customer will draw his cheques with due care so that he does not facilitate fraud. When a customer made out a cheque in such a way that the amount could be readily altered, he was liable to the bank for the full amount paid out on a cheque which had been fraudulently increased by a third party (*London Joint Stock Bank* v *Macmillan* [1918] AC 777).

The injured party may break the chain of causation with his own negligence. That was the situation in *Quinn* v *Burch Bros (Builders)* [1966] 2 QB 370 where the defendants breached their contract with the plaintiff plasterer by failing to provide him with a step ladder. The plaintiff was injured when he tried to use an unsecured trestle instead of a step ladder. Paull J held that his negligence had broken the chain of causation (see also *Lambert* v *Lewis* [1982] AC 225).

The actions of the injured party, and their effect upon his claim to damages, are also considered in the context of the duty to mitigate and the problem of contributory negligence (see below).

7. Mitigation

"[Mitigation] imposes on a plaintiff the duty of taking all reasonable steps to mitigate the loss consequent on the breach; and debars him from claiming any part of the damage which is due to his neglect to take such steps" (*British Westinghouse Electric and Manufacturing Co Ltd* v *Underground Electric Railways Co of London* [1912] AC 673 *per* Lord Haldane at p 689).

Mitigation is frequently discussed in terms of a "duty" to mitigate, as it is in the quotation, but this can be misleading. There is no "duty" as such, but merely a limitation upon recoverable damages (*Sotiros Shipping Inc* v *Schmeiet Solholt; (The Solholt)* [1983] 1 Lloyd's Rep 605 at p 608). The question of what steps are reasonable is one of fact (*Payzu* v *Saunders* [1919] 2 KB 581 at p 586). The burden of showing a failure to mitigate is on the party in breach (*James Finlay & Co* v *NV Kwik Hoo Tong HM* [1928] 2 KB 604 at p 614).

Three aspects to mitigation can be identified. First, if there are reasonable steps which the injured party could take to reduce his loss, and if he does not take those steps, then the damages awarded to him will be limited to what he would have lost had he acted reasonably. Secondly, the expenses reasonably incurred in dealing with the breach will be recoverable. Thirdly, if the injured party takes action which in fact reduces his loss then the damages payable will be reduced accordingly.

(a) Reasonable steps to limit loss

The "duty" to mitigate means that the injured party cannot recover damages for any loss which he could have avoided by taking reasonable steps. There was no failure to mitigate in *James Finlay & Co* v *NV Kwik Hoo Tong HM* [1929] 1 KB 400 where the steps suggested by the party in breach would have damaged the injured party's commercial reputation. In that case, the facts were as follows:

> The plaintiffs contracted to purchase sugar from the defendants. The contract stated that it was to be shipped in September. It was shipped in October but, wrongly, the bill of lading stated that it had been shipped in September. Being unaware of the breach the plaintiffs contracted with sub-buyers for the sale on of the sugar. The contract with the sub-buyers stated that the bill of lading should provide

"conclusive evidence" of the date of shipment. The sub-buyers rejected the goods because of the inaccuracy of the bill of lading.

The plaintiffs sued the defendants. The defendants claimed that the plaintiffs were entitled only to nominal damages as the plaintiffs should have mitigated by enforcing the sub-sale, on the basis of the "conclusive evidence" clause. It was held that the plaintiffs did not have to mitigate in that way. Once they knew the truth, enforcing the sub-contract would not have been in the ordinary course of business and would have damaged their business reputation (see also *London & South of England Building Society* v *Stone* [1983] 1 WLR 1242).

In *Pilkington* v *Wood* [1953] Ch 770, again there was no failure to mitigate. The steps to reduce loss suggested by the party in breach were not reasonable. There the injured party had purchased land with a defective title because of his solicitor's negligence. When he sued his solicitor the court held that the injured party was not expected to have undertaken "a complicated and difficult piece of litigation", against the vendor of the land, to try to mitigate his loss. That was the case even though the solicitor was prepared to indemnify him in respect of the cost of that litigation.

The duty to mitigate was not satisfied in *Brace* v *Calder* [1895] 2 QB 253. There it was considered that it would have been reasonable to accept another contract from the party in breach as a means of reducing loss. In that case, the facts were as follows:

> The four defendants carried on business in partnership as Scotch whisky merchants. They contracted with the plaintiff for him to manage their office business for two years. Before the expiry of the two years the partnership was dissolved on the retirement of two of the partners. The other two partners carried on the business. The plaintiff stated that the dissolution of the partnership had terminated his contract. He claimed the salary that he would have earned during the remainder of the two years. The remaining partners wished to employ him on the same terms as the original agreement.

The Court of Appeal accepted that there had been a wrongful termination of the plaintiff's contract but held that he was entitled only to nominal damages. He could have mitigated his loss. It would have been reasonable to accept the alternative employment with the two partners. The situation would have been different had the plaintiff's technical dismissal on the termination of the original contract been more than that, if, for example, he had been dismissed in humiliating circumstances.

> "It is plain that the question of what it is reasonable for a person to do in mitigation of his damages cannot be a question of law but must be one of fact in the circumstances of each case. There may be cases where as a matter of fact it would be unreasonable to expect a plaintiff to consider any offer made in view of the treatment he has received from the defendant. If he had been rendering personal services and had been dismissed after being accused in the presence of others of being a thief, and if after that his employer had offered to take him back into his service, most persons would think he was justified in refusing the offer, and that it would be unreasonable to ask him in this way to mitigate the damages in an action for wrongful dismissal" (*Payzu* v *Saunders* [1919] 2 KB 581 (see below) *per* Bankes LJ at p 586).

The duty to mitigate was held to cover the new contract offered by the party in breach in *Payzu* v *Saunders* [1919] 2 KB 581. In that case, the facts were as follows:

The plaintiff had contracted to purchase crêpe de Chine from the defendant. The defendant was to supply it, as required, over a nine month period. The plaintiff was to have the goods on credit, payment to be made within one month of each delivery. Owing to a cheque going astray, the first payment was late and the defendant wrongly claimed to be able to terminate the contract. The defendant offered to continue to supply the plaintiff under a new contract on the same terms, except for the single change that payment was to be made on delivery. The plaintiff was in a position to pay on delivery but he refused the offer. The market price of the goods had risen.

The plaintiff claimed that the wrongful termination of the original contract entitled him to damages to cover the rise in the market price above the contract price. It was held that the plaintiff should have mitigated the loss by accepting the defendant's offer of a "cash on delivery" contract at the original price. Had the plaintiff accepted that offer, he would have obtained the goods at the original contract price but not on credit terms. In other words he would have avoided having to pay the increased market price and, on that basis, the court held that he was entitled to recover only for the loss of a month's credit on each order — ie the only loss he would have made had he accepted the defendant's offer. The court thought that there was nothing to make this a case in which it was not reasonable to avoid the increased market price by accepting the new offer from the party in breach. Scrutton LJ thought that "in commercial contracts it is generally reasonable to accept an offer from the party in default" (at p 589). See also *The Solholt (Sotiros Shipping Inc v Schmeiet Solholt)* [1983] 1 Lloyd's Rep 605.

However, there has been criticism of the approach taken in *Payzu v Saunders* (and *The Solholt*) to the claim to damages based on the rise in the market value of the goods between contract and delivery date. The effect of the court's decision was to transfer the benefit of that rise in the market from the injured party to the party in breach. The plaintiff's refusal of the defendant's offer meant that the defendant could realise the rise in value of the goods in the market. If the court had decided differently on the mitigation point that rise in value would have been paid in damages to the plaintiff — the original contract allocation of the market risk would have been maintained. As the court decided that the mitigation rule prevented the plaintiff from recovering that sum, the rise in market price of the goods was left with the defendant, who had lost it under the original contract allocation of the market risk (see Bridge (1989) 105 LQR 398).

(b) Expenses incurred

The above cases concern the argument that the injured party has failed to act as the reasonable man would have done to reduce his loss. In addition, where the injured party has incurred expenses in reacting to the breach, the party in breach may argue that those expenses are not recoverable because they were unreasonably incurred. *Banco de Portugal v Waterlow & Sons* [1932] AC 452 provides an example of a case where the expenditure was held to have been reasonable, and Lord Macmillan stated that the injured party's actions "ought not to be weighed in nice scales at the instance of the party whose breach of contract has occasioned the difficulty" (at p 506). In that case, the facts were as follows:

Waterlow contracted to print a series of "Vasco da Gama" 500 escudo bank notes for the bank. In breach of contract they printed and delivered a second batch to Marang, in the mistaken belief that he had the bank's authority. Marang and his associates formed the Banco de Angola e Metropole in Portugal to put the notes into circulation. When the Banco de Portugal discovered what had occurred, they called in all "Vasco da Gama" 500 escudo notes and redeemed both the authorised and unauthorised notes.

The Banco de Portugal claimed the cost of printing the notes and also the cost of redeeming the unauthorised notes. Waterlow contended that, as the authorised and unauthorised notes could be distinguished, the bank need not have paid out on the unauthorised notes. The House of Lords held that the bank could recover that sum. It had acted reasonably to maintain confidence in the currency.

Expenditure which is not reasonably incurred cannot be recovered. If the injured party takes out a loan to obtain the release of his ship, which has been detained in breach of contract, and the loan is at a very high rate of interest the interest charge will not be recovered where it is unreasonably incurred (*The Borag (Compania Financiera "Soleada" SA v Hamoor Tanker Corp Inc)* [1981] 1 All ER 856).

(c) Benefit gained

There is said to be one further aspect of mitigation, namely that the injured party cannot recover for a loss which he has avoided. Benefit derived from the breach is taken into account in calculating the loss it has caused.

> "This. . . does not impose on the plaintiff an obligation to take any step which a reasonable and prudent man would not ordinarily take in the course of his business. But when in the course of his business he has taken action arising out of the transaction, which action has diminished his loss, the effect in actual diminution of the loss he has suffered may be taken into account even though there was no duty on him to act" (*British Westinghouse Electric and Manufacturing Co Ltd v Underground Electric Railways Co of London Ltd* [1912] AC 673, *per* Viscount Haldane LC at p 689).

In *British Westinghouse Electric and Manufacturing Co Ltd v Underground Electric Railways Co of London Ltd* [1912] AC 673, there was a contract for the sale of turbines. The turbines supplied were not of the efficiency stated in the contract, and they were more expensive to run. Before the turbines were worn out, the purchaser replaced them with new turbines which were much more efficient than those originally contracted for. The extent of their increased efficiency was such that their purchase price was covered by the savings in the running costs which would have been incurred had the other machines been of the efficiency contracted for. The purchaser could not recover the cost of the new machines as part of its damages claim against the seller of the original machines. The purchaser was regarded as having mitigated (see also *Laverack v Woods of Colchester Ltd* [1967] 1 QB 278).

(d) Anticipatory breach[5]

The further difficulty occasioned in relation to anticipatory breach was considered above (see page 432).

(e) Economic efficiency

Mitigation has obvious links with the issue of causation. However, in not including in the injured party's damages a loss which he would not have incurred had he acted reasonably, the mitigation rule can be seen as a means of preventing resources from being wasted. In that context it can also be viewed as an incentive to breach — it is not a disincentive to do so. It can be seen as part of the promotion of the "efficient breach" which it has been argued is economically desirable.

> "In some cases a party would be tempted to breach the contract simply because his profit from breach would exceed his expected profit from completion of the contract, and if damages are limited to loss of expected profit, there will be an incentive to commit a breach. There should be. The opportunity cost of completion to the breaching party is the profit he would make from the breach, and if it is greater than his profit from completion, then completion will involve a loss to him. If that loss is greater than the gain to the other party from completion, breach would be value maximising and should be encouraged" (Posner, *Economic Analysis of Law*, 2nd ed at pp 89–90).

The rationale is that the injured party is satisfied because damages provide him with the benefit he would have derived from the contract. If the party who breached can pay those damages and, after doing so, make a profit in excess of that which he would have derived from the contract, then it is economically efficient to encourage him to breach. A greater benefit has been derived from the breach than would have followed from performance. The mitigation rule can be seen as part of the encouragement to efficient breach[(6)].

8. Taxation

In *British Transport Commission* v *Gourley* [1956] AC 185 damages were awarded in tort for loss of earnings due to personal injury. Had the injured party been able to earn that money, it would have been taxed. The award of damages was not subject to tax. The court decided that the damages should be reduced to represent his post-tax rather than his pre-tax earnings. *Gourley* was a tort case but the same approach has been taken to reduce contract damages, such as damages for wrongful dismissal: *Beach* v *Reed Corrugated Cases Ltd* [1956] 1 WLR 807. The basic principle behind contract damages is to put the injured party in the position that he would have been in had the contract been performed. From that the courts have also taken the view that damages should not put him in a better position than he would have been in had the contract been performed; in this regard account must be taken of tax, although it is not always clear which method should be used (*Parsons* v *BNM Laboratories Ltd* [1964] 1 QB 95; *Shove* v *Downs Surgical* [1984] 1 All ER 7; Lee 47 MLR 471).

9. Contributory negligence

The injured party may have contributed to his injury through his own negligence. One question which needs to be considered is whether damages can be reduced in contract, as in tort, on the basis of the injured party's contributory negligence. In tort, reduction of damages — on the basis of the injured party's negligent contribution to his own injury — is dealt with by the Law Reform (Contributory Negligence) Act 1945. The question here concerns the applicability of that Act to an action in contract.

The Law Reform (Contributory Negligence) Act 1945 applies where "any person suffers damage as the result partly of his own fault and partly of the fault of any other person". Where that is the situation, the damages recoverable "shall be reduced to such an extent as the court thinks just and equitable having regard to the claimant's share in the responsibility for the damage" (s 1). "Fault" is defined in s 4, which states that it "means negligence, breach of statutory duty or other act or omission which gives rise to a liability in tort or would, apart from this Act, give rise to the defence of contributory negligence".

The current law, on the applicability of the 1945 Act in relation to a breach of contract, basically requires a threefold division of the cases:

"1. Where the defendant's liability arises from some contractual provision which does not depend on negligence on the part of the defendant.
2. Where the defendant's liability arises from some contractual obligation which is expressed in terms of taking care (or its equivalent) but does not correspond to a common law duty to take care which would exist in the given case independently of contract.
3. Where the defendant's liability in contract is the same as his liability in the tort of negligence independently of the existence of any contract."
(*Forsikringsaktieselskapet Vesta* v *Butcher* [1986] 2 All ER 488 *per* Hobhouse J at p 508).

With the definition of fault in s 4, the Act clearly seems inappropriately worded to cover cases in the first category and *Vesta* indicated that it would only be applied to the third category and that is the line that has been taken (eg *Barclays Bank* v *Fairclough* [1995] 1 All ER 289, *Rataflac* v *Eade* [1999] 1 Lloyd's Rep 506, *Barclays Bank* v *Fairclough* (*No 2*) [1995] IRLR 605). The Law Commission has recommended that contributory negligence should be applicable in both categories 2 and 3 (Law Com Rep No 219 (1993)). Of course, since the decision in *Henderson* v *Merrett Syndicates* [1995] 2 AC 145 concurrent liability, bringing the situation within category 3, is more likely to be found and the problem diminished. However, the point has been made that "the ebbing and flowing of the tort of negligence should not be affecting the ambit of contributory negligence in contract" and that it would be sensible to amend the law, as the Law Commission suggested, to make it simpler and fairer (Burrows *Understanding the Law of Obligations* at p 150). However, the High Court of Australia has taken a completely different view of the appropriateness of recognising contributory negligence in the contractual setting, concluding that their equivalent legislation (s 27A, Wrongs Act 1936 (SA)) should not be used to reduce contract damages on the basis of contributory negligence even in a category 3 case (*Astley* v *Austrust Ltd* (1999) 73 ALJR 403).

10. Penalties, liquidated damages, advance payments and forfeiture

(a) Penalties and liquidated damages

Given the complexity of the above rules, it is hardly surprising that the parties should sometimes choose to include a term in their contract stating what damages are to be available upon the occurrence of a particular breach or breaches. Such a clause is known as a "liquidated damages" clause. The fixing of liability by such a clause has the benefit of introducing certainty into the question of damages. It makes it easier for the parties to calculate the risks involved in the contract and to insure appropriately. It may even help to avoid a dispute reaching the point where it is litigated. There is much to be said for such clauses and the courts will enforce them.

However, the courts have had to deal with the question of whether a clause fixing a sum to be paid on breach is a liquidated damages clause or a penalty clause. A liquidated damages clause is a genuine pre-estimate of loss. A penalty clause is "a payment of money stipulated as *in terrorem* of the offending party" (*Dunlop Pneumatic Tyre Co Ltd* v *New Garage and Motor Co* [1915] AC 79 at p 86). In other words, a penalty clause is an attempt to coerce performance by setting an excessive sum to be paid on breach. This conflicts with the view taken by English law that damages merely compensate the injured party and do not punish the party in breach. The injured party will not recover the sum specified in the penalty clause but will be limited to recovering his actual loss. The clause is not struck out of the contract but will not be enforced beyond the sum which represents the actual loss of the injured party (*Jobson* v *Johnson* [1989] 1 All ER 621 at p 633).

Although the above discussion centres on consideration of clauses requiring the payment of a sum of money, in *Jobson* v *Johnson* [1989] 1 All ER 621 the Court of Appeal treated as a penalty clause a clause requiring the transfer of property, and the court refused to enforce it on that basis.

The EC Directive and the 1999 Regulations on Unfair Terms in Consumer Contracts should be noted in the context of this discussion of penalty and other clauses. As will be seen, in the consumer context, the Regulations may avoid some of the difficulties in the borderlines of the applications of the rules on penalty clauses (see page 494).

(b) Distinguishing penalty and liquidated damages clauses

An obvious problem created for the courts in this area is to distinguish penalty clauses and liquidated damages clauses. They may take the same form and an express label, placed upon them by the parties, by no means determines the issue. Any such label may not have been used in its technical sense. "Though the parties to a contract who use the words 'penalty' or 'liquidated damages' may *prima facie* be supposed to mean what they say, yet the expression used is not conclusive. The court must find out whether the payment stipulated is in truth a penalty or liquidated damages" (*Dunlop Pneumatic Tyre Co Ltd* v *New Garage and Motor Co* [1915] AC 79 at p 86). (See also *Clydebank Engineering and Shipbuilding* v *Castenada* [1905] AC 6.)

It is a matter of construing the contract to determine whether the clause is a genuine pre-estimate of damages on the basis of the circumstances known, or which should have been known, at the time of contracting. In *Dunlop Pneumatic Tyre Co Ltd* v *New Garage and Motor Co* [1915] AC 79 Lord Dunedin set out four "tests" to help with this question. He said (at pp 87–88):

"(a) It will be held to be a penalty if the sum stipulated for is extravagant and unconscionable in amount in comparison with the greatest loss that could conceivably be proved to have followed from the breach.

(b) It will be held to be a penalty if the breach consists only in not paying a sum of money, and the sum stipulated is a sum greater than the sum which ought to have been paid. . . .

(c) There is a presumption (but no more) that it is a penalty when a single lump sum is made payable by way of compensation, on the occurrence of one or more or all of several events, some of which may occasion serious and others but trifling damage.

On the other hand:

(d) It is no obstacle to the sum stipulated being a genuine pre-estimate of damages, that the consequences of the breach are such as to make precise pre-estimation almost an impossibility. On the contrary that is just the situation when it is probable that pre-estimated damage was the bargain between the parties."

In that case Dunlop sold motor car tyres to dealers who in turn sold them on. In return for a discount, the dealers had undertaken not to tamper with the marks on the goods, not to sell the tyres to private customers below Dunlop's list price, not to sell to anyone whose supply Dunlop had suspended, and not to exhibit or export any of the tyres. It was stated that they were to pay £5 as "liquidated damages" for a breach. The dealers sold a tyre below list price. Dunlop's business was carried on through sales to dealers, and all the dealers to whom they sold were required to sign the agreement. There was evidence that if a dealer undersold, it had the effect of forcing other dealers to buy elsewhere, thereby reducing the number of outlets for Dunlop's goods.

The House of Lords decided that the clause requiring £5 "liquidated damages" was indeed a liquidated damages clause and not a penalty. This was largely on the basis of (d) above. There was evidence that failure to maintain the price would cause the manufacturers damage on a broad scale, through reduction of their retail outlets, but it was not clear how much loss would result from one specific underpriced sale. It was regarded as reasonable for the parties to estimate that loss, and the clause was upheld as the figure was not extravagant. In addition, the fact that the same sum was payable in relation to different breaches did not mean that it had to be labelled as a penalty. The test in (c) above did not mean that the clause in the particular case was a penalty clause. All the prohibitions on dealers related to the same type of broad potential damage to Dunlop. In addition, the loss from breach of any one was uncertain and such things "could not be weighed nicely in a chemical balance". The court thought that it was a matter of whether the loss from one particular breach could clearly never reach the specified sum, and that was not the case.

The loss arising from a particular breach may vary according to a particular factor. If the clause indicating the sum to be paid on breach is one which varies the amount appropriately in accordance with this factor, that may indicate that the clause is a liquidated damages clause. It may be, for example, that the breach is one which can continue for a period of time and the loss will increase as the time passes. A clause increasing the sum to be paid with the increasing period of time may well be found to be a liquidated damages clause (*Clydebank Engineering and Shipbuilding Co* v *Castenada* [1905] AC 6). On the other hand, it may be that the variation of the sum payable does not relate to likely variations in the loss suffered, but is an arbitrary variation in relation to likely loss. Such arbitrary variation indicates that the clause was not a genuine pre-estimate of damage (*Public Works Commissioner* v *Hills* [1906] AC 368). The situation is even more extreme and more clearly indicative that the clause is a penalty where the loss varies in exactly the opposite way to the variation in the clause: a penalty clause is indicated where there is "a sliding scale of compensation but a scale that slides in the wrong direction" (*Bridge* v *Campbell Discount Co* [1962] AC 600 at p 623).

One final, and more general, point should be made here as to the basic approach to the construction of a clause which states the amount of damages to be paid upon a breach or breaches occurring. In *Philips Hong Kong Ltd* v *A-G of Hong Kong* (1993) 9 Const LJ 202 the Privy Council emphasized the usefulness of the liquidated damages clause because of the certainty it creates for both parties and, against that background, the point was made that the courts' power to deal with penalty clauses was one which "was always recognized as being subject to fairly narrow constraints" and not one giving a general jurisdiction to rewrite the parties' bargain (see also *AMEV-UDC Finance Ltd* v *Austin* (1987) 68 ALR 185; *Robophone Facilities Ltd* v *Blank* [1966] 1 WLR 1428 at p 1447). In particular, the point was made that although the nature of the clause had to be assessed against what could be foreseen at the time of contracting, the courts would not find a clause to be a penalty clause just because some hypothetical examples of its use could be found in which there would be a gap between the sum specified under the clause and the loss suffered. The likelihood of the losses in question had to be considered as well. Lord Woolf, delivering the judgment of the court, said:

"Arguments of this nature should not be allowed to divert attention from the correct test as to what is a penalty clause provision — namely is it a genuine pre-estimate of *what the loss is likely to be?* — to the different question, namely are there possible circumstances where a lesser loss would be suffered?" (emphasis added).

Thus Lord Dunedin's third "test" to assist in determining whether a clause is a penalty clause must be read in the light of this, but more generally the point can be made that the Privy Council clearly indicated that the courts should not be too ready to label a clause as a penalty clause. The Privy Council even treated the fact that the clause did not arrive at an inappropriate sum in the instant case as "valuable evidence" of what could reasonably be foreseen as the loss at the time of contracting and that the clause was thus not a penalty clause. However, there was an emphasis upon the idea that an approach tending to non-intervention was justified because the clause had been accepted by both parties. It can be suggested that a different line might be taken if there was a significant inequality of bargaining power between the parties. Reflecting this point and the more general non-interventionist approach, Lord Woolf said:

"Except possibly in the case of situations where one of the parties to the contract is able to dominate the other as to the choice of the terms of a contract, it will normally be insufficient to establish that a provision is objectionably penal to identify the situations where the application of the provision could result in a larger sum being recovered by the injured party than his actual loss. Even in such situations so long as the sum payable in the event of non-compliance with the contract is not extravagant, having regard to the range of losses that it could reasonably be anticipated it would have to cover at the time the contract was made, it can still be a genuine pre-estimate of the loss that would be suffered and so a perfectly valid liquidated damage provision."

(c) Avoidance of the rule on penalties

The limits of the application of the rules on penalty clauses are technically drawn and there is considerable scope for evasion of those rules by the use of an appropriate form of clause. To an extent, that is being mitigated in relation to deposits by the common law (see page 493) and, in the consumer context, more broadly by the Unfair Terms in Consumer Contracts Regulations 1999 (see page 494). Those points will be considered below, but further consideration must first be given to the scope of the rules as to penalty clauses and the means of evading their operation through careful drafting.

The first point to emphasise is that the rule about penalty clauses only applies where the sum specified in the clause in question becomes payable on breach. The courts have had to decide whether payment is due upon breach or other circumstances. If the sum specified becomes payable under circumstances which are not a breach then the rule as to penalty clauses does not apply. An example is provided by *Alder* v *Moore* [1961] 2 QB 57:

> The Association Football Players' and Trainers' Union took out an insurance policy on behalf of their members. It provided for payment of £500 if a player suffered permanent disablement preventing him from playing professional football. Brian Moore was a professional footballer with West Ham. He received an injury which permanently deprived him of 90 per cent of his vision in one eye. It was thought that he would never be able to play professional football again and the insurance company paid him £500. The policy required him to sign a declaration on receiving such a payment. The declaration stated that "in consideration of the [£500] I hereby declare and agree that I will take no part as a playing member of any form of professional football and that in the event of infringement of this condition I will be subject to a penalty of [£500]". Mr Moore's sight did not return but he started to play professional football again, on a part-time basis, with Cambridge United. The insurance company claimed the £500.

The Court of Appeal (with Devlin LJ dissenting) held that he had not committed a breach on playing professional football again. The insurance company was entitled to the £500 as it was merely payable upon the resumption of professional football. The clause was not subject to the rule on penalties.

Specifying a condition upon which a payment must be made, and ensuring that it is not a breach, may provide a means of evading the operation of the rules on penalties. This can be seen more clearly in the case of *Bridge* v *Campbell Discount Co* [1962] AC 600 where Lord Denning said (at p 629):

> "equity commits itself to this absurd paradox: it will grant relief to a man who breaks his contract but will penalise the man who keeps it".

In that case, the facts were as follows:

> Mr Bridge had obtained a car on a hire purchase basis. The contract contained an
> option for him to give notice to terminate the hiring and return the car at any time.
> However, it also contained a clause requiring him to pay "compensation" for
> "depreciation" upon termination of the contract. The clause was effectively one to
> insure a minimum payment. It required a payment to make up two-thirds of the hire
> purchase price when combined with the money already paid. Mr Bridge returned
> the car after he had made only one of the required thirty-six monthly payments.

The Court of Appeal found that returning the car did not involve a breach as
Mr Bridge had merely exercised the option and, on that basis, the requirement
as to the payment of compensation could not be subject to the rule on penalty
clauses. The House of Lords avoided this conclusion by construing the return
of the car not as an exercise of the option but as a breach. It was then able to
find that the clause was a penalty clause. A decreasing sum could not be
genuine compensation for depreciation. The depreciation would increase as the
amount payable under the clause decreased. The hire purchase company was
not able to recover the amount specified in the penalty clause, but only its
actual loss. See also *Export Credit Guarantee Department* v *Universal Oil
Products Co* [1983] 1 WLR 339; *Transag Haulage Ltd* v *Leyland DAF
Finance plc* [1994] 2 BCLC 88.

The rules on penalty clauses may be avoided by drafting a clause in a different
form; the court is then faced with a problem of form and substance. It is the
same type of problem as was indicated above in relation to exemption clauses
and the ambit of the Unfair Contract Terms Act 1977 (see page 194). The
Court of Appeal identified the problem before it as one of form and substance
in relation to penalty clauses in *Lombard North Central* v *Butterworth* [1987]
1 All ER 267 (see above, page 130). The judges thought that they were forced
to arrive at a different result from that in the earlier case of *Financings Ltd* v
Baldock [1963] 2 QB 104 (see above, page 129) on the basis of form rather
than substance.

In *Financings* v *Baldock*, the facts were as follows:

> Mr Baldock acquired a van from Financings Ltd under a hire purchase agreement.
> He paid £100 and was to pay monthly instalments of £28 for two years. Clause 8
> provided that Financings had a right to terminate the contract if any instalment was
> more than ten days overdue. Clause 11 gave Financings the right to recover
> two-thirds of the total amount to be paid on any termination by them under clause
> 8. Mr Baldock failed to make the first two payments on time and Financings
> terminated the contract and took back the van under clause 8. Financings sold the
> van for £140.

Prima facie, clause 11 gave Financings a right to a minimum sum on
termination but clause 11 was held invalid as a penalty clause. It was regarded
as requiring payment of an arbitrary sum rather than a genuine pre-estimate of
damage. The question was what damages Financings could claim. Were they
restricted to the instalments due when the contract was terminated? They
argued that, as the contract had been terminated for breach, they had a right to
recover their loss for the non-performance of the rest of the contract. In effect,
they were making a common law claim similar to that provided for in clause
11. The court held that clause 8 gave Financings the right to terminate, but it
was not a right to terminate for breach of condition. The giving of an express

right to terminate did not make punctual payment a condition. In addition, there would not have been a right to terminate simply on the basis of the seriousness of the breach. Clause 8 merely gave an express right to terminate where there would otherwise have been no such right. The court regarded termination as Financings' choice and found that the loss due to termination was due to that choice, and not Mr Bridge's breach. By this interpretation of events the court prevented Financings from producing, through clause 8 and the decision to terminate, an effect like that of the penalty clause. Financings were confined to recovery of the sums due at the time of termination. They did not recover damages relating to the loss of the contract for the future.

The Court of Appeal in *Lombard North Central* v *Butterworth* [1987] 1 All ER 267 had to consider whether the finance house there had found a way to avoid the result in *Financings* v *Baldock*. The court reluctantly concluded that good draftsmanship had succeeded in achieving a different result. The court felt that Lombard had achieved the same result as it would have done under its penalty clause, had it been effective, by making it a condition of the contract that payment of each instalment should be on time. In that case:

> Mr Butterworth obtained a computer from the finance company. The transaction was, in effect, one of hire purchase. Mr Butterworth was to pay £584 initially, followed by nineteen quarterly instalments of the same amount. Clause 2(a) made punctual payment "of the essence". Clause 5 stated that failure to make due and punctual payment entitled the finance company to terminate the contract. Clause 6 provided that, on termination, the finance house was entitled to all arrears and to all future instalments which would have fallen due had the contract not been terminated. In the second year Mr Butterworth's payments were late but there was only one outstanding when the finance company terminated the contract under clause 2(a). The computer was resold for only £172.88.

Clause 6 was construed as a penalty clause and could not be enforced. The question was whether the finance house could recover only for the instalment overdue at the time of termination or whether it could recover for the loss of the rest of the contract. The Court of Appeal found that clause 2(a) made punctual payment a condition. As termination had occurred for breach of condition, and not merely on the basis of an express right, the finance house could recover for the loss of the rest of the contract. In other words, the finance house substantially recovered at common law what it could not recover under clause 6, clause 6 being a penalty clause. The difference between this case and *Financings* v *Baldock* was that here the court accepted that the finance house had succeeded in making the clause regarding punctual payment a condition. Nichols LJ acknowledged that the difference between the contract in the instant case and in *Financings* v *Baldock* was one of "drafting form and not substance", but he could see no escape from a drafting form which emasculated *Financings* v *Baldock* (at p 280). He even regarded clause 6 as helping to show that punctual payment was a condition. Mustill LJ also saw the artificiality of the distinction being drawn because clause 2(a) was being construed as a condition but he thought that to treat that clause as a penalty would have been "to reverse the current of more than a hundred years' doctrine, which permits the parties to treat as a condition something which would otherwise not be so" (at p 273)[(7)].

There are other means of achieving much the same result as would follow from a penalty clause if it was allowed to take effect. In other words, there are other ways of avoiding the rule on penalty clauses. The contract may, for example, provide a discount for prompt payment rather than a penalty for late payment. Where the contract requires payment in instalments, there is the possibility of using an acceleration clause which provides that if one payment is not made on time then all the instalments immediately become due, and such a clause is effective (*Proctor Loan Co* v *Grise* (1880) 5 QBD 529 but see *O'Dea* v *Allstates Leasing Systems (WA) Pty Ltd* (1983) 57 ALJR 172). In addition, the position of deposits, and provisions for the forfeiture of instalments paid, must be considered.

(d) Deposits, instalment payments and forfeiture

The rules governing penalties now need to be compared with the approach taken by the courts to deposits and forfeiture.

The basic rule in relation to an advance payment is that it has to be determined whether it is a deposit or a part payment. Was it meant to secure performance or merely to partly discharge the contract price? Basically, a part payment will be recoverable if there is a total failure of consideration by the seller (*Dies* v *British and International Mining and Finance Corporation* [1939] 1 KB 724)[8] but, until recently, a deposit was not recoverable as it was required to secure performance (*Howe* v *Smith* (1884) 27 Ch D 89)[9]. The fact that a deposit could not be recovered, no matter how little relationship it had to any loss caused by the failure to perform, made an uneasy contrast with the rules in relation to penalties. In effect the law's treatment of deposits provided a means of avoiding the rules on penalties. However, this anomaly was noted and, to an extent, mitigated by the Privy Council in *Worker's Trust and Merchant Bank Ltd* v *Dojap Investments Ltd* [1993] 2 All ER 370 (Beale (1993) 109 LQR 526). The approach taken there was that it was anomalous that the rules on penalties did not apply to deposits and that that should only be the case if the sum specified was "reasonable". However, the assessment of whether the sum was "reasonable" was carried out on an, admittedly, illogical basis. The simple line taken was that the long-standing, customarily required deposit was 10 per cent of the purchase price, and anything in excess of that would be regarded as "unreasonable" unless it could be shown to be justified by special circumstances. In the instant case, the sum demanded had been 25 per cent of the purchase price, and the vendor claimed to be entitled to retain it when the buyer failed to complete the purchase within the time specified. The Privy Council ordered that, subject to the vendor's claim for damages, the entire sum should be returned by the vendor. As the entire sum was not to be viewed as a deposit, but a penalty, the vendor could not even retain 10 per cent.

The approach of the Privy Council in *Worker's Trust and Merchant Bank Ltd* v *Dojap Investments Ltd* has mitigated the effects of the distinction drawn between penalties and deposits, although it was conceded by Lord Browne-Wilkinson, delivering the judgment of the court, that a reasonable deposit could contain an element that was penal and which would thus not be subject to attack by the courts. The differences in the approach to penalty clauses and deposits are still highlighted by the fact that a sum payable on breach will be subject to the rules on penalties and the "genuine pre-estimate of loss" test, whereas if the same sum is payable as a deposit it will be merely asked if it is "reasonable".

THE LAW OF CONTRACT

Another difficult distinction in this area is required because of the rules on relief from forfeiture. We have seen that *prima facie* an advance payment will not be recoverable if it is a deposit. Similarly, if the contract requires a series of payments, *prima facie* they will not be recoverable by the party in breach if there is a forfeiture clause in the contract. (A contract for the sale of property, for example, may provide that the property is to be returned to the seller and the sums so far paid are forfeit.) However, where the contract is one which required the transfer of property rights, the party in breach may be granted relief from forfeiture. If the breach is a failure to make timely payment, the court has a discretion to grant an extension of the time in which payment is to be made. The situation in relation to the granting of other relief, such as the return of payments made, is less clear. Denning and Somervell LJJ suggested in *Stockloser* v *Johnson* [1954] 1 QB 476, that the court might give relief against forfeiture by ordering the return of money paid (subject to the other party's loss) where the forfeiture was penal and unconscionable. Romer LJ took a much more restrictive approach (and contrast *Galbraith* v *Mitchenall Estates* [1965] 2 QB 473 and *Else* v *Parkland Holdings* [1994] 1 BCLC 130). In any event, this is an area where the trends in the development of the law are difficult to identify. As has been indicated, granting relief from forfeiture is discretionary and, in considering the breadth of that discretion, in *Union Eagle Ltd* v *Golden Achievement Ltd* [1997] 2 All ER 215 Lord Hoffmann, delivering the judgment of the Privy Council, emphasised the importance of restricting it in the interests of certainty in the business context. He said (at p 218):

"In many forms of transaction it is of great importance that if something happens for which the contract has made express provision, the parties should know with certainty that the terms of the contract will be enforced."

Of course, with the decision in *Worker's Trust* v *Dojap* [1993] 2 All ER 370 it must also be asked whether the rules as to penalties should be extended to cover these types of contracts as, to a limited extent, they have been extended to cover deposits (and see also *Jobson* v *Johnson* [1989] 1 All ER 621). In *Worker's Trust* v *Dojap* the Privy Council specifically did not extend its considerations to the situation in which "a party is seeking relief from forfeiture for breach of a contract to pay a price by instalments, the party in default having been let into possession in the meantime" (at p 376). However, the view has been taken that:

"The penalty jurisdiction being an inroad on freedom of contract which is inflexible compared with the equitable rules of relief against forfeiture, ought not to be extended." (*Else* v *Parkland* [1994] 1 BCLC 130 Hoffman LJ at p 144.)

Some contrast can be made between this approach and the line indicated above as to the undesirability of a wide discretion to relieve from forfeiture because of the uncertainty which would be generated.

(e) Unfair Terms in Consumer Contracts Regulations 1999

The point has been made above that there is considerable scope for avoiding the rules as to penalty clauses by setting out to achieve the same end (a disincentive to non-performance) by a different form of clause and this can produce anomalies. However, in the consumer context there is considerable potential to mitigate that problem through the use of the Unfair Terms in Consumer Contracts Regulations 1999 because the application of the fairness test under the Regulations is not dependent upon the form of the clause. The fulfilment of that potential will, however, depend upon an appropriate approach being taken to the identification of the "core" of the contract, which is exempt from the fairness test provided it is in "plain intelligible language". These points require further consideration.

As has been indicated, the 1999 Regulations generally apply a fairness test to non-individually negotiated terms in contracts between consumers and sellers or suppliers (see Chapter 11). "Core terms", which state the price or define the main subject matter of the contract, are not, however, subject to the fairness test unless they are not in plain intelligible language (reg 6(2)). A term is regarded as unfair if "contrary to the requirement of good faith, it causes a significant imbalance in the rights and obligations of the parties arising under the contract to the detriment of the consumer" (reg 5(1)). In addition, there is a "grey list" of terms which "may be unfair" in Sch 2, and two of the elements of the grey list should be noted here. It encompasses:

"1 Terms which have the object or effect of—

. . .

(d)   permitting the seller or supplier to retain sums paid by the consumer where the latter decides not to conclude or perform the contract, without providing for the consumer to receive compensation of an equivalent amount from the seller or supplier where the latter is the party cancelling the contract;

(e)   requiring any consumer who fails to fulfil his obligation to pay a disproportionately high sum in compensation".

It can be seen that (e) readily encompasses penalty clauses and (d) deposits. However, it should be noted that the elements of the grey list are not identified by their form but by their "object and effect". So the devices identified above as being used to achieve the same "object and effect" as a clause in the form of a penalty clause could also be seen as falling within the grey list. In addition, even if the scope of the grey list is seen as more form dependent. It should be emphasised that terms do not have to fall within the grey list to be unfair. "Exclusion from the [grey list] cannot be seen as forming any sort of "white list". Any standard term will be seen as being unfair whether or not it appears in . . . the list, if it fails the test" of unfairness in Regulation 5 (OFT Bulletin 5 at p 10). It can be suggested that whatever the form of the clause if it gives the seller or supplier disproportionate compensation for breaches, or analogous acts of the consumer, it will be regarded as unfair.

However, the extent to which the Regulations are capable of mitigating the problems of the difficult borderlines of the application of the rule as to penalty clauses, depends upon the scope of the "core exclusion". As has been indicated, basically this takes outside the application of the fairness test, terms stating the price or defining the main subject matter of the contract, provided they are in plain intelligible language (reg 6(2) — see page 225). It was indicated in *Director General of Fair Trading* v *First National Bank plc* [2000] 1 All ER (Comm) 371 that too wide an approach to the "core" should not be taken (at para 25). However, it is easy to exemplify the difficulties which might be encountered in seeking to use the Regulations to mitigate the arbitrary scope of the rule as to penalties.

It was indicated above that in relation to a clause imposing an extra sum upon late payment, the rule as to penalties can be avoided if the clause is in the form of a concessionary rate for timely payment. In substance both types of clause achieve the same end — providing the consumer with an incentive to pay on time — and it is arbitrary if only one is subject to the rules on penalties and unenforceable if it does not constitute a genuine pre-estimate of the supplier's loss. However, the line might be taken that the Regulations do not apply to the term stating the concessionary rate on the basis that it states the price and is core. That is not the line taken by the Office of Fair Trading, which has said that (OFT *Non Status Lending — Guidelines for Lenders and Brokers* (revised November 1997) OFT 192):

> "a term providing for a higher rate of interest on default cannot be a core term . . . regardless of how the term is drafted and whether the higher rate of interest is expressed to be the ordinary rate. The term providing for the higher rate of interest is in substance a term making provision for payment of compensation upon a breach of an obligation and not, therefore a core term".

However, it must be conceded that a different line was taken by the Northern Ireland court in *Kindlance* v *Murphy* (12 December 1997, Lexis) where one of the terms which the court was asked to consider provided that mortgage payments were at a "concessionary rate" as long as the borrower paid promptly but if he failed to pay on time the much higher "standard rate" became payable. The court considered the term to be "core" as it "concern[ed] the adequacy of price and remuneration". The approach of the court in *Kindlance* v *Murphy* carries over the formalistic distinction used to determine the scope of the penalty rules into the use of the Regulations. The line taken by the OFT does not, and is to be preferred. It is in keeping with the "grey list" identifying terms by reference to their "object or effect" rather than their form (see page 236). It should also be noted that, in the light of the OFT's views, the City Mortgage Corporation agreed with the Director General to stop using dual interest rate clauses (OFT Bulletin 5 at pp 8–9) and a term allowing for a discounted rate as long as prompt payment was made was assumed to be subject to the fairness test by HH Judge Elystan Morgan in *Falco Finance Ltd* v *Michael Gough* [1998] Tr L Rep 526.

Provided an appropriate approach is taken to the "core exclusion", in the consumer context, the 1999 Regulations on Unfair Terms in Consumer Contracts can considerably mitigate the impact of the formalistically based scope of the rules as to penalty clauses.

B. Action for an agreed sum

A contract will often require one party to pay money as that party's performance. If one party has fulfilled all contractual requirements for the money to be due to him, then if the other party refuses to pay, he may be able to claim the sum due under the contract rather than damages. An action for the sum due under the contract is a form of specific enforcement of the contract but, as it involves only the payment of money, it is not hedged round with the same restrictions as an action for specific performance or an injunction. In addition, it is not subject to the uncertainty and restrictions of the rules on damages.

Where the contract has been terminated after the duty to pay has arisen, the action for the price may be maintained. The price cannot be claimed where termination has occurred before the duty to pay has arisen. Where the party to be paid has to decide whether to terminate in the light of the other party's wrongful refusal to perform, he will often have no effective choice. He will probably not be able to continue to perform without the co-operation of the other party. However, if he can continue to perform, so that the other party's duty to pay arises, he will then be able to claim the price rather than damages. That was what occurred in *White and Carter* v *McGregor* [1962] AC 413 (see above, page 432). We have already noted how uncomfortably this case fits with the duty to mitigate, which operates when damages are being claimed, and the fact that Lord Reid suggested that the action for the price should not be available where there is "no substantial or legitimate interest in completing performance" (at p 431).

C. Specific performance and injunctions

1. Specific performance

An order for specific performance has the effect of ordering a contracting party to do what he has undertaken to do. However, an award of damages is the main remedy for breach of contract; it is available as of right whereas there are restrictions on the availability of the equitable remedy of specific performance and it is subject to the court's discretion. Sometimes, an injunction may, in effect, enforce performance of the contract; when it would have that effect, it is subject to the same limitations as specific performance.

(a) Adequacy of damages[10]

Damages provide the primary remedy for breach of contract, and specific performance is not available where damages would provide an adequate remedy (*Harnett* v *Yielding* (1805) 2 Sch & Lef 549 at p 553). The basis of the precedence is historical, in that the courts of equity would provide a remedy only where the remedy available at common law was inadequate. However, the question of adequacy of damages continues to be the first hurdle to be overcome by a plaintiff asking for specific performance although there are *dicta* to be found which could indicate a move away from the adequacy test and towards the question of the appropriate remedy. In *Beswick* v *Beswick* [1968] AC 58, Lord Reid looked to the question of "a just result" in considering whether specific performance should be ordered (at p 77), and Lord Hodson considered which remedy was appropriate (at p 83; see also Lord Pearce at p 88). In *Marine (CN) Inc* v *Stena Line A/B and Regie Voor Maritiem Transport (Stena Nautica (No 2))* [1982] 2 Lloyd's Rep 336, the majority of the Court of Appeal applied the adequacy test, but May LJ thought that "the court has to ask whether in the circumstances it is just that the plaintiff should be left to his remedy in damages"[11]. In *Tito* v *Waddell (No 2)* [1977] Ch 106 Sir Robert Megarry VC thought the question was whether specific performance will "do more perfect and complete justice than an award of damages" (at p 322). More recently, in *Rainbow Estates Ltd* v *Tokenhold Ltd* [1998] 2 All ER 860 it was said that specific performance "should be available when damages are not an adequate remedy or, in the more modern formulation, when specific performance is the appropriate remedy" (at p 868).

The question of whether damages will be an adequate remedy for a breach of contract is often put in terms of whether the injured party would be able to purchase a substitute performance if given damages. A contract for the sale of shares which are freely available on the market will not usually be specifically enforced. The injured party can buy substitute shares (*Cud* v *Rutter* (1720) 1 P Wms 570). But replacement shares will not always be available. Specific performance might be ordered where, for example, the contract relates to shares determining the controlling interest in a company (*Harvela Investments Ltd* v *Royal Trust Co of Canada* [1985] 2 All ER 966). In contrast, the courts always seem to assume that any piece of land, no matter what it is wanted for, is unique, and damages will always be an inadequate remedy. This even applies where it is the seller, rather than the buyer, who is asking for specific performance.

Section 52 Sale of Goods Act 1979 provides that the courts have a discretion whether to award specific performance to a purchaser of specific or ascertained goods, but the courts still apply the common law test of adequacy to the question of whether to award specific performance under s 52[12]. In relation to a sale of goods contract, damages are nearly always considered to be adequate. A substitute is usually available. Occasionally, the goods will be considered to be unique and damages inadequate.

"Unique" goods are usually thought of as being those with some artistic merit, such as the Chinese vases in *Falcke* v *Gray* (1859) 4 Drew 651 where Kindersley V-C said:

> "In the present case the contract is for the purchase of articles of unusual beauty, rarity and distinction, so that damages would not be an adequate compensation for non-performance."

The argument has sometimes been successful in relation to essentially commercial goods.

In *Société des Industries Metallurgiques SA* v *Bronx Engineering Co Ltd* [1975] 1 Lloyd's Rep 465 the goods were not considered to be unique and specific performance was not ordered.

> The buyer had ordered a machine from the seller. A dispute had occurred and the seller contended that he was entitled to treat the contract as ended. The buyer was trying to prevent the seller sending the machine abroad to another purchaser before the trial of the main action. The buyer could obtain a substitute machine but only after 9–12 months' delay

The court was immediately concerned with whether to award an interim injunction. It decided that an interim injunction would not be awarded if specific performance would not ultimately be available if the buyer was successful in the main action. On that basis, the court considered the adequacy test and concluded that damages were adequate because a substitute was available. The long delay, before another machine could be obtained, was not seen as preventing that conclusion. A similarly restrictive approach to the question of adequacy of damages was taken in *Stena Nautica (No 2) (Marine*

(CN) Inc v *Stena Line A/B and Regie Voor Maritiem Transport)* [1982] 2 Lloyd's Rep 336. That case concerned the sale of a ship. In breach of contract the seller was refusing to deliver the *Stena Nautica* to the buyer. In deciding that damages were adequate the court placed reliance upon the availability of a substitute ship, despite the fact that the substitute was "substantially less convenient" for the buyer (at p 342).

In contrast with *Bronx Engineering* and *Stena Nautica (No 2)*, is the decision in *Behnke* v *Bede Shipping Co Ltd* [1927] 1 KB 649. In that case, specific performance was ordered of a contract for the sale of a ship on the basis that the ship was:

> "of peculiar and practically unique value to the plaintiff. She was a cheap vessel, being old, having been built in 1892, but her engines were practically new and such as to satisfy the German regulations, and hence the plaintiff could as a German ship-owner, have her at once put on the German register. A very experienced ship valuer has said that he knew of one other comparable ship, but that could now have been sold" (Wright J at p 661).

The plaintiff wanted a ship for immediate use and Wright J concluded that damages would not be an adequate remedy. Specific performance was ordered. On the basis of the "uniqueness" of the goods involved, there seems to be little to distinguish the three cases. Perhaps the main point to make is simply that specific performance will rarely be awarded where the contract is one for the sale of goods.

In *Sky Petroleum* v *VIP Petroleum* [1974] 1 All ER 954 the question of substitute goods was considered in the context of the sale of commodities, which were usually readily available, but which events had rendered scarce. The *Sky* case concerned a contract for the supply of petrol under which the suppliers were refusing to continue to supply. An interlocutory injunction was ordered, against the supplier, after the court applied the adequacy test. The test was applied as the circumstances were such that an injunction would be equivalent to specific performance (at p 956). Damages were found to be inadequate because the oil crisis at the time meant that the purchaser could not obtain supplies of petrol elsewhere and there was a serious danger that he would be forced out of business if the seller did not deliver (see also *Howard Perry & Co* v *British Railways Board* [1980] 2 All ER 579).

There is a further difficulty, in addition to that of the question of adequacy, where the contract is one for the sale of goods which are not specific or ascertained. As was indicated above, s 52 Sale of Goods Act 1979 envisages specific performance being available where the contract is one for the sale of specific or ascertained goods. Basically, goods are specific if identified and agreed upon at the time the contract is made (s 61 Sale of Goods Act 1979) and ascertained if they have been identified subsequent to the making of the contract, ie goods are specific or ascertained if it is known exactly which goods are to be used to fulfil the contract. Where the contract is for the sale of a quantity of oil, or steel, or citrus pulp pellets, the goods may not be specific and may not have been ascertained by the time specific performance is requested. The question is whether specific performance is possible if the case does not fall within s 52 — it has been indicated that it is not (*Re London Wine Co (Shippers)* [1986] PCC 121, but see *Sky Petroleum* at p 956).

Focusing on the availability of a substitute emphasises that the adequacy rule helps to prevent the remedy of specific performance from rendering the duty to mitigate largely meaningless. We saw above that an injured party will not recover, in damages, any sum which he would not have lost had he behaved reasonably when the breach occurred (see page 481). If specific performance was readily available, this incentive for the injured party to take reasonable steps to limit his loss would be removed. Under the present, restricted, approach to the availability of specific performance, if there is a substitute contract which a reasonable man would make, a substitute within the duty to mitigate, then damages will be adequate. Specific performance will not then be available and the duty to mitigate will not be circumvented (see Treitel [1966] JBL 211).

The test of adequacy of damages is often translated into the question of whether a substitute can be acquired from another source, but that question is not always helpful. In *Beswick* v *Beswick* [1968] AC 58 the problem was whether specific performance should be awarded because the privity rule would have produced an award of nominal damages. In that case:

> Peter Beswick was a coal merchant. He handed over his business to his nephew on the basis that the nephew would pay him £6 10s a week during his lifetime and £5 a week to his widow after his death.

The nephew ceased payment on the death of Peter Beswick. The question was whether any remedy was available to meet the nephew's breach of contract. The widow could not sue on the contract personally, as she was not a party to it. However, the widow was also the administratrix of Peter Beswick's estate and she could sue, in that capacity, for the estate. The problem with the estate suing was that the loss was not to the estate but to the third party, the widow, and the estate could only have recovered nominal damages. To meet that problem, and avoid the difficulty caused by the privity rule, the House of Lords ordered specific performance of the contract and the nephew had to perform. The fact that damages were nominal did not mean that they were an adequate remedy in the instant case. (A promise for the benefit of a third party to a contract may now be directly enforceable by the third party under the Contracts (Rights of Third Parties) Act 1999 — see Chapter 18.)

The adequacy of damages limitation on specific performance has been examined in terms of economic efficiency (see Burrows, *Remedies for Torts and Breach of Contract* (1994)). The non-availability of specific performance can be seen as economically efficient. It is part of the efficient breach theory (see above, page 485). It allows the breaching party merely to pay damages, where that is an adequate remedy for the other party, and keep the additional profit, the prospect of which led him to breach in the first place. The argument is that if specific performance was generally available he would not have been able to make that extra profit. He would have been inefficiently held to his contract. In answer to that it can be argued that the greater availability of specific performance would not lead to inefficient performance, but merely to the party wanting to breach having to pay a proportion of his extra profit to the other party as a way of negotiating his way out of the readily available specific performance. However, it is not easy to say where economic efficiency truly lies because of the transaction costs. There are costs involved in the party wishing to breach having to negotiate his way out of the contract. There are also transaction costs involved in an award of damages and it is not clear which are likely to be the greater. In other words, there is no obvious economic justification for the adequacy rule[13].

(b) Supervision

If the contract requires performance over a period of time, so that an order of specific performance would involve the court in constant supervision, then that has been seen as a reason why an order of specific performance should not be made. In *Ryan* v *Mutual Tontine Westminster Chambers Association* [1893] 1 Ch 116:

> The lease of a flat obliged the landlord to provide a resident porter who would be "constantly in attendance". The landlord employed someone who was absent for several hours each day while he worked elsewhere as a cook.

The Court of Appeal refused to specifically enforce the landlord's obligation to have a porter "constantly in attendance". Such an order would have involved the court in constant supervision.

More recently, in *Co-op Insurance* v *Argyll Stores* [1997] 3 All ER 297 the House of Lords reaffirmed that specific enforcement would not normally be granted where it would require persons to carry on a business, and considered and explained the question of "constant supervision".

In *Co-op Insurance* v *Argyll*:

> The plaintiffs had leased the largest unit in a shopping centre to the defendants for 35 years for the purposes of operating a supermarket. There was a covenant that it be kept open during the usual hours of business. The supermarket became unprofitable for the defendants, and they shut it. The plaintiffs were concerned that the closure would impact upon other trade in the shopping centre and sought specific enforcement. That was refused at first instance, granted on appeal and then refused by the House of Lords.

Lord Hoffmann, with whom the other members of the court agreed, explained that specific enforcement would not normally be granted when it would require someone to carry on a business and would thus require "constant supervision". He pointed out that it could lead to the need for an indefinite number of rulings by the courts, and that was undesirable. He explained that the only means available to the court to enforce its rulings was the "quasi-criminal procedure of punishment for contempt of court" and that meant that the situation was unsuitable for specific enforcement. He said (at pp 302–303):

> "The heavy-handed nature of the enforcement mechanism is a consideration which may go to the exercise of the court's discretion in other cases as well, but its use to compel the running of a business is perhaps the paradigm case of its disadvantages ...
>
> The prospect of committal or even a fine, with the damage to commercial reputation which will be caused by a finding of contempt of court is likely to have two undesirable consequences. First, the defendant, who *ex hypothesi* did not think it was in his economic interest to run the business at all, now has to do so under a sword of Damocles ... This is, as one might say, no way to run a business ...
>
> Secondly, the seriousness of a finding of contempt for the defendant means that any application to enforce the order is likely to be a heavy and expensive piece of litigation. The possibility of repeated applications over time means that, in comparison with a once and for all inquiry as to damages, the enforcement of the remedy is likely to be expensive in terms of the costs to the parties and the resources of the judicial system."

In other words, it is inappropriate to use the threat of contempt proceedings to compel someone to run a business that they had decided should be discontinued — and the possibility that the "constant supervision" might require repeated recourse to such proceedings also makes specific enforcement too costly, in terms of the resources of the parties and of the courts.

Lord Hoffmann also explained why specific enforcement in such cases as *Co-op Insurance* v *Argyll* is usually refused, at a more general level. He pointed out that the likely result of ready availability of such an order would be that the parties would negotiate so that the plaintiff would eventually accept, instead of actually enforcing the obligations, a sum of money which would be far higher than if specific enforcement had not been available and which may be in excess of any loss caused by non-performance. Lord Hoffmann pointed out that "the purpose of the law of contract is not to punish wrongdoing but to satisfy the expectations of the party entitled to performance". He regarded as "unjust" a "remedy which enables [the plaintiff] to secure, in money terms, more than the performance due to him" (at p 305).

However, Lord Hoffmann distinguished between contracts requiring someone to carry on an activity over a period of time and contracts for results. In the latter type, the same possibilities of repeated applications to the courts would not generally arise. The court could usually simply view the end result. This distinction was used to explain the fact that specific enforcement has been ordered in relation to building and repairing contracts (see eg *Wolverhampton Corporation* v *Emmons* [1901] 1 KB 515, *Jeune* v *Queens Cross Properties Ltd* [1973] 3 All ER 97). The point can also be made that such contracts often specify the work to be done with precision. Another factor indicating that cases in which a defendant has contracted to carry on a particular activity will normally be unsuitable for specific performance, is that of uncertainty. If specific enforcement is to be granted, it must be clear what the defendant must do to comply, and the obligations in such contracts are often not set out with that degree of certainty (*Co-op Insurance* v *Argyll* at pp 303–304). Building contracts, on the other hand, are usually set out with the required degree of certainty.

(c) Personal services

The general rule is that the court will not order specific performance of a contract requiring personal services, for example a contract of employment. If specific performance were readily available in relation to such a contract, it would place too great a restriction upon the freedom of the individual. In relation to an order of specific performance against an employee, the restriction upon making such an order is embodied in statute. Section 236 Trade Union and Labour Relations (Consolidation) Act 1992 states that no court shall compel any employee to do any work by ordering specific performance of, or granting an injunction in relation to, a contract of employment. However, exceptional cases, where it is appropriate to give specific enforcement against an employer, have been identified. In *Hill* v *C A Parsons & Co Ltd* [1972] 1 Ch 305:

> Mr Hill was sixty-three and had worked for the defendant for thirty-five years. The defendant made a closed shop agreement with a union, DATA. Mr Hill refused to join DATA and, at the insistence of the union, the defendant purported to terminate

his employment on one month's notice. Until the dispute, Mr Hill had every expectation of continuing in that employment until he retired. The relationship between employer and employee had not broken down. Union pressure was the only reason for the dismissal of Mr Hill.

The Court of Appeal (Stamp LJ dissenting) gave Mr Hill an interlocutory injunction in circumstances which made it equivalent to temporary specific performance. The court ordered the defendant to continue to employ Mr Hill for the proper period of notice which he should have been given (ie six months). This may seem to be a very short-term benefit, but Mr Hill was hoping to postpone the ending of his employment long enough for the Industrial Relations Act 1971 to come into force and provide him with protection against the closed shop agreement. Sachs LJ emphasised that the relationship between employer and employee had not broken down.

Hill v *Parsons* is regarded as an exceptional case (*Chappell* v *Times Newspapers Ltd* [1975] 1 WLR 482 at pp 501 and 503) — specific enforcement of a contract of employment will not normally occur. The lack of breakdown of the relationship of employer and employee in *Hill* has been emphasised as the key factor in justifying the exception:

> "Very rarely indeed will a court enforce. . . a contract for services. The reason is obvious: if one party has no faith in the honesty, integrity or the loyalty of the other, to force him to serve or to employ that other is a plain recipe for disaster" (*Chappell* v *Times Newspapers Ltd* [1975] 1 WLR 482 at p 506 *per* Geoffrey Lane LJ).

However, there may also be room for limited specific enforcement where the relationship of trust and confidence has broken down, if the order is so limited that it will not produce a situation where such trust and confidence is required (*Robb* v *London Borough of Hammersmith & Fulham* [1991] IRLR 72: see below, page 504).

Great importance was placed upon the continued trust and confidence between employer and employee in *Powell* v *London Borough of Brent* [1988] ICR 176 where it was seen to require not only that the employer should view the employee as competent but also as able to work sufficiently well with fellow employees. In that case, the facts were as follows:

> Mrs Powell was employed by the authority as a Senior Benefits Officer. She applied for the post of Principal Benefits Officer. After the interviews she was informed that she had been appointed and she should take up the new post. However, after a query by another candidate, the authority decided that its selection procedure might have been in breach of its equal opportunity policy and informed Mrs Powell that it was going to re-advertise the post. The authority claimed that Mrs Powell had never been appointed to the post, and that she should return to her job as Senior Benefits Officer and re-apply for the post. She claimed that she had been appointed. When Mrs Powell commenced legal action the authority gave an undertaking that it would treat her as a Principal Benefits Officer for a month. The pattern of events was then such that she had been working as a Principal Benefits Officer, without complaint from her superiors, for four months, by the time the court came to consider the granting of an interlocutory injunction, to order the authority to treat her as a Principal Benefits Officer and to restrain it from filling the post before the trial of the main action.

The Court of Appeal granted the interlocutory injunction because it thought that specific enforcement, by a full injunction, might be granted when the main action came to trial. The four month period provided evidence that Mrs Powell could perform the duties of the Principal Benefits Officer and there was no evidence of a breakdown in her relationship with those she would be working with. The authority was ordered to continue employing her as a Principal Benefits Officer until the trial of the main action (see also Wishart v National Association of Citizens' Advice Bureaux [1990] IRLR 393).

In Powell the court took the view that the question, of whether there has been a breakdown in the confidence required to exist between employer and employee, should encompass consideration of the employee's working relationships. Ralph Gibson LJ said (at p 194):

"Sufficiency of confidence must be judged by reference to the circumstances of the case, including the nature of the work, the people with whom the work must be done and the likely effect upon the employer and the employer's operations if the employer is required by injunction to suffer the plaintiff to continue to work."

In the particular case that point was met by the fact that the plaintiff was working successfully with those she would have to work with. A much narrower view of what the court should look at, to decide if the relationship between employer and employee has broken down, was taken in Irani v Southampton and South West Hampshire Area Health Authority [1985] ICR 590. However, that case should be viewed in the light of the limited nature of the order made. An interlocutory injunction was granted in circumstances which made it equivalent to temporary specific performance, but conditions were placed upon it. Mr Irani had been dismissed from his post as a part-time ophthalmologist at an eye clinic after a dispute with the consultant who ran the clinic. The dismissal was in breach of contract. The health authority had failed to follow the prescribed disputes procedure. The purpose of the order was to ensure that the prescribed procedure was carried through. Warner J thought that there had not been a breakdown of the necessary confidence between employer and employee. He took that view on the basis that there was no complaint about Mr Irani's conduct or professional competence. His dismissal was simply a matter of incompatibility with the particular consultant. However, it was a condition of the court's order that Mr Irani would not attempt to carry on working. In effect, the authority was merely being ordered technically to continue to employ him so that he could have the benefit of the correct disputes procedure.

In Irani the court took a more limited view than Powell of what was required for the necessary confidence still to exist between employer and employee. However, in Powell the employee was asking to continue to work. More recently, in Robb v London Borough of Hammersmith and Fulham [1991] IRLR 72 Morland J took the line that where the contract is to be kept alive in only a limited way, it does not matter whether confidence still exists between employer and employee. Under those circumstances, the enforcement envisaged would not produce a situation which required confidence to exist. In that case:

Mr Robb was employed as the borough's director of finance. In May 1990 the council invoked the disciplinary procedure relating to capabilities in para 41 of his conditions of service. He was suspended on full pay while an investigation was conducted in accordance with para 41. However, negotiations were also started with regard to the terms of a possible agreed termination of Mr Robb's contract. In the light of those negotiations, but before they were completed, the investigation was discontinued. Unfortunately no agreement was reached for the termination of Mr Robb's contract and, in breach of contract, the council then summarily dismissed him.

Mr Robb sought an injunction to restrain the council from giving effect to the purported dismissal until the proper disciplinary procedures had been carried out under para 41. He was willing to give undertakings that he would remain suspended on full pay, as he had been from the commencement of the para 41 procedure. Morland J thought that, to obtain an injunction, there was no need to show continued trust and confidence, where all that was being asked for was the right to have disciplinary procedures properly carried through, without any actual work being done by the employee.

The basic exception to the normal refusal to grant specific enforcement of a contract of employment is where the necessary trust and confidence has not broken down between employer and employee. This seems to require that the employer should have confidence not only in the ability of the employee to carry out the specific tasks of that employment but also, in appropriate cases, in the ability of the employee to work sufficiently well with others. However, the question of trust and confidence need not arise if all that is being asked for is a technical enforcement of the contract to allow a dispute or disciplinary procedure to operate, and there is no question of the employee actually working whilst that procedure is undertaken.

There are other situations where an inroad has been made upon the general prohibition on specific enforcement of contracts requiring personal services. For example, dismissal from an office in breach of the rules of natural justice may be invalid and restrained by an injunction (*Ridge* v *Baldwin* [1964] AC 40; *Vine* v *National Dock Labour Board* [1957] AC 488). In addition the employee's primary remedy for wrongful dismissal is now reinstatement or re-engagement (Employment Protection (Consolidation) Act 1978) although, of course, this will have to bow to the practicalities of an employer's refusal to implement it.

Another inroad on the basic restriction on specific enforcement in this area is where an injunction is granted to enforce a negative term in a contract for personal services. However, it should be noted that such an injunction will not be granted where its effect would be to compel specific performance of a contract in relation to which specific performance, as such, is not regarded as appropriate. An injunction will not be granted where the negative term states that the employee is not to take up any other employment (*Whitwood Chemical Co* v *Hardman* [1891] 2 Ch 416). Enforcement of such a negative term would, in effect, leave the employee with no option but to continue to perform the positive terms of the contract of employment. However, the courts have not always taken the same approach as to which negative terms can be enforced without, effectively, coercing the employee to keep his or her contract with a particular employer. In *Lumley* v *Wagner* (1852) 1 De GM & G 604, the facts were as follows:

> Mlle Wagner had contracted to sing at Mr Lumley's theatre, Her Majesty's Theatre, on two nights a week for three months. She had also contracted, negatively, that she would not sing elsewhere during that time without Mr Lumley's permission. Mlle

Wagner was offered a better rate of pay by Mr Gye. She decided to break her contract with Mr Lumley and to contract with Mr Gye to sing at the Royal Italian Opera, Covent Garden.

The court granted an injunction to prevent Mlle Wagner from breaching the negative covenant not to sing elsewhere during the three month period. Specific performance of the obligation to sing at Her Majesty's Theatre could not have been granted, but the injunction was not regarded as doing indirectly what could not be done directly. It did not matter that the injunction might persuade her to fulfil her contract with Mr Lumley.

The approach taken in *Lumley* v *Wagner* was followed in *Warner Bros Pictures Inc* v *Nelson* [1937] 1 KB 209. In that case:

Mrs Nelson, who was known professionally as Bette Davis, had contracted to render her services as an actress exclusively for Warner Bros for a number of years and, during that time, not to perform for anyone else. In breach of that contract she agreed to act for a third party.

Warner Bros could not obtain specific performance of the obligation to act for them or an injunction which would have the same effect. Branson J said (at p 216):

"true to the principle that specific performance of a contract of personal service will never be ordered, [the court will not] grant an injunction in the case of such a contract to enforce negative covenants if the effect of so doing would be to drive the defendant either to starvation or to specific performance of the positive covenants."

However, in the instant case, an injunction was granted to prevent Bette Davis from acting for anyone else. That was not regarded as indirect specific performance. The court was not persuaded by the argument that she would be compelled to perform for Warner Bros because of the difference between what she was likely to earn acting in films and doing anything else. The court thought that, although the injunction might tempt her to perform the contract with Warner Bros, it was not equivalent to granting specific performance. She could earn a living without breaching the injunction. The case seems all the more extreme because of the time span involved. *Lumley* v *Wagner* concerned a covenant for three months, whereas the covenant in *Warner Bros* v *Nelson* related to a period of years.

A more realistic approach to the question of whether an injunction would amount to indirect specific performance was taken in *Page One Records Ltd* v *Britton* [1968] 1 WLR 157. In that case:

The Troggs, a pop group, had contracted to employ the plaintiff as their manager for five years. The Troggs covenanted not to employ anyone else as their manager for that period. The group broke that agreement by employing another manager.

The court refused to grant an injunction preventing the Troggs from employing anyone but the plaintiff as their manager. It was recognized that they could not function as a pop group without a manager and that any such negative injunction would effectively amount to specific enforcement of the contract of employment.

The decision in *Page One Records* v *Britton* clearly takes a more realistic line than the previous decisions on what will effectively amount to specific performance. The court did not take the view that the Troggs would not, effectively, have to continue to employ the plaintiff, because they could always have taken up some occupation other than that of pop group. Stamp J distinguished *Lumley* v *Wagner* on the basis of the type of obligation undertaken by the plaintiff who was asking for the injunction. He said that the obligation of the plaintiff in *Lumley* v *Wagner* was simply to pay money. In the instant case, the obligations involved mutual trust and confidence on both sides. On that basis also, it would be undesirable to put pressure on the Troggs to continue to employ the plaintiff.

In *Warren* v *Mendy* [1989] 3 All ER 103 the Court of Appeal preferred the approach taken in *Page One Records* to that of *Warner Bros* v *Nelson* which was regarded as a very extreme case. In *Warren* v *Mendy*:

> The boxer, Nigel Benn, made a contract with Warren for Warren to act as his manager for three years. The contract contained a covenant that Benn would not enter into an agreement with anyone else to carry out the functions of a manager for that period. Within a few months of the agreement being signed, Benn claimed that he was not bound by it. He made an agreement with Mendy for Mendy, effectively, to act as his manager.

Warren sought an injunction to restrain Mendy (a) from inducing a breach, by Benn, of the contract with Warren and (b) from acting as Benn's manager. The Court of Appeal refused to grant the injunction. It took the line that the question to consider was, basically, the same as the one which it would have had to address had Warren chosen to try to enforce the negative covenant in the contract against Benn — ie was the court being asked to make an order which would have the same effect as an order for specific performance, compelling Benn to perform his contract with Warren? The court thought that:

> "Compulsion may be inferred where the injunction is sought not against the servant but against a third party, if either the third party is the only other master or if it is likely that the master will seek relief against anyone who attempts to replace him".

The judge at first instance had gained the impression that Warren would take action against anyone in Mendy's position. On that basis, the question of "compulsion" had to be considered more generally, and in the same way as it would have been looked at had Warren taken action against Benn. The court looked at "compulsion" in the context of a contract for personal services, "inseparable from the exercise of some special skill or talent". Nourse LJ, delivering the judgment of the court, said (at p 114):

> "Compulsion is a question to be decided on the facts of each case, with realistic regard for the probable reaction of an injunction on the psychological and material, and sometimes the physical, need of the servant to maintain the skill or talent. The longer the term for which an injunction is sought, the more readily will compulsion be inferred."

In other words, the court thought that the need to work to maintain a particular skill, or talent, might effectively compel an employee to perform a contract if he was prevented from exercising his talents otherwise. This is akin to the line taken in *Page One Records*. It is very different from the suggestion in *Warner Bros* v *Nelson* that Bette Davis would not be forced to act for Warner Bros because she could always take up some employment other than acting. The reference to the length of time covered by an injunction should also be noted; it was indicated above that the time involved was one factor making *Warner Bros* an extreme case.

In *Warren* v *Mendy* the court made the point that it was considering a contract which related to the use of a particular skill or talent. If a particular skill or talent is involved, it may need to be exercised if it is not to decline or be lost and, even without that, there is every reason not to take the line that the employee should be required either to waste his skill or talent for a time or to perform the contract. The view has been taken that this should apply even where there is no question of the employee starving because the employer is willing to pay him to do nothing, provided that he does not work for anyone else for the contract period. It is suggested that it applies even where the skills are not those of the artist or sportsman but of the chartered accountant:

> "The employee has a concern to work and a concern to exercise his skills. That has been recognized in some circumstances concerned with artists and singers who depend on publicity, but it applies equally, I apprehend, to skilled workmen and even chartered accountants" (*Provident Financial Group plc and Whitegates Estate Agency* v *Hayward* [1989] 3 All ER 298 *per* Dillon LJ at p 304. See also restraint of trade).

However, some consideration should be given to *Evening Standard Co* v *Henderson* [1987] ICR 588. At first sight, it might be seen as supporting the approach taken in *Warner Bros* v *Nelson*. In *Evening Standard* v *Henderson*:

> Mr Henderson worked as a production manager for *The Evening Standard* newspaper. His contract specified that twelve months' notice of termination was required on either side. It also stated that he would not work for anyone else, without permission, while he was an employee of *The Evening Standard*. He decided to take a job with a new newspaper, which would compete with *The Evening Standard*, and he gave *The Evening Standard* two months' notice.

The Evening Standard sought an interlocutory injunction to prevent him from working for a rival until the full twelve months' notice period had expired. The Court of Appeal granted an interlocutory injunction. However, it is important to note first that, even if he did not work, *The Evening Standard* was willing to continue to pay him for the rest of the notice period. There was no question of the injunction forcing him to choose between starvation and fulfilling the positive terms of his contract. Secondly, he had continued to work for *The Evening Standard* until the day before the Court of Appeal's consideration of the matter, and *The Evening Standard* was happy for him to continue to do so. The relationship between employer and employee had not broken down. They could continue to work together satisfactorily. Lawton LJ emphasised those two factors in coming to his decision to grant the injunction, and those factors mean that the case is not out of line with the other recent authorities. The court may, in the short term, have been effectively granting specific performance of a contract of employment, if Mr Henderson was not to sit idly by and waste his skills. However, we have already noted that specific performance will be granted of a contract of employment where there is no breakdown in the relationship of employer and employee. As Mr Henderson had continued to work for *The Evening Standard*, the case can be seen as fitting within that exception. On that basis too much regard should not be paid to the *obiter dictum* of Balcombe LJ that he was:

"inclined to accept the alternative ground of appeal raised by [*The Evening Standard*] that the evidence before the judge was not such as to indicate that there was no alternative employment, even in some other field, open to the defendant."

To that extent, Balcombe LJ "would have followed *Warner Bros v Nelson*", but the other reasons for the decision in the case, and the decision itself, should not be seen as out of keeping with the move away from *Warner* in other recent cases. However, there is a difficulty with this view of the case, and its reduction of the support for *Warner Bros v Nelson*. The problem is that, once the case is perceived as one of specific enforcement, it conflicts with the statutory bar which is now contained in s 236 Trade Union and Labour Relations (Consolidation) Act 1992 as the order was made against an employee, rather than an employer. It would be unfortunate, however, if the avoidance of that statute promoted the use of reasoning which appeared to favour the line taken in *Warner Bros*. It should also be emphasised that the order was only for a limited period.

(The cases considered above may also be seen to have an anti-competition element and it may be necessary also to consider the doctrine of restraint of trade — see page 340.)

(d) Discretion[(14)]

Specific performance is an equitable remedy. It cannot be asked for as of right. It is a discretionary remedy, but the discretion is not arbitrary or capricious. It is governed, as far as possible, by fixed rules and principles (*Lamare v Dixon* (1873) LR 6 HL 414, at p 423). On that basis, factors affecting the court's decision can be identified. For example, the court will consider whether there has been a delay in asking for specific performance (*Milward v Earl of Thanet* (1801) 5 Ves 720; *Lazard Brothers & Co Ltd v Fairfield Properties Co (Mayfair) Ltd* (1977) 121 SJ 793). It will consider whether the person seeking specific performance is himself prepared to perform his side of the contract (*Chappell v Times Newspapers Ltd* [1975] 1 WLR 482). The court will weigh the difference between the benefit one party will gain from specific performance and the cost of performance to the other. If the cost is disproportionate to the benefit, that is a factor against the making of an order of specific performance (*Tito v Waddell (No 2)* [1977] Ch 106, at p 326). Further consideration is given below to some of the factors identified as relevant to the exercise of the court's discretion. It should be noted that the parties cannot fetter the courts' discretion in their contract (*Quadrant Visual Communications Ltd v Hutchison Telephone UK* [1993] BCLC 442).

(i) Hardship

The person against whom specific performance is being sought may argue that it should not be granted because it will cause him substantial hardship. In *Denne v Light* (1857) 8 De GM & G 774 specific performance was refused of a contract for the sale of land. After making the contract the purchaser refused to continue with the purchase because he discovered that the land in question was "landlocked" and the vendor refused to guarantee that he would have a right of way over any of the surrounding land.

Specific performance has been refused because of the substantial hardship which it would cause to the party refusing to perform, even, in exceptional circumstances, where that hardship arises from circumstances which occur after contracting (see Harris, *Remedies in Contract and Tort* (1988) p 146). The hardship was sufficient to justify a refusal of specific performance in *Patel* v *Ali* [1984] 1 All ER 978. In that case:

> In July 1979 Mrs Ali contracted to sell her house to Mr Patel. At that time she had one child and was in good health. Mrs Ali spoke English very badly. Through neither party's fault, completion was initially delayed. By the time the court came to consider whether Mr Patel should be granted specific performance, Mrs Ali had two more children, and cancer had resulted in the amputation of her leg. She claimed that specific performance would cause her great hardship. She would have to move and her poor English, coupled with her disability, made her very reliant upon assistance from friends and relations who lived close by the home she had contracted to sell.

Goulding J exercised his discretion not to order specific performance. However, his refusal was subject to Mrs Ali paying a sum of money into court to ensure that Mr Patel would receive his damages, once they had been calculated. In deciding to exercise his discretion, and to refuse specific performance, Goulding J acknowledged (at p 981) that:

> "in the majority of cases the hardship which moves the court to refuse specific performance is either a hardship existing at the date of the contract or a hardship due in some way to the plaintiff."

However, he was satisfied that the court's discretion was wide enough to refuse specific performance in other cases of hardship. In the particular case, although the hardship was not caused by Mr Patel, specific performance was refused because, in the circumstances, it would inflict a "hardship amounting to injustice" to grant it. The delay was not due to the fault of either party and an order of specific performance would force Mrs Ali to move in circumstances very different from those which she contemplated when contracting.

(ii) Consideration

It is said that "equity will not assist a volunteer" and specific performance will not be granted of a contract which is merely under seal and for which there is no consideration as such, or of a contract for which the consideration is purely nominal (*Jefferys* v *Jefferys* (1841) 1 Cr & Ph 138, [1835–42] All ER Rep 81). It also seems that inadequacy of consideration may be relevant to the exercise of the court's discretion, particularly where it supports other factors indicating that specific performance should not be granted (*Falcke* v *Gray* (1859) 4 Drew 651).

(iii) The party claiming specific performance

Specific performance was refused in *Walters* v *Morgan* (1861) 3 De GF & J 718 because it was thought that the contract had been obtained by unfair means. The defendant bought land and was immediately hurried into granting the plaintiff a mining lease over the land, before he had time to discover its true value. By "contrivance of the plaintiff the defendant was surprised and was induced to sign the agreement in ignorance of the value of the property" (at p 723). In many cases irregularities in formation will now be covered by duress, undue influence, misrepresentation or mistake.

In *Shell UK* v *Lostock Garage* [1977] 1 All ER 481, Shell was refused specific enforcement of its contract with Lostock. Shell had acted unfairly in its performance of the contract and had inflicted hardship on Lostock. In that case:

> Shell had contracted to supply petrol to Lostock Garage on the basis that Lostock would not obtain petrol from any other supplier. The agreement could be terminated on twelve months' notice. During a petrol price war, Shell subsidised the other garages which it supplied in the same area as Lostock. Shell did not subsidise Lostock but charged it the full price. Without the subsidy Lostock could not sell petrol at a price which would not make a loss. Lostock told Shell that it would obtain petrol elsewhere. It found a supplier from whom it could buy petrol at a price which would enable it to make a profit.

Shell asked for an injunction to prevent Lostock from breaking their agreement not to buy petrol from any other supplier. Shell was effectively asking for specific performance of the tie agreement. On the basis of Shell's discriminatory treatment of Lostock, and the hardship it had caused Lostock, the Court of Appeal refused to grant the injunction.

In *Lamare* v *Dixon* (1873) LR 6 HL 414 a contract had been made for the lease of some cellars. Before the making of the contract, the owner promised that he would make them dry. The promise was not a term of the contract and it was not regarded as a misrepresentation (it related to the future). Nevertheless, the owner's failure to make the cellars dry led to a refusal of specific performance.

(iv) Mutuality[15]

It has been thought that, in order for one party to obtain specific performance, the remedy must have been one which could have been available to the other party from the time when they contracted. On that basis, mutuality meant that if the obligation of one party, X, was such that it could not be specifically enforced then X could not obtain specific performance. That was so, even if the obligation of the other party was one which was otherwise appropriate for specific performance. At its most extreme, mutuality meant that specific performance was not available even when the party asking for specific performance had already performed. In that situation there would be no possibility of the other party performing, as ordered, and then finding himself able to ask only for damages in the face of a breach (*Fry on Specific Performance* 6th ed 1921). However, in *Price* v *Strange* [1977] 3 All ER 371, the Court of Appeal made it clear that mutuality is to be tested at the time when the court has to consider whether to grant specific performance. In addition, it seems that the question of mutuality is more appropriately regarded as a factor relevant to the exercise of the court's discretion rather than as a bar to specific performance. In *Price* v *Strange*, the facts were as follows:

> Mr Price was the tenant of a maisonette and Miss Strange was the lessor. Mr Price's lease came to an end and Miss Strange agreed to renew it if he carried out certain repairs to the building. He carried out some of the repairs but Miss Strange prevented him from completing them. Miss Strange refused to grant him the new lease. She completed the repairs herself.

Mr Price asked for specific performance of Miss Strange's promise to grant him a new lease. Miss Strange argued that he could not obtain that remedy as she could not have specifically enforced his obligation to repair, ie that there was no mutuality. The Court of Appeal stated that the question of mutuality had to be considered when the action came to court. By that stage the repairs had been completed and Mr Price was willing to reimburse Miss Strange for the cost of the repairs. There was no question of Miss Strange being ordered to perform only to find that Mr Price was refusing to repair and could not be ordered to do so. However, Buckley LJ went further than simply considering the time at which the potential non-performance of the plaintiff's obligations should be assessed. He thought that where damages would provide an adequate remedy, if the plaintiff failed to perform, then that might satisfy mutuality. He said (at p 392):

"the court will not compel a defendant to perform his obligations specifically if it cannot at the same time ensure that any unperformed obligations of the plaintiff will be specifically performed, unless, perhaps, damages would be an adequate remedy for the defendant for any default on the plaintiff's part".

In the particular case, the potential sufficiency of a damages remedy to satisfy mutuality did not have to be considered. The repairs had already been carried out. However, the line taken by Buckley LJ seems appropriate. There should be no difficulty with the question of mutuality, and an order of specific performance against one party, if damages would provide an adequate remedy for that party. It also seems that mutuality should be regarded as a factor in the court's decision on the proper exercise of its discretion, rather than as a bar on specific performance. Goff LJ said (at p 381):

"want of mutuality raises a question of the court's discretion to be exercised according to everything that has happened up to the decree".

2. Injunctions

An injunction may be used to prevent a breach of a negative undertaking in a contract. As indicated above, where such enforcement would effectively compel performance of the positive contractual obligations, the question of granting the injunction will be considered in the same way as an order for specific performance. Where an injunction would not amount to effective specific performance, it is readily available (*Doherty* v *Allman* (1878) 3 App Cas 709 at p 720).

A mandatory injunction may be used to order the undoing of a breach which has already occurred. The granting of such an injunction will be subject to the "balance of convenience" test, ie the court will weigh the benefit to the injured party and the detriment to the other party from the order (*Sharp* v *Harrison* [1922] 1 Ch 502).

An injunction may provide the means of securing relief until the trial of the main action. An interlocutory injunction is basically granted in the light of the principles stated by the House of Lords in *American Cyanamid Co* v *Ethicon Ltd* [1975] AC 396.

3. Damages as an additional remedy

When the jurisdictions of the common law and equity were divided between different courts, damages could not be awarded by the Court of Chancery, the court to which a plaintiff would have to go to obtain an injunction or specific performance. Lord Cairns' Act (Chancery Amendment Act 1858) provided for the awarding of damages in addition to, or in substitution for, specific performance (s 50 Supreme Court Act 1981). However, as an injured party may now ask for both the common law remedy of damages and an injunction or specific performance in the same court, there is little need for the additional damages remedy (s 49 Supreme Court Act 1981).

Footnotes

(1) Macauley, *Non-Contractual Relations in Business*, (1963) 28 Am Soc Rev 55; Beale and Dugdale, *Contracts Between Businessmen: Planning and the Use of Contractual Remedies* (1975) 2 Br J Law and Soc 45.

(2) On the timing of the calculation of damages in sale of goods cases, see *Shearson Lehman Hutton Inc* v *Maclaine Watson & Co Ltd (No 2)* [1990] 3 All ER 723.

(3) Of course care must be taken to ensure that such damages have not effectively been encompassed in some other head — *Bigg* v *Howard Son & Gooch* [1990] 1 EGLR 173 at p 174.

(4) For example, contrast *Satef-Huttenes Alberns SpA* v *Paloma Tercera Shipping Co SA* [1981] 1 Lloyd's Rep 175 at pp 183–4; *Weld-Blundell* v *Stephens* [1920] AC 956 at p 980; *GKN Centrax Gears Ltd* v *Matbro Ltd* [1976] 2 Lloyd's Rep 555 at p 580.

(5) See page 428.

(6) But see Harris *Remedies in Contract and Tort* at pp 84–87.
Bridge, (1989) 105 LQR 398, states at p 408 that the mitigation rule is based on:
"several impulses that mollify the strictness of contractual obligation and that are hard, perhaps impossible to rationalise in their totality. The rules of mitigation may well express the law's concern to avoid economic waste, but it would be a mistake to believe that this represents entirely the law's concern in the matter".

(7) See also Opeskin (1990) 106 LQR 293; Wilkin (1990) LMCLQ 16; Beale (1988) 104 LQR; Bojczuk [1987] JBL 353.

(8) *Hyundai Shipbuilding and Heavy Industries Co* v *Papadopoulos* [1980] 1 WLR 1129; *Rover International Ltd* v *Cannon Film Sales Ltd* [1989] 1 WLR 912 (see page 529).

(9) A statutory discretion is provided in relation to a contract for the sale of land — s 49(2) Law of Property Act 1925.

(10) Burrows, *Remedies for Torts and Breach of Contract* (1994).

(11) At p 348. See also *Anders Utkilens Rederi A/S* v *O/Y Lovisa Stevedoring Co A/B and Keller Bryant Transport Co* [1985] 2 All ER 669 at p 674; *Evans Marshall & Co* v *Bertola SA* [1973] 1 All ER 992 at p 1005.

(12) For example, *Société des Industries Metallurgiques SA* v *Bronx Engineering Co Ltd* [1975] 1 Lloyd's Rep 465 at p 469; *Stena Nautica (No 2) (CN Marine Inc* v *Stena Line A/B and Regie Voor Maritiem Transport)* [1982] 2 Lloyd's Rep 336.

(13) See Burrows, *Remedies for Torts and Breach of Contract* (1994); Posner, *Economic Analysis of Law* (2nd ed) pp 88–93 and 95–97; Beale, *Remedies for Breach of Contract* (1980) pp 13–14 and 142; Goetz and Scott (1977) 77 Col LR 554; Macneil (1982) 68 Va LR 947.

(14) Burrows, *Remedies for Torts and Breach of Contract* (1994); Harris *Remedies in Contract and Tort* (1988) pp 141–154.

(15) Burrows, *Remedies for Torts and Breach of Contract* (1994).

Chapter 22

An outline of the law of restitution

Restitution is a large subject in its own right. This chapter is intended to provide an outline of the area. Further reading could include:

Goff & Jones, *The Law of Restitution* (5th ed, 1998)
Burrows, *The Law of Restitution* (1993)
Birks, *An Introduction to the Law of Restitution* (1989)
Beatson, *The Use and Abuse of Unjust Enrichment* (1991)
Burrows, ed, *Essays on the Law of Restitution* (1991)
Finn, ed, *Essays on Restitution* (1990)
Burrows & McKendrick, *Cases and Materials on the Law of Restitution* (1997).

A. Introduction and basic principles

1. Background

The law of restitution is concerned with those situations in which the defendant, D, has been unjustly enriched at the expense of the claimant, P[1]. It should basically be seen as part of the law of obligations, alongside contract and tort, although it also includes elements of property law.

However, restitution has not always been recognized as providing a distinct claim based on unjust enrichment. Historically, restitution was linked with contract because, at a time when the thinking of English lawyers was dominated by the forms of action, many of the cases which we would now regard as restitutionary, were brought within the action of assumpsit, the normal remedy for breaches of contract. This created difficulties once lawyers sought to move beyond simple lists of cases falling within a particular form of action. Claims based on contract were recognized as such but, for the most part[2], those based on unjust enrichment were not. The historical connection led to the label "quasi-contract" and to the idea that the cases which we would now regard as restitutionary were based on implied contract as in, for example, the decision of the House of Lords in *Sinclair* v *Brougham* [1914] AC 398. Of course, the "implied agreement" rationale was not uniformly accepted, but it is only in very recent times that its artificiality has been fully recognized and the basis of restitution identified. In *Lipkin Gorman* v *Karpnale Ltd* [1992] 4 All

ER 512 and *Woolwich Building Society* v *Inland Revenue Commissioners (No 2)* [1992] 3 All ER 737, the House of Lords recognized unjust enrichment as the principle behind all restitutionary claims and in *Westdeutsche Landesbank Girozentrale* v *Islington LBC* [1996] 2 WLR 802 it overruled *Sinclair* v *Brougham*. In the *Woolwich Building Society* case Lord Browne-Wilkinson said (at p 780):

"Although as yet there is in English law no general rule giving the plaintiff a right of recovery from a defendant who has been unjustly enriched at the plaintiff's expense, the concept of unjust enrichment lies at the heart of all the individual instances in which the law does give a right of recovery."

It is worth emphasising that this dictum indicates not only the principle underlying restitution but also that the principle by itself does not lead to a right of recovery. It is necessary to consider whether a case falls within one of the particular heads of recovery (see below, page 519).

2. The basic principle

As we have seen, the basic principle on which restitution is based is that D should not be unjustly enriched at the expense of P. In *Banque Financière de la Cité* v *Parc (Battersea) Ltd* [1998] 1 All ER 737 (at p 740) Lord Steyn indicated that four questions arise:

"(1) Has [D] benefited or been enriched?
(2) Was the enrichment at the expense of [P]?
(3) Was the enrichment unjust?
(4) Are there defences?"

(1)–(3) are considered as (a)–(c) in this section and some further matters (d) will also be dealt with. Defences are addressed below (see page 537).

(a) Enrichment[3]

Enrichment may be positive or negative. It is positive if, for example, D has acquired money or property from P or if P has improved D's property. It is negative if P has saved D an expense. The clearest form of enrichment is the situation in which D has been positively benefited by the receipt of a sum of money from P. Equally, there is no difficulty in establishing enrichment if P is simply seeking the return of property from D, which D has retained. The difficulties arise if property cannot simply be returned in its original form or if services are involved. Under those circumstances, any benefit will have to be valued so that P can receive a money sum. However, whilst P may argue that he has conferred a benefit upon D and enriched him, D may argue that, whatever the objective assessment might be, he has not been benefited. Surely D should have a right to choose how he uses his limited resources and should not necessarily be regarded as enriched simply because P has conferred upon him something which would commonly be regarded as a benefit? In *Taylor* v *Laird* (1856) 25 LJ Ex 329 Pollock CB said (at p 332):

"Suppose I clean your property without your knowledge, have I then a claim on you for payment? How can you help it? One cleans another's shoes; what can the other do but put them on."

Clean shoes might generally be regarded as a benefit, but D might have preferred dirty shoes rather than to pay for their cleaning. Should the law regard the cleaning as a benefit and force him to "pay" for that "enrichment" through allowing P a restitutionary claim?

There is a tension between what would objectively be regarded as a benefit and D's right to choose how to allocate his limited resources. Both Birks and Goff & Jones take the view that, in general, D has a right to choose how to use his resources, but they also recognize that that right should be denied in certain circumstances. Birks (pp 109–132) explains the problem in terms of the exceptional circumstances in which D will be unable to rely upon his "subjective devaluation" (from the objective valuation) in order to deny that he has been enriched, and that terminology was adopted by Hoffmann LJ in *Ministry of Defence* v *Ashman* (1993) 66 P & CR 195. Basically[4] both Birks and Goff & Jones (pp 16–27) see D as being unable to deny enrichment where there is:

(i) incontrovertible benefit, or
(ii) free acceptance.

These situations need to be considered further.

(i) Incontrovertible benefit

Although it may be seen as inherent in earlier cases, the principle of incontrovertible benefit was expressly accepted by Hirst J in *The Manila (Proctor & Gamble Philippine Manufacturing Corp* v *Peter Cremer GmbH)* [1988] 3 All ER 843, where, on the facts, it was held not to be present.

The basic idea is that there is incontrovertible benefit, and enrichment, if no reasonable man in D's position would deny his enrichment (Birks at p 116). Money is an obvious incontrovertible benefit. However, a narrow or wide view can be taken of what constitutes incontrovertible benefit. Thus, for example, in relation to positive benefits, such as improvements to D's property, Birks sees it as merely covering realized benefits (ie those which D has turned into money (pp 121–124)), Burrows would extend it to those benefits which it is reasonably certain D will realize (pp 10–11), and Goff & Jones include readily realizable benefits, basically drawing a line between chattels and land (ie work done on D's chattel is basically regarded as a realizable benefit but work done on D's land is not — p 23).

A wide or narrow view of incontrovertible benefit can similarly be taken when a negative benefit is in question. It could simply be said that an incontrovertible negative benefit is established if P discharges an obligation which D would otherwise necessarily have incurred. However, the question of what amounts to "necessity" also provides scope for a wide or a narrow approach. Birks has taken the line that in determining "necessity", there should be an exclusion of "unrealistic or fanciful" possibilities of D not incurring the liability that P has discharged (at p 120). On that basis, incontrovertible benefit would encompass not only such cases as the legal necessity of *Exall* v *Partridge* (1799) 8 TR 308 but also the type of "factual necessity" encountered in *Craven-Ellis* v *Canons Ltd* [1936] 2 KB 403. In *Exall* v *Partridge*:

D, a coach maker, rented premises from W. He fell behind in his rent and W distrained, taking possession of P's carriage which was on the premises at the time.

P paid D's arrears of rent to recover his carriage. P had benefited D by discharging his legal obligation to W and P obtained restitution.

There was no necessity in the sense of legal obligation in *Craven-Ellis* v *Canons*, but the case can be seen as one of factual necessity if necessity is not viewed too rigidly. In that case, P performed the services of a managing director for a company. He was acting under the mistaken belief that he had a valid contract with that company. The court took the view that the services he had provided were necessary to the functioning of the company, and so he received a *quantum meruit* award. In the strictest sense P's services were not necessary — the company could have ceased to function.

Before leaving the question of negative benefit, we should briefly refer to the limited situations in which P's payment to X, to discharge D's debt to X, will succeed in doing so. Obviously, if P's payment does not discharge D's debt then D has not been benefited, and such a payment will discharge D's debt in limited circumstances only. It would seem that a payment by P to X will discharge D's debt to X if P is acting with D's actual or apparent authority (*Lloyd's Bank plc* v *Independent Insurance Co Ltd* [1999] 2 WLR 986), if D adopts the payment (*Simpson* v *Eggington* (1855) 10 Exch 845, *Belshaw* v *Bush* (1851) 11 CB 191), if P has an interest in property belonging to D and makes the payment to protect that interest (*Kleinwort Benson Ltd* v *Vaughan and Vaughan* [1996] CLC 620), or if D made the payment under legal compulsion (*Exall* v *Partridge* (1799) 8 TR 308 above, and see contribution and recoupment at page 526).

(ii) Free acceptance

In this context, "free acceptance" is being considered as a means of denying D's subjective devaluation. However, it should be noted that it will be considered below as a factor showing that D's enrichment is unjust (see below, page 527).

In the context of services, Goff & Jones formulate thus the situation in which D will be held to have "freely accepted" (at p 18):

"In our view, he will be held to have benefited from the services rendered if he, as a reasonable man, should have known that the plaintiff who rendered the services expected to be paid for them, and yet he did not take a reasonable opportunity open to him to reject the proffered services."

The basic idea is that D will be taken to have "freely accepted" and been enriched by services rendered by P if, knowing that the services were intended to be paid for, D did not stop P when he had the opportunity to do so. Under those circumstances, D cannot then deny his enrichment. In *Leigh* v *Dickeson* (1884) 15 QBD 60, in relation to a claim for reimbursement of expenditure on repairs by one co-owner against another, Brett MR said (at p 65):

"Sometimes money has been expended for the benefit of another person under such circumstances that an option is allowed him to adopt or decline the benefit: In this case, if he exercises his option to adopt the benefit, he will be liable to repay the money expended: but if he declines the benefit he will not be liable. But sometimes, the money is expended for the benefit of another person under such circumstances that he cannot help accepting the benefit, in fact that he is bound to accept it: in this case he has no opportunity of exercising any option and he will come under no liability."

In the particular case, the co-owner was not seen as having a choice in adopting the repairs. It is important that the "acceptance" be "free". The action or inaction on the part of D which can be construed as an acceptance must be one about which he had an effective choice. In other words, if D stands back and allows P to mistakenly paint his, D's, house, knowing that P expects to be remunerated, it is seen as acceptable to deny D's appeal to "subjective devaluation". The situation is different if D arrives home only to discover that P has mistakenly painted his, D's, house. D then has no effective option but to adopt P's work, in the sense of continuing to use the house. Under those circumstances there is no free acceptance and D can rely upon subjective devaluation, ie he can succesfully contend that he does not have to pay P as he can deny his enrichment by saying that he does not regard himself as having been benefited.

Controversy

The idea of enrichment being identified by reference to incontrovertible benefit and free acceptance is not uncontroversial. Beatson (Ch 2) would adopt a much more restricted view of enrichment, basically looking for "exchange value". Such an approach would encompass incontrovertible benefit in a narrow sense. However, it is in complete contrast with the idea of free acceptance, which Beatson regards as enlarging the scope of restitution inappropriately, so that it trespasses into areas where liability should rather be governed by, for example, contract.

In contrast with Beatson, Burrows does not take such a narrow view of enrichment, but he does view free acceptance as inappropriately wide[5]. He views it as merely indicating D's indifference to the objective benefit being conferred by P, and he argues that mere indifference should not be enough to overcome D's right to allocate his own resources. Instead, Burrows would require D to have "bargained for" the objective benefit in question, thus requiring the manifestation of a positive desire and willingness to pay for it. However, Burrows would also recognize D's enrichment where D acquired the objective benefit through a "reprehensible seeking out" of it. This would cover those cases where D clearly valued the objective benefit conferred by P, but equally clearly did not intend to pay for it as, for example, when the objective benefit is conferred by P under duress.

(b) At the expense of the plaintiff

Birks has identified two basic situations to be considered here[6]:

  (i) enrichment by subtraction;
  (ii) enrichment by a wrong to P.

(See the analysis in *Halifax Building Society* v *Thomas* [1996] 2 WLR 63; see also *Banque Financière* v *Parc* [1998] 1 All ER 737, Lord Steyn at p 740.)

(i) Enrichment by subtraction

Enrichment by subtraction covers those cases where there is an enrichment of D which is derived from a loss to P. So, for example, this covers the situation where

P has suffered a loss through supplying money, goods or services to D, which have enriched D. P's claim will be restricted to the amount which can be said to be both D's gain and P's loss. If D's gain is less than P's loss, P's recovery will still be restricted to the amount of D's gain and will be similarly restricted to P's loss if D's gain is greater. This is merely to emphasize that P's recovery is not simply of D's gain but of D's gain at his expense. However, the same restrictions do not apply in relation to enrichment by a wrong (see below).

(ii) Enrichment by a wrong

In the case of enrichment by a wrong, P's loss, or the absence of it, is not relevant. What matters is simply that D gained through a wrong done to P. So, for example, in *Reading* v *Attorney-General* [1951] AC 507 the sum claimed by the Crown was the money which Sergeant Reading had received, in breach of duty, as a bribe for travelling with smugglers to assist them to go through road blocks in Cairo. The money did not represent a reduction in the property of the Crown. Sergeant Reading obtained it at the expense of the Crown in the sense that it had come from the breach of his duty to the Crown.

It should be emphasized that not all legal wrongs by which D gains will give rise to a restitutionary action. However, some legal wrongs do, and when that is the case, P's claim is not restricted to any sum which he has lost. This second type of enrichment is concerned with the gain which D has derived from his wrong, rather than P's loss as such. The wrongs in question are, for example, some torts, or the profits made by a fiduciary in breach of his fiduciary obligations. Unjust enrichment through a wrong is returned to below (see page 534).

(c) Is the enrichment "unjust"?

As with the question of whether D has been enriched at the expense of P, the question of whether the enrichment is unjust ("the unjust factor") can be considered in relation to:

- (i) enrichment by subtraction; and
- (ii) enrichment by a wrong.

Within both categories, there can be no simple consideration of whether an enrichment is "unjust" in some abstract sense. In both cases, it is a matter of looking at which situations the law has identified as containing an "unjust factor". In relation to the two types of enrichment, the unjust factors are dealt with below and form the bulk of this chapter (see page 521).

(d) Other matters

Before moving on to the next section and looking at the situations in which D's enrichment will be regarded as unjust, two further matters should be mentioned briefly.

(i) Remedies

The historical legacy of the forms of action survives in this context in the language used and so, rather than simply claiming, for example, "damages for unjust enrichment", the different counts of assumpsit must be referred to, ie:

- "money had and received"
  This covers claims, for example, for money paid by mistake or under duress, for a consideration which has totally failed, and where P's action is based on D's wrong in the "waiver of tort" cases (see below).
- "money paid at D's request"
  This covers the situation where P has paid money to a third party at D's request, or, by extension, where P has to pay D's debt.
- *quantum valebat* and *quantum meruit*
  These counts deal with the cases in which P is claiming for the value of goods supplied (*quantum valebat*) or services rendered (*quantum meruit*) to D.

The above claims are at common law, but equity may also be relevant. It would, for example, provide a remedy in relation to profits made by a fiduciary through his position.

Most cases involving unjust enrichment are concerned with personal remedies, with P claiming that D is under a personal obligation to pay a sum of money representing his unjust enrichment. Proprietary remedies are also used on occasion, with P claiming that he has a right in property. However, the extent to which proprietary claims should be recognized is controversial. Proprietary remedies are very important. They give priority in insolvency — it is disputed as to when a restitutionary claim should enable P to gain priority over others who are claiming against an insolvent D[7].

D's unjust enrichment may sometimes be held on constructive trust for P (eg where a fiduciary D profits from trust property). The constructive trust has itself been seen as a proprietary restitutionary remedy[8].

(ii) Tracing and subrogation[9]

These are two techniques by which P may establish that a restitutionary remedy is appropriate.

In certain circumstances, the rules on tracing allow a legal or equitable owner to identify property as his although it has changed hands and even been converted into a different form. For example, if P gives D £5,000 by mistake, he can recover the money from D, but the rules relating to tracing will need to be considered to determine whether P has rights in the £5,000 if D gives the money to T or, if D uses it to buy a car, whether P has rights in the car.

Tracing can occur at common law or in equity and the rules at common law and in equity differ and give rise to different rights against the property in question, ie tracing in equity will only give rise to an equitable right but at common law a legal right is established.

Subrogation is "the technique by which one party (P) steps into the shoes of another party (X) so as to have the benefit of X's rights and remedies against another party (D)" (Burrows at p 76). Thus, for example, subrogation allows an indemnity insurer, P, to take over the rights of the assured, X, against D. (For subrogation as a restitutionary remedy see *Banque Financière* v *Parc* [1998] 1 All ER 737.)

B. Unjust enrichment

Consideration must now be given to the situations in which D will be found to be unjustly enriched.

1. Mistake[10]

In looking at restitution for mistake, three types of situation must be considered:

(a) mistaken payments;
(b) benefits in kind conferred under a mistake;
(c) benefits conferred under a contract mistakenly made.

As category (c) would indicate, the first two categories deal with the situation where the relevant benefits have not been conferred under a contract. In the contractual context, a greater security of transaction has been seen as required and a more restrictive approach taken to intervention by the courts.

(a) Mistaken payments

Traditionally, mistakes of law could not generally found a restitutionary claim. That position has now been changed by the House of Lords in *Kleinwort Benson Ltd* v *Lincoln City Council* [1998] 4 All ER 513, but the scope of such a claim is still in the process of being worked out. The discussion below will start by looking at payments made under a mistake of fact before moving on to consider the situation in relation to mistakes of law.

(i) Mistake of fact

Initially, to ground a restitutionary claim, a mistake of fact had to be a mistake as to P's liability to make the payment in question (*Kelly* v *Solari* (1841) 9 M & W 54 at p 58; *Aiken* v *Short* (1856) I H & N 210 *per* Bramwell B at p 215). However, recovery for mistake of fact was extended beyond such cases, to the situation in which P did not believe that he was liable to D, but to a third party (eg *R E Jones Ltd* v *Waring and Gillow Ltd* [1926] AC 670), and even to the situation in which P believed that he was merely under a moral obligation to make the payment (*Larner* v *LCC* [1949] 2 KB 683) and to gifts. It has been suggested that the mistake must be fundamental (e.g Tettenborn *Law of Restitution* (1993) pp 27–28). However, *dicta* supporting this tend to arise from an equation of the non-contractual and contractual cases (eg *Norwich Union Fire Ins Soc* v *Price* [1934] AC 455 Lord Wright at p 463) and, on the whole these cases have been kept distinct, as a greater security of transaction is seen as required in the contractual context. In the context of non-contractual mistaken payments, the better view would seem to be that there is a *prima facie* right to recover simply on the basis that the mistake caused the payment — in the sense that the payment would not have been made but for the mistake (Goff & Jones pp 191–192; Burrows pp 99–103; Birks pp 155–159). In *Barclays Bank Ltd* v *W J Simms & Cooke (Southern) Ltd* [1980] QB 677, Robert Goff J said (at p 695):

"If a person pays money to another under a mistake of fact which caused him to make the payment he is, *prima facie*, entitled to recover it under a mistake of fact".

However, a broad, basic approach to restitution for mistake, nevertheless, requires appropriate limitations, or defences, and Robert Goff J was concerned to make that clear in *Barclays Bank v Simms*. He said (at p 695):

"His claim may however fail if (a) the payer intends that the payee shall have the money at all events whether the fact be true or false; or is deemed in law so to intend; or (b) the payment is made for good consideration, in particular if the money is paid to discharge, and does discharge, a debt owed to the payee ... or (c) the payee has changed his position in good faith or is deemed to have done so."

(ii) Mistake of law

Traditionally, mistake of law would not generally found a restitutionary claim (*Bilbie v Lumley* [1802] 2 East 469). However, the situation was anomalous. Exceptions were developed and the courts were inventive in finding that what was in question was a mistake of fact, rather than one of law. In addition, the general bar on claims based on mistake of law had been dispensed with in Canada, Australia and New Zealand, and here, the Law Commission criticised the then approach of English law and basically recommended that the distinction between mistakes of fact and law be removed (Law Commission No 227). There had been a fear of the floodgates opening if mistake of law was generally recognised as a restitutionary ground and there was great concern about the undermining of good faith compromises and submissions to claims. The law could not cope with the prospect of every payment to settle a dispute being capable of being re-opened on the basis that it was made under a mistake of law. However, what was required was a recognition of the general right to recover for mistake of law but hedged round by sufficient defences. In the *Kleinwort Benson* case Lord Goff took the view that the removal of the bar on recovery for mistake of law was inevitable given (at p 530):

"first, recognition that there exists a coherent law of restitution founded upon the principle of unjust enrichment, and second, within that body of law, recognition of the defence of change of position".

The general availability of a defence of change of position had been accepted by the House of Lords in *Lipkin Gorman v Karpnale Ltd* [1991] AC 548. The question of other limits on a restitutionary claim of mistake of law remains to be fully considered. It is clear that there will be no recovery where P has entered into a compromise or assumed the risk of a mistake and in *Kleinwort Benson* the court rejected the idea of a defence arising from the fact that D had honestly believed that he was entitled to retain the payment. In addition, a majority rejected the claim that the payment should not be recoverable where it had been paid under a settled view of the law (Lord Browne-Wilkinson and Lord Lloyd dissenting) — a point which requires some further explanation.

There is a particular problem — unique to the issue of mistake of law, which makes all the greater the risk to apparent settlements of claims and to the finality of transactions in general. The particular problem is an aspect of identifying when a mistake of law has occurred — the problem of identifying what the law is. It is a problem which is severely aggravated by what are, in effect, judicial changes in the law, but which the theory of the declaratory nature of judicial decision-making says merely state the law as it has always been. Should a payment be regarded as made under a mistake of law if it was made to be in keeping with the law as it was perceived at the time, but a subsequent decision has taken a different line? The Law Commission's proposed Restitution (Mistakes of Law) Bill had stated (cl 13):

"(1) An act done in accordance with a settled view of the law shall not be regarded as founding a mistake claim by reason only that a subsequent decision of a court or tribunal departs from that view.

(2) A view of the law may be regarded for the purpose of this section as having been settled at any time notwithstanding that it was not held unanimously or had not been the subject of a decision by a court or tribunal."

There would be obvious difficulties in determining what amounted to a "settled view of the law". As has been indicated, the majority of the House of Lords in *Kleinwort Benson* took the approach that there would be a mistake of law even where the payment had been made in compliance with the then perceived view of the law which was subsequently held to be wrong by the courts.

Other questions still remain to be fully explored in relation to restitution for mistake of law: whether the mistake must be as to "liability to pay", or "fundamental" or merely the cause of the payment (*Nurdin & Peacock plc v D B Ramsden & Co Ltd* [1999] 1 All ER 941); whether any special rules are required in relation to a "payment of taxes and other similar charges" (*Kleinwort Benson*, per Lord Goff at pp 532, 537–538); whether any of the specific exceptions to the general non-availability of restitution for mistake of law survive, with their own specific limitations (eg that established in *Re Diplock* [1951] AC 251, [1948] Ch 465 (CA)).

(b) Benefits in kind conferred under a mistake

The situation is more complex if D does not simply receive money but, rather, where P improves D's property, performs some other service for D, or, unless it is returnable, where P hands over property to D. As was indicated above, it will then be necessary to give careful consideration to the question of whether D has been enriched, and to determine whether D has been incontrovertibly benefited or freely accepted the goods or services (see above, page 515).

The mistaken improvement of personal property can be considered in the light of *Greenwood v Bennett* [1973] QB 195. In that case:

A car dealer, Bennett, delivered a Jaguar car, to Searle in order for him to carry out repairs. Searle crashed the car and sold it to Harper. Harper repaired it, in the belief that he was the owner of it. He then resold it to Prattle. Bennett reported the loss to the police who then recovered the car and took action to ascertain who the owner was.

The county court ordered the car's return to Bennett, who sold it for £400. However, the Court of Appeal said that a condition should have been placed on its return, that Bennett should pay Harper the £226 he was claiming for the work and materials which had improved the car.

Phillimore and Cairns LJJ considered the mistaken improver's recovery only in relation to the reimbursement of expenditure when an owner sued to recover his property or in analogous cases. However, the reasoning of Lord Denning MR was wider, encompassing a restitutionary claim generally for someone in Harper's position. He said (at p 202):

> "There is a principle at hand to meet the case. It derives from the law of restitution. The plaintiffs should not be allowed unjustly to enrich themselves at his expense. The court will order the plaintiffs, if they recover the car, or its improved value, to recompense the innocent purchaser for the work he has done on it. No matter whether the plaintiffs recover it with the aid of the courts, or without it, the innocent purchaser will recover the value of the improvements he has done to it."

It should be noted that the Court of Appeal did not analyze the question of Bennett's enrichment. There was no question of free acceptance, as he had not known what was occurring. In relation to incontrovertible benefit, the sum awarded by the court must be queried — any enrichment would seem to be linked to the improved value of the chattel or the cost saved (ie the dealer might have repaired it more cheaply), rather than the £226 claimed by the garage owner. In addition, there is a difficulty with finding the enrichment here. The approach of Goff & Jones could be followed (ie the "readily realizable approach" — see page 516), and the line basically taken that someone is expected to sell an improved chattel, to realise their enrichment, where an unjust factor is present. However, if that line is not to be taken, it should be emphasised that the benefit of the improvement had in fact been realized in the instant case. The car had been sold before the Court of Appeal had to decide upon the case. In addition, it should also be emphasised that, in any event, the owner in question was a car dealer, whose business was buying and selling cars. Applying the "readily realizable" approach to enrichment in that context would not necessarily indicate its use in other circumstances (Burrows pp 9–11, 120–121; Birks pp 124–125; Matthews [1981] CLJ 340). It should be noted that s 6(1) Torts (Interference with Goods) Act 1977 now provides some assistance to the mistaken improver of goods.

Historically, the mistaken improver of land has been treated differently from the improver of personal property. However, some relief may be available for P in equity, if D has behaved unconscionably, under the doctrine of estoppel by acquiescence or proprietary estoppel (Goff & Jones pp 240–245, but see Burrows pp 122–123).

(c) Benefits conferred under a contract mistakenly made — mistake and misrepresentation

In this situation questions of restitution arise once the invalidity of the contract has been established. Thus restitution for mistake can be granted if the contract is, for example, void for mistake or voidable, and is rescinded for mistake or misrepresentation (which can be viewed as induced mistake) (see Chapters 12 and 13). The mistake provides the basis for the claim that D's enrichment is "unjust", and rescission itself may operate as a restitutionary remedy. The limitations on which mistakes and misrepresentations can affect the contract were considered above (see Chapters 12 and 13).

2. Ignorance

Although not expressly recognized by the courts, ignorance may be seen as a more extreme case for restitution than mistake. Mistake is seen as negativing voluntariness and so providing a basis for claiming that D's enrichment was unjust. Ignorance can be seen as a stronger ground for denying the voluntariness of D's enrichment, and it can similarly be argued that it should be recognized as grounding a restitutionary action[11]. Obiter, in *Kleinwort Benson* v *Lincoln City Council* [1998] 4 All ER 513 Lord Hope said (at p 562) "the concept of mistake includes cases of sheer ignorance as well as of positive but incorrect belief".

3. Duress and undue influence

We have already seen that duress and undue influence may render a contract voidable (see Chapter 14), and similarly they may provide the basis of a restitutionary claim. Unlike mistake, the courts have not distinguished contractual and non-contractual cases.

4. Necessity[12]

Generally, English law provides no remedy, such as recovery of expenses, for one who intervenes to assist another in circumstances of necessity (eg preserving that other's life or property). In *Falcke* v *Scottish Imperial Insurance* (1887) 34 Ch D 234 Bowen LJ said (at p 248):

"The general principle is, beyond all question, that work and labour done or money expended by one man to preserve or benefit the property of another do not according to English law create any lien on the property saved or benefited, nor, even if standing alone, create any obligation to repay the expenditure. Liabilities are not to be forced upon people behind their backs any more than you can confer a benefit upon a man against his will."

However, there are exceptional situations in which the intervener, in circumstances of necessity, has been granted a remedy. Of some importance are the cases in which the "agent of necessity" has been reimbursed his expenditure (see page 548). Additionally, there are cases concerning the reimbursement of funeral expenses by the individual who had, at least, a strong moral obligation to bury the deceased (eg *Jenkins* v *Tucker* (1788) 1 Hy Bl 90), cases concerning the supply of necessaries to those lacking contractual capacity, and cases like *The Zuhal K* [1987] 1 Lloyd's Rep 151 concerning the reimbursement of a guarantor who had acted in circumstances of necessity (see also *Re Berkeley Applegate (Investment Consultants) Ltd* [1989] Ch 32).

Reference should be made here to the law of salvage which basically deals with the preservation of ships or cargo at sea[13]. Commonly salvage will now be dealt with by a contract but, even in the absence of a contract, a salvor will be awarded a sum by the courts if he acted without legal obligation, in a situation of necessity, and his actions were successful[14]. However, it is not clear that the sum awarded by the courts necessarily bears any relationship to a restitutionary award. Such an award would be calculated on the basis of the benefit received by D at P's expense.

The courts' award in the context of salvage will be based upon such matters as the value of what has been saved, whether the salvor was a professional, and the work and danger involved for the salvor.

Against the background of exceptional recovery by the intervener in circumstances of necessity, it has been argued that an "unjust factor" might be found which would justify restitution more generally in cases of necessity. Birks argues that the unjust factor is that of "moral compulsion", ie something akin to duress, but in this case no illegitimate threat affects P's decision to act, rather it is the "moral compulsion" of D's necessity (pp 192–196). There is a difficulty in bringing the salvage cases within this view (apart from the calculation of the award) in that "moral compulsion" does not seem to have been felt by those salvors who were prepared to stand by until the right price had been agreed to (Birks pp 304–308). However, the courts have seen recovery by the salvor as a matter of the public policy of encouraging salvage (eg Willmer J in *The Telemachus* [1957] P 47 at p 49) and Burrows has suggested that such a policy is the basis in all cases of recovery by the intervener in circumstances of necessity (pp 242–246). If an "unjust factor" can be found then the question of whether D has been enriched would seem to be answered by reference to the idea of "incontrovertible benefit".

5. Legal compulsion — recoupment and contribution[15]

(a) Recoupment[16]

Here we are concerned with the situation in which T, by exercising, or threatening to exercise a legal right, "compels" P to discharge D's obligation to T. P himself may have been under an ancillary liability to T or he may not have been under any liability to T at all. The situation is akin to duress but here T exerts pressure by legitimate means and P's action is not against T but against D. D has been enriched through the discharge of his liability to T (see page 517). D has been incontrovertibly benefited. The unjust factor lies in the way that P's choice was affected when he decided to discharge a liability for which D had, at least, greater responsibility. Restitution is here referred to as recoupment or reimbursement.

Exall v Partridge (1799) 8 Term Rep 308 provides an example of the type of case in which P was under no obligation to T (see above, page 516). The second type of situation to be considered here is where P has discharged D's debt to T despite the fact that P's liability was only ancillary. *Moule v Garrett* (1872) LR 7 Exch 101 provides an example. In that case:

> T was the landlord of premises which had been leased to P. P had assigned them to B who had assigned them to D. D failed to comply with the covenant to repair and T sued and recovered from P, as the original lessee.

The question was whether P could recover from D, and it was held that he could. There was no contract between D and P, as P had not directly assigned to D, but D had to reimburse P as the liability to T was primarily D's. It was D who was occupying the premises when the breach of the repairing covenant occurred. However, "where a person guarantees the debt of another, he cannot claim a right of indemnity against the other if the guarantee has been given officiously or purely at the request of the creditor" (Goff & Jones at p 446, and see *Owen* v *Tate* [1976] QB 402)[17].

(b) Contribution

P seeks recoupment where he was not liable to T at all or his liability was ancillary to D's. If, however, he is liable in the same degree as D, but he has discharged the debt alone (or more than his share of it) then he will seek contribution from D. If P and D are both liable to pay compensation to T for some damage caused to him (eg by a tort or breach of contract), contribution is covered by s 2(1) Civil Liability (Contribution) Act 1978. The court will decide what contribution is "just and equitable" having regard to the person concerned's "responsibility for the damage in question". The common law still applies where P and D are both liable to pay the same debt. The *prima facie* rule is that of equal contribution, but if co-sureties, for example, were sureties for different amounts then contribution is proportionate[18].

6. Total failure of consideration and free acceptance

Here we are concerned with benefits which P conferred upon D under a contract which has been discharged or under a contract which was void, incomplete or otherwise ineffective. Additionally we shall be looking at the non-contractual situation in which a benefit has been conferred upon D conditionally and the condition has failed. We are not looking at situations in which a valid contract has continued to exist between the parties and which relates to the benefit in question. To that extent, restitution is not interfering with the parties' bargain.

The "unjust factor" or ground for restitution, which we are looking at in this context, is clearly total failure of consideration when the benefit in question is a money benefit. However, historically, a division was made between money benefits and benefits in kind because of the legacy of the forms of action. Total failure of consideration was linked to the claim for money had and received but it was not associated with the *quantum meruit* and *quantum valebat* claims for benefits in kind. Against that background, when benefits in kind are in question, the basis of the restitutionary claim has been seen as a request by D or, more broadly, free acceptance by D (see above, page 517; Goff & Jones pp 42–44, Ch 19; Birks Ch 8). However, it has been argued that the basis of restitution in relation to benefits in kind should mirror that for money benefits and that, although the courts have not acknowledged it, that ground is failure of consideration, with partial failure sufficing in this context (Burrows (1988) 104 LQR 576; Birks, "In Defence of Free Acceptance" in *Essays* (Burrows ed)). This should be borne in mind in looking at the various situations considered below.

Contracts discharged for frustration or breach

When dealing with the restitution of benefits supplied under contracts subsequently discharged for frustration or breach, the common law basically dealt with the two forms of discharge in the same way. However, for most contracts, the situation after frustration is now dealt with by statute — the Law Reform (Frustrated Contracts) Act 1943 (see page 454).

Contracts discharged by breach

The first situation to be considered here is where the innocent party is seeking to recover a payment made under a contract which has been discharged because of the other's breach. P will only succeed where the failure of consideration is total. In *Whincup* v *Hughes* (1871) LR 6 CP 78:

> Whincup had paid a sum of money to a watchmaker for his son's six year apprenticeship. The watchmaker died after one year but none of the money was recoverable. There had not been a total failure of consideration.

This requirement of total failure is arbitrary and would seem to have stemmed from the common law's reluctance to value the non-money benefits conferred by the other party. It means that, unless P can restore to D any contractual performance which D carried out prior to discharge, P will be unable to recover his payment. Further examination of the requirement of total failure of consideration is required.

We should look at the meaning of "consideration" in the context of "total failure of consideration". The first point to be made is that it does not mean contractual consideration. It does not extend to the promise itself. In *Fibrosa Spolka Akcyjna* v *Fairbairn Lawson Combe Barbour Ltd* [1943] AC 32 Lord Wright said (at p 65):

> "The payment was originally conditional. The condition of retaining it is eventual performance. Accordingly, when that condition fails, the right to retain the money must simultaneously fail."

The argument simply is that the payment was only made on the basis that D's promised performance would happen. Once it is clear that D will not perform, the basis of retention of the payment is removed. Thus contractual promises do not, in themselves, constitute consideration in this context, and the contrary misconception was laid to rest in *Fibrosa* v *Fairbairn*. In that case:

> The plaintiffs were a Polish company who had contracted with the defendant English company in July 1939 for the purchase of machinery. The contract price was £4,500 but the plaintiffs paid £1,000 in advance. Before any machinery was supplied, war broke out and the contract was frustrated.

The question was whether the Polish company could recover its advance payment. The House of Lords held that the money could be recovered as there had been a total failure of consideration. The defendants' contention that their contractual promises prevented there being a total failure of consideration was dismissed. Viscount Simon said (at p 48):

> ". . . in the law relating to formation of contract, the promise to do a thing may often be the consideration but when one is considering the law of failure of consideration and of the quasi-contractual right to recover money on that ground, it is, generally speaking, not the promise which is referred to as the consideration, but the performance of the promise".

Basically, in this context, a promise itself does not prevent consideration failing. The contract does not have to be wiped out *ab initio* in order for there to be total failure of consideration.

In determining whether the failure of consideration is total, difficulties can arise in relation to P's use of the subject matter of the contract prior to discharge. In *Rowland* v *Divall* [1923] 2 KB 500[19], there was held to be a total failure of consideration despite P's considerable enjoyment of the chattel which D had purported to sell to him. In that case:

> P bought an "Albert" motorcar from D on 19 May 1922. In September 1922, it was discovered that the car had been stolen from its true owner to whom it was then returned by the police.

The question was whether P could recover the price he had paid for the car. P contended that there had been a total failure of consideration. D claimed that there was consideration because P had temporarily had the use of the car. The Court of Appeal rejected D's argument. It was held that P had not received what he bargained for, the title and right to possession of the car. (See also *Barber* v *NWS Bank plc* [1996] 1 All ER 906.)

The *Rowland* v *Divall* approach to total failure of consideration may be seen as having produced an appropriate result in the instant case. D was not the owner of the car and P's use of it was not, therefore, at his expense[20]. More generally, in being ready to find that there has been a total failure of consideration in artificial circumstances the courts may be seen to be diminishing the importance of the requirement that the failure of consideration must be total (see also *Rover International Ltd* v *Cannon Film Sales Ltd (No 3)* [1989] 1 WLR 912, Burrows pp 254–257 and *Ferguson* v *Sohl* (1992) 62 Build LR 95. It may be that the courts will become willing to accept that failure of consideration need not be total, provided there can be restoration of any benefit conferred by D (see *Goss* v *Chilcott* [1996] AC 788, *per* Lord Goff at p 798. See also *Westdeutsche Landesbank* v *Islington LBC* [1996] AC 669 at p 682, in the context of a void contract).

One further aspect of the question of whether the consideration has totally failed should be noted here. *Thomas* v *Brown* (1876) 1 QBD 714 indicates that there will not be a total failure of consideration if D is still ready and willing to perform. The case was concerned with a deposit paid by P under a contract to purchase land which was unenforceable under The Statute of Frauds. P claimed the return of his deposit. Quinn J said that consideration could not be regarded as having failed as long as D was willing to perform.

Consideration should now be given to the position of the party in breach. Whether the party in breach can recover payment made on the basis that there has been a total failure of consideration depends initially on whether the payment was intended as a deposit, in the sense of a guarantee of performance. In *Dies* v *British and International Mining and Finance Corporation* [1939] 1 KB 724, P contracted to purchase arms. He paid £100,000 in advance of delivery but was then unable to take delivery. The pre-payment was recoverable, it was not a guarantee of performance. (For relief in relation to deposits through the application of the rules on penalties where the sum specified is "unreasonable", see above page 493.)

However, in deciding whether there has been a total failure of consideration in this context, a distinction also needs to be made between a case like *Dies*, where the contract was simply for the guns and ammunition, as goods, and one for work and materials as well as the end product. In *Hyundai Heavy Industries* v *Papadopoulos* [1980] 1 WLR 1129 Hyundai had contracted to build a ship for the buyer. Payment was to be made in instalments. Papadopoulos guaranteed the buyer's payments. The buyer failed to make a payment and Hyundai terminated the contract. Hyundai took action against Papadopoulos to recover the payment that the buyer had failed to make. The court held that Hyundai could recover. The buyer remained liable to pay the instalment due before the contract was discharged and so did the guarantor, Papadopoulos. The buyer could not argue that had the payment been made, it could have recovered the payment after discharge for total failure of consideration. There had been no total failure of consideration for the instalment. It was not simply a contract for goods, like *Dies*, but was for the building of the ship. (See also *Stocznia Gdanska SA* v *Latvian Shipping Co* [1998] 1 WLR 574.)

We should now look at the situation in which the benefit in question is not money, but a benefit in kind. Historically, as was noted above, a total failure of consideration has no role in this area and restitution may be seen as based upon D's free acceptance. Nevertheless, it has been argued that the ground for restitution is failure of consideration (see page 527). One example of recovery is provided by *Chandler Bros Ltd* v *Boswell* [1936] 3 All ER 179. In that case, the innocent party recovered a *quantum meruit* in relation to work done in excavating a tunnel. The other party had wrongfully terminated the contract. However, it should be noted that in this context there is controversy as to whether any restitutionary recovery should be restricted by the contract price[21]. In the well-known United States case of *Boomer* v *Muir* 24 P 2d 570 (1933) the *quantum meruit* awarded was $257,000 when the unpaid contract price was only $20,000.

The party in breach seeking to recover for his part performance is frequently prevented from recovering by the finding that the contract is entire. In *Sumpter* v *Hedges* [1898] 1 QB 673 and *Bolton* v *Mahadeva* [1972] 1 WLR 1009, the parties in breach were denied *quantum meruits* in relation to the building work done in the former case and the installation of central heating in the latter. The Law Commission has recommended that there should be recovery for the work done, subject to the contract price and the parties' right to contract out of the availability of such a remedy (Law Com Rep No 121 (1983)).

Void contracts

A contract may be void for many reasons (such as mistake). The reason why it is void may provide a basis for restitution. More generally it would seem that restitution should depend upon a total failure of consideration or free acceptance (see above, page 527 — in relation to contracts *ultra vires* companies or public authorities, see page 532).

However, it is contentious in this situation whether what is in question is "failure of consideration" or "no consideration". Does "failure of consideration" presuppose an initially valid contract? (See *Westdeutsche Landesbank Girozentrale* v *Islington LBC* [1994] 4 All ER 890, *per* Hobhouse J; [1994] 1 WLR 938 (CA); [1996] 2 WLR 802 (HL); *Guiness Mahon* v *Kensington and*

Chelsea RLBC [1999] QB 215; Birks (1993) UWALR 195; Burrows [1995] RLR 15.)

Incomplete or anticipated contracts[22]

P may carry out work, or despatch goods, in advance of a completed contract with D because he anticipates the making of a contract which will provide for payment for the work or the goods. When the expected contract is not concluded, the question may arise as to whether P has any claim against D. There will be difficulties in the way of P's claim in restitution. P may find it difficult to establish that D was benefited. In the absence of a concluded agreement, D may be able to argue that there was no free acceptance. In any event, should P recover when there was an inherent risk in acting before the conclusion of the contract?

It has already been indicated that total failure of consideration as a ground for restitution does not refer to consideration in the contractual sense. Total failure of consideration may provide a ground for restitution in relation to incomplete or anticipated contracts.

> "The link between 'consideration' and contracts makes it easy to suppose that 'total failure of consideration' must always refer to a failure of contractual reciprocation, whereas that is only the most common species of genus so described. In the law of restitution the word 'consideration' should be given the meaning with which it first came into the common law. A consideration was once no more than a matter considered and consideration was the matter considered in forming the decision to do it." (Birks p 223.)

As was indicated above (see page 527), where the benefit for which P seeks restitution is a benefit in kind, it is disputed whether the basis of a restitutionary remedy should be seen as free acceptance or failure of consideration[23].

William Lacey (Hounslow) Ltd v Davis [1957] 1 WLR 932[24] provides an example of recovery in this area. In that case:

> P had submitted the lowest tender for some building work for D. On that basis they were led to believe that a contract would be made and, at D's request, they carried out considerable extra work on estimates and revised estimates. Such work went beyond that normally performed by a builder in relation to a tender. The work would have been paid for under the completed contract but no contract was ever made because D sold the premises in question.

P claimed for the extra work done at D's request. It was held that they could recover.

However, a difficult borderline exists here between the law of contract and the law of restitution. A restitutionary remedy must not be given too readily if the latter is not to infringe inappropriately upon the former. If, in carrying out work, P has taken the risk that no contract will be concluded, then no restitutionary remedy should be granted. In *Regalian Properties plc v London Docklands Development Corp* [1995] 1 WLR 212, the parties had reached agreement "subject to contract" and Rattee J saw that as allocating, to each party, the risk of their own expenditure until the contract was made. He said (at p 231):

"Each party to such negotiations must be undertaken to know ... that pending the conclusion of a binding contract any cost incurred by him in preparation for the intended contract will be incurred at his own risk, in the sense that he will have no recompense for those costs if no contract results."

However, that is not necessarily the conclusion to be drawn from the use of the phrase "subject to contract" (cf *Chillingworthe* v *Esche* [1924] 1 Ch 97; *Brewer Street Investments* v *Barclays Woollen Co* [1954] 1 QB 428). It must be considered whether the parties had intended it to allocate the risks (or all the risks) involved in pre-contractual expenditure.

Other situations

The same approach as that indicated above is also applicable in relation to the situation where, for example, P hands over money to D on the clear understanding that D's retention of it is conditional on the happening of a specific event such as the making of a contract (eg *Chillingworth* v *Esche* [1924] 1 Ch 97). It has already been indicated that "consideration" in this context should not be seen as contractual but as the condition upon which the benefit was covered on D.

For restitution in relation to illegal contracts see below.

7.   Capacity

Minors' mental incapacity and companies — see Chapter 17.
Public authorities and *ultra vires* — see below.

8.   Illegality[(25)]

Contracts are generally unenforceable when illegality is present (see Chapter 15), and restitution is similarly generally denied. Illegality generally provides a defence to a restitutionary action. However, there are exceptional situations in which restitution is granted (see page 365). Basically these are:

- where the parties are not *in pari delicto* (eg *Kiriri Cotton Ltd* v *Dewani* [1960] AC 192);
- where P has appropriately withdrawn (eg *Taylor* v *Bowers* (1876) 1 QBD 291; *Tribe* v *Tribe* [1996] Ch 107);
- where P can establish that D has property belonging to him without relying upon the illegal contract (eg *Bowmakers Ltd* v *Barnet Instruments Ltd* [1945] KB 65; *Tinsley* v *Milligan* [1993] 3 All ER 65).

9.   Ultra vires and public authorities

Where public authorities make payments which were not due, or demand and collect payments that they were not owed, then the question whether those payments can be recovered is often dealt with by statute. Nevertheless, not all such payments are dealt with by statute — here we shall consider the common law.

Payments by public authorities

It appears that an *ultra vires* payment made by a public authority is recoverable. This seems to be based upon the public policy of protecting the public purse by allowing restitution where a payment was made without the power to do so (*Auckland Harbour Board* v *R* [1924] AC 318). However, the policy of protecting the public purse may be taken to extremes. It was held in *Commonwealth of Australia* v *Burns* [1971] VR 825 that D could not use the defence of estoppel in relation to a claim by a public authority based on *ultra vires*.

Payments to public authorities

Traditionally[26], the person trying to recover a payment made as a result of an *ultra vires* demand has had to make out a claim of restitution based on mistake or duress[27]. As mistake of law was not generally regarded as grounding a claim until the late 1990s (see page 522), this had led to recovery being very limited. However, although the exact extent of the impact of the decision is not yet clear, in *Woolwich Building Society* v *IRC (No 2)* [1992] 3 All ER 737 the House of Lords seems to have recognized the right to recover money paid under an *ultra vires* tax demand simply because the demand was *ultra vires*. In that case:

> The revenue issued a demand to the building society under the Income Tax (Building Societies) Regulations 1986. The society disputed the validity of the 1986 regulations but paid the amount assessed. The next day, it applied for judicial review of the regulations and also a writ to recover the amount paid as money had and received. Judicial review declared the regulations to be *ultra vires*. The question which ultimately had to be decided by the other action was whether the society had a right to restitution of the money paid.

By a majority, both the Court of Appeal and the House of Lords held that the society should recover. This seems to have been based on a restitutionary right which arose simply because of the *ultra vires* nature of the demand.

In justifying its innovative conclusion, the House of Lords emphasised both the unconstitutionality of an *ultra vires* tax demand and also the relative powerlessness of the taxpayer faced with such a demand. Lord Goff said (at pp 759–760):

> "... the retention by the state of taxes unlawfully exacted is particularly obnoxious, because it is one of the most fundamental principles of our law — enshrined in a famous constitutional document, the Bill of Rights (1688) — that taxes should not be levied without the authority of Parliament; and full effect can only be given to that principle if the return of taxes exacted under an unlawful demand can be enforced as a matter of right. ... when the Revenue makes a demand for tax, that demand is implicitly backed by the coercive powers of the state and may well entail (as in the present case) unpleasant economic and social consequences if the taxpayer does not pay."

It was also noted that, if such recovery was not allowed, there was an unattractive comparison with the reverse situation. A public authority can recover *ultra vires* payments it has made. In addition, the point was made that under European Community law, if a person pays charges levied by a member state contrary to the rules of Community law, then there is a right to recover those charges. There are issues which remain to be determined, such as the bodies to which this restitutionary recovery applies and the availability of additional defences as a matter of public policy (but see *AEM (Avon) Ltd* v *Bristol City Council* [1999] LGR 93; *Marks & Spencer* v *Commissioner of Customs & Excise*, 19 January 2000, *The Times*.

See, further, Law Com No 227, *Restitution: Mistakes of Law and Ultra Vires Public Authority Receipts and Payments*; Burrows & McKendrick at pp 545–568; Goff & Jones Ch 27; Beatson (1993) 109 LQR 401; Birks (1992) PL 580.

10. Restitution for wrongs[28]

Introduction

In relation to the grounds for restitution considered above, P was seeking to recover the benefit D had gained at P's expense in the sense that D's gain stemmed from P's loss. However, here we are solely concerned with the benefit that D has acquired from his wrong. We are not concerned with P's loss. In this situation the enrichment is said to be at P's expense in the sense that it arises from a wrong done to P. Such a claim may well be attractive to P if he has suffered no loss as such, and compensatory damages would be nominal. However, there is no clearly identifiable principle indicating when restitution of this type is, or should be, available[29]. Consideration will be given to the situations in which D's wrong is:

   (a) tortious;
   (b) a breach of contract;
   (c) equitable.

(a) Tort

There is no generally available restitutionary claim based on the fact that D has benefited through a tort against P. There are some cases in which such a claim may be possible. It is, however, by no means clear in which cases P *should* be able to claim D's gain when P has suffered no loss[30].

In some cases, P may make a claim through "waiver of tort" using the action for money had and received. The terminology "waiver of tort" is historically based and is potentially confusing. In this context it should simply be seen as indicating that particular type of action rather than an action for damages in tort (see *United Australia* v *Barclays Bank* [1941] AC 1). The claim seems mainly to have been used where the tort is concerned with property, such as conversion (eg *Chesworth* v *Farrar* [1967] 1 QB 407), trespass to land (*Powell* v *Rees* (1837) 7 Ad & EL 426) and to goods (*Oughton* v *Seppings* (1830) 1 B & Ad 241). The terminology "restitutionary damages" has been seen as more suitable here and more generally in the cases considered below (Law Com No 247 paras 3.82–3.84).

The remedy of account of profits may also be seen as restitutionary in its stripping of D of the profits made through a wrong committed against P. It is available in relation to torts protecting intellectual property rights either at common law (eg *My Kinda Town Ltd* v *Soll and Grunts Investments* [1982] FSR 147) or by statute (eg Copyright, Designs and Patents Act 1988).

In addition, it may be that damages can be awarded on a restitutionary rather than compensatory basis. In *Penarth Dock Engineering Co Ltd* v *Pounds* [1963] 1 Lloyd's Rep 359, D trespassed in P's dock through failing to remove their pontoon. P did not lose an opportunity to let their dock to anyone and they suffered no loss as such through D's trespass. Nevertheless, Denning J awarded damages on the basis of the benefit obtained by D in using the berth, ie the money saved through not paying rent at another dock[31].

(b) Breach of contract[32]

It is generally said that damages for breach of contract are compensatory and if P has suffered no loss as a result of a breach of contract, the award of damages will be purely nominal. D's profit from his breach is generally regarded as irrelevant. Indeed, it is argued to be economically efficient for D to breach when he can make a greater profit through doing so, despite having to compensate P for any loss due to the breach (see page 485). However, building generally on such cases as those in which a property right has been infringed, and a sum awarded relating to D's gain, rather than P's loss (above), and those cases in which an account of profits has been ordered from a fiduciary or on the disclosure of confidential information, in *Attorney-General* v *Blake* [2000] 4 All ER 385 the House of Lords recognised that in exceptional cases P may be awarded the profits of D's breach of contract.

In *Blake* the more specific basis for recovery based on D's profits in contract was *Wrotham Park Estate Co* v *Parkside Homes Ltd* [1974] 2 All ER 321. That case was seen as shining as "a solitary beacon, showing that in contract, as well as tort, damages are not always narrowly confined to recoupment of financial loss" but that in a suitable case, recovery for breach of contract "may be measured by the benefit gained by the wrongdoer from the breach" (*Blake* at p 396). In that case:

> In 1971 land was sold to D with a covenant restricting building on that land in favour of P's land. Without knowledge of the covenant and in breach of it, D began building on the land. In early 1972, P issued a writ claiming an injunction to prevent further building in breach of the covenant and to order the demolition of such building as had occurred. The action came for trial in 1973, by which time 14 homes had been built.

Unsurprisingly, Brightman J refused to order the wasteful destruction of 14 houses. However, despite the lack of any loss to P through the breach, he granted damages in lieu of an injunction under the Chancery Amendment Act 1858 (Lord Cairn's Act). It was held that D should pay P the hypothetical sum which P might have obtained through bargaining for the release of the covenant, although it was clear that P would not have entered into such a bargain. The sum to be awarded was arrived at as a proportion of the profit which D obtained from the breach.

However, in *Blake* the House of Lords was asked to go further and in effect give P an account of profits to cover all of D's gain. In *Blake*:

Blake had been employed as a member of the Secret Intelligence Service from 1944 to 1961, at which point it was discovered that he had been betraying secrets to the Soviet Union since 1951. He was convicted and sentenced to 42 years imprisonment, but he escaped to Moscow in 1966. In 1989 he wrote his autobiography and it was published in 1990. The action arose out of the amount he was to be paid by the publishers in this country.

By the time Blake wrote his autobiography, the information contained in it had ceased to be confidential and recovery of his profits was not available on that basis. However, when he joined the Secret Intelligence Service, Blake had signed a contractually binding undertaking that he would not disclose official information in the press or in book form. He had, therefore, breached a contract in making some of the disclosures in the book. On that basis, the House of Lords (Lord Hobhouse dissenting), held that the Attorney-General was entitled to succeed in recovering the profits of Blake's autobiography. It was made clear that such an award would only be made in exceptional cases. Lord Steyn emphasised the close relationship of the case to those in which there is disclosure of confidential information. Lord Nicholls, with whom Lord Goff and Lord Browne-Wilkinson agreed, saw no reason why, in practice, "the availability of the account of profits need disturb settled expectations in the commercial or consumer world". He emphasised that "normally the remedies of damages, specific performance and injunction, coupled with the characterisation of some contractual obligations as fiduciary, will provide an adequate response to breach of contract". He made it clear that it would only be in exceptional cases, where those remedies are not adequate, that "any question of an account of profits will arise". He then gave some indication of what might make a case sufficiently exceptional. He said (at p 398):

> "No fixed rules can be prescribed. The court will have regard to all the circumstances, including the subject matter of the contract, the purpose of the contractual provision which has been breached, the circumstances in which the breach occurred, the consequences of the breach and the circumstances in which relief is being sought. A useful general guide, although not exhaustive, is whether the plaintiff had a legitimate interest in preventing the defendant's profit-making activity and, hence, in depriving him of his profit."

In the particular case, Lord Nicholls took the view that the "Crown had and has a legitimate interest in preventing Blake profiting from the disclosure of official information, whether classified or not, while a member of the service and thereafter" (at p 399). He emphasised that members of the security services should not have any incentive to reveal information. He viewed it as of "paramount importance that members of the service should have complete confidence in all their dealings with each other, and that those recruited as informers should have the like confidence" (at p 399). On that basis an "absolute rule against disclosure, visible to all, makes good sense" (at p 400).

(c) Equitable wrongs[33]

In contrast to the above cases, the primary remedy for breach of a fiduciary duty and breach of confidence is restitutionary. D has to account for the profit caused by his wrong.

(i) Breach of fiduciary duty

Basically, a fiduciary must not put himself in a position where his interests conflict with those of his principal, and he must not profit from his position without the consent of his principal. Trustees, for example, must disgorge unauthorised profits made out of their position, and that duty is strictly applied. Their good faith is irrelevant, as is the fact that the trust would not itself have made the profits concerned. In *Boardman* v *Phipps* [1967] 2 AC 46:

> The trust had a minority shareholding in a company. D, solicitors of the trust, advised that, to increase the value of the shares, the trust should acquire a majority holding in the company and improve its running. The trust decided against that course. D bought the shares themselves and made their own shareholding, and the trust's, profitable. One of the beneficiaries claimed D's profit on the basis of D's fiduciary relationship.

D's knowledge of, and opportunity to purchase, the shares had arisen through their fiduciary position. D had to disgorge their profits, despite their bona fides, and the trust's refusal to purchase the shares itself. The House of Lords recognized their bona fides to the extent of making them an allowance for their work and skill.

It should be emphasised that in *Boardman* v *Phipps* D were said to be constructive trustees of their profit for the beneficiaries. On that basis the beneficiaries would be protected in the event of D's insolvency. In addition, in *Attorney-General for Hong Kong* v *Reid* [1993] 3 WLR 1143 the line was taken that a benefit obtained by a fiduciary through a breach of duty belongs to the principal in equity. However, an extensive proprietary remedy is controversial because of the impact upon other creditors of the fiduciary if he is insolvent[34].

(ii) Breach of confidence

Deliberate breaches of confidence give rise to a right to an account of profits as in the "Spycatcher" case, *Attorney-General* v *Guardian Newspapers Ltd (No 2)* [1990] 1 AC 109. There is also some indication of the possibility of a damages award based on the restitutionary measure (*Seager* v *Copydex (No 2)* [1969] 1 WLR 809; *Universal Thermosensors Ltd* v *Hibben* [1992] 3 All ER 257).

C. Defences

In this section consideration will not be given to all the possible defences which a defendant might use. Rather, those of particular relevance in the restitutionary area will be looked at.

1. Change of position[35]

Traditionally, English law refused to recognize a defence of change of position, requiring instead an estoppel to be established (*Bayliss* v *Bishop of London* [1913] 1 Ch 127), with the difficulty that entailed in the need to prove a representation from P to D (see below). However, in *Lipkin Gorman* v *Karpnale Ltd* [1992] 4 All ER 512, the House of Lords recognized the availability of a general defence of change of position. In that case:

C, a partner in a firm of solicitors, P, was authorised to draw cheques on its client account. However, on the occasions in question, he did so for unauthorised reasons, using them to fund his gambling at D's casino. The gaming contracts were void under s 18 Gaming Act 1845.

The question for the court was whether P could recover from D. The House of Lords held that P had a *prima facie* right to restitution of the money from D, but D had a defence of change of position to the extent that they had paid out winnings to C. P could recover the amount C had used at D's club minus C's winnings.

Lord Goff stated the defence of change of position in the broadest terms, leaving future cases to work out its limitations. He said (at p 534):

"At present I do not wish to state the principle any less broadly than this: that the defence is available to a person whose position has so changed that it would be inequitable in all the circumstances to require him to make restitution, or alternatively to make restitution in full."

The first point to emphasise is that this is not an "all or nothing" defence. If P has paid a sum to D and has a *prima facie* right to restitution then D's change of position may prevent the recovery of some or all of that money, depending upon how much of it was affected by the change of position. Despite Lord Goff's reluctance to set the limits of the defence, he did think that some points were clear. He said (at p 534):

"It is, of course, plain that the defence is not open to one who has changed his position in bad faith, as where the defendant has paid away the money with knowledge of the facts entitling the plaintiff to restitution, and it is commonly accepted that the defence should not be available to a wrongdoer."

Whilst "bad faith" appears to relate to the time of D's change of position, the question of whether D is a "wrongdoer" would seem to bring in the "unjust factor". The idea would seem to be that the basis on which P is claiming restitution may indicate that D was a "wrongdoer" in obtaining the money and so should not be able to rely on his own change of position to resist the claim.

It is clear that a causal connection will be required between the payment and D's change of position. Lord Goff said (at p 534):

"the mere fact that the defendant has spent the money, in whole or in part, does not of itself render it inequitable that he should be called upon to repay, because the expenditure might in any event have been incurred by him in the ordinary course of things."

In other words, D cannot rely upon a defence of change of position if he has spent the money on something which he would have purchased even had the payment not been made.

More generally, what is required for a change of position is illustrated by *Scottish Equitable plc* v *Derby* [2000] 3 All ER 793. In that case:

Through an error in record keeping, the claimant paid out to the defendant a much larger pension fund than he was actually entitled to. He used it to reduce his mortgage, purchase an annuity and spent £10,000 improving his lifestyle generally.

The only sum in relation to which D could establish change of position was the £10,000. The mortgage was a debt which D had to pay in any event and he retained the benefit of the payment in the form of an increased equity of redemption. The company which had supplied the annuity was prepared to undo the transaction. In effect when the court took the view that D's only change of position was in relation to the lifestyle expenditure, it merely left D ceasing to enjoy benefits which he had never been entitled to, and left him no worse off than he would have been without the mistaken windfall payment. It would seem that where what is sought is restitution of a sum of money paid to D, D's change of position will be considered in terms of his overall wealth reduction. The point should be made, however, that a broad-brush approach has been taken to addressing the question of increased lifestyle expenditure consequent on mistaken periodic payments. In *Philip Collins Ltd v Davis* [2000] 3 All ER 808, where what was in question was the overpayment of periodic royalties to musicians, the judge was unable to find that "any particular item of expenditure was directly referable to the overpayments of royalties" (at p 829). However, the judge nevertheless concluded that "the overpayments caused a general change of position by the defendants in that they increased their level of outgoing by reference to the sums so paid" (at p 830).

Some consideration must be given to the relationship of change of position and estoppel. As has been indicated, change of position allows the courts merely to reduce the amount recovered, rather than denying restitution at all. In contrast, if estoppel is established, the claimant's right is denied in its entirety (see below). Against that background, it may be that D will be denied the right to rely on estoppel where the defence of change of position is, in principle, available in relation to such a restitutionary claim as that in question (*Scottish Equitable v Derby* [2000] 3 All ER 793 at pp 804–807, *Philip Collins v Davis* [2000] 3 All ER 808 at p 826).

It should be emphasised that although *Lipkin Gorman* was concerned with a money payment, and the discussion above has similarly been in terms of D having received a money payment, there appears to be no reason to confine the defence to that type of enrichment. The point should also be made that recognition of a general defence of change of position makes it easier for the courts to ensure a principled development of the grounds for restitution. The development of the grounds for restitution (the unjust factors) need not be restricted by the fear of hardship to D through a change of position after his enrichment (Lord Goff at p 534). This was indicated above in relation to the recognition of the general availabilty of restitution for mistake of law (see page 522).

2. Estoppel[36]

The defence of estoppel is not unique to restitution but it should be compared here with the restitutionary defence of change of position which, as has been indicated, may have displaced it. The defence basically requires a representation of fact by P and a bona fide change of position by D in reliance upon that representation, in circumstances making it unjust for P to deny the representation. The defence has basically been used in relation to restitutionary claims for payments made under a mistake. This may be accounted for by the unlikelihood of finding the generally required representation in other cases, and there seems to be no reason in principle why the defence should not be generally available, although in some cases D's involvement in the "unjust" element of the restitutionary claim should prevent him relying on the defence (eg if the restitutionary claim is based on duress).

When P makes a mistaken payment to D, there is no representation simply in that act. Something more will be required to ground an estoppel, as for example where D has queried the payment and been informed that it was due to her (*Avon County Council* v *Howlett* [1983] 1 All ER 1073; see also *Holt* v *Markham* [1923] 1 KB 504). However, in exceptional cases, no such representaton will be required if P has breached a duty owed to D. In *Skyring* v *Greenwood* (1825) 4 B & C 281, for three years before his death Major Skyring had been paid too much by the army paymasters. His administratrix took action when they deducted the overpayment from the sum owing to his estate on his death. The question arose as to whether they could have recovered the overpayments in an action during his lifetime. It was held that they would not have succeeded because they had failed to inform him of the overpayments for three years after they had been informed by the Board of Ordnance, and he had changed his position in reliance upon the money being his. The court regarded it as the duty of the army paymasters to communicate the information received from the Board.

The estoppel will require a bona fide change of position in reliance upon the representation. There can be no estoppel if D did not believe that he was entitled to the payment in question or if he would have incurred the same expenditure had the payment not been made. In *United Overseas Bank* v *Jiwani* [1976] 1 WLR 964, the bank, P, mistakenly credited D's account with a payment, of $11,000, twice. When the second, mistaken payment was reclaimed, no defence of estoppel was open to D because he could not have believed that he was entitled to the payment, and also because he used the money to invest in a hotel which was an investment he would have made even without the mistaken payment.

Unlike the change of position defence considered above, estoppel is regarded as an "all or nothing defence". On this basis, if D's change of position relates only to part of the sum concerned, P's restitutionary action nevertheless fails in relation to the whole sum. The Court of Appeal came to that conclusion in *Avon County Council* v *Howlett* [1983] 1 WLR 605 on the basis that estoppel simply prevented P from disputing the fact he had represented, and thus had to apply to the whole sum once reliance upon any part of it had occurred.

3. Bona fide purchaser[37]

We have already seen that property cannot be recovered from a bona fide third party purchaser for value without notice even though B, who sold it to him, had acquired it from A through a contract which was voidable for misrepresentation (see page 301). This is one example of the defence provided for the bona fide third party purchaser for value without notice. A proprietary restitutionary claim will normally be defeated by the defence and exceptionally it may be relevant to a personal claim.

4. Submission to an honest claim[38]

As we have seen, it has been recognised that it is important that restitutionary recovery for mistake be limited by appropriate defences. The recognition of the defence of change of position was seen as important in the development of restitutionary recovery for mistake of law. Similarly, in that context, and elsewhere, it is important to recognise that there should be no recovery of a payment made in submission to an honest claim. So, in the context of mistake, P should not be able to recover a payment made on the basis that P accepted the risk that D's claim to it might be based on a mistake.

Footnotes

(1) For discussion of contrasting views see Burrows at pp 1–6, and see Atiyah, *Essays on Contract* at pp 47–52, Stoljar *The Law of Quasi-Contract* (1989), Beatson ch 2, Muir, "Unjust Sacrifice and the Officious Intervener", in *Essays* (Finn, ed).

(2) But see, eg *Moses v Macferlan* (1760) 2 Burr 1005. Lord Mansfield said (at p 1012): "The gist of this kind of action is that the defendant, upon the circumstances of the case, is obliged by the ties of natural justice and equity to refund the money".

(3) Burrows at pp 6–16, Goff & Jones at pp 16–36, Birks at pp 109–132.

(4) Goff & Jones would also allow for the case of necessitous but unsuccessful intervention by P to assist D, and Birks recognizes that there may be "other" residuary cases in which D will be regarded as enriched.

(5) pp 11–16 and (1988) 104 LQR 576, Garner (1990) 10 OJLS 42 and contrast Birks, "In Defence of Free Acceptance" in *Essays* (Burrows ed).

(6) See Birks at pp 23–25, 39–44 and 132–139. For criticism of Birks approach see Beatson ch 8.

(7) See Burrows at pp 40–46, Goff & Jones ch 2, Birks at pp 378–386, Burrows & McKendrick ch 14, Gummow, "Unjust Enrichment, Restitution and Proprietary Remedies" in *Essays* (Finn ed), Goode, "Property and Unjust Enrichment" in *Essays* (Burrows ed). See also *Attorney-General for Hong Kong v Reid* [1993] 3 WLR 1143; *Westdeutsche Landesbank Girozentrale v Islington LBC* [1996] 2 WLR 802.

(8) For discussion of this see Burrows at pp 35–40.

(9) Burrows ch 2, Goff & Jones ch 3, Mitchell [1992] LMCLQ 483.

(10) Butler, "Mistaken payments, Change of position and Restitution", in *Essays* (Finn ed).

(11) Birks at pp 140–146, [1989] LMCLQ 296, [1991] LMCLQ 473, [1993] LMCLQ 218. Burrows ch 4, McKendrick (1992) 55 MLR 377, Harpum in Birks (ed) *The Frontiers of Liability* (1994) vol 1, 9–25, Gardner (1996) 112 LQR 56, Swaddling [1996] LMCLQ 63, Virgo (1996) TLI 20, Grantham & Rickett [1996] LMCLQ 463, Bant [1998] LMCLQ 18. But see Goff & Jones at pp 175–177.

(12) Rose (1989) 9 OJLS 167, Goff & Jones at pp 461–482, Muir "Unjust Sacrifice and the Officious Intervener" in *Essays on Restitution* (Finn ed).

(13) The preservation of life and aircraft is included by statute (Merchant Shipping Act 1894, Civil Aviation Act 1982).

(14) See generally *Kennedy's Law of Salvage*. Goff & Jones at pp 483–498, Birks at pp 304–308, Burrows at pp 236–238.

(15) See also the law relating to general average (contributors to loss during a voyage by ship and cargo owners) Goff & Jones at pp 429–436.

(16) Sutton, "Payments of debts Charged upon Property" in *Essays* (Burrows ed).

(17) See Burrows at pp 213–216, Goff & Jones at pp 446, 467. But see *The Zuhal K* [1987] 1 Lloyd's Rep 151.

(18) *Dearing v Earl of Winchelsea* (1787) 2 Bos & P 270. See also eg *North British and Mercantile Ins Co v London, Liverpool and Globe Ins Co* (1876) 5 Ch D 569 (co-insurers), *Re Royal Bank of Australia, Robinson's Executors Case* (1856) De G.M. & G. 572 (partners), *Commercial Union Assurance Co Ltd v Hayden* [1977] QB 804.

(19) See also *Butterworths v Kingsway Motors* [1954] 1 WLR 1286, *Warman v Southern Counties Car Finance Corporation* [1949] 2 KB 576. But contrast *Hunt v Silk* (1804) 5 East 449.

(20) See Goff & Jones at p 528. Burrows at pp 264–265, Law Com Rep No 160, *The Sale and Supply of Goods*, paras 6.1–6.5. However, in the recent DTI consultation document (Transfer of Title: Sections 21 to 26 of the Sale of Goods Act 1979 (1994)) it was proposed that the recovery by the innocent purchasers should be restricted. They would not recover

the full contract price but would have to set off an amount on account of any benefit or enjoyment of the goods.

(21) See Burrows at pp 268–271, Birks, "In Defence of Free Acceptance" in *Essays* (Burrows ed) at p 136, Goff & Jones at pp 530–534, Beatson at pp 12–15, (1989) 2 Jo of Contract Law 65, Law Com Consultation Paper No 132, part vii.

(22) Jones (1980) 18 Univ Western Ontario LR, Carter "Ineffective Transactions" in *Essays* (Finn ed), Farnsworth (1987) 87 Col LR 217, McKendrick (1988) 8 OJLS 197, Ball (1983) 99 LQR 572, McKendrick in *Restitution Past, Present and Future* (Cornish *et al* eds), Hedley in *Restitution Past, Present and Future* (Cornish *et al* eds).

(23) See eg Goff & Jones ch 26 and Burrows at pp 293–299 respectively.

(24) See also *Way* v *Latilla* [1937] 3 All ER 759, *British Steel Corp* v *Cleveland Bridge and Engineering Co* [1984] 1 All ER 504.

(25) Goff & Jones ch 24, Burrows at pp 331–334, Grodecki (1955) LQR 254, Beatson (1975) 91 LQR 313, Merkin (1981) 97 LQR 420, Dickson, "Restitution and Illegal Transactions" in *Essays* (Burrows ed). Enchong (1994) 14 OJLS 295, Cohen [1994] LMCLQ 163, Law Com Consultation Paper No 154 (1998).

(26) For criticism of the traditional position see *Restitution of Payments made under a Mistake of Law* (Law Com No 120), Birks, "Restitution from the Executive: A Tercentenary Footnote to the Bill of Rights" in *Essays* (Finn ed), Cornish (1987) 14 JMCL 41, Burrows, "Public Authorities, Ultra Vires and Restitution" in *Essays* (Burrows ed).

(27) The reference is often to cases on demands made *colore officii*, eg *Morgan* v *Palmer* (1824) 2 B & C 729, *Steele* v *Williams* (1853) 8 Exch 625, *T & J Brocklebank Ltd* v *R* [1925] 1 KB 52.

(28) Law Com Consultation Paper No 132 Part VII, Law Com Rep No 247 (1999).

(29) For discussion of possible basic principles see eg Jackman (1989) CLJ 302, Birks at p 326.

(30) Goff & Jones at pp 781–786, Burrows at pp 393–397, Jackman (1989) CLJ 302, Birks, *Introduction* at pp 326–333, Beatson, *Use and Abuse of Unjust Enrichment* at pp 206–243.

(31) See also *Whitwham* v *Westminster Brymbo Coal & Coke Co* [1896] 2 Ch 538, *Strand Electric and Engineering Co Ltd* v *Brisford Entertainments Ltd* [1952] 2 QB 246, *Bracewell* v *Appleby* [1975] Ch 408, *Swordheath Properties Ltd* v *Tabet* [1979] 1 WLR 285, *Carr-Saunders* v *Dick McNeil Associates Ltd* [1986] 2 All ER 888. And see *Ministry of Defence* v *Ashman* [1993] 2 EGLR 102, [1993] 40 EG 144; *Ministry of Defence* v *Thompson* [1993] 2 EGLR 107, [1993] 40 EG 148; *Inverugie Investments Ltd* v *Hackett* [1995] 1 WLR 713.

(32) Goff & Jones at pp 412–417; Burrows at pp 397–403; Birks at pp 334–336 (1987) LMCLQ 421, (1993) 109 LQR 518; Jones (1983) 99 LQR 443; O'Dair [1993] Restitution Law Review 31; Jackman (1989) CLJ 302; Farnsworth (1985) 94 Yale LJ 1339; Stoljar (1989) 1 Jo of Contract Law 1, Beatson (1989) 2 Jo of Contract Law 74; Sharpe and Waddams (1982) 2 OJLS 290; Waddams "Restitution as Part of Contract Law" in *Essays* (Burrows ed); Goodhart [1995] RLR; Law Com No 247, McGregor in *Wrongs and Remedies in the Twenty-First Century* (Birks ed); Beale in *Wrongs and Remedies in the Twenty-First Century* (Birks ed).

(33) McDermott (1992) 108 LQR 652, Gummow J, "Unjust Enrichment, Restitution and Proprietary Remedies" in *Essays* (Finn ed). Goff & Jones chs 33, 34.

(34) See Birks at pp 387–389, Goff & Jones at pp 668–669, Needham (1979) 95 LQR 536; Goode, "Property and Unjust Enrichment" in *Essays* (Burrows ed), Millett (1993) 1 RLR 7.

(35) Goff & Jones at ch 40, Burrows at pp 421–431.

(36) Goff & Jones at ch 40, Burrows at pp 431–439, Birks at pp 402–410.

(37) Goff & Jones at ch 41, Burrows at pp 472–475.

(38) Goff & Jones pp 53–58, 197–200, 214–215, 234–235, 347–351.

Chapter 23

Agency

1. Introduction

The relationship between principal and agent will frequently be contractual but that is not the reason why the topic of agency is dealt with here. Merely as one type of frequently occurring contract it would not merit such discussion. The reason why some consideration is given to the law of agency is because of the important role which it plays in the making of many contracts. Agency provides the means by which numerous contracts are made and, as such, students of contract law should be aware of the basics of agency law. For more detailed treatment the student is referred to such books as:

FMB Reynolds, *Bowstead & Reynolds on Agency* (16th ed)
Fridman, *The Law of Agency* (7th ed, 1996)
Markesinis & Munday, *An Outline of the Law of Agency* (4th ed, 1998)
Sealy & Hooley, *Text and Materials in Commercial Law* (1994).

2. Types of agency — Authority

There have been numerous attempts to define agency. Fridman, for example, sees agency as:

"the relationship that exists between two persons when one, called the *agent*, is considered in law to represent the other, called the *principal*, in such a way as to be able to affect the principal's legal position in respect of strangers to the relationship by the making of contracts or the disposition of property." (Fridman *The Law of Agency* (1996) p 9.)

This definition is helpful to an extent. It focuses attention on the important effect of an agency relationship, ie an agent can affect the principal's legal position in relation to third parties. In fact, agency can simply be seen as a "power-liability" relationship. Thus (Dowrick (1954) 17 MLR 24 at p 36):

"The essential characteristic of an agent is that he is invested with a legal power to alter his principal's legal relations with third persons: the principal is under a correlative liability to have his legal relations altered."

Obviously, the aspect of the agent's ability to affect his principal's legal relations with third parties with which we are particularly concerned is the agent's ability to bring his principal into a direct contractual relationship with a third party. The agent can create a contract between his principal and a third party.

However, although Fridman's definition can be used to emphasise the important effect of the agency relationship, and it also has the advantage of being able to encompass the different types of agency considered below, it does not tell us everything we want to know. It does not reveal anything about how any agency relationship is created. In contrast, other definitions look to the way in which an agency relationship is created. Bowstead (art 1(1)), for example, defines agency as:

> "the fiduciary relationship which exists between two persons, one of whom expressly or impliedly consents that the other shall act on his behalf, and the other of whom similarly consents so to act or so acts."

This definition focuses upon consent to the relationship by the parties. The situations in which consent exists may provide the "paradigm case" of agency (Bowstead p 4), and the definition does indicate how an agency relationship may arise. However, as will be seen, because of this definition's focus on consent, it does not encompass all of the different types of agency. No one definition is entirely satisfactory. Basically, we have to be content with the idea that agency means that the agent can affect the principal's legal position with respect to others, but we must also consider the various ways in which the different types of agent derive their power to do this. The different types of agency need to be considered and they can be identified by the different forms of authority which are involved. We need to consider agency where the agent has:

(a) actual authority — express or implied;
(b) apparent authority;
(c) authority by operation of law;
(d) no authority at the time of acting but there is subsequent ratification by the principal.

Brief consideration will also need to be given to the special regime for "commercial agents" under the Commercial Agents (Council Directive) Regulations 1993 (SI 1993 No 3053 as amended by SI 1993 No 3173, SI 1998 No 2868) which were made to implement the EC Directive on the Co-ordination of Laws of the member states Relating to Self-Employed Commercial Agents (OJ 1986, L382/17). The definition of a "commercial agent" falling within these regulations is considered at the end of this section. The principal effect of the Regulations is on the rights and duties between principal and agent, in particular, the agent is given extensive rights against the principal. The Regulations are considered at appropriate points in the text.

(a) Actual authority — express or implied

> "An 'actual' authority is a legal relationship between principal and agent created by a consensual agreement to which they alone are parties. Its scope is to be ascertained by applying ordinary principles of construction of contracts. . .." (*Freeman & Lockyer* v *Buckhurst Park Properties* [1964] 1 All ER 630 *per* Diplock LJ at p 644).

The basis of actual authority is consent. The principal confers actual authority on the agent. Commonly this is done through a contract, but a non-contractual agreement will suffice. No formalities are required to appoint an agent unless the agent is to execute a deed. Even if the agent is required to make a contract which must itself be in writing, his appointment can be oral (*Heard* v *Pilley* (1869) LR 4 Ch App 548). (However, if the agreement falls within the 1993 Regulations on commercial agents, each party may demand of the other a written statement of the terms of the agency agreement (reg 11)). Express authority is that which is conferred by the express words of the agreement between the principal and the agent. As Diplock LJ stated in *Freeman & Lockyer*, determining its extent is a matter of construction of the agreement.

If there is ambiguity in a contract between principal and agent, then the agent may be held to have been acting within his authority even where he has understood, and acted upon, the agreement in a way which is different from that intended by the principal (*Ireland* v *Livingstone* (1872) LR 5 HL 395). However, modern methods of communication will normally mean that it is reasonable for the agent to seek clarification. If it is, and he does not do so, it would seem that he will not be held to have acted within his authority if he acts upon the agreement in a way not intended by the principal (*European Asian Bank AG* v *Punjab and Sind Bank (No 2)* [1983] 2 All ER 508).

However, actual authority may be express or implied.

> "It is *express* when it is given by express words such as when a board of directors pass a resolution which authorises two of their number to sign cheques. It is *implied* when it is inferred from the conduct of the parties and the circumstances of the case." (*Hely-Hutchinson* v *Brayhead Ltd* [1968] 1 QB 573 Lord Denning MR at p 583.)

The agent's actual authority may be wholly express or it may be wholly implied or, more commonly, there may be implied authority to supplement express authority. It was wholly implied in *Hely-Hutchinson* v *Brayhead* [1968] 1 QB 573. In that case:

> Brayhead had not appointed anyone as managing director but the Brayhead board allowed its chairman, R, to act as if he was the managing director. He made various contracts on behalf of Brayhead and simply reported back on them to the board. Brayhead decided to buy some shares in Perdio Electronics, a company which was then experiencing difficulties. It did so with a view to eventually obtaining control of Perdio. H, the managing director of Perdio, became a member of the Brayhead board. Subsequently, R discussed the possibility of H putting more funds into Perdio. H did so after R agreed that Brayhead would indemnify him for any loss he might make.

The question which had to be decided was whether Brayhead was bound to indemnify H. At first instance it was held that R had had apparent authority as a managing director. The Brayhead board's treatment of R was held to have made a representation to H that R had such authority. (On apparent authority see page 546.) However, the Court of Appeal concluded that R had the actual implied authority to do what a managing director would usually do and Brayhead was bound to indemnify H. The board's treatment of R was held to have impliedly given him that actual authority.

More commonly, implied authority arises in the situation where someone is appointed to a particular post or office and, subject to contrary indications, they will then impliedly have the actual authority which someone in that office or position usually has. An example is when "a board of directors appoint one of their number to be a managing director. They thereby impliedly authorise him to do all such things as fall within the usual scope of that office" (*Hely-Hutchinson v Brayhead* Lord Denning MR at p 583). Such authority will not be implied where an express contrary restriction has been put upon the agent's powers. A solicitor usually has the authority to compromise a claim on behalf of his client (provided the compromise does not involve a matter collateral to the action). However, in *Waugh v Clifford* [1982] 1 All ER 1095 the solicitor did not have actual authority to compromise the particular claim on the terms in question. His power to compromise had been expressly restricted. (On the finding that the solicitor nevertheless had apparent authority to make the compromise and that his client was therefore bound, see page 547.)

There may be implied authority when an agent is appointed to carry out a specific task. The agent will impliedly be given the authority to do what it is necessary to do to carry out that task. In *Rosenbaum v Belsen* [1900] 2 Ch 267 an agent, who was instructed to sell property, impliedly had authority to sign an agreement of sale. It was necessary for the agent to have that authority if he was to carry out his appointed task of selling the property. In contrast, the agent in *Hamer v Sharp* (1874) LR 19 Eq 108 had no such implied authority. He had been expressly appointed merely to "find a purchaser" and it was held not to be necessary to that task that he should have the power to conclude a contract of sale.

Authority may be implied by custom when an agent is appointed to deal in a particular market. The agent will be taken to have impliedly been given authority to act in accordance with the customs of the market, (*Pollock v Stables* (1848) 12 QB 765).

(b) Apparent authority

Here the agent's authority is not real — it is labelled as "apparent" or "ostensible", and is not derived from the consent of the principal and agent. It is a product of the principal's representation to the third party that the agent has authority as an agent. The position was clearly explained by Diplock LJ in *Freeman & Lockyer v Buckhurst Park Properties* [1964] 1 All ER 630. He said (at p 644):

> "An 'apparent' or 'ostensible' authority . . . is a legal relationship between the principal and the contractor created by a representation, made by the principal to the contractor, intended to be and in fact acted on by the contractor, that the agent has authority to enter on behalf of the principal into a contract of a kind within the scope of the 'apparent' authority, so as to render the principal liable to perform any obligations imposed on him by such contract. To the relationship so created the agent is a stranger."

In other words, whereas actual authority arises from the relationship of the principal and the agent (see page 544), apparent authority stems from the relationship of the principal and the third party. It can be viewed as "agency by estoppel" — basically it arises from a representation of the agent's authority by the principal to the third party which is relied upon by the third party and causes the third party to change his position (*Rama Corp Ltd v Proved Tin and General Investments Ltd* [1952] 2 QB 147 Slade J at pp 149–150).

The principal's representation of the agent's authority can arise in different ways. It commonly stems from the appointment of the agent to a post, or office. That appointment normally carries with it actual authority to do what someone in that position usually has authority to do, but the appointment is also a representation that the person so appointed is an agent with that same "usual" authority. That may result in an apparent authority which is the same, in extent, as the agent's actual implied authority. However, the actual authority may be restricted and the apparent authority may be more extensive than the agent's actual authority, if the representation is unrestricted. In *Waugh* v *Clifford*, for example, the actual authority of the solicitor had been expressly restricted, but the principal was still bound by the compromise agreed by the solicitor with the third party. The solicitor had apparent authority to make the compromise agreement. It was within the scope of what a solicitor would usually have authority to do. His appointment was a representation that he had the authority a solicitor would usually have, and the third party had no notice of the restriction upon the solicitor's actual authority. Similarly, in *Hely-Hutchinson* v *Brayhead*, Lord Denning MR provided an example (at p 583):

> "when the board (of a company) appoint the managing director, they may expressly limit his authority by saying he is not to order goods worth more than £500 without the sanction of the board. In that case his *actual* authority is subject to the £500 limitation, but his *ostensible* authority includes all the usual authority of a managing director. The company is bound by his ostensible authority in his dealings with those who do not know of the limitation."

It is worth emphasising that no confusion should arise from any reference to "usual" authority in the context of both actual and apparent authority. In both cases, the use of the term "usual" merely indicates the extent of the authority (ie what is usual for someone in that post or office) — it does not indicate anything about the basis of the authority, which is consent in the case of actual authority and representation and reliance in the case of apparent authority.

A representation that the agent has authority may arise from the principal's past conduct. In *Summers* v *Soloman* (1857) 7 E & B 879, the facts were as follows:

> An uncle employed his nephew as the manager of his jewellery shop. The nephew regularly ordered jewellery from S for resale in the shop and the uncle paid for it. The nephew left his uncle's employment and ended his actual authority to make contracts on behalf of his uncle. However, the nephew obtained further jewellery from S.

The question was whether the uncle was liable to S for the price of the jewellery. It was held that he was. His past payments for the jewellery ordered by the nephew had created a representation which had not ceased just because, without S's knowledge, the nephew had left his uncle's employment.

As indicated above, apparent authority generally arises where there is a representation by the principal. In some cases there will be a representation not by the principal himself but by an agent. A company, for example, as a legal but not an actual person, must do everything through agents. It has been indicated that the representation must be made by the principal or someone with actual authority to make the representation (*Freeman & Lockyer* Diplock LJ at p 645), but apparent authority to make such a representation should be equally effective. Of course, in general, an agent cannot generate his own apparent authority by his own representation (*Armagas Ltd v Mundogas SA; (The Ocean Frost)* [1986] 1 AC 717). A representation by the principal, or which can be traced back to the principal through his agents — that the person concerned has authority — is the basis of apparent authority. However, this cannot be seen as an absolute rule. To some extent apparent authority may depend upon the agent's representation. For example, the situation may be such that it is usual for a person in the position of the agent to have authority to do certain things only if a given background factor is present. It would seem that the third party can rely upon the agent's statement as to whether that factor is present. For example, a solicitor may purport to give a guarantee on behalf of a client. The giving of such a guarantee would fall within the authority which a solicitor would usually have if his firm was holding money for the client. Against that background, the solicitor may be seen to have represented his own authority when the third party is allowed to rely upon his express or implied assertion that the firm is holding money for that client (*United Bank of Kuwait Ltd v Hammoud* [1988] 1 WLR 1051).

However, in *First Energy (UK) Ltd v Hungarian International Bank Ltd* [1993] 2 Lloyd's Rep 194, if the case is not confined to its facts, considerable inroads were made upon the basic idea that generally an agent cannot represent his own authority. The case was concerned with the arrangement of *ad hoc* finance for a client of the bank. The senior manager of the bank in Manchester did not have authority to make any such agreement but he wrote a letter to the client which purported to communicate the decision of his superiors that such a loan was available. The bank was held liable on the basis that the senior manager had, at least, apparent authority to communicate the approval of the loan and the offer. It can be seen that taking this view of the impact of the senior manager's authority to write letters on behalf of the bank makes considerable inroads on the general rule requiring the representation of the agent's authority to stem from the principal (see Reynolds (1994) 110 LQR 21).

(c) Authority by operation of law

The situations to be considered here are those in which there is said to be agency despite the absence of consent or even of any representation. These are circumstances in which the law has concluded that an agency relationship should be found to deal with what has occurred.

(i) Necessity

Agency of necessity originated in the situation where a ship's master had to act in an emergency to save his ship or cargo (eg *The Argos* (1873) LR 5 PC 134). He was then regarded as an agent of necessity. It has been disputed as to how far beyond that case it can extend[1], but it would seem to apply where perishable goods or livestock are being carried or stored on land[2]. If the situation is one in which an agency of necessity can be found, a number of factors are required for it to be established in the instant case.

(a) Circumstances of necessity are required. This does not mean that there must be an "irresistable compelling power" — rather the situation must be such that "the force of circumstances determines the course a man ought to take" (*Australian Steam Navigation Co* v *Morse* (1872) LR 4 PC 222 at p 230).

(b) "It must be practically impossible to get the [principal's] instructions in time" (*Sims & Co* v *Midland Ry Co* [1913] 1 KB 103 Scrutton J at p 112).

(c) The agent must act *bona fide* in the interests of the principal (*Prager* v *Blatspiel, Stamp and Heacock* [1924] 1 KB 566).

(d) The agent's actions must be reasonable (*F* v *West Berkshire Health Authority* [1989] 2 All ER 545 Lord Goff at p 566).

It has been indicated that a distinction should be drawn between cases where a third party is involved and those in which the "agent" is merely seeking reimbursement or indemnity from the "principal" — the former being cases of agency and the latter being more appropriately dealt with under the law of restitution (*China Pacific SA* v *Food Corporation of India* [1982] AC 939 at p 958. See *Bowstead and Reynolds*, Chapter 4).

(ii) Cohabitation

The courts recognized a presumption that a wife has the authority of her husband to contract on his behalf for the supply of household necessaries on credit (*Debenham* v *Mellon* (1880) App Cas 24 at p 36). This also applies to unmarried female cohabitees (*Ryan* v *Sams* (1848) 12 QB 460) and is clearly anachronistic.

(d) Subsequent ratification by the principal

Here we are concerned with the situation where the agent initially acts without authority but the principal then ratifies the transaction. Once ratification has occurred, from the perspective of the relationship of the principal and the third party it is as if the agent had actual authority at the time he acted — the agent may remain liable to the third party for breach of warranty of authority and to his principal for breach of duty, although that will normally have been waived with the principal's ratification (*Suncorp Insurance and Finance* v *Milano Assicurzion* [1993] 2 Lloyd's Rep 225 at pp 234–235).

In order for there to be a valid ratification, at the time of contracting the agent must have made it clear that he intended to act on behalf of a principal, and the principal must be in existence and have capacity both then and at the time of ratification. (Ratification could not be used to solve the problem of contracts purportedly made on behalf of a company before the company was incorporated — *Kelner* v *Baxter* (1866) LR 2 CP 174.) The attempt to ratify was ineffective in *Keighley, Maxsted & Co* v *Durant* [1901] AC 240 because A did not make it clear that he was not simply intending to contract on his own behalf but for P. At the time that he contracts, the agent must have made the "principal" identifiable, although he need not have named him (*Watson* v *Swann* (1862) 11 CBNS 756; *Southern Water Authority* v *Carey* [1985] 2 All ER 1077; but see *National Oilwell (UK) Ltd* v *Davy Offshore Ltd* [1993] 2 Lloyd's Rep 582 at p 596). This contrasts with the situation in which an agent has actual authority. He may then act effectively as an agent without disclosing his status as an agent (see below in relation to undisclosed agency — page 557). However, undisclosed agency is anomalous in itself and is not extended to the context of ratification (*Keighley, Maxsted & Co v Durant*).

The principal may state that he is ratifying, or his actions may indicate that to be the case. If ratification is implied, then it must generally have occurred with full knowledge of the unauthorised acts of the "agent" (*In re The Bonita; The Charlotte* (1861) 1 Lush 252). However, P's adoption of A's acts will not be sufficient to amount to ratification if P had no effective choice but to adopt them. In *Forman & Co Pty Ltd v The Liddesdale* [1900] AC 190 the sale of the ship did not amount to ratification of the repairs which the ship's master had exceeded his authority in undertaking. There was no unequivocal act by the owners which amounted to ratification. They had no effective choice but to take the benefit of the repairs.

In *Keay v Fenwick* (1876) 1 CPD 745, after ratification, the agent was entitled to his commission from the principal. However, perhaps the most extreme effect of the retroactive nature of ratification occurs when the third party has attempted to withdraw an offer after there has been acceptance by the purported agent but before ratification. It has been held that the third party is bound (*Bolton Partners v Lambert* (1889) 41 Ch D 295). The retroactive nature of the ratification means that, after ratification, it is as if there was a valid acceptance which had occurred before the attempt to withdraw the offer (an offer cannot be withdrawn once it has been accepted). This is illustrated by *Bolton Partners v Lambert* in which the facts were as follows:

> T made an offer which A purported to accept as agent for P. T then purported to revoke the offer. After that, P ratified. The question was whether T's revocation was effective. It had occurred before P's ratification.

The court held that T was bound. Once an offer is accepted, it cannot be revoked (see above, page 29). The ratification meant that it was as if the offer had been accepted by P at the time when A purported to accept on his behalf.

The retroactive effect of ratification means that a third party offeror is left in a situation in which he cannot revoke although there is a time during which the "principal" is not bound. From the perspective of the third party this is open to criticism. However, there are limitations upon it. If acceptance is made subject to ratification, then there will be no binding acceptance before ratification and the third party can revoke effectively before ratification (*Watson v Davies* [1931] 1 Ch 455). In addition, in order for the ratification to be effective it would seem that it must occur within any time set for acceptance (*Dibbins v Dibbins* (1876) 2 Ch 348) or within a reasonable time (*Metropolitan Asylums Board Managers v Kingham* (1890) 6 TLR 217). (But see *Presentaciones Musicales SA v Secunda* [1994] 2 All ER 737.)

(e) Commercial agents

The final point to be considered in this section is different from those looked at above. The previous points outlined the different types of authority and thus the different basic types of agency stemming from them. Here we are not considering a type of agency in that sense. Here we need briefly to look at when an agent will come within the definition of "commercial agent" within the Commercial Agents (Council Directive) Regulations 1993 and, thus, when an agent will fall within the regime set out by the Regulations (see Reynolds [1993] JBL 260). It is, basically, actual authority which is in question here.

A commercial agent is defined by reg 2(1) as:

"a self-employed intermediary who has continuing authority to negotiate the sale or purchase of goods on behalf of another person (the 'principal'), or to negotiate and conclude the sale or purchase of goods on behalf of and in the name of that principal."

The Regulations apply only to self-employed intermediaries, and they do not apply if the agent's activities are unpaid (reg 2(2)). There are a number of stated exclusions from the regulatory regime (eg officers of companies, agents in commodity exchanges and markets — reg 2(1), (2)). A person is not a commercial agent unless he makes contracts, for the principal, for the sale or purchase of goods or he negotiates for the sale or purchase of goods. This requires the person concerned to be acting as an agent in negotiating the sales or purchases. "If a person buys or sells himself as principal he is outside the ambit of the Regulations. That is so because in negotiating that sale or purchase he is acting on his own behalf and not on behalf of another" (*AMB Imballaggi Plastici Srl* v *Pacflex Ltd* [1999] 2 All ER (Comm) 249 at p 252). The meaning of "negotiate" was considered by the Court of Appeal in *Parkes* v *Esso Petroleum Co Ltd* [1998] Eu LR 550. The case was concerned with sales at a self-service petrol station where the plaintiff licensee of the petrol station received a commission on the petrol sales. The court took the view that whilst the use of the word "negotiate" in the regulation did not require a process of bargaining "in the sense of invitation to treat, offer, counter offer and finally acceptance, or more colloquially" haggling, it did require more than the "self-service by the customer followed by payment in the shop of the price shown on the pump". The reference to "goods" in reg 2(1) precludes those who act as agents in relation to the sale or purchase of services or anything which is not "goods". However, in *Tamarind International Ltd* v *Eastern Natural Gas (Retail) Ltd* [2000] CLC 1397 it seems to have been assumed that agents acting in relation to the sale or purchase of gas and electricity could fall within the Regulations. The reference to "continuing authority" would seem to preclude agents contracted to negotiate a single sale or purchase. There is a specific exclusion from the scope of the Regulations of anyone whose activities as a commercial agent are considered to be "secondary" (reg 2(3), (4)). The approach taken to the meaning of "secondary" in Sch 1 does not embody any of the natural assumptions which would be made about the scope of such an exclusion and it has been questioned whether it conflicts with the Directive from which the Regulations derive[3].

Regulation 13 states that each party is entitled to receive from the other "a signed written document setting out the terms of the agency contract". Other rights and liabilities dealt with by the Regulations are referred to below.

3. Relations with third parties

An agent can bring a principal into direct contractual relationship with a third party. We should now give more detailed consideration to the effect upon the third party. However, the distinction must first be made between disclosed and undisclosed agency, ie between the situations where there is a disclosed and an undisclosed principal. There is a disclosed agency where it is known that the agent is contracting on behalf of a principal, rather than simply on his own behalf. The principal may be named or unnamed. He need not be identified, provided that it is made clear that the agent is contracting as an agent. In contrast, undisclosed agency is where there is an undisclosed principal and the third party thinks that he is contracting with the agent personally, ie it is not known that the agent is contracting as an agent.

(a) Disclosed agency

Where there is actual authority, the normal rule is that the agent drops out and the third party can sue, and be sued by, the principal as if no agent had been involved (*Montgomerie v United Kingdom Mutual Steamship Assn* [1891] 1 QB 370).

(i) Settlement with the agent

Once the agent has brought the principal and the third party into a direct contractual relationship, the agent usually plays no further part in the contract. However, cases have arisen in which the principal or the third party have sought to claim that they have discharged an obligation to pay the other party through payment to the agent. Difficulties arise when the agent does not pass the payment to the party for whom it was intended, and the question is whether the payer remains liable under the contract.

If payment is by the third party, then the question of whether he remains liable is simply a matter of whether the agent had authority from the principal to receive the payment. If there was no such authority, the third party's payment to the agent does not affect the principal who may sue the third party. In *Butwick v Grant* [1924] 2 KB 483, the facts were as follows:

> An agent obtained, for his principal, an order for coats from a tradesman. The coats were dispatched with the principal's invoice. The tradesman paid the agent.

It was held that the agent had not had authority to receive payment and that the third party was still liable to pay the principal.

Where payment by the principal to the agent is in question, then generally the principal cannot rely upon any such payment to defeat a claim by the third party. However, it has been held that the principal will have a defence to a claim by the third party if the third party induced the principal to believe that the agent had already discharged the principal's obligation.

> "If the conduct of the seller would make it unjust for him to call upon the buyer for the money; as for example, where the principal is induced by the conduct of the seller to pay his agent on the faith that the agent and seller have come to a settlement on the matter, or if any representation to that effect is made by the seller either by words or conduct, the seller cannot afterwards throw off the mask and sue the principal" (*Heald v Kenworthy* (1855) 10 Exch 739, Parke B at p 746).

The basis of the restriction upon the third party's right to sue the principal in these circumstances would seem to be estoppel.

Despite his payment to the agent, the principal remained liable to pay the third party in *Irvine & Co* v *Watson & Sons* (1880) 5 QBD 414. In that case the facts were as follows:

> W employed an agent to purchase oil. Having revealed that he was acting for a principal, but without naming W, the agent contracted with I, for the purchase of oil. There was a term in the contract stating that payment was to be by "cash on or before delivery". I delivered casks of oil to the agent without requiring payment. W paid the cost of the oil to the agent, assuming the agent had paid to obtain delivery. The agent did not pass the payment on to I.

The question was whether I could still claim the price of the oil from W. It was held that they could. Delivery without payment was not regarded as sufficient to mislead W into believing that the agent had paid I for the oil. It was indicated that the situation might have been otherwise if it had been an invariable trade custom to insist on payment before delivery.

The third party was prevented from pursuing the principal for payment in *Wyatt* v *Marquis of Hereford* (1802) 3 East 147. In that case the third party took security for the principal's payment from the agent but gave the agent a receipt as if the agent had actually paid the sum due. When the principal paid the agent, the receipt meant that the third party was unable to pursue the principal further for payment.

(ii) The agent's liability and right to sue on the contract

Where the agent has actual authority, the general rule is that the agent drops out and it is the principal and the third party who can sue and be sued on the contract. It is as if the contract had been made without the assistance of an agent.

> "There is no doubt whatever as to the general rule as regards an agent, that where a person contracts as agent for a principal the contract is the contract of the principal, and not that of the agent; and *prima facie*, at common law the only person who may sue is the principal, and the only person who can be sued is the principal." (*Montgomerie* v *United Kingdom Mutual Steamship Assn* [1891] 1 QB 370 Wright J at p 371.)

However, there are exceptional cases in which it will be found that the agent can sue or be sued on the contract either instead of, or in addition to, the principal. For example, there are special rules dealing with the situation where an agent has signed a deed or a bill of exchange or the principal is a company and the signatory is a company officer (see Markesinis & Munday pp 188–190).

It may be intended that the agent is to be a party to the contract. It used to be presumed that the agent did not bring the third party and the principal into a direct contractual relationship if the principal had a foreign domicile, ie it was presumed that the agent alone became a party to the contract with the third party (eg *Elbinger AG für Fabrikation von Eisenbahn Material* v *Claye* (1873) LR 8 QB 313). However, in *Teheran-Europe Co Ltd* v *ST Belton (Tractors) Ltd* [1968] 2 All ER 886, it was recognized that this should no longer be the case and that a principal's foreign domicile should simply be regarded as one factor to be considered in determining the parties' intentions. It has also been indicated that the agent should be presumed to be personally liable when the principal, although disclosed, is unnamed. However, again, in *N & J Vlassopoulos Ltd v Ney Shipping Ltd; (The Santa Carina)* [1977] 1 Lloyd's Rep 478 it was stated that there is no such presumption and that it is simply a matter of looking at all the facts to determine the parties' intention.

Generally, when a contract is in writing and signed by the agent in his own name, he will be deemed to have contracted personally on it unless a contrary intention appears in the document (*Parker v Winslow* (1857) 7 E & B 942; see also *Seatrade Groningen BV v Geest Industries Ltd* [1996] 2 Lloyd's Rep 375). It may be made clear in the body of the document that the agent is not contracting personally. In *Gadd v Houghton* (1876) 1 Ex D 357 the brokers had signed the contract of sale in their own name but they were not held liable on the contract. It was said, in the body of the contract, "we have this day sold to you *on account of* James Morton & Co . . ." (emphasis added). The phrase "on account of" was seen as clearly indicating that the brokers were not contracting personally but purely as agents for James Morton & Co. Of course, such a phrase will not be determinative in every case — the contract has to be seen as a whole (see *Tudor Marine Ltd v Tradax Export SA; (The Virgo)* [1976] 2 Lloyd's Rep 135).

The leading case of *Universal Steam Navigation Co Ltd v J McKelvie & Co* [1923] AC 492 shows the importance of some qualification of capacity added to the agent's signature. In that case, the agents were referred to in the body of the contract as "charterers" but they were held not to be personally liable on the charterparty when sued by the owners. The agents had signed the contract in their own name but then added "as agents". The House of Lords viewed that addition to the agents' signature as clearly showing that they were not contracting personally.

It should be emphasised that the agents in the *Universal Steam Navigation* case did not merely add the description "agents" to their signature but "as agents". If an addition to a signature is to be used to deny personal liability then it must not be such that it could merely be seen as descriptive. It must show that the person signing was doing so in a representative capacity.

> "Where it is stated in the contract that the person makes it 'as agent for', or 'on account of' or 'on behalf of' or simply 'for' a principal, or where words of that kind are added after such a person's signature, he is not personally liable . . .. Where such words are not used but the person is merely stated to be an agent, or the word 'agent' is just added after his signature, the result is uncertain, because it is not clear whether the word is used as a qualification or merely as a description . . ... In general, it would seem that in such a case the person does not avoid personal liability . . .." (*Bridges & Salmon Ltd v The Swan (Owner); (The Swan)* [1968] 1 Lloyd's Rep 5).

If there is nothing on the face of a written contract to contradict the presumption that an agent signing in his own name contracts personally, then he may wish to introduce evidence extrinsic to the document to show that he merely signed as an agent. However, when that is the case, the agent will be faced with the restrictions of the parole evidence rule (see eg *Higgins v Senior* (1841) 8 M & W 834).

On occasion an agent has purported to contract on behalf of a non-existent or fictional principal. It is generally a matter of construction to determine if the agent is personally liable on the contract. However, the situation in which this is most likely to occur is where the agent has purported to contract on behalf of a company which was not incorporated at the time the contract was made. That case is now dealt with by statute (s 36C(1) Companies Act 1985, as inserted by s 130(4) Companies Act 1989). Unless a contrary intention is clearly expressed in the terms of the contract, the agent will be personally liable on it. (But see *Coral (UK) Ltd* v *Rechtman* [1996] 1 Lloyd's Rep 235.)

There have been cases where although someone has made the contract as if he was an agent acting on behalf of someone else, in reality he has been contracting for himself. Under these circumstances, the purported agent has been recognized as a party to the contract and been allowed to sue in cases where he has not named a principal (*Harper* v *Avery* [1909] 2 KB 549; *Schmaltz* v *Avery* (1851) 16 QB 655). Where no principal has been named, the view can be taken that the identity of the principal was unimportant to the third party who is not therefore prejudiced when the supposed agent is recognized as the contracting party. The same argument does not apply if the purported agent has named a "principal", and in *Bickerton* v *Burrell* (1816) 5 M & S 383 the "agent" was not allowed to sue. He had stated that he was acting on behalf of his housekeeper. However, in *Rayner* v *Grote* (1846) 15 M & W 359, the court allowed the supposed agent to assert that he had in reality contracted personally, despite naming a "principal". It would seem that that will be the case if the third party has continued to perform after discovering the truth or if the identity of the other contracting party was not material to the third party. The supposed agent should not be able to sue if the contract is one in which the skills or creditworthiness of the person named as "principal" were vital to the third party's decision to contract (*Gewa Chartering BV* v *Remco Shipping Lines Ltd; (The Remco)* [1984] 2 Lloyd's Rep 205).

(iii) Election and merger

In those exceptional cases in which both the principal and the agent are liable on the contract, it is said that the third party will be prevented from suing one of them if he has already elected to hold the other liable (eg *Debenham's Ltd* v *Perkins* (1925) 133 LT 252). It is questionable what actions by the third party, short of obtaining a final judgment, will constitute an election, although certainly they must be clear and unequivocal (*Calder* v *Dobell* (1871) LR 6 CP 486). But, once judgment has been obtained against either the principal or the agent, it is said that action against the other is prevented by merger (*Priestly* v *Fernie* (1865) 3 H & C 977). It has, however, been argued that the cases dealing with election can be explained on different grounds and that, in any event, the doctrine is founded on the mistaken assumption (see eg *Debenham's Ltd* v *Perkins* (1925) 133 LT 252 Scrutton LJ at p 254) that contracts are made on the basis that the liability of the principal and agent is alternative when it is far more likely to be intended that the liability should be joint and several (Reynolds (1970) 86 LQR 318, [1994] JBL 149; *LC Fowler & Sons Ltd* v *St Stephen's Board of Governors* [1991] 3 NZLR 304).

(iv) Liability to the third party of the agent without authority — breach of warranty of authority

It has been seen that normally the agent simply drops out of the picture once he has concluded a contract with the third party on behalf of the principal.

Exceptionally the contract may be such that the agent is personally liable on it. However, if the agent acted without authority, and the principal is not bound by the contract which the agent purported to make on his behalf, that in itself cannot make the agent liable on the contract. In *Lewis* v *Nicholson and Parker* (1852) 18 QB 503, the facts were as follows:

> N and P were solicitors for the assignees of a bankrupt. L was a mortgagee of the bankrupt's property. N and P purported to make an agreement with L on behalf of the assignees. They had no authority to make the agreement. Under it the property was to be sold and L paid out of the proceeds. The property was sold but L did not receive payment. As N and P had not had authority to make the agreement and the assignees were not bound, L attempted to sue N and P personally on the agreement.

Construing the contract, the court held that it had only been intended to create contractual relations between L and the assignees. That had not occurred because of the lack of authority of N and P, but N and P were not personally liable on it.

However, an agent who purports to act on behalf of a principal despite his lack of authority may be liable to the third party in tort for deceit or for negligent misstatement. In addition, the purported agent may be liable, without fault, for breach of warranty of authority. In *Collen* v *Wright* (1857) 8 E & B 647, the facts were as follows:

> W was a land agent for G. He purported to lease some of G's land to C for a period of twelve and a half years. W lacked authority to make a lease for that period of time. C sued W.

Willes J, delivering the judgment of the Court of Appeal, said (at p 658):

> "a person, professing to contract as agent for another, impliedly if not expressly, undertakes to or promises the person who enters into such a contract upon the faith of the professed agent being duly authorised, that the authority which he professes to have does in point of fact exist. The fact of entering into the transaction with the professed agent, as such, is good consideration for the promise."

The warranty of authority may extend beyond the third party contracting with the principal to other third parties dependent upon that contract. Where a solicitor thought that he had the authority of both husband and wife to carry out the sale of their property, he was liable to the building society (which had advanced money to the purchasers) when it transpired that the wife knew nothing of the sale and had given the solicitor no authority to act for her (*Penn* v *Bristol and West Building Society* [1997] 3 All ER 470).

The liability for breach of warranty of authority is seen as contractual and strict. In *Yonge* v *Toynbee* [1910] 1 KB 215 it was reaffirmed that liability for breach of warranty of authority is strict. In that case, the solicitors' (who were the agents) lack of authority arose because, unknown to them the principal had become insane. His loss of capacity meant that the agency was automatically ended. Despite the solicitors' lack of fault they were liable for breach of warranty of authority.

The warranty of authority may be express or implied, but the agent can prevent it occurring by informing the third party that he lacks authority or is unsure if he has authority (*Halbot* v *Lens* [1901] 1 Ch 344). It also seems that the agent will avoid liability where the third party should have known that he was not warranting his authority (*Lilly Wilson & Co v Smales, Eeles & Co* [1892] 1 QB 456). (The possibility of the Unfair Contract Terms Act 1977 applying to any disclaimer should be borne in mind.)

(b) Undisclosed agency

There is undisclosed agency when the third party believes that he is simply contracting with the agent on his own behalf. Undisclosed agency can only occur where the agent has actual authority and intends to act on the principal's behalf (*Siu Yin Kwan v Eastern Insurance Co Ltd* [1994] 1 All ER 213 Lord Lloyd at p 220). There cannot be a representation creating apparent authority when the very existence of the principal is unknown to the third party[4] — and there is no scope for ratification (*Keighley, Maxsted & Co v Durant* [1901] AC 240 — see above, page 549). Where an agent makes a contract without disclosing that he is acting as an agent, the contract is simply made between the third party and the agent. The third party can sue the agent or, on discovering his existence, the principal. He will not be able to pursue actions against both of them to judgment, but at some stage will have to make an election (see below). The agent can sue on the contract until the principal intervenes. The principal is able to sue on the contract if he can intervene, but, as we shall see, there are some restrictions on his intervention (*Welsh Development Agency v Export Finance Co* [1992] BCLC 148 at pp 173, 182).

The development of recognition of undisclosed agency may be explained historically (Goodhart & Hamson (1932) 4 CLJ 320) but it is anomalous in terms of legal principle. There have been various attempts to explain it, for example, using trusts (Ames (1909) 18 Yale LJ 443) or the idea of assignment (Goodhart & Hamson *op cit*; Rochvarg (1989) 34 McGill LJ 286). Whilst assignment may be the closest analogy, none of the explanations is entirely satisfactory and should not be taken too far — the courts tend merely to regard the doctrine of undisclosed principal as commercially convenient (*Siu Yin Kwan v Eastern Insurance Co Ltd* [1994] 1 All ER 213 at pp 220, 223). In *Keighley, Maxsted & Co v Durant* [1901] AC 240 Lord Lindley said (at p 261):

> ". . . as a contract is constituted by the concurrence of two or more persons and by their agreement to the same terms, there is an anomaly in holding one person bound to another of whom he knows nothing and with whom he did not in fact intend to contract. But middlemen, through whom contracts are made, are common and useful in business transactions and in the great mass of contracts it is a matter of indifference to either party whether there is an undisclosed principal or not. If he exists it is, to say the least, extremely convenient that he should be able to sue and be sued as a principal, and he is only allowed to do so upon terms which exclude injustice."

The doctrine of the undisclosed principal must be considered further.

(i) Restrictions on the principal's intervention

The principal's intervention may be excluded expressly by the terms of the contract (*United Kingdom Mutual Steamship Assurance Association v Nevill* (1887) 19 QBD 110). More commonly it will be argued to be impliedly excluded. In *Humble* v *Hunter* (1848) 12 QB 310 the principal was held to be impliedly excluded from intervening in a charterparty which referred to the agent as the "owner" of the vessel that was the subject matter of the contract (see also *Formby Bros* v *Formby* ((1910) 102 LT 116). However, referring to the agent as "tenant" (*Danziger* v *Thompson* [1944] KB 654), or "charterer" (*F Drughorn Ltd* v *Rederiaktiebolaget Trans-Atlantic* [1919] AC 203) has been held not to have excluded the principal, and it has been indicated that a restrictive approach should be taken to arguments that the undisclosed principal is precluded, in this way, from intervening (*Siu Yin Kwan* v *Eastern Insurance Co Ltd* [1994] 1 All ER 213 at p 222. But see also *Asty Maritime Co Ltd* v *Rocco Guiseppe & Figli SNC; (The Astynax)* [1985] 2 Lloyd's Rep 109).

It has been held that the principal cannot intervene where the third party "made the contract for reasons personal to the agent which induced the third party to contract with the agent to the exclusion of his principal or any one else" (*Greer* v *Downs Supply Co* [1927] 2 KB 28, Scrutton LJ at p 35). In *Greer* the third party was held to have intended to contract only with the agent because he had a set off against the agent which he wished to use in relation to the contract. On that basis, the undisclosed principal was not allowed to intervene. More commonly, the kind of example which is given to illustrate when this argument will prevent the principal from intervening is of a contract requiring personal skills, such as portrait painting. That example was given in *Siu Yin Kwan* v *Eastern Insurance Co Ltd* [1994] 1 All ER 213, and it was distinguished from the contract in the instant case. The case was concerned with a contract providing indemnity insurance for an employer against claims by its employees in relation to their personal injury or death in the course of their employment. The particular contract had been made by a shipping agent, R, with the actual authority of the shipowner, X, in relation to X's potential liability to its employees, the crew of *The Osprey*. R had made the contract without disclosing that it was acting as an agent, and the question was whether X could claim on the indemnity insurance or whether the contract was such that an undisclosed principal could not intervene. The Privy Council held that the indemnity insurance contract was not one which was so personal that the principal could not intervene. The insurers had been given all the information that they required in relation to the ship and the crew and, on that basis, they were not concerned with whether R was acting on its own behalf or as an undisclosed agent. The Privy Council distinguished the instant case from that of a car insurance contract based on one driver's record. Obviously, another driver could not claim to be the undisclosed principal in such a case (at p 223). More generally, the point was made that in ordinary commercial contracts it could not normally be assumed that the third party was willing to make a contract with only the agent and with no one else (at p 221). See also *Teheran-Europe Co Ltd* v *ST Belton (Tractors) Ltd* [1968] 2 All ER 886 Diplock LJ at p 890; Tettenborn [1994] CLJ 223).

There are cases in which it has been argued that the principal should not be able to intervene because the third party would not have made a contract with him. In *Dyster* v *Randall & Sons* [1926] Ch 932, the facts were as follows:

> Dyster wished to buy some land from Randall & Sons but knew that they would not sell to him. Dyster arranged for C to make the purchase without revealing that he was acting for Dyster. After contracting, Randall & Sons discovered the truth and the question was whether they could resist an action for specific performance.

It was held that there was no personal element in the contract which would deny specific performance to Dyster. The situation is different if there is any misrepresentation by the agent to conceal the principal's existence. If that is the case, then the third party can rely upon the misrepresentation itself to rescind the contract (*Archer* v *Stone* (1898) 78 LT 34). However, it was the personal element which was held to be "strikingly present" and to prevent the principal from intervening in *Said* v *Butt* [1920] 3 KB 497. That case concerned the purchase of a theatre ticket by an agent. The theatre's management had already twice refused to sell one directly to the principal, a theatre critic. When the principal tried to use the ticket, he was refused admittance to the theatre. He was also unsuccessful when he attempted to sue for breach of contract. The performance was a first night of a new play — it was regarded as a special event at which the management wanted to get the right first reaction to the play. The management had refused to sell the principal a ticket because they were already in dispute with him over allegations that he had made concerning their ticket sales. Despite the court's conclusion, the personal nature of the contract would seem doubtful.

(ii) Election

Once the third party has discovered the existence of the principal, then he can decide to sue the principal rather than the agent. However, the liability of the undisclosed principal and the agent is regarded as alternative — at some stage the third party must elect "to avail themselves of one of those inconsistent rights and abandon the other" (*Clarkson Booker Ltd* v *Andjel* [1964] 2 QB 775). An election occurs once the third party knows all the facts and indicates unequivocally that he is going to avail himself of his rights against one party and not the other. Once judgment is obtained, then further action against the other party is said to be prevented by merger (*Priestly* v *Fernie* (1865) 3 H & C 977). It is not clear what action by the third party, short of obtaining judgment, will prevent him pursuing the other party, on the basis of election. In *Clarkson Booker Ltd* v *Andjel* [1964] 2 QB 775 it was unsuccessfully argued that an election had occurred. In that case, the facts were as follows:

> Clarkson Booker sold airline tickets to Andjel on credit. The tickets were not paid for. Clarkson Booker discovered that Andjel had made the purchase on behalf of an undisclosed principal (Peters & Milner Ltd). Clarkson Booker sent letters to both Andjel and Peters & Milner, threatening to take action. Clarkson Booker then started proceedings against Peters & Milner but did not pursue them on being informed that Peters & Milner were insolvent. The question was whether it was still open to Clarkson Booker to sue Andjel or whether an election had occurred which prevented them from doing so.

It was held that no election had been made. The court indicated that, in some circumstances, commencing an action against the principal or the agent might indicate an intention to proceed purely against that party, but such an intention was not regarded as unequivocally indicated on the facts of the instant case. Commencing an action was regarded as *prima facie* evidence of an election, but no election was found on the facts of the instant case. Although the case was regarded as borderline, the view was taken that commencement of an action against Peters & Milner, the principal, should be viewed against the background of the letters sent to both parties.

It has been argued that it is a misconception to talk of a doctrine of election in this context, but that rather what is in question is an estoppel (Reynolds (1970) 86 LQR 317, [1994] JBL 149. See also *LC Fowler & Sons Ltd* v *St Stephen's Board of Governors* [1991] 3 NZLR 304).

(iii) Set-off[5]

In the context of undisclosed agency, it is often said that any defence which the third party may have against the agent is available against his principal (eg *Siu Yin Kwan* v *Eastern Insurance Co Ltd* [1994] 1 All ER 213 at p 220) provided that the defence accrued before the third party became aware of the principal's existence (*Browning* v *Provincial Insurance Co of Canada* (1873) LR 5 PC 263 at pp 272–273; *Rabone* v *Williams* (1785) 7 Term Rep 360). This idea provides some comfort when it is pointed out how anomalous it is to allow the principal to intervene on a contract which the third party made with an agent who appeared to be contracting on his own behalf. However, when the right against the agent is one of set-off, an unduly restrictive view seems to have been taken of the circumstances in which the third party can set-off any monies owed to him by the agent against his (the third party's) liabilities under the contract. In *Cooke & Sons* v *Eshelby* (1887) 12 App Cas 271 the House of Lords indicated that the third party could only rely upon a right of set-off that he had against the agent if the principal was estopped from denying that right. It would seem inappropriate to impose any such general limitation upon set-off by the third party.

(iv) Settlement with agent

If the third party pays the contract price to the agent before discovering that the agent did not contract on his own behalf, then that payment should discharge the third party's liabilities. However, in *Coates* v *Lewes* (1808) 1 Camp 444 the line was taken that that would only happen where the principal had induced the third party to pay the agent. Any such requirement seems inappropriate where the existence of the principal was unknown before the payment.

In the case of a disclosed principal it has been seen that the principal's payment to the agent will only prevent the third party from continuing to pursue the principal for payment if the third party has induced the principal to make the payment to the agent (see above, page 552). However, the line has been taken that any payment by an undisclosed principal to the agent will discharge the principal (*Armstrong* v *Stokes* (1872) LR 7 QB 598). This may be seen as "logically indefensible" (Markesinis & Munday at p 171. But see Reynolds (1983) 36 CLP 119).

4. Rights and obligations between principal and agent

(a) Duties of the agent

Equity recognised the vulnerability of those who entrust others with the power to act on their behalf. That vulnerability was protected by the imposition of fiduciary duties upon those in whom such trust and confidence was reposed.

The duties of fiduciaries "stem from the extension ... of the duties and responsibilities imposed by courts of equity upon express trustees" (Bowstead at 6-033) and what is required in any given case will depend upon the particular relationship — "the fiduciary duties owed by an express trustee are not the same as those owed by an agent" (*Henderson* v *Merrett Syndicates Ltd* [1995] 2 AC 145 at p 214). However, the fiduciary relationship and the duties imposed were described generally by Millett LJ in *Bristol and West Building Society* v *Mothew* [1996] 4 All ER 698 (at pp 711–712):

"A fiduciary is someone who has undertaken to act for or on behalf of another in a particular matter in circumstances which give rise to a relationship of trust and confidence. The distinguishing obligation of a fiduciary is the obligation of loyalty. The principal is entitled to the single-minded loyalty of his fiduciary. This core liability has several facets. A fiduciary must act in good faith; he must not make a profit out of his trust; he must not place himself in a position where his duty and his interest may conflict; he may not act for his own benefit or the benefit of a third person without the informed consent of his principal. This is not intended to be an exhaustive list, but it is sufficient to indicate the nature of fiduciary obligations. They are defining characteristics of the fiduciary."

It should be emphasised that the fiduciary duties arise independently of any contract and will apply to a gratuitous agent. If there is a contract, then the fiduciary duties may be incorporated into it, or varied, or excluded by it (*Henderson* v *Merrett Syndicates Ltd* [1995] 2 AC 145 at pp 214–215). The point should also be made that "not every breach of duty by a fiduciary is a breach of fiduciary duty". A breach of the agent's duty to use due care and skill in carrying out his instructions, for example, may not involve any breach of fiduciary duty (Millett LJ in *Bristol and West Building Society* v *Mothew* [1996] 4 All ER 698 at p 710). The fiduciary duties are considered further below.

Where the agent is a "commercial agent" within the Commercial Agents (Council Directive) Regulations 1993, both principal and agent are under an obligation to act dutifully and in good faith (regs 3, 4), and terms inconsistent with those duties are void (reg 5). Both parties are also under more specific duties, such as in relation to the communication of certain information to the other. However, principally the Regulations provide rights for "commercial agents", particularly on termination of the agency. Whilst harmonising the laws of Member States to assist competition may be the first purpose of the Directive on Commercial Agents, from which the Regulations derive, the second has been identified as "one ... of social policy, that commercial agents are a down-trodden race, and need and should be afforded protection against their principals" (*Page* v *Combined Shipping and Trading Co Ltd* [1997] 3 All ER 656 at p 660).

(i) Duty to carry out instructions — due care and skill

An agent will be liable for exceeding his authority (*Fray* v *Voules* (1859) 1 E & E 839). If the agency is contractual, he may be liable simply for failing to do what he has undertaken to do (*Turpin* v *Bilton* (1843) 5 Man & G 455). If the agent is gratuitous, there is no contractual liability if he fails to do what he agreed to do and there is unlikely to be liability in tort for merely failing to act. He may be liable in tort if he acts and is negligent. A contractual agent who acts and fails to exercise due care and skill may be liable either in tort or contract (eg *Henderson* v *Merrett Syndicates Ltd* [1994] 3 All ER 506). The fact that an agent is gratuitous or paid is one factor in determining the standard of care required (*Chaudhry* v *Prabhakar* [1988] 3 All ER 718). An agent is not liable for failing to carry out his agreement with the principal if what it required was illegal or null and void (*Cohen* v *Kittel* (1889) 22 QBD 680).

(ii) Duty not to delegate

The agency relationship is, in general, a personal one of trust and confidence and the agent does not normally have authority to appoint a sub-agent but must carry out his tasks in person (*De Bussche* v *Alt* (1878) 8 Ch D 286). This is often expressed by the use of the Latin maxim *delegatus non potest delegare*. However, there are situations in which the agent will be found to have authority to delegate. It may be a trade custom that the agent should have authority to delegate (*Solley* v *Wood* (1852) 16 Beav 370), or the circumstances of the particular agency agreement may indicate that the principal and agent must have intended there to be delegation (*De Bussche* v *Alt* (1878) 8 Ch D 286; *Calico Printers' Association* v *Barclays Bank* (1931) 145 LT 51). In addition, delegation is normally allowed where the act is purely ministerial rather than one requiring the personal skills of the agent. In *Allam & Co* v *Europa Poster Services Ltd* [1968] 1 All ER 826 the agents were held to have acted within their authority in delegating, to their solicitor, the mere service of a notice. The act was not one which needed to be performed by the person in whom the principal had placed confidence (the agent). It was merely ministerial.

When delegation is authorised and the agent appoints a sub-agent, the sub-agent is not normally brought into a direct contractual relationship with the principal, ie the agent is not generally authorised to create privity between the principal and the sub-agent even if he is permitted to delegate (*Calico Printers' Association* v *Barclays Bank* (1931) 145 LT 51). In the absence of such privity, the principal cannot sue the sub-agent in contract if the sub-agent does not act with due care. The principal's contractual action will be against the agent who will himself be in breach of his obligations through the sub-agent's default (*Calico Printers' Association* v *Barclays Bank*; *Mackersy* v *Ramsays, Bonars & Co* (1843) 9 Cl & Fin 818. But see *Thomas Cheshire & Co* v *Vaughan Bros & Co* [1920] 3 KB 240, Atkin LJ at p 259). The principal may be able to take action against the sub-agent in tort (*Henderson* v *Merrett Syndicates Ltd* [1994] 3 All ER 506). The Contracts (Rights of Third Parties) Act 1999 does allow direct enforcement by the third party beneficiary of a contract. However, if the contract does not expressly provide that it is to be enforced by the third party (here the principal), the fact that a chain of contracts has been used may be seen as showing that there was not intended to be direct enforcement by the third party, and the Act will not then provide such enforcement (s1 (2) and see Law Com No 242, para 7.18).

(iii) Agent's duty not to put himself in a position where his interests conflict with his duties to his principal

As a fiduciary, the agent is under an obligation not to put himself in a situation where his interests are in conflict with his duties to the principal (*Aberdeen Ry*

Co v *Blaikie Bros* (1854) 1 Macq 461 Lord Cranworth at p 471). The most obvious example is where the agent purchases property from the principal (*McPherson* v *Watt* (1877) 3 App Cas 254) or sells his own property to the principal (*Armstrong* v *Jackson* [1917] 2 KB 822). A purchaser has an interest in paying the lowest price he can, but it is in the seller's interest that the highest price be obtained. The agent selling on behalf of his principal will be under a duty to get the best price reasonably obtainable. There is a conflict of interests where the purchaser is the agent. In fact, the law will react even to the potential for conflict so that the transaction may be affected where there is "a real sensible possibility of conflict" (*Boardman* v *Phipps* [1967] 2 AC 46 Lord Upjohn at p 124)[6].

If there is a conflict of interests, or a potential conflict, then the principal may rescind the contract (unless rescission is barred) or the principal may affirm the contract and either claim the agent's profit or damages. In *Bentley* v *Craven* (1853) 18 Beav 75 Romilly MR said (at p 76):

"Two principles with relation to the doctrine of principal and agent have been recognised from the earliest times. One is, that an agent employed to purchase cannot legally buy his own goods for his principal; neither can an agent employed to sell, himself purchase the goods of his principal. If he should do so, and thereby make a profit, the principal may either repudiate the transaction altogether or adopt it and claim for himself the benefit made by his agent."

The law will not intervene in the transaction if the principal consented to it, after being fully informed of the agent's position, and it was at the best price reasonably obtainable. Of course, as is generally the case with the fiduciary duties, the agent's duty not to put himself in a conflict of interests situation may be restricted by the terms of the contract between principal and agent (*Kelly* v *Cooper* [1993] AC 205; *Henderson* v *Merrett Syndicates Ltd* [1994] 3 All ER 506).

(iv) Duty not to take bribes

The agent is under a duty not to accept any bribes from the third party. A bribe was defined in *Industries & General Mortgage Co Ltd* v *Lewis* [1949] 2 All ER 573. Slade J said (at p 575):

"For the purposes of the civil law a bribe means the payment of a secret commission, which only means (i) that the person making the payment makes it to the agent of the other person with whom he is dealing; (ii) that he makes it to that person knowing that person is acting as the agent of the other person with whom he is dealing; (iii) that he fails to disclose to the other person with whom he is dealing that he has made that payment to the person whom he knows to be the other person's agent."

It is not necessary to establish any corrupt motive[7]. It is said to be "irrebuttably presumed" that the bribe was given to induce the agent to act favourably to the person giving the bribe and unfavourably to the principal and that the agent was so influenced (*Industries & General Mortgage Co Ltd* v *Lewis* [1949] 2 All ER 573).

If an agent takes a bribe, he will normally lose his commission (*Andrews* v *Ramsay & Co* [1903] 2 KB 635). If the agent was, for example, making a sale on behalf of the principal, then it would seem that the third party was willing to exceed the contract price by at least the amount of the bribe and the agent cannot normally claim to have fulfilled his obligation to get the best price reasonably obtainable, and so cannot have earned his commission (but see *Hippesley* v *Knee Bros* [1905] 1 KB 1).

In addition, the principal can terminate the agency and recover the bribe (*Boston Deep Sea Fishing and Ice Co* v *Ansell* (1888) 39 Ch D 339). In fact, the agent will hold the bribe on constructive trust for the principal, and the principal will be able to claim any profits that the agent may have made with the bribe (*A-G for Hong Kong* v *Reid* [1994] 1 All ER 1). The principal can also rescind the contract made with the third party — this does not prevent his recovery of the bribe (*Logicrose Ltd* v *Southend United Football Club Ltd* [1988] 1 WLR 1256). The point should also be made that both the agent and the third party may be liable to the principal for fraud. However, it has been held that the principal cannot recover both damages for fraud and the bribe (*Mahesan S/O Thambiah* v *Malaysia Government Officers' Co-operative Housing Assn Ltd* [1979] AC 374).

(v) Duty not to profit from the position as agent, the principal's property or confidential information

The agent is under a duty not to profit from his position as agent, or from the principal's property, or from confidential information. Again, this duty basically can be regarded as a particular example of the agent's general duty not to put himself in a position where his interests conflict with those of the principal. It is strictly applied and does not require any bad faith on the part of the agent. It is simply that any such profit must be accounted for to the principal, and may be regarded as held on trust for the principal[8], unless the informed consent of the principal is obtained. In *Boardman* v *Phipps* [1967] 2 AC 46, the facts were as follows:

> A trust owned shares in a certain company. The agents of the trustees attended a shareholders' meeting and otherwise gained information on the company through acting as the agents of the trust. The agents decided that the company could be made much more profitable if they controlled it. The trust did not want to acquire any more shares in the company. The agents bought shares themselves and made money both for the trust and themselves. The agents had not concealed what they were doing but they had not obtained the consent of all the trustees.

The House of Lords held that the agents had to account for their profit to the trust. Their good faith was recognized to the extent that they were allowed payment for their expenses and their services (see also *Target Holdings Ltd* v *Redferns* [1994] 2 All ER 337; Heydon (1994) 110 LQR 328).

In *Lamb* v *Evans* [1893] 1 Ch 218 the canvassers employed by the publisher of a trade directory were not allowed to use, in another publication, the confidential information they had gained in that employment.

(vi) The duty to account

The agent may receive property simply as a debtor of the principal, or it may be entrusted to the agent on behalf of the principal, depending on the intentions of the agent and principal. Where receipt is on behalf of the principal, the agent is under a duty to keep the property separate from his own. If it becomes mixed with his own property then the principal will be entitled to all of the property unless the agent can establish what is his own (*Lupton v White* (1808) 15 Ves 432). If the agent disposes of the principal's property, the principal can trace it into whatever the agent has converted it into, provided that it remains identifiable (*Re Hallett's Estate* (1880) 13 Ch D 696). The agent is normally treated as if he was trustee of the property for the principal (*Foley v Hill* (1848) 2 HL Cas 28 at pp 35–36).

The agent must keep full accounts of the transactions which he carries out on behalf of the principal. If he fails to do so the court may "presume everything most unfavourable to him" (*Gray v Haig* (1855) 20 Beav 219).

(b) Rights of the agent

(i) Remuneration

If there is a contract between the principal and the agent, then the agent maybe entitled to remuneration. There may be an express or implied term entitling the agent to remuneration[9]. None can be implied if there is an express contradictory term, even if that leaves the agent without any remuneration (*Kofi Sunkersette Obu v Strauss & Co Ltd* [1951] AC 243).

The remuneration of commercial agents within the Commercial Agents (Council Directive) Regulations 1993 is dealt with by regs 6–12. If there is no express agreement as to remuneration, the principal must pay the customary remuneration for an agent dealing with the relevant type of goods in the place where the agent carries on his activities. If there is no such "customary" remuneration then the agent is entitled to a "reasonable remuneration" (reg 6(1)).

If there is a term entitling the agent to payment under certain circumstances then he will only become so entitled once those circumstances have been fulfilled (*Giddy and Giddy v Russell* (1904) 48 Sol Jo 415). If the payment is to be made upon a particular result being achieved, if, for example, property is to be sold, then the agent will only be entitled to payment if he was the effective cause of the sale (*Millar, Son & Co v Radford* (1903) 19 TLR 575). In relation to transactions concluded during the period of the agency contract, a commercial agent is entitled to commission "where the transaction has been concluded as a result of his action" (reg 7(1)(a)), which may be less stringent than the common law requirement of effective cause. In addition, the commercial agent is also entitled to commission where the "transaction is concluded with a third party whom he has *previously* acquired as a customer for transactions of the same kind" (emphasis added) (reg 7(1)(b)). In other words, the commercial agent is entitled to commission on repeat orders.

On occasion, the acts of the principal may prevent the occurrence of the event upon which commission is to be become due to the agent. The question then becomes whether the agent can claim that there has been a breach of an express or implied term that the principal would not so act. The courts are generally unwilling to imply such a term (*Luxor (Eastbourne) Ltd v Cooper* [1941] AC 108, *French & Co Ltd v Leeston Shipping Co Ltd* [1922] 1 AC 451). However, in *Alpha-Trading Ltd v Dunnshaw-Pattern Ltd* [1981] QB 290, where the principal's actions involved a breach of the contract with the third party, the court was willing to imply a term that the principal would not breach the contract made with the third party and thereby prevent the agent from earning his commission. In relation to commercial agents, when there is a failure to perform the contract with the third party, the principal can only escape from the payment of commission if that failure "is due to a reason for which the principal is not to blame" (reg 11(1)).

(ii) Indemnity

There will normally be an express or implied term of a contract giving the agent, acting within the scope of his authority, a right to recover his expenses from his principal and also to be indemnified for losses and liabilities thereby incurred (eg *Chappell* v *Bray* (1860) 6 H & N 145; *Rhodes* v *Fielder, Jones and Harrison* (1919) 89 LJKB 15). The agent must act in a manner authorised by his principal — he will not, for example, be indemnified for expenses incurred through his own negligence (*Lage* v *Siemens Bros & Co Ltd* (1932) 42 Ll L Rep 252).

If the agency is not contractual, the agent may have a restitutionary right of recovery in relation to payments which the principal would otherwise have had to make himself (see Chapter 22).

(iii) Agent's lien

The agent is given a lien (a right to retain the principal's property in his possession) until the principal has satisfied the claims which the agent has against him for, for example, indemnity or commission. It is normally only a particular, rather than a general, lien — ie the sum due must relate to the particular goods retained (see Markesinis & Munday, *An Outline of the Law of Agency* pp 136–140).

5. Termination of agency[10]

It is necessary to consider termination by act of the parties and termination by operation of law.

(a) Termination by act of the parties

There are certain exceptional situations in which the agency is said to be irrevocable. That is, where the agency is coupled with an interest ie the agency was created to protect an interest of the agent (*Frith* v *Frith* [1906] AC 254), where the authority is executed ie where the agent has incurred liability for which the principal must indemnify him (*Chappel* v *Bray* (1860) 6 H & N 145), or where certain statutory restrictions on revocation apply eg s 4 Powers of Attorney Act 1971.

In general, the agency may end when the agent has completed the particular task required or when he was to be an agent for a stated period and that has ended. If the agency was created by agreement the parties may agree to end it or one party may give notice and terminate it although, if it is contractual, generally a notice period will be required (*Martin-Baker Aircraft Co Ltd* v *Canadian Flight Equipment* [1955] 2 QB 556), unless there has been a repudiatory breach. Generally the principal may revoke the agent's authority at any time before the agent has completed performance of his obligations (*Campanari* v *Woodburn* (1854) 15 CB 400), although he may need to comply with a contractual notice period if he is not to be in breach of contract thereby (*Martin-Baker Aircraft Co Ltd* v *Canadian Flight Equipment* [1955] 2 QB 556). If there is a breach, then there will be an action for damages.

The Commercial Agents (Council Directive) Regulations 1993 have provided extensive rights for commercial agents on termination, treating them more like employees than independent contractors. The idea being that the principal will continue to benefit from the prior work of the commercial agent and the good will in his business which has been built up by the commercial agent. Under a commercial agency contract for an indefinite period the Regulations set out minimum notice requirements (reg 15(1)). The commercial agent is entitled to commission on transactions entered into after the termination of his agency if they are "mainly attributable to his efforts during the period covered by the agency contract and if the transaction was entered into within a reasonable period after the contract terminated" (reg 8) — there are apportionment provisions where a new commercial agent has been appointed (reg 9). Regulation 17 provides for the payment of, what may be, significant sums to the agent on termination by way of "compensation" or "indemnity" on termination. The notions of compensation and indemnity referred to are not related to the meaning they might *prima facie* be given in English law. They stem from the Directive which derived them from French and German law respectively and the English courts will need to consider their usage in those systems in order to give them meaning (*Moore* v *Piretta PTA Ltd* [1999] 1 All ER 174). The parties can state in the agency contract whether the agent is to receive compensation or indemnity on termination, but if no statement is made the agent will receive compensation (reg 17(2)). The recovery of an indemnity does not preclude the commercial agent also from recovering damages (reg 17(5)), if the termination was such as to give rise to a damages claim. The indemnity is based upon the extent to which the agent has brought the principal new customers, or has substantially increased his volume of business with existing customers, and factors such as the commission lost by the agent on the business transacted with such customers (reg 17(3)) — there is a limit placed on recovery based on an average year's remuneration for the agent (reg 17(4), *Moore* v *Piretta*). Under reg 17, "compensation" is awarded to cover the "damage" to the agent due to the termination. In particular damage is deemed to occur when the circumstances of termination:

"(a) deprive the commercial agent of the commission which proper performance of the agency contract would have procured for him whilst providing his principal with substantial benefits linked to the activities of the commercial agent; or

(b) have not enabled the commercial agent to amortize the costs and expenses that he had incurred in the performance of the agency contract on the advice of his principal" (reg 17(7)).

The recovery of compensation or indemnity is precluded where the principal has terminated the contract because of default by the agent which would justify immediate termination, or where it was the agent who terminated the agency contract unless such termination was justified. The commercial agent's termination of the contract will be justified if, for example, the termination is "justified by circumstances attributable to the principal" or it is done on the grounds of age, infirmity or illness (reg 18). (See *Page* v *Combined Shipping & Trading Co Ltd* [1997] 3 All ER 656; *King* v *Tunnock* [2000] IRLR 569; *Duffen* v *FRA BO SpA* (1998) Tr LR 460; Saintier (1997) JBL 77).

(b) Termination by operation of law

Agency is regarded as a personal relationship and, unless it is irrevocable, it is terminated automatically on the death of either party (*Campanari* v *Woodburn* (1854) 15 CB 400), or the insanity of either party (*Drew* v *Nunn* (1879) 4 QBD 661 — subject to the Enduring Powers of Attorney Act 1985) or, if the agency is contractual, on frustration of the contract (*Marshall* v *Glanville* [1917] 2 KB 87) — see also reg 18 of the Commercial Agents (Council Directive) Regulations 1993. The bankruptcy of either party may also terminate the agency but special rules apply in that context.

Footnotes

(1) *China Pacific SA* v *Food Corpn of India; (The Winson)* [1981] 3 All ER 688, *Prager* v *Blatspiel* [1924] 1 KB 566, *Jebara* v *Ottoman Bank* [1927] 2 KB 254.
(2) *Great Northern Ry Co* v *Swaffield* (1874) LR 9, *Sachs* v *Miklos* [1948] 2 KB 23.
(3) *AMB Imballaggi Plastici Srl* v *Pacflex Ltd* [1999] 2 All ER (Comm) 249 at p 254. But see *Tamarind International* v *Eastern Natural Gas (Retail) Ltd* [2000] CLC 1397 at p 1404.
(4) But see the anomalous case of *Watteau* v *Fenwick* [1893] 1 QB 346; "The Demise of *Watteau* v *Fenwick: Sign-O-Lite Ltd* v *Metropolitan Life Ins Co*", Fridman (1991) 70 Can Bar Rev 329.
(5) Reynolds (1983) CLP 119, Derham [1985] CLJ 384.
(6) The duty not to put oneself in a conflict of interest situation may persist for some time after the relationship of principal and agent has technically ended if the trust and confidence of the relationship remain — *Allinson* v *Clayhills* (1907) 97 LT 709.
(7) Corruption is required for a criminal conviction under the Prevention of Corruption Act 1906 (ss 1, 2).
(8) *A-G for Hong Kong* v *Reid* [1994] 1 All ER 1 but see *Industrial Development Consultants* v *Cooley* [1972] 1 WLR 443, *Lister & Co* v *Stubbs* (1890) 45 Ch D 1.
(9) If there is no contract then the agent may be able to recover in restitution.
(10) See Markesinis & Munday Ch 6.

Index